Buddhist Religions

A Historical Introduction

Buddhist Religions

A Historical Introduction

Fifth Edition

RICHARD H. ROBINSON
Formerly of the University of Wisconsin

WILLARD L. JOHNSON
San Diego State University

THANISSARO BHIKKHU (GEOFFREY DeGRAFF)
Metta Forest Monastery

WADSWORTH
CENGAGE Learning™

Australia • Brazil • Japan • Korea • Mexico • Singapore • Spain • United Kingdom • United States

WADSWORTH
CENGAGE Learning™

Buddhist Religions: A Historical Introduction, Fifth Edition
Richard H. Robinson, Willard L. Johnson, and Thanissaro Bhikkhu (Geoffrey DeGraff)

Publisher: Holly J. Allen
Philosophy Editor: Steve Wainwright
Assistant Editors: Lee McCracken and Anna Lustig
Editorial Assistant: Barbara Hillaker
Marketing Manager: Worth Hawes
Marketing Assistant: Annabelle Yang
Advertising Project Manager: Bryan Vann
Print Buyer: Rebecca Cross
Permissions Editor: Joohee Lee
Production Service: Shepherd, Inc.
Copy Editor: Terri Winsor
Cover Designer: Margarite Reynolds
Cover Image: Photograph by John C. Huntington, Courtesy of The Huntington Archive
Compositor: Shepherd, Inc.

Library of Congress Control Number: 2004106988

ISBN-13: 978-0-534-55858-1

ISBN-10: 0-534-55858-5

Wadsworth
20 Davis Drive
Belmont, CA 94002
USA

Printed in the United States of America
4 5 6 7 14 13 12 11 10

To Sītā and Neil,
my daughter and my son,
kuladuhitre ca kulaputrāya
(RHR)

In this life, hate is never
calmed by hatred,
but by love.
This is the primordial dhamma.
Dhammapada, 5
(WLJ)

To Donald K. Swearer,
My first ācarya in things Buddhist
(TB/GFD)

Contents

2 THE BUDDHA AS TEACHER AND POWER FIGURE 22

3 THE DEVELOPMENT OF EARLY INDIAN BUDDHISM 43

Preface

This edition of *Buddhist Religions* represents a thorough rethinking of the book with the aim of bringing it more up-to-date with current scholarship and making it more useful to the student. One change will be readily apparent: The title *The Buddhist Religion,* used for the first four editions, has now been changed, for reasons explained in the Introduction. For anyone familiar with those earlier editions, other changes will become apparent as you go through the book. In particular, the chapters on Indian Buddhism have been radically revised and reorganized, with two chapters—four and five—entirely new. All of the remaining chapters contain major revisions as well, which we hope will make this edition a major advance over what has gone before.

The revision process was set in motion by two thorough and helpful critiques of the previous edition—one, of the entire book, by Jan Nattier of Indiana University; and another, of the last five chapters, by Peter Gregory of Smith College. As the manuscript for the new edition was in progress, Jan Nattier also provided valuable feedback on many of the chapters; John McRae of Indiana University, Richard Seager of Hamilton College, Karma Lekshe Tsomo of San Diego University, Gil Fronsdal of the Sati Center for Buddhist Studies, and Clark Strand, formerly of *Tricycle: The Buddhist Journal,* offered advice in their respective fields of expertise. Sarah Dubin-Vaughn and Thomas Patton read through many of the chapters and offered helpful comments. Helen Newmark also offered assistance. At Wadsworth, our editor Anna Lustig provided constant encouragement; and Terri Winsor, our copy editor, helped bring clarity and consistency to the book.

We are also grateful to the Wadsworth reviewers: Jonathon R. Herman, Georgia State University; Harry Krebs, Dickinson College; James P. McDermott, Canisius College; and James Santucci, Fullerton State College.

We would like to express our sincere gratitude to all of these people for their assistance; the book is much, much clearer and more accurate because of their help. Any errors that remain in the book, of course, are our own.

Willard L. Johnson
San Diego State University

Thanissaro Bhikkhu (Geoffrey DeGraff)
Metta Forest Monastery

KUCHA
TUNHUANG
KHOTAN
BAMIYAN
GILGIT
AFGHANISTAN
PESHAWAR
TAXILA
KASHMIR
TIBET
GANDHARA
TASHILHUNPO
Tsangpo
Mt. Kailasa
LHASA
SHIGATSE
SAMYE
NEPAL
SAKYA
GYANTSE
PAKISTAN
DELHI
KATHMANDU
Indus
SAMKASYA
Ganges
LUMBINI
MATHURA
Jumna
SRAVASTI
KAPILAVASTU
KUSINAGARI
Irawaddy
SARNATH
VAISALI
BANGLADESH
Chambal
BHARHUT
PATNA
Salween
NALANDA
BURMA
(Myanmar)
BODHGAYA
SANCHI
CALCUTTA
MANDALAY
Narmada
PAGAN
AJANTA
PROME (Sri Kshetra)
INDIA
BOMBAY
CHIANGMAI
PEGU
LAMPHUN
AMARAVATI
BAY OF
BENGAL
SUKHOTHAI
ARABIAN
SEA
THAILAND
Krishna
LOPBURI
RANGOON
AYUTTHAYA
THATON
NAGARJUNAKONDA
BANGKOK
ANGKOR
CAMBODIA
KANCHI
PHNOM PENH
SRI LANKA
MIHINTALE
ANURADHAPURA
POLONNARUVA
COLOMBO
KANDY
MALAYSIA
INDIAN OCEAN
SUMATRA

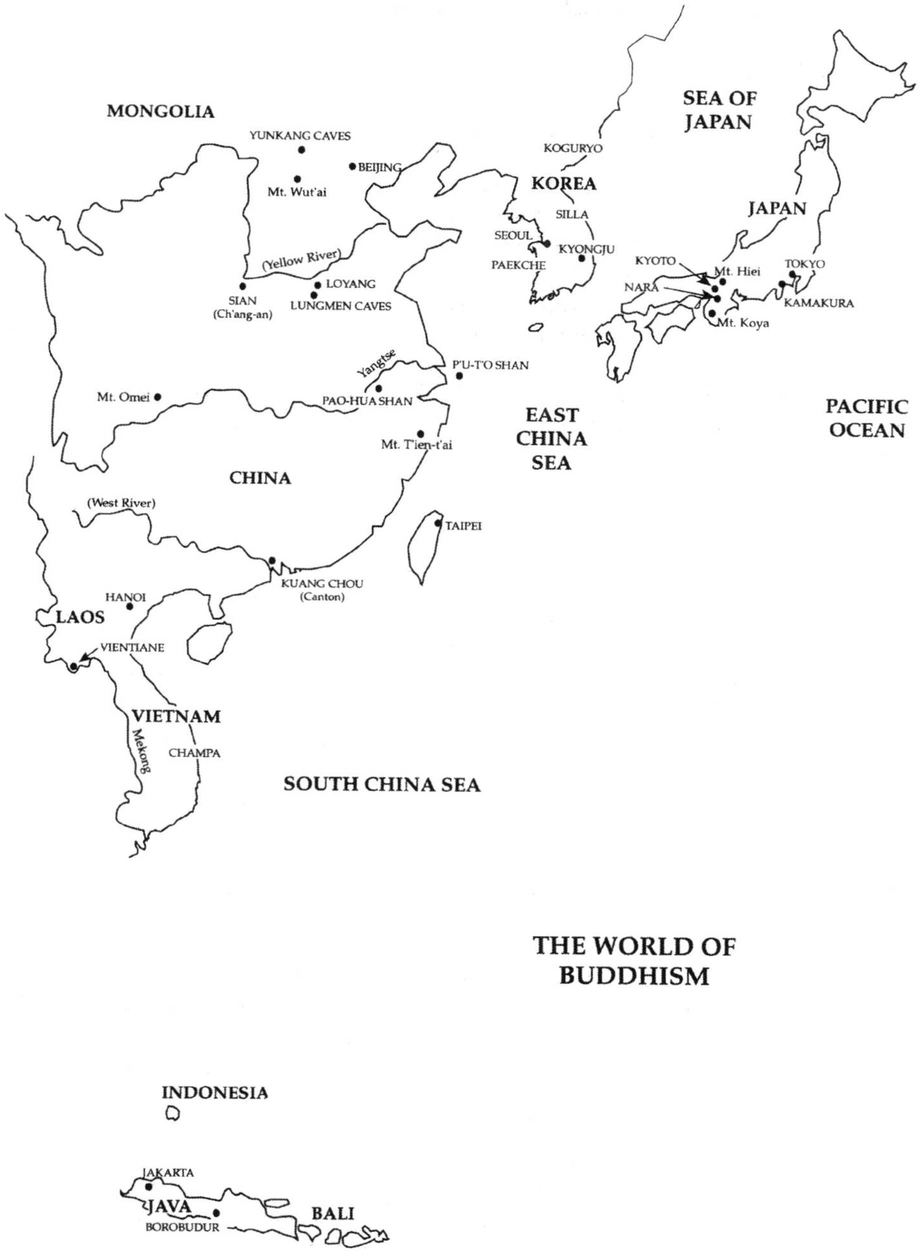
MONGOLIA
YUNKANG CAVES
BEIJING
Mt. Wut'ai
(Yellow River)
SIAN
(Ch'ang-an)
LOYANG
LUNGMEN CAVES
KOGURYO
SEA OF JAPAN
KOREA
SILLA
SEOUL
KYONGJU
PAEKCHE
JAPAN
KYOTO
Mt. Hiei
TOKYO
NARA
KAMAKURA
Mt. Koya
Yangtse
P'U-T'O SHAN
Mt. Omei
PAO-HUA SHAN
EAST CHINA SEA
PACIFIC OCEAN
Mt. T'ien-t'ai
CHINA
(West River)
TAIPEI
KUANG CHOU
(Canton)
HANOI
LAOS
VIENTIANE
VIETNAM
Mekong
CHAMPA
SOUTH CHINA SEA
THE WORLD OF BUDDHISM
INDONESIA
JAKARTA
JAVA
BOROBUDUR
BALI

Abbreviations

Texts from the Pali Canon:

AN	*Aṅguttara Nikāya*
Cv	*Cullavagga*
DN	*Dīgha Nikāya*
MN	*Majjhima Nikāya*
Mv	*Mahāvagga*
SN	*Saṁyutta Nikāya*
Sn	*Sutta-Nipāta*

References to DN and MN are to Sutta. References to Mv and Cv are to section and subsection. References to the remaining texts are to section (*saṁyutta, nipāta,* or *vagga*) and *Sutta.*

Other texts:

Aṣṭa	*Aṣṭasāhasrikā-prajñāpāramitā Sūtra*
Kośa	*Abhidharmakośa*
Laṅka	*Laṅkāvatāra*
MMK	*Mūla-madhyamaka-kārikā*
Pañca	*Pañcaviṃśatisāhasrikā-prajñāpāramitā Sūtra*
Pratyutpanna	*Pratyutpanna-buddha-saṃmukhāvasthita-samādhi Sūtra*
Tattvasaṃgraha	*Sarvatathāgatatattvasaṃgraha*

Introduction

B*uddhism*—as a term to denote the vast array of social and cultural phenomena that have clustered around the teachings of a figure called the Buddha, the Awakened One—is a recent invention. It comes from the thinkers of the eighteenth century European Enlightenment and their quest to subsume religion under comparative sociology and secular history. Only recently have Asian Buddhists come to adopt the term and the concept behind it. Previously, the terms they used to refer to their religion were much more limited in scope: the *Dharma,* the *Buddha's message,* or the *Buddha's way.* In other words, they conceived of their religion simply as the teaching of the Buddha—what the earliest Buddhist sources call *Dharma-Vinaya,* Doctrine and Discipline. Whereas *Dharma-Vinaya* is meant to be prescriptive—advocating a way of life and practice—*Buddhism* is descriptive, in that it simply denotes the actions of people who follow a vision of Dharma-Vinaya, without passing judgment on the validity of that vision or suggesting that the reader accept that vision or follow it.

This is a book about Buddhism. Although it will describe the various ways that Buddhists over the centuries have defined Dharma-Vinaya in their words and actions, it will not attempt a definition of its own. Its purpose is to portray the thoughts and actions of the large segment of the human race who have called themselves followers of the Buddha. The authors have felt that this would be a worthwhile enterprise in exploring part of the range of the human condition. As Socrates once said, an unexamined life is not worth living. One of the best ways to begin the examination of one's own life is to examine the lives and beliefs of others, so that one's unconscious assumptions can be thrown into sharp relief by the perspective offered by the assumptions, unconscious and conscious, of the rest of humanity. This book is meant to help provide a part of that perspective.

The serious study of Buddhism in the West began in 1844, when the French philologist Eugene Burnouf came to the conclusion that certain religions encountered by European explorers and traders in East Asia, Tibet, India, Sri Lanka, and Southeast Asia were in fact branches of a single tradition whose home was in India. Burnouf's discovery of the connecting thread among these Buddhist traditions was such a major intellectual feat that it has continued to shape perceptions about those traditions: that despite their superficial differences, they share a common core. Thus the West has perceived Buddhism as a single religion, much like Christianity or Islam, with the differences among its various permutations analogous to the differences among Protestant, Catholic, and Eastern Orthodox Christians. For more than a century after Burnouf's discovery, Buddhologists—scholars of the Buddhist tradition—tried to delineate the essential characteristics of that common core, but the data refused to fit into any clearly discernible mold. As the Thais would say, it was like trying to gather live crabs into an open basket: The old crabs kept crawling out faster than any new ones could be caught and thrown in.

To deal with this great variety, scholars tried to define an "ideal Buddhism," against which actual forms of Buddhism could be measured to see how well they managed to embody the ideal. The arbitrary nature of this process was best revealed by the lack of agreement on how the ideal could be found. Some scholars defined the ideal in terms of the earliest teachings: What the historical Buddha taught must be the most authentic Buddhism; any tradition deviating from that must be degenerate or corrupt. This approach ran into the problem that there is no unassailable account of what the Buddha taught; thus the ideal turned out to be little more than a product of each scholar's attempt at reconstruction. Other scholars defined the ideal form of Buddhism in terms of a doctrine they found particularly advanced or insightful, such as the doctrines of emptiness or original Awakening, but this too was an arbitrary choice, based on the individual scholar's personal preferences or nationalistic sentiments. In either case, it ultimately became obvious that the definition of an ideal Buddhism was less a useful rubric for organizing knowledge than a means for passing judgment on what one did or didn't like about Buddhist traditions.

More recently, the reaction against this search for an ideal Buddhism—called "essentialism"—has led scholars to define Buddhism simply as that which anyone who calls him- or herself a Buddhist does and believes. This approach—which might be termed "inclusionism"—has the advantage of allowing a wider range of Buddhist activities to be studied without prejudice. But when combined with the perception that Buddhism is a single religion, it has the consequence of privileging those Buddhist traditions that are also inclusionistic—enclosing the largest range of Buddhist beliefs and practices in their framework—as the most complete expressions of the religion. This is unfortunate, in that it implicitly denigrates less inclusionistic forms of Buddhism as partial or incomplete, suggesting that they would best achieve completeness by submitting to the rubric provided by another, very different Buddhist tradition. For a scholar to tell practicing Buddhists that the particular tradition to which they have devoted their lives is incomplete is as great an error as telling them that their tradition is degenerate or corrupt.

To avoid this error, it seems better to regard the term *Buddhism* as describing a family of religions, each with its own integrity, much as *monotheism* covers a family of religions that are related but so inherently different that they cannot be reduced to a common core. How can we prove that the different forms of Buddhism are actually different religions? Unfortunately, there is no universal set of criteria to decide whether the differences between two particular traditions are great enough to class them as different religions rather than different sects within the same religion. Historically, these decisions in the West have been shaped more by political forces than by clearly articulated standards. Still, a few general criteria for designating two traditions as separate religions would include the following:

1. They are institutionally separate.
2. They cite different sources of inspiration as providing the final word on their doctrines and practices. If they have some sources in common, at least one of the traditions must state that the common sources provide only a partial expression of the truth, whose complete expression is to be found in sources exclusive to it.
3. They have different views of the ultimate nature of the primary focus of their veneration. In monotheistic religions, this would involve radically different notions of the Godhead. In Buddhist religions, this would involve radically different notions of who or what, in an ultimate sense, the Buddha is.
4. They have different views on the goal of their practice and the legitimate means used to attain that goal. Again, if they have some views in common on these matters, at least one of the traditions must maintain that the common elements are only a partial or inferior vision of the religious life, whose complete expression is found in the exclusive elements of its vision.

When these criteria are applied to the living Buddhist traditions of the modern world, it becomes clear that at least three separate Buddhist religions can be delineated: the Theravāda tradition centered on the Pali Canon; the East Asian tradition, centered on the Chinese Canon; and the Tibetan tradition, centered on the Tibetan Canon. Arguments have been advanced that these religions contain subtraditions that should also be classified as separate religions, but for the purposes of this book we will limit our classification to these three. Each of the three religions is derived from one of the three "courses" or "vehicles"—visions of the path of Buddhist practice—that developed in India. Theravāda is dominated by the Śrāvaka-yāna, or Disciple Course; East Asian Buddhism by the Mahāyāna or Great Course; and Tibetan Buddhism by the Vajrayāna or Adamantine Course. However, it would be a mistake simply to equate each of these religions with its dominant course, for each contains elements of all three courses. Still, the dominant course in each case provides the framework that assigns meaning to the elements of the other courses, meanings that vary drastically from one of these religions to the next. Thus, even though they derive from common sources, the structural differences in the way they interpret those sources makes them separate.

When the three courses had become delineated in the Indian Buddhist tradition by the seventh or eighth centuries C.E., the last three of the previously noted criteria for classifying separate religions were already in place. The first, however, was not, in that the institutions of monastic Buddhism encompassed all three courses. However, when the Buddhist homeland in the Ganges Valley was decimated in the thirteenth century, Buddhists in other parts of Asia began to develop their own independent interpretations of what they had inherited from India, at the same time developing their own separate monastic institutions. At that point, the break into separate religions was complete. The discussion in this book will treat in detail how this happened.

The advantages of viewing these three traditions as separate religions are many, but here we will focus on two. (1) Each tradition is granted its own integrity, without invidious comparisons as to whether it is a corrupt, partial, or primitive expression of what it "should" be. (2) Students of comparative religion are alerted to the fact that no one tradition speaks for all of Buddhism. Just as it is obvious that there is no point in asking about "the monotheistic position" on a particular moral, political, or spiritual issue, there is no point in asking about "the Buddhist position." When the religions of the world are compared, for whatever purpose, then at the very least representatives of all three Buddhist religions should have a place at the table.

Some people, especially in the West, may feel uncomfortable at the idea of dividing Buddhism into different religions, for division among the monotheistic religions has often been underscored by pogroms, genocide, and war. To divide Buddhism into separate religions would thus seem like an invitation for more violence and disharmony in the world. However, many Asian Buddhists have long commented that, on encountering other forms of Buddhism, they are struck by how radically different they are, as if they did not belong to the same tradition. Yet they have never felt motivated by this observation to wage war on the other forms. Thus in viewing the different traditions as separate religions and yet noting how those religions have never turned violent on one another, we gain examples of how different religions can maintain their differences and yet live together in peace.

Despite their differences, however, it is instructive to view the Buddhist religions as a family, to see how those differences developed and where the family resemblances lie: thus this book. There is a tendency in books on Buddhism to engage in what might be called the amoeba fallacy: to view the tradition as an entity with a will to live that moves into a society and adapts itself to its surroundings in order to survive. Here we have tried to avoid that fallacy, and instead have depicted Buddhism as a body of traditions handed down from generation to generation. Although the existence of a tradition may influence the way a particular group of people define their perceived religious needs, they are the active agents in bringing about change in the tradition, just as their embrace or rejection of parts of the tradition brings about changes in them. In using the tradition to meet their own needs, they have applied it to questions and purposes that in some cases it may have never been applied to before. As these new applications are tested in experience and found useful, they become part of the tradition handed down to the next generation. Thus Buddhism has developed, not as a willful entity, but as a result of the contributions of many human beings with varying needs and agendas. In our discussion, we have tried to keep this human element always in mind.

Our presentation here tries to cover five main aspects of the Buddhist religions in a relatively balanced way: ritual, devotionalism, doctrine, meditation practice, and institutional history. The five aspects fit rather neatly with the Triple Gem—the Buddha, Dharma, and Sangha—which, in varying definitions, serves as the basis of all the Buddhist religions. Ritual and devotionalism relate to the respect accorded the Buddha and bodhisattvas (Buddhas-to-be); doctrine and meditation practice correspond to the Dharma; and institutional history corresponds to the Sangha.

The balance among these elements varies from chapter to chapter partly because of the authors' interests, and partly because the available sources concerning that particular period or country may tend to be weighted in one direction more than others. We have chosen what might be termed a "block and bridge" approach to the material, delving into a particular block of material in detail, and then skimming over large areas before delving into another block. In trying to cover a topic as large as Buddhism in the small space of a book, this approach has the advantage of bringing some occasional depth to the discussion. However, the fact that a particular topic has been skimmed over does not mean that it is unimportant, simply that it did not meet our—admittedly subjective—notions of what is interesting and useful to know. In many cases we have given more emphasis to the Dharma than to other aspects of Buddhism, both because of its intrinsic interest and because of its pervasive influence on those other aspects. Rituals and institutions have meaning only when interpreted in light of the doctrine through which that meaning is articulated. In choosing this emphasis, we are honoring an assumption common to all Buddhist religions: that the mind is the primary shaper of the world, rather than vice versa. Readers who prefer to approach the tradition from its more material aspects, such as its economic history, are directed to the bibliography.

The book falls into two parts: the first six chapters covering the history of Buddhism in India; the latter six, Buddhism outside of India. The emphasis on India is due to the fact that Indian Buddhism forms the common stock from which all other Buddhist traditions stem. To understand the relationship between, say, Japanese and Burmese Buddhism, it is necessary to trace back through events in India. In both parts we have tried to cover what the most reliable recent historical scholarship has been able to unearth of what actually happened in the past, as well as how Buddhists in those times and places viewed their own history. We have also touched on some of the grand doctrinal syntheses—the work of Asaṅga, Buddhaghosa, Chih-i, Fa-tsang, Kūkai, and Tsongkhapa, among others—to show how Asian Buddhists themselves tried to deal with the bewildering wealth of their tradition. In addition, we have covered in detail the history of the meditation and devotional traditions now coming to the West, so that this book will be useful to students not only of Buddhism past, but also of Buddhism present and yet to come.

1

The Buddha's Awakening

1.1 THE SOCIAL AND RELIGIOUS CONTEXT OF EARLY BUDDHISM

Buddhism began with the Awakening of the Buddha, whose title means "Awakened One." The location of his Awakening—at Bodhgaya, in the Ganges River plain of northeastern India—is known with some certainty. The date is not. A Sri Lankan tradition places it at 589 B.C.E., whereas modern scholarly conjecture places it later in the fifth or sixth century B.C.E. For Buddhists, the truths to which the Buddha awakened transcend the conditions of space and time. However, there is no denying that the social and cultural context in which he lived influenced the way he expressed his teachings and the way his contemporaries understood them. Thus the history of Buddhism must begin with an account of the events prior to the Buddha's Awakening that helped shape that context.

The sixth century B.C.E. was a period of great social and intellectual ferment in the Ganges plain. Absolute monarchs were developing new urban centers of economic and political power. Their economic power was based on a monetary economy supported by a rising class of merchants and property owners; their political power was based on growing bureaucracies and professional armies. In this manner, they were supplanting the clan-based agrarian republics of the traditional aristocratic and religious elites. As often happens when elites are being disenfranchised, many sensitive members of society began questioning traditional values and proposing new answers concerning the ultimate meaning and goal of life. The religious traditions that shaped the debates on these issues fell into two broad camps: those within the Vedic tradition and those without.

The *Vedas* were religious texts of the Indo-Aryans, who had come to dominate the local population after entering northwest India over the Khyber Pass beginning sometime after 1600 B.C.E. These texts had been memorized by a hereditary Aryan priestly caste called *brahmans,* who engaged in philosophical speculation and conducted rituals—often involving animal sacrifice—to bend the will of the gods in their pantheon to the wishes of their clientele.

As Vedic tradition developed on Indian soil, the patterns of the ritual came to eclipse the gods in importance, as the belief developed that the gods had no choice but to obey a ritual properly performed. This belief is reflected in the *Brāhmaṇas,* ritual and speculative texts that were composed in the first millennium B.C.E. and that best depict the many currents of the Vedic tradition at the time of the Buddha. Although the Brāhmaṇas were largely concerned with *orthopraxy* (rules of ritually proper behavior), they included a body of texts called *Upaniṣads,* which contain speculations on the origin and nature of the cosmos. In addition to these canonical Upaniṣads, so many noncanonical Upaniṣads were composed that they came to form a separate body of texts. Although these Upaniṣads contain a wide variety of teachings, several strands of thought tie them together. One is that the cosmos is derived from Brahmā—conceived either as an anthropomorphic god or as a living principle—who gave birth to the cosmos through a process analogous to that of the Vedic ritual. Thus the ritual represents an order of being prior to that of the cosmos itself. Another strand is that the brahmans as a caste are descended from the mouth of Brahmā, whereas other castes are descended from lower parts of his body. Thus the brahmans are a higher order of being than the rest of humanity and hold a monopoly not only on ritual knowledge but also on knowledge of all ultimate truths.

The second broad camp were the *śramaṇas* (literally, strivers), who rejected the basic claims of Brahmanism and asserted what they saw as truths of nature that human beings of any caste could discover through reason or meditation. Although their original leaders were non-brahmans, they managed to attract some brahmans to their cause. Whether the śramaṇas were a resurfacing of a pre-Aryan religious movement, an anti-Vedic upsurge from within the Aryan tradition, or a combination of both, no one knows for sure. They abandoned the family and its ritual life, generally giving up normal work and social status to live as mendicants. Many of these strivers lived as wanderers, dwelling outside the villages and towns in forest *āśramas* (places of spiritual striving). There they formed fluid communities around masters who propounded a wide diversity of teachings, including extreme asceticism, skepticism, fatalism, materialism, and hedonism. Siddhārtha Gautama—the Buddha-to-be—became a śramaṇa at the age of 29 and eventually became one of the masters in the movement, founding early Buddhism and changing the face of Indian spiritual culture.

1.2 ISSUES IN EARLY NORTH INDIAN THOUGHT

Early Buddhist thought was defined not only by the answers it gave to the questions of its day, but also by its choice of which questions to answer and not to answer. For example, several early accounts list the more popular questions debated by the Buddha's contemporaries as: Is the cosmos eternal or not? Finite or not? Is the soul the same thing as the body or something separate? Do people who have reached the religious goal exist after death? Do they not exist? Both? Neither? One text (SN.XII.48) adds two more metaphysical questions: Does everything exist? Is everything a oneness or a plurality? Another (MN.2) adds a list of personal questions: Do I exist? Do I not exist? What am I? In every instance, the accounts say that the Buddha refused to answer these questions on the grounds that they did not lead to freedom from suffering.

The prime area where the Buddha did take a stance, and that the texts cite repeatedly as the position distinguishing Buddhism most markedly from other schools of thought, was on the issue of *karma,* or intentional action: Is action real? Does it give results? What determines the nature of those results? Are human beings responsible for their actions, or does an outside power act through them? How far can action go toward bringing about lasting happiness? To understand the early Buddhist answers to these questions, we must first look at the answers fielded by other groups at the Buddha's time.

By the first millennium B.C.E., north Indian thought had accepted the notion—based on astronomers' calculations of planetary cycles—that time is measured in aeons, incomprehensibly long cycles that repeat themselves endlessly. The thinkers of the time presented their views on the potential of human action against this vast temporal frame, but differed widely in their interpretations of its role. The primary differences centered on two issues:

1. *Personal identity.* Most Brahmanical and śramaṇa schools assumed that a person's identity extends through countless lifetimes in a vast cycle of repeated birth, death, and rebirth called *saṁsāra,* or the wandering-on. There was some disagreement, however, as to what exactly constituted that identity, and whether it would change from life to life or remain the same. Although a few early Vedic hymns had expressed a positive attitude toward the idea of rebirth, by the time of Siddhārtha Gautama most of those who believed in rebirth felt that true happiness could be found only through release from the otherwise endless cycle. However, a śramaṇa band of hedonist materialists called *Lokāyata* denied the existence of any identity beyond death. A person, they said, was simply a combination of physical elements and mental faculties, with no self to survive death. They thus insisted that happiness was to be found by indulging in the pleasures of the senses here and now.
2. *Causality.* Vedic thinkers and some of the śramaṇa schools accepted the idea that human action played a causal role in providing for one's happiness both in this lifetime and on into future lives. Views about how this causal principle

worked, however, differed. For some Vedists, the only effective action was ritualistic: sacrifices to the gods, following rigid instructions as to what was done and said, and gifts to the priests themselves. The Jains, one of the śramaṇa schools, taught that all action fell under linear, deterministic causal laws and acted as a bond to the recurring cycle. The past shaped the present, which in turn shaped the future. According to them, the only escape from the cycle lay in a life of nonviolence and inaction, culminating in suicide by starvation. Some Upaniṣads expressed causality as a morally neutral, purely physical process of evolution. Others stated that moral laws are intrinsic to the nature of causality, rather than being mere social conventions, and that the morality of an action determines how it affects one's future course in the round of rebirth. There is no way of knowing, though, whether these last texts were composed before or after Buddhist texts expressing this view. At any rate, all pre-Buddhist thinkers who accepted the principle of causality—however they expressed it—viewed it as a strict linear process: x causes y, which in turn causes z, but neither y nor z feed back to have an influence on x.

On the other side of the question, the Lokāyatas insisted that no causal principle acts between events, and that all events are self-caused. Thus actions have no consequences, and one may safely ignore morality and ritual orthopraxy in one's pursuit of sensual pleasure. Another śramaṇa school, the Ājīvakas, who specialized in astrology and divination, insisted that human life was entirely determined by impersonal, amoral fate. One branch of the Ājīvakas insisted that human action and agency were unreal: In the act of killing, there was no killer and no one being killed, simply a knife slipping between impersonal atoms. Another branch maintained that action was real but totally predetermined, playing no role in providing for one's happiness or misery. Morality, both branches said, was purely a social convention. Escape from the round of rebirth came only when the round worked itself out. Peace of mind could be found by accepting one's fate and patiently waiting for the round, like a ball of string unwinding, to come to its end.

The divergent viewpoints on these two issues formed the backdrop for Siddhārtha Gautama's quest for ultimate happiness. In fact, his Awakening may be viewed as his own resolution of these issues, which provided a view of the role of human action, seen in the light of personal survival and causal principles, that proved influential for many centuries afterward, both in northern India and beyond.

1.3 THE QUEST FOR AWAKENING

The earliest accounts of the Buddha's life are fragmentary reports scattered through the *Sūtras* (Discourses) and *Vinaya* (Disciplinary Rules) in the canons of the early Buddhist communities. These reports were designed to illustrate points of doctrine or to explain the origin of some of the rules. Not until at least 400 years after the Buddha's death were full-length biographies of his life composed for their own sake, to glorify him as an epic hero and to celebrate his deeds, in line with the literary conventions of the times. And ever since, Buddhists have continued to produce lives of the Buddha for a variety of purposes. Some accounts, in order to inspire faith in the reader, stress the miraculous acts of the Buddha; others focus more on his personal qualities as models for Buddhists to emulate; still others try to establish a universal pattern for how Buddhas come about. The early canons tell us "our" Buddha is one of a long line of Buddhas, and our aeon is a particularly auspicious one: Gautama is the fourth of the five who will appear.

The quest for the historical Gautama is predestined to a measure of failure. We cannot get behind the portraits drawn by the early communities; their reports are all we have. Although the *Sangha* (Community) formulated the image of the Buddha, the Buddha had established the Sangha and exhorted his disciples to imitate him. What they found valuable in the training they received, they transmitted as a model for later generations to emulate. Although the process of formulation may have entailed some distortion, the purpose of transmission ensured a measure of fidelity. And, although the historical truth of the accounts may never be proven, the accounts themselves are undoubtedly of historical importance, as they have inspired Buddhists by the millions over the past two and one-half millennia.

The following account is based largely on two sources: the fragmentary biographical information in the Pali Canon as preserved by the *Theravāda* school (see Section 3.2) and the *Buddhacarita* (Acts of the Buddha), an epic retelling of the legend composed by the poet-monk Aśvaghoṣa in approximately the first century C.E., partially extant in Sanskrit, and fully preserved in the Buddhist canons of China and Tibet. The purpose of this account is threefold: to introduce episodes of the Buddha-narrative common to most schools of Buddhism, to provide a narrative framework for some of the early core Buddhist teachings, and to indicate motifs from the Buddha-narrative that have had a long-term impact on Buddhist religions.

1.3.1 The Birth and Youth of the Bodhisattva

The *Śākyas,* the Buddha's ancestors, were members of a noble *kṣatriya* (warrior) class living on the northeastern Ganges River plain just below the Himalayan foothills. Their clan name was *Gautama:* descendents of the sage Gotama. The Bodhisattva's father, Śuddhodana, was a leading aristocrat in the town of Kapilavastu, which archaeologists have identified with remains on the present-day border between India and Nepal. During the later period when monarchies had become the norm in India, Buddhist chroniclers—including Aśvaghoṣa—portrayed Śuddhodana as a king, but the earlier texts present him as simply one of a council of rulers of the Śākyan agrarian republic. His republic, like many republics at that time, was eventually annexed by the nearby kingdom of Kosala toward the end of the Buddha's life.

According to legend, Śākyamuni (the Sage of the Śākyans, an epithet for the Buddha) was conceived when his mother, Māyā, dreamed that a white elephant entered her body through the side. Aśvaghoṣa reports that as her delivery time approached, she was overcome with a desire to retire to the forest, foreshadowing her son's later flight into the wilderness. So, together with her retinue, she journeyed to the wooded garden of Lumbini, near Kapilavastu. There, standing with her upstretched right hand on the branch of a tree, she gave birth to the Bodhisattva. The newborn child stood up, strode seven paces, and declared that this was his last birth: He was destined for Awakening. Shortly thereafter, Asita, an aged sage, examined the infant and prophesied that he would become a Buddha. Other accounts specified that he would attain Awakening only if he chose to leave the palace to become a wandering ascetic; otherwise, he would rule as a universal monarch over the entire Indian subcontinent. The parents named the boy Siddhārtha, "he who has achieved his goal."

Seven days after giving birth, Māyā died. Śuddhodana married her sister, Mahāprajāpati, who brought up the young Bodhisattva. When he came of age, he was married to a bride (named Yaśodharā in most of the accounts) whom his father had selected. In due course Yaśodharā bore Siddhārtha a son, whom they named *Rāhula* (Obstacle), an indication that the young father's heart was already turning away from the household life.

1.3.2 The Great Renunciation

The Pali Suttas (Sūtras) describe Prince Siddhārtha's youth and renunciation in simple terms. He lived a life of extreme luxury, with a separate mansion for each of the three Indian seasons. On gaining maturity, however—and realizing that he, like other beings, was subject to aging, illness, and death—he lost all intoxication with youth, health, and life. Shaving off his hair and beard while his parents looked on with tearful faces, he left home for the life of an ascetic wanderer in order to seek the "unaging, unailing, deathless, sorrowless, undefiled, unexcelled security from bondage, *nirvāṇa*" (AN.III.38; MN.26—see Abbreviations, p. xviii).

Later accounts provide a more dramatic rendition of the events. Aśvaghoṣa relates how King Śuddhodana, from the very beginning, had tried to prevent his son from leaving the palace by ensnaring him with sensual pleasures, not only arranging his marriage but also surrounding him with young song-and-dance women and every other delight a man might desire. One day the young prince, longing to see the outside world, went out for a chariot ride through the capital city. There, for the first time, he saw a decrepit old man. Shocked, he asked his charioteer about the man's condition; the charioteer replied that this was the destiny of all human beings. The prince turned back to the palace and brooded, taking no relish in the gaiety around him. On a second ride, he saw his first diseased man and reflected that people are foolish to revel under the constant shadow of illness. On the third trip, he saw his first corpse. Dismayed, he marveled that people could live heedlessly, forgetting the certainty of death.

Employing the conventions of Sanskrit drama, Aśvaghoṣa's poem exploits Siddhārtha's life of princely pleasure as a counterpoint to the traumatic encounters with impermanence and suffering. In an artfully composed dialogue, the king's counselor advises the young prince to disregard his disturbing encounters and to follow the example of ancient heroes and sages in pursuing the pleasures of erotic love. The Bodhisattva's reply is an eloquent statement of the ascetic case against the sensual life. Sensual joys are fleeting; death always casts its long shadow over life, blighting all transient pleasures. The only true happiness would be one not subject to change. The pursuit of any lesser pleasure cannot be held up as a fulfilling or noble ideal.

The prince rode out again, saw peasants plowing, and—unlike the ordinary patrician—was moved to grief at the suffering of the toilers and oxen, and even at the slaughter of worms and insects by the plow. Retiring to a nearby grove, he meditated alone until a forest śramaṇa wandered past. Questioning the man, he learned a brief explanation of the renunciate life: "I dwell wherever I happen to be, at the root of a tree or in a deserted temple, on hill or in forest, wandering without expectations or ties, in search of the highest good." The prince—confident that this way of life offered the only opportunity to find the happiness he sought—made up his mind to leave home for the forest.

Aśvaghoṣa poignantly describes how, in the deep of night, the prince took one last look at his sleeping wife and infant son, mounted his horse, and rode out of the city, accompanied by his charioteer. After a fair distance he dismounted, sent his charioteer back to Śuddhodana with his ornaments and a message, then cut off his hair and exchanged clothes with a passing hunter.

The core of this episode, the Great Renunciation, is the conflict between the life of the householder and that of the forest renunciate. In this, it foreshadows a theme that has played itself out in Buddhist religions up to the present: the tension between the merits of civilization and those of the wilderness. Although the wilderness is definitely favored as the place for testing oneself and discovering the truth, the duties of civilized life are not entirely denied. At each crucial juncture prior to his flight, Siddhārtha recognizes his familial duty and expresses strong affection toward his father. If he transcends birth and death, he promises to return to teach his discovery to his family. This parallels the position that Buddhist thought and life have assumed over the centuries, straddling the line between civilization and the wilderness. The verse portions of the Pali Canon, for example, contain some of the world's first wilderness poetry, alongside verses detailing the duties and joys of a happily married life. The monastic Sangha, as we will see, has been composed both of wandering forest meditators and settled city-dwellers ministering to the needs of the laity. The tradition's ability to bridge the gap between the city and the wilds in this way has proven to be a source of enduring strength.

The story of the Great Renunciation also introduces two emotions that have played a major role in Buddhist religions throughout the centuries. The first is *saṁvega,* the emotion the prince felt on his first encounter with aging, illness, and death. Saṁvega covers a broad range of feeling, ranging from the simple act of coming to one's senses after a bout of foolish carelessness, to a more extreme sense of alienation, awe, shock, and dismay over the futility of life as it is normally lived, combined with a strong sense of urgency in trying to find escape from the trap of futility. Its companion emotion is *prasāda,* the emotion the prince felt on encountering the forest śramaṇa: a clear sense of serene confidence that one has found the way out. As the word *prasāda* is also used to describe the clarity of a calm lake, the implicit image is that saṁvega "stirs up" the mind, whereas prasāda makes it calm. The two emotions provide proper balance for each other: saṁvega keeps prasāda grounded in reality; prasāda keeps saṁvega from turning into hopelessness. Both emotions have formed a common thread among branches of Buddhism that have otherwise diverged widely in terms of doctrine and practice. Texts in many Buddhist traditions have advised their readers to cultivate both as the primary spur to the religious life.

1.3.3 The Bodhisattva's Studies and Austerities

The new mendicant, then 29 years old, went first to an ascetic teacher named Ārāḍa Kālāma, who taught a form of meditation leading to the "dimension of nothingness." Gautama practiced the method, quickly attaining the goal, and Kālāma then set him up as his equal and co-teacher. Gautama, however, concluded that this teaching did not lead to nirvāṇa—a term that literally means the extinguishing of a fire (see Section 1.4.2), but figuratively the highest happiness, freedom, and peace. So he left in search of a better teaching. Studying under another ascetic leader, Udraka Rāmaputra, he mastered a higher state, the "dimension of neither perception nor nonperception." Udraka then proclaimed Gautama to be his teacher, but the latter was again dissatisfied with his attainment and so set out to practice on his own.

Going eastward to Uruvela near Bodhgaya, he found a pleasant forested spot by a river and settled down to try the path of austerities. Suppressing his breath in order to induce trances, he was undeterred by the resulting violent headaches. Fasting, he came as close as he could to eating nothing at all, becoming utterly emaciated. He was joined in his strivings by five ascetics and continued in this painful course until the sixth year after the Great Renunciation. Then, seeing that this severe mortification had not led him to liberating knowledge, and having exhausted the various forms of ascetic practice current in his day, he tried to think of another way. He remembered an incident in his childhood: While sitting under a shady tree as his father was performing a royal plowing ritual, he had entered the first *dhyāna* (a rapturous state of concentration). Perhaps, he surmised, this might be the path. Although he had seen that mental absorption did not constitute liberation, it might act as part of the path to that goal. His body, however, was too weak to regain that blissful concentration.

Aśvaghoṣa goes on to say that Gautama then sat under a sacred tree. A woman named Sujātā had vowed a yearly offering to the deity inhabiting the tree if she bore a son. Her wish having been fulfilled, she was preparing to offer a fine bowl of rice cooked in milk. Her maid came upon the Bodhisattva sitting there, mistook him for the spirit of the tree, and reported the apparition to her mistress, who came and presented the food to Gautama herself. A Pali Sutta (MN.36) states simply that Gautama took rice and barley gruel. In so doing, he took the first step on the Middle Way toward Awakening, a way that became a central feature of the *Dharma* (or doctrine) he later taught. The five mendicants, however, left him in disgust, saying that he had given up striving and was living in abundance.

1.3.4 Temptation by Māra

After accepting the meal from Sujātā, Gautama sat under another tree, in retrospect called the *Bodhi* (Awakening) *Tree*, facing east and resolving not to arise until he had attained his goal. The birds and beasts of the forest fell quiet in anticipation. Māra (the personification of death and temptation) grew alarmed at the prospect of the Bodhisattva's escaping from his realm, and so tried to divert him—an episode that later tradition embellished lavishly over the centuries, following the early texts in freely blurring the lines between psychology and allegory. The Pali Canon (Sn.III.2) states that Māra tempted the Bodhisattva in two stages, first trying to plant doubts in the Bodhisattva's mind and then calling up his armies to assault him. The Bodhisattva, however, recognized Māra's ten armies for what they were—sensuality, discontent, hunger and thirst, craving, sloth and lethargy, fear, doubt, hypocrisy, self-exaltation, and the desire for fame—and this was enough to dispel them. Māra's daughters—Discontent, Delight, and Craving—then volunteered to seduce the Bodhisattva, but they too failed. Aśvaghoṣa adds little to the legend, aside from depicting Māra's armies in grisly detail and attributing the Bodhisattva's victory over them to his persistent resolve. Legends postdating Aśvaghoṣa, however, add that Māra finally challenged the Bodhisattva's right to Awakening, in response to which the Bodhisattva touched Mother Earth to bear witness to his merit. She rose up and squeezed an ocean of water out of her hair, symbolic of the cooling waters of his many past good deeds, washing the armies away. The heavens then cleared—in Aśvaghoṣa's words, "shining with the moon like a maiden with a smile"—and a shower of sweet-smelling flowers rained down. The Bodhisattva returned to his quest.

1.3.5 The Awakening

A Pali Sutta (SN.XII.70) divides the knowledge of Awakening into two steps: "First there is the knowledge of the regularity of phenomena (the laws underlying all action), then there is the knowledge of nirvāṇa." Another Sutta (MN.19) describes the Bodhisattva's discovery of the first step as follows: The Bodhisattva first divided his thoughts into two sorts—those leading to affliction for himself or others (these, he determined, were thoughts imbued with sensual passion, ill will, or harmfulness) and thoughts free from sensual passion, ill will, and harmfulness, which lead to no affliction for anyone. When thoughts of the first sort arose in his mind, he obliterated them. When thoughts of the second sort arose, he allowed them free rein. In doing so, he experienced a mind-state free from affliction. But even nonafflictive thinking, he concluded, tires the mind, and so he steadied his mind in concentration—one tradition states that he focused on his in-and-out breathing—and ascended the four stages of dhyāna.

The first dhyāna is a meditative absorption produced by detaching from sensual thoughts and unskillful attitudes. The mind attains unity while evaluating the object to which it consciously directs its attention, giving rise to a sense of rapture and ease born of seclusion. The second stage is free from evaluation and directed thought. There is singleness of mind and internal assurance, with rapture and ease born of composure. The third stage—equanimous rather than rapturous—is mindful and alert, with a feeling of bodily ease. The fourth consists of pure equanimity and mindfulness, free of pleasure and pain.

This fourth stage can serve as foundation for six *abhijñā* (superknowledges): (1) psychic powers (such as levitation and walking on water); (2) the divine ear, or psychic hearing; (3) knowledge of others' minds; (4) memory of one's former lives; (5) the divine eye, or clairvoyance; and (6) the ending of the *āsrava* (binding effluents or pollutants of the mind)—namely, sensual desire, becoming (states of being), views, and ignorance. The first five superknowledges are mundane, as they do not release the mind from its defilements. Only the sixth is supramundane, as it opens the mind to the deathlessness of nirvāṇa.

Both the Suttas and Aśvaghoṣa describe Gautama's progress toward the deathless in terms of three cognitions identical with three of the superknowledges. During the first watch of the night (dusk to 10 P.M.), he acquired the first cognition, which is identical with the fourth superknowledge (that of recollecting his previous lifetimes over many aeons) seeing: "There I had such a name, belonged to such a clan, had such an appearance. Such was my food, such my experience of pleasure and pain, such the end of my life. Passing away from that state, I re-arose there. There, too, I had such a name, belonged to such a clan, had such an appearance. Such was my food, such my experience of pleasure and pain, such the end of my life. Passing away from that state, I re-arose here."

Struck by the meaninglessness of his chain of lifetimes, the Bodhisattva during the second watch (10 P.M. to 2 A.M.) turned his mind to the second cognition and fifth superknowledge (knowledge of the death and rebirth of living beings everywhere). The entire cosmos, Aśvaghoṣa says, appeared to him as in a spotless mirror. He saw that good karma, under the influence of right views, leads to a happy rebirth on the upper realms of existence; whereas evil karma, under the influence of wrong views, leads to a miserable one in the realms of deprivation.

Dismayed at the suffering inherent in this endless cycling through death and rebirth, the Bodhisattva during the third watch (2 A.M. to dawn), turned his mind to the third cognition and sixth superknowledge (that of the ending of the āsravas). According to Aśvaghoṣa, this involved realizing the principle of *pratītya-samutpāda* (dependent co-arising; see Section 1.4.1), the interdependent pattern of twelve preconditions whereby the āsrava of ignorance gives rise not only to *duḥkha* (personal suffering) but also to the experience of the world of rebirth as a whole. By meditating on this pattern as it displayed itself directly to his awareness, Gautama was able to unravel it and gain release.

The Pali account is more terse: "When the mind was thus concentrated . . . I directed it to the knowledge of the ending of the āsravas. I discerned, as it actually was, that 'This is duḥkha. . . . This is the origination of duḥkha. . . . This is the cessation of duḥkha. . . . This is the way leading to the cessation of duḥkha. . . . These are the āsravas. . . . This is the origination of the āsravas. . . . This is the cessation of the āsravas. . . . This is the way leading to the cessation of the āsravas.' My heart, thus knowing, thus seeing, was released from the āsrava of sensual desire, released from the āsrava of becoming, released from the āsrava of views, and released from the āsrava of ignorance. With release, there was the knowledge, 'Released.' I discerned that, 'Birth is ended, the holy life fulfilled, the task done. There is nothing further for this world.' This was the third knowledge I attained in the third watch of the night. Ignorance was destroyed; knowledge arose; darkness was destroyed; light arose—as happens in one who is heedful, ardent, and resolute."

With this knowledge—as the new day dawned—Gautama completed the first step of Awakening, the knowledge of the regularity of phenomena, and arrived at the second step of Awakening, the unconditioned bliss of nirvāṇa. According to Aśvaghoṣa, the natural world celebrated the event with miracles.

The earth swayed, thunder rolled, rain fell from a cloudless sky, and blossoms fell from the heavens. The beings of the world, for the moment, were at peace, with none giving way to anger, passion, or intoxication. The beings of the heavens showed reverence to Gautama—now the Buddha—and sang his praise.

1.4 THE LESSONS OF AWAKENING

One memorable Sutta (SN.LVI.31) indicates that the account of the Buddha's Awakening only hints at what he actually experienced. Walking one day through a forest grove, he picks up a handful of leaves and tells the monks that what he has taught is comparable to the leaves in his hand, whereas what he experienced in his Awakening is comparable to all the leaves in the forest. He has not taught the whole forest of leaves because it would not help them in their Awakening; instead, he has taught just the handful of leaves that would lead them to nirvāṇa. Thus the account of the Awakening, though autobiographical in form, had a didactic intent. What lessons did the early Buddhists draw from it?

The most basic lesson was the possibility of mastering a skill leading to happiness. This carried important implications for understanding the nature of action. Action (*karma*) is real and it gives results that follow discernible patterns. It is determined by the mind, and the quality of the results is determined, not by ritual correctness, but by the intention motivating the action. Those results can be experienced in the present as well as the future, and they can head in two directions: mundane, leading to continued existence in the cycle of death and rebirth; and supramundane, leading to release from the cycle. On the mundane level, karma falls under laws of moral causality. The supramundane level is achieved through a type of karma that puts an end to karma. The thrust of all these teachings is that it is not only possible but also desirable to train the mind so that its intentions become more skillful, leading to better results on both the mundane and supramundane levels. In the following sections we will review the incidents in the Awakening narrative to see how they illustrate these points, at the same time drawing on other teachings from the Pali Suttas to expand on them.

1.4.1 The Regularity of Phenomena

The beginning of the Pali account—in which the Bodhisattva develops a sense of mental ease by skillfully controlling his thoughts and then attains the dhyānas—illustrates the principle that action is not illusory, that it gives results, and that those results follow regular patterns. Were it not for the regularity of the patterns, he would not have been able to develop mental skill—or any skill—for his actions would not have given consistent results. This skill also illustrates the point, made elsewhere in the Suttas (AN.VI.63), that action is intention, and that the quality of the intention is what determines the quality of the results. The bliss of nonaffliction comes directly from the Bodhisattva's intention to avoid affliction for himself and others. Finally, this account shows that actions yield results in the present: The mental stability and ease that the Bodhisattva experienced by mastering these mental skills could be attributed to his present intentions.

The first and second cognitions illustrate the point that the pattern of cause and effect connecting actions and their results is not limited to the immediate present, or even to one lifetime. In addition to influencing the present, actions shape one's future even after death. Unskillful intentions, expressed through body, speech, and mind, lead to miserable destinations; skillful intentions, expressed in the same three ways, lead to good destinations. The quality of the intention, in turn, is influenced by one's views. Mundane right view, which inspires actions leading to a good destination, is defined in a standard formula (MN.117) as conviction that good and bad deeds bear fruit in good and bad results; that there is a next world after death, and that there are priests and contemplatives who, practicing rightly, proclaim that world having directly experienced it through their meditation. This view, the texts say, counsels an attitude of care and responsibility, for there is no such thing as an action without results. Wrong views, according to the same Sutta, deny the results of karma and the existence of a life after death, and so inspire careless and irresponsible behavior, leading to undesirable results.

Narrative and Cosmology. The first cognition illustrates the principle of life after death through an autobiographical narrative of lives before birth. The second cognition, however, expresses this point in terms of cosmology, a picture of the cosmos as a whole and the principles underlying its operation.

The Pali texts present no account of creation of the cosmos, because saṁsāra's origin in time cannot be discerned and—for the purpose of ending suffering—is ultimately irrelevant. More important is to understand the constant re-creation of the round through one's intentions in the present, for then one can escape the round.

The cosmos as a whole consists of three realms: in ascending order, the sensual realm, the realm of form, and the realm of formlessness. Within these realms are located the six major destinations: hell, hungry ghosts, animals, *asuras* (angry demons), human beings, and *devas* (spirits, deities, gods). The first five destinations all fall within the sensual realm; the devas are split among all three realms, with the inhabitants of the realms of form and formlessness sometimes called Brahmās, or great gods. Rebirth in the four lower destinations results from evil acts; the two upper destinations reward good.

The most degraded beings are the inhabitants of the hells, hot and cold subterranean places of suffering that lasts for many aeons. However, Buddhist hells are purgatorial, not places of everlasting retribution. Once the ripening of their evil karma is complete, the beings of hell can ascend again to the higher realms. Just above the beings of hell are the hungry ghosts. These haunt the earth's surface, tormented by hunger. They stand outside walls and gates, invisible to all but a few human beings, pleading to be fed. The realm of animals ranks just above the hungry ghosts. This is the only realm of deprivation whose inhabitants are visible to human beings at large, although its lines are somewhat blurred by the occasional inclusion of the *nāgas* (magical serpents, capable of assuming human form); their enemies, the *garuḍas* (half human, half bird of prey); and other hybrid beings. Above the animals are the asuras, former deities who once fought the devas for control of heaven and lost.

The two upper destinations reward good karma. Of these, the human destiny is the lowest but also the most important, for it is the primary level where virtue and wisdom can be increased. In the lower realms, beings are too overcome with suffering to practice the Dharma; in the higher realms, they are often—but not always—too immersed in their pleasures to care.

The highest sensual destinies are those of the sensual devas. These destinations are inhabited by a diversity of beings, but again all are there by virtue of their karma and, when the fruit of their merit runs out, are subject to rebirth.

Buddhists inherited a diverse tradition of spirits and celestial beings from their Aryan and non-Aryan predecessors, and the Pali texts offer no standard list of "who's who" in the lower deva realms. The lowest level contains the spirits inhabiting the earth's surface and the lower atmosphere. Prominent among these are the *yakṣas* and *gandharvas.* The yakṣas were primarily tree spirits, the chief divinities of a popular non-Vedic fertility cult. The gandharvas in the *Ṛg Veda* were spirits of the clouds and waters, also associated with fertility. In the Pali account, gandharvas are the adolescents of the deva worlds, obsessed with sex, music, and playing tricks on hapless human beings.

The celestial levels of devas are considerably more orderly than the earthly ones. The first is that of the Four Great Kings, also called World-Protectors, each of whom rules one of the cardinal points and a race of earthly devas. The most prominent of these kings is Kubera, also called *Vaiśravana,* ruler of the North and of yakṣas. He was widely worshiped as the god of wealth, and the Suttas portray him as vowing to protect anyone who practices the Dharma in the wilderness. The second rank of celestial devas are the Gods of the Thirty-Three, the old pantheon of the *Ṛg Veda,* headed by Indra, more generally called *Śakra* in Buddhist texts. He, too, reveres the Buddha and Dharma. Above the Thirty-Three, the Suttas list four more tiers of devas, of which only the second—*Tuṣita* (Satisfied)—plays an important role in Pali accounts. The Bodhisattva spends his next-to-last life in this realm before returning to the human world to become a Buddha. His mother is reborn there after giving birth to him.

At the upper limit of the cosmos lie the Brahmā/deva worlds of form and formlessness, numbered in the Suttas as more than 1,000. Later accounts divide them into 20 levels, 12 in the realm of form—corresponding three each to the first four dhyānas—and the remaining ones in the realm of formlessness, corresponding to the formless levels of dhyāna. Somewhat confusing this neat classification are the Brahmās who are totally unconscious from having put themselves in an unconscious trance while on the human level and a special set of worlds called the Pure Abodes, whose inhabitants are destined to full Awakening after having perfected the practice of dhyāna and reached the level of nonreturn (see Section 2.3.2) while still on the human level. In general, rebirth in the Brahmā/deva worlds results from great virtue, including celibacy; meditation; and the development of the four Brahmā Attitudes: unlimited goodwill, compassion, sympathetic joy, and equanimity. These are the only heavenly worlds in which there is no gender. Only rarely do their inhabitants interact with human beings (see Section 2.2).

The Suttas are remarkable for the sense of easy familiarity they display between the human and spirit worlds. Theirs is an attitude of polite respect for spirits, but not worship. They take the existence of spirits for granted but do not consider them especially sacred. Spirits, after all, are subject to passion, aversion, and delusion, and thus to the law of karma. In this, they are inferior to the Buddha and arhats who have overcome all mental defilements and thus create no further karma. Even the great gods of the popular religion of the time, Indra and Brahmā, were not regarded by the Buddhists as eternal persons but merely as individuals born into those positions and destined to fall from office when their karma ran out.

This gave the spirit world an ethical basis, rendering it rational and more benign. Malicious spirits were not to be appeased with sacrifice, or condemned to damnation, but rather tamed and converted through a holy individual's mental powers and goodwill. This is how Buddhists over the centuries have understood Buddhism's interaction with the spirit cults it encountered in every land to which it spread. As for the benign spirits, the Pali texts treat their foibles with a gentle humor entirely devoid of awe. For example, one of the more entertaining exchanges in the Suttas (DN.21) is between the Buddha and a gandharva who relates how on the night of the Buddha's Awakening, when all the other deities were breathlessly awaiting the outcome, he was able to sneak off and seduce the nymph of his dreams. In another story (SN.I.25), a female tree deva propositions a handsome young monk whom she spies half-naked after his bath in a river. Yet another passage (DN.11) depicts the Great Brahmā as a pompous hypocrite intent on hiding his ignorance from his adoring retinue. Thus the spirit world is not radically different from the human world. Even its refined pleasures are doomed to pass away when the power of the individual's karma runs out.

Just as an individual being's identity within the cosmos is fluid, so too does the cosmos as a whole undergo change, evolving and devolving through repeated aeons of cosmic expansion and contraction. At the end of an aeon, the entire cosmos except for the very highest Brahmā worlds and lowest hells is consumed with flame. Most beings at that time are reborn in the *Appassarā* (Radiant) Brahmā world. Then, through the ripening of their karma, the cosmos reevolves. Tempted by a playful desire to "taste" the pleasures of the new cosmos, they find themselves reborn within it. The first to be reborn in the new cosmos becomes the Great Brahmā for the ensuing aeon. Just as he starts feeling lonely in his new abode, other beings take birth within it. He assumes himself to be their creator, as do they. This, in two sentences, is the Pali explanation for theistic creation accounts. But as with individual destinies, karma—influenced by right and wrong views—is the force determining the waxing and waning of the cosmos as a whole. There is even variation in the pattern of the aeons: in many, no Buddhas will appear to teach the Dharma; only in fortunate aeons will Buddhas appear. Gautama is the fourth of five Buddhas destined to discover and teach the Dharma in our aeon. The fifth, Maitreya (Pali: Metteyya), will appear only after Gautama's teachings have been forgotten. During the periods between Buddhas, however, any number of Private Buddhas (*pratyeka-buddhas*) may gain Awakening, but without being able to formulate the Dharma to teach anyone else.

As mentioned previously, the Suttas' accounts of cosmology are somewhat haphazard, perhaps because they function as illustrations for the teaching on karma, and not as topics of interest for their own sake. The emphasis is on identifying the simple principle underlying the complexity of karmic destinations. One Sutta (AN.IV.71) quotes the Buddha as saying that the results of karma are so complex that any attempt to trace them all out would lead to insanity. Most of the cosmological discussions in the Suttas end with a reminder that the many pleasures and pains of the various realms all result from the one principle of karma. If the listeners are interested in experiencing those pleasures, or if they want release from the round of saṁsāra entirely, they should thus focus on training their minds.

Emptiness. Whereas the second cognition illustrates the outcome of right and wrong views on the mundane level, the third cognition illustrates a transcendent level of right view that leads to freedom from saṁsāra. As our two sources have shown, this form of right view is expressed either as dependent co-arising or as the Four Noble Truths, which as the following analysis will show are related doctrines.

Mundane right view forms the context for transcendent right view, for it explains why one would look for a way out of saṁsāra, and points to where one should look for that way: to the mind. Nevertheless, to move from the mundane to transcendent right view requires a major shift of mental gears. Although there is a logical connection between the two—having seen the role of the mind in shaping the experience of the cosmos, Gautama turned to look at the pattern of action within his mind—still the switch in frame of reference is sharp. This is one reason why Buddhist traditions regard Gautama's leap from the second cognition to the third as earthshaking.

Unlike the autobiographical narrative form of the first cognition, which deals in terms of "self" and "others," or the cosmological form of the second cognition, dealing in terms of "living beings" and "cosmos," the transcendent right view of the third cognition deals in categories devoid of those concepts, simply in terms of the direct experience of the present. In modern Western philosophy, this approach is called radical phenomenology, the description of reality as it is directly experienced, without reference to the question of whether there is any subject or object underlying the experience. In the Suttas, this approach is called an "empty" mode of perception, in which nothing is added to or taken away from what is immediately experienced.

For the purpose of understanding the cause of suffering, the Suttas formulate several modes of analyzing direct experience, based on the insights the Buddha gained in the course of the third watch of the night.

According to the most basic mode, experience can be divided into two spheres: that which is fabricated (*saṅkhata*) by action and that which is not. Unfabricated (*asaṅkhata*) experience is discussed in Section 1.4.2. Here we will focus on fabricated experience, which falls into two classes: *nāma* and *rūpa,* name and form, that is, mental and physical phenomena. These classes are in turn divided into two patterns. The first pattern is that of the six sense fields: the senses of sight, hearing, smell, taste, touch, and ideation, together with their respective objects. The first five sense fields belong to the category of form, and ideation to the category of name. In the second pattern, the five *skandhas* (aggregates), form is one category, whereas name is divided into four: feelings—pleasure, pain, and neither-pleasure-nor-pain; perception or recognition—the mental act of labeling things; mental fabrications—thoughts, intentions, and so forth; and consciousness of the six sense fields.

Because the unfabricated is by definition uncaused, the only way to experience it would be by unraveling the fabricated from within and bringing it to cessation. To do so, one needs to know the pattern in which the various categories of fabricated experience depend on one another. The most complete explanation of this pattern, called "dependent co-arising," is best understood as an analysis of how the sense fields and aggregates go about grouping, disbanding, and regrouping in various configurations as they influence one another in giving rise to suffering and to the fabricated world as a whole. This last point is one of the most distinctive insights of the Buddha's Awakening: the realization that personal experience and the entire fabricated cosmos all boil down to this single pattern, whose factors work over time but can also be directly experienced at the mind in the present.

Dependent co-arising is most commonly expressed as twelve *nidāna* (preconditions). These are (1) ignorance, (2) fabrications, (3) consciousness, (4) name-and-form, (5) the six sense fields, (6) contact, (7) feeling, (8) craving, (9) clinging-sustenance, (10) becoming, (11) birth (that is, rebirth), and (12) aging and dying, with their attendant suffering. Most of the early canonical accounts trace these factors from condition back to precondition, as follows:

12. *Aging and dying depend on birth (that is, rebirth).* If there were no birth, there would be no process exhibiting aging and death. It is important to note here, and in the following causal links, that "birth," "aging," and "dying" refer not only to the arising, decay, and passing away of the body, but also to the repeated arising, decay, and passing away of momentary mental states.
11. *Birth depends on becoming.* If there were no coming-to-be (through karma) of the conditions of the sensual realm, the realm of form, or the formless realm, there would be no locus for rebirth. Again, these realms refer not only to levels of being, but also to levels of mental states. Some mental states are concerned with sensual images, others with forms (such as the form of the body experienced in dhyāna), and still others with formless abstractions, such as space or nothingness.
10. *Becoming depends on clinging-sustenance.* The image here is of a fire remaining in existence by clinging to and appropriating sustenance from its fuel. The process of becoming takes its sustenance from the five skandhas, whereas the act of taking sustenance is to cling to these skandhas in any of four ways: through sensual intentions, through views, through precepts and practices, or through doctrines of the self. Without these forms of clinging, the sensual, form, and formless realms would not come into being.
9. *Clinging-sustenance depends on craving.* If one did not thirst for sensuality, for coming-to-be, or for no change in what has come to be, then there would be no grasping after the fuel for becoming.
8. *Craving depends on feeling.* If pleasant, neutral, and painful feelings were not experienced, one would not thirst for continuing experience of the pleasant and neutral, or for cessation of the unpleasant.
7. *Feeling depends on contact.* Without contact there is no pleasure or pain.
6. *Contact depends on the six sense fields.* If either the senses or their objects were absent, there would be nothing to make contact.

5. *The six sense fields depend on name-and-form.* "Name" here is defined as feeling, perception, attention, contact, and intention. With the inclusion of intention in this factor, this is where karma fits into dependent co-arising. "Form" includes the physical elements of wind, fire, water, and earth.
4. *Name-and-form depends on consciousness of the six sense fields.* Without this kind of consciousness, the physical birth of the individual, which is composed of the skandhas, would abort, whereas on the level of momentary mental birth there would be nothing to activate an experience of the skandhas.
3. *Consciousness of the six sense fields depends on the forces that bring about the fabrication of the body, speech, and mind.* On the level of physical birth, the phrase "fabrication of the body, speech, and mind" refers to volitional forces from the previous birth that engender the conditions taken on by sensory consciousness in the new life. On the level of momentary mental birth, the breath is the force that fabricates the body; directed thought and evaluation are the forces that fabricate speech; and feeling and perception are the forces that fabricate the mind. Without these forces, sensory consciousness would have no basis for growth.
2. *Fabrications come into play only because there is ignorance of the Four Noble Truths, that is, one does not view the cosmos in terms of transcendent right view.* The Four Noble Truths are suffering, its origination (craving), its cessation, and the path of practice leading to its cessation. The knowledge that does away with this ignorance not only knows what the four truths are, but also knows the duty appropriate to each, along with the fact that one has completed that duty (see Section 2.3.1). Without this knowledge, it would be impossible to disband any force or fabrication that would lead to suffering.
1. *Ignorance: not viewing the cosmos in terms of transcendent right view.*

The prescription is as follows: When ignorance ceases, fabrications cease, and so on, until aging and dying cease. Thus is the cessation of the entire mass of suffering. This is also called knowledge of the ending of the āsravas, because the four āsravas are sensual intentions and views, both of which would fall under the category of clinging-sustenance, along with becoming and ignorance. These āsravas all cease with the unraveling of the causal process, leaving simply the experience of the unfabricated.

If ignorance is not overcome, however, the process of dependent co-arising gives rise to repeated suffering indefinitely because of its many feedback loops. For instance, the suffering of birth, aging, and death would count as feeling; as long as ignorance remains operative, this feeling could reenter the series as a mental fabrication (precondition 2), a factor of name-and-form (precondition 4), or as feeling itself (precondition 7). This adds a complex cyclic dimension to the series. Later commentaries attempted to make the causal pattern into a simple circle by asserting that the sorrow of aging and dying gives rise to ignorance. Although one Sutta does note that there are times when suffering can lead to bewilderment (AN.VI.63), the series has so many points of feedback that the image of a circle does little justice to its complexity. The Suttas never characterize the series as a wheel, but instead compare it to streams flowing down the mountains to fill lakes, which in turn fill rivers, which lead to the ocean

(SN.XII.21). This description provides a more fluid image of the interplay of interdependent forces.

The formal complexity of the series is shown by its synopsis as given in the Suttas (SN.XII.23), called this/that conditionality (*idappaccayatā*):

1. When this is, that is.
2. From the arising of this comes the arising of that.
3. When this isn't, that isn't.
4. From the cessation of this comes the cessation of that.

As a theory of causation, this formula is both linear and synchronic. The linear pattern (taking 2 and 4 as a pair) connects events over time; the synchronic pattern (1 and 3) connects phenomena in the present moment. This combination of two causal patterns—influences from the past interacting with those occurring in the immediate present—combines Gautama's insights into the immediate results of karma, which he gained in bringing his mind to dhyāna, with his vision of the long-term results of karma that he saw in the second cognition on the night of his Awakening. It also accounts for the complexity and diversity of causal explanations given in the Pali Canon. At the same time, these two causal patterns distinguish the Buddhist interpretation of causality from the deterministic teachings of some of its early rivals. Even though the past may influence the present, the possibility of modifying that influence through present action creates an opening for free will. At the same time, however, events are not totally random: Each specific *this* in experience is connected to a specific *that*. Experience is regular enough to be mastered as a skill.

Furthermore, the combination of the two patterns explains features of Gautama's Awakening itself. On the one hand, the synchronic pattern of causality explains why he experienced the Deathless at the very moment he was able to overcome ignorance of the Four Noble Truths and did not have to wait for some future time for his previous karma to run out. On the other hand, the linear pattern explains why he did not die at the moment of Awakening. Although he no longer created any karma, he lived out the remainder of this life on the strength of previous karma. Old karma entered the process of dependent co-arising at the conditions of name-and-form or the six sense fields, but with no ignorance or craving to reiterate the process, it could go no further than feeling.

The teaching of dependent co-arising resembles a medical diagnosis in several ways. By showing that the ailment depends on a series of conditions, dependent co-arising indicates the points at which the series can be broken and a cure achieved. Craving and ignorance are the two most important links in this regard, and in the next chapter we will analyze the duties appropriate to each of the Four Noble Truths in order to show how the overcoming of ignorance and the abandoning of craving must occur simultaneously. In pointing out these causal links, the pattern of dependent co-arising counteracts the theory that suffering is a fortuitous happening for which there would be no remedy. It also opposes the view that the ultimate cause of suffering is some entity outside the process, such as a god or an immutable soul.

The Suttas state that dependent co-arising inextricably entails suffering and stress. Happiness based on causal conditions is inherently unstable and unreliable.

However, although there is no refuge to be found within the interdependent dance of causally produced things, one can use the dynamics of dependent co-arising to follow a path to gain release from causality to the unfabricated sphere, and thus beyond suffering altogether.

The formula of conditionality gives a hint of how this might be done. If present experience is composed of the results both of past actions (intentions) and present actions (intentions), what would happen if no present intentions were fabricated by the mind? A Sutta (MN.137) recommends bringing the mind to ever more subtle levels of equanimity and equilibrium until it reaches a point called "nonfashioning" (*atammayatā*), in which no present intention is added to what is experienced. The skill here, of course, is how to drop the intention not to have an intention, and yet not replace it with another intention. This is one of the reasons why Buddhist teachings place so much emphasis on tactical skill. When the skill is mastered, experience of the present moment disbands, followed by a realization of nirvāṇa.

1.4.2 Nirvāṇa

The word *nirvāṇa* (in Pali, *nibbāna*) literally means extinguishing (as of a fire). Why the Buddha would use such a term to describe the goal of his teachings has long puzzled Western scholars, largely because they have viewed it in light of their own notions of what happens to fire when it goes out. Viewed in light of the physics of the Buddha's time, however, the term is much less puzzling.

Modern etymology derives the word *nirvāṇa* from verbal roots meaning "blowing out." A Pali commentary, however, derives it from roots meaning "unbinding." This relates to the fact that the Suttas described fire as being in a state of agitation, dependency, and entrapment as it burned, then growing calm, independent, and released as it went out. A number of Pali idioms reflect these notions: To start a fire, one had to "grasp" the fire-potential latent in the fuel; when a fire went out, it was "freed."

Thus the term *nirvāṇa* carried no connotations of "going out of existence." In fact, there were occasions when the Buddha used ancient Vedic notions of fire—which held that fire did not go out of existence when it was extinguished, but rather went into a diffuse, indeterminate, latent state—to illustrate the notion that a person who has attained the goal is beyond all description. Just as a fire that has gone out cannot be described as having gone in any particular direction, so the person who has attained the goal cannot be predicated as existent, nonexistent, both, or neither. As for the experience of nirvāṇa, it is so free from limitation that there is no means of saying whether there is a person having the experience. There is simply the experience, in and of itself.

Thus, in the time of the Buddha, the word *nirvāṇa* conveyed primarily the notion of freedom. As experienced in this life, it meant freedom from any attachment or agitation in terms of passion, aversion, or delusion; after death—when the results of all karma created prior to one's Awakening had finally worked themselves out, and input from the senses cooled away—it meant freedom from even the most basic notions or limitations that make up the experience of the describable universe. Other names the Buddha used metaphorically to indicate the goal (there are more than thirty in all) carry similar connotations, implying a subtle experience of utter transcendence and freedom from change, disturbance, danger, insecurity, or unhappiness of any sort. Other, more technical names, include consciousness without feature or surface, the sphere where the six sense fields cease, and the Deathless.

Because nirvāṇa is unfabricated, it is not divided into categories. The Buddha rarely described it, for description would count as a perception to which one could easily become attached, thus blocking the possibility of experiencing the unfabricated. Language, being fabricated, is adequate for describing the fabricated, but inadequate for describing the unfabricated. Even terms such as *all, exists, doesn't exist, both exists and doesn't exist,* and *neither exists nor doesn't exist,* the Buddha said, could apply only to the fabricated. What could be usefully said about the unfabricated was that it transcended suffering and stress, that it was worth experiencing, and that there was a method for experiencing it.

Thus the Pali texts are quite clear that the fabricated and unfabricated are radically separate. Nirvāṇa is thus not the ground of being or the source of the universe. Duḥkha (suffering) is inherent in the stressful nature of fabricated phenomena, whereas the unfabricated is totally free from suffering. Suffering could not possibly be produced by absolute freedom from suffering; because the nature of conditioning is such that causes are in turn influenced by their effects, the unfabricated could not itself function as a condition.

At the same time, the practice leading to nirvāṇa does not cause nirvāṇa. It simply opens the way there. This may explain why the practice is called a path. Just as a path to a park does not cause the park, and may not even resemble the park, nevertheless one can get to the park by following the path.

1.4.3 The Awakening as Paradigm

As mentioned previously, there is no way of knowing how historically accurate the accounts of the Buddha's Awakening may be. Nevertheless, the accounts themselves have been of great historical importance. Their content has provided a religious ideal for many millions of individuals. Some, inspired by Gautama's first and second cognitions, have tried to improve their lot in the mundane realm by creating good karma. Others, inspired by the third cognition, have tried to tease out its philosophical implications for understanding reality and the mind. Still others, inspired by the account of nirvāṇa, have tried to see if they, too, might put an end to suffering. The interconnections among the various stages of the Awakening have ensured a measure of symbiosis between these groups of people. Those who do not feel ready to bow out of saṁsāra have been inspired to give support to those who do; those determined to leave saṁsāra have responded to this support with the gift of teaching. At the same time, the tensions among the stages of Awakening have foreshadowed some of the tensions that have developed over the centuries within this symbiotic relationship.

In formal terms, the account of the Awakening has had a pervasive effect on Buddhist thought. Buddhist writings fall into the modes of the three cognitions: narrative, cosmological, and "empty," that is, analyses of immediate experience. As mentioned previously, the Sutta accounts of the first two modes tend to be sketchy, and aim at interesting the reader/listener in the third mode. For example, in the Sutta used as a basis for our narrative of the Awakening (MN.19), the Buddha ends by encouraging his monks to practice dhyāna for the sake of putting an end to suffering. Another Sutta (DN.26) ends its cosmological sketch of kingly power with a strong dose of saṁvega and a reminder that a monastic's highest power lies in overcoming Māra and destroying the āsravas. In what appear to be later texts—both within the Pali Canon and elsewhere—there is an attempt to fill in the sketches, providing complete narrative cycles of the Buddha's many lives along with those of his disciples, comprehensive maps of the cosmos, and systematic analyses of mental and physical phenomena. Of special interest in the narrative mode are the many first-person accounts of Awakening experiences and of individuals' paths to those experiences. In this respect, Buddhist writings are unique in Indian literature, where first-person accounts of this sort are fairly rare. This genre can easily be traced to the Buddhist understanding of karma—great insights come from what people *do*—and to early canonical accounts in which the Buddha's Awakening is presented in first-person terms.

Another legacy of the Awakening account is that the different modes of the three cognitions deal in such different terms. As we have noted, the first cognition deals in terms of "self" and "others"; the second, in terms of "living beings" and "cosmos"; the third, in terms devoid of those concepts. Some Buddhist writers have attempted to overcome the inconsistencies and paradoxes among these modes, trying to reduce everything to a single mode of ultimate truth. Others, content to let the paradoxes stand, actually flaunt them in recognition that words are to be used as tools to get beyond words. Although these two impulses head in opposing directions, they are both shaped by tensions present in the narrative of the Awakening. Just as Buddhism started with the Buddha's Awakening, Buddhist literature can be said to have its seeds in the Awakening account.

2

The Buddha as Teacher and Power Figure

2.1 THE RESPONSE TO THE AWAKENED ONE

The Pali Canon informs us that the Buddha gained Awakening at age 35, and then taught the Dharma for another 45 years before passing away at the age of 80. The texts reporting the events of his teaching career focus not only on what he taught and how he taught it, but also on how others received his teachings. Some people and devas treated his teachings with respect; others did not. Among those who showed him respect, there were essentially two responses. Some, treating the Buddha as a figure of power, simply followed the etiquette of respect commonly shown to religious figures in India at the time. Others, treating him as a teacher as well, put his teachings into practice to the point where some of them gained Awakening themselves.

Modern Western interpretations of the early response to the Buddha's teachings usually assume a sharp divide between these two roles—power figure and teacher—and argue as to which of the two was more authentic. Some, focusing on the rationality of the teachings reported in the texts, view the Buddha primarily as a philosopher whose heritage was vulgarized into a religion when absorbed into the cultic mentality of people at large. Others—focusing on the miracles present in the earliest Buddhist narratives, and the cultic nature of the earliest archeological evidence of Buddhist practices—argue that the Buddha was primarily a figure of religious power whose teachings, much like those of Jesus, were later distorted into a systematic philosophy at odds with the original message.

There is reason, however, to doubt whether the radical split between philosophy and religion posited by both sides of this question applies in the Buddhist case. Although the Buddhist tradition reports a certain tension between the two ways of viewing the Buddha, it sees no sharp divide. Part of the reason is specific to Indian culture. Traditionally, a student not only took lessons from a teacher, but also acted as his attendant and treated him with a clearly defined etiquette of respect. In return, the teacher not only shared his knowledge, but also provided the student with "safety in all directions"—which, if he had psychic powers, was an especially valuable part of the relationship. Thus the teacher was both instructor and protector. A passage in the Pali Canon (DN.31) indicates that Buddhists adopted this traditional attitude of the roles of student and teacher, and passages in the Vinaya flesh out these mutual duties for Buddhist monastics in great detail.

Not all śramaṇa schools adopted these traditional attitudes toward respect. When Pali Suttas describe rival śramaṇa schools, they often criticize them for being disrespectful not only to outsiders but also among themselves. Students are shown being disrespectful to their teachers. Their group meetings are described as raucous, noisy, and out of control. All of this is then contrasted with the way Buddhists conduct their meetings in mutual courtesy and respect. This suggests that the Buddhists were free to reject the common customs of respect but consciously chose not to.

This choice is directly related to the principle of causality at the heart of the Buddha's Awakening. If experience were totally predetermined or random, respect would play no role in the pursuit of happiness, for it would have no effect on the success of one's pursuit. But given the Buddhist view of causality, in which true happiness is to be found by skillfully mastering a complex causal pattern, an attitude of respect for those who have already mastered that pattern makes perfect sense. Without the proper level of respect, one cannot open one's mind to learn from them, while they—sensing disrespect—might feel disinclined to share their valuable knowledge. And given the gulf between success in their skill—the bliss of nirvāṇa—and failure—endless rounds of suffering through birth after birth, death after death—it is easy to understand why anyone hoping for success would treat his or her teachers with a level of respect edging into reverence and veneration.

So to understand the Buddha's teaching career and the traditions that it engendered, it is important to understand the varied ways in which his role as teacher shaded over into that of protector; and how his followers' respect for him as a teacher shaded over into respect for him as a figure of power.

For this purpose, the Pali Canon is the more useful of the two sources we have been using so far. Aśvaghoṣa's main concern in portraying the Buddha's teaching career is to refute the various Brahmanical philosophical positions extant in his day. Thus he emphasizes the philosophical side of the Buddha's teaching role almost—albeit not entirely—to the exclusion of the religious side. The Pali Canon, however, offers a wealth of detail on both the philosophical and religious sides of the Buddha's teaching role and the reactions of his students. Thus our discussion here will focus on the Pali sources.

Although the Pali Canon is filled with incidents from the Buddha's teaching career, they contain only two extended narratives from that period. One (Mv.I) covers the year or so immediately following the Buddha's Awakening; the other (DN.16), the last year before his *parinirvāṇa* (final passing away). Neither is a simple chronicle of events. Rather, each serves a purpose. Thus, to understand what is included in these narratives and how it is presented, we must keep their original purposes in mind.

2.2 THE BUDDHA BEGINS TEACHING

The first narrative—by connecting the Awakening with the Buddha's placing the Sangha in charge of ordaining its new members—is aimed at legitimizing the Sangha's authority as an institution. Its first order of business is to establish the legitimacy of the Buddha's Awakening and his ability to induce it in others. Beginning with his contemplation of dependent co-arising on the night of the Awakening, it proceeds to the four subsequent weeks, during which he sat in meditation for one-week intervals at four places near the Bodhi tree, experiencing the bliss of release. During each interval memorable events occurred, most of them showing that the spirit world was the first to recognize the Buddha's achievement. For instance, a deity directs two merchants—relatives in a previous life—to give alms to the Buddha; the Four Great Kings provide him with a bowl into which to receive the alms; the merchants then take refuge in the Buddha and his Dharma. A nāga coils up around the Buddha, covering him with his hood, to protect him from a storm.

At the end of the four weeks, the Buddha contemplates the subtlety of the Dharma he has discovered, and—reflecting that humanity is overcome with passion and aversion—inclines his mind against trying to teach them. Immediately, Sahampati Brahmā leaves his Brahmā world and, appearing before the Buddha on bended knee, entreats him to teach: There are beings with only a little dust in their eyes, he argues, who will suffer if they do not hear the Dharma but will benefit if they do. The law of karma is such that it is possible to help other beings; and the specific karma of some beings is such that they are ripe for a Buddha's help. The Buddha then surveys the world with his Buddha-eye and perceives its beings as a pool of lotuses: Some of the lotuses will stay immersed in the water, some have reached the surface, while some have risen up out of the water and are undefiled by it. These last are the few who will understand the Dharma. Out of compassion, he decides to teach.

2.2.1 The First Encounter

The Buddha first thought of telling his two former teachers, but a deity informed him that Ārāḍa Kālāma had died a week before, and Udraka Rāmaputra the previous night. The Buddha confirmed this with his superknowledge, then thought of the five mendicants who had been his attendants throughout his austerities. With his divine eye he saw that they were now near Varanasi, so he set out to teach them the way to Awakening.

On the road he met an ascetic who, remarking on his clear eyes and radiant complexion, asked who his teacher was. The Buddha declared that he had no teacher; he was a victor who had attained nirvāṇa and was on his way to "beat the drum of the Deathless." The ascetic answered, *hupeyya*—"it may be so" or "let it be so"—shook his head, and walked away. Gautama's first proclamation of his Buddhahood was disregarded, but his presence was such that even a nonbeliever was stopped in his tracks.

2.2.2 Setting the Wheel of Dharma in Motion

The Buddha walked by stages to Varanasi, about 130 miles from Bodhgaya. Four miles north of the city, in the Deer Park at Sarnath, the five mendicants saw him coming and resolved not to show more than minimal courtesy to the backslider who had taken to the easy life. But his charisma was too strong for them. Against their own resolve they saluted him, took his bowl and robe, prepared his seat, and gave him implements with which to wash his feet. Again, the effect of his presence preceded any word.

Still, they called him "Friend Gautama," but he told them not to do so, as he was now a *Tathāgata* (see the Glossary); an arhat (one worthy of reverence); rightly self-awakened. He declared that he had attained the Deathless; that he was going to teach the Dharma; that if they practiced as taught, they would quickly realize it for themselves. The five were dubious, protesting that one who had quit striving could not have attained the transcendent. The Buddha denied that he had given up striving, reasserted his claim, and asked them if he had ever made such a claim before. Eventually they admitted that he hadn't, and so agreed to listen receptively.

The Blessed One began by condemning each of two extremes, saying that sensual indulgence is low, domestic, common, ignoble, and useless, whereas self-torture is painful as well as ignoble and useless. The Tathāgata, by avoiding these extremes, had discovered the Middle Way that produces vision (literally, an eye: *cakṣu*) and knowledge, leading to peace, higher knowledge, Awakening, and nirvāṇa. This Middle Way is the Noble Eightfold Path: (1) right view, (2) right resolve, (3) right speech, (4) right action, (5) right livelihood, (6) right effort, (7) right mindfulness, and (8) right concentration.

The Buddha then declared the Four Noble Truths, the framework for right view. The first is the truth of duḥkha (suffering), experienced in birth, aging, death, grief, lamentation, pain, distress and despair, conjunction with the hated, separation from the dear, and not getting what one wants. In short, the five skandhas (aggregates) when conjoined with clinging are suffering. The second truth is that of the origination of suffering: the thirst or craving that leads to renewed becoming, endowed with passion and delight for this thing and that; in other words, craving for sensuality, for becoming, and for nonbecoming. The third is the truth of the cessation of suffering: When, through dispassion, craving ceases and is relinquished, suffering ceases. The fourth is the truth of the path of practice leading to cessation of suffering, the Noble Eightfold Path.

Each of these truths entails a task. Suffering must be thoroughly understood, the origination of suffering abandoned, cessation realized, and the Noble Eightfold Path developed. The Buddha testified that he attained unexcelled, right self-awakening when—and only when—he had acquired purified true knowledge and vision of these Four Noble Truths as they actually are, and had completed the task appropriate to each. As a result, he knew that his release was unassailable, that this was to be his last birth, and that for him there was no further becoming.

The five mendicants welcomed the discourse, and one of them, Kauṇḍinya, while listening to it, acquired the pure Dharma-eye, seeing that whatever is subject to origination is subject to cessation. This was a momentous incident in the history of Buddhism. It indicated that the Buddha could teach the Dharma to others in such a way that they would learn from it and taste the results for themselves. As a result, the Buddha declared, "Kauṇḍinya knows! Kauṇḍinya knows!" Kauṇḍinya asked the Buddha for full ordination, which he received with the simple formula, "Come, bhikṣu, the Dharma is well proclaimed. Follow the chaste course to the complete end of suffering." Thus he became the first member of the *Bhikṣu Sangha*—the Order of Monks.

The texts assert that at the conclusion of the discourse, the earth deities announced to the higher heavens that the Buddha had set rolling the unsurpassed wheel of Dharma that could not be stopped by anyone in the cosmos. On hearing this, the higher levels of deities took up the proclamation until it reached the Brahmā worlds. The earth quaked, and a dazzling light illuminated the cosmos momentarily, indicating that the first teaching of the Dharma, like the other major events in the Buddha's life, was cosmic in its importance.

The reference to the wheel of Dharma is a play on words. On the one hand, it refers to a passage in the discourse in which the Buddha collates two sets of variables—the Four Noble Truths and the three levels of knowledge appropriate to each: knowing the truth, knowing the task it entails, and knowing that one has completed the task. He then lists all 12 permutations of the two sets (not to be confused with the 12 conditions of dependent co-arising). This sort of schema, in Indian legal and philosophical traditions, is called a wheel. In this case it has 12 spokes, uniting at the hub of knowledge and vision of things as they actually are. Early Indian sculptures of the Dharma wheel have many more than 12 spokes, however, which may be their way of indicating in a stable medium that the wheel is in motion.

The wheel also has political connotations. The wheel-turning monarch is one whose power is so universally acknowledged in the Indian subcontinent that the wheel of his chariot can drive unimpeded from one ocean to the other. The implication here is that the Buddha's authority as a religious leader is equivalent to the power of such a monarch; his first discourse is the establishment of that authority. Later movements in Buddhism adopted the turning-of-the-wheel image to indicate what they regarded as momentous developments in the Buddhist tradition—the rise of the Perfection of Discernment school, the Yogācāra school, and Vajrayāna—but more conservative traditions recognize only one turning of the Dharma wheel, the discourse we have just reviewed.

On the days immediately following the first discourse, the other four mendicants took turns begging alms for the group and listening to the Buddha's instruction. Very soon all four attained the Dharma-eye and received admission to the Sangha.

The Buddha then preached a discourse on the five skandhas, briefly mentioned earlier under the First Noble Truth. Here he switched from the declaratory style of his first teaching to a dialogue. With regard to each of the five skandhas, he asked: Is it constant or inconstant? Inconstant. Is what is inconstant easeful or stressful? Stressful. And is it appropriate to view what is inconstant and stressful as "This is me. This is my self. This is what I am"? No.

During this dialogue, the five monks became disenchanted with and dispassionate toward the five skandhas. Thus freed from the āsravas, they too were now arhats.

2.3 AN ANALYSIS OF THE FIRST DISCOURSE

All Buddhist traditions refer to the Buddha as a doctor who treats the spiritual ills of the world (M.75), and this reference provides a convenient metaphor for understanding the form and content of his teaching. To understand the metaphor's implications, we should look at how an ideal doctor was viewed in the Buddha's time. A Vinaya text (Mv.VIII) contains a portrait of such a doctor—Jīvaka Komārabhacca, the Buddha's own physician—whom it praises for his tactical skill, not only in knowing cures for unusual diseases, but also in getting his patients to undergo difficult treatments. So it is not surprising that the texts often extol the Buddha's skill in parallel ways: He knew not only the cure for suffering, but also the means for inducing others to take it. But in defining true health—nirvāṇa—in such absolute terms, he was presented with two tactical challenges that no medical doctor ever had to face.

The first was that, because his listeners had never experienced this health, they would have to take the most important point of his teaching on faith. Thus he first had to win their trust and respect. In the case of the five mendicants, he prefaced his teachings by insisting on his Awakened status, for only if his listeners were receptive to his words would they benefit from them. In other cases (see Section 2.4.1), he had to subdue his listeners' pride with a display of psychic powers. In either event, his motive seems not to have been vanity but rather a desire to prepare his listeners to receive the doctrine. He did not teach until his listeners were ready to admit his integrity and give his words a fair hearing.

2.3.1 The Four Noble Truths

The Buddha's second tactical challenge was that, because nirvāṇa was unfabricated, it played no role within the causal process. Absolute health could thus not be used to lead to absolute health. This meant that he had to find a way to utilize fabricated experience to lead to the unfabricated. He did this with his formulation of the Four Noble Truths. Dividing fabricated experience into three truths—the first (suffering), the second (craving), and the fourth (the path to the cessation of suffering)—he left the unfabricated as the third (the cessation of suffering). Then he assigned a task for each: Suffering was to be comprehended, its cause abandoned, its cessation realized, and the path to its cessation developed.

What this means is that the Four Noble Truths, together with their respective tasks, are not simply propositions. Instead, they are phenomenological categories—a framework for classifying the processes of experience as they are directly present to the awareness—strategically designed to lead to an experience of the unfabricated. And because the fabricated is transcended in the experience of nirvāṇa, this further means that when the cure is effected, the medicine of the Four Noble Truths can be placed aside. The Suttas illustrate this point with another analogy: After using a raft to cross a river, one would be foolish to carry it over dry land. Instead, one should put it down.

To understand how this happens in practice, we can look at the truths one by one.

The formula for dependent co-arising states that craving acts as a condition for clinging, which is equated with suffering. If, however, the mind can be liberated from its ignorance that the objects of craving are unworthy of clinging, the cycle can be broken. These objects are precisely where the First Noble Truth is aimed: the five skandhas (aggregates), which cover the whole of describable reality (DN.15). As the brief formula for the first truth states, clinging to any of these five aggregates constitutes the essence of duḥkha. Duḥkha is a term with no one equivalent in the English language. Suffering, stress, pain, disease, and distress come close, but whatever the equivalent chosen, the important point is that the skandhas are unworthy of clinging because they provide no unalloyed happiness.

Buddhism has frequently been charged with pessimism because of its emphasis on suffering, but this charge misses the fact that the first truth is part of a strategy to attain freedom from suffering. In this sense, the Buddha was similar to a doctor, focusing on the disease he wanted to cure. Contrary to a popular misperception, he never stated that life is suffering, nor did he deny that life has its measure of happiness. Still, the happiness of the human and heavenly worlds is stressful in that it is inconstant and impermanent. Because it is stressful, it does not lie completely under one's control, and thus does not deserve to be identified as one's self, as "me" or "mine." These three characteristics—inconstancy, stressfulness, and "not-selfness"—lie at the heart of the diagnosis provided by the First Noble Truth. If one clings to anything marked with these characteristics, suffering follows.

Like the teaching on suffering, the teaching on not-self has been controversial from early on. Opponents of Buddhism have regarded it as a metaphysical doctrine denying the existence of a self or a soul, and even many Buddhists (including Aśvaghoṣa—see Section 4.5) have come to view it in that light. In the Suttas, however, the Buddha pointedly refuses to answer the metaphysical question as to whether or not there is a self. He simply points out the inconsistencies of various self or soul theories and states the rewards of focusing on the not-selfness of the five skandhas. In fact, he asserts that the belief "I have no self" is as much an obstacle to Awakening as the belief "I have a self" (MN.2). To believe in a permanent self, he says, is to deny the possibility of spiritual self-change. To deny the existence of a self is to deny the worth of a moral or religious life. To cling to the perception even of an impermanent self is to cling to one of the five skandhas, which would prevent a realization of the unfabricated that comes only when the skandhas are relinquished.

Thus the Suttas suggest that a person seeking Awakening should entirely drop the question of the existence of the self and focus instead on the categories of the Four Noble Truths so as to avoid the pitfalls entailed in any view asserting the existence or nonexistence of the self. For a person well advanced on the

Path, the Buddha says, the question of whether or not there is a self simply would not occur. Such a person would be more involved in observing phenomena as they arise and pass away. All of this indicates that the not-self doctrine, like the teaching on suffering, is to be regarded as a strategy for undercutting craving and clinging in the formula of dependent co-arising. The meditator is taught simply to observe the five skandhas as they occur and to let go of them by noting that they are not-self. This would open the way for the experience of the unfabricated, to which labels of "self" or "not-self"—which, as perceptions, would count as a skandha—would not apply.

As stated in the first discourse, the First Noble Truth—suffering—is to be comprehended. Once it is comprehended, the Second Noble Truth—craving—has no object to latch onto and so can be abandoned. Here we must note that the word craving covers not all desire, but only the desire leading to further becoming. (It should be noted, though, that craving for nonbecoming—which later commentaries define either as annihilation or a freezing of the processes of becoming—can produce further becoming as well.) The desire to escape from the cycles of becoming and nonbecoming is part of the Path; without such a desire, there would be no motivation to follow the Path or reach nirvāṇa. When nirvāṇa is reached, though, even this desire is dropped, just as a desire to walk to a park is dropped when the park is reached.

Once the Second Noble Truth is abandoned, the third—cessation of suffering—is realized. "Cessation of suffering" is a description of the goal of the practice, but its negative form does not mean that the goal is experienced in negative terms. The standard metaphor is one of cooling. Just because cold is technically the absence of heat, that does not mean that it cannot be positively enjoyed. This point is supported by the many passages in which noble disciples express in intensely joyous terms the freedom of having reached the goal.

This goal is realized by developing the fourth truth, the Noble Eightfold Path, which can be subsumed under a shorter formula, the Three Trainings: discernment (right view and resolve), virtue (right speech, action, and livelihood), and concentration (right effort, mindfulness, and concentration). We have already seen all three as strands in the Awakening. Discernment here means clear understanding of the Four Noble Truths and the consequent intention to act skillfully in light of the law of karma. Virtue goes beyond mere self-denial because it involves developing positive qualities—such as mindfulness, compassion, and understanding—that prevent acting on harmful intentions. Concentration includes the proper effort and mindfulness leading to the dhyānas.

The Three Trainings are mutually dependent. Some Suttas portray a linear progression among the three, with virtue leading to concentration leading to discernment, whereas others describe a spiraling or interdependent pattern. *Right view* on the preliminary level, as mentioned in Section 1.4.1, begins with the belief that skillful and unskillful deeds bear fruit in good and bad results, that there is a next world after death, and that there are priests and contemplatives who, practicing rightly, proclaim that world having directly experienced it through their meditation. *Right resolve* follows naturally on this belief because the quality of an act is determined by the intention motivating it. Anyone who intends to act skillfully must begin by resolving to abstain from sensual desire, from ill will, and from harming others or oneself; these three resolves form the definition of this factor of the Path.

The training in virtue follows from these three resolves. *Right speech* means abstaining from four unskillful verbal deeds: lying, divisive tale-bearing, harsh or abusive language, and idle chatter. *Right action* means abstaining from three unskillful bodily deeds. All the early texts agree on two of the three—taking life and stealing—but disagree as to whether the third is sexual misconduct (such as adultery) or sexual intercourse of any sort. *Right livelihood* is abstention from occupations that harm living beings—for example, selling weapons, liquor, poison, slaves, or livestock; butchering, hunting, fishing; soldiering; fraud; soothsaying; and usury.

When one's speech, actions, and livelihood are free from harm, the mind is free from remorse, and this opens the way for the smooth practice of concentration. This practice begins with *right effort,* which means persistence in avoiding and eliminating evil and unskillful mental qualities, and nurturing skillful ones in their place. This involves right mindfulness, inasmuch as mindfulness is the primary skillful mental quality, necessary for the development of such qualities as discernment, vigor, serenity, concentration, and equanimity. *Right mindfulness* consists of focusing on any one of four foundations or frames of reference: the body in and of itself, feelings in and of themselves, mind-states in and of themselves, and mental qualities in and of themselves. In the beginning stages of the practice, this means simply observing events as they occur in the course of one's attempts to master concentration. As one's mastery grows, one gains a clearer perception of causal patterns underlying these events. This provides an understanding of how unskillful mental qualities may be undercut, and skillful ones fostered. Acting on this understanding leads to fuller mastery of the four dhyānas, which constitute *right concentration.* Right concentration in turn leads to a transcendent level of right view—insight in terms of the Four Noble Truths—and the Path spirals to a higher level.

The practical relationship between dhyāna and transcendent right view has been a major point of controversy in Buddhist philosophical and meditation circles over the centuries. The Pali Suttas present the following scenario:

The proper practice of dhyāna develops two qualities in tandem: tranquility (*śamatha*) and insight (*vipaśyanā,* Pali: *vipassanā*). The meditation method that the Suttas recommend most frequently and in most detail—mindfulness of in-and-out breathing (MN.118)—illustrates how this is done. The meditator is to find a solitary spot, sit cross-legged, and begin focusing on the breath by noticing whether it is long or short. He or she then develops a whole-body awareness while focusing on the breath, and then lets the breath grow calm. At this point, if the focus is steadily maintained, feelings of rapture and ease arise. These the meditator allows to permeate and suffuse the entire body, leading to the states of dhyāna that constitute right concentration. When the rapture and ease subside with the attainment of the fourth dhyāna, the meditator is left with a bright awareness filling the body in a state of pure mindfulness and equanimity.

At this point, attention shifts to the sense of bright awareness together with the breath, rather than just to the breath itself. The meditator then works at developing skill in steadying, gladdening, and releasing the mind in the various stages of absorption. This provides a solid internal basis of pleasure and equanimity that the meditator can use to pry away any attachment to sensual pleasures.

The meditator then turns to reflect on the processes of dhyāna itself. One text (AN.V.28) describes an intermediate reflective stage of absorption, in which a meditator can analyze the various mental components of each stage of dhyāna without destroying the integrity of the stage, and some of the texts (MN.111; AN.IX.36) indicate that talented meditators can do this in great detail. Further contemplation brings about a realization of the impermanence, stress, and lack of self not only in the pleasures of mental absorption but also in the insights arising from reflection, all of which count as subtle forms of the five skandhas. This realization leads the mind to perceive these phenomena in terms of the Four Noble Truths, inducing a sense of dispassion, cessation, and letting go. Ultimately, even right view and the other factors of the Path are abandoned as the last step in gaining total release. One Sutta (AN.X.93) makes the point that right view is the only form of view whose development leads to the abandoning of attachment to all views, itself included. Thus is the raft set aside. Once these subtlest attachments are gone, no fetters remain to bind one to saṁsāra, and the mind experiences Awakening.

2.3.2 The Stages of Awakening

The Suttas describe some of the Buddha's disciples as becoming arhats (attaining total release from saṁsāra) immediately in a single experience of Awakening, whereas others attain total release in as many as four stages. These in ascending order are: stream-entry (i.e., entering the "stream" to nirvāṇa), once-returning, nonreturning, and arhatship. The texts, while terse about the content of these Awakening experiences, are explicit about their function in all three modes of Buddhist discourse. In terms of the emptiness mode, each awakening experience cuts through specific fetters binding the mind to saṁsāra: stream-entry cuts through self-identity views, uncertainty, and attachment to precepts and practices; once-returning weakens passion, aversion, and delusion; nonreturning cuts through sensual passion and irritation; and arhatship cuts through passion for form, passion for formlessness, conceit, restlessness, and ignorance. In terms of the cosmological and narrative modes, stream-enterers (*srotāpanna*) are destined to reach total Awakening in no more than seven lifetimes without falling below the human level in the interim; once-returners will return to this world once more before attaining total nirvāṇa; nonreturners will be reborn in the Pure Abodes, there to attain total nirvāṇa without returning to this world; and arhats, totally awakened, are utterly freed from the processes of renewed becoming and birth. Kauṇḍinya, on hearing the Buddha's first discourse, became a stream-enterer through the arising of the Dharma-eye (the realization that all things subject to origination are subject to cessation). Other texts (Mv.I.23.5) make clear that this vision involves a glimpse of the Deathless. Only in contradistinction to what is not subject to origination would the concept of "all things subject to origination" occur to the mind. In Kauṇḍinya's case, as with the rest of the five mendicants, he did not have to wait the full seven lifetimes to become an arhat, for he gained total Awakening only a few days later upon listening to the Buddha's second discourse.

2.4 THE SPREAD OF THE RELIGION

After the second discourse there were six arhats in the world, counting the Buddha himself. Soon Yaśas, son of a rich merchant of Varanasi, waking up during the night in a state of anxiety, went out to Sarnath, where the Buddha comforted him and taught him a graduated Dharma suitable for lay people, namely, the merits of generosity and virtue, the rewards of generosity and virtue to be enjoyed in heaven, the drawbacks of even heavenly sensual pleasures, and the blessings of renunciation. Then he taught the Four Noble Truths to the young man, who soon afterward attained arhatship and took full ordination as a monk. Meanwhile, Yaśas's father came looking for his son, happened to find the Buddha, listened to his teaching, attained the Dharma-eye, and took refuge in the Triple Gem—the Buddha, Dharma, and Sangha—for life. Thus he became the first *upāsaka* (lay devotee) in the strict sense, inasmuch as the two merchants who had brought offerings to the Buddha at Bodhgaya had not been able to take refuge in the Sangha prior to its existence. Eventually, Yaśas's mother and sisters took the Three Refuges and became the first *upāsikā* (female lay devotees).

At present, the word *Sangha* is used in the West as a collective term for all Buddhists, but the Pali Canon uses the word *parisā* (Sanskrit, *pariṣad*) for the larger Buddhist community—the monks, nuns, lay men, and lay women who have taken the Three Refuges—reserving "Sangha" for a more restricted use. In Pali usage, the Sangha in its *ārya* (ideal) sense consists of all people, lay or ordained, who have acquired the pure Dharma-eye, gaining at least a glimpse of the Deathless. In a conventional sense, Sangha denotes the communities of monks and nuns. The two meanings overlap but are not necessarily identical. Some members of the ideal Sangha are not ordained; some monastics have yet to acquire the Dharma-eye. When Yaśas's family took refuge in the Sangha, all of the bhikṣus in the conventional Sangha were also members of the ideal Sangha, so for them the two senses of the word completely overlapped. This became the standard formula for taking refuge, even as the two meanings of the term began to diverge in the course of the Buddha's career. When the divergence became noticeable, the standard formula for taking refuge continued to refer to the conventional Sangha, whereas the formula defining faith and conviction in the Three Refuges was worded to refer specifically to Sangha in the ideal sense.

2.4.1 Taking Refuge

The act of taking refuge, in traditional Indian culture, was a formal act of allegiance, submitting to the preeminence and claiming the protection of a powerful patron, whether human or divine. As this act became standardized in its Buddhist form, it did not necessarily imply an understanding or acceptance of the basic points of the Buddha's Dharma; nor did it mean aligning oneself exclusively with the Triple Gem. Some people took refuge in the Triple Gem only after an Awakening experience sparked by the Buddha's words, whereas many others took refuge after a short dialogue that touched on none of the essential points of his teaching. The true meaning of refuge is best indicated by the standard formula used to announce it: After stating that one was taking refuge, one asked to be remembered as a follower who had gone for refuge in the Triple Gem for life. The request to be remembered indicates the nature of what "refuge" meant: a request for protection. As mentioned earlier, the traditional Indian view of the student–teacher relationship included the teacher's duty to protect the student. In announcing oneself as a follower through taking refuge, one was asking the Triple Gem to take on the duty of protector.

The Buddha's role as protector, as depicted in the early portions of the Pali Canon, is complex. A predominant theme in the early texts is that one is one's own true protector (*nātha*). Only in later parts of the Canon, which we will discuss in the next chapter, is the Buddha explicitly called a nātha. Still, the early texts do frequently show him acting as a protector, even if they do not use the word. And because people can be taught, the idea of self as protector and Buddha as protector are not entirely at odds. In the most general sense, the Buddha gives protection by formulating teachings that protect anyone who follows them from the dangers of bad karma. In the words of a Pali verse, the Dharma protects those who practice it. For instance, one passage (AN.IV.28) states that anyone who follows the four customs of the noble ones—having the right attitude toward one's clothing, food, and shelter, and taking delight in developing skillful qualities and abandoning unskillful ones—will not be conquered by discontent in any of the four directions. In another passage (MN.66), a monk—citing many amusing mishaps that befell the monks before the Vinaya rules were formulated, such as stumbling over cows while on almsround at night—details how the Buddha, through formulating the rules, has given protection to any monk who follows them.

However, the early texts also show the Buddha giving protection of a more personal sort. In many passages, when he detects through telepathy that a monk is about to go off-course in his meditation, he uses his psychic powers to appear right in front of the monk to give him the needed instruction. There are also passages in which the Buddha teaches the Dharma to sick monks who, as they reflect on the teaching, immediately recover. Perhaps the most famous instance of the Buddha's personal protection is when, with a show of psychic powers, he induces the murderous bandit Aṅgulimāla (MN.86) to give up his life of crime and eventually to become an arhat, thus protecting him from staying in the round of rebirth where he otherwise would have boiled in hell.

Thus, although the texts may state repeatedly that the individual is his or her own protector and refuge through making the choices that shape his or her own life, the Triple Gem also acts as protector and refuge by intervening to shape those choices skillfully.

2.4.2 The Development of the Sangha

When Yaśas's family became Buddhists, word spread to Yaśas's friends. Many of them came, listened to the Buddha, took ordination, and gained full Awakening. There were then 61 arhats in the world. Once the Buddha had consolidated a cadre of 60 Awakened monks, he sent them out as missionaries, charging them to travel and proclaim the Dharma for the benefit of the many, out of compassion for the world and for the welfare of divine and human beings. Those with keen faculties would attain liberation if, and only if, they heard the doctrine.

The 60 missionaries were soon so successful that many converts traveled long distances to receive ordination. The Buddha, noting the hardship this entailed, granted his monks permission to confer ordination themselves wherever they went.

He then spent the first three-month rainy season after his Awakening at Sarnath, as the heavy rains made travel impractical. This Rains retreat, generally observed by śramaṇas at the time, became a Buddhist institution that has been observed to the present day in Theravāda countries. After the rains, the Buddha returned to Uruvela, where he had earlier practiced austerities. The Vinaya relates that there he encountered and converted three brothers of the Kāśyapa clan, leaders of a sect of fire-worshipping ascetics, together with their one thousand disciples.

This tale demonstrates how the six superknowledges (see Section 1.3.5) played a role not only in the discovery of the Dharma but also in its propagation. Although the Buddha forbade his disciples from demonstrating their powers before the laity, there were occasions when he himself found it necessary to exhibit his powers to put his audience in the proper frame of mind to accept his teachings. The eldest Kāśyapa believed in his own arhatship, so the Buddha used a display of powers to subdue his pride. He tamed the nāga living in Kāśyapa's fire-ritual shrine; he vanished from one spot and appeared instantly in another; devas attended to him as he took a bath; he prevented Kāśyapa and his disciples from chopping wood for their fires, but then caused the wood to be instantaneously chopped when they complained.

Finally, Kāśyapa saw the Buddha part the waters of a flooding river to walk in the dust of the riverbed; when he asked the Buddha to enter his boat, the latter did so by first levitating into the air. Even then Kāśyapa remained convinced of his own spiritual superiority, so the Buddha, reading his mind, confronted him, saying that he was not even on the Path to the state he believed himself to have achieved. This shocked Kāśyapa so profoundly that he asked for ordination into the Buddhist Sangha. His followers quickly followed suit. The Buddha then taught them the Fire Discourse, in light of their previous worship of fire, saying that the six senses and their objects are on fire with passion, aversion, and delusion, with birth, aging, and death, with sorrows, lamentations, pains, distresses, and despairs. The disciple of the noble ones, recognizing these fires, thus grows dispassionate to the senses and their objects, and experiences release. When Kāśyapa and his followers listened to this exposition, their minds were released from the āsravas.

The Buddha then went to Rajagrha, capital of Magadha, where he was greeted by King Bimbisāra and a large crowd. Kāśyapa made a public announcement of his conversion to the Buddha's teachings, after which the Buddha gave a graduated discourse similar to the one given to Yaśas. This enabled the king, together with the majority of the crowd, to attain the Dharma-eye. On the following day, the king provided a meal for the Buddha and his followers, after which he donated the Bamboo Grove Park just outside the gates of the city for the Sangha's use.

Soon afterwards, Asvajit—one of the original five monks—went for alms in Rajagrha. There his clear countenance attracted the attention of Śāriputra, a wanderer from the nearby town of Nalanda. After hearing Asvajit's brief summary of the Buddha's teachings—"Whatever phenomena arise from cause: their cause and their cessation. Such is the teaching of the Tathāgata, the Great Contemplative"—Śāriputra attained the Dharma-eye. Returning to his āśrama, he taught the same summary to his fellow wanderer, Maudgalyāyana, who attained the Dharma-eye as well. This double Awakening was of crucial importance in the development of the Sangha, for it showed not only that Awakening could be experienced outside of the Buddha's presence, but also that it could be sparked by the words of a person who had never even met the Buddha. Śāriputra and Maudgalyāyana, together with 250 of their fellow wanderers, then went to the Buddha. As the latter saw them coming, he told the monks that these two would be his foremost disciples. Śāriputra became renowned for his discernment, Maudgalyāyana for his psychic powers.

At this point, the narrative in Mv.I shifts its focus from the Buddha to the Sangha. The monastic Sangha grew so fast, it says, with so many inexperienced new members, that they needed a system whereby each new monk would be trained by a preceptor. Eventually, the Buddha stopped giving ordination himself and instituted a formula whereby the Sangha gave ordination as a community transaction. This was the first step toward allowing the Sangha to function independently of the Buddha. Fittingly, Śāriputra was chosen to be the first preceptor under the new formula.

2.5 THE MIDDLE YEARS

Scattered passages in the early canons tell of events during the Buddha's teaching career without giving an overall chronology. The general picture is that the Buddha journeyed around the central Gangetic plain for 45 years, receiving all callers: devas and human beings; men, women, and children; ascetics, brahmans, royalty, commoners, outcastes, and lepers. He answered their questions, displayed miraculous powers, taught the Dharma, and aided followers in spiritual growth. Here we will point out a few prominent events in the development of the Buddha's following prior to his last year.

The Buddha opened membership in his Sangha to members of all castes—and to outcastes as well—stipulating that they abandon their caste ranking on becoming ordained and not even mention caste rank in their internal dealings. Śāriputra and Maudgalyāyana were among the many brahmans who become prominent in the Sangha. Another prominent brahman was Kātyāyana, a court priest who became the father of Buddhist exegesis, praised by the Buddha as "foremost of those who analyze at length what has been stated in brief." Still another was Mahākāśyapa, a stern figure, foremost in observing the ascetic rules and in mastering dhyāna. Upāli, the barber of Kapilavastu, was one of the members of the lower castes who also became prominent in the Sangha. His specialty was in remembering the Vinaya.

Members of Gautama's own family also joined the Sangha. His son, Rāhula, became an arhat, unrivaled in his desire for training; while his cousin, Anuruddha, also an arhat, was unrivaled for the power of his clairvoyance. Another cousin, the genial Ānanda, attained the Dharma-eye and served as the Buddha's constant attendant for the last 20 years of the latter's life. In later centuries, Ānanda developed a cultic following among Buddhist nuns for having interceded with the Buddha on behalf of the latter's aunt and foster mother, Mahāprajāpatī, to allow full ordination for women (see Section 3.3.4). Mahāprajāpatī and her attendants became the first nuns. One of Bimbisāra's queens, Kṣemā, joined the Order of Nuns and, like Śāriputra, became renowned for her discernment. Utpalavarṇā, like Maudgalyāyana, was renowned for her psychic powers.

The early lay converts included, in addition to members of the common classes, an array of kings, queens, princes, and wealthy merchants. Of the last, Anāthapiṇḍika donated the land for the famous Jetavana Monastery at Sravasti. Two wealthy lay women also donated land to the Sangha, the courtesan Āmrapālī giving her orchard at Vaisali, and the housewife Viśākhā giving land for a monastery near Sravasti.

Thus, even during the Buddha's lifetime, his Sangha became a wealthy landowner. Arrangements were made, however, for the original donors of the land to watch over it. This left the monks free to come and go, enjoying the advantages of having established places to stay, yet unburdened with administrative responsibilities aside from helping to keep their simple dwellings in repair. With the passing centuries, though, as more and more elaborate buildings were constructed on Sangha land, converting them from parks to monasteries, the custodial and administrative responsibilities associated with the monasteries fell increasingly to the monks. This made them, in effect, some of the most extensive landowners in a society where land was the primary measure of political power.

Even while the Buddha was still alive, the growth of the Sangha as an institution had its social and political repercussions. The Gangetic plain at the time was divided into small city-states. For the rulers of these states—especially the absolute monarchs—the growth in their midst of a religious institution transcending caste and political barriers was a matter of concern. Thus the Buddha, like other successful śramaṇa leaders, had to work out an arrangement whereby the Sangha would not be perceived as a political threat and yet would not have to sacrifice its independence to the powers that be. The possible sense of threat was somewhat defused when he won as disciples the kings of two of the most powerful states in the Ganges Valley: Bimbisāra of Magadha and Prasenajit of Kosala. The Buddha also advocated that his lay and monastic disciples lead their lives in line with strict moral principles, a teaching that appealed to kings not only in his time, but also for many centuries after, in that it lightened their job of maintaining law and order. At the same time, the Buddha empowered the Sangha to banish any of its monks or nuns who delivered messages or ran other errands for lay people, thus discouraging the Sangha from getting involved in political activity.

Nevertheless, the Buddha did not simply capitulate to the status quo. He realized that the smooth practice of the religion required a stable and peaceful society, which in turn depended on the wide distribution of material wealth among the people. Thus, absolute monarchies, in which kings were free to confiscate and hoard wealth at whim, did not provide an environment conducive for the religion to prosper. Therefore, the Buddha praised the ideal society as one in which the king obeyed the law and freely dispensed grants of money for his subjects to use in setting themselves up in business. Interestingly enough, the Suttas never depict him mentioning this ideal to the kings who were his followers. Instead, he taught the ideal to people at large, perhaps secure in the knowledge that it would have a grassroots effect. This in fact did occur approximately two hundred years after his death, when King Aśoka—who had ascended to the throne of an empire covering almost all of India—began putting the Buddha's social and political agenda into practice, at the same time fostering the spread of the Sangha beyond the Indian cultural sphere (see Section 3.4).

2.6 THE LAST DAYS AND BEYOND

The Mahāparinibbāna (Great Final Nibbāna) Sutta (DN.16) recounts the Buddha's final year. Like the narrative of the first year of his teaching career, this text is not a simple chronicle of events. Instead, it functions on many levels, primarily as a devotional text, justifying in particular the cult of the Buddha's relics that developed after his death, and more generally the practice of Buddhist devotionalism. It depicts the Buddha as a figure worthy of devotion, reports his own reputed words on the topic, shows the varied ways in which his contemporaries expressed devotion to him and to his relics, and accounts for the original set of stūpas, or reliquary mounds, built to house his relics and provide focus to a devotional cult. The picture that emerges is full of contrasting ideas. In this, the text prefigures not only specific Buddhist devotional practices, but also the contrasting attitudes toward devotion that have marked the Buddhist tradition up to the present day.

The Sutta's narrative is episodic and disjointed. In this, it reflects real life—reality rarely follows a coherent plot—but it also has led many modern scholars to suspect that at least some of the episodes were inserted at later dates. Thus, instead of prefiguring later practices, the Sutta may have been rewritten to justify those practices as they arose. Still, as with the Awakening account, the historical influence of the Sutta is undeniable, even though its historical accuracy cannot be ascertained.

The basic narrative is this: In his seventy-ninth year, the Buddha sets out from Rajagrha to Vaisali, where he spends his final Rains retreat. After the retreat, while staying in a forest shrine, he tells Ānanda that through the development of the four bases of attainment, he could—if he so desired—stay alive for a *kalpa* (aeon). Blind to the hint, Ānanda fails to request him to do so. The Buddha then goes alone to a quiet spot, where Māra approaches him, saying that the time has come for his *Parinirvāṇa* [total nirvāṇa, final release from saṁsāra]: He has established the Dharma and the fourfold pariṣad in line with his aspiration. The Blessed One responds, "Enough, Evil One. Very soon the Tathāgata's Parinirvāṇa will take place. Three months from now he will be totally unbound." This relinquishment of the forces of life, as it is called, triggers another earthquake, which startles Ānanda. Going to the Buddha, he asks what caused it. When he learns the answer, he requests the Blessed One to live on for an aeon, but the latter tells him that the time for such a request is past: Once a Tathāgata has abandoned something, he cannot take it up again.

That night, after calling a meeting of the monks, the Buddha lists the essential teachings in the message he has been promulgating for the past 45 years. This list has come to be named the *bodhipakṣya-dharma* (Wings to Awakening) and is common to many schools of Buddhism. It consists of seven sets of dharmas: (1) the four foundations of mindfulness, (2) the four right exertions, (3) the four bases of attainment, (4) the five strengths, (5) the five faculties, (6) the seven factors of Awakening, and (7) the Noble Eightfold Path. Set 1 is identical with right mindfulness, set 2 with right effort, and we have already discussed set 7 in detail. Set 3 concerns types of concentration: based on desire, on vigor, on attention, and on discrimination. Sets 4 and 5 are identical: conviction, vigor, mindfulness, concentration, and discernment. Set 6 is mindfulness, analysis of mental qualities (which the texts equate with discernment), vigor, rapture, serenity, concentration, and equanimity. The sets obviously overlap, and as the Suttas explain, the full practice of any one set involves the practice of the others. What is striking about the sets is that they contain no tenets about the nature of reality or the cosmos. Rather, they deal entirely with the development of mental qualities. The Buddha is portrayed as confident that whoever develops these qualities, focuses them on the present with reference to the foundations of mindfulness, and categorizes what is experienced in terms of the Four Noble Truths is sure to reach Awakening. The teaching will survive, he concludes, as long as his followers agree about these qualities and put them into practice. The preservation of the teachings is now their responsibility.

Then, together with Ānanda and a large community of monks, he heads toward Pava. There he takes his last meal at the home of Cunda, a silversmith, and soon afterward contracts a severe case of food poisoning. The text identifies the offending food with a word that could mean either tender pork or "piglet" mushrooms. Enduring his pains calmly, the Blessed One walks a considerable distance to Kusinagari, where he lies down between two sāla trees. After nightfall he receives the wanderer Subhadra, who questions him about the Awakened status of the teachers of other sects. Only in a religion that teaches the Noble Eightfold Path, the Buddha responds, could members of the ideal Sangha be found. Ānanda then receives this last of the Buddha's converts into the Bhikṣu Sangha.

The dying Buddha then asks the assembled monks three times whether they have any last doubts or questions regarding the teaching, but all remain silent. Then, as dawn approaches, he delivers his final exhortation: "Conditioned things are perishable by nature. Be heedful in seeking realization." He then dies a Buddha's death, composed and alert in meditation. Entering the first dhyāna, he ascends to the fourth and then on through the formless dhyānas—focused on the infinitude of space, the infinitude of consciousness, nothingness, and neither perception nor nonperception—up to the ninth, the cessation of perception and feeling. Then he returns, step by step, to the first dhyāna, and then up again to the fourth. While leaving the fourth, he passes immediately into parinirvāṇa. Just as he had been born and gained Awakening in the forest, that is where he dies.

Earthquakes mark the moment of death. Brahmā and Śakra recite stanzas, and the monks except for the arhats burst into lamentation until the Buddha's cousin Anuruddha reminds them of the impermanence of all fabricated things.

The people of Kusinagari come the next day and hold a six-day wake for the Blessed One. They dance, sing, and make music, offering garlands and scents. On the seventh day, eight chiefs of the Malla clan carry the body to a shrine east of the town. There they wrap the body in alternate layers of cloth and cotton batting and place it on a pyre in an iron bier filled with oil, as would befit a wheel-turning monarch. When they try to light the pyre, however, it won't catch fire. On asking Anuruddha why, they learn that the devas want to delay the cremation until Mahākāśyapa's arrival. When the latter arrives with a following of 500 monks, he circumambulates the pyre with hands raised in añjali and worships the Blessed One's feet with his head. The pyre then bursts spontaneously into flame.

After the body is consumed, the Mallans gather the bone relics and worship them for seven more days with song, dances, and so on, as before. Then there arrive the chiefs of seven other kingdoms and republics, demanding a share of the relics. The Mallans refuse and prepare for war to keep all the relics themselves until a brahman named Droṇa convinces them that doing so would not accord with the Dharma. So they agree to his dividing the relics into shares for each of the contestants. When this is completed, Droṇa is given the empty relic urn. Then more chieftains arrive, demanding their share of the relics, but as the division is finished, they are offered the embers of the pyre instead. Thus ten *stūpas,* or burial mounds, are built in ten locations: eight for the relics, one for the urn, and one for the embers. "That," concludes the Sutta, "is how it was in the past."

2.6.1 Buddhist Devotionalism

As stated previously, the Great Final Nibbāna Sutta narrates events in a way that depicts the Buddha as deserving the highest devotion. This it does first by showing the extent to which his contemporaries revered him. Kings ask his advice, wealthy donors vie with one another for the honor of presenting him with offerings, devas shower him on his deathbed with heavenly flowers, incense, and song.

More impressive to the modern mind is the Sutta's portrait of the Buddha in action: noble, composed, and compassionate to the end. Unlike a "close-fisted" teacher, he does not save any important teachings to the last moment. The many teachings given throughout the Sutta are all recapitulations, together with instructions as to how his followers are to distinguish Dharma from non-Dharma once he is gone: Anything consistent with what they already know to be Dharma and Vinaya should be accepted; anything inconsistent, no matter what authority the speaker may claim, should be rejected.

Even on his deathbed, the Blessed One is portrayed as exhibiting great nobility. He patiently explains the Dharma to his last convert; comforts the grieving Ānanda; and sends word to Cunda that the latter should not regret having provided the meal that brought on the Buddha's final illness, inasmuch the offering of a Buddha's final meal entails the highest possible merit that the offering of a meal can provide. At the moment of death, he gives a final display of his full mastery of concentration. Perhaps most impressive is his response to the extreme devotion shown to him. He patiently reminds those who express grief at his passing that they do not need him: He has fully explained the Dharma, and all they need is to practice it. He directs his followers to regard the Dharma and Vinaya as their teacher in his place. He describes to Ānanda how the devas are worshipping him with heavenly songs, flowers, and sandalwood powder, and then comments, "But not to this extent is a Tathāgata worshipped, honored, respected, venerated, or revered. Rather, the monk, nun, upāsaka, or upāsikā who . . . keeps practicing the Dharma in accordance with the Dharma is the person who worships, honors, respects, venerates, and reveres the Tathāgata with the highest homage." Thus in every case, he deflects devotion away from himself and toward the practice of the Dharma.

Many scholars have read these comments as attempts to discourage personal devotion to the Buddha, and have deemed the Sutta an antidevotional text. To do so, however, is to take the comments out of context, for the Sutta also portrays the Buddha as encouraging an attitude of devotion toward himself and his relics. While on his deathbed, he drives away an attendant monk sitting in front of him, so as to oblige the devas who want their last glimpse of him. He has Ānanda inform the Mallans of his imminent demise, so that they will have a chance to pay him their last respects. He stipulates how his body is to be cremated and the relics placed in a stūpa as would befit a wheel-turning monarch. And he recommends the practice of making pilgrimages to four locations connected with his life and teaching: the places of his birth, his Awakening, his first discourse, and his Parinirvāṇa.

Given the context of the Buddha's "antidevotional" remarks, the question arises as to their proper interpretation. Buddhist traditions have offered three answers: (1) they are to be taken at face value as deflecting devotion away from the Buddha and toward practice; (2) they are signs of the Buddha's noble, selfless character, and thus further proof that he deserves veneration; and (3) both. Prevalent in most traditions is answer (3), and this seems to be the attitude of the Sutta's authors, as symbolized in the way Mahākāśyapa's veneration of the Buddha's body enables its cremation. Known both for his fierce personal devotion to the Buddha and for his strict practice of the Dharma, Mahākāśyapa embodies the principle that Buddha-devotion and Dharma practice go together. The Pali texts recognize that some forms of devotion are inappropriate, with the Suttas condemning animal sacrifice, and the Vinaya discouraging the offering of sexual favors and gifts of liquor. But, as noted at the beginning of this chapter, respect and devotion in acceptable forms make the practice of the Dharma possible. As our text notes, the practice itself can be seen as an expression of devotion, thus erasing the distinction between the two.

2.6.2 The Etiquette of Devotion

Our Sutta indicates what the etiquette of acceptable devotion might be. Parts of this etiquette are attributed to the Buddha himself. Pilgrims to the four locations associated with his life, he says, should gaze at these places and develop feelings of saṁvega and prasāda. Visitors to his stūpas should offer garlands, scents, or perfume powders, bow down, or develop feelings of prasāda. The merit they acquire in doing so will be for their long-term well-being and happiness.

Other aspects of the Buddhist devotional etiquette are modeled in the depiction of how the Buddha's contemporaries revere him during life and his relics after death. Four aspects deserve special mention, as they have characterized Buddhist devotionalism up to the present.

Circumambulation. When Mahākāśyapa circumambulates the Buddha's pyre (keeping the pyre to his right), he is following an ancient Indian custom for taking leave of a revered person. At the same time, he is prefiguring a common Buddhist way of showing respect to sacred objects and places. Over the centuries, stūpas throughout the Buddhist world have been built with pathways to facilitate circumambulation, some even with roofs to allow it in inclement weather. To this day, on Buddhist holidays in the Theravādin world, crowds flock to circumambulate stūpas while carrying candles, flowers, and incense. In Tibet, some devotees go even further when circumambulating sacred objects, measuring out the entire path in full-body prostrations.

Gazing at the Eye. Just prior to the Buddha's death, devas hoping for their last glimpse of him complain that "the One with Eyes" will soon disappear from the world. This is a common epithet for the Buddha, based on the role that clear vision plays in his teachings. We have already encountered references to the Blessed One's Buddha-eye and divine eye, as well as to the Dharma-eye. However, references to the Eye also carry connotations going back to Vedic scriptures, where a deity's power was said to reside in his or her eyes, and in a sense the deity was "all eyes"—to see the deity was to be seen by the deity, so that the deity's power could enter through the devotee's eyes. Thus, to see a deity was highly auspicious. Thus one of the epithets for the Buddha in the earliest Suttas is "the all-around Eye," and we often read in the Suttas of people obsessed with the desire to see the Buddha. In one passage (SN.XXII.87), the Buddha dismisses this desire, explaining that the true way to see him is to see the Dharma, but his words can also be read the other way around: seeing him, one sees the Dharma. Throughout the history of South Asian Buddhism the desire to see the Buddha has been a common theme. Worshippers have visited stūpas and performed acts of merit in monasteries, philosophers have constructed their theories, all in hopes of gaining a vision of him. When Buddha images became widespread (see Section 4.3.1), a common meditation practice was to gaze at them, a practice that eventually spread to other parts of Asia. Some scholars believe that the eyes painted on all four sides of the Svayambhunātha stūpa in Nepal relate to this tradition as well.

Enough devotees gained meditative visions of the Buddha to engender a controversy over how these visions should be explained. Did the Buddha somehow continue to exist in a way that he could enter such a vision? Or was the vision simply the fruit of the devotee's meritorious intention? This became a major issue in Buddhist philosophy, and is an example of how some philosophical issues grew, not from dry theorizing, but from devotional experiences.

Declaring One's Name. When the Mallans come to pay their last respects to the Buddha, Ānanda has them call out their names to the Buddha, family by family, to save time. The Suttas (e.g., MN.89) show, without explaining why, that calling out one's name was a common way of showing respect. Two possible explanations come to mind: (1) the devotee is asking to be remembered, as in the act of taking refuge; (2) the devotee is showing the sincerity of his or her respect by declaring it publicly. In either event, this practice took on an unusual form as the cult of the stūpa developed in India. Donors' names would be inscribed on stone bas-reliefs and other offerings, even on offerings to be placed inside the stūpa or high off the ground where no one would ever see the names. This suggests that the inscribing of the name was not an act of vanity, but one of devotion. This practice continues in many Buddhist countries to the present day.

Song and Dance. The Buddha does not commend the devas for worshipping him with song and music, but neither does he condemn or try to stop them. Similarly, when the Mallan lay people of Kusinagari spontaneously conduct his wake with song, music, and dance, the monks do not interfere. In this, the devas and Mallans prefigure the practice of stūpa festivals, reported by Chinese pilgrims to India and persisting in such events as the annual celebration of the Tooth Relic in Kandy, Sri Lanka, and the many temple fairs throughout the Buddhist world. Observers have often commented on the joyous atmosphere on these occasions and—in the period when Buddhism was considered pessimistic—found this joy paradoxical, part of a perceived gap between the Great Tradition of the ancient canons and the Little Tradition of Buddhism on the ground. However, as prasāda is the emotion to be developed at a stūpa, joy in this case is perfectly consistent with the teachings of the Suttas. And as our Sutta maintains, Buddhists have good reason to rejoice. The Parinirvāṇa did not bring their relationship to the Buddha to a full stop. As teacher, he has the Dharma and Vinaya acting in his stead, still capable of showing them the way to release from suffering. As power figure, he survives in the form of his relics. Regardless of how his followers show their devotion to him—through Dharma practice, the cult of the relics, or both—the Sutta encourages them to be confident that it will lead to their long-term well-being and happiness.

3

The Development of Early Indian Buddhism

3.1 SOURCES

Our most reliable sources for the history of early Indian Buddhism are of two types: *textual,* the canons of the early Buddhist monastic lineages; and *archaeological,* inscriptions and remnants of religious edifices. Both types have their limitations, with two major limitations in common. (1) Both were produced by elites—intellectual and literary in the first case, and financial in the second. Thus they speak for only small segments of the total Buddhist population of the time. (2) Both are fragmentary. The general ravages of time, and the particular destruction that accompanied the Muslim invasions of India in the eleventh and twelfth centuries, have left only a small fraction of what once existed.

In addition, each type has its specific limitations. The canons of the early lineages cannot be precisely dated, and some of the texts show evidence of having been tampered with over time; thus, we cannot with total certitude read them as reports of actual behavior. Regardless of how accurate they may be, the historical method limits us to reading them as *norms* for behavior: a central part of religious history to be sure, but not the whole picture.

The inscriptions can be dated with a little more accuracy, but—with the exception of the edicts of King Aśoka, which are discussed separately—they are short and terse, the lithic equivalent of sound bites. Only by putting them in context can they provide more than the most rudimentary information, but there is currently little agreement on how to construct that context. Modern scholars, by providing their own contexts for reading these inscriptions, have been able to make them say many contradictory things.

Some scholars have tried to work around these limitations, in particular by trying to use textual and archaeological evidence to date various parts of the canons, but so far without success. The philological arguments based on the textual evidence assume that the earliest parts of the canons must have been composed in a regular language following clear grammatical or philological rules. Thus any passage that breaks those rules must be a later addition. This, of course, is more an assumption than a proof, and is tantamount to saying that a great poet like Shakespeare would not write anything ungrammatical, and thus all the ungrammatical passages in his plays must be later interpolations.

As for the arguments based on archaeological evidence, these tend to focus on the composition of the Vinayas of the various lineages. All the extant Vinayas presuppose large, settled monastic communities, but the earliest known archaeological remains from such communities—stone inscriptions and brick foundations—date no earlier than the beginning of the common era. Thus it has been suggested that the Vinaya texts were composed in the first to fourth centuries C.E., and that they cannot provide us with a record of the earlier life of the community. This suggestion, however, ignores the fact that the typical "permanent" buildings described in the Vinayas are wattle and daub with dirt floors, a type of construction that would leave no archaeological traces. Thus, although brick and stone remains can tell us roughly when brick and stone monasteries first became fashionable, they cannot tell us when the first wattle and daub monasteries were built, or when the Vinaya texts were composed.

Nevertheless, although no absolute chronology can be determined for the early canons, there is general scholarly agreement that a relative chronology can be discerned within the canons themselves. Each of the extant canons falls into several strata, and a common method for calculating the relative ages of the strata is this: If stratum *B* seems to assume the preexistence of stratum *A*—either explicitly, through direct quotations, or implicitly, through assuming that the reader has a knowledge of the material in *A*—and then uses that material to address questions not even mentioned in *A,* we can generally assume that *B* is later than *A*.

When this approach is applied to the early canons, we find that the most important differences in the texts lie, not among the different lineages, but among different strata within the texts of each lineage. Furthermore, these differences are parallel in all the lineages for which we have evidence. Each starts with a core of Dharma texts and disciplinary rules treating the issues of suffering—and the graduated Dharma leading up to those issues (see Section 2.4)—with a variety of tools drawn from all three modes of discourse we found in the Awakening account: narrative fragments, cosmological fragments, and "emptiness" fragments. From this core, they expand in several directions to encompass a wider variety of issues, at the same time developing more complete narrative cycles, cosmologies, and philosophies of emptiness. In doing so, they generated controversies that have marked the Buddhist tradition ever since, at the same time establishing some conceptual frameworks that have crossed sectarian lines to shape Buddhism's many subsequent forms.

Secondly, when we compare the results of this analysis with the archaeological evidence, we find interesting points of congruence. A current scholarly fashion is to use archaeological evidence to contradict what is found in the canons, the implication being that the canons are unreliable accounts of what was happening on the ground in India at the time. A careful reading of the texts, however, shows that the archaeological evidence simply points to portions of the canons that have previously been ignored. For instance, scholars long liked to portray Buddhist monastics prior to the common era as spiritual virtuosos with little concern for the devotional practices of the laity. Then, when archaeological evidence surfaced that Buddhist monastics in the first century B.C.E. made offerings and dedicated the merit to their dead ancestors, just like lay Buddhists, this was offered as proof that the canons had misrepresented the actual behavior of monks and nuns. However, the Pali canon contains, in one of its later strata, a text (the *Petavatthu*) advocating just this practice, with no less a monk than Śāriputra depicted as the exemplar in how it is to be done.

Thus the lesson to be drawn here is that, although our sources for this period are limited, they are most fruitful if viewed in conjunction with one another. And even though a precise chronology cannot be calculated for the canons, their relative chronology provides a narrative line for how an ever-widening variety of people looked to Buddhism to address their wants and questions, and in so doing gave it a shape that it was to maintain not only for the remainder of its career in India, but also for much of its career in other countries ever since.

3.2 THE FORMATION OF THE CANONS

All our sources agree that the Buddha left no written record of his teachings, and no centralized authority to govern the monastic Sangha after his death. These are perhaps the most important facts in shaping the development of the Dharma-Vinaya (the doctrine and discipline) that he founded. With no written record, his followers had nothing to rely on but their own memories of his teachings. Because he had addressed many different groups of people on many different occasions, no one person could claim a complete memory of what he had taught. The situation was further complicated by the fact that the monks memorized his teachings in their own dialects, and the Buddha himself may have been multilingual. With no central authority, there was no place where an authoritative version—or authoritative translations—of his teachings could be compiled.

The Buddha is said to have foreseen part of this difficulty, and the Mahāparinibbāna Sutta quotes him as establishing standards for judging whether a report of his teachings was to be accepted or not: The decisive factor was, not the authority of the person reporting it, but its consistency with what one already knew of the Dharma-Vinaya. This, of course, opened the possibility that one group might accept a teaching as consistent while another might not. And that is exactly what happened. There has never been a single, standard version of what the Buddha taught. What is remarkable, though, is that the early lineages differed so little in their accounts of his teachings.

3.2.1 The Early Monastic Lineages

Traditional accounts tell us that the Sangha produced 18 separate monastic lineages in the first centuries after the Buddha's death. Although the accounts are unanimous on the number 18, the various lists of 18 contain different names. When the lists are collated together with archaeological references to the lineages, the total number is considerably higher. Perhaps 18 was the number of lineages at one prominent point in the history of the religion—the reign of Aśoka is often offered as a possibility—or else it was chosen for its symbolic value as a sign of completeness. To get a sense of what did and did not divide the lineages, we must first look at the canons they preserved.

Each lineage maintained its own canon of Dharma-Vinaya, composed either of two *Piṭakas* (literally basket or collection)—a *Vinaya Piṭaka* and *Sūtra Piṭaka*—or of three, the third being an *Abhidharma Piṭaka,* composed of texts that analyzed *mātṛkā* (lists) of essential teachings drawn from the Sūtras.

Each lineage claimed that its canon preserved the most direct line to the Buddha's teachings, but there is no way that such claims can be proven. To begin with, the canons were memorized and transmitted orally for centuries. Chronicles tell us that none of the canons were written down until the first century B.C.E.; and the earliest extant manuscripts, which are very fragmentary, date only to the first century C.E. Secondly, there is the question of language. We do not know what language(s) the Buddha spoke, but his native tongue was probably the precursor of the Magadhi dialect in which many of Aśoka's inscriptions are couched. The only complete canon extant in an Indic language is that of the Theravāda lineage, which has been preserved in Pali, a literary language similar to Magadhi based on a vernacular thought to have been spoken in western India. Fragments of canons in other languages similar to Magadhi, offering slightly variant readings, also survive.

The Vinayas of all the lineages are divided into two sections: the *Sūtra Vibhaṅga* (Analysis of the Text) and the *Skandhaka* (in Pali, *Khandhaka*—Groupings). The Skandhakas contain miscellaneous material on personal and institutional matters, including instructions on how community transactions—such as ordination—are to be handled. The Sūtra Vibhaṅga contains the rules of the *Prātimokṣa* (in Pali, *Pāṭimokkha*—Codes of Discipline), which were to be recited in assemblies of monks and nuns on the *Poṣadha* (in Pali, *Uposatha*—Observance Day), the last day of each lunar half-month. The Sūtra Vibhaṅga also provides background material on each rule, together with a detailed analysis of the factors determining whether an action that might come under the purview of the rule would in fact count as an offense. In the Pali recension, the five factors used in the analysis are perception, object, intention, effort, and result. The text thus encourages the individual monastics to take a persistently mindful and analytical attitude toward all of their actions. This indicates that the disciplinary code was to be observed not only as an external exercise for harmony within the community, but also as an integral part of training the mind in the skills needed for meditation.

Comparative analysis shows only minor differences among the extant Prātimokṣas of the different lineages. Complete, detailed comparisons of all the extant Skandhakas have yet to be made, but more limited studies have shown considerable variation in the minor rules.

The Sūtra Piṭakas of the early lineages were divided into sections called *Nikāyas* or *Āgamas*. Four Nikāyas were recognized by all the early lineages: the Long (in Sanskrit, *Dīrgha;* in Pali, *Dīgha*), the Medium (*Madhyama/Majjhima*), the Connected (*Saṁyukta/Saṁyutta*), and the Numerical (*Ekottara/Aṅguttara*). Some of the lineages—such as the *Sthaviravādins, Sarvāstivādins,* and *Dharmaguptakas*—also collected a Little (*Kṣudraka/Khuddaka*) Nikāya. The *Little Nikāya* is unusual in that it contains some of the earliest as well as some of the latest strata in the Sūtra Piṭaka. At present we have only one complete Sūtra Piṭaka, that of the Sthaviravādins, in an Indic language. The Chinese canon contains extensive translations of the first four Āgamas, based on Sarvāstivādin, Dharmaguptaka, and Mahāsaṃghika versions. Although Sarvāstivādin treatises mention that their lineage also had a Little Āgama, the Chinese have only a few scattered works from this collection.

The Sūtras are chiefly prose discourses and dialogues, except for stanzas interspersed through the first four Nikāyas and the anthologies of verse (Dhammapada, Sutta-nipāta, and so on) in the fifth Nikāya. The prose texts betray their original oral style through their many repetitions and standardized passages describing the basic teachings. Although most of the Sūtras simply report Dharma teachings, some of them tell extended narratives, and many of the longer Sūtras are polished literary creations.

Sectarian preferences undoubtedly led to distortions in, additions to, and omissions from the Sūtras, but a large core—including all the major Buddhist doctrines—is common to all extant versions. Whether that core goes back to the Buddha himself, no one can say.

Because the Abhidharma Piṭakas were a later development, we will discuss them in Section 3.5, where we will draw some conclusions about the differences that Abhidharma issues came to define among many of the lineages.

We lack definite knowledge of how the various lineages split off from one another. No contemporary accounts of the divisions are preserved; most of the traditional accounts date from centuries later. In some cases, the splits seem to have been intentional. For example, the apparent first split, some time after the Second Council (see Section 3.2.2), occurred when a large assembly of monks met and took issue with the teachings of a group identified only as "the elders." This gave rise to the first two lineages: the doctrine of the elders (*Sthaviravāda,* Pali: *Theravāda*) and the Great Assembly (Mahāsaṃghika). Later Theravādin writers maintained that the original Mahāsaṃghikas deleted parts of the canon and rearranged the remainder, taking passages out of context. Later Mahāsaṃghika writers maintained that the split occurred because the elders had added new material to the canon. Of course, neither claim can be evaluated, for we have no access to a canon predating the split.

In other cases, however, the splits seem to have been unintentional. Groups in different localities, separated by geography and dialect, gradually grew further apart as they independently collated the teachings available in their own areas and dialects.

Some of the splits seem to have been amicable; others less so. The early Vinayas contain rules for how monks of other lineages should be treated, with clear distinctions between the treatment accorded to those who advocate what each lineage considered to be the true Dharma and those who advocate what they considered to be false. Thus, tolerance was encouraged, but not to the point of ignoring genuine differences.

3.2.2 The Early Councils and the Attitude toward Sectarianism

All of the Vinayas tell of two councils (*saṅgīti,* or recitation) held shortly after the Buddha's death, which offer two differing paradigms for how differences should be handled. Whether or not the councils actually occurred as reported, the accounts clearly show the Sangha's attitudes toward controversies in their midst.

The First Council was reportedly held in Rajagrha during the Rains retreat immediately following the Parinirvāṇa. Five hundred arhats met, led by Mahākāśyapa, who questioned Upāli about the Buddha's words on Vinaya and Ānanda about the Buddha's words on Dharma. The remaining arhats then memorized their responses. Soon after the meeting dispersed, another arhat—named Purāṇa—arrived at Rajagrha with a following of 500 monks. He was told to memorize the teachings as standardized by the council, but responded: "The Dharma-Vinaya has been well standardized by the elders, but I will remember the Dharma-Vinaya as I heard it in the Blessed One's presence." In this case, the disagreement was handled amicably. Purāṇa recognized the validity of the council's work, while the elders recognized the purity of his motives in not submitting to the council's decisions.

The Second Council is traditionally dated to 100 years after the Parinirvāṇa, when wilderness elders learned that monks in the eastern city of Vaisali had formulated what the elders regarded as aberrant and lax interpretations of the monastic code—some relatively minor (for example, making it permissible to store salt to add flavor to bland alms meals) and others more significant (allowing the use of gold and silver). A council was convened in Vaisali to address nine points of discipline and the one point of principle that underlay all of the Vaisalian practices: that it was permissible to take one's personal teacher's practices as a guide. A committee of elders was appointed to consider the issues, which they resolved by unanimously denouncing all nine of the Vaisalian practices and limiting the scope of the underlying principle. The council concluded by chanting the Vinaya to establish commonality.

This is an account with clear heroes and villains. The wilderness monks are loath to engage in controversies, for fear that it will disturb their meditation, but they eventually agree to put aside their personal comforts for the sake of the Dharma-Vinaya. The city monks, however, are portrayed as unscrupulous, trumping up charges against their opponents and trying to influence the elders with bribes. Only through a long and concerted campaign do the wilderness elders prevail.

The combined lesson of these two accounts is that differences based on pure motives should be tolerated and respected, while deviations based on impure motives should not. This lesson coincides with the various rules for handling a split in the Sangha: Such a split can be properly healed only if both sides have met and ascertained the intentions at the root of the split. This further coincides with the emphasis placed on intention in the doctrine of karma.

There is no way of knowing the extent to which these lessons affected the actual splits in the early community, but their existence in the texts of all the lineages has proven influential through many centuries of the Buddhist tradition. Thus—as with the life story of the Buddha—the historical accuracy of the accounts of the first councils may be open to question, but their historical impact is not.

3.3 NORMS FOR RELIGIOUS LIFE

Before dealing with the known issues that divided the early lineages, we should look at some of the teachings they held in common. We have already discussed the most central of those teachings in the context of the Buddha's life. Here we will focus more on norms for religious life set out for the major divisions of the Buddha's parisad: the monastics and the laity. The Vinaya Piṭaka prescribes the correct life for the monks and nuns and describes, in the origin stories for the rules, the colorful abuses against which the Order had to protect itself. In doing so, it paints a detailed and quite realistic picture of the monastic community, along with its relations with the laity. At the same time, passages from the Vinaya and Sūtra also formulate norms for lay Buddhist practice.

3.3.1 The Code of Discipline for Monks

The *Bhikṣu Prātimokṣa* (in Pali, *Bhikkhu Pāṭimokkha*), the central code of discipline in the Vinaya Piṭaka, defines five classes of offense, prescribes rules of deportment, and establishes procedural guidelines for the peaceful running of the monks' community in a way conducive to the individual training of the mind. A similar code governed the lives of nuns. The following account draws from the Pali and Mahāsaṃghika versions, which differ only in minor details.

Two dominant ethical concerns of the code are nonviolence and celibacy, which derive from the principles of right resolve in the Noble Eightfold Path (see Section 2.3.1). These principles are clearly illustrated in the four offenses that constitute immediate and permanent expulsion: sexual intercourse, grand larceny, killing a human being (this includes recommending abortion), and falsely claiming spiritual attainments.

Thirteen offenses require a formal meeting of the Sangha chapter and are punished with probation. The most prominent of these concern sex: intentional ejaculation, touching a woman with lustful intent, speaking suggestively to her, telling her that she would benefit spiritually by yielding sexually to him, and serving as a matchmaker. In each case, a formal meeting of the Sangha is called and the offending monk is placed under probation for at least six days. The probationer forfeits many privileges. He must not allow monks in good standing to offer salutation, provide seats for him, or carry his robe or bowl. Every day he must announce to the monks in the monastery the reason for his probation, repeating this announcement whenever newcomers arrive. He must always take the lowest seat, the worst bed, the worst room, and sit at the end of the line when food is distributed. He may not leave the monastery unless accompanied by four monks of good standing. When the probation period is over, he may be reinstated only by an assembly of 20 monks or more.

This class of rules is followed by two rules dealing with how to handle a case when a monk has been sitting in private with a woman and is accused of an offense. The assembly must meet to review the case, deciding what penalty, if any, is called for.

Thirty rules deal with improper use or acquisition of an article, requiring confession and forfeiture of the article involved. For the most part the rules concern robes, alms bowls, and sitting-rugs. The monk must not have more than one of each (or one set of three robes) at a time. However, when his begging-bowl develops five cracks, he may exchange it for a new one. He must not get a nun to do his laundry, give him a robe (except in exchange), or prepare wool for a rug. He may store medicinal foods for only seven days. He may not receive gold or silver, buy, sell, or barter.

Ninety-two of the rules require simple confession. The list is quite miscellaneous: lying, verbal abuse, divisive tale-bearing, stealing another monk's sleeping space, sporting in the water, or eavesdropping while other monks quarrel. A monk may not dig the ground or destroy plant life. These rules, ostensibly to protect plant and small animal life, also keep the monks from engaging in agriculture or becoming solitary hermits, growing their own food. Another group of rules prohibits the monk (except for good cause) from going near an army drawn up for battle, staying with an army for more than two or three nights, and watching other military activities. These prohibitions protect a monk from accusations of engaging in espionage or diplomatic intrigue. A monk must not deliberately kill an animal or even use water containing living things that would die from his using it. He must not eat food after noon or before dawn, nor is he to store food overnight. Drinking liquor—even as much as the tip of a blade of grass—is an offense to be confessed.

A monk who tells a lay person of his actual spiritual attainments commits an offense requiring confession, as does one who informs an unordained person of a fellow monk's grave offense. Nevertheless, every monk is duty-bound to inform the assembly of any serious transgression committed by a fellow monk because an unconfessed sin is considered an affliction that grows aggravated the longer it goes unabsolved. However, the code forbids false accusations or harrying another with insinuations that he is transgressing.

Rules of etiquette—75 in the Pali, 67 in the Mahāsaṃghika recension—regulate the conduct of the monk when entering inhabited areas, receiving alms, eating, and excreting. He must at all times be properly clothed, keep his eyes downcast, not sway his limbs or body, refrain from loud laughter and noise, and observe good table manners: neither stuffing his mouth, smacking his lips, nor talking with his mouth full. He must not excrete while standing up, onto cultivated plants, or into potable water. This set also includes rules forbidding a monk from preaching Dharma to a listener who shows disrespect.

Some of the rules of etiquette may seem trivial, but we must remember that the Sangha accepted recruits from all backgrounds, and so had to train them to a common standard for the sake of communal harmony. People may often be more offended by breaches of etiquette than by transgressions of civil law. Thus the rules teach the sons of peasants to eat politely, and the sons of brahmans to wipe themselves after going to the bathroom. Etiquette alone does not suffice, of course, but it forms a necessary part of the complete discipline that shapes character and attracts outsiders to the Dharma.

A noteworthy feature of the Vinaya rules is the utter absence of the taboos common in Brahmanical and Near Eastern law books. There is no idea that certain foods are impure, that bodily wastes pollute spiritually, that certain acts or objects are lucky or unlucky, or that certain plants and animals are taboo because of their association with particular divinities. Also noteworthy is the Vinaya's approach to living in the wilderness. All of the activities that have historically defined domesticity as apart from wilderness life—farming, animal husbandry, trading, storing food—are forbidden to the monks. Although not all monks were wilderness dwellers, and later communities found ways to circumvent these prohibitions, the original vision for the monks' life seems to have been one of hunting and gathering, with a civilized twist. Instead of taking life or plucking plants, the monks were to hunt and gather in a sustainable fashion from the generosity of the laity. As a verse from the Dhammapada (49) puts it:

> As a bee—without harming
> the blossom,
> its color,
> its fragrance—
> takes its nectar and flies away:
> so should the sage
> go through a village.

Anthropologists have noted that hunters and gatherers have more free time than do people in an agricultural or industrial economy. Monks living in this alms economy thus had the free time needed to devote to the practice of the Dharma.

Another noteworthy feature is the prominent role the Vinaya gives to intention, in line with the general Buddhist teachings on the importance of intention in shaping one's experience of the cosmos. In most cases, an unintentional infraction of a rule does not count as an offense.

3.3.2 Communal Governance

The Vinaya does not view the monk as working out his own salvation unaided (see Section 2.4.1). Rather, each monk is his brother's keeper. When the ordinand joins the Sangha, he surrenders some liberties and submits to the collective authority of the community. The Skandhakas lay down disciplinary procedures for enforcing this authority. Because "friendship with admirable people is the entirety of the holy life" (SN XLV.2), the punishments meted out by these procedures entail varying degrees of ostracism, from censure to suspension from the Sangha. All these punishments end when the offender has mended his ways.

In allowing these extra punishments, the Skandhakas insist on due process of law. The offender is warned, reminded of the rules, and, if his unacceptable behavior persists, is formally charged and tried by the whole community. He may not be penalized for an act he does not admit doing, cannot be tried in absentia, and may speak in his own defense. Once a unanimous sentence has been passed in line with the proper procedure, however, he must accept it and try to mend his ways.

The discipline presupposes a high degree of willingness and maturity. For this reason, full *upasampadā* (ordination) is granted only to those who are at least 20 years of age and who have formally requested admission to the Sangha. Eight years, however, is the minimum age for the *pravrajyā* (novitiate ordination), which even adult candidates must undergo—albeit briefly—before proceeding to full ordination. In the "going forth" ceremony, the ordinand has his head shaven, is given the ochre robes, and takes the Three Refuges and Ten Precepts to abstain from (1) taking life; (2) stealing; (3) sexual intercourse; (4) lying; (5) drinking liquor; (6) eating after noon; (7) watching dancing, singing, and shows; (8) adorning himself with garlands, perfumes, and ointments; (9) using a high bed or seat; and (10) receiving gold and silver. The ordinand is thereafter a novice and has left the household life. If under the age of 20, he must live with a preceptor until he returns to lay life or gains full ordination upon coming of age. The preceptor must have passed 10 years since full ordination and must be of good character, knowledgeable, and competent.

Full ordination is conferred by an assembly consisting of a quorum of at least ten monks if held in the middle Ganges Valley, and five anywhere else. The ceremony is quite simple. The candidate is questioned to make sure that he is fully qualified; if unanimously accepted by the assembly, he is publicly announced as ordained. The preceptor then gives the new monk an exhortation, telling him that henceforth his four basic requisites are alms for food, old rags for clothing, the shade of a tree for shelter, and urine-medicine. He mentions, however, that more luxurious requisites are also allowed, and monastic life often entails the allowances. The new monk is then informed of the four offenses requiring expulsion and told to avoid them for the rest of his life.

Once ordained, the new monk is to live in apprenticeship to a mentor—his preceptor or another teacher—for at least five years. He is to regard his mentor as his father and treat him accordingly, acting as his personal attendant and applying himself diligently to a life of study and meditation. In return, the mentor is to regard the new monk as his son and to provide for his needs and training. The new monk, however, does not take a vow of obedience to his mentor. If he feels mistreated, he is free to search for another mentor. Only when his knowledge of the Dharma-Vinaya is sufficiently extensive, and his behavior sufficiently reliable, is he freed from apprenticeship and allowed to set out on his own.

A Buddhist nun's ordination was similar in most respects to a monk's except that she had to be accepted twice: once by the assembly of nuns with whom she planned to live, and again by the local assembly of monks. She, too, had to undergo a period of apprenticeship to a senior nun, although hers was for four years: two as a postulant before her ordination, and an additional two afterward.

3.3.3 The Life of the Monks

From the very beginning of the tradition, the life of the monks combined two modes: *eremitic* (solitary wandering) and *cenobitic* (settled communities). The Vinaya presents a picture in which the ideal monk followed both modes by wandering during the dry season of each year and then settling down with fellow monks during the Rains. During the dry season he might live—alone or with small groups of his fellows—under a tree, in a cave, on a hillside, in a glen or forest glade, in a thatched hut, or even in the shade of a haystack. Naturally, he stayed near a village or town for his alms. His possessions were kept simple and few so that he could travel light, "like a bird, with its wings as its only burden" (DN.2). Ideally, he owned only one set of clothing: an under robe, upper robe, outer cloak, and belt. The robes, donated by the laity or made by the monk from thrown-away rags, were dyed reddish brown. He also wore sandals and carried a begging-bowl, a razor, tweezers, nail clippers, a water filter, a needle, and a bag of medicines. He was allowed an umbrella against the sun and a fan against the heat. At least once every other month he shaved his head without using a mirror; mirrors were forbidden to him, as were adornments, cosmetics and perfumes, music and song. The ideal Buddhist nun's personal possessions were equally meager.

During the three months of the rainy season—July to October (*varṣa;* in Pali, *vassa*)—open-air living became difficult, and travel impractical, so the Vinaya required that the monks settle for the period in dwellings sufficiently closed off to protect them from the elements. There they could pursue their spiritual development, learn from one another, and conduct communal business relatively undisturbed. The sites selected for such dwellings had to be isolated enough to ensure a proper atmosphere for meditation, but close enough to a village or town for alms-going. The return of the dry season was marked by ceremonies at which the laity presented gifts of cloth and other necessities to the monks, who then set out on their solitary wanderings, perhaps leaving a few of their number to maintain the dwellings.

With the passage of time, these temporary dwellings developed into settled monasteries. According to the Vinaya texts, this process began during the Buddha's lifetime, when wealthy donors made permanent gifts of land to the Sangha and erected buildings on them (see Section 2.5). Scholars have debated whether the texts can be believed on this point, the argument boiling down not to any firm evidence but simply to the question of whether such a process could conceivably have occurred during the 45 years of the Buddha's teaching career. Modern experience with the "domestication" of wilderness monks (see Section 7.5.2) indicates that such a time frame is entirely possible. At any rate, the Vinaya provides detailed rules for running such communities on a year-round basis. Although some monks continued their dry-season wanderings, others settled down more or less permanently. This resulted in the distinction between town-dwelling monks and wilderness-dwelling monks that has continued to the present in Theravāda countries.

Town-dwelling monks were involved in the daily routine of the monastery and its service to the people, functioning as scholars, teachers, preachers, administrators, doctors, and even politicians (see Section 6.1). Although they were exhorted to keep their personal possessions to a minimum, none of the monks took a vow of poverty. The list of possessions forbidden to them was much shorter than the list of possessions allowed. In many cases, gifts that monks were forbidden to accept for their personal use, such as servants, vehicles, and land, were given to monasteries on an institutional basis. Thus some town and city monasteries became lavishly endowed, and the life of their monks quite luxurious. Although individual monks were not allowed to handle money, their stewards could keep accounts for them, and some seem to have become very wealthy. The Vinaya tells of monks sponsoring the construction of entire monasteries; archaeological evidence shows that they were major contributors to the construction of stūpas.

Wilderness-dwelling monks, by contrast, were less encumbered with social entanglements, and were thus freer either to pursue their spiritual goals with more rigor or, lacking community surveillance, to break or ignore the Vinaya. If they developed a reputation for meditative or psychic powers, their hermitages, like the town monasteries, might become laden with donations as well.

The early records indicate that each group acted as a counterweight to the abuses of the other. An incident reported in both the Sūtras and the Vinayas (Mv.X) contrasts the quarrelsome city monks of Kausambi with the harmony of a small forest hermitage. Later legends that grew up around such charismatic figures as Upagupta and Piṇḍola Bhāradvāja suggest that wilderness meditators might use their psychic powers to attract personal followings, ignoring the strictures of the Vinaya and in effect seceding from the Order. In such cases, scholarly monks from the towns might be called in to reassert communal authority. A recurring theme throughout the history of Buddhist monasticism is that the Order as a whole thrives when town and wilderness monks find a harmonious balance, and suffers when that harmony breaks down. The ideal monastic is one who successfully combines the meditative prowess of the wandering ascetic with the social concern and communal loyalty of the settled monastic. Maudgalyāyana, for instance, was repeatedly praised for devoting his psychic powers not to his own aggrandizement but to the well-being of the monastic community and its supporters.

3.3.4 The Life of the Nuns

The Buddha is said to have instituted the *Bhikṣuṇī Sangha* (Order of Nuns) at the request of his aunt and foster mother, Mahāprajāpatī, and upon the intercession of Ānanda, on the condition that the nuns accept eight *garudharma* (vows of respect), strictly subordinating them—institutionally but not spiritually—to the Order of Monks. The vows were as follows: A nun shall honor every monk as her senior, even if she has been ordained for a hundred years, and he one day; during the Rains she shall not reside in a district where there are no monks; the nuns shall schedule their Observance Day in line with the monks; a nun shall invite criticism at the end of the Rains from both the nuns' and the monks' assemblies; she shall undergo penance (temporary probation) for a serious offense before both assemblies; a female postulant must undergo a two-year novitiate and then seek ordination from both assemblies; a nun shall not verbally abuse a monk; and whereas monks are allowed formally to reprove nuns, nuns may not reprove monks.

The Buddha is said to have stipulated this strict subordination of the nuns to the monks because, "Just as a clan in which there are many women and few men is easily plundered by robbers and bandits, in the same way, in whatever Dharma-Vinaya women get to go forth, the holy life does not last long" (Cv.X.I.6). Not long after the founding of the Bhikṣuṇī Sangha, Mahāprajāpatī asked the Buddha to release the nuns from the first vow. This the Buddha refused to do, as it would erase the boundaries between the two Orders, jeopardizing the public perception of their vows of celibacy. If, however, the Orders were so radically separated that all contact between them was precluded, their interpretations of the teaching would have diverged. Thus for practical reasons, one Order had to be placed under the other; the rationale given for placing the monks' Order over the nuns'—and scholars debate heatedly over whether this decision was made by the Buddha or later generations of monks—was that the religion would be more likely to survive if the monks outnumbered the nuns.

To prevent the nuns' position in the hierarchy from being abused or misconstrued, the Vinaya contains rules to keep the monks in check. For instance, monks were forbidden from requesting that nuns perform menial tasks for them, and nuns had the right to publicly boycott any monk who treated them in an unseemly manner. Apart from the fortnightly exhortation, the two Orders rarely met. The nuns had their own separate lineage of teachers, and—for the most part—conducted their business independently of the monks.

The formal subordination of the Order of Nuns to the Order of Monks was clearly not meant as an indication of spiritual inferiority. The *Verses of the Women Elders* (the Pali Canon's *Therīgāthā*)—an anthology of 73 poems memorized by monks and nuns for many centuries—demonstrates that the early Buddhists and their descendents recognized women as having attained a liberation equal to that of the Master's. In fact, it is first text in world history to report the religious experiences of women, apparently in their own words. One of the more famous verses is Muttā's (I.11):

> So freed! So thoroughly freed am I!—
> from three crooked things set free:
>   from mortar, pestle,
>   and crooked old husband.
> Having uprooted the craving
> that leads to becoming,
> I'm set free from aging and death.

Another is Soṇā's (V.8):

> Ten children I bore
> from this physical heap.
> Then weak from that, aged,
> I went to a nun.
> She taught me the Dhamma:
>   aggregates, sense spheres, and elements.
> Hearing her Dhamma,
> I cut off my hair and ordained.
> Having purified the divine eye
> while still a probationer,
> I know my previous lives,
> where I lived in the past.
> I develop the theme-less meditation,
> well-focused oneness.

I gain the liberation of immediacy—
from lack of clinging, unbound.
The five aggregates, comprehended,
stand like a tree with its root cut through.
I spit on old age.
There is now no further becoming.

Although the arrangement formalizing relations between the monks and nuns may offend modern sensibilities, the early canons were careful to provide female disciples, both nuns and lay women, with opportunities for spiritual advancement. For example, a Sutta (SN.XXXVII.34) encourages education for female lay disciples; this one text may account for the Buddhist countries of Southeast Asia having had the highest female literacy rates in the premodern world.

The rules governing the life of the nuns were similar to those for the monks. Their Prātimokṣas tended to be longer than the Prātimokṣas of the monks. For instance, the Pali Bhikṣuṇī Prātimokṣa contains 311 rules, to the bhikṣus' 227. Some of the rules appropriate only for men—such as the rule against intentional ejaculation—were deleted from the nuns' code, and others—such as rules against ordaining pregnant or nursing women—were added.

One important difference was that, whereas a senior monk could act as preceptor to any number of new monks at any one time, a senior nun could act as preceptor to only one new nun every two years. This kept the number of nuns smaller than that of the monks. A candidate for nun's ordination had to undergo a two-year period of probation during which she observed the ten precepts of the novice. If she broke any of the first six precepts during that time, her two-year probation began anew.

Because Utpalavarṇā, the nun foremost in psychic powers, had been raped while alone in a forest, nuns were forbidden to sleep alone or to wander alone into the wilderness. Their nunneries had to be situated within town or city walls. To compensate for this restriction, all nuns were required to go as groups on a wilderness tour once a year after the Rains. Still, their normal confinement to the towns and cities meant that their lives were similar to those of town monks. Donative inscriptions indicate that some nuns were honored for their mastery of the *Tripiṭaka,* and that some were either independently wealthy or had large followings. The early Vinayas report cases where individual nuns sponsored the construction of entire nunneries and monasteries. Of course, being confined to the towns had its disadvantages. Later Indian literature often portrays Buddhist nuns as involved in political intrigue; their stereotypical role in Sanskrit plays—even when portrayed favorably—is as matchmakers, in violation of their rules. At the same time, the Bhikṣuṇī Sangha as a whole was more affected than the Bhikṣu Sangha by the rise and fall of nation-states, flourishing when the cities prospered, declining when they fell.

3.3.5 The Laity

Buddhist adherents who did not opt for the monastic life were taught a level of Dharma appropriate to their duties as householders. In their search for happiness in this life, they were advised to be diligent in their work, to care for their possessions, to keep their expenditures in line with their income, and to associate with good people. For happiness in the next life, they were to develop conviction in the principle of karma, generosity, virtue, and discernment. These last four qualities boil down to the three means for acquiring *punya* (karmic merit)—giving, virtue, and meditation—that have formed the basic framework for lay Buddhist practice to the present day.

Although lay people were encouraged to be generous with one another and with mendicants of other religions, they were also taught that generosity to the Bhikṣu and Bhikṣuṇī Sanghas earned the highest merit. Without the generosity of the laity, the monastic Orders would have perished. In return, the monastics instructed the laity in Dharma, through word and example, assuring them in part that their generosity would win them wealth and the love of their fellow living beings both in this life and in the next.

As for virtue, both men and women householders were encouraged to take five *śīla* (precepts) as a constant practice. Śīla is defined as intentionally abstaining from unskillful conduct of body and speech. The first precept is to refrain from killing living beings, meaning all sorts of animals but not plants. The precept is broken if, knowing that something is a living being and intending to kill it, one attempts to do so and succeeds.

The second precept is to refrain from taking what has not been given; that is, from taking the property of another by force or by stealth. The offense is committed when one knows that the object belongs to another, attempts to steal it, and succeeds in moving it from its place.

The third precept is to refrain from sexual misconduct, which is defined following the double standard of the mores of the time. For a man, this means intercourse with the wife of another, a woman under the care of a guardian, a betrothed woman, or a woman under a vow of celibacy. As a commentary points out, visits to courtesans are thus not forbidden under this precept. The same commentary maintains that, for an unmarried woman under the protection of her family or her religious vows, all men are forbidden under this precept; for a married woman, all men except her husband. For an unmarried woman living independently—a rarity in those days, aside from courtesans—the only men forbidden are those observing vows of celibacy.

The fourth precept is to refrain from lying speech. This precept is broken when one intentionally misrepresents the truth to another person, even in jest. The fifth precept is to refrain totally from taking intoxicants that lead to heedlessness.

These precepts were to be observed in the context of interpersonal relationships marked by reciprocal duties. For instance, children were to support their parents in old age in return for having been supported during their childhood; they were to help their parents in their work, carry on the family line, behave so as to deserve their inheritance, and make meritorious gifts to the religion in their parents' name after the latter's death. In response, parents were to restrain their children from doing evil, encourage them to do good, provide for their education, find them spouses, and in due time turn over their inheritance. A husband was to honor his wife's good name, be faithful to her, give her complete authority in running the household, and provide her with adornments. She, in return, was to organize her work well, be faithful to her husband, honor his relatives and guests, be skillful at home crafts, and protect his earnings. Similar reciprocal patterns governed relations between teacher and student, master and servant, lay person and monastic, friend and friend (DN.31).

Lay Buddhists were assured that their virtue would guarantee them a fine reputation, confidence in public gatherings, a calm and unbewildered death, and rebirth in a heaven. Those desiring to enhance their virtue were encouraged to observe the eight precepts—formulated in such a way as to cover the same ground as the first nine of the novice monk and nun's ten precepts (see Section 3.3.2)—either on a constant basis or on the lay Poṣadha: the days of the full moon, new moon, and two half moons. Those following this practice would dress in white and spend the day learning about the Dharma and practicing meditation.

All the early lineages agreed that the laity could attain the first three degrees of Awakening and remain in the household life. Some lineages, such as the Theravāda, maintained that, although lay people could attain arhatship, lay arhats had to ordain or else die within seven days after their attainment, for the lay state could not support an arhat's purity.

The early canons tell us little of the life-cycle ceremonies of the early Buddhist laity. The Vinayas inform us simply that monks were regularly invited to teach Dharma at weddings and housewarmings. However, if modern-day Theravāda practice can be taken as a guide, the monks did not officiate at such ceremonies. They simply provided the sponsors the opportunity to gain merit, leaving the remainder of the ceremony to the sponsors and the ritual experts hired for the occasion. Unlike such experts, the monks were treated as honored guests.

3.4 AŚOKA

In 321 B.C.E., Candragupta Maurya succeeded to the throne of Magadha. His primary adviser, Kauṭalya, was the author of a treatise on political power that, because of its amoral approach to power, has earned him the name of the "Machiavelli of India." Kauṭalya's advice was apparently very astute, for by 303 B.C.E. Candragupta had gained control of territory from Bengal to eastern Afghanistan and as far south as the Narbada River. His son, Bindusāra, acceded to the throne in 297 B.C.E. and conquered the Deccan and Mysore in central India, and the Tamil country in the far south. Bindusāra died in 272 B.C.E., succeeded by his son Aśoka, who was crowned four years later after eliminating other claimants to the throne.

Although Bindusāra was a supporter of the Ājīvaka sect, whose denial of morality fit well with his approach to power, Aśoka converted to Buddhism—perhaps for political reasons, perhaps at the behest of his first wife—nine years into his reign. By his own admission, the religion did not mean much to him personally until two and a half years later, after his conquest of Kalinga in northeast India, the only major area of the subcontinent still refusing to submit to his rule. The extensive bloodshed and destruction caused by the conquest filled him with remorse. He began to study the teachings of various sects, visited monks frequently, learned from them, and formally dedicated himself as an adherent to the Sangha. As a result, he began making drastic changes both in his personal life and in his administrative policies, abandoning the amoral maxims taught by Kauṭalya and undertaking a great experiment in applying Dharma to the running of his empire, thus earning for himself a lasting reputation in world, as well as Indian, history.

For centuries the only records of Aśoka's reign were the Buddhist chronicles, which claimed him as an exemplary supporter of the Sangha. Then in the nineteenth century, Aśokan edicts were discovered and deciphered, providing in his own words a history of his reign. In these edicts, Aśoka expresses his support for all the major religions of his time: Buddhism, Brahmanism, Jainism, and the Ājīvaka sect. On the basis of this fact—together with the fact that Aśoka's expressed conception of Dharma makes no mention of particularly Buddhist doctrines such as the Four Noble Truths—some scholars have questioned whether Aśoka was actually Buddhist. The case for regarding him as Buddhist, however, rests on much stronger evidence in the edicts. To begin with, there are the many edicts addressed intramurally to Buddhists; in one, Aśoka declares himself an upāsaka; in another, he shows a close familiarity with Buddhist texts. No edicts addressed intramurally to members of other religions have been found. Second, there are the Aśokan rock pillars erected at Buddhist holy sites, an honor he did not extend to the holy sites of other religions. Although caves donated by Aśoka to the Ājīvakas have been discovered, his continued support of the Ājīvakas fits into the Buddha's instructions to major lay converts from other sects that they continue giving alms to their previous sect as before (MN.56; Mv.VI.31).

As for the edicts addressed to the populace at large, they are aimed at lay people, and it should be remembered that the Buddha himself rarely taught abstract doctrine to the laity. Aśoka's purpose was to formulate an ideology that would bring his empire together. Had he tried to force his beliefs on members of other religions, it would have proven politically divisive. Thus, in these edicts he generally focuses on themes that members of all religions would accept, such as truthfulness, nonviolence, and respect for teachers and elders. Still, his language, modes of expression, and injunctions betray a Buddhist orientation. Dharma, for him, refers to moral values as well as the qualities of heart that underlie moral action. This is a specifically Buddhist use of the term. The only other religion of the time that used Dharma in anywhere near this sense was Brahmanism, which defined it as the moral rules and ritual behavior enjoined by the Vedas. The Vedic rules, however, make no reference to qualities of the heart, and Aśoka's belittling of rituals in one of his edicts, together with his outlawing of animal sacrifices, indicates that he was not looking to the Vedas for guidance. In fact, the ideals he espouses correspond to the first three steps of the Buddha's graduated discourse (see Section 2.4). The attitudes he expresses fall under the four Brahmā Attitudes (see Section 1.4.1). On the whole, we can safely assume that Buddhists have been correct in claiming Aśoka as one of their own.

By Aśoka's own analysis, his domestic Dharma policy had three prongs: personal Dharma practice on his own part, administration in line with the Dharma, and Dharma instruction for the populace. In terms of his own practice, Aśoka cut back on the slaughter of animals in the royal kitchens (allowing only two peacocks and one deer a week) and abandoned the sport of royal hunting excursions, replacing them with Dharma excursions on which he would take pilgrimages to holy spots, visit śramaṇas and brahman priests, give donations to religious mendicants and to the aged, and discuss Dharma with the general populace. Appropriately, his first Dharma pilgrimage was to Bodhgaya, the site of the Buddha's Awakening. Later in his reign he visited Lumbini, the site of the Buddha's birth, where he erected a commemorative pillar that still stands today. In the same region in 253 B.C.E., he ordered the enlargement of the stūpa dedicated to the former Buddha Konamakamuni. The inscription recording this act is the earliest datable evidence for the cult of Buddhas who had lived prior to Gautama. Aśoka's first wife came from Vidisa, which is apparently why he sponsored the first stage of construction of the still-famous stūpa on the nearby hill of Sanchi, the most extensive and perhaps loveliest of all early Buddhist structures still standing in India.

Tradition maintains that Aśoka opened nine of the ten original stūpas (see Section 2.6) and distributed the relics they contained among 84,000 stūpas throughout his kingdom. But even the more modest tally of history and archaeology abundantly testifies that honoring the Buddha ranked as highly as ethical conduct in Aśoka's personal religious beliefs. As stated previously, Aśoka made donations to all sects, but his support for the Buddhist Sangha was prodigious, reportedly causing recruits to flock to the Order and demonstrating the oft-repeated rule that the survival and prosperity of Buddhism have usually depended on rulers' support.

Aśoka's administrative reforms were aimed at facilitating redress of grievances against petty officials. Inspectors were sent out to check on the fair administration of justice, especially in the newly conquered area of Kalinga. Special officials were appointed with the power to convey petitions from the populace to the king at any time, even when he was in his women's quarters. Dispensaries and medicinal herb gardens were set up for the treatment of human and animal diseases, wells were dug, and highways improved. Aśoka noted that previous kings had also provided public works of this last sort for their subjects, but that his provisions differed inasmuch as his motivation was directed at the Dharma. This difference in motivation suggests that he was inspired by the Buddhist maxim that the practice of the Dharma fares best in a stable society, and that societies are most stable when prosperity is widely shared (see Section 2.5).

Aśoka's policy of Dharma instruction for the general populace was the most original part of his policy. According to him, it took two forms: Dharma injunctions and Dharma persuasion. The injunctions included laws forbidding animal sacrifice; prohibiting the killing of many kinds of animals, in particular those not used for food; and outlawing wasteful festivals. The persuasion consisted of the presentation of edifying performances containing moral themes for the populace, portraying the heavenly rewards of virtue, and an extensive set of royal messages aimed at persuading his subjects to live more moral lives. In 254 B.C.E. Aśoka had a series of 14 edicts on topics related to the Dharma engraved on rocks throughout his empire, and he instructed his officials to read them to the public on festival days. Thirteen years later he began issuing a similar series of seven edicts, which were inscribed on polished stone pillars. These inscriptions are the earliest surviving compositions of a Buddhist lay follower, and their perspective on the Dharma affords an interesting contrast to the monastic perspective recorded in the canons.

Dharma for Aśoka meant both moral action and skillful mental qualities. The actions he recommended to his subjects included honor for and obedience to one's parents, teachers, and other elders; generosity to relatives, acquaintances, and religious persons; abstention from killing animals; moderation in spending wealth; kindness to servants; and above all, the gift of Dharma, that is, mutual admonition among friends and family members as to what is right and wrong. Mental qualities he recommended included self-control, gratitude, devotion, compassion, forgiveness, impartiality, and truthfulness. He warned against irascibility, cruelty, anger, spitefulness, and pride. The Dharma of his edicts, however, is not just humanistic morality. Aśoka repeatedly asserted that his aim was to enable others to find happiness in the next world.

In addition to promulgating edicts, Aśoka formed a new branch of the government devoted to Dharma instruction, sending Dharma officials throughout the empire to carry his message to the populace and to supervise religious activities. His interference in the life of the religious sects, Aśoka said, was motivated by a desire that each sect develop fine traditions and its religious "essence," which to him meant tolerance: not praising one's own sect to the disparagement of others. He recommended that the different sects listen to and learn from one another. To honor other sects, he said, was to honor one's own. Paradoxically, in spite of his support for tolerance, there is epigraphic evidence that Aśoka became involved in a split that was dividing the Buddhist community at this time, ordering the faction he saw as deviant to leave the community or be forcibly disrobed.

Five years after attacking Kalinga, Aśoka proclaimed a new foreign policy, one of peaceful Dharma-conquest rather than military conquest. Dharma officials were sent to proclaim Aśoka's domestic policy of Dharma practice, administration, and instruction to the people of kingdoms bordering his own—especially the Greek kingdoms on his western frontier, and the Colas and Sinhalese kingdoms to his south. A bilingual Greek-Aramaic Aśokan inscription found at Kandahar in Afghanistan records, for the benefit of the people in his neighboring kingdoms, the measures he had taken so that "during their present life and in their future existence, people will live better and more happily together in all things." Aśoka aimed his policy of Dharma-conquest at inspiring other kingdoms to follow his example. This, he said, would be a source of greater joy than military conquest could ever provide. One of his edicts states that in 256 and 255 B.C.E. he sent Dharma-envoys to the Greek rulers of Syria, Egypt, Macedonia, Cyrene, and Epyrus, as well as to the Tamils in south India. Buddhist tradition records that he also sent missions to Sri Lanka and Southeast Asia. His missionaries left no clearly documentable impression on the Mediterranean world, but they had greater impact closer to home. In particular, his mission to Sri Lanka appears to have been an outstanding success. Legend reports that he sent not only Dharma-officials but also his own son and daughter—Mahinda and Saṅghamittā—who went as monk and nun, respectively, and succeeded in converting the king, thus setting in motion a process that converted the entire island to Buddhism.

Scholars have debated the possible ulterior motives for Aśoka's Dharma policies. Although his edicts convey sincere concern for the welfare of his own and his neighbors' subjects more convincingly than any other royal pronouncements of the ancient world, it would be a mistake to regard Aśoka as a starry-eyed idealist with his feet planted firmly in the clouds. He had inherited a large, multicultural empire, and thus needed a transcultural policy, inculcating moral behavior in his subjects, that would tie it together more firmly than could the cynical maxims of amoral statecraft. In addition, his strong bureaucratic state not only regulated commerce, industry, and agriculture, but also acted as an entrepreneur itself. Buddhism, along with the other śramaṇa religions, was popular among craftsmen and merchants, whose interests were tied to the state enterprises. Thus Aśoka, in supporting Buddhism, was strengthening a bond with an already loyal class. In pursuing a policy of Dharma-conquest, he ensured the peace and stability needed for the profitable functioning of the government enterprises. In formulating and propagating a Dharma policy that transcended any particular religion, he created a common ideology that could tie his far-flung empire together.

According to tradition, Aśoka's successors discontinued his policies, and his dynasty fell half a century after his death. Aśoka's main success was in his contribution to the Buddhist tradition. His social ideals served as a model of the well-run Buddhist polity, and he himself served as a model for the dedicated lay supporter—models that later Buddhists never forgot. Thus, alongside the Sangha and its monastic ideals, there developed a parallel tradition whose goals involved achieving the Dharma's ends in social and political contexts.

3.5 ABHIDHARMA

As the early lineages amassed large collections of Sūtras, they felt a need to supplement them. Although the Sūtras were useful for showing how specific Dharma teachings could be applied to specific contexts—or, to use our medical analogy, how they could treat specific ailments of the mind—they proved cumbersome for general teaching purposes. Thus the early lineages supplemented them with pedagogical tools to present the Dharma in more universal terms: treatises on how to interpret ambiguous passages, textbooks to collate different descriptions of the path found in the Sūtras, and catechisms based on lists (*mātṛkā*) of central topics. Over time, these tools grew in importance, as they proved the most efficient way of training new students in basic Dharma and defending the Dharma from attacks from non-Buddhist opponents. The early lineages gathered some of these tools into their Sūtra Piṭakas, while some of the lineages also fashioned them into a third Piṭaka: an *Abhidharma* (Pali: *Abhidhamma*) *Piṭaka* or "Higher Dharma" collection.

Of the many Abhidharma Piṭakas, we have only one complete version in an Indic language—the Abhidhamma of the Theravādins—and one nearly complete version—the Abhidharma of the Sarvāstivādins—in Chinese translations. We also have assorted treatises of other schools, including what may be a Chinese translation of the Dharmaguptaka Abhidharma, but the Theravādin and Sarvāstivādin versions proved by far most influential over the long run. The Theravādin Abhidhamma provided the foundation for Buddhist scholastic philosophy in Sri Lanka and Southeast Asia; and the Sarvāstivādin Abhidharma, the foundation of Buddhist scholastic philosophy in Tibet and East Asia.

We have to stress the word "foundation" here, for although Abhidharma is often presented as systematic philosophy, Buddhist philosophical systems did not develop until several centuries after the canons closed. The canonical Abhidharmas were less concerned with system than with taxonomy: principles for classifying the wide variety of teachings found in the Sūtras into orderly categories. Philosophical controversies arose—and are recorded in the Abhidharmas—as the process of taxonomy gave rise to questions around points where the Sūtras were silent or ambiguous. However, not until generations later were the taxonomies and their controversial points worked into what we would recognize as coherent systems built on philosophical principles. Instead, what we find in the canonical Abhidharmas is a strong concern for organization. Lists of teachings are compiled, their members precisely defined, and then the lists are analyzed against each other to make the distribution of terms even more precise. This methodical quest for precise placement is the hallmark of early Abhidharma.

By including Abhidharma treatises in their canons, the early lineages were placing them on the level of the word of the Buddha, and one of the duties of the later commentaries was to justify this position. The Theravādin commentators claimed that six of their seven Abhidhamma treatises were actually spoken by the Buddha himself. According to their account, he spent an entire Rains retreat teaching the Abhidhamma to his mother, who had been reborn as a male deva in the Tuṣita heaven. Every day after his meal the Buddha descended from heaven to a lake in the Himalayas, where Śāriputra was waiting to wash his bowl, and there he repeated to Śāriputra what he had taught his mother the previous day. As for the Sarvāstivādins, they insisted that their seven Abhidharma treatises, although composed by monks, were the Buddha's word because the authors had simply collated material already present in their canon. Thus, while the Abhidharmists made many original contributions to the Buddhist tradition, they were loath to claim originality. The habit of using stories to hide an original contribution was to continue unabated throughout Buddhism's lifetime in India and in other countries as well.

3.5.1 The Lists (Mātṛkā)

Although the Theravādin and Sarvāstivādin Abhidharmas each contain seven treatises, only two of their earliest treatises—the Theravādin *Vibhaṅga* (Analysis) and the Sarvāstivādin *Dharmaskandha* (Aggregate of Teachings)—are in any way similar. However, both Abhidharmas take as their point of departure similar lists of teachings drawn from the Sūtras; and, although the taxonomies they derived from these lists developed in different directions, they began with a similar method of derivation. This method is what we will discuss here.

The lists fall into three major sets drawn from what we have identified as the "emptiness" mode of the Sūtras. The first set might be called lists of *topics,* including such things as the five aggregates, the twelve sense spheres, the Four Noble Truths, the four dhyānas, the twelve factors of dependent co-arising, and the thirty-seven wings to Awakening. The second set of lists might be called *categories:* various ways of dividing realities into two or three types. Some examples include: skillful, unskillful, and indeterminate; conjoined with pleasure, conjoined with pain, conjoined with neither pleasure nor pain; internal, external; fabricated, unfabricated. The third set of lists concerns *conditional relationships* that, instead of being directly drawn, are inferred from the Sūtras. Some of the relationships are formal, such as: condition existing prior to effect, condition arising simultaneously with effect, and two factors conditioning each other. Others are more specific, such as: the relationship of nutriment to what is nourished and the relationship of a sense object to the corresponding sense organ. The final treatise in the Theravādin Abhidhamma—the *Paṭṭhāna* (Conditioned Relationships)—identifies 24 types of these relationships; the final treatise in the Sarvāstivādin Abhidharma—the *Jñānaprasthāna* (Foundation of Knowledge)—identifies six.

How these lists are converted into complete taxonomies can be illustrated by looking at three of the Theravādin treatises: the *Dhammasaṅginī* (Compilation of Dhammas), the *Vibhaṅga,* and the *Paṭṭhāna.*

The *Dhammasaṅginī* focuses on the second type of lists, the categories. It identifies 22 triads (sets of three categories) and 100 dyads (sets of two). Some of these categories cover only mental phenomena, while others cover both physical and mental phenomena. Starting with the first set—skillful, unskillful, and indeterminate—the treatise follows the form of a catechism (the basic form of all the Abhidhamma treatises), asking for and then giving precise definitions of each term. The catechism continues, asking how all the major terms in the Sūtras fall into each category. The treatise's treatment deviates from the Sūtras in that it classifies the unfabricated as one of the twelve sense spheres—as an object of the intellect—and as part of the category of name (see Section 1.4.1). The Sarvāstivādin treatises classify the unfabricated in the same way, a fact that scholars have attributed to the Abhidharmists' eagerness to capture in the net of their taxonomies all the knowledge of an awakened mind, even in areas that the Sūtras regarded as beyond classification.

The *Vibhaṅga* is organized around the first type of lists, the topics. Each set of topics is first defined with the most technical and precise terms used in the Sūtras. This is then followed by a second set of definitions, even more precise, based on a collation of all relevant material drawn from the Sūtras and the *Dhammasaṅginī,* noting areas where the Sūtras are vague. For instance, the authors seem undecided as to whether greed, anger, and delusion should come under the first noble truth or the second. The topics are then further analyzed in terms from one to ten. For example, in what ways do all feelings belong to one class? Two classes? Three? And so on. Finally, each topic is analyzed in terms of the triads and dyads from the *Dhammasaṅginī,* forming enormous wheels (see Section 2.2.2). The *Vibhaṅga* as a whole concludes with its "Heart," a definitive map of the various levels of the cosmos—something the Sūtras had not provided—with each level analyzed in terms of the topics just covered. In this way, the treatise subsumes the cosmological mode of the Sūtras under the emptiness mode in an effort to arrive at an ultimate mode of truth applicable to all types of discourse. (A Sarvāstivādin treatise, the *Prajñaptibhāsya,* analyzes the various stages in the narrative of the Buddha's life into "emptiness" terms in a similar attempt to arrive at a mode of speech universally true in the ultimate sense.)

The *Paṭṭhāna,* by far the largest of the Abhidhamma treatises, creates a much larger set of wheels by asking how 24 types of causal relationship, in all imaginable combinations, operate among the members of the *Dhammasaṅgiṇī*'s triads and dyads. The treatise does not list every member of the resulting wheels, but simply outlines how the method should be applied. Theravādin commentaries differ in their calculation of how many questions would be asked if all the permutations of the method were worked out. Some say slightly more than 400 billion; others, slightly less.

At first glance, it might seem that the Abhidharmists had converted the Dharma into a numbers game, with wheels upon wheels spinning farther and farther away from the path of actual practice. And—given the emphasis the Sūtras lay on being sensitive to the right time and place to make a statement—there is the question of whether taking the teachings out of context inevitably distorts them. Nevertheless, the simple fact that the Abhidharmists had placed the various Sūtra teachings on the table all at once opened many new lines of inquiry. On the one hand, it inspired efforts to compose definitive treatises on the Dharma that would subsume all the variations of the Sūtra teachings into a single whole. Particularly prominent were efforts to eliminate the redundancies in the Abhidharma taxonomies to create a more streamlined picture of ultimate truths, along with efforts to formulate definitive maps of the path of practice that would apply in all contexts. On the other hand, the new all-embracing context sparked new types of questions as factors previously isolated from one another were now side by side. This last tendency is what provoked the formation of distinct schools of thought in the Buddhist community, as the various lineages mined their Sūtras for answers to questions that the Sūtras had not proposed to ask. Here we will discuss two of these questions that had the most far-reaching effect on Buddhist thought.

3.5.2 Points of Controversy: The Nature of the Individual

A treatise in the Theravāda Abhidhamma, the *Puggalapaññati* (Descriptions of Individuals) tabulates the Buddha's many statements about the different types of individuals existing in the world. For example, there are individuals who are like a mark in water (their anger easily fades), those who are like a mark in the dirt, those who are like an inscription in stone (they bear long grudges); and so forth. This tabulation is apparently what sparked the question: How does the concept of "individual" fit into the other taxonomies? Is it an ultimate truth like other topics? The Abhidharmists began to split between those who answered "Yes" to this question, and those who answered "No."

The standard Theravādin position became "No," and one of their treatises—the *Kathāvatthu,* or Points of Controversy—contains their arguments to support this negative position, as well as their record of their opponents' arguments for the affirmative. Both sides manage to quote passages from the Sūtras to support their positions, but the Theravādin speakers generally avoid stating precisely how they regard the concept of the individual, and devote their efforts simply to attacking their opponents' concept. To avoid the implication that their individual is simply a disguised assertion of "self," the *Pudgalavādins*—"those who teach [the existence of] the individual"—are forced into an awkward concept of person that is neither identical with nor separate from the five aggregates; neither fabricated nor unfabricated; and cannot be directly experienced, like the aggregates, but can only be inferred from them. This, for the Theravādins, shows that the concept of individual as an ultimate truth is self-contradictory, and thus untenable.

However there is one set of arguments where the Theravādins state their own positive assertions on the issue, and here they deviate from their own Sūtras no less than do their opponents. The arguments concern the nature of karma and they focus on two questions that the Buddha as portrayed in the Sūtras refused to answer, on the grounds that they did not conduce to the ending of duḥkha. The questions are these: Given that there are actions and their results, is there anyone who does the action? Is there anyone who experiences the result? The Pudgalavādins answer "Yes" to both questions, and then are charged with creating an infinite regress (having to further infer the doer of the doer, the experiencer of the experiencer, and so one). However, the Theravādins answer "No" to both questions, and although they do not portray themselves as encountering any difficulties, they have actually adopted a doctrine similar to an Ājīvaka position attacked in the Sūtras (see Section 1.2): that in the ultimate sense there are no agents and no one acted upon. In the succeeding centuries, most Buddhist schools adopted this position and were bedeviled by the natural follow-up questions: How can moral responsibility be more than a social convention if there are no agents? What does it matter if actions are skillful and unskillful if no one experiences their results?

The debates between the Pudgalavādins and their opponents reached an impasse that lasted for centuries, as each side developed increasingly sophisticated arguments to bolster its position. The Pudgalavādins formed their own lineage, which survived until Buddhism was wiped out of northern India in the beginning of the thirteenth century C.E. Their major offshoot, the *Sāmmitīyas*, flowered in the seventh and eighth centuries C.E., largely through the patronage of the great Buddhist king, Harṣavardhana (see Section 5.1), whose sister, Rājyaśrī, joined the school as a bhikṣuṇī. According to Chinese pilgrims at the time, it was the dominant sect in the Ganges Valley. The school also had an outpost in what is now Vietnam. Only a few of its texts survive, however, mostly in Chinese translations.

3.5.3 Points of Controversy: The Nature of Existence

The controversy with the Pudgalavādins raised further issues that we at present would classify under the headings of epistemology, cognitive psychology, and ontology: How are ultimate facts known? How is knowledge of anything formed? How do things exist in an ultimate sense? Full-fledged answers to these questions would not develop for centuries, but in the early period two important theories coalesced that provided the foundation for a major school of Buddhist philosophy, the Sarvāstivādin. The name of the school means "those who teach that everything exists," the "everything" here meaning things past, present, and future.

The theory of "everything existing" grew from discussions of how dharmas (facts) exist, how they can influence one another, and how they can be known. One of the peculiarities of the word *dharma* is that it can mean both teaching and phenomenon, in the same way that *fact* can mean a statement about a truth, as well as the truth itself. In the context of Abhidharma discussions, dharmas listed in the mātṛkās thus came to be seen both as classes of facts and as individual events. The question arose: How does an individual fact or event exist in the present? The general agreement was that mental facts had only a momentary existence, but were physical facts equally momentary? The Sarvāstivādin position began when someone said "Yes." The seeming permanence of mountains, for instance, is simply an illusion caused by many similar physical form-events happening in rapid succession.

The difficulties entailed by this position are many. If everything is equally momentary, how can anything be present long enough to be known through the long cognitive process from sensory impression to concept? How can an action done at one time give results in another? The answer was that things exist through all time frames but act as events only in the present. The details of this position weren't worked out until centuries later, but because those details have been very influential in the history of Buddhist thought, a brief summary might be useful here: Dharmas exist as real entities or substances (*dravya*) in all three time periods, each defined by an intrinsic nature (*svabhāva*) and marked by an intrinsic identifying characteristic (*svalakṣana*). Given appropriate conditions, they manifest a particular activity (*kāritra*), which makes them present. But even when not acting in the present, they can serve as conditions for other dharmas to act.

The standard Theravādins opposed these theories, saying that physical events endure for longer periods than mental events, and that things past and future, by definition, do not currently exist. Another group, whose lineage is unknown, adopted a qualified position between the Theravādins and Sarvāstivādins, maintaining that two kinds of events exist: present ones and past ones that have yet to yield their karmic results. Because they made this distinction, the Sarvāstivādins called them *Vibhajyavādins* (Distinctionists).

The Sarvāstivādin position came to dominate Buddhist philosophy in northern India for many centuries, perhaps because its inherent difficulties set combustible intellects on fire with the desire to resolve them. Most of the Sarvāstivādin treatises were written in Kashmir, and were further adopted by another monastic lineage—the *Mūlasarvāstivādins*—centered in Mathura.

The Sarvāstivādins also established a center in Gandhara in northwest India. This put them—together with their offshoots, the *Dharmaguptakas* and *Mahīśāsakas*—in a favorable position to spread their teachings to the cities on the northern branch of the Central Asian trade route and on into China. Traces of Sarvāstivādin traditions have also surfaced in Burma and northern Thailand. As for the Mūlasarvāstivādins, they maintained a strong presence in the Ganges Valley, from which their Vinaya spread into Tibet.

3.6 PAST-LIFE NARRATIVES

As the Abhidharmists were attempting a definitive map of the Buddhist tradition in its emptiness mode, other monastics were attempting a full record of its narrative traditions, filling in the blanks and accounting for the anomalies in the Sūtra narratives. Interest centered on questions related to the previous lives of the

Buddha and his arhat disciples: What particular actions during their long saṁsāric journey enabled them to reach Awakening in their final lives? How had they been related to one another in past lives? How were their careers related to those of previous Buddhas? And the question that was to have the most far-reaching influence on the future of Buddhist thought: How, in general, did the career of a bodhisattva differ from that of an arhat-to-be, and how did both differ from the Private Buddha? (See Section 1.4.1.)

The narratives answering these questions fall into two genres: the *jātaka,* or Birth-story; and the *avadāna* (Pali: *apadāna*), or Lesson. Both try to establish a pedigree for the Buddha and his arhat disciples, but in different ways. The typical jātaka focuses on the pedigree of the Buddha's and arhats' virtues: how they had striven to perfect their character in preparation for Awakening. The typical avadāna focuses on the pedigree of the Buddha and arhats in relation to previous Buddhas: how their connections to the long line of previous Buddhas had helped them on their way to Awakening. The two genres are not always mutually consistent—nor are the tales within a particular genre—but they developed important concepts. From the jātakas came the concept of the *pāramitās* (Pali: *pāramīs*), the perfections of character that constitute the path to a Buddha's or arhat's Awakening. From the avadānas came the concept of the Buddha-field (*buddha-kṣetra;* Pali, *buddha-khetta*), the fertile ground surrounding a Buddha or his relics that enables "seeds" of merit to bear abundant fruit. Together, these concepts have exerted an enormous influence—much greater than the speculations of the Abhidharmists—on the worldview of Buddhists of all levels over the centuries.

3.6.1 Jātakas and the Perfections

The jātakas are the older genre of the two. Scattered examples are found in the oldest strata of the canons, but the most famous jātakas are those added to the canons after the time of Aśoka. The Theravādin canon, for instance, contains a large collection of 547 sets of jātaka verses, each set associated with a narrative contained in the lineage's later commentaries. Although the commentaries in general postdate the canon, most of the narratives seem to be very old, and there is no understanding the verses without them. Some of the narratives, in fact, predate the time of the Buddha, which suggests that the monastics who collected and added them to the Buddhist canons had a second pedigree in mind. By identifying the Bodhisattva and arhats-to-be with the heroes and heroines of old Indian folk tales, they provided them with a cultural pedigree, a connection with the traditions of folk-wisdom that Indians had learned from early childhood. Indian Buddhist converts could thus view their religion as the culmination, rather than the repudiation, of their pre-Buddhist cultural heritage.

The typical jātaka tale follows a simple pattern: first, a narrative of the present, that is, an event in the last life of the Buddha or an arhat; then a narrative of the past, in which the Buddha recounts events in a previous life to explain the present event, after which he identifies the characters in the past narrative with characters in the present. Most often, the stories center on the Buddha himself, and the narratives of the past show him in a variety of roles: as a common animal, a merchant, a prince, an ascetic, very occasionally a deva, but never—in the Theravāda collection—a Brahmā or a woman.

Curiously, the tales do not always portray the Bodhisattva in the best light. He occasionally breaks his precepts (although never the fourth, against lying), and there is even a tale in which, as an ascetic invited to teach the ladies in a palace harem, he tries to seduce the queen (Yaśodharā in a previous birth). She, however, reminds him of his responsibilities. Chastened, he returns to his austerities in the forest, never again to seek fortune or fame.

In the vast majority of the stories, however, the Bodhisattva evinces a high level of wisdom and integrity, sometimes to superhuman extremes. In his penultimate life, for instance—as Prince Vessantara—he vows to give his belongings to anyone who asks for them. As a result, he forfeits his kingdom and is forced to relinquish his children to a cruel brahman who treats them like slaves. Fortunately, the story has a happy ending, as his kingdom and family are restored, but the lesson is clear: The path to Buddhahood is not for the faint-of-heart. In fact, most of the jātakas in which the Bodhisattva is a lay person end with him leaving home and taking up the life of a forest ascetic.

Not in all cases, though, is the Bodhisattva the hero of the tale. In fact, the Jātakas depict the path to Awakening as something of a group effort, in which friends and relatives, in a kaleidoscope of shifting relationships, work together through many lifetimes. In one of the tales, for instance, the Bodhisattva and Yaśodharā-to-be are a pair of kinnarīs (half-bird, half-human creatures) sporting in the Himalayas. A passing deva, smitten with Yaśodharā, kills her husband and tries to take her as his wife. She, however, refuses his advances, and her protests force Indra, the king of the devas, to descend to the earth and restore the Bodhisattva to life. Yaśodharā's loyalty in this instance is said to have earned her the right to be the Bodhisattva's wife in his last existence and to gain Awakening from his teachings.

From this mass of narratives, Buddhist monastics tried to extract the elements of a path to Buddhahood, and the result is the theory of the *paramitās,* or perfections of character needed for Awakening. The Sarvāstivādins found six perfections illustrated in their collection—giving, virtue, endurance, energy, dhyāna, and discernment—a list that shaped Mahāyāna thought in later centuries. The Theravādins found ten perfections illustrated in their collection—giving, virtue, renunciation, discernment, energy, endurance, truth, determination, good will, and equanimity—and organized their jātaka collection to end with ten stories to illustrate each in its ideal form. What is noteworthy about these lists is that all their elements can be found in sūtra descriptions of the path to arhatship. This fact raised an important question: How do the perfections differ from the qualities developed by an arhat? The Theravādins gave their answer to this question in the *Cariyapiṭaka,* a late addition to their Khuddaka Nikāya, stating that all three paths to Awakening—as a Teaching Buddha, a Private Buddha, and a *srāvaka* (disciple) arhat—require all the perfections, but in differing strengths: a srāvaka arhat develops perfections on an ordinary level, a Private Buddha on a heightened level, and a Teaching Buddha on an ultimate level. How these levels differ was not clearly stated. The original theory seems to be that they differ only in intensity, and not in kind, but this interpretation raised a practical problem: What was to prevent a person aiming at Full Buddhahood from slipping into arhatship when the ordinary level of perfections had been fulfilled? One possible answer—which gained support from many lineages—was provided by the avadāna literature: At one's first aspiration to Awakening, one should determine one's goal with a vow. How this was supposed to work is best understood within the context of the avadāna genre as a whole.

3.6.2 Avadānas and the Buddha-Field

Because the avadānas were originally associated with the stūpa cult, they are among the earliest texts whose dating can be indicated by archaeological evidence. The Pali apadānas mention details of stūpa architecture using a vocabulary found only in the inscriptions dating from the second century B.C.E. to the first century C.E., during the reign of the *Sātavāhana* dynasty, centered in the West, and the *Śunga* dynasty, centered in Magadha. Other collections of avadānas, roughly contemporary, include those collected in the Vinayas of the Mūlasarvāstivādins and the Lokottaravādins (an offshoot of the Mahāsaṃghikas), along with the *Avadānaśataka,* a more polished literary text compiled by the Sarvāstivādins.

Like the jātakas, avadānas aim at inspiring a sense of devotion toward the Buddha and his arhat disciples by relating stories from their previous lives, but with a different strategy. Instead of emphasizing the strength of character required by the path to Awakening, they stress the abundant rewards that come from doing service (*adhikāra*) to a Buddha or his relics. By showing how the Buddha or an arhat received an extraordinary boost on the path to Awakening by planting a "seed" in the merit-field surrounding a previous Buddha or his relics, they encourage their listeners to plant similar seeds in the merit-field still available to them in the relics of the current Buddha.

The notion of a *merit-field* dates to the earliest strata of the canon, where the noble (ārya) Sangha is said to be the unexcelled merit-field for the world. In other words, offerings given to members of this Sangha bear greater fruit than offerings given to anyone else. In this way, an arhat's spiritual accomplishments give not only individual benefits to the arhat, but also collective benefits to everyone who shows respect or gives the arhat material support.

With the development of the three-path theory mentioned above, the idea grew that the Teaching Buddha's merit-field was the most fertile of all. To distinguish this field from that of the arhat, it was termed the Buddha-field. Although the idea of the Buddha-field appears in a handful of other canonical texts, the avadānas added three important contributions to the idea: (1) the Buddha-field surrounding a relic of the Buddha is equally fertile to that surrounding a living Buddha; (2) there are innumerable Buddha-fields in every direction beyond the limits of our cosmos; and (3) a Buddha-field is absolutely necessary to the path of Awakening, for only by planting a merit-seed in such a field can one embark on the path of Awakening at all. Thus the Buddha-field becomes the ground from which further awakened beings will grow. All three of these ideas proved influential in later Buddhist history, but the third was probably the most revolutionary, in that it marked a radical revision of the role of the Buddha and the nature of the path to Awakening.

As mentioned in Section 2.4.1, the early strata of the canons depict the Buddha as both teacher and protector, with the emphasis on the former. With the avadānas, however, the stress shifts markedly the other way. These are the first texts where the Buddha is explicitly called a *nātha,* or protector, and they give him a twofold role. Having developed his perfections, (1) he is endowed with a dazzling appearance ("like a fearless lion-king," "like a lightning flash,"), impressive psychic powers, and an ability to teach marvelous Dharma, all of which are aimed at inspiring prasāda in beings at large; (2) he provides a Buddha-field in which beings moved by their prasāda can plant seeds of merit. Because his Dharma is aimed at inducing prasāda rather than understanding, his role as teacher is subsumed to that of protector. His main purpose is to provide the inspiration and the means for his followers to gain abundant fruit from their all-important merit-seeds.

In this version of the path, the most decisive religious acts are the services that a follower performs immediately on being impressed with the Buddha. The service may be a material gift (flowers, food, perfumed bricks for a stūpa), the gift of a skill (plastering a new stūpa, cleaning an old neglected one, ferrying a Buddha across a river), or an act of homage (praising a Buddha, taking the Triple Refuges in his presence, raising one's hands in añjali over the heart). All of these services are seeds in that they inevitably bear fruit as nirvāṇa aeons hence, and most of them guarantee a painless route through saṁsāra along the way. A typical passage reads, "Through that well-done action, on dropping the human body I went to the heaven of the Thirty-three. Eighty times I was lord of the devas; 1,000 times, a wheel-turning monarch. I enjoyed abundant local sovereignty countless times. For the 100,000 aeons since doing that action, I never experienced the lower realms."

These services also function like seeds in that their particulars determine the particular characteristics of individual arhats. Thus Bhadrakāpilanī, Mahākāśyapa's wife, was invariably born with a beautiful complexion because she had covered a stūpa with gold bricks. Tinipadumiya (Three-Lotus) was born in a ruby-red deva palace because the flowers he first presented to a Buddha were red. Even the distinctive talents of the great arhats were determined by their first act of service: Among Gautama's disciples, Śāriputra was foremost in discernment because, aeons past, he had praised the discernment of the Buddha Anomadassī. Anuruddha was foremost in clairvoyance because he had presented the Buddha Sumedha with lamps that burned nonstop for seven days.

The simple act of service is enough to guarantee Awakening, but if one desires special distinctions, the act must be accompanied by a vow. Thus Mahākāśyapa was foremost in his ascetic practices because he had directed the building of a stūpa to that aim. If the Buddha receiving the act of service was still alive and informed of the vow, he would confirm it with a prediction: "In so-and-so many aeons, in the dispensation of Gautama, you will be so-and-so, foremost among bhikṣus or bhikṣuṇīs in the talent you desire." As might be guessed, the vow to become a Buddha must accompany an extraordinary act of service. In the *Buddhāpadāna,* the Bodhisattva Gautama's act is so extraordinary that it can only be imagined: He visualizes a lavish, multistoried palace built of precious substances and furnished with every luxury, invites all Buddhas of the past and present for a sumptuous meal, and then provides them with rooms to rest, teach, or meditate at their leisure. This type of mental offering later became widespread in Indian Buddhist practice, and is fundamental to Tibetan practice even today.

By emphasizing the inevitability of Awakening after an act of service, the avadānas downplay all other factors of the path. This point is illustrated by the *Subhūtittherāpadāna,* in which Subhūti-to-be meditates in a forest, subduing all lust, for 30,000 years, and then has the chance to pay homage to the Buddha Padumuttara for seven days. The meditation serves only to attract the Buddha to visit him; the merit decisive for Awakening comes entirely from the act of homage. Also noteworthy in the avadānas is the predominance of prasāda as the distinctive emotion. Saṁvega is mentioned only rarely, as an afterthought, and is often depicted not as a fearful emotion but as a rapturous one.

As one scholar has noted, the avadānas promote Buddhism as a feel-good religion. Minimal effort is promised maximum rewards in terms of mundane and supramundane pleasures: a long, scenic joyride through saṁsāra before going out in a blaze of glory. The rich can buy their way into nirvāṇa; the poor can get there with a bow. We have noted the feel-good side of Buddhism from the earliest strata of texts (see Section 2.6.2), but the avadānas emphasize it to an extreme. And if we look at the social context for these narratives, the reason for this emphasis is not hard to surmise. By the second century B.C.E., King Aśoka had dispersed Buddha relics in stūpas throughout his realm; the Sātavāhana and Śunga dynasties witnessed a period of renewed prosperity. Thus a likely motive for the composition of the avadānas may have been to attract donations for the upkeep of the many new stūpas and their surrounding monasteries.

Scholars are divided in how they view this new development. Some regard it as a valuable step in making Buddhism a universal religion, in that it gives heightened value to the activities of lay religious life. Others regard it as a perversion of the religion's original aims, selling the doctrine of karma so as to support the monastics' material comfort. Either way, the avadānas were undeniably important in shaping Buddhist devotionalism from their time onward. Their portraits of devotional practices and beliefs influence Theravādin devotionalism even today. And they formed the conceptual and emotional backdrop for the next major development in Indian Buddhism, the rise of the Mahāyāna as a distinctive body of practice and thought.

3.7 THE STŪPA CULT

Because the avadānas are directly related to the stūpa cult, they offer a rare opportunity for collating the textual and archaeological sources of early Indian Buddhism. Stūpas—with their unusual structure, their bas-reliefs and inscriptions—provide a datable but terse record of the beliefs and practices of early Indian Buddhists. The avadānas and other related texts help give context to these records. Together, they help us reconstruct a fuller picture of early Indian Buddhists and their religion than either type of source could provide alone.

Ancient sources—both written and engraved—show that early Buddhists regarded the stūpa both as a symbol of the Buddha's absence, inspiring saṁvega, and as a residence of his presence, inspiring prasāda. Modern scholars have tried to pin down the way in which this presence was conceived—as personal or impersonal—but the records are largely noncommittal on this point. One ambiguous early inscription says that the relic is endowed with "breath." More commonly, inscriptions describe the relic as "infused" with the Buddha's virtue or compassion, using the same word commonly used to describe the way a perfume infuses or leaves its scent in a hamper. Written sources are more explicit in implying or stating outright that the Buddha is not personally present in the relic. Narrators in the avadānas face or bow down to the relic "as if" it were the Buddha himself. An early Mahāyāna text—the *Aṣṭa* (see Section 4.3.2)—compares the quality of the Buddha's discernment enshrined in the relic with the radiance of a magical gem that, even after the gem has been removed, continues to emanate from the basket that once held it.

These statements on the *nature* of the presence felt in the relic, however, are overshadowed by explicit assertions focused on the *power* of that presence. The physical form of the early relic stūpa confirms this focus. A dome resting on a square or circular base, topped with an altar sheltered by a stone umbrella, the abstract nature of the form allows a wide variety of interpretations. In the context of ancient Indian symbolism, it can be read as a symbol of cosmic power, royal power, or the power of fertility, with the sense of power the constant factor no matter what the interpretation. The impression that the stūpa was intended to be a power center is further confirmed by the placement of the relics in the stūpa at the two power points traditional in Indian temple architecture: the center of the base and the summit of the building. And even the name *stūpa* indicates a power center: It is named after the topknot that brahmans wore at the crown of the head, where divine inspiration was believed to enter the body.

The architectural details and inscriptions often found at the stūpas help to articulate the type of power that early Buddhists sensed there, along with the personal benefits they hoped to gain by tapping into it. Circumambulation paths, stone railings, gates, and other architectural adornments associated with royalty surround the stūpa, along with bas-reliefs depicting jātaka tales or religious celebrations attended by human beings, devas, and nāgas. Many of these adornments are marked with donative inscriptions, saying, "Gift of so-and-so." Occasionally the inscriptions have more to say, indicating that the donor was dedicating the merit of the gift to his or her deceased parents, to the recovery of a friend's illness, or to his or her own attainment of nirvāṇa. Sometimes the donors are individuals—lay or monastic—and sometimes whole villages, guilds of merchants, or royal families.

At present these sites are often deserted: mere stone remnants of what must have been intense human activity. To imagine that activity, we can look at the avadānas and related texts. Although there is no way of knowing if a particular set of avadānas was connected with a particular stūpa, the avadānas as a whole give us the best grounding available for imagining the human side to these stone monuments, and for further articulating the sense of power they were believed to contain.

Some of the stūpas' inscriptions can be explained by reference to the earliest strata of the canons. Thus the concept that merit can be dedicated to present and future worldly aims, as well as to nirvāṇa, coincides with the exclusively Buddhist aspects of the doctrine of karma. The simple act of inscribing one's name on one's gift can be explained by the practice, noted in Section 2.6.2, of calling out one's name as an act of reverence.

Other inscriptions, however, can be explained only with reference to later strata of texts. Thus the practice of dedicating merit to the deceased can be related to the *Petavatthu,* which tells of meditating monastics who gain visions of hungry ghosts suffering in the afterworld until relatives make merit with the Sangha and dedicate the merit to them. And of course the avadānas' doctrine of the Buddha-field can explain why the stūpas were built and adorned with so many gifts in the first place. But they also explain more. The avadānas are celebratory texts—filled with wonder, drama, and humor—addressed to large crowds of people. Most likely they were recited at the festivities marking the completion of a stūpa or the adornment of a stūpa with a new gift. Many avadānas describe such festivals, and their descriptions match the religious celebrations depicted in the stūpas' bas-reliefs. Pennants fly, music resounds, monks recite avadānas, lamps are lit all around the stūpa. Rich guilds and individuals vie with one another to make the most lavish donations, people of all levels of society are welcome and have their place in the gaiety—a happy change from the caste divisions of day-to-day life. Workers who actually built the stūpa are promised the same rewards as the wealthy royal or mercantile sponsors who paid for them. Devas and nāgas also participate in the merit-making, sometimes entering into the human participants to "laugh a great laugh." Even the children who tag along with their parents are promised a smooth path to nirvāṇa, together with their friends, simply by delighting in the spirit of the occasion.

Thus the stūpa festival served as a paradigm for the ideal cosmos: a happy society of beings voluntarily cooperating in acts of merit that benefit everyone, all united by the stūpa at the center of their activity, and surrounded by the beneficent power of the Buddha-field emanated by the relic it contains. Passages in the avadānas indicate that, for merit-making purposes, this field is functionally equivalent to that surrounding a living Buddha. And the power of this field would have been directly apparent to the participants in the stūpa festivities as they saw how the merry/merit-making surrounding the relic could transform people from their ordinary petty selves into an ideal, happy society.

As we read of the remaining centuries of Indian Buddhism, we must keep this vision of the stūpa festival in mind, for it was apparently the gentle, joyous context in which many people were first exposed to Buddhism as children and continued to express their devotion to the Buddha throughout life.

4

The Period of the Three Vehicles

4.1 SOCIAL BACKGROUND

Buddhists from the period from the first century B.C.E. through the second century C.E. forged great changes in their tradition. Various groups among them actively spread their religion into Central, East, and Southeast Asia; developed a cult around the future Buddha, Maitreya; sponsored the carving of Buddha and bodhisattva images; wrote down their canons, sometimes translating them into Sanskrit; composed original plays, poems, and prose literary works on Buddhist themes; formulated instructions on how to pursue the bodhisattva path to full Buddhahood; and debated the technical issues that arose in formulating a coherent philosophy from the old canonical writings, at the same time debating the validity of trying to formulate such a philosophy in the first place.

Attempts to explain these developments have traced their roots in two directions: to contemporary developments in Indian society at large, and to precedents within the Buddhist tradition itself. And because India during this period was exposed to a wide variety of foreign cultural influences, there is the added question of whether these influences also played a role in shaping the new Buddhist developments. Unfortunately, our knowledge of the external influences is sketchy at best, and so—aside from a few obvious cases—any attempt to gauge their role in the developments within Buddhism has to remain speculative. It's much easier to point to the internal aspects of the Buddhist tradition that either inspired new internal developments or provided a foothold for the external influences to take root within the tradition. Still, it's useful to have at least some knowledge of social and political developments during this period, in order to have a sense of who these new generations of Buddhists were and the general situation to which they were responding.

The first century B.C.E. saw the demise of the Magadhan empire, as the Sātavāhanas attacked the Śungas from the south and west, and a series of "barbarians"—Greeks, Scythians, and Parthians—battled one another for control of the northwest. In the early part of the first century C.E., however, another Central Asian tribe—the Kushans—took decisive control of Gandhara and other parts of the northwest, establishing capitals in Peshawar and Mathura, and placing underlords over the Ganges kingdoms of Kosala and Kasi. Under the rule of the Kushan emperor, Kaniṣka I in the late first or early second century C.E., India settled down to two centuries of relative peace and abundant prosperity. The Sātavāhanas maintained control of the south and west, while the Kushans governed an empire—the Kushanshahr—stretching from northern India back to their homelands in Central Asia. This gave them effective control of the major trade routes connecting the great civilizations of the time—Rome, Persia, India, and China—at the same time exposing them to cultural influences from the people with whom they traded.

Kaniṣka is remembered as a great patron of the Sangha: a second Aśoka in the eyes of many Buddhists. The evidence for his personal religious affiliation lies mainly in legends, and there is some indication that his support for the Sangha was simply part of a broader policy of support for all the major religions in his realm: Buddhism, Brahmanism, Persian religions, and even Greek religions. However, Peshawar contains the remains of an enormous stūpa dating from the Kushan period, its size indicating either that it received royal sponsorship or required royal permission for its construction. Legends report that it was more than 600 feet tall, and contemporary terra cotta plaques show its multitiered umbrella dwarfing the hemispheric dome. This was apparently the first of the new towering stūpas whose influence can still be seen today in the pagodas of China and Japan, as well as the tall tapering cetiyas of South and Southeast Asia. There is no telling which Kushan king was involved in the stūpa's construction, or why it was built so tall, but a possible motive may have derived from an avadāna telling of a king who, having placed a limit on the height of a stūpa built by his subjects, was reborn as a dwarf.

Archaeological records show that the combined effects of royal patronage and general prosperity funneled unprecedented wealth into Buddhist monasteries throughout India and the Kushanshahr. The earliest remnants of stone-built monasteries date from this time, and the sort of issues that surround large, wealthy monasteries found their way into texts believed to date from this time as well. For example, the *Divyāvadāna,* a Sarvāstivādin avadāna collection, contains an interesting new wrinkle on the doctrine of karma: Anyone who destroys a tree or wall in a monastery is destined for rebirth as a tree or a wall. An early Mahāyāna polemic, favoring the traditions of wilderness monks, denounces monks living in lavish monasteries: Having abandoned their true duties in recitation and meditation, these "worthless monks" devote themselves to the cult of the relics and Buddha images for the sake of acquisitions and honors, renown, reputation, and fame. For its part, the Mūlasarvāstivādin Vinaya denies wilderness monks the right even to take up temporary residence in a monastery. To maintain an attractive, cheerful atmosphere around monastic stūpas, it forbids monks wearing robes made of cast-off cloth (often found in cemeteries) from approaching them.

In addition to fostering prosperity, the new political situation brought a measure of peace and security to the major trans-Asian trade routes, thus allowing Buddhists to spread their religion into Central Asia and China. Buddhist traders are believed to have played the predominate role in the spread of the Dharma, as they established monasteries in the trading centers where they took up residence and invited monks from their homelands to staff them. However, the Kushan royal house may have played an active role diffusing the Dharma as well, for the Chinese report that their emperor received the gift of a Buddhist text from a Kushan prince.

Many scholars treat this story as mere legend, but the reference to a "text" points to another major development of this time: Buddhists had begun putting their canons and other teachings into writing. Sri Lankan histories state that Theravāda monks on their island wrote down their canon in the first century B.C.E. in response to a wartime situation. After Sri Lankan forces had repelled an invasion from southern India, monks were gathered to recite the entire canon, and only one monk who had memorized an obscure part of the Khuddaka could be found. Thus they decided to write down their canon to prevent the sort of loss that could have easily occurred had that monk been killed. Whether their brethren in northern India made a similar decision during the invasions of the first century B.C.E., or decided during the peace of the following century to write down their texts to aid in disseminating the Dharma to new lands, no one knows for sure.

We do know that the oldest known Buddhist manuscripts, found in what is now Afghanistan, date from the first century C.E. And we also know that, once the monks had decided to write down their canons, they were freed to write more independent commentaries on the canonical teachings. The composition of new sūtras, purporting to be the word of the Buddha, also continued during this period, and the adoption of the written medium allowed the authors greater latitude in composing longer and more elaborate texts. This parallels a contemporary development in Indian fine literature: Literary poetry, drama, and prose became markedly more extravagant in style and length. Buddhists often led the field in this direction, some of the greatest poets and prose stylists of this period—Aśvaghoṣa, Mātṛceta, and Ārya Śūra—being Buddhist monks.

Sanskrit's revival as a literary and not purely religious language meant that it was now used as an universal medium of discourse among the educated classes throughout the Indian subcontinent. To speak to these classes, many of the monastic lineages, in the course of writing down their canons, translated them into a hybrid form of Sanskrit that contained traces of the vernaculars from which they were translated. Many of the new sūtras were written in this language as well.

Most of these new sūtras focused on an issue raised by the jātaka and avadāna literature: the nature of the bodhisattva path to full Buddhahood. The canons give explicit instructions on how to become an arhat, and the avadānas stress that

Buddhas are needed throughout the *multiverse*—the multiple universes in the ten directions—because a Buddha's merit-field is necessary for anyone who wants the merit needed for Awakening. But if people are inspired to meet this need, or to take advantage of the glorious opportunity to acquire their own Buddha-fields, where should they go for instructions on how to become Buddhas themselves? The texts answering this question gave a new name to the bodhisattva path: the *Mahāyāna,* meaning the Great Course or the Great Vehicle. In later centuries, the term *Mahāyāna* came to denote a movement self-consciously distinct from what some of its adherents called the *Hīnayāna,* or Lesser Vehicle, their derogatory term for the mainstream that denied the authority of the Mahāyāna sūtras and continued to adhere to the goal of arhatship. But evidence from the period under consideration here shows that the authors of the early bodhisattva sūtras saw the Mahāyāna not as a separate social or sectarian movement, but simply as one of three soteriological options, all well within the traditional fold. Thus the title of this chapter: If we view each of these options as a vehicle, then the Buddhism of this period was a chariot stable large enough to hold all three in relative harmony.

4.2 THE CULT OF MAITREYA

One prominent pan-Buddhist trend during this period was the growth of the cult of Maitreya, the next Buddha to appear in our world. As mentioned in Section 1.4.1, the early canons contain accounts, not only of the present Buddha, but also of past and future Buddhas. The earliest archaeological evidence for a cult of past Buddhas dates from the time of Aśoka; the earliest for Maitreya's cult dates from the first century B.C.E.

The Pali canon (DN.26) contains a brief account of the conditions leading up to Maitreya's coming: Life will grow shorter as human beings become less virtuous, culminating in a "sword-interval" when people with a life expectancy of ten years will hunt one another like animals. A few of them, however, will hide in the wilderness to escape slaughter, and on emerging from their hideouts will resolve to take up a life of virtue. The revival of virtue, over the generations, will increase the natural human life span until it peaks at 80,000 years. At that point, human beings will know only three diseases: desire, lack of food, and old age. Maitreya will come to Earth, gain Awakening, and lead a Sangha composed of thousands of monks, compared to the mere hundreds in Śākyamuni's.

The first archaeological traces of Maitreya's cult date from the first century B.C.E., when images of Maitreya, carved from stone, begin to appear. Some of the images are massive, protective figures, obviously objects of worship. Others are bas-reliefs showing Maitreya in the Tuṣita heaven—following the pattern of earlier Buddhas in their penultimate lives—dressed in monk's robes and wearing the jewelry of royalty, watching Śākyamuni's activities. No first-century explanations of the cult are extant, so to interpret these images we must rely on later accounts.

One of the earliest written accounts comes from Fa-hsien, a Chinese pilgrim who traveled to India in the late fourth and early fifth centuries. Fa-hsien reports seeing a massive sandalwood statue of Maitreya in a sanctuary at Darel, in the upper Indus valley. Told that the erection of the statue marked the beginning of the spread of the Dharma to the people of the East, he himself remarks, "If Maitreya bodhisattva were not the successor of the Śākyan, who would there be to cause the Triple Gem to spread everywhere and frontier people to understand the Dharma?" As an example of Maitreya's activities, he cites the legendary dream that inspired the Han emperor Ming-ti (r. 58–71 C.E.) to take an interest in Buddhism.

Thus one of Maitreya's first recorded roles was as an agent in helping the Dharma to spread to new lands. This role corresponds with the fact that most of the early evidence of his cult comes from outside the Ganges Valley. Some scholars have argued that his cult was inspired by messianic expectations—originating probably in present-day Iran—that spread through India and the Mediterranean world after 200 B.C.E. This, however, ignores the early evidence for Maitreya's cult in areas more isolated from Western Asian influences, such as Sri Lanka and Southeast Asia. Perhaps a better explanation for his early role relates to the fact that frontier areas lacked the sense of Buddha-presence that people in the Ganges Valley derived from the stūpas all around them. The cult of Maitreya provided this sense of awakened presence in outlying lands before stūpas could be built there.

Over the centuries, Maitreya's cult developed four dimensions, corresponding to the ways his devotees hoped to tap into this presence. These dimensions can be placed under a fourfold rubric—here/now; here/then; there/now; and there/then. In the *here/now* dimension, devotees hoped to gain visions or dreams of Maitreya here in the present life. In some cases, simply having the vision was considered auspicious, in line with the belief that the mere sight of a holy figure was a blessing. In other cases, devotees would hope to receive *dhāraṇīs* (mnemonic protective spells), to hear the Dharma, or to request material boons from the vision. (In later centuries, especially in East and Southeast Asia, the here/now dimension of the Maitreya cult also came to include millennial cults centered on individuals who, claiming to be Maitreya, led uprisings against the established political order.) In the *here/then* dimension, people who had difficulties practicing the Dharma under present conditions could dedicate the merit of their current practice to being reborn on Earth in Maitreya's time to practice under more favorable conditions. In the *there/now* dimension, devotees would meditate or practice austerities in hopes of being taken up into the Tuṣita heaven to meet with Maitreya and ask him questions about the Dharma. The philosopher Asaṅga (see Section 5.3.2) is said to have solved his doubts about Dharma in this way. Finally, in the *there/then* dimension (a variant of here/then), devotees would make merit in hopes of being reborn in the Tuṣita heaven as part of Maitreya's retinue, thus escaping the sword-interval and other horrors of human degeneracy, finally returning to Earth along with Maitreya and attaining arhatship or furthering their bodhisattva careers under his tutelage. Of the four dimensions, this last was—and still is—the most pervasive, as part of a recurrent motif in many Buddhist countries: the belief that the current age is too degenerate for the practice of the Dharma. Prominent Buddhists as diverse as the warrior-king Duṭṭhagāmiṇi (second century B.C.E., Sri Lanka) and the pilgrim-scholar Hsüan-tsang (seventh century, China) dedicated the merit of their lives to being reborn in Tuṣita with Maitreya.

The Maitreya cult, over time, provided the pattern for other bodhisattva cults and the cults of the celestial Buddhas, whose Buddha-fields are located in other universes. We will consider some of these cults in Sections 4.4.2 and 5.2.2.

Once widely popular in China and Japan, Maitreya's cult inspired local variants, including that of the "fat Buddha" or "laughing Buddha": Pu-tai Ho-shang (Hemp-bag monk; in Japanese, Hotei), who is more accurately described as Maitreya in a previous birth. Since the thirteenth century, Maitreya's cult has been eclipsed in China and Japan by that of another bodhisattva, Avalokiteśvara (Kuan-yin). However, it remains strong in Korea, Sri Lanka, and Southeast Asia.

4.3 MONUMENTS TO THE TRIPLE GEM

Another pan-Buddhist development in this period is the growth—both in numbers and in kinds—of new monuments (*cetiya*) to the Triple Gem. A Sri Lankan text, said to have been completed in the second century C.E., classifies these monuments into four types: relic monuments, item-of-use monuments, "dedicated" monuments, and Dharma monuments. Relic monuments include relics not only of a Buddha but also of his arhat disciples. Item-of-use monuments include objects that a Buddha used, such as his bowl, robes, and staff, along with the sites of important events in the narratives of his lives. "Dedicated" monuments are Buddha images. Dharma monuments are written passages of Dharma. Fa-hsien indicates that all four types of monuments were prevalent in India and Central Asia during the time of his travels, and that all were perceived as power centers, receiving the sorts of services and devotion that the avadānas advocated for Buddha relics. Although Fa-hsien's visit falls into a later period, the customs he observed were probably current in the period under discussion here.

4.3.1 Buddha and Bodhisattva Images

Archaeology and written legends give conflicting reports on the origins of the Buddha image. The earliest surviving stone Buddha and bodhisattva images date from the first century B.C.E. All previous stone representations of the Buddha were aniconic, representing him not in human form but by an abstract symbol, such as a lotus or a pair of footprints. Arguing from the archaeological record, scholars have long debated as to why Buddhists suddenly switched to iconic representations at this time. Because the earliest iconic images have been found in northwest India—primarily in Mathura and Gandhara—much of the speculation has centered on Mediterranean and Western Asian influences brought in during the barbarian invasions. The Gandhara images show clear signs of Hellenistic influence in their modeling, a reflection of the fact that the Parthians, who ruled Gandhara for part of the first century B.C.E., had a well-documented taste for Greek religion and sculpture. The Mathura images, however, with their warmer modeling, suggest a more native Indian inspiration for the Buddha image. Mathura had long specialized in producing images of *yakṣas* and *yakṣiṇīs,* male and female deities of superhuman power and size, worshiped by devotees seeking worldly protection and benefits. The Mathura Buddha resembled the yakṣa images both in form and function. The earliest sculptors invariably represented him as massive and strong, with his right hand raised in a gesture of offering protection, and his eyes wide open, so as to better share in a gaze with his devotees.

Stone images of great bodhisattvas appeared concurrently with images of the Buddha. No images were identified with specific bodhisattvas until the following century. In the second century C.E., a standardized iconography of bodhisattva images began to appear, along with the first image of a celestial Buddha, Amitābha (see Section 5.2.2), dated 104 C.E.

Written legends, however, make no mention of an aniconic period, claiming that the first Buddha images were created during the life of the Buddha himself. Fa-hsien, at Jetavana (see Section 2.5), for instance, saw a sandalwood image of the Buddha said to have dated from the time of the Buddha. Based on this and similar legends, some scholars have suggested that Buddha images made of perishable materials may have predated the earliest stone images, and that the first century B.C.E. simply marked the date when stone suddenly became acceptable for depicting a likeness of an Awakened One. However, no incontrovertible evidence has surfaced to support these legends. No Buddhist texts contain evidence of taboos against stone, and the earliest texts mentioning Buddha images cannot be dated with any certainty prior to the first century C.E. There is also the question of why—if perishable Buddha images predated stone ones by centuries—the iconography of Buddha images was not established until well after the first stone images were made.

Still, whatever the origins of the Buddha image, archaeological and written records are unanimous in showing that Buddha images were viewed as power centers, much like stūpas, from their very inception. In Fa-hsien's legend, the first Buddha image was such a realistic embodiment of the Buddha's qualities that when the Buddha first encountered it, it stood up in an act of homage. Many of the early Gandhara images—especially of bodhisattvas—portray in their pediments the implements of the pre-Buddhist *homa* fire sacrifice, in which precious scents and grains are burned in a fire while devotees chant petitionary formulae. Some of the pediments depict worshippers engaged in the sacrifice. This indicates that the image was either employed as an adjunct to such sacrifices or was thought to contain a power equivalent to them. No contemporary records explaining the roles of an image in such a sacrifice survive, but a text translated into Chinese in the sixth century C.E. suggests three: (1) the sacrifice was part of a ceremony in which the qualities of the Buddha were infused into the image (much as relics were said to be naturally infused with those qualities); (2) the image helped empower a sacrifice aimed at gaining a meditative vision of a Buddha or bodhisattva (see Section 4.4); and (3) the sacrifice was aimed at calling a bodhisattva or celestial Buddha into the image, to ask for boons, to give teachings, or to grant dhāraṇīs.

The fire sacrifice has not been a universal feature in the worship of Buddha images. At present, it is found only in Tantric traditions from Japan and the Tibetan cultural area. But many of the above activities—infusing the new image with the Buddha's qualities, using the image as an aid in gaining a vision of the Buddha, and using it to petition a Buddha's or bodhisattva's presence, however that presence is conceived—have had a long history in all Asian Buddhist countries. And although the explanation of an image's power will vary from Buddhist to Buddhist, the sense of this power has been a constant throughout Buddhist history. Fa-hsien relates many miraculous powers attributed to specific images in the late fourth century, and similar stories abound in Buddhist countries today.

4.3.2 The Cult of the Book

As soon as the Dharma was written down, the written texts themselves were also treated as centers of power. Fa-hsien reports that monasteries in Mathura and lands to the south would contain three stūpas: one each dedicated to the Vinaya, the Sūtras, and the Abhidharma, each with its yearly festival day. A pan-Buddhist tradition has long held that the act of copying a Dharma text is a strong act of merit, and that a finished text should be treated with the same respect due to a relic. In this way, Dharma texts provide a merit-field that, much like that of a Buddha relic, amply repays acts of service.

The strongest statements of this principle come from some of the more radical early texts devoted to the bodhisattva path. A prime example is the earliest version of the *Aṣṭasāhasrikā-prajñāpāramitā Sūtra,* the Perfection of Discernment Sūtra in 8,000 lines—the *Aṣṭa* for short—translated into Chinese in 179 C.E. It recommends that devotees worship copies of the sūtra with añjali, praise, flowers, incense, parasols, banners, bells, and rows of lamps all around. The act of copying the text is also considered an act of worship. The spot of earth on which the text is placed becomes a *cetiya,* attracting devas, nāgas, and so on, from every direction, who will worship it by gazing at it, bowing down to it, listening to it, memorizing it, and reciting it. They will also protect the house or room in which the text is placed, so that no evil beings can enter and no harm can come to the devotee, except through past bad karma. The sūtra concludes with an avadāna in which a written text of the sūtra takes the place of a Buddha relic. Written in melted lapis lazuli on golden tablets, placed in a box made of four large gems, it is surmounted with a tower made of seven precious substances, ornamented with gems. People from all directions come to worship it and chant its praise.

The sūtra maintains that the cult of the book is not extraneous to the practice of the perfection of discernment. Because this perfection is a difficult state of mind to accept, to say nothing of its attainment, the devotee's mind should first be nurtured in that direction by expressing devotion and praise for the sūtra's physical text. Although some passages in the sūtra make a clear distinction between the perfection of discernment as a mental state and the words that describe it, others blur the distinction. Thus praise for the sūtra is equivalent to praise for the mental state; the virtues of the mental state are ascribed to the spoken and written text. A constant theme throughout the sūtra is that, because Buddhas owe their Buddhahood to the perfection of discernment, it is the mother of all Buddhas. As such, the merit engendered by worshipping it—both text and mental state—is superior to the merit engendered by worshipping a Buddha relic. And a large portion of the sūtra is devoted to passages that could easily be used in a worship service directed to the perfection of discernment—both mental state and text.

In addition to advocating the worship of the text, the *Aṣṭa* also advocates performing *adhikāra* (services) for the person who possesses the text and from whom one wants to learn it. In the concluding avadāna, the bodhisattva *Sadaprarudita* ("Perpetually Weeping") is told in a meditative vision to learn the perfection of discernment from the bodhisattva Dharmodgata, who has taught him this perfection in many past lifetimes. Because of this debt, Sadaprarudita would never be able fully to repay Dharmodgata, even if he were to carry him around on his head for aeons, providing him with all the sensory pleasures of the universe. He should regard Dharmodgata as the Buddha himself; and should he ever entertain the thought that his teacher actually enjoys the services being performed for him, he should understand that the thought is inspired by Māra. In actuality, Dharmodgata only pretends to enjoy them, as part of his tactical skill. When Sadaprarudita and his retinue finally meet Dharmodgata, they first worship the text of the perfection of discernment and then Dharmodgata by scattering flowers over him and playing heavenly music for him on their instruments.

The *Aṣṭa* is not alone among early bodhisattva sūtras in advocating the cult of the book, and in extending the focus of the cult to include those who possess it. The *Pratyutpanna-buddha-saṃmukhāvasthita-samādhi Sūtra* (The Sūtra on the Concentration for Direct Encounter with the Buddhas of the Present—*Pratyutpanna* for short) makes similar assertions, adding that, before being allowed to study the text, a student should be willing to give years of slave-like service to the teacher possessing it. None of the teacher's demands should be regarded as too extravagant. This contrasts sharply with the system of checks and balances that the Vinaya places on the student–teacher relationship.

There is no way of knowing how many people actually followed these book-cult prescriptions, although some aspects of the cult survive to the present day. A strong belief in the merit that comes from copying a Dharma text is universal in the Buddhist world, as is the habit of placing texts in stūpas. Each Buddhist culture has its own etiquette for showing respect for Dharma texts, and when an old text becomes too worn for use there are detailed instructions for how to dispose of it respectfully. The transference of the cult of the book to teachers who possess the book—in which the teacher is treated with the same respect as a Buddha—is still practiced in Tibet.

4.3.3 The Topography of Sacred Narrative

Fa-hsien reports that the Ganges plain in his time was studded with stūpas marking the location of important events from the Buddha's life. This is hardly surprising. What is more intriguing is that he reports traces of the Buddha's lives in areas where the Dharma spread only many centuries after the Buddha's passing away. Belief in these traces show the desire of Buddhists in frontier lands to have their vicinity marked by his presence: When marked in this way, the landscape around them tells a sacred narrative, which in turn imbues the land with meaning.

These traces are of two sorts. The first are spots identified with particular jātaka tales. Arriving in Swat, Fa-hsien was shown a spot where the Buddha, in a previous life, had given his flesh to ransom a dove caught by a hawk. In Gandhara, he was shown spots where the Buddha had made a gift of his eyes, cut off his head, and given his body to feed a starving tiger. All four locations, he reports, were marked with stūpas that attracted constant offerings and devotion.

Traces of the second sort are those related to miraculous journeys that the Buddha was reputed to have made during his last lifetime. In Nagarahara, for instance, he was shown a stone dwelling on the side of a mountain with a permanent golden shadow on the wall, said to have been left by the Buddha himself. As Fa-hsien remarks, the likeness was most realistic when viewed from a distance of ten paces. Viewed close up or from far away, the effect was destroyed.

This use of topography to tell a sacred narrative is common to many religions, and in Buddhism has not been confined to northwestern India. Many Sri Lankans are convinced that the Buddha visited their island three times during his lifetime, leaving marks of his visits at various locations, including a footprint on top of Adam's Peak. Northern Thais possess a chronicle detailing a similar visit to their part of the world. The spot where the Buddha reportedly landed after levitating from India is still marked with a temple, and many northern Thai temples contain Buddha images in a distinctive stance—standing with his arms straight, angled slightly away from his sides—to commemorate the event. Secular education has led some Asians to discount these legends, but in others it has fostered a desire for more traces of sacred presence in their lives. Thus, at the end of the twentieth century, when a Sri Lankan politician dismissed the Buddha's Sri Lankan visits as a myth, the resulting uproar forced him to retract his statement.

4.4 THE SEARCH FOR THE MAHĀYĀNA

Speculation about the bodhisattva path—the path to full Buddhahood—continued during this period, building on earlier accounts found in the jātakas and avadānas. Two important innovations in this speculation were the composition of sūtras attributing to the Buddha detailed descriptions of how this path should be ascertained and followed; and the introduction of the term *Mahāyāna,* the Great Course or Great Vehicle, as a name for this path.

Our best sources for understanding these new bodhisattva sūtras are Chinese translations made of them during the second and third centuries C.E. The Indian epigraphical record from the period is silent about them; the extant Sanskrit texts of the sūtras date from later centuries and have obviously been expanded and reworked. Of course, there are obvious methodological problems in using Chinese translations to study Indian Buddhism. Aside from possible mistakes in the translations, the fact that a particular sūtra made its way to China does not guarantee that it is representative of what was happening in India at the time. However, the translations have compensating advantages. To begin with, they carry dates that, within a fair degree of certitude, can be verified. Although these do not tell us precisely when the sūtras were first composed in India, they at least tell us the date before which the sūtras must have been composed. And there are ways of cross-checking the texts to ferret out mistranslations.

More importantly, even though they may not provide a complete picture of the bodhisattva writings during this period, they show a wider spectrum of that literature than is otherwise available. In fact, when combined with what we know of the jātakas and avadānas, they help to forge what has long been a missing link in the story of the development of Indian Buddhism. Until recently, scholars have tried to understand this period by comparing later Sanskrit Mahāyāna texts or present-day Mahāyāna practices in East Asia with the earliest strata of the original canons and Abhidharma treatises. The radical differences between these two bodies of data have led to myriad speculations as to what sorts of people, with what sorts of motivations, would have created such a radically innovative form of Buddhism. When compared with the jātakas and avadānas, however, the early Chinese translations of the bodhisattva sūtras show that the Mahāyāna developments in this period grew organically and incrementally from what went immediately before.

In fact, the connections among the jātakas, avadānas, and bodhisattva sūtras are so organic that their relative chronology is hard to determine. When taken as genres, the jātakas and avadānas obviously provided an important set of assumptions from which many of the bodhisattva sūtras derived their teachings: the doctrine of the perfections, the use of the Buddha-field as a means of maximizing merit, the importance of gifts and predictions in embarking on the path to Awakening, and the role of vows in mentally determining the precise destination of one's path. However, some individual avadānas, describing the path of the bodhisattva (the Theravādin *Buddhāpadāna* is a prime example), share so many features with the bodhisattva sūtras that scholars have been unable to determine which came first. For instance, the bodhisattva avadānas and bodhisattva sūtras share a belief in the existence of innumerable Buddha-fields outside of our own universe, and of the importance of relating to the Buddhas in those fields for the purpose of maximizing one's merit toward the goal of full Awakening. This doctrine obviously derives from a more basic avadāna concept of Buddha-fields, but no one knows whether the sūtras borrowed this concept from the avadānas, or vice-versa, or if they both borrowed it from texts or oral discussions that have not been preserved. In any case, the important point is that the authors of both the *Buddhāpadāna* and the bodhisattva sūtras were living in similar mental worlds. In later centuries, the *Buddhāpadāna* was accepted into a traditional canon while the bodhisattva sūtras were not. But at the time of their composition, there seems to have been no radical division between them.

Whatever the relative chronology of specific avadānas, however, it is clear that the authors of the early bodhisattva sūtras had inherited from earlier traditions two paradigms for viewing the bodhisattva path: what might be called the jātaka paradigm and the avadāna paradigm. The widely differing versions of the bodhisattva path offered in these sūtras can be attributed to the practical problems the authors encountered in trying to implement the sketchy areas where these two paradigms agree in their vision of the bodhisattva path, and to resolve the inconsistencies where they don't.

The jātaka and avadāna paradigms agree on two points. (1) The terms with which they describe the bodhisattva path—the perfections and acts of merit—differ only quantitatively from the factors constituting the arhat's path: The bodhisattva simply needs more of both. (2) They maintain that a Buddha can arise in a particular universe only when the teachings of the preceding Buddha have been forgotten. Both points present a practical problem for an aspiring bodhisattva. First, if the qualities required for both paths differ only quantitatively, then what is to prevent a bodhisattva from aborting his or her career by slipping unintentionally into the attainment of arhatship when an arhat's level of perfections and/or merit have been attained? The *Buddhāpadāna* suggests that one's initial vow is enough to prevent this from happening, but the authors of the bodhisattva sutras seem to know, from practical experience, that it wasn't. Second, if no one can currently become a Buddha in our universe, where will the aspiring bodhisattva draw the strength to forswear any hope for Awakening in this lifetime?

The inconsistencies between the jātaka and avadāna paradigms lie primarily in the relative role they give to self-power versus other-power along the path. The jātakas emphasize the solitary nature of the bodhisattva's path. Although they portray a group of closely related people joining the bodhisattva in their quest for Awakening, each person in the group has to be self-reliant in developing his or her personal perfections, preferably in the solitude of the wilderness, where the difficulties are both physical and mental. The avadānas, however, emphasize the need to rely more on the power of another: the merit-field of a living Buddha or his relics. Thus they downplay the need for solitude and emphasize a right relationship to preexisting Buddhas as the crucial element in following the path to Awakening. The bodhisattva avadānas expand the avadāna paradigm to include the Buddha-fields of the ten directions, to which one relates in a visionary way, performing services for their reigning Buddhas and listening to their Dharma. The difficulties of this path are more mental than physical, in requiring strong powers of concentrated visualization.

To understand the early bodhisattva sūtras' attempts to solve these problems, we can place them on a spectrum running from those siding with the jātaka paradigm, through those encompassing both paradigms, to those focused more on exploring the possibilities opened by the avadāna paradigm. Once we understand what these sūtras have to say about the bodhisattva path—and how they treat one another's visions of the path—we can draw some conclusions about the who and the why behind them. Although, chronologically, some sūtras translated into Chinese in the third century C.E. might belong in this section, they represent developments that came to full flower only in later centuries, so they will be discussed in the next chapter. Here, to focus on the roots of the bodhisattva sūtras in earlier texts, we will focus exclusively on sūtras translated into Chinese in the second century C.E.

4.4.1 The Ugraparipṛcchā

An example of a sūtra siding with the jātaka paradigm is the *Ugraparipṛcchā*—Ugra's Inquiry—translated into Chinese between 180 and 190 C.E. Ugra is a wealthy householder who asks the Buddha how to follow the bodhisattva path. The Buddha's answer falls into two parts: the practices for a lay bodhisattva and those for a monk bodhisattva. Because the solitude of the wilderness is the best environment to develop the perfections that will enable the bodhisattva to teach multitudes in later lifetimes, the Buddha's instructions for the lay bodhisattva focus primarily on how to disentangle himself from his lay responsibilities and ordain as quickly as possible; once ordained, he should head for the wilderness as soon as he can. In the meantime, prior to ordination, he is to develop a set of qualities derived from the early canons, the four "bases for fellowship"—giving, endearing speech, helpful behavior, and consistency—with the emphasis on the giving. Unlike early canonical sūtras, which focus on generosity to the Sangha, *Ugra's Inquiry* follows the jātakas in focusing on heroic generosity toward beggars. It also contains advice on how Ugra is to develop dispassion toward his wife and children, and to teach the Dharma to his wayward neighbors. The only avadāna elements in the text are instructions on how mentally to convert all one's merit to the goal of Buddhahood, and how to pay homage on a daily basis to the Buddhas of the ten directions, asking their forgiveness for any transgressions. There is no mention of the cult of the stūpa.

When the discussion switches to the career of a monastic bodhisattva, all avadāna elements disappear, and the text focuses primarily on how to face the dangers of the wilderness. When the bodhisattva monk returns to monasteries, his purpose should be to hear the Dharma and to perform other monastic duties, and not to acquire material gain. He is to be especially careful about pride: Having chosen the highest and most difficult spiritual path, he is nevertheless not to look down on those who have chosen the relatively easy path of arhatship. Instead, he should reflect, "When I become a Buddha, my role will be to lead others to arhatship, so it is not fitting that I despise those who aspire to that goal." His other main social duty is to the teacher who shows him the bodhisattva path: To that teacher he owes a debt that even aeons of service will never fully repay. However, the text makes no mention of any social grouping of lay or monastic bodhisattvas. Each bodhisattva must tread the path in solitude. This, however, does not deter Ugra, who—together with 500 other householders—receives ordination at the conclusion of the sūtra.

4.4.2 The Akṣobhya-Vyūha

An example of a text straddling the line between jātaka and avadāna paradigms is the *Akṣobhya-Vyūha,* translated into Chinese in 186 C.E. This text details the career of the bodhisattva who has now become Akṣobhya, the Buddha presiding over the Buddha-field in the eastern direction, showing how the vows he fulfilled as a bodhisattva have resulted in an ideal Buddha-field in which people aspiring to arhatship or Buddhahood can practice with ease. The text combines both jātaka and avadāna approaches to the bodhisattva path by treating that path from two angles. The first angle focuses on Akṣobhya's own vows and practices, which follow the jātaka paradigm: He vowed to become a wilderness monk in every lifetime; to observe strict ascetic practices above and beyond the rules of the Vinaya, such as eating only one meal a day and not lying down; and to sacrifice even his own life for the sake of others. Following a cosmological principle enunciated in the early canons, the accumulated power of these fulfilled vows created the universe in which Akṣobhya finally gained Awakening and now presides as Buddha.

The second angle focuses on the practices of the bodhisattvas reborn in Akṣobhya's realm, which follow the avadāna paradigm. In addition to performing services for Akṣobhya and hearing his Dharma, these bodhisattvas are able to travel easily to infinite numbers of other Buddha-fields to perform services and hear the Dharma of all the Buddhas in the multiverse, thus fulfilling the merit and knowledge qualifications required to form Buddha-fields of their own.

The text states that an aspiring bodhisattva must have developed many of the perfections of the jātaka model before qualifying for rebirth in Akṣobhya's realm. In this, it parallels what came to be the mainstream solution to the inconsistencies between the jātaka and avadāna paradigms: Whether one wanted to become an arhat or a Buddha, one first had to develop perfections along the jātaka model in order to qualify for a Buddha's irreversible prediction of one's future Awakening. And it's worth noting that the cult of Akṣobhya was open, not only to potential bodhisattvas, but also to mainstream Buddhists aiming at arhatship: another sign of the harmony between the mainstream and aspiring bodhisattvas at this point in time. In fact, one of the great ironies of Buddhist history is that the *Akṣobhya-Vyūha* provided the model for one of the more radical developments of Buddhist thought and practice—what came to be known in East Asia as the "Pure Land" schools—and yet the text itself is quite conservative. Although its descriptions of the splendors of Akṣobhya's realm seem extreme, they have precursors in the early canonical portraits of an earthly Northern Paradise. And its accounts of the bodhisattva path add nothing new to what had gone before.

4.4.3 The Perfection of Discernment in 8,000 Lines

A more novel approach to the bodhisattva path—one that further explores the implications of the avadāna paradigm—is exemplified by the Perfection of Discernment in 8,000 Lines (the *Aṣṭa*), mentioned in Section 4.3.2. Although the text seems to be a patchwork, composed by what scholars call an "authorial community," it focuses consistently on a handful of related issues. The primary issue parallels that of the *Buddhāpadāna:* how to negotiate the practical problem, facing every aspiring bodhisattva, of needing to make as much merit as possible by performing services to a Buddha, countered by the need not to allow that merit to issue in arhatship in any Buddha's dispensation. And, like the *Buddhāpadāna,* the *Aṣṭa's* solution is twofold: to treat the problem as an issue of tactical skill, and to redefine the bodhisattva's perfection of discernment as qualitatively—and not just quantitatively—different from that of the arhat. In the *Buddhāpadāna,* the bodhisattva's perfection of discernment consists of the tactical skill required to plant seeds of merit in the fields of all Buddhas—past, present, and future—through the power of visualization. The *Aṣṭa,* however, provides a more comprehensive redefinition of the perfection of discernment, challenging the basic suppositions of the entire Abhidharma approach to discernment. Its solution proved to be such an elegant resolution of the bodhisattva's double bind that it formed the basis for a major school of Mahāyāna thought and practice that has lasted to the present.

For the authors of the *Aṣṭa,* the perfection of discernment is exemplified in the thought of Awakening (*bodhi-citta*)—one's first aspiration for Awakening prior to one's decisive act of service to a Buddha—which they define as a state of no-thoughtness, free from modification and discrimination. They advise the bodhisattva to "course" in this state of no-thoughtness, maintaining it in all activities. Because there can be no thoughts of existence or nonexistence in a state of no-thoughtness, a person coursing in this state will have no concept of dharmas arising or ceasing, no concept of beings, no concept of attainment. Thus the ideal bodhisattva courses in the perfection of discernment like a bird through space, with no sense of path or attainment, viewing all dharmas, beings, and so on, as mirages, dreams, illusions, empty of any individual reality. For such a person, the Suchness of all things—the reality underlying all concepts of things—is one and the same, without differentiation. The concepts have reality only as words and names. The name for this insight of radical nominalism is "the nonarising of dharmas."

The beauty of this no-thought-coursing, from an avadāna standpoint, is that it vastly multiplies one's store of merit while—as it negates the active analysis of dharmas, which lies at the essence of the srāvaka path—it blocks the possibility of that merit's issuing in arhatship. This balancing act, in which the bodhisattva creates enormous merit while delaying its fruition, lies at the essence of the *Aṣṭa's* definition of the bodhisattva's "tactical skill" (*upāya-kauśalya*—sometimes translated as *skill in means*). The multiplication of merit happens in two ways: The aspiring bodhisattva currently incapable of coursing in the perfection of discernment can worship the perfection of discernment, both the written text describing that perfection and the perfection itself. Because this perfection is the mother of all Buddhas, its merit-field is vastly more productive than that of all the Buddhas and Buddha's relics in the ten directions. As for the bodhisattva capable of coursing in the perfection of discernment, the state of no-thoughtness automatically multiplies the merit of any act performed while in that state. When one then dedicates the merit toward Awakening, one sees that there is no reality to "merit" or "Awakening." This insight leverages the merit to an astronomical level.

The authors of the *Aṣṭa* do not disguise the fact that this teaching breaks one of the cardinal early Buddhist standards for judging what is and is not Dharma, in that it is totally inconsistent with the teachings transmitted by the srāvakas. In fact, the authors view this inconsistency as proof of the truth of their vision of the bodhisattva path. Because a bodhisattva's perfection of discernment is qualitatively different from that of a srāvaka, no srāvaka could possibly understand it. The authors emphasize this point by giving Śāriputra, the early Buddhist personification of discernment, the role of ignorant listener throughout the text. And they revel in the paradoxes that their redefinition of discernment creates: For example, a bodhisattva vows to save all beings, while at the same time realizing that no beings exist to be saved.

The question, then, is what authority the authors of the *Aṣṭa* cite for their ideas. Although they give fleeting reference to a number of possible answers, their primary authority is what we at present would call channeled speech: They assert that it is possible to speak under the Buddha's power to people here in the present. This point is illustrated repeatedly in the sūtra by Subhūti, the interlocutor who expounds the bodhisattva path without faltering and who insists repeatedly that he is speaking, not under his own power, but through the inspiring power (*anubhāva*) of the Buddha.

There is second possible source of authority, only touched on by the *Aṣṭa,* but so frequently cited in other bodhisattva sūtras—both contemporary and later—that it deserves mention here. That is the possibility of contacting the innumerable Buddhas of the multiverse, through the practice of concentration, and of hearing the Dharma from them. The earliest known sūtra to explore this possibility was the *Pratyutpanna* (see Section 4.3.2), which was translated into Chinese by the same monk who translated the *Aṣṭa*. This sūtra contains detailed instructions for inducing such a concentration, involving visualizations, long periods of going without sleep, and the practice of not sitting down except when taking meals. When the desired visions arise, one may ask questions of a far-away Buddha and receive teachings that earthly canons could never contain.

Although the *Aṣṭa*'s authors celebrate the gracefulness of the bodhisattva's path, they do not disguise the mental and physical difficulty it involves. Hard are the sacrifices needed to be worthy of receiving instructions in the perfection of discernment, and even harder is the endurance needed to accept the counterintuitive principle of the nonarising of dharmas. Still more difficult is the ability to stay the full course to full Awakening, for when the srāvaka path is still available, the temptation to abandon such a far-off ideal is great. Yet there is consolation. All the Buddhas of the ten directions are ready to offer help if one will simply allow them to do their work in driving the doubts inspired by Māra from one's mind. They will grant protective dhāraṇīs—the Perfection of Discernment being the highest dhāraṇī of all. Dreams, visions, and disembodied voices will also offer instruction. In addition, one can take confidence in the various signs guaranteeing that one has already received irreversible prediction of Buddhahood from a Buddha in a past lifetime. Perhaps the most dramatic test for one's bodhisattva vow is an assertion of truth: If one encounters a person possessed by a spirit, one can order the spirit to depart by declaring the truth of one's irreversible bodhisattva vow. If the spirit actually leaves, one can rest assured that the declaration is true.

In addition to promises of help, the *Aṣṭa's* authors also issue warnings to keep a bodhisattva on the path: The bad karma of abandoning the Mahāyāna and reverting to the Srāvaka path, they assert, is the worst possible karma that anyone can incur.

4.4.4 The Bodhisattva Elites

What do these texts tell us about the bodhisattva movements during this period? Primarily that they were movements only in the sense of a trend. They were not organized around a common cult or doctrine, nor did they draw exclusively on any one lineage or other subcommunity within the larger Buddhist community. Some of the texts borrow from one another—the *Aṣṭa* contains an interpolation extolling Akṣobhya's Buddha-field—while others contain irreconcilable differences. The *Aṣṭa,* for instance, reserves some of its most sarcastic similes for bodhisattvas, like those portrayed in *Ugra's Inquiry,* who take guidance from the early canons. It is also the only text portraying bodhisattvas in organized groups, although its portrait is a dreamlike fable, which may have had no correspondence in reality. The divisions among bodhisattvas are indicated not only by the *Aṣṭa*'s criticisms of wrong-headed bodhisattvas but also by its repeated appeals that bodhisattvas not criticize one another. This lack of cohesion has characterized bodhisattva movements to the present.

Both lay and monastic bodhisattvas are portrayed in the texts: wilderness monks in *Ugra's Inquiry*, urban monks in the *Aṣṭa*. Contrary to one current theory, that the bodhisattva movement originated among wilderness monks who flouted the Vinaya, the wilderness monastics portrayed in *Ugra's Inquiry* and other similar texts are more scrupulous in their Vinaya observance than are their city confreres. For its part, the *Aṣṭa* makes deprecatory remarks about wilderness monks. As for gender, some of the texts focus exclusively on male bodhisattvas, while those that speak of female bodhisattvas often assure them that they will never again take a female birth.

These early texts are unanimous, however, in presenting the bodhisattva ideal as appropriate only for a select elite: those able to endure the hardships of the most difficult spiritual path. Not until later centuries was the bodhisattva path promoted as a universal ideal. And, in another contrast to later Mahāyāna texts, the early texts rarely mention compassion as a motivating factor in undertaking the path. Instead, they appeal to the potential bodhisattva's heroic instincts: The bodhisattva is a warrior, buckling on his armor, embarking on the most glorious adventure of all. The character flaw they warn most against is the hero's susceptibility to pride.

Epigraphic evidence and the reports of non-Indian visitors to the subcontinent indicate that Mahāyāna groups were never more than small minorities in Indian Buddhism. Their future lay more outside of India. And there is no evidence that mainstream Indian Buddhists regarded the bodhisattvas in their midst as anything more than harmless eccentrics or saints. There are, for instance, no extant Indian anti-bodhisattva tracts. The bodhisattvas regarded themselves, however, as the elite of the Buddhist world. This is another constant that has characterized the movement from its diverse beginnings up to the present day.

4.5 TWO LEVELS OF TRUTH

The rise of literate culture in India inspired Buddhists to compose literary works presenting their philosophical ideas in a polished style to appeal to educated audiences. Two of these works composed toward the beginning of the common era—Aśvaghoṣa's *Buddhacarita* (see Section 1.3) and the *Milinda-pañhā (King Milinda's Questions)*—illustrate developments in Buddhist philosophy at this time. In particular, their treatment of the not-self teaching shows how Buddhist thinkers at this time had fastened on two questions that the early canons had recommended avoiding on the grounds that they did not conduce to Awakening. Those questions concern the metaphysics of personal identity ("Who am I?" "Is there a self?") and the metaphysics of karma ("By what mechanism are the results of actions transmitted from one lifetime, or one moment, to the next?"). Although Buddhist thinkers over the succeeding centuries have taken up a multitude of questions, these two have perhaps had the most important role in shaping the development of Buddhist philosophy from the beginning of the common era to the present day.

The *Buddhacarita* is among the earliest extant Buddhist texts to state explicitly that there is no self. Aśvaghoṣa includes this statement in an argument designed to refute non-Buddhist doctrines of the self, asserting that any idea of self, whether permanent or temporary, is inherently self-contradictory. Thus, he concludes, there is no self, but he does not address the potential objections that the idea of there being no self might entail contradictions as well.

The *Milinda-pañhā*—which portrays a series of philosophical dialogues between the Bactrian king Menander and a Buddhist monk, Nāgasena—has come down to us in a Pali version (perhaps a translation from a northwest Indian Prakrit) and several Chinese translations. Nāgasena, who successfully argues the Buddhist position throughout, never states that there is no self, but he does explore the issues raised when he introduces himself as Nāgasena, but adds provocatively that there is no person corresponding to the name. First, the question of truth: If concepts such as *Nāgasena* or *person* had no truth at all, then any reference to them would be a lie. To avoid accusations of uttering falsehood (and to protect the Buddha as recorded in the canons from similar accusations), Nāgasena introduces a teaching developed from the anti-Personalist arguments: that there are two levels of truth, conventional and ultimate. On an ultimate level, there are simply aggregates arising and passing away. The conventional term *person* arises in response to a particular stream of aggregates, in the same way that the term *chariot* arises in response to a particular assemblage of parts. Just as *chariot* is not a lie, *person* is not a lie even though it does not properly describe what is happening on the ultimate level.

Second, to explain the continuance of karma in such a stream of aggregates, he uses the image of writing a letter at night by torchlight. Even though the torch may get extinguished after the letter has been written, the letter still exists. In the same way, even though aggregates may pass away, the work they have accomplished does not get annihilated.

Because these works present popular, rather than systematic, philosophy, they leave many questions unanswered. But the fact that these teachings—the denial of a self and the theory of two levels of truth—made their way into popular works suggests that their influence had become pervasive in intellectual Buddhist circles. When we turn to look at more technical philosophical works produced during this period, we find that this was indeed the case. We also find, however, that Buddhist philosophers were unable to reach consensus on how to work out the implications of these teachings.

4.5.1 Vaibhāṣikas and Sautrāntikas

Legend has it that the Sarvāstivādins, under Kaniṣka's patronage, held a Fourth Council to resolve points of controversy within their lineage. As a result, they produced a massive commentary on the *Jñānaprasthāna,* the final treatise in their Abhidharma. This commentary, called the *Mahāvibhāṣā,* collated opinions on the controversial questions of the time, concluding with the orthodox Sarvāstivādin position on each. Other schools of thought continued to develop within the Sarvāstivādin lineage, but the monks who stuck by the *Mahāvibhāṣā* as authoritative were called *Vaibhāṣikas.*

Whatever the truth of the legend of the council and its patron, there is an extant Chinese translation of the *Mahāvibhāṣā.* Although the content of certain passages show that it was composed after Kaniṣka's time, it is still an important document for ascertaining the philosophical discussions of the Kushan period.

As opposed to Aśvaghoṣa's categorical denial of the self, the *Mahāvibhāṣā* gives a qualified denial. "There are two kinds of self," it says, "the dharma-self, which exists, and the person-self, which does not." This statement admits two possible interpretations. One is that personal identity can be defined on the ultimate level as an assemblage of impersonal dharmas—the five skandhas—but that there is no entity corresponding to our conventional notion of person. This is the position adopted by the Theravādins in the Sinhalese commentaries composed during this time, the position adopted by later Sarvāstivādin commentators, and apparently the position intended by the authors of the *Mahāvibhāṣā* itself. A second interpretation—that a person does not have a self, but that dharmas do—is what later Mahāyāna commentators chose to read into this statement as part of their attack on Mainstream—"Hīnayāna"—philosophy. For them, this statement shows that Hīnāyānists do not understand what came to be a cardinal tenet among Mahāyāna philosophers: that even dharmas have no self-nature.

The *Mahāvibhāṣā* devotes more attention to what it regards as the prime expression of ultimate truth: dependent co-arising. It delineates four ways of understanding the relationships among the factors in the causal chain: *momentary,* in which all twelve factors occur in a single moment of action; *serial,* in which the factors cause one another to arise in rapid succession as they themselves then pass away; *static,* in which the factors represent distinct stages in the relationships among the aggregates, which maintain continued existence before and after those relationships come and go; and *prolonged,* in which the whole sequence of causation occurs over three lifetimes. The Vaibhāṣikas maintain that only the static interpretation is valid, for unlike the first two it allows a mechanism for karmic consequences to last over time; unlike the last, it doesn't require that the ending of suffering take more than one lifetime.

The Theravādins and a dissident subschool of the Sarvāstivādins, however, adopted the serial interpretations of dependent co-arising, another subschool adopted the momentary interpretation, and the Theravādins held to the prolonged interpretation as well. All these groups rejected the static interpretation on the grounds it contradicts the canonical summary of dependent co-arising that portrays the factors in the causal sequence as actually coming in and going out of existence depending on the existence or nonexistence of their preconditioning factors. This controversy took the sort of hair-splitting technical turn for which the Abhidharmists are famous when the Vaibhāṣikas countered that the dharmas going in and out of existence are actually secondary dharmas—the stages of appearing, remaining, and passing away of each momentary relationship—but that the aggregates maintain their existence in all three time frames. Their opponents countered that admitting secondary dharmas would lead to an infinite regress: There would have to be the arising of the arising, the arising of the arising of the arising, and so forth. The Vaibhāṣikas admitted such dharmas up to a tertiary level, but denied any further regress, and the discussion reached an impasse.

One group of dissident Sarvāstivādins was to have a long-term influence in Buddhist philosophy. Called the *Dārṣṭāntikas,* the "Example Methodologists," in the *Mahāvibhāṣā,* their views were taken up by a group called the *Sautrāntikas,* "Those Who Follow the Sūtras" (as opposed to following the Abhidharma treatises as well). The relationship between the two groups is unclear. Perhaps their opponents called them by the first name, while they preferred the second; or perhaps the second group was simply influenced by the first. Although no Sautrāntika writings are extant, we know from later sources that although they claimed to take the sūtras as their only guide, they addressed many of the questions formulated by the Abhidharmists, especially the question of how best to understand ultimate reality. As a result, they formulated an Abhidharma-like philosophy of their own. From the Sarvāstivādins they adopted the principle that present existence is an activity—to be is to act—but they rejected the idea that past and future dharmas somehow exist. Existence, they said, is only momentary. In fact, the moment of a dharma's existence is so short as to be indivisible, with no duration. The arising and passing away of a dharma happen simultaneously. Canonical references to duration between arising and passing away, they said, were simply a concession to unenlightened mentalities. To counter the objection that momentary existence would not allow a substratum for karmic consequences, they drew on the canonical image of karmic consequences as seeds. Each momentary dharma, they said, "perfumes" the series of momentary dharmas with a karmic seed, which will sprout later in the series. To allow for the possibility of Awakening, they said that each dharmic series comes prescented with the potential for Awakening. Nirvāṇa, however, is not a dharma, but simply the cessation of all dharmas.

We don't know how the Sautrāntikas answered their opponents' objections that they were teaching a doctrine of annihilationism, but we do know that their teachings on momentary existence, the perfuming action of karmic seeds, and the innate potential for Awakening had a strong impact on later Buddhist philosophy, particularly among Mahāyānists. We also know that their example in declaring independence from the Abhidharma opened the way for philosophers of later generations to formulate philosophical positions increasingly independent from that of the ordination lineages to which they belonged.

4.5.2 Nāgārjuna

One of the greatest and most provocative of these independent philosophers—Nāgārjuna—was also one of the earliest. Reportedly a native of southern India, he is believed to have taught at Nalanda in the latter half of the second century. Many works have been ascribed to his name, and although modern scholars agree that one central work is genuinely his, they do not agree on how many of the remaining works are genuine. Here we will focus on the one work universally accepted as his.

Although Nāgārjuna addressed many of the issues raised by the Sarvāstivādins and Sautrāntikas, he did not join in their attempt to articulate a view of ultimate truth. In fact, he noted that the Buddha taught the Dharma for the purpose of relinquishing all views. Thus, within the context of Buddhist practice, a philosopher's duty is to formulate views only to the extent that they can then be used to deconstruct attachment to any and all views. This is the project that Nāgārjuna sets for himself in his greatest work, the *Mūla-madhyamaka-kārikā* (MMK), The Root-Middle Kārikās. A *kārika* is a shorthand verse summary of a philosophical argument, written as a memory aid, to which the writer then usually appends a prose self-commentary to fill out and explain the verse. For some reason Nāgārjuna never composed a self-commentary for the MMK, which is unfortunate, for the arguments in the verses are very compressed and open to many interpretations. Still, some of the verses clearly describe the overall shape of his project, which is the deconstruction of views for the purpose of attaining nirvāṇa.

The primary tool Nāgārjuna uses for the sake of this deconstruction is the concept of emptiness. To understand emptiness and its meaning, however, he says that one must first understand its aim. And to explain the aim of emptiness, he cites the teaching of the two levels of truth: ultimate and conventional. To attain nirvāṇa one must understand ultimate truth, but ultimate truth cannot be taught without relying on conventional truth. However, unlike earlier philosophers, who equated ultimate truth with dependent co-arising, Nāgārjuna treats dependent co-arising as a conventional truth; and it is in the context of dependent co-arising that Nāgārjuna introduces his conventional use for emptiness. In fact he equates the two: dependent co-arising and emptiness are the same thing.

What this means is that, contrary to the Sarvāstivādin teaching, dependently co-arisen dharmas must be empty of any own-nature (*svabhāva*) that could be described as existing or not. If they had an existing own-nature, they could not arise or pass away, for they would always have to exist by nature. If their nature were not to exist, then again they could not arise or pass away, for nothing could bring them into being without violating their nature. Thus they must be empty of any inherent nature, and cannot be described in any intelligible way as existing or not existing. To say that they both exist and do not exist is also inappropriate, for that simply compounds the difficulties of both positions. To say that they neither exist nor not exist would be meaningful only if there were anything in experience that could rightly be described as existing or not. But because there is no such thing, the terms are meaningless.

If Nāgārjuna's analysis had stopped here, he would have ended with a view of the emptiness of dharmas. However, in a fairly standard discussion of the factors in dependent co-arising, he focuses on the factor of clinging: "When clinging exists, the becoming of the clinger is set in motion; if he were to be a non-clinger, he would be released and there would be no further becoming." Thus, because clinging to views is one of the four types of clinging, the next step for anyone who desires release is let go of views. This explains Nāgārjuna's second meaning for emptiness: On the ultimate level, emptiness means the relinquishing of all views. If one simply holds to the conventional meaning of emptiness, one cannot reach the ultimate meaning of emptiness. In fact, Nāgārjuna maintains that anyone who holds to a view of emptiness is incorrigible. One must use the conventional meaning as a tool to relinquish all views. However, if one did not understand the conventional truth about the role of clinging in causing suffering, one would not understand the purpose of relinquishing views. Thus the need for both levels of truth in the Buddha's teaching.

In practice, the interdependence of conventional and ultimate truths means that ultimate truth is less a specific view than a process of using conventional truths to dismantle views. Most of the MMK is devoted to a demonstration of this process in action, as Nāgārjuna employs the implications of his emptiness arguments to dismantle a wide range of views, showing not only that specific positions on particular questions are untenable but that all possible positions, when examined closely, are untenable. Either they are absurd and self-contradictory, involve infinite regress, or deviate from the teachings of the early canons. In some instances, he explains why the Buddha, in the early sūtras, refused to take a position on a wide range of non-Buddhist views (see Section 1.2). In others, he dismantles the views of the Sarvāstivādins, Sautrāntikas, and other contemporary Buddhists on the mechanics of karma and the nature of conditioned reality, showing that no possible answer to the questions they have framed could make any sense. In others, he explores the basic concepts from which any and all views might be constructed—such as causality, motion, time, agents—to show that they, too, do not withstand close scrutiny.

Because the purpose of this process of deconstruction is to dismantle clinging, Nāgārjuna doesn't stop at arguing for the meaninglessness of all views about the potential objects of clinging. He also argues for the meaninglessness of any views about the existence or nonexistence (or both or neither) of clinging or the person doing the clinging. Similarly, he deconstructs views about the saṁsāra that result from clinging, and the nirvāṇa attained when clinging is abandoned. Finally, he turns his tools on themselves and deconstructs the concept of the emptiness of dharmas: "If dharmas are not empty, how could they arise and cease? If dharmas *are* empty, how could they arise and cease?" Thus, starting with the emptiness of existents, he ends up asking, "Where, to whom, which, and why would views such as 'eternal,' etc., occur? I bow down to Gautama who, out of compassion, taught the Dharma for the abandoning of all views."

This is a bravura performance. And, more than with any other Indian Buddhist philosopher, modern philosophers still take this performance as a living challenge to their thought. Yet, it is possible to cite precedents in the early canons for even some of Nāgārjuna's most radical statements. He himself explicitly cites an early canonical sūtra—the *Kātyāyanāvavāda* (Pali: *Kaccāyanagotta Sutta,* SN XII.15)—to support his assertion that dependently co-arisen dharmas cannot properly be described as existing or not existing. As for one of his more radical statements of deconstruction—that the ontological status of nirvāṇa (which cannot be described as existing, not existing, both, or neither) is no different from that of saṁsāra: This too occurs in the context of an argument drawn straight from an early sūtra (SN XXII.85 in the Pali Canon) discussing the ontological status of a Buddha before and after death. His deconstructive method has numerous canonical precedents and his twofold meaning for emptiness, as a quality of dharmas and as a state of mind, has canonical precedents as well.

But when we compare his two levels of emptiness with the two reported in the early canons, we can see precisely where he has developed them in new directions. Emptiness as a quality of dharmas, in the early canons, means simply that one cannot identify them as one's own self or having anything pertaining to one's own self. For Nāgārjuna, it means that they have no self of their own. Emptiness as a mental state, in the early canons, means a mode of perception in which one neither adds anything to nor takes anything away from what is present, noting simply, "There is this." This mode is achieved through a process of intense concentration, coupled with the insight that notes more and more subtle levels of the presence and absence of disturbance (see MN 121). For Nāgārjuna, the ultimate level of emptiness is the relinquishing of all views, and it is attained, not with the aid of concentration, but through logical analysis. These two innovations in the meaning and method of emptiness were to prove influential in later centuries.

Nāgārjuna did not succeed in putting an end to the Abhidharma quest to formulate ultimate truth. Perhaps the possibility of pinning ultimate reality down in words was too appealing for potential Abhidharmists to heed his warnings. Or they may have objected—in common with some modern commentators—that he misinterpreted the meaning of *svabhāva* and played fast and loose with his logic.

However, Nāgārjuna had an enormous impact on Mahāyāna thought, particularly in the interpretation of the Perfection of Discernment literature. In fact, Mahāyānists have long claimed him as one of their own—the first great Mahāyāna philosopher—and have maintained that his purpose in writing the MMK was to explain the Perfection of Discernment concept of emptiness. Modern scholars are sharply divided over these claims. The argument for accepting them relies on interpreting Nāgārjuna through the eyes of later Mahāyāna commentators and on accepting a number of explicitly Mahāyāna writings attributed to him as being genuinely his. The argument against accepting these claims relies on the principles of consistency and context. To begin with, the Mahāyāna writings attributed to Nāgārjuna follow the *Aṣṭa* in saying that the purpose of discernment is to build the merit of Buddhahood while preventing Awakening in this lifetime, whereas the MMK states that its purpose is to deconstruct views so as to end clinging and attain nirvāṇa here and now. Second, the Mahāyāna writings attributed to Nāgārjuna conflate the MMK teaching on emptiness with the *Aṣṭa's* teaching on the nonarising of dharmas, saying that emptiness means both that dharmas lack inherent existence and that they do not arise or pass away. Although a few statements in the MMK, when taken out of context, might be used to support the principle of the nonarising of dharmas, there are many more central passages in which Nāgārjuna's arguments and conception of emptiness would make no sense unless dharmas do actually arise and pass away. Later Mahāyāna commentators noticed this discrepancy and explained it with recourse to the two levels of truth: Emptiness as lack of inherent existence, they said, applies to conventional truth; emptiness as the nonarising of dharmas applies to ultimate truth. Because this explanation presents ultimate truth as a description of the true nature of dharmas, however, it created a further difficulty, for the MMK presents ultimate truth, not as a description of reality, but as a process in which all descriptions are deconstructed. Bhāvaviveka, a sixth-century follower of Nāgārjuna (see Section 5.3.3), attempted to resolve this discrepancy by identifying two types of ultimate truth—that which can be described and that which can't—but it is hard to imagine the author of the MMK accepting this explanation.

A further difficulty with some of the Mahāyāna writings attributed to Nāgārjuna is that they contain refutations of the Yogācāra school of Mahāyāna thought (see Section 5.3.2), which did not come into existence until approximately a century after Nāgārjuna's commonly accepted dates. Mahāyāna traditions explained this discrepancy by ascribing magical powers to Nāgārjuna: A doctor of extraordinary skill, he was able to prolong his life to hundreds of years. A few scholars have suggested that more than one writer may have gone by the name Nāgārjuna, but scholars generally have not given this question the attention it deserves.

Whatever Nāgārjuna's personal religious aims, his terse and provocative style made his writings a fertile source for a wide variety of conflicting interpretations in later centuries. Still, there is unanimous agreement that he provided an important example in taking the deconstructive tradition of early Buddhist thought—in which non-Buddhist questions unconducive to Awakening are dismantled—and turning it on what he regarded as similar questions that had developed in the Buddhist tradition itself.

5

Early Medieval Indian Buddhism

5.1 PORTRAITS OF A BUDDHIST EMPIRE

Starting with the third century, in the declining years of the Kushan and Sātavāhana empires, Indians developed a form of government that can best be described as feudal. Large, centrally administered empires were replaced with smaller hereditary kingdoms, which, if subject to an imperial authority, simply owed tribute to the authority without handing over the right to local administration. This pattern continued until the Muslim invasions in the eleventh to thirteenth centuries. During the early part of this medieval period—from the third to seventh centuries—the political and cultural center of northern India shifted back to the Ganges Valley. Literature and the arts flourished especially under the Gupta dynasty (fourth to sixth centuries). Although the Guptas were not Buddhist, they provided support to Buddhist monasteries, as did their feudatories. Because Indian sculpture in general reached its pinnacle during the Gupta era, the loveliest Indian Buddha images date from this period. During the fifth and sixth centuries, the Hephthalite Huns established themselves in Gandhara, and Gupta kings repeatedly had to repel their invasions. After the Huns were finally expelled from Gandhara in the sixth century, that area—together with Central Asia in general—experienced a Buddhist revival. Simultaneously with this revival, the last of the great Indian Buddhist emperors, Harṣavardhana (606–647 C.E.), gained control of northern India.

Harṣa's reign is unique in the annals of Indian Buddhism for the number of surviving contemporary documents describing Indian Buddhism from an outsider's perspective. These allow us a better sense of the "look" of Buddhist practice at that time than can be derived from written and archaeological evidence produced by Indian Buddhists themselves. One of these documents is Harṣa's biography, a masterpiece of Indian fine literature, written by Bāṇa, a brahmanical admirer of the king. The climax of the biography accounts for Harṣa's Buddhist affiliation: After the death of his father, his brother-in-law was murdered and his sister was forced to wander destitute through the wilderness. Through the agency of a Buddhist forest monk, Harṣa saved her from suicide in the nick of time. As a result, he swore his allegiance to Buddhism for the remainder of his life, taking a vow of celibacy to boot.

Bāṇa's description of the monk's forest hermitage is the earliest such account. Some of the details are blatantly fanciful, in keeping with Bāṇa's general style—monkeys worship the stūpa, parrots and mynahs lecture on Abhidharma and Vinaya, pacified lions lounge around the forest master's seat—but the description contains a more believable detail found in no other document: The master's students include śramaṇas of every school who are free to continue practicing and teaching the doctrines of their original schools. This example of Buddhist tolerance in the wilderness, if accurate, contrasts strongly with the evidence for strong partisanship in the urban monasteries of the time.

An even more valuable document from this time is Hsüan-tsang's account of his travels in India. Although other Chinese monk-pilgrims also recorded their impressions of the subcontinent, Hsüan-tsang's are by far the most detailed, highlighting both continuities and new developments in the Buddhism of this period. He describes in detail the ritual calendar, which by his time already varied from lineage to lineage. For instance, the Sthaviravādins celebrated the Buddha's birth in May; the Sarvāstivādins, in November. All sects celebrated the Buddha's Awakening and Parinirvāṇa in May, but the Sarvāstivādins observed these events on the waxing half moon, while the others did so on the full moon.

Hsüan-tsang's depiction of stūpa festivals hardly deviates from the descriptions in the early avadānas or from what can be observed at any stūpa festival in South or Southeast Asia today: Thousands of people flocked to the events, pennants flew, parasols formed a network around the stūpa, music played, clouds of incense rose to block out the sun and moon, while flowers were scattered like rain. Although his tone is uncritical, Hsüan-tsang confirms the accusations, recorded in sūtras praising the forest monk's life, that some monasteries exploited relic worship for material gain. He reports that a prominent temple, home to a tooth-relic, was so inundated by crowds on festival days that, in order to dissuade the crowds, it was forced to charge one gold piece per person to view the relic. Even then, thousands were willing to pay the price.

Hsüan-tsang also describes cults surrounding great bodhisattvas, such as Maitreya, Avalokiteśvara, Tārā, and Mañjuśrī. Statues of Avalokiteśvara in particular were famous as oracles. Devotees would fast and pray in front of them for days on end in hopes of receiving visions of the bodhisattva and answers to their questions. Contemporary documents and archaeological evidence point to a similar cult surrounding Buddha images. Every monastery would contain a "perfumed chamber" in which such an image would be placed. Devotees would make gifts and perform acts of service along the lines prescribed in the avadānas, often receiving visions of the Buddha as a reward. One medieval avadāna explains these visions as the combined results of a vow made by the Buddha while he was alive, together with the power of the merit of the devotees' acts of service. However, given the fact that such images were called "Buddhas," rather than "Buddha images," it is likely that, for some devotees, at least, the line between image and the person imaged was blurred. Even today, this terminology causes problems of interpretation. Vinaya passages dealing with the objects donated to these images state simply that the "Buddha" owned the objects. Scholars analyzing these texts argue as to whether the objects were believed to belong to the image, in the same way that objects donated to stūpas belonged to the stūpas, or somehow were believed to belong to the person of the Buddha himself.

Hsüan-tsang was fortunate enough to witness the ceremonies surrounding the installation of such an image in a monastery built by King Harṣa. The procession carrying the image to the monastery was modeled on the story of the Buddha's return to Earth after having spent a Rains retreat in heaven, teaching his mother. With the image placed on an elephant's back, the king dressed as Indra went along on its left, carrying a parasol over it, while his viceroy, dressed as Brahmā, went along on the right, carrying a whisk. Long escorts of elephants carrying musicians on their backs preceded and followed them, and the king scattered pearls and other precious items to the crowds lining the route. After arriving at the monastery, he gave the image a ritual bath and then carried it himself to its chamber in a tower. The remainder of the day until sundown was given over to sermons.

Hsüan-tsang spent most of his sojourn in India studying in the university at Nalanda. He reports legends that the first monastery at this location dated from soon after the time of the Buddha. By Hsüan-tsang's time, it had grown to a complex of monasteries constituting the world's first university, with thousands of students, rigorous admissions standards, vast libraries, and an organized curriculum covering not only the various schools of Buddhism but also the Vedas, grammar, linguistics, logic, philology, medicine, music, belles-lettres, literary criticism, art, architecture, sculpture, astronomy, and the Sāṁkhya system of philosophy. The development of this university reflected the continuing importance in India of public philosophical debates. These debates served as means for defining orthodoxy within one's own religious/philosophical tradition, triumphing over the positions of opponents both within and without that tradition, and perhaps attracting the support of rulers and other influential people who attended the debates. Within the context of the debate, religion came to be seen as a philosophical system that had to be logically consistent and verbally nimble in order to carry the day. To maintain his position in such an environment, a debater had to be well versed not only in the ground rules of logic and dialectic (the science of argument), but also in the texts of his own and his opponent's traditions. This sort of background required full-scale training, and Nalanda was the first Buddhist institution to rise to the task of filling this need.

The combined contexts of debate and university lectures fostered a new type of Buddhist literature that, more than any previous Buddhist writing, fits the modern definition of systematic philosophy. The philosophers who best exemplify this trend were two Sautrāntika monks: Dignāga, who taught at Nalanda in the fifth century, and his commentator, Dharmakīrti, who taught there in the seventh. Dignāga's main fields of interest were logic and dialectics. His works in these fields were so revolutionary that they rewrote the ground rules for debate and had a wide influence even on non-Buddhist philosophers. More important historically, however, was his contribution to epistemology, the theory of knowledge. Prior to his time, epistemology had been taught in Buddhist circles as an adjunct to logic, and logic as an adjunct to the study of the Sūtra and Abhidharma. Dignāga's writings, however, endowed epistemology with foremost importance, stating that the pursuit of true knowledge first requires familiarity with the criteria or means of knowledge. Thus the study of these criteria should come first so that the texts could be judged against them. In this way, Dignāga wrote the rules for how debaters from different traditions could find common ground on which to debate. In the seventh century, Dharmakīrti wrote commentaries on Dignāga's thought, defending it against critics and reworking it so skillfully that he came to eclipse Dignāga as the major authority in the field of epistemology.

Although this sort of philosophizing may seem far removed from the religious life of ordinary people, Hsüan-tsang insists that it was not. Traveling debaters were famous throughout India, and large crowds would flock to any debates that promised to be educational or entertaining. At the same time, the great philosophers were not regarded as mere academicians. In the popular mind, their command of logic was viewed as a sign of mental power that could easily shade into psychic power. This follows the pattern we noted in the story of the Buddha himself. Hsüan-tsang recounts many legends surrounding the great Buddhist philosophers, including Nāgārjuna's reputed powers as a doctor, noted in the last chapter. His most dramatic story, though, is that of the sixth-century Mahāyāna philosopher, Bhāvaviveka.

In his search for an authoritative account of the Mahāyāna, Hsüan-tsang reports, Bhāvaviveka wished to encounter Maitreya face to face. Unlike other Mahāyānists, though, he was not content to visit Maitreya in meditative visions or dreams, or to wait until after death to ascend to Maitreya's heaven. He wanted, in this very body, to encounter Maitreya in the flesh. Thus for three years he fasted and chanted dhāraṇīs before a statue of Avalokiteśvara, who finally appeared to him and tried to dissuade him from his quest, but without success. So the bodhisattva taught him another dhāraṇī, with instructions to recite it before a certain rock-faced mountain. After Bhāvaviveka had followed these instructions for three years, a *Vajrapāṇi* (thunderbolt-handed) spirit appeared to him, informing him that the mountain contained an asura's palace in which he could dwell until Maitreya's arrival on earth. If he recited a certain dhāraṇī, the mountain would open, giving him access to the palace. Again, Bhāvaviveka chanted the dhāraṇī for three years, without allowing "even a mustard-seed's gap" in the recitation. The mountain opened as predicted, revealing many bizarre sights, but Bhāvaviveka was undeterred. He called on his entourage to follow him into the mountain, but only six complied. The mountain then closed behind them. According to the story, they are still there, awaiting Maitreya's coming.

5.2 MAHĀYĀNA SŪTRAS

Buddhists in the early medieval period continued the practice of composing new Sūtras and avadānas to answer questions they brought to the Buddhist tradition as it had been handed down to them. The extant avadānas from this period—which would probably tell us a great deal about both Mainstream and Mahāyāna practices of this time—have received little scholarly attention. However, the Mahāyāna sūtras from this period have been studied in great detail, so this is the aspect of early medieval Indian Buddhism that we will focus on here.

During this period, followers of the Mahāyāna path came to consider themselves a distinct type within the Buddhist community. Inscriptions as early as the fourth century show monks, nuns, and lay people on the Mahāyāna path referring to themselves as *śākya-bhikṣus, śākya-bhikṣuṇis* (Śākyan monks/nuns), *paramopāsakas* and *paramopāsikās* (foremost lay followers). By the sixth century, they came to refer to themselves in their inscriptions as *Mahāyānists.* Also, during this period, the term *Mahāyāna* itself came to take on new meanings. In the preceding centuries, *Mahāyāna* was simply the name of a soteriological option: the path to becoming a Buddha, rather than an arhat. By the fourth century, however, Asaṅga (See Section 5.3.2) established the trend of using the term Mahāyāna to refer to a body of literature: the sum total of all the writings prescribing the bodhisattva path. Thus when Buddhist individuals started calling themselves *Mahāyānists* in the sixth century, they could be stating, not only their commitment to a particular path of practice, but also their acceptance of at least part of the Mahāyāna body of literature as their guidance on that path.

The word *part* is a necessary qualification here, for this literature had become even more diverse over time, and there is no indication that Mahāyānists ever constituted a single, unified group. Bhāvaviveka's story, related in the previous section, illustrates the central problem that militated against unanimity among Mahāyānists: By definition, there could be no living person who had completed the aeons-long path they were speculating about. Thus there was no living authority who could refute or verify their speculations. With some of the earlier Mahāyāna texts encouraging individual bodhisattvas to search for inspiration in meditative visions, and stating that new inspirations did not have to be consistent with previous visions or texts in order to be authoritative, Mahāyāna practices, beliefs, and texts naturally continued to develop in new and sometimes contradictory ways.

Most of the major Mahāyāna Sūtras were composed by the fourth century, but that did not mean that they had reached their final form by then. Many of the important Sūtras were translated several times into Chinese during the medieval period, and the translations show how the Sūtras continued to grow and develop over time. These changes show two tendencies: an effort to generate new, original ideas, and an effort to consolidate material from other Mahāyāna Sūtras to provide a coherent synthesis. Later translations of *Ugra's Inquiry,* for instance, illustrate both of these tendencies. On the one hand, the text was rewritten so that Ugra praises the lay bodhisattva's path as superior to the monk's. On the other, the revised Sūtra incorporated elements from the *Aṣṭa* and/or similar Sūtras, such as the inclusion of channeled speech, the definition of tactical skill, and the doctrine of the nonarising of dharmas as the bodhisattva's distinctive form of discernment.

Given the changeable and diverse nature of this literature, it is impossible to recreate a chronology or give a comprehensive survey of its development. Thus, instead, we will give a thematic introduction to some of its highlights. In the broadest terms, this literature can be divided into two categories based on their relationships to the Sūtras discussed in the preceding chapter: (1) works taking up jātaka and avadāna issues that were not treated by those Sūtras; and (2) works developing themes already introduced by those Sūtras. In the first category, the most prominent example is the *Daśabhūmika Sūtra*. As for the second category, there are many subcategories. Some Sūtras, such as the *Samādhi-rāja* (Concentration-King) *Sūtra,* follow the *Pratyutpanna* in outlining meditation practices that lead to knowledge about and encounters with Buddhas and bodhisattvas in the various Buddha-fields of the multiverse. Others, such as the *Ratnarāśi* (Jewel-Heap) and *Ākāśagarbha* (Space-Womb) Sūtras, follow *Ugra's Inquiry* in detailing the duties of monastic and lay bodhisattvas. Still others follow the *Akṣobhya-vyūha* in portraying the glories of the Buddha-fields in other universes. Finally, a large array of Sūtras develop themes set forth in the *Aṣṭa,* such as the content of the bodhisattva's perfection of discernment, the nature of tactical skill, dhāraṇīs, and the question of the bodhisattva's irreversibility. Here we will discuss some of the most important Sūtras in these various categories.

5.2.1 The Daśabhūmika Sūtra

Early avadānas repeatedly stated that, after the vow to follow the path of Awakening, the devotee pursued a long path, of many aeons, developing the perfections and never reborn—except by choice—in any of the realms lower than the human. However, none of the texts had provided a systematic map of what happened during those aeons. The authors of the *Daśabhūmika Sūtra* set out to make up for this lack by tracking a systematic account of the stages of bodhisattva practice across the levels of the Buddhist cosmos. To the Sarvāstivādin list of six perfections—giving, virtue, endurance, energy, dhyāna, and discernment—they added four more: tactical skill, aspiration, strength, and knowledge. Then, to correspond to the resulting ten perfections, they formulated ten stages in the bodhisattva path that began after the generation of *bodhicitta.*

The stages were named the Joyful, the Stainless, the Refulgent, the Radiant, the Difficult-to-Conquer, the Presence, the Far-going, the Immovable, the Good Thought, and the Dharma-cloud. Each stage was associated with a particular level of the cosmos. The first two were on the human level, where a bodhisattva on the first stage would tend to be a king; and on the second stage, a universal emperor. The remaining stages ascended through the deva and Brahmā realms to the realm of the Great God—*Maheśvara*—on the tenth. Although each stage entailed the development of all ten perfections, the bodhisattva was expected to focus special attention on the perfection appropriate to that particular stage. Thus a Joyful king bodhisattva focused on giving; a Stainless emperor bodhisattva, on virtue.

The ten stages provided an organizational framework, not only for the perfections, but also for other Dharma teachings and practices. The first six stages covered teachings that bodhisattvas shared in common with Mainstream Buddhists. Thus they mastered all 37 Wings to Awakening on the Radiant stage, the Four Noble Truths in the Difficult-to-Conquer stage, and dependent co-arising on the Presence stage. The Presence stage, however, served a double function, in that it introduced the first distinctively Mahāyāna insight, into the unity of all things, erasing any duality between self and other, or existence and nonexistence. The remaining four stages entailed insights and abilities exclusive to bodhisattvas. On the Far-going stage, bodhisattvas realized that all Buddhas are identical in terms of their cosmic body. On the Immovable stage they achieved endurance toward the teaching of the nonarising of dharmas, at the same time being initiated by Buddhas into the omniscience that prevented their premature entrance into nirvāṇa. On the Good Thought stage they learned how to emit voices through every pore, using one sound to teach many different Dharmas to beings with different needs. Finally, on the Dharma-cloud stage, beams of light from the heads of all the Buddhas entered the bodhisattva's head, pervading him with a million concentrations and dhāraṇīs. This consecration would enable him to create the Enjoyment Body in which he would gain Awakening in the Pure Abodes, and in the meantime to emit innumerable magical Emanation Bodies that returned to human realms to act out the lifework of a Buddha in human form.

Although other versions of the ten stages were found in other Mahāyāna texts, the idea of a ten-stage development formed one of the most pervasive models for the bodhisattva path, both in Sūtras and in philosophical treatises.

5.2.2 The Sukhāvatī-Vyūha Sūtras

The most influential of the Buddha-field (or to use the Chinese term, *Pure Land*) Sūtras were the larger and smaller *Sukhāvatī-Vyūha* sūtras, dedicated to the Buddha-field of Amitābha located one hundred trillion Buddha-fields to the west of ours. Whereas the *Akṣobhya-vyūha* focused primarily on the course of practice that Akṣobhya had to follow to achieve his own Buddha-field, the *Sukhāvatī-vyūha* Sūtras focus on the wonders of Amitābha's Sukhāvatī, or Land of Bliss. The primary lesson here is less on how to generate one's own Buddha-field than on how to gain rebirth in the best Buddha-field possible.

As the Sūtras explain, the spiritual development of Amitābbha began countless aeons ago, when—as a monk named Dharmākara (Dharma Treasury)—he aroused bodhicitta while hearing a sermon from the Buddha Lokeśvararāja. He implored Lokeśvararāja to teach him the way to supreme Awakening and the qualities of an ideal Buddha-field, so Lokeśvararāja taught him the amenities of innumerable Buddha-fields for 10 million years. Dharmākara then made a series of vows, determining not to reach final Awakening until his Buddha-field embodied the best qualities of every field. The different versions of the Sūtras differ in their descriptions of these qualities, and the many Chinese translations made of these Sūtras show that, over time, the list of qualities kept growing. Because of its many attractions, Sukhāvatī came to eclipse all other Buddha-fields in the Buddhist imagination.

Unlike Akṣobhya's Buddha-field, which is primarily a garden paradise for monks and nuns, Sukhāvatī is a more urban paradise with buildings made of jewels, interspersed with parks filled with jeweled trees and jeweled lotus ponds.

Another difference between the two Buddha-fields is that anyone reborn in Sukhāvatī becomes a man. Many of Sukhāvatī's amenities are designed to appeal to people who grew up on stūpa festivals: Music is always playing, flowers fall like rain, and there is the opportunity, after the morning meal, to visit the Buddhas of 100 trillion Buddha-fields, shower them with heavenly flowers, and return home for the midday nap. Birds, magically created by Amitābha, gather to sing three times a day, and their song conveys the Dharma.

The most controversial issue surrounding Sukhāvatī is how to get there. Chinese translations of the Sūtra showed that theories about Dharmākara's vows on this point changed over time. In a (fifth-century?) Chinese version of the Sūtra, Dharmākara's eighteenth vow states that all living beings in the ten directions who with sincere faith desire rebirth in his land will attain it by recollecting this desire only ten times. Only those who have committed atrocities such as matricide, or who have slandered the True Dharma, are excluded. The nineteenth vow states that all living beings in the ten directions who arouse bodhicitta, cultivate all the virtues, and wholeheartedly vow to be reborn in Sukhāvatī will, at death, see Amitābha and a large welcoming retinue before them. The twentieth vow states that if living beings in the ten directions hear Amitābha's name, fix their thoughts on his land, plant the roots of virtue, and wholeheartedly dedicate the resulting merit to rebirth there, their desire will be fulfilled. These vows formed the basis of the Chinese and Japanese Pure Land sects that grew up around Amitābha.

However there is no indication that a cult exclusive to Amitābha ever took root in India. Instead, rebirth in Sukhāvatī became a generic aspiration throughout Indian Mahāyāna circles. Many texts, even those devoted to other celestial Buddhas—such as Bhaiṣajyaguru, the "Medicine Buddha"—promised that the simplest forms of adhikāra, such as copying a text or sweeping a shrine, would result in rebirth in Sukhāvatī.

The existence of these Buddha-field Sūtras sparked a question: Why did Śākyamuni appear in our inferior, imperfect world, rather than in an ideal Buddha-field of his own? Various answers were attempted, but two became prominent. The first was that, in the scheme of the *Daśabhūmika Sūtra,* Śākyamuni—like all Buddhas—achieved Awakening in his Enjoyment Body in the Pure Abodes, which is where his Buddha-field is. The Śākyamuni perceived on earth was simply an Emanation Body projected from that Buddha-field. The second answer—proposed by the *Saddharma-puṇḍarīka* (Lotus), *Vimalakīrtinirdeśa,* and *Gaṇḍavyūha* Sūtras—was that this world actually is a pure Buddha-field. It seems impure and inferior only to our defiled perceptions. When one's perception is pure, one sees the world as blissful and pure. Śākyamuni designed his Buddha-field in this way out of compassion and as a tactical skill, to illustrate the principle that there is no difference between saṁsāra and nirvāṇa.

5.2.3 Issues in the Perfection of Discernment

The *Aṣṭa* spawned a large body of literature, as new generations of authors sought to refine its teachings. Among the primary topics they developed were: emptiness, tactical skill, dhāraṇīs, and the relationship between the bodhisattva's and the arhat's path.

A. Emptiness. A series of new Perfection of Discernment Sūtras were composed to augment the *Aṣṭa*'s teachings on the nonarising of dharmas. These included, among others, Perfection of Discernment Sūtras in 25,000 and 100,000 lines, which are essentially versions of the *Aṣṭa* interspersed with new material. Still other texts, such as the *Heart* and *Diamond* Sūtras, condensed the teachings into a more manageable form. The version in 25,000 lines—the *Pañcaviṃśatisāhasrikā-prajñāpāramitā Sūtra,* or *Pañca* for short—made important advances over the *Aṣṭa* in its treatment of compassion and its definition of discernment. These advances became emblematic of the Perfection of Discernment literature as a whole, as other Perfection of Discernment texts simply explored their implications. Even later versions of the *Aṣṭa* were rewritten to accommodate the new teachings. These later versions are the ones that currently underlie most translations and discussions of the *Aṣṭa* in English.

Whereas the earliest extant version of the *Aṣṭa* rarely mentions compassion as a motivating force for undertaking the bodhisattva path, the *Pañca* makes it primary: The arousing of bodhicitta is an act of infinite compassion for all beings, and the bodhisattva path entails myriad acts of compassion for the material and spiritual well-being of others. As for discernment, the *Pañca* defines the bodhisattva's perfection of discernment as the comprehension of emptiness. The earliest version of the *Aṣṭa* mentions emptiness only rarely, and almost always in a completely ordinary sense. The *Pañca* mentions it repeatedly, and in a dual technical sense: both as the principle of the nonarising of dharmas and as the lack of any own-nature in dharmas. In this way, the *Pañca* conflates two very different anti-Abhidharma teachings, and two radically different types of discernment—the nonreflective, nonanalytical discernment of the *Aṣṭa,* and the actively analytical discernment of the MMK—under one term. However, it does not work out the implications of this conflation. Later commentators, following the lead of the Mahāyāna texts attributed to Nāgārjuna (see Section 4.5.2), explained the relationship between these two forms of discernment in terms of the two levels of truth: emptiness as the absence of own-nature in dharmas applied to the conventional level of truth, whereas emptiness as the nonarising of dharmas applied to the ultimate level. In other words, dharmas when viewed on the conventional level are empty of own-nature in that they arise and pass away; when viewed on the ultimate level, they don't really arise and pass away at all.

Although this interpretation attracted a number of adherents and formed the basis for one of the two major Mahāyāna philosophical schools in India—the *Madhyamaka* (see Section 5.3.3)—other Mahāyāna thinkers found it unsatisfactory. The main objection was that it seemed too nihilistic. If the data of experience are empty of any essence and, on the ultimate level, do not actually take place, then experience has no more value or meaning than a magic show. And because these data are not only the building blocks of the experience of the world "out there," but also of one's own sense of worth "in here," the nihilistic implications would seem to undercut any motivation to undertake any path of practice at all, much less the demanding path of the bodhisattva. The Perfection of Discernment authors insisted that this was simply an unskillful reading of their teaching, but other Mahāyāna authors felt the need for a new interpretive framework for the teaching on emptiness. Thus they composed texts to provide the

Perfection of Discernment definition of emptiness with a context that would reveal the unity underlying its apparent duality, at the same time erasing its nihilistic connotations.

One of the most ambitious attempts at this task was the *Sandhinirmocana* (Resolution of Enigmas) *Sūtra,* which aimed not only at giving a definitive account of the meaning of emptiness, but also at resolving the conflicts between the Perfection of Discernment Sūtras and the Mainstream canons. It did this by proposing three different ways in which dharmas are empty of own-nature *(svabhāva):* in terms of their origination, in terms of their characteristics, and in ultimate terms. First, following the MMK: The distinguishing characteristics of dharmas are not self-caused, but are instead other-dependent (*paratantra*—literally, "woven together by others"). Thus, to say that they are empty in terms of their origination means that they have no inherent existence. Second, following the Perfection of Discernment literature in general, and the *Aṣṭa* in particular: The distinguishing characteristics of dharmas are mere linguistic conventions—attributed, imputed, imagined *(parikalpita).* Thus, to say that dharmas are empty in terms of their characteristics is to say that their distinguishing characteristics ultimately don't exist, and thus don't really arise or cease. Third—and here is where the *Sandhinirmocana* claims to be breaking new ground—when dharmas are purified of their imagined characteristics, what remains is perfected *(pariniṣpanna):* the ultimate, all-pervasive, unitary, uncompounded. Thus, to say that the perfected is empty in the ultimate sense means that it is empty of any characteristics of dependency. In other words, the perfected is simply the other-dependent stripped of the imagined. This doctrine, although it concerns three meanings of emptiness, is called the *three svabhāvas.*

At first glance, the last two meanings of emptiness may not sound that much different from what is found in the *Aṣṭa,* with the "imagined" another way of saying that dharmas are mere concepts and, as such, do not really arise, and the "perfected" as another name for Suchness. However, the *Sandhinirmocana* claims that the true meaning of the emptiness of the perfected is only implied in the Perfection of Discernment literature, and that people might easily miss it. Thus this third meaning needs to be explicitly spelled out: Dependent co-arising applies only to the linguistic conventions that have built up around the stream of experience, and not to experience itself. The inherent not-selfness of dharmas means that they are not distinct from one another, and thus are all part of a seamless unity. For this reason, all experience in its ultimate sense is already nirvāṇa, already activity-free, and only the imputed/imagined conventions need to be cleared away for there to be purity. This insight, according to the *Sandhinirmocana,* is what distinguishes bodhisattvas from arhats. Arhats, perceiving the other-dependent aspect of all phenomena, abandon everything: not only the imagined aspect but also the perfected. This leads them to a release in which they are unable to use the perfected aspect for the good of other beings. Bodhisattvas, however, abandon only the imagined, and so are able to use the perfected for the benefit of all. Thus the importance of understanding the third aspect of emptiness: Without this perspective, a person listening to the Perfection of Discernment literature might take the teaching on the nonarising of dharmas too far and slip into the path to arhatship.

To further explain this doctrine, the *Sandhinirmocana* elaborates four ways in which Awakening is embodied. Regardless of which path one is following—that of the arhat, Private Buddha, or bodhisattva—one attains a Liberation body on Awakening. However, only a bodhisattva also attains the Dharma body, which is totally free from elaborative thinking and manifest activity, and yet capable of projecting (1) Emanation bodies to teach the arhat path on earth, and (2) the Enjoyment body to teach the bodhisattva path to beings visiting his Buddha-field.

The *Sandhinirmocana* states that this teaching is so important that it constitutes a third and final turning of the wheel of Dharma (see Section 2.2.2), in which everything in the teaching is finally spelled out. The first turning of the wheel—the teaching of the Four Noble Truths—set out the path for śrāvakas. The second turning—the teachings on lack of own-nature and the nonarising of dharmas—set out the path for bodhisattvas. This third turning—the three svabhāva doctrine—provides a comprehensive view for all paths, and is thus the definitive teaching. All other teachings should be interpreted in its light. Any Sūtra passage apparently at odds with this teaching should be understood as an expedient means for dispelling a particular type of misunderstanding, and not as definitive in its own right. An entire school of Mahāyāna philosophy, the Yogācāra (see Section 5.3.2), developed around this principle of interpretation and became the predominant Mahāyāna school in India.

Other Mahāyāna authors proposed other ways of qualifying the Perfection of Discernment doctrine of emptiness, and three of their distinctive doctrines proved especially important in later Mahāyāna thought.

The first is the teaching of the *tathāgata-garbha.* We have already encountered the word *tathāgata* as an epithet for the Buddha. *Garbha* has two sets of meanings. The first covers such things as a womb, an inner room, or the calyx of a flower. The second set covers the contents of the womb or calyx: an embryo, fetus, or seed. In the most basic terms, the tathāgata-garbha is the Buddha-potential in every being, a potential that remains after everything else is abandoned in Awakening. The precise status of this potential, though, was a matter of controversy. The earliest Sūtra to discuss it—the *Tathāgata-garbha Sūtra*—illustrated the concept with a series of similes: an excellent child in the womb of a poor woman; honey in a beehive; gold fallen into the mud. Some of these similes, such as the honey or the gold, suggest something already pure. Others, like the child, suggest something that needs to be conceived and nurtured. Still others, like the womb, suggest a nurturing power. Later Mahāyānists, both in India and beyond, worked out the practical implications of each of these ways of conceiving the potential for Buddhahood, and divided into broad camps over which concept provided the most reliable guide to meditation practice.

There was also the question of how this doctrine related to the doctrine of not-self. Some of the tathāgata-garbha Sūtras, such as the Mahāyāna *Mahāparinirvāṇa Sūtra,* stated flatly that this potential was one's true self. Others, such as the *Lion's Roar of Queen Śrīmālā,* denied that this potential is a self, for it is impersonal: the womb/embryo of the Dharma realm, the Dharma body, the transcendent. Furthermore, this Sūtra claims that this womb/embryo must be assumed for the path to Awakening to be possible. If, following the Abhidharmists, one were to assume that a person is nothing but a conglomeration of momentary dharmas arising and passing away, what is there in momentary dharmas to sense suffering or to seek the path to its ending? Only if there is something permanent within each individual can suffering be perceived and the desire to turn away from suffering conceived.

Still, the impression that the tathāgata-garbha was simply a way of sneaking a permanent self in the back door of Buddhist thought seems to have persisted, for another Sūtra—the *Laṅkāvatāra* (Descent into Laṅka)—takes up just this question. It employs the canonical image of the Buddha as doctor to explain how Dharma teachings should be understood: in terms of their intended purpose in bringing the mind to Awakening, just as medicine can be properly understood only in terms of its purpose in curing illness. In the same way that different illnesses require different medicine, different mental defilements require different teachings. Thus the *Laṅka* explains the tathāgata-garbha teaching in terms of its purpose: to assuage the fears of those who are disconcerted by the not-self teaching. As for the not-self teaching, its purpose is to clear away the mind's habit of imputing imagined categories to reality. Ultimately, however, all doctrines must be abandoned to allow for an experience of Awakening, which is totally inexpressible.

The *Laṅka* then goes on to propose its own tactical way of redefining the tathāgata-garbha, with the purpose of pointing the aspiring bodhisattva away from abstract theorizing and toward an "emptiness" mode of perception, seeing the realm of experience simply as an interplay of different types of consciousness. Thus it explains the tathāgata-garbha as a "storehouse" *(ālaya)* consciousness present in every being. As with the tathāgata-garbha, this concept serves the dual function of (1) proposing a solution to a problem inherent in the Abhidharma doctrine of momentariness and (2) defining what is left over after the bodhisattva realizes the nonarising of dharmas. In this case, the Abhidharma issues center on the question of how karmic seeds are maintained—in fact, this is where the consciousness gets its "storehouse" name. If one were to assume, along with the Sautrāntikas, that dharmas exist only long enough to arise and pass away, then what mental dharmas can perform the function of passing on karmic seeds? Moments of consciousness at the eye, ears, and so on, are too short to carry on the simultaneous functions of registering sense impressions and passing on karmic seeds, so there has to be another mental function serving just this purpose. This is where the storehouse consciousness steps in: receiving seeds from acts of the mind-faculty *(manas),* and then transmitting them to the consciousness at the six senses.

This model is used to explain both aspects of the emptiness teaching. On the one hand, the dharmas of experience possess no own-nature, for they are caused by mind and made of mind. Their nonarising does not mean that they do not happen, simply that they do not happen outside of the mind, nor do they refer to any extramental reality. The experience of a color, for instance, is to be viewed just as an experience, and not as a representation of something outside of the mind.

Despite the name of the storehouse consciousness, the Sūtra's primary image for explaining it is the ocean. The water in the ocean is inherently pure. Karmic impulses are like waves in the ocean—neither identical with the water nor separate from it—which stir up the water and make it murky. The ocean is momentary in the sense that, when there are waves, it is never still for a moment; but inherently it is not momentary, for it is always water, and not even the murkiness can turn it into not-water. When one understands experientially that all the contents of experience are simply mind-made, this brings an end to impure karmic impulses, which are based on the assumption that objects in experience have their own existence "out there." When these impure impulses are pacified, that is like the stilling of the waves that make the water murky. What remains is the water, together with waves free from āsravas (see Section 1.3.5), which do not disturb the water's innate purity. This state is neither empty nor nonempty, for while it is empty of defiling waves, it is not empty of pure water and pure waves.

The way in which the *Laṅka* defines all experience in terms of consciousness has led some modern scholars to interpret it as an early form of ontological idealism, or the theory that nothing exists except the mind and its contents. And some of the Sūtra's traditional interpreters in Asia have seen it in just that light. Other modern scholars, however, have interpreted the *Laṅka*'s approach more as a type of phenomenology, focusing on experience in and of itself for the purpose of ending defilement, without concern for abstract theorizing beyond that purpose. Given the Sūtra's provisional, tactical approach to the Dharma, this interpretation seems closer to its actual intent.

Together with the *Sandhinirmocana,* the *Laṅkāvatāra* became a foundational text for the Yogācāra school (see Section 5.3.2).

A third way of explaining the implications of the doctrine of emptiness in a nonnihilistic way is found in the *Gaṇḍavyūha Sūtra,* a discourse in the form of a long novel relating a bodhisattva's quest. Whereas the *Sandhinirmocana* and *Queen Śrīmālā* Sūtras offer an ontological resolution to the question of emptiness, and the *Laṅkāvatāra Sūtra* a psychological one, the *Gaṇḍavyūha*'s resolution is aesthetic. And instead of trying to shy away from the impression that the teaching of emptiness turns the world of experience into a magical illusion, the *Gaṇḍavyūha* embraces it head-on. In the Sūtra's final scene, the bodhisattva Sudhana meets with Maitreya and gains a glimpse of Maitreya's pavilion, which is essentially a vision of the universe as seen by the Awakened. Although the pavilion appears small on the outside, when viewed from within it fills the entire universe. Each atom of the pavilion contains more pavilions within pavilions, where, in a moment of thought, Sudhana can see Maitreya assuming millions of Emanation bodies to spend aeons of time bringing millions of beings to Buddhahood in millions of Buddha-fields. Then, as quickly as the vision appears, it vanishes.

This vision has many implications, but a few of them are these: Emptiness does not mean that dharmas are not present, simply that they have no boundaries to separate them from one another in space, and no boundaries to mark their arising and passing away in time. Thus they can interpenetrate without interfering with one another. Because space and time are also empty, they can interpenetrate on many scales at once. A single spot can contain many worlds and exist in many different interpenetrating worlds. A moment of time on one scale can encompass aeons on others. Thus the ramifications of a single meritorious thought, focused in a single spot, cannot be counted. Because of this, emptiness means the exact opposite of lack, and interdependence the opposite of duḥkha. Although Maitreya's pavilion seems illusory, the overwhelming plenitude of the illusion is meant to counteract any sense that it is nihilistic. In other words, the *Gaṇḍavyūha*'s message is that the emptiness of experience doesn't matter as long as that emptiness is so full. This magical view was especially influential in East Asian Buddhism, where the *Gaṇḍavyūha* was studied as the final chapter of the immense *Avataṃsaka Sūtra,* which formed the basis for a major philosophical school, the *Hua-yen* (see Section 8.5.2).

B. Tactical Skill. The doctrine of tactical skill *(upāya-kauśalya)* developed in many different directions within the Mahāyāna Sūtras. For the *Aṣṭa,* tactical skill was primarily a bodhisattva's inner ability to balance the two requirements of the bodhisattva path: the need to make as much merit as possible, coupled with the need not to allow that merit to issue in a premature Awakening as an arhat. When the *Pañca* redefined the two poles of the bodhisattva path as discernment and compassion, it also redefined tactical skill to accommodate these new poles. In its new definition, tactical skill is the ability to gain discernment into the teaching of emptiness without abandoning compassion for all living beings, and vice versa. In other words, tactical skill is the ability to pursue two potentially contradictory motivations without being attached to either one in a way that its implications would interfere with the other. The *Pañca* also states—without explanation—that the bodhisattva uses tactical skill to teach other beings. Compared to the *Aṣṭa*'s teachings on tactical skill, this is a major expansion in the range and function of the concept. Instead of being a purely internal ability, tactical skill now becomes one of the bodhisattva's social tools for helping others as well.

The Sūtras that expanded on this concept approached it from two directions: tactical skill as used in the teaching activity of (1) a Buddha and (2) a bodhisattva. The *Lotus Sūtra* stated the most general principle about a Buddha's use of tactical skill: Only a Buddha can know the Dharma as it actually is. Because it is inexpressible, he must use various tactical skills to induce others to gain a Buddha's knowledge and vision of that Dharma. In fact, the array of tactical teaching skills at his disposal is infinite. At times he is required to say contradictory or even false things, but because his motives are compassionate he is not guilty of deception. For example, the *Lotus* claims, the teachings on the Three Vehicles are to be regarded simply as tactical skills. In reality, there is only the One Vehicle, the Mahāyāna, a point we will discuss further in this chapter.

Other Sūtras used tactical skill as an interpretive principle for explaining apparent contradictions among Mahāyāna doctrines attributed to the Buddha. In some cases, the purpose was to establish one doctrine as more definitive than another. Thus, as we have seen, the *Sandhinirmocana* used the idea of tactical skill to explain how the doctrine of the nonarising of dharmas was simply a tactical expedient, whereas the doctrine of the three svabhāvas was definitive. In other cases, the doctrine of tactical skill was used to argue that all teachings are expedients meant for specific purposes, and that their mutually contradictory implications are not to be taken seriously. The *Laṅka*'s treatment of the tathāgata-garbha, the doctrine of not-self, and its own teaching on the storehouse consciousness is a case in point.

As for a bodhisattva's use of tactical skill in teaching others, two Sūtras in particular give graphic examples. The first is the *Upāya-kauśalya*—Tactical Skill—*Sūtra,* which interprets tactical skill as the ability to transmute unskillful mental states and activities into the roots for desirable results. It proposes two ways in which a beginning bodhisattva may employ this sort of tactical skill to help others along the path. The first is in framing one's vows. A bodhisattva (whom the Sūtra assumes must be male) is required to develop the merit-qualifications that will yield the handsome physical body of a Buddha. However, the danger here is that, as his physical appearance improves along the path, women will be sexually attracted to him. Thus he should vow that their lust will be transformed into a skillful basis for them to be reborn as male devas who aspire to Buddhahood.

The second application of tactical skill proposed by the *Upāya-kauśalya* is more controversial, and is based on an innovative reading of the jātaka tales. As we noted in Section 3.6.1, some of the canonical jātaka stories show the Bodhisattva breaking the five precepts (although never the fourth, against lying). The traditional interpretation for these lapses was that the Bodhisattva was still learning the ropes; once he became the Buddha, his behavior was ethically perfect and never transgressed the precepts. The *Upāya-kauśalya* proposes instead that the Bodhisattva fully knew what he was doing, and that his lapses were actually examples of tactical skill in teaching or helping other living beings. It illustrates this principle with a jātaka of its own: An evil man threatened to kill a crowd of people on a ship, so the Bodhisattva killed him instead, both to protect the crowd and to save the man from the evil karma he was planning to incur. Because the Bodhisattva's motives were compassionate, he suffered only a moment in hell before being reborn in the Brahmā worlds. The *Upāya-kauśalya* then extrapolates a principle from the story: A bodhisattva's tactical skill means that a transgression is not a transgression, that any activity based on compassionate motives can be a means to Awakening.

The *Vimalakīrtinirdeśa Sūtra* offers another interpretation of tactical skill as a bodhisattva's teaching tool. Echoing the *Pañca,* it defines tactical skill as the ability to fulfill all the requirements of the bodhisattva's path without being attached to them. It depicts its hero, the lay bodhisattva Vimalakīrti, as consorting with people in brothels, taverns, and places of government—all off-limits to monks—as an expression of his compassionate desire to lead people of all sorts to the Dharma. However—and here the *Vimalakīrtinirdeśa* differs from the *Upāya-kauśalya*—Vimalakīrti's own personal ethical conduct is flawless.

His most distinctive use of tactical skill, however, lies in using the teachings of emptiness to deconstruct the teachings of Mainstream Buddhism. This skill is illustrated in a series of anecdotes, a typical example being this: Kātyāyana, the arhat disciple foremost in explicating brief Dharma teachings, is explaining the meaning of impermanence, suffering, emptiness, not-self, and nirvāṇa to his students. Vimalakīrti appears and admonishes him for using arising and ceasing thoughts to teach about what, in ultimate terms, does not arise and cease. He then uses the doctrine of the nonarising of dharmas to deconstruct all the concepts Kātyāyana has been explaining, claiming for example that nirvāṇa means that events have never arisen and will never cease. As a result of this admonition, Kātyāyana's students all gain release.

Although this passage illustrates Vimalakīrti's use of tactical skill as a teaching tool, it also makes an important statement about tactical skill as an inner attitude in one's progress along the bodhisattva path: *Nonattachment* means deconstructing all the concepts on which the path is built, and the teachings on emptiness are the tools for implementing that deconstruction. In fact, deconstruction itself becomes the path. This attitude differs sharply from the early canonical definition of nonattachment to the path, illustrated by the raft simile (see Section 2.3.1): One uses the raft to cross over the river and then sets it aside upon reaching the further shore. Vimalakīrti's attitude can be illustrated by the raft simile as presented in the *Diamond Sūtra:* One crosses the river by letting go of the raft.

C. Dhāraṇīs. Many of the early bodhisattva Sūtras stated the bestowal of *dhāraṇīs,* or mnemonic protective spells, was one of the distinctive gifts of advanced bodhisattvas granted to devotees and beginning bodhisattvas. Some of the Sūtras, such as the *Aṣṭa,* maintained that they themselves were dhāraṇīs, or offered short, more practical dhāraṇīs as a parting gift to the listener. Other Mahāyāna Sūtras throughout the early medieval period continued this tradition. The *Bodhisattvabhūmi* (Stages of the Bodhisattva), a scholastic treatise ascribed to the late fourth or early fifth century, lists four types of dhāraṇīs found in the Mahāyāna Sūtras. The first two—*dharma-dhāraṇīs* and *artha-dhāraṇīs*—are formulae designed to aid in the memorization, respectively, of Dharma passages and their meaning. The third type, *mantra-dhāraṇīs,* are protective charms to appease the worldly sufferings of living beings. An example would be the spells included in the *Puṣpakuṭadhāraṇī* (Flower Peak Spell) *Sūtra* for protecting one's home. All three of these dhāraṇīs have parallels in Mainstream Buddhist texts. However, the fourth type—*bodhisattva-kṣānti-labhāya dhāraṇīs* for gaining the receptivity of a bodhisattva—are a distinctively Mahāyāna practice. The bodhisattva is supposed to contemplate these dhāraṇīs, which are usually strings of meaningless syllables, as a way of becoming receptive to the reality of emptiness. Seeing that their meaning lies precisely in their meaninglessness, the bodhisattva then extends this insight, by analogy, to all phenomena, realizing that their significance lies in their ineffability.

This use of spells as an aid to transcendent discernment became increasingly popular in Mahāyāna circles with the passage of centuries, and remained one of the major points of controversy dividing the Mahāyāna from Mainstream points of view. Bhāvaviveka, in the sixth century, wrote a rebuttal to the Mainstream assertion that the repetition of mere words could not possibly succeed in cleansing the mind of the roots of unskillful behavior. His rebuttal, however, was based entirely on Mahāyāna Sūtras, and so carried no weight in Mainstream circles. Within Mahāyāna circles, however, it lent the weight of his authority to the theory that the letter and syllables of mantras embodied an intrinsic power. Those who accepted this theory, however, differed as to whether this power was intrinsic in the letters themselves or embodied the *anubhāva* of the Buddha or bodhisattva who bestowed the mantra. We will discuss this issue further in Section 6.2.

D. The Bodhisattva versus the Arhat Path. Many of the teachings in the *Aṣṭa* deal with the fear of slipping from the bodhisattva path and ending up as an arhat. Medieval Mahāyāna Sūtras, however, rarely mention this fear, perhaps because of a new teaching called the *ekayāna,* or One Vehicle. Although

Mahāyāna thinkers interpreted this teaching in various ways, the implication in any case was that no aspiring bodhisattva would be trapped unwillingly in the arhat's path.

The interpretation that proved most influential in East Asia was formulated in the *Lotus Sūtra:* There is only one path, the Buddha-path, which all beings will eventually follow. Arhatship is simply a way station along this path. Śākyamuni was forced to teach the doctrine of the Three Vehicles as an expedient means because his contemporaries were corrupt and lacking in merit, and would respond only to a less demanding goal. The Sūtra illustrates this point with a parable: A fire breaks out in a mansion belonging to a rich householder, but his 20 sons are too engrossed in their playing to notice the flames and do not respond when he calls them to come out. So, as a stratagem, he tells them that toy carts—bullock carts, goat carts, and deer carts—await them outside. The boys come out, safe from the flames, and find one kind of cart, a magnificent bullock cart.

The Sūtra maintains that the father is not guilty of lying, as his aim was to save his children, and that the Buddha, in promulgating the Three Vehicles, is not guilty of lying either, as he is simply expressing his fatherly compassion for the world. Just as the rich man gave each of his sons the best of carts, so the Buddha leads all beings to the same supreme Awakening.

The Sūtra goes on to show that this Awakening is a path without a goal. Śākyamuni actually attained Awakening trillions of aeons ago and, despite his show of entering total nirvāṇa, he currently resides on Vulture's Peak, outside Rajgir, teaching the Dharma. He will continue to assume various forms to help living beings for an inconceivably long period of time. Thus the One Vehicle, which all beings will eventually follow, is an ongoing path of doing good for the entire world.

Despite its popularity in East Asia, where it formed the basis for one of the major Mahāyāna philosophical schools, the *Lotus* seems to have had little impact in India. A vision of the One Vehicle more influential there was formulated in the *Sandhinirmocana Sūtra.* According to this Sūtra, all three vehicles are one in that they follow the same pattern: letting go of the imagined nature imputed in the other-dependent nature, so that only the perfected nature remains (see Section 5.2.3a). The turning point where this happens in the practice is called the *āśraya-parāvṛtti* (reversal of the basis). Although all practitioners go through this turn, they receive differing results due to differences in their innate spiritual *gotra* (lineage or clan). Those in the Buddha lineage, because of their great compassion, can negotiate the turn and come out in a nonabiding nirvāṇa, that is, established neither in saṁsāra nor nirvāṇa. From this position they can follow the career of a bodhisattva. Those in the arhat lineage, however, because of their limited compassion and great fear of suffering, fall off the vehicle when it makes the turn and thus end up in a totally separate nirvāṇa. Asaṅga, in commenting on this Sūtra, adds that if arhats see this nirvāṇa as inferior (implying that they are actually members of the Buddha lineage), they can abandon it and take another try at the turn, assured that their more developed compassion will put them on the bodhisattva path. If, however, they are happy where they are, they are free to stay.

The *Lotus Sūtra*'s version of the One Vehicle, in particular, is a radical departure from Mainstream Buddhist teachings, as it denies the validity of the Triple

Gem as previously conceived. The career of the historical Buddha is said to be simply a show; any comprehensible expression of the Dharma inherently inadequate; and the noble Sangha of the great human disciples as-yet-unawakened. The Mainstream goal of total, final release is an illusion. For some of the *Lotus*'s adherents in medieval East Asia, this total break with the *Hīnayāna,* or Inferior Vehicle, was part of its appeal: In following it, they could rest assured that their practice was in no way contaminated with Hīnayāna ideals. In addition, the *Lotus* and other medieval Mahāyāna Sūtras far outdo the *Aṣṭa* in the contempt they show for arhats, the Mainstream ideal. The *Ākāśagarbha* even makes it a heinous sin for a bodhisattva to encourage others to take up the arhat's path. The later *Sukhāvatīvyūha* Sūtras, as opposed to the earlier versions, expel arhats from Amitābha's land, replacing them with "One-birth Remaining" bodhisattvas, on the grounds that arhats would be undesirable elements in the best of Buddha-fields.

The question thus arises: To what extent do these Sūtras represent the beginning of a Buddhist religion separate from the religion of Mainstream Buddhism? The apparent answer is that they represent the seeds of separate Buddhist religions that would develop as Buddhism spread to other lands, but in India they remained part of one large but increasingly fractious religion. To begin with, the Mahāyāna Sūtras themselves did not represent a monolithic movement, and their authors often directed *ad hominem* arguments not only at Hīnayānists, but also at one another. The authors of the *Sandhinirmocana,* for instance, announced that anyone who accepts the Perfection of Discernment doctrines but not the three svabhāvas is basically dishonest by nature, and will suffer rebirth for hundreds of millions of aeons before gaining entry to the bodhisattva path. Secondly, different Sūtras show different attitudes toward Mainstream teachings and adherents. Some are fairly extreme in their denunciation—the Mahāyāna *Mahāparinirvāṇa Sūtra,* for instance, condemns any Hīnayānist who does not accept it as the word of Buddha to a particularly miserable hell—but others, like the *Sandhinirmocana,* are more conciliatory, holding that Mahāyāna teachings do not contradict Mainstream teachings, but instead encompass them and bring them to perfection. Finally, and most importantly, Mahāyāna monastics never seem to have made a complete institutional break with the Mainstream. Hsüan-tsang reports that although many monasteries in India were either exclusively Mainstream or Mahāyāna in their allegiance, others contained Mahāyāna and Mainstream monastics living together. We can assume that they were living in peace, but the seeds for separate religions were already in place.

5.3 SCHOLASTIC PHILOSOPHY

With the rise of Nalanda as a university, teaching monks confronted the challenge that faces all modern professors: how to organize the growing body of their subject matter in a comprehensive but coherent way. Because many of the students were preparing for the public debates staged outside the universities, they also needed to have their knowledge packaged in convenient, easy-to-remember forms. These factors inspired the growth of the first truly systematic philosophy in the Buddhist tradition, which found its expression both in encyclopedic treatises and in more compact summaries meant to organize and clarify the vast body of literature that the Buddhist tradition had produced over the centuries. In many cases, the summaries were arranged around *kārikas* (see Section 4.5.2), shorthand verses composed as memory aids, with prose commentaries to fill in their blanks. Some sets of kārikas proved so useful that many writers over the centuries offered their own, sometimes conflicting, commentaries and subcommentaries to them. In this way, different schools of thought developed around particular Sūtras or philosophical texts. There is a frequent tendency to reduce each of these schools to a set of doctrines to which all the followers of the school supposedly adhered, a tendency that the scholastic philosophers themselves indulged in when trying to point out the weak points of other schools or to define true orthodoxy in their own. However, this tendency does not do justice to the fact that individual thinkers would sometimes stamp their own genius on the schools to which they belonged, causing the schools to change radically from generation to generation. A better way to conceive of these schools is as long, ongoing conversations on particular topics, the list of topics being the factor that best defines the school. Thus, instead of trying to define the standpoint of the major schools here, we will focus on a handful of individuals who set the agenda for each school, together with a few of the issues that proved controversial within that agenda.

The schools fell into two major camps: Mainstream and Mahāyāna. Mahāyāna philosophers often borrowed from their Mainstream counterparts—particularly in the area of epistemology and dialectics—and disputed points in Mainstream philosophy. For instance, a common Mahāyāna criticism of Mainstream philosophers was that they were incapable of understanding the principle of the not-selfness of dharmas, the teaching that dharmas have no inherent nature; if they understood it, they would convert to the Mahāyāna. Mainstream thinkers, on the other hand, left no record of their stands on specifically Mahāyāna issues. Our only grounds for speculating about Mainstream responses to Mahāyāna thought are the objections that the Mahāyānists address in their own writings. In some cases, the Mahāyānists argue against the objections, in others they are content to leave them as paradoxes that separate the sheep from the goats: Only a bodhisattva, they say or imply, would have the courage not to be deterred by such paradoxes. Asaṅga, for instance, follows both methods in treating two objections raised by his doctrine of Buddhahood. The first objection is this: If infinite Buddhas have been working for the good of beings since beginningless time, why is there still poverty in the world? His answer: If beings had all their material needs met before they were spiritually advanced, they might use their wealth in unskillful ways. The second objection is this: If the realization of all Buddhas, past and future, is already identical, beginningless, and infinite, then why must individual bodhisattvas exert effort for the sake of Awakening? This paradox Asaṅga allows to stand.

Early Mahāyāna philosophers themselves were split over the question of how best to win converts from the Mainstream camp: whether to stress the orthodoxy of their ideas by showing their continuity with Mainstream ideas, or to stress the superiority of their ideas by emphasizing discontinuities. Over time, the second approach became dominant. Thus, for instance, Buddhapālita argued in the fifth century that Mainstream texts contained, in embryo form, the doctrine of the not-selfness of dharmas, thus proving the orthodoxy of this teaching. In the sixth century, however, Bhāvaviveka heaped ridicule on Buddhapālita's position, asserting that the superiority of the Mahāyāna lay precisely in its exclusive claim to this teaching. Bhāvaviveka's position carried the day.

5.3.1 Vasubandhu and the Abhidharmakośa

The earliest extant systematic presentation of Buddhist philosophy dates from the third century, when the Sarvāstivādin thinker, Dharmaśrī, composed the *Abhidharmasāra,* or Abhidharma Essence, in which he tried to encompass all Buddhist thought in a coherent framework. The framework is this: Starting with the basic components of experience, the five skandhas, he moved on to show how these components arise, not in isolation, but in conjunction with one another. Here he touched on the mental properties, the theory of physical atoms, the doctrine of time, and causality: the six conditions recognized by the Sarvāstivādins and the four ways of conceiving dependent co-arising (see Section 4.5.1). Then came the doctrine of karma, to show how causality plays a role in human action, followed by a doctrine of release: an explanation of the tendencies *(anuśaya)* that entangle one in saṁsāra, the knowledge that brings release by putting an end to those tendencies, and the types of knowledge and concentration that enable one to develop that knowledge. Unfortunately, Dharmaśrī was unable to incorporate all the important Buddhist teachings into this framework, and so ended with three miscellaneous chapters. For two centuries, however, his work served as the standard text on Sarvāstivādin Abhidharma, and inspired thinkers in other schools to compose compact, organized texts on their own doctrines.

In the fifth century, a new set of Sarvāstivādin kārikas was composed, following Dharmaśrī's basic framework, but incorporating the miscellaneous material throughout. The major changes involved a discussion of cosmology after the discussion of causation, and a concluding chapter on the ontological status of the "person." This set of kārikas was called the *Abhidharmakośa* (Abhidharma Sheath), or *Kośa* for short. Its authorship is uncertain, but two important commentaries based on it are still extant. The first, composed by Vasubandhu in the fifth century, used the verses as a framework for discussing controversies among the various Buddhist schools, sometimes siding with the Sarvāstivādins and sometimes against them. Vasubandhu is often classified as a Sautrāntikan—particularly because he rejected the Sarvāstivādin doctrines on time and dependent co-arising—but he also took issue with earlier Sautrāntikan doctrines as well. He thus illustrates a trend toward more independent thinking among Buddhist scholastics.

Nevertheless, his treatment of the "person" gives a fairly standard summary of the position held in common by the Sarvāstivādins, Sautrāntikas, and other anti-Pudgalavādins on the doctrine of not-self. The "self," he says, is simply a conventional designation for a series of skandhas, and does not exist in and of itself. Because there is no direct perception or inference of a self independent of the skandhas, we can conclude that a real self does not exist. In response to the observation that the Buddha, in the early Sūtras, refused to answer the question of whether a self did or did not exist, Vasubandhu maintains that, had his listener understood dependent co-arising, the Buddha would have told him that the conventional self exists, but the real self doesn't. And in response to the objection that this doctrine is a form of annihilationism, Vasubandhu maintains that only two doctrines qualify as annihilationism: the doctrine that there is nothing there at all, and the doctrine that there is a permanent soul that can suffer annihilation.

Vasubandhu's attack on the Sarvāstivādin positions inspired a Sarvāstivādin philosopher, Saṅghabhadra, to write a much longer commentary on the *Kośa* in their defense; and apparently there were other, later thinkers who used the *Kośa* as a framework for advancing their own opinions as well. The *Kośa* was so well known that Bāṇa, in his description of the forest monastery, could refer to parrots discoursing on the *Kośa* and expect his reader to smile in recognition. Of all the commentaries, however, Vasubandhu's remained the most prominent, largely because of his student, Dignāga (see Section 5.1). In his revision of the ground rules for epistemology and dialectics, Dignāga incorporated material from Vasubandhu's work, thus keeping it alive for several centuries.

5.3.2 Asaṅga and the Yogācāra

Asaṅga was the father of systematic Mahāyāna philosophy, the first philosopher to take the disparate Mahāyāna Sūtras of his time and work out a coherent framework for encompassing them all. Little is known of his personal history. He is assumed to have lived in the fourth century, and Hsüan-tsang reports that he was a Mahīśāsaka monk converted to the Mahāyāna by a Maitreyanātha. There is debate as to whether this Maitreyanātha was a human being or the great bodhisattva himself. Hsüan-tsang assumes that it was the bodhisattva, and other legends tell of how Asaṅga encountered the great being: After meditating for 12 years in a cave to gain a vision of Maitreya, all in vain, he one day noticed a wounded dog lying at the mouth of the cave. Feeling compassion for the dog, he wanted to dress its wound but noticed that the wound was infested with maggots. This created a quandary: If he removed the maggots, they would die. So he cut off a piece of his own flesh to provide them with another place to live, but this presented another challenge: how to move the maggots without injuring them. After rejecting various means, he concluded that he had to move them one-by-one with his tongue. Closing his eyes in disgust, he proceeded to move the first maggot. At that point the dog vanished and was replaced by Maitreya, who rewarded Asaṅga's compassion by taking him to his heaven and revealing five texts to him, which were to form the basis of Asaṅga's great compilation of Mahāyāna philosophy. Modern scholars, of course, doubt the story, and note that the Maitreya texts, as we have them, differ considerably both in style and substance from Asaṅga's own works.

Asaṅga was a prolific writer, compiling enormous, Abhidharma-like texts to absorb all of Buddhist thought, both Mainstream and Mahāyāna, into a Mahāyāna framework. Following Dharmaśrī's example, however, he also wrote shorter works to present his thought in outline form, the most compact being the *Mahāyāna-saṃgraha,* or *Summary of the Great Vehicle.* The structure of the *Summary* parallels that of the *Abhidharmasāra,* and a comparison of the two texts highlights the gulf that had come to separate Mahāyāna from Mainstream speculative thought by the fourth century.

Asaṅga places his discussion of Dharmaśrī's first three topics—the skandhas, dependent co-arising, and karma—in the context of the "knowable" (what can be directly experienced) and the "support of the knowable" (what has to be assumed as underlying experience). The *knowable* he defines as the three svabhāvas, which cover the skandhas and all other dharmas of experience. The *support of the knowable* is the storehouse consciousness, which contains all karmic seeds. Dependent co-arising is the process whereby seeds of language in the storehouse consciousness give rise to all knowable dharmas; whereas the three svabhāvas are simply dependently co-arisen phenomena. In this scheme, the twelve factors of Mainstream dependent co-arising do not actually give rise to one another. They are simply the products of the maturing of karmic linguistic seeds in the storehouse consciousness.

In place of Dharmaśrī's description of the path to liberation, Asaṅga presents the Mahāyāna path as one of "entry into the knowable." In other words, whereas the arhat enters into conditioned phenomena only in the practice of concentration, followed by a total release from all conditioned phenomena through discernment, the bodhisattva's path is one of immersion into the Suchness of conditioned experience with the purpose of staying there in an undeluded way. This path grows from seeds originating, not in the storehouse consciousness, but from the *Reality Realm of the Buddhas,* in the form of words and images of the Mahāyāna teachings. As the practitioner nourishes these seeds through the right conditions—fostering the roots of skillful behavior, rendering adhikāra to innumerable Buddhas, and so on—they lead to a "reversal of the basis" (see Section 5.2.3d), in which the storehouse consciousness ends and the Reality Realm itself becomes the basis for the seeds of all further actions. This enables one to undertake the path, which Asaṅga describes as the six perfections, the ten stages (see Section 5.2.1), and the three trainings of virtue, concentration, and discernment, showing precisely where the bodhisattva's practice of these trainings resembles that of the arhat and where they differ. The *Summary* closes with a description of the Three Bodies of a Buddha: the Dharma body, the Enjoyment body, and the Emanation bodies (see Section 5.2.3a).

Asaṅga's discussion of discernment, dividing it into three phases, set the pattern for its treatment by all subsequent Mahāyāna philosophers, even those who did not join his school. The first phase is *preparatory discernment,* in which one meditates on the teachings of the storehouse consciousness and the three svabhāvas, to see that all dharmas are mere constructs of consciousness *(vijñapti-mātra),* that all experiences are like the colors perceived in meditative practice, unrelated to anything outside. Seeing that there is nothing "out there" to grasp and no one "in here" to do the grasping, all grasping falls away, and this leads to the second phase of discernment, the *nonimagined phase,* which constitutes the reversal of the basis. At this point, one drops all the concepts of the preparatory phase, including the concept of "mere constructs of consciousness," and enters into the Dharma body, which is beyond the scope of the intellect. The Dharma body is described, however, as the Suchness of the perfected nature; the initial purity of all dharmas; and the experience of nonduality—of existence and nonexistence, conditioned and unconditioned, unity and multiplicity. This phase of discernment is followed by a *subsequent phase,* in which one resumes action in the phenomenal world, but without delusion. The attainment of nonimagined discernment recurs with each stage of the bodhisattva path, until—through the attainment of diamond-concentration on the tenth stage—it yields in the non-abiding nirvāṇa of Buddhahood. At this point, one no longer engages in action or encounters obstacles, but one's Enjoyment and Emanation bodies continue to function through the anubhāva of one's previous vows. In this way, one's actions continue without end for the liberation of all.

Asaṅga compared these three phases of discernment to training in magic: In the first phase, one is trying not to be fooled by a magician's trick; in the second phase, one sees through the trick; in the third phase, one becomes a magician oneself, working magic for the good of all beings.

Asaṅga inspired a school of Mahāyāna thought, called the *Yogācāra* (Practice of Meditation) school because of the role it gave to meditation practice in developing preparatory discernment. The school was also called the *Mere Constructs of Consciousness* school and the *Mere Mind* (or *Mind-Only*) school, for its analysis of dharmas. One of the major issues in the development of the school was in how to interpret the tathāgata-garbha in the light of its treatment of the storehouse consciousness. Asaṅga insisted that the storehouse consciousness was simply a momentary stream, rather than a permanent entity, and he had broken ranks with the *Laṅka* by insisting that it was abandoned rather than purified with the reversal of the basis. Thus there was no way he could identify the storehouse consciousness with the tathāgata-garbha. For him, the tathāgata-garbha was simply another term for the discernment experienced with the reversal of the basis. Later thinkers in the school, however—including his brother, Vasubandhu (apparently not the Vasubandhu who commented on the *Kośa,* although this is a controversial point)—modified Asaṅga's position on this topic, and equated the storehouse consciousness with the tathāgata-garbha.

5.3.3 Bhāvaviveka and the Madhyamaka

Nāgārjuna developed a Mahāyāna following, including a direct pupil—Āryadeva—and later commentators, such as Buddhapālita in the fifth century. In the fifth century, a commentary on the *Pañca,* attributed to Nāgārjuna, was translated into Chinese, but most scholars doubt the attribution, as no Sanskrit or Tibetan reference to the work is known. However, not until Bhāvaviveka, in the sixth century, did a genuine school of thought develop around Nāgārjuna's work. In fact, Bhāvaviveka (also called Bhavya) was largely responsible for creating the notion of "schools" of thought in Buddhist philosophy to begin with, defining his own school—the *Madhyamaka*, or *Middle Way* school—as well as competing schools in terms of their distinctive doctrines or approaches.

Bhāvaviveka adopted Asaṅga's analysis of discernment into three phases, as well as the analogy of the magician to describe them, but he differed sharply with Asaṅga on the nature of the first phase. Simply put, he proposed a different way of using the doctrine of dependent co-arising as a means of arriving at non-dual discernment. Rejecting the concepts of storehouse consciousness and the three svabhāvas as counterproductive, he advocated using Nāgārjuna's method of deconstructive analysis as presented in the MMK. Thus, for him, the work of preparatory discernment was less meditative and more analytical: destroying all viewpoints by exploring the implications of the lack of own-nature of dharmas. This would lead to the second phase, or nondual awareness which, following the Mahāyāna writings attributed to Nāgārjuna, Bhāvaviveka identified with the discernment of the nonarising of dharmas. In the subsequent phase, one's discernment would embrace both levels of emptiness, so that one could continue the work of a bodhisattva.

In order to make the method of analysis employed in the first phase more effective for his day and time—when the logical theories of Dignāga had been accepted—Bhāvaviveka emphasized the need to present Nāgārjuna's arguments in the newly accepted form. This required that each argument clearly state the logical assumptions on which it was based. Thus Bhāvaviveka wrote an extensive commentary on the MMK, explicitly stating the logical assumptions underlying each of Nāgārjuna's arguments.

In the seventh century, another Madhyamaka thinker, Candrakīrti, rejected this approach, and his arguments highlight an interesting question in the issue of tactical skill: To what extent is it skillful to work within the presuppositions of the people one wants to draw to one's point of view; and to what extent must one embody one's position in one's actions to achieve the same end? Bhāvaviveka believed that to be logically persuasive, Nāgārjuna's arguments had to be cast in the form acceptable to one's audience. Candrakīrti, however, felt that this was a betrayal of the Madhyamaka approach. In casting Nāgārjuna's arguments in terms of their logical assumptions, Bhāvaviveka—in Candrakīrti's eyes—was guilty of a two-fold error: (1) To assume that words have necessary implications is to endow them with an inherent nature; (2) to set out one's assumptions is to establish a philosophical system, which is precisely the sort of thing that the Madhyamaka approach is meant to deconstruct. To counter the first error, Candrakīrti noted that, "Words are not like policemen on the prowl: We are not subject to their independent authority. . . . They take their meaning from the intention of the person using them." In other words, they carry logical implications only if employed to construct a view about reality. If employed to destroy attachment to views, they carry no necessary meanings beyond their intended use. To counter the second error, Candrakīrti identified the Madhyamaka with a particular style of argumentation, called *prasaṅga,* in which one deconstructs one's opponent's statements simply by exposing their own logical inconsistencies, without proposing any independent views of one's own. Any other style of argumentation, he claimed, was not true to the Madhyamaka and thus did not properly belong to the school. As far as he was concerned, Bhāvaviveka was not a true Madhyamaka, but simply a logician dabbling in Madhyamaka ideas.

Candrakīrti's approach was fairly uninfluential in India, perhaps because it contradicted the MMK in two ways: (1) Nāgārjuna himself had not restricted himself to prasaṅga arguments; and (2) Nāgārjuna had taught the necessity of views on the conventional level on the grounds that, if one did not have a view that encouraged the deconstruction of attachment to views, one would have no reason to accept the deconstructionist approach to begin with.

Later Indian Madhyamaka thinkers tended to follow Bhāvaviveka's example, expressing their arguments in the logical fashions of the times. In Tibet, however, Candrakīrti became the more influential of the two thinkers. Tsongkhapa, the great fourteenth-century scholar, divided all Madhyamaka thought into two schools: the *Independent Argument (Svātantrika)* school, exemplified by Bhāvaviveka; and the *Prasaṅga Adherent (Prāsaṅgika)* school, exemplified by Candrakīrti. Tsongkhapa championed Madhyamaka as the highest expression of Buddhist thought, and Candrakīrti as the highest expression of the Madhyamaka method, and thus Candrakīrti's teaching has dominated Tibetan philosophy to this day.

6

Buddhism in Late Medieval and Modern India

6.1 THE CULTURE OF BELLIGERENCE

Bāṇa's biography of Harṣavardhana closed with a spectacular bloodred sunset, symbolizing the many violent wars that marked Harṣa's reign. This sunset can also be taken as a symbol of the period from the end of Harṣa's reign in the late seventh century to the Muslim invasions at the beginning of the thirteenth. The sunset stands for the fact that this was Buddhism's final phase as a living, creative presence in its original homeland, the Gangetic Plain. The blood-red stands for the fact that, politically, this was a period of incessant internecine warfare among small states, none of which were able to achieve lasting dominance of the subcontinent. The political situation was so unstable, and war so prevalent, that they fostered what one scholar has called a "culture of belligerence" that glorified war, bloodshed, and the unabashed pursuit of power. The arts, literature, and inscriptions of the time celebrated the warrior-king in erotic terms. Violence—often depicted in gruesome detail—was an aspect of his erotic play; the cities he had conquered swooned at his feet like a woman impatient to be ravished. Unlike heroes of earlier periods, who were glorified for sacrificing their immediate benefit for the sake of moral principle, here the values were inverted: The hero was glorified for pursuing his immediate gain by overthrowing the shackles of social convention.

Perhaps this inversion was due to the fact that the majority of the new kings were not from the noble warrior caste. Many had risen from lower castes, and based their claims to legitimacy, not on birth, but on the fact that they or their ancestors had offered patronage to *siddhas,* ritual adepts often dwelling on the fringes of society, devoted to the cult of *vidyādharas,* or wizards, whose empowerment rituals employ what has been termed *transgressive sacrality:* the pursuit of spiritual power through defying and inverting conventional religious practices and social norms.

These developments affected the development of Buddhist thought and practice during this period in both general and specific ways. In general, many members of the cultural and political elites came to regard traditional social conventions as outmoded and discredited. The fact that power could be gained by flouting those conventions led people on many levels of society to call them into question and to look outside them for guidance. In some ways, this trend paralleled the time of the Buddha, although this time traditional Buddhist ideals were part of the established culture being called into question. Two previously disreputable groups of society now became models for how to work free of the strictures of traditional religion: siddhas and tribal people. Siddhas were now publicly sought for their support, and their pattern of practice was adopted in many circles. A parallel trend was the development of a cult of spontaneity, in which members of the political and cultural elites self-consciously adopted what they believed were the customs of tribal people in defiance of traditional social and ethical norms. Both of these trends influenced developments in all the major religions of India: Jainism, Buddhism, and the devotional cults surrounding Viṣṇu, Śiva, and Śaktā.

Other social developments had a more specific effect on Buddhists. To begin with, Buddhist monasteries now faced intense competition for royal patronage, both from ascetic orders in other religions and among themselves. The external contenders for royal patronage included the Śaivite and Śaktā ascetics, most prominently the Pāśupata Śaivites, who patterned many of their practices on siddha models. One practice particularly popular with rulers was a ritual in which they would assume the identity of the god Śiva. Their divine identity would then justify the violence of their military campaigns as an aspect of Śiva's erotic play.

In most of India, kings and princes withdrew their support from Buddhists and—desperate for capital to support their wars—often plundered or seized Buddhist monasteries or monastic lands. One major exception to this trend was in the northeast, where the Pāla dynasty in Bengal and Bihar (eighth to eleventh centuries) and the Bhaumakara dynasty in Orissa adopted Buddhism as their religion. Both dynasties established many new universities modeled after Nalanda, but their support of these universities was uneven, both because of the waxing and waning of each dynasty's fortunes in war, and because of royal favoritism for one university over another. The politicization of the universities was heightened by the fact that many monks, after receiving university education, would disrobe to seek employment in the courts of princes and kings. Others would serve as diplomats even as they remained in the robes. Thus, not only their royal sponsors but also those of their students who sought to use the Sangha as a means of social advancement were pressuring the monasteries to find new ways of meeting the Śaivite challenge.

One interesting side effect of the universities' unstable financial condition was that many of them sent emissaries to Buddhist kingdoms outside India to teach and send donations back to their home institutions. Inscriptions show that they succeeded in attracting support from kings in such faraway places as Java and Tibet. Thus economic problems at home provided impetus for the exportation of the new teachings developing in India during this time.

Buddhists responded to the development of this unsettled cultural environment in a variety of ways. Some ignored the new political situation entirely, practicing and theorizing in line with trajectories already set by earlier centuries of the tradition. In the major universities, Mainstream and conservative Mahāyāna scholars continued the work of consolidating and refining the theories of their predecessors. For example, the eighth-century Madhyamaka philosopher, Śāntarakṣita, used Dharmakīrti's epistemological teachings to resolve two contradictions: one between Madhyamaka and Yogācāra interpretations of the conventional meaning of emptiness, and the other between the Madhyamaka's own conventional and ultimate meanings of the term. Dharmakīrti had argued that words apply not to realities but to our ideas about reality. From this argument, Śāntarakṣita argued further that the dharmas to which words apply are mere concepts and as such do not exist as realities even on the conventional level, much less on the ultimate level. Thus, because they are mere concepts, they lack any nature of their own; because they are not realities, they do not really arise and pass away. Thus the three major interpretations of the meaning of *emptiness*—"mere constructs of consciousness," "lack of own-nature," and "the nonarising of dharmas"—all come down to the same thing. Another eighth-century thinker, Śāntideva, in his popular poem, the *Bodhicaryāvatāra (Appearance of Awakening Practice),* broached a problem that had long occupied Mahāyāna philosophers: If all dharmas are without self, why did the Buddha introduce the apparently redundant teaching that persons are also without self? Śāntideva's solution was simple: The teaching on the not-selfness of individuals was a meditative reflection on the lack of separateness among individuals intended to arouse compassion for all. Both Śāntarakṣita's and Śāntideva's solutions of these issues proved enduring in Mahāyāna philosophical circles. What is striking about them, considering the growth of entirely new Buddhist movements in response to the belligerent atmosphere of their time, is that the works of neither thinker show any influence from those movements.

In general terms, compassion was the Buddhist ideal most out of step with the glorification of violence, and even some non-Buddhist writers, appalled at the state of affairs around them, looked to Buddhism to provide a compassionate alternative. A prime example was the eleventh-century brahman Kṣemendra, who tried to spark new interest in the compassionate ideals of the jātaka and avadāna tales by recasting them in the sophisticated literary style of the day. Still, there is evidence that some Buddhists began to explore the possibility that belligerent action might be a legitimate expression of compassionate intentions. This trend is exemplified even in the Mainstream cult of Śākyamuni. Images of him in the "Earth-touching" mudrā—depicting the moment of his victory over Māra, the most warlike incident in the traditional biography—achieved an unprecedented popularity during this period.

Some Mahāyāna Buddhists went even further, exploring the possibility that compassion could find expression in ritual acts of subjugating others and, in some cases, in the psychology of violent eroticism. This exploration opened the way for them to embrace the models set by the siddhas, Śaivites, and tribal religions as means of attaining Buddhist goals. The most prominent of these models was the ritual of *sādhana,* the invocation of a deity by an initiate through the use of mantras, mudrās (hand gestures), and the visualization of maṇḍalas—stylized realms representing the deity's field of power. Once the deity was invoked, the initiate would then assume the identity of the deity, together with the deity's knowledge and powers.

In the Buddhist context, the sādhana method was focused on attaining the knowledge and powers of a Buddha or bodhisattva. The texts describing these rituals were remarkably varied, particularly in the extent to which they did or did not adopt the more extreme transgressive methods of the siddhas. In adopting the sādhana method into their practice, Buddhists who were attracted to this approach not only formulated a wide variety of rituals but also rethought the theories and values underlying their own practice. Thus, in addition to ritual texts, they also produced new theories to explain how these practices related to their views of karma and causality, and to their religious goals.

Scholars disagree as to when the sādhana method was first introduced into Buddhism. Given the general secrecy that surrounded siddha practice, a firm date may be impossible to determine. The earliest clear mention of non-Buddhist siddhas dates from the first two centuries of the common era, and some siddhas may have independently adopted the Buddha as their patron deity quite early on. We have already noted the use of mantras in earlier Mahāyāna Buddhism, particularly in the dhāraṇī Sūtras, and scholars have found maṇḍala-like elements in Mahāyāna Sūtras dating back at least to the fourth century. However, none of these earlier writings contain the essential element of Buddhist sādhana practice, the ritual step of assuming a Buddha's or bodhisattva's identity together with control over the attendant maṇḍala. For example, the *Suvaṃaprabhāsottamarāja Sūtra* (The Highest King of Golden Radiance), translated into Chinese in the early fifth century, is sometimes cited as an early instance of sādhana practice. However, its "maṇḍala" is actually the opposite of a maṇḍala, in which the meditator surrounded by four Buddhas housed in a palatial setting is their supplicant, rather than their ruler. In this, the Sūtra differs in no way from other early Mahāyāna devotional texts. In fact, the Buddhas depicted in this Sūtra, instead of yielding their knowledge to the supplicant, refuse to answer his questions. The earliest datable Buddhist texts in which the meditator achieves identity with a divine being—together with control over that being's maṇḍala, knowledge, and powers—come from the seventh century. Thus, that is the date we will take as the beginning of the movement.

The other controversial issue surrounding these new practices is whether they were absorbed directly from siddhas or through Śaivism. The existing evidence supports the first interpretation in some instances, and the second in others.

In the following sections we will focus on these new developments, but it should be remembered that not all Buddhists embraced the new practices. In fact, medieval Tibetan historians insisted that, even to the end of the twelfth century, Indian Buddhists were overwhelmingly devoted to Mainstream practices, while the innovators and their followers were a distinct if vocal minority, even within the Mahāyāna. Still, the new practices achieved an international influence throughout the Buddhist world. Although that influence has waned—and even been suppresed—in some Buddhist countries, traces are still present in all. These practices underlie the Shingon and Tendai sects in Japan, and constitute the dominant form of Buddhism in the Tibetan cultural sphere, from which their influence has recently spread once again throughout Asia and also into the West.

6.2 VAJRAYĀNA

The results of these new developments were consolidated in the *Vajrayāna,* or Adamantine Vehicle. Sometimes presenting itself as a simple development of ideas already inherent in the Mahāyāna and sometimes as a radically different vehicle, the Vajrayāna claimed to be a faster, more direct path to Buddhahood than that outlined in older avadāna and Mahāyāna texts. Calling the more traditional path the "cause" path, in which one had to develop the *pāramitās* before being able to taste the fruit of Awakening, advocates of the Vajrayāna presented their path as a "result" path, in which one could tap directly and immediately into the Awakening of already Awakened beings. This was accomplished by using ritual means to return to the emptiness that serves as the common source of all beings and, from there, using further rituals to emerge with the identity, together with the knowledge and powers, of Buddhas and/or bodhisattvas. Some Vajrayāna texts proposed that the result path was simply a faster alternative to the cause path; others, that it was the only true path to Buddhahood.

Central to the practice of the Vajrayāna was proper initiation by a qualified guru, or teacher. Only a guru who already attained ritual identity with a Buddha or bodhisattva was qualified to induct another into the ritual. And because of the guru's heightened identity, the initiate was to treat the guru with the highest respect, observing all the taboos that the guru required. Thus, under the Vajrayāna, the guru assumed the role of the Buddha under the avadāna/Mahāyāna model, in that the guru's acceptance of the initiate was the necessary prerequisite for accessing the path. Because initiation was usually secret, Vajrayāna is often labeled as *esoteric Mahāyāna,* as opposed to the cause path to Buddhahood, which is labeled as *exoteric Mahāyāna.*

The new vehicle was named after *Vajradhātu* (the Adamantine Realm), its term for the emptiness that formed the ground of Buddhahood. In adopting the symbolism of the *vajra* (diamond/thunderbolt), the new vehicle was laying claim to a tradition with deep roots in Indian religion, for the vajra was the weapon wielded by the Vedic storm god Indra (see Section 1.4.1). As both a diamond and a thunderbolt, the vajra stood for two aspects of supreme power: total invincibility and unfettered spontaneity. However, in keeping with the new vehicle's multivalent use of language, the vajra carried additional layers of symbolism as well. In the royal rites on which many Vajrayāna texts were based, the vajra was the king's scepter. The *vajrapañcara,* or scepter cage, was the impregnable fortress at the center of the king's maṇḍala. In the more transgressive rites, the vajra stood for the male sexual organ, which in most texts was an analogue for compassion, which could remain firm only when combined with the female organ, an analogue for the discernment of emptiness.

Another term for the new vehicle was the *Mantrayāna,* or Incantation Vehicle. We have already encountered incantations in earlier dhāraṇī Sūtras, which prior to the seventh century had been classed as *Mantranaya,* or the Incantation Path, which was said to augment the *Pāramitānaya,* or Perfection Path of practice. In fact, ritual incantation texts date back to the early canons. The Pali Canon, for instance, contains texts for recitation to protect against evil spirits and dangerous animals. Unlike the Mantrayāna texts, however, these early texts do not claim that their words have an inherent power of coercion. Most of them, such as the *Mettā Sutta* (Sn.I.8), derive their power from the compassion in the reciter's mind; the good karma produced by thoughts of goodwill is what protects the reciter from danger. In another discourse, the *Āṭānāṭiya Sutta* (DN. 32), the deva Vaiśravana (see Section 1.4.1) promises that if any practicing Buddhists are harassed by spirits under his jurisdiction, they need only chant his mantra and he will deal with the offenders. In this case, the power of the incantation comes from Vaiśravana's voluntary offer to fellow Buddhists; this is the pattern followed by the incantations given in the early Mahāyāna texts.

With the Mantrayāna, however, the words themselves are said to derive their power directly from the Vajradhātu, enabling them to coerce deities and other forces on a lower ontological level to do one's bidding. In this respect, Mantrayāna linguistic theory is closer to Brahmanical linguistic theory—according to which, sacred words are identical with Brahmā, embodying a level of being and power prior to that of the material cosmos—than to earlier Buddhist linguistic theory, in which words are simply social conventions.

Given their ontological status, mantras were the most basic element in the new rituals. *Seed mantras* were used to generate the maṇḍala and its inhabitants; *heart mantras,* to contemplate the deity and to perform his/her functions. Different texts explained the stages in the process in different ways, sometimes augmenting the recitation with mudrās and a practice of internal yoga to clear "knots" from the internal energy channels in the body, leading to a stage of completion *(niṣpannakrama),* formless and awakened, from which the initiate emerged fully identified with the deity to relieve the sufferings of sentient beings.

6.2.1 Tantras

Another, more modern name for the Vajrayāna, is *Tantric Buddhism,* after the *Tantras,* the principal texts containing the new vehicle's ritual instructions. Because the same genre of texts was used in similar movements in other Indian religions at the time, the entire ritual trend of this period has been called *Tantrism.* This term has become controversial in scholarly circles, largely because its modern meaning tends to be equated with sexual rituals, which formed only a part of the new movement. Another difficulty stems from the fact that Indian Buddhists, Jains, Śaivites, and so on, themselves used the term *Tantra* in a variety of inconsistent ways. However, despite the difficulties surrounding the term *Tantrism,* there is no other term to describe the general development of ritual practice across religious lines in India during this period, and so we will use it for that purpose in this book.

The term *tantra* literally means *weave.* Originally, as a literary genre, a Tantra was a text with at least two levels of meaning, depending on the context in which it was interpreted. Just as a Sūtra, literally a *thread,* carried a thread of meaning, a Tantra was an interweaving of at least two threads in a single text. Because sādhana practice carried many levels of symbolic meaning—political, sexual, and religious—Tantras were the ideal genre for conveying ritual instructions. Over time, the term *Tantra* was expanded to denote the ritual itself as well, in the sense that it wove a new reality.

An additional difficulty in ascertaining the meaning of *Tantra* lies in the fact that Buddhists themselves have produced many different interpretations of which texts qualify as Tantras. An eighth-century commentary defines three types: *Kriyā* (Action) *Tantras, Caryā* (Performance) *Tantras,* and *Yoga* (Union) *Tantras.* A twelfth-century text divides the last category into three: *Yoga, Yogottara* (Higher Union), and *Yoganiruttara* (Unexcelled Union). The last two categories were also known as *Mahāyoga* (Great Union) and *Yoginī* (Female Yogin) *Tantras,* for reasons we will discuss later. To make matters more complicated, later Tibetan exegetes combined the last two categories into one, the *Anuttarayoga* (Unsurpassed Union). For the purpose of our discussion, we will employ the twelfth-century classification, as it is native to India.

Kriyā Tantras are essentially dhāraṇī Sūtras, although some of them contain references to simple maṇḍalas. In fact, scholars disagree as to whether they really qualify as Tantras. Many of the texts included in this category were written prior to the eighth century—some date back to the third—and yet none of the texts with that early a date actually call themselves Tantras, nor do they contain the essential element of sādhana practice, the assumption of a deity's identity. Perhaps eighth-century commentators classified them as Tantras to show that the new movement had old roots in the Buddhist tradition. At any rate, Kriyā Tantras written in the eighth century and later do occasionally refer to themselves as Tantras, and although they lack initiatory rites, later commentators interpreted them as preparatory to sādhana. These texts limit themselves to mantras devoted to worldly ends, classified into four functions: pacifying, fostering, subjugating, and destroying. The influence of royal rites on these Tantras can be seen in the fact that these four functions correspond to the four functions of a king. A king would pacify dissent and insurrection, whereas a *tantrika*—a practitioner of Tantra—would pacify illness or a quarrel; a king would foster prosperity, a tantrika merit or crops; a king would destroy criminals, a tantrika dangers, crops, buildings, or roads; both would subjugate enemies, although the tantrika might subjugate enemies in both the spiritual and physical realm.

Caryā Tantras also focus on worldly ends, but they center on rites in which the initiate identifies with Vairocana, the cosmic Buddha that the *Gaṇḍavyūha* and *Daśabhūmika Sūtras* identify as embodied in the universe as a whole. In principle, the efficacy of these Tantras depended on the ability to take on Vairocana's own enlightened view of the cosmos which, as represented in the *Gaṇḍavyūha Sūtra,* was multivalent and infinitely malleable. From this vantage point, one could ritually affect events on the material level through the medium of Vairocana's identity with the cosmos as a whole.

Yoga Tantras took the process of identification with Vairocana one step further in that they presented the ritual as a means not only of gaining worldly powers, but also of gaining full Buddhahood. An important text in this category is the *Sarvatathāgatatattvasaṃgraha,* or Compendium of the Truths of All the Tathāgatas (*Tattvasaṃgraha* for short), believed to date from the late seventh or early eighth century. This text established the Vajradhātu maṇḍala, which was to be adopted by many other Tantras, with Vairocana occupying a palace in the middle surrounded by other Buddhas in the cardinal directions: Akṣobhya to the east, Ratnasaṃbhava to the south, Amitābha to the west, and Amoghasiddhi to the north. Each of these Buddhas was associated with a clan or retinue, specializing in different functions. Thus Akṣobhya's Vajra or Thunderbolt clan specialized in subjugating, while Amitābha's Padma or Lotus clan specialized in pacifying.

The Vajradhātu maṇḍala replicated in cosmic terms the political theory behind the royal rites of medieval India. The architectural details of Vairocana's dwelling were described using terminology used for palaces, rather than temples or monasteries; and the assignment of clans or retinues to the cardinal directions corresponded to the way feudatories were arranged to protect a king.

Mahāyoga Tantras follow the pattern of Yoga Tantras, although they tend to adopt more of the transgressive elements from the siddha tradition. In the *Guyhasamāja* (Secret Congress), believed to date from the early eighth century, Akṣobhya and his fierce Vajra family move to the center of the maṇḍala, thus paving the way for the fierce and semifierce deities that dominate later Vajrayāna in India. Another emblematic change is that the Buddhas in the maṇḍala are depicted in sexual union with their consorts. Although a few Yoga Tantras include descriptions of sexual intercourse, these descriptions are a defining feature of the Mahāyoga Tantras. Thus the *Guyhasamāja* features, in the initiatory ritual, sexual intercourse with a partner from another caste, along with the consumption of substances conventionally viewed as forbidden or impure: urine, feces, and sexual fluids. Other Mahāyoga Tantras also prescribe the consumption of human flesh. The rationale behind these taboo-breaking recommendations is twofold: to tap into the power held by the forbidden, and to erase dualistic mind states, together with the pride that surrounds conventional purity. Two schools of monastic exegesis quickly developed around the *Guyhasamāja,* one insisting on the importance of interpreting the symbolism of the Tantra in line with traditional Mahāyāna doctrine (thus the transgressive elements were only to be visualized), the other insisting that the true interpretation of the ritual had to be passed down orally, so as not to be revealed to the uninitiated.

Yoginī Tantras add further transgressive elements from siddha practice. In these Tantras the royal symbolism of the Yoga and Mahāyoga Tantras is replaced with symbolism drawn from cemeteries. Thus, for instance, the major figures of a Yoginī maṇḍala often show gruesome expressions, wear flayed animal skins and ornaments made of bones, drink from human skulls, and engage in intercourse while standing on corpses. Another distinctive feature of these maṇḍalas is the prominent role played by female figures. In some cases, ḍākinīs (female sky dancers, often ferocious looking) encircle the central figures; in others, female figures occupy the central position of the maṇḍala alone. Many Yoginī rituals climax in a blissful, nondual state called *Mahāmudrā,* or Great Seal (in the sense of a king's seal of authority), in union with one's consort. This is then equated with the *Mahāsukha,* or Great Bliss, that characterizes the experience of Awakened cognition. Among the most prominent Yoginī Tantras are the *Hevajra, Caṇḍamahāroṣana* (Fierce Great Infuriating), and the *Kālacakra* (Wheel of Time) Tantras.

6.2.2 Siddhas

Beginning with the ninth century, the Mahāyoga and Yoginī Tantras eclipsed others in importance, as the Vajrayāna fully embraced the siddha ideal. Hagiographies appeared, extolling the Buddhist siddha as the ideal model for Awakened behavior. In these hagiographies, tales of the siddhas were organized in one of two ways: either in terms of their personal lineages or as members of a loosely defined group. The first pattern reflects the importance of the guru-bond in Vajrayāna practice; the second, the importance of *gaṇacakras,* or ritual feasts, in which groups of Buddhist siddhas participate after their initiation. The most famous work of siddha hagiography is the eleventh-century *Caturaśītisiddhapravṛtti* (*Lives of the Eighty-four Siddhas),* attributed to Abhayadattaśrī. Scholars doubt the historical accuracy of these hagiographies—and with good reason, as the tales ascribed to the most famous siddhas vary widely from one compilation to the next. Still, they are important sources for studying the values of the siddha movement.

The individuals depicted in Abhayadatta's work came from all stations of life, much as in earlier Buddhist times. Among them were former kings, princes, monks, and brahmans; the wealthy and poor; the handsome, ugly, young, and old. Many came from such despised occupations as clothes washer, rag scavenger, beggar, rope maker, bird catcher, hunter, and smith. Some were even thieves. Those who came from higher castes were usually required to take on low-caste occupations as a way of subduing their pride.

Typically in these legends, the potential siddha faces a personal crisis, arousing a sense of saṁvega. Troubled, he or she may go to a cremation ground for respite or, during a visit by a wandering mendicant-yogin or ḍākinī, request teaching. The teacher directly addresses the karmic knot causing the person's distress and sings a verse stating the appropriate antidote. When the person responds appropriately to the song, the teacher gives initiation into a sādhana. Some students attain realization immediately, but most practice from 6 months to 12 years to erase their defilements, climaxing in an experience of Mahāmudrā, which in the context of these tales includes both the Awakening to the state of nonduality and the gaining of *siddhis,* or mundane psychic powers, which the initiates then use during their long careers as siddhas.

The *Subāhuparipṛcchā Tantra,* (Subāhu's Questions) translated into Chinese in 726, lists these siddhis as eight: the ability to delight deities through one's practice of mantras; the ability to find the palaces of the asuras and either gain treasure or to live there for an aeon (see Section 5.1); the ability to ingest magical medicines from the elements or from beings' bodies, thereby gaining longevity; the ability to bring about a continuous bestowing of gems; the ability to find treasures in the earth; the ability to find wells of gold and silver; and two separate abilities for transmuting base metals into gold. Other texts list further abilities, such as the power to cure diseases by exorcising disease-bearing spirits, to bring rain, and to turn back fire.

Having experienced Mahāmudrā, Abhayadatta's siddhas would spend the rest of their lives—sometimes up to 700 years or more—in compassionate service to untold numbers of beings, aiding the good and subjugating the evil. Finally, they would rise, often in bodily form and with their disciples, to the Paradise of the Ḍākinīs, a Buddha-field presided over by a female Buddha, there to enjoy eternal bliss.

An interesting study in contrasts is offered by the story of Nāropā (1016–1100), whom the Tibetan Kagyü sects (see Section 11.2.2) recognize as the source of their lineage. In their version of his life, he is a Bengali brahman of towering intellectual gifts who becomes the abbot of Nalanda university, only to be chastised by a ḍākinī in a vision for knowing nothing of what he taught. As a result of the vision, he leaves his monastic position and finds his guru only after enduring visions that undermine such conventional values as honesty, humanity, morality, and purity. As part of his training, he suffers further acts of humiliation, including being forced to steal delicacies from a wedding feast and getting caught for the theft, for which he is subsequently beaten to within an inch of his life. These humiliations form his initiation, putting his mind in the proper state to receive his teacher's more subtle instructions. In Abhayadatta's version of the story, however, Nāropā is a simple Kashmiri woodcutter who attends to his guru for many years, receiving instruction only after having proven his full devotion to the guru by a successful theft from the wedding feast. Although the details of these two versions of the story differ, their values show a commonality: the need for the siddha to give full devotion to the guru, to risk social approbation, and to disregard social conventions. These values are common to the tales of most of the siddhas. In this pattern, Buddhist siddhas may have been imitating their Pāśupata Śaivite rivals, as members of that sect in one stage of their training had to act in ways that provoked ridicule, feigning insanity and courting dishonor, while in another they had to dwell in cemeteries.

As for Nāropā, whatever the details of his early career, a visiting Tibetan monk had a brief audience with him in his later years and left one of the few eyewitness accounts we possess of a Buddhist siddha at this time. Nāropā, the monk said, was corpulent, well dressed, and carried on a palanquin by four men. He gave audiences to great princes and was so surrounded by devotees that the monk was able only briefly to touch his foot in homage before being pushed away by the crowd.

The monk also mentions that Nāropā was dwelling in a monastery, which raises the question of the extent to which monastics were active in the siddha movement. At first glance, the sexual nature of the Mahāyoga and Yoginī Tantras, and their antinomian attitude toward moral strictures would seem to have precluded monastic participation in the movement, but such was not the case. From the beginning of the movement, monastics wrote commentaries on Tantras, and may even have composed Tantras themselves. The question was: To what extent could a monastic participate in the Tantras without violating his or her monastic vows? Scholastic monks gave four responses to this question. The first held that the Tantras were totally incompatible with the Buddha's teachings, and that monks should have nothing to do either with Tantric texts or practices. The remaining three approaches viewed the Tantras as compatible with traditional Buddhist teachings, but differed in their view of the extent to which monastics could participate in the initiation ritual. The first of the three is exemplified in the writings of Atiśa, a tenth-century monk famous for teaching Vajrayāna in Tibet, who claimed that the sexual elements in Tantric initiation were essential to the empowerment ritual, and that a monk could therefore not participate in such rituals, although he could teach Tantric texts and participate in rituals that did not compromise his monastic vows. The second approach, exemplified in the writings of Munidatta, stated that the sexual elements in the empowerment were superfluous, and that a monk could use a *jñāna-mudrā,* or knowledge (i.e., imagined) partner, rather than using a *karma-mudrā,* or action (i.e., flesh and blood) partner. In fact, the former mode of practice was superior to the latter, which was intended only for those of inferior spiritual capacities. In this interpretation, all textual references to intercourse, sexual fluids, and so on, were purely symbolic. The third approach, typified by Abhayākaragupta, the eleventh-century author of the last major philosophical synthesis of Indian Buddhist thought prior to the Muslim invasions, was that the sexual aspects of the empowerment ritual were essential to the ritual, and that a monk could participate fully in them as long as he had a proper understanding of the teaching on emptiness. All three of these last approaches found adherents in the monastic practice of Vajrayāna in Tibet.

As for nuns and Buddhist lay women, their participation in Indian Vajrayāna is a matter of scholarly controversy. On the one hand, some texts have credited women with having helped to found the movement and to have authored important texts. For instance, Tibetan traditions credit Princess Lakṣmīṅkarā and her circle of followers with having composed seven root texts of the Vajrayāna. Among these texts is a short piece by Sahajayoginīcintā, a female wine seller, who claimed that sensual pleasure is essentially no different from religious bliss. She thus advocated the use of the erotic arts in sexual yoga as a way of creating an experience of pleasure so intense that one's sense of a separate self dissolves. Abhayadatta's hagiographies feature two women, and many of the men received transmission from female adepts. Nāropā's female students were said to far outnumber his male students. At the same time, siddha vows required adepts to treat women with the greatest respect.

On the other hand, none of the extant Tantras were written for women. The tantrika is always male, and women figure only as aids in the ritual. As many scholars have noted, elaborate codes of etiquette and respect for women, such as those found in the Tantras, have often been means for disguising oppression. Given our present sources, there is no way of knowing whether the exalted position of women in the texts translated into a similar position in day-to-day reality.

The Pāla period as a whole was not supportive of nuns. Although queens continued giving donations to monasteries until the Muslim invasions, the last inscription recording the building of a nunnery was dated in the late ninth century. A play written in the eighth by the great brahmanical playwright, Bhavabhūti, features a nun who trains her disciple in Tantric practice for compassionate ends, but this play is our only evidence that nuns may have been involved in the Vajrayāna.

6.2.3 Sahaja

In the ninth or tenth century, as the siddha model was becoming more prevalent in Buddhist circles, an antisiddha movement took the process of inversion inherent in the Vajrayāna one step further by denouncing the use of Tantras and mantras in favor of completely spontaneous action. This movement is sometimes called the *Sahajayāna* (Spontaneous Vehicle), although it was ultimately absorbed into the Vajrayāna. *Sahaja* denotes the world of freedom naturally born *(ja)* with every moment *(saha),* thus indicating that every moment offers the opportunity to realize the absolute. Advocates of this movement denounced the siddhas for lacking two essential Buddhist virtues: In their egotistical pursuit of power, they lacked the virtue of compassion; and in their attachment to their mantras and Tantras, they lacked the virtue of nonclinging. Instead, followers of the sahaja movement proposed that a simple life of spontaneous pleasure, freed from the duality of right and wrong, would enable one to experience the nonduality of Awakening. This movement took its inspiration from what cultured Indians understood to be the values of tribal people, although anthropologists have learned that this view was highly romanticized. Sahaja devotees expressed their teachings in vernacular songs, sung to folk tunes. Recorded in the Indian literary vernacular Apabhramśa, these songs became very popular.

Sahaja values can be illustrated by the hagiography of Saraha, one of the movement's most famous figures: Saraha, originally a brahman priest, became a Buddhist monk with a propensity to drink. Once, while he was in a drunken stupor, a bodhisattva appeared to him, directing him to seek out a low-caste female arrow maker. At their first meeting, she presented him with the image of her humble craft: making arrows perfectly straight. Using two eyes (dualistic vision), she could not straighten the arrow shaft, but using one eye (nonduality), she could. Saraha immediately intuited her message, abandoned his monastic status, and became her disciple and companion, taking on her low caste and occupation as a way of expressing his transcendence of dualism. In one of his songs, he declared: "Here there's no beginning, no middle, no end, no saṁsāra, no nirvāṇa. In this state of supreme bliss, there's no self and no other." For him, the Awakened person was beyond good and evil, Path and attainment.

6.2.4 The Vajra Cosmos

In addition to formulating rituals, the Vajrayāna created a theoretical context to accommodate those rituals into the Buddhist tradition. This involved composing texts in the three modes noted in Chapter 1: narrative, cosmology, and emptiness. Because of the wide differences among the Tantras, however, no single, unified position was taken on any of the issues involved in this process. Instead, the texts offer a plethora of creative approaches.

Two issues dominated the narrative accounts: (1) how to square the traditional accounts of the Buddha's Awakening with the ritual Awakening propounded in the Tantras; and (2) how to account for the obvious elements that Buddhist Tantrism had in common with other Tantric movements. To deal with the first issue, the authors of the Tantras offered new versions of the Awakening story. The *Tattvasaṃgraha,* for instance, provides an account in keeping with the practice of the Yoga Tantras. In this account, Sarvārthasiddhi (rather than Siddhārtha), is seated under the bodhi tree when a host of Tathāgatas visit him to inform him that he is striving for Awakening the wrong way. When he asks to be taught the right way, they have him chant mantras that establish a series of visions in his heart that stabilize bodhicitta. The Tathāgatas then enter his heart to empower him with their combined discernment, thus making him a Tathāgata as well, with the name Vajradhātu. They then take him to the summit of Mt. Meru, where they seat him on a lion throne and surround him with four Tathāgatas in the cardinal direction, thus creating a maṇḍala. Afterwards he returns to the bodhi tree, and the traditional account resumes. The *Caṇḍamahāroṣana,* on the other hand, provides an account more in keeping with the Yoginī Tantras. In this account, Gautama actually attains Buddhahood while still living in his palace, engaged in ritual sexual intercourse with his wife Gopā. Afterwards he follows the ascetic quest, doing battle with Māra simply for the benefit of those who would be inspired by such an example.

To explain how non-Buddhist (primarily Śaivite) elements found their way into Buddhist Tantras, compilers provided two types of narratives. The first type maintains that these elements were Buddhist to begin with, were then forgotten by Mainstream Buddhists and stolen by the Śaivites, but now were restored to their proper tradition. The second type of narrative depicts the Buddha engaging Śiva in battle and subjugating him, after which Śiva goes to the Buddha for refuge, converting all the elements in his tradition to Buddhism as well. Thus, for example, the half-moon mark on Śiva's forehead is explained as a sign of subjugation coming from the Buddha's big toenail.

In terms of cosmology, we have already noted that the Vajrayāna added a new type of Buddha-field, the Ḍākinī Paradise, to the Buddhist multiverse, which it presented as a vast maṇḍala. However, there was no one standard version of how this maṇḍala was arranged. In some texts, it is presented as the emanation of an overarching Buddha-clan, in a sense the source of all Buddhas, headed by Vajradhara or Vajrasattva, who in some cases is presented as a being and in others as a principle. Different Tantras also peopled this multiverse with a wide variety of Vajra beings; new Buddhas and bodhisattvas, male and female, who express their compassion not only in gentle but also in seemingly fierce and violent ways; beings adopted from siddha cosmologies, such as the ḍākinīs and vidhyādharas, together with the gods and goddesses of the Śaivite, Śakta, and Vaiṣṇava religions.

In terms of the emptiness mode, Vajrayāna practice represented two primary departures from traditional Buddhist doctrines. The first is rather abstract, concerning the place of analogy in efficacious action. For earlier Buddhist texts, both Mainstream and Mahāyāna, analogy is simply a means of explaining abstract teachings. In Vajrayāna, however, it becomes a means of influencing analogues. What this means is that elements of the ritual are interpreted as being analogous to other beings, objects, or principles. Because of this relationship, when the ritual element is manipulated, the action is then transferred to the analogue, placing it under the initiate's power. This is a radically new interpretation of the doctrine of karma. The second departure concerns the range of skillful action. Unlike earlier Buddhist traditions, some Vajrayāna texts advocate exciting passionate mind states and erasing the distinction between good and evil as means of overcoming attachment and gaining Awakening.

To bring these departures into line with traditional Buddhist doctrines, Vajrayāna authors made use of four important Mahāyāna concepts: emptiness, nonduality, the reversal of the basis, and tactical skill. Emptiness and nonduality were used to explain the power of analogous action. Because dharmas have no inherent nature, and because they are nondual, the person who ritually makes contact with their underlying nonduality can thus manipulate them, even when seeming to act from a great distance on the causal chain. The stages of the ritual leading to that power were explained with reference to the Yogācara doctrine of the reversal of the basis (see Section 5.2.3d). For example, by contacting nondual emptiness, mantras could undergo a reversal of the basis and be converted into the appearance of deities, which further mantras could convert into subsequent stages of the ritual through the same mechanism. And all the transgressive elements of Vajrayāna practice—the breaking of taboos, the glorification of subjugation as a form of compassion, the transcending of moral rules—were explained as a form of tactical skill. Thus the use of strong passions was explained as a means for clearing out the "knots" in the body's energy channels, for only then could the body be a proper vehicle for Awakening.

In some cases, the explanations for tactical skill were equivocal, as individual texts gave conflicting interpretations of exactly how the tactic was supposed to work. For example, a Tantra might advocate breaking moral rules, but then would explain its statements in at least two different ways. On the one hand, it would claim that the statements were to be taken symbolically, not literally, and were intended only for their shock value. This would follow a pattern set in the early canons, as in Dhammapada 294, where the phrase "killing one's mother and father" is a reference to eliminating craving and conceit. However, the same Tantra in another passage would say that there might be occasions where the compassionate course of action would actually be to break the moral rule, in line with the position asserted in the *Upāya-kauśalya Sūtra* (see Section 5.2.3b). The discrepancy between these two interpretations would itself then be explained as an example of tactical skill, meant to induce a realization of the emptiness of words and to free the mind from attachment to their "right" and "wrong" meanings, thus fostering a nondual attitude conducive to Awakening.

These doctrines were drawn mostly from the Mahāyāna, which is why Vajrayāna practice was able to present itself as a natural outgrowth of the Mahāyāna, and why Mahāyāna scholars of the late medieval period were able to include it under that rubric in their grand syntheses of Buddhist philosophy and practice. Mainstream traditions, however, were not reconciled to the Vajrayāna. Although there are some extant Theravāda Tantras, none of them include transgressive elements, and by Vajrayāna standards are rather tame. Instead of advocating the act of taking on the identity of a Buddha or bodhisattva, they teach the ritual act of taking on the power of dhyāna or nirvāṇa. The standoff between Mainstream and Vajrayāna practitioners is illustrated in the taboo that many Vajrayāna siddhas observed against associating with "Hīnayānists." Because of this divide, and because of the way Vajrayāna inverted many central Mainstream teachings and practices, it can be argued that Vajrayāna came as close as possible, within the still-cohesive institution of the Indian Sangha, to becoming a genuinely separate Buddhist religion.

6.3 THE DECIMATION OF INDIAN BUDDHISM

Muslim Turks began attacking western and northwestern India in the eighth century, destroying the great Sthaviravādin university at Valabhi. Through a long series of bitterly fought battles, they encroached further and further into Indian territory until they sacked Mathura in the mid-eleventh century. There they were held in check for 150 years. The utter destruction caused by this Turkish warfare was something totally new to the Indians, who were more familiar with war as a chivalrous spectator sport among kings. The Turks followed a scorched-earth policy, looting and destroying thousands of temples and putting the populace to the sword. Huge numbers of refugees, lay and monastic, fled east to the Buddhist homeland in the Gangetic Plain, where the Pāla empire offered shelter. The main centers of Buddhist strength in the Pāla empire were its great universities. These high-profile institutions, however, required high maintenance, and as we have already noted, Pāla support for the universities varied from reign to reign. Thus the universities, too, were in a precarious position.

In 1162, the Senas seized power from the Pālas, and the empire fragmented into small states, opening the way for the Turks to come sweeping though the Gangetic Plain at the end of the twelfth and the beginning of the thirteenth century. The universities were left defenseless: their wealth plundered, their inhabitants massacred, their buildings and libraries put to the torch. Because the universities had been the repositories not only of Buddhist traditions but also of secular arts and sciences, their annihilation was a devastating blow to Indian culture as a whole. Indian Buddhism never recovered, although it continued to subsist in isolated pockets, such as Andhra and Orissa until the sixteenth century, and the Nepal Valley, Ladakh, and eastern Bengal until the present. The Tibetan historian Tāranātha reports that Buddhist refugees also fled to Southeast Asia and Tibet. A few monks remained in the ruins of the monasteries into the next century, but repeated raids by the Turks made their position untenable.

Miraculously, the great temple at Bodhgaya survived unscathed, as did holy sites in more out-of-the-way places, such as Sanchi and Ajanta. Mostly, though, Buddhist shrines were demolished. What the Turks did not destroy, centuries of scavenging has leveled to the ground. Even today, bricks from the ancient monasteries, stamped with Buddhist symbols, can be found in village buildings and wells near where the great Buddhist centers used to be.

Scholars are divided in their opinions as to why Buddhism succumbed to the Muslim invasion when it had survived previous ones, such as the Kushan annexation of the northwest and the Hun attacks on the Gupta empire. Part of the answer lies in the nature of the invaders. The Turks, unlike the Kushans, were not open to conversion; unlike the Huns, they settled down to rule and pursued a policy of religious suppression to boot. For them, the Buddhists were idolators; the Muslim word for idol, *but/budh,* actually derives from "Buddha." Thus, they viewed the destruction of Buddhism as a religious duty.

Other reasons for the demise of the Indian Sangha as an institution, however, relate more to the nature of Buddhism itself during this period. Five centuries of

Tantrism had served to blur the line between Buddhism and its fellow Indian religions, as each religion absorbed elements of its competitors to attract their followers. Thus it was an easy matter for Vaiṣṇava, for example, to claim that the Buddha was an avatar of Viṣṇu, and in this way absorb many Buddhists into its fold. And the reason why Buddhism was the absorbed, rather than the absorber, relates to the centrality of the Sangha to the Buddhist community. The religions of Śiva, Viṣṇu, and Śaktā lost their philosophical schools and ascetic orders in the Muslim invasions as well, but because these orders were not central to their devotionalism, they managed to survive.

The destruction of the Buddhism in its homeland had a profound effect on Buddhism in other countries, which we will examine in detail in the following chapters. In general, it forced Buddhists in each country to become independent in their interpretation of the Dharma-Vinaya, rather than looking to India for guidance. This allowed for the arising of Buddhist religions that were truly separate, both institutionally and doctrinally, as the Buddhist pariṣad fragmented into three main cultural areas having limited contact with one another: Sri Lanka and Southeast Asia; East Asia; and the Tibetan cultural sphere.

However, the disappearance of the Sangha from its homeland did not mean that Buddhist doctrines disappeared from India without trace. We have noted how Buddhism was influenced by other Indian religions during their many centuries of coexistence; influences went the other way as well. The Advaita Vedānta school founded by Gauḍapāda and Śaṅkara in the sixth and seventh centuries applied Yogācāra ideas to the interpretation of Vedic texts. The Sahajayāna movement influenced the Bengali minstrel saints, including the fifteenth-century mystic Kabir, and the Bengali Bauls. In a more pervasive manner, the Buddhist notion of karma as a moral rather than a ritual force had permeated Indian thought, as had the notion of Dharma as rectitude of the mind rather than Vedic orthopraxy. The measure of how quietly pervasive these Buddhist ideas remained in Indian society is indicated by what happened when the Aśokan edicts were deciphered and translated in the late nineteenth century (see Section 3.4). According to many Indians, there was nothing particularly Buddhist about Aśoka's message, for it conveyed what they regarded as the basic ideals of Indian morality as a whole. Perhaps the best symbol of the continuing Buddhist influence on Indian life is the Dharma wheel that the Indians placed in the middle of their flag on gaining independence from the British. It was the only symbol that all segments of Indian society would accept as a sign of what united them.

6.4 BUDDHISM IN NEPAL

The Nepal Valley presently contains some of the few surviving remnants of medieval Indian Buddhism. In the material sense, these remnants fall into two areas: texts and the arts. Unlike the Tibetans, the Nepalese have continued to use Sanskrit texts for their studies and rituals; thus their libraries have preserved the Sanskrit originals for many Indian Buddhist texts that were otherwise lost. In terms of art, the monastic buildings still surviving in Patan seem to be faithful replicas of the great Indian universities; Nepalese painting and statuary preserve the medieval Pāla style. In the social sense, however, the picture is more complex, as the Nepalese have evolved new patterns to replace the monastic Sangha and have developed their own distinctive way of defining Buddhist religious identity.

Inscriptions reveal that Buddhist monasteries were present in the valley in the fifth century C.E. In the seventh century, I-ching heard reports that the valley was home both to Mainstream and to Mahāyāna adherents. Vajrayāna later became predominant at an unknown date and absorbed all other forms of Buddhism into its fold. From the 1200s to 1768, the Hindu Malla dynasty controlled the valley and, like many preconquest Hindu dynasties in India, provided support to Buddhist institutions. Gradually, however, the economic base for the monasteries began to shrink. This economic trend, together with the influence of lay Buddhist Tantric adepts, led to a process whereby the Sangha began to adopt the Hindu model of a married, hereditary priesthood. This process was already under way by the end of the fourteenth century, when King Jayasthiti Malla (r. 1382–1395) established a caste system for his Buddhist subjects, in which upper-class Buddhist lay people were classified as the *u-dai* caste, and married Buddhist priests were divided into two subcastes: *vajrācārya,* descended from Tantric adepts, and *śākya-bhikṣu,* descended from married Buddhist monks. This adoption of the Hindu pattern apparently took several centuries, for as late as the seventeenth century the city of Patan boasted more than 20 celibate monasteries in its immediate vicinity.

In 1768, the Mallas were ousted by the Gurkhas, a militant Hindu clan descended from Rajasthani refugees. The Gurkhas established their own dynasty, which has lasted to the present, and set about to transform the local Newari culture. As part of this program, they withdrew support from Buddhist institutions and promoted Hinduism as an element of Nepalese political identity. This policy formally ended in 1951, when Nepal was opened to the outside world, but there are reports that it has died hard. Theravāda Buddhism has been reintroduced from Sri Lanka and Thailand, and the influx of refugees from Tibet has brought about the establishment of Tibetan monasteries in the valley. These newly imported forms of Buddhism remain a small minority, however, with native Nepalese Buddhism largely impervious to their influence.

The focus of Nepalese Buddhism lies in the act of homage. This begins in the home, to one's parents and elders, and extends beyond the home in acts of homage to priests and deities. Religion is thus less a matter of beliefs than of proper etiquette in showing respect to others on the human and celestial planes. We have already noticed how Vajrayāna in India absorbed elements from Śaivism, and this tendency has continued in Nepal. Buddhist and Hindu groups have each found ways of including the deities of the other in their own pantheons. Hindus regard Śākyamuni as an avatar of Viṣṇu, whereas Buddhists view Śiva and Viṣṇu as bodhisattvas. Forms of ritual and worship are also similar, with the care and feeding of Buddhist icons following the Hindu pattern. This means that the act of homage is somewhat noncommittal, as the same deity may be worshiped in either his or her Buddhist or Hindu form. Some members of the priestly castes, secure in their command of ritual knowledge, declare themselves to be exclusively Hindu or Buddhist in their allegiance, but most Nepalese are loath to define their acts of homage in such an exclusive way. They feel it wiser to stay on good terms with all the powers that be, in case they ever need to ask or negotiate with a particular power for help. As is frequently the case in matters of etiquette, they consider it poor form to be too inquisitive about the personal preferences that may lie behind another person's good behavior, or too explicit about their own.

Buddhist identity is viewed as a matter of caste. Buddhists observe the obligatory rites of homage traditional to their caste, but in terms of optional acts of homage they are free to offer respect to any deity they please. As we shall see in the following chapters (Sections 7.5.1, 8.7.3), a fluid sense of religious identity is common throughout Buddhist countries, but the Nepalese pattern of determining religious identity by birth is clearly non-Buddhist in origin. Buddhists assume their caste identity not only in their dealings with Hindus but also among themselves. Only members of the vajrācāryas and śākya-bhikṣu castes, for instance, are allowed to live in temple compounds. Vajrācāryas form the ritual and scholarly elite, whereas the śākya-bhikṣus hold a more limited ritual role, many of the men earning their livelihood working in precious metals. Young boys from both castes are ordained for a period of four days, after which they renounce their vows and return to lay life. Vajrācāryas then undergo secret Tantric initiation as well. Vajrācāryas can give Tantric initiations to members of other Buddhist castes, but the new initiates from those castes do not then become Vajrācāryas themselves. Thus, not only is one's identity as a Buddhist a function of caste, but so is one's role within the religion.

6.5 THE BUDDHIST REVIVAL

Since the latter part of the nineteenth century, when the British consolidated their hold over India and instituted a policy of religious tolerance, there have been several attempts at fostering a rebirth of Buddhism in its original home. In the 1890s, a group of Sri Lankans led by Anagārikā Dharmapāla (see Section 7.4.1) founded the Maha Bodhi Society with the purpose of reintroducing Buddhism to India. Although the society was able to establish centers in cities and at ancient Buddhist sites, and to petition the British Raj to give Buddhists control over the great temple at Bodhgaya, it has had little success in winning converts.

The European "discovery" of Buddhism in the nineteenth and twentieth centuries helped revive interest in the religion among India's educated classes as they were attempting to recover their national heritage as part of their move toward independence. Again, this trend won no converts to the religion, although it did influence the Bengali author Rabindranath Tagore and others in their interpretation of Hinduism.

In 1956, Bhimrao Ramji Ambedkar, the late leader of Maharashtra's Dalits ("Untouchables"), led 600,000 of his followers in a mass conversion to Buddhism on the grounds that it was the Indian religion whose doctrines were least demeaning to their caste. The few native Indian temples set up in various parts of the country in response to this conversion have followed the example of the Christian missionaries and are engaged primarily in charitable work, establishing schools, clinics, and orphanages for the poor. The teaching of meditation has been left largely to lay people. Among both Dalits and non-Dalits, the most popular meditation movement is that headed by S. N. Goenka, an Indian student of the lay Burmese Vipassanā master, U Ba Khin (see Section 7.5), who began leading retreats in the 1960s. His enormous Vipassanā center outside of Mumbai, the world's largest, now has branches worldwide. Goenka presents Vipassanā as a scientific—rather than religious or sectarian—method of mind-training, and has had great success in teaching it to prison inmates and to others outside the Buddhist fold. There is little likelihood, however, that this movement will translate into a revival of the monastic Sangha, as Goenka not only tends to shun the Buddhist label but also actively discourages his followers from making a lifelong commitment to monasticism.

In 1959, Tibetan Buddhists fleeing the Chinese invasion of their homeland began to establish themselves in India, both in the north (Dharamsala) and in the south (Mysore). They have succeeded in establishing monasteries and nunneries, and are fighting valiantly to preserve their scholastic curriculum. Still, they are losing many of their young to the attractions of modern materialism. Buddhists from many other Asian countries have flocked to Buddhist pilgrimage centers in India, setting up temples representative of their cultures both to house pilgrims and to engage in missionary work, which has had limited success.

However, Buddhism was able to establish firm roots in other countries long before the Muslim invasions, and in many of those countries it is still strong. The story of how it developed from an Indian religion to a family of world religions will be the subject of the remainder of this book.

7

Buddhism in Sri Lanka and Southeast Asia

7.1 THE ECONOMY OF MERIT

As cultural areas, Sri Lanka and Southeast Asia are vastly different. What they have in common is that, beginning from the eleventh century, Buddhists in Sri Lanka have worked together with those on mainland Southeast Asia to maintain Theravāda as their dominant religious tradition. Prior to that point in time, Theravāda had been merely one among many forms of Buddhism—including other Mainstream schools, Mahāyāna, and Vajrayāna—practiced in this region along with Hinduism and indigenous animist cults. Although Theravāda is a conservative tradition—the only living Buddhist religion adhering strongly to an early canon—its rise to prominence involved absorbing many elements from the other traditions in its milieu.

Modern scholars have often tried to identify the various threads of influence in the resulting mix, but they have frequently mislabeled many of them because of their unfamiliarity with the Pali Canon as a whole. Most of them equate "classic" Theravāda with the early Suttas and Abhidhamma. This view has been ascribed both to Western scholars' subconscious Protestant tendency to regard the earliest records of a religion as its only true form, and to the historical accident that Westerners first encountered Theravāda in Sri Lanka at a time when Sri Lankans themselves had recently revived interest in the earliest layer of Suttas as the truest expression of the Buddha's teachings. Whatever its causes, the result of this viewpoint is that many elements of modern Theravāda with roots in other parts of the canon—the cult of relics, the sense of Buddha-presence in stūpas and

Buddha images, even the portrayal of thousands of Buddhas in temple murals—are wrongly labeled as non-Theravādin in provenance.

As we noted in Chapter 3, the Pali Canon—like all the early Buddhist canons—contains many differing layers. Thus any Buddhist looking to it for religious guidance has a choice as to which layers to take as his or her primary guide. While the majority of Buddhists in Sri Lanka and Southeast Asia give formal pride of place to the Suttas and Abhidhamma, and some individuals and groups have focused exclusively on this layer for their religious inspiration, most Theravādins in practice follow the layer defining the Buddhist path in terms of the accumulation of merit and perfections: the jātakas, the apadānas, and texts such as the *Petavatthu,* which focuses on the issue of dedicating merit to one's dead ancestors. *Puñña* (merit) and *pāramī* (perfections)—defined in accordance with this latter layer—are among the most common words in the everyday religious vocabulary in the Theravādin world, far more common than the terms associated with the earlier strata of Suttas, such as *path* or *nibbāna.* People build monasteries to develop their perfections; they make gifts to monastics, follow the precepts, and meditate as a way of making merit. Whether they are dedicating their merit and perfections to Buddhahood or arahantship—either in the dispensation of Gautama Buddha or of Maitreya—is purely a matter of individual choice. As we noted in section 3.6.1, Theravāda views the difference between the two paths as quantitative, rather than qualitative, so from the outside the practice of these paths looks the same.

The vocabulary of merit and perfections even enters the political realm: The legitimacy of a particular ruler is judged by his or her merit and perfections as evidenced in events coincident with his or her time in power. Thus, for example, in the nineteenth century, when cholera ravaged Bangkok during the reign of King Rāma III, the king—whose ascent to the throne had been clouded by palace intrigue—responded with a massive campaign of temple building throughout the city to augment his accumulated perfections. Even today, government officials and business executives in the Theravādin world are said to possess (or, in unfortunate cases, to lack) the perfections needed to maintain their positions. Given this use of the term *perfection,* it has come to take on connotations of *influence,* although the influence here is more than social or political, covering every area of experience to which the law of kamma extends.

According to the layer of the Pāli Canon most concerned with making merit, acts of merit are most fruitful when planted in the appropriate "field": either the Buddha-field surrounding a relic (or, by extension, a Buddha image); or legitimate members of the monastic Sangha. The importance of the Buddha-field explains the cults of stūpas, Buddha images, and Buddha amulets that thrive in the Theravādin world. The importance of the monastic Sangha as a field of merit explains the devotional cults surrounding individual monks or nuns who are believed to be noble disciples. It also explains, at least in part, the recurrent attempts throughout Theravādin history to "cleanse" the Sangha by reestablishing pure ordination lineages, often through sending monks to reordain in another Theravādin country and to return with both a new ordination lineage and a higher standard of Vinaya practice.

On the surface, the story of these repeated attempts at purifying the Sangha may not make for the most intriguing reading. However, an understanding of the dynamics behind these attempts gets to the heart of the economy of merit that forms the matrix for Theravādin practice. This economy is primarily an economy of gifts: Lay people donate the necessities of life to monastics; monastics respond by teaching the Dhamma and, more importantly, practicing the Dhamma so that the necessities that make their practice possible will bear the donor great fruit. Like any economy, the economy of merit thrives on trust and breaks down when that trust is betrayed. One of the most common causes for this betrayal is greed on both sides of the equation: Donors hoping for a great deal of merit make unwise donations to monastics who, instead of practicing the Dhamma in a trust-inspiring way, misuse the donations to lead a life of luxury. When this abuse becomes endemic, trust in the Sangha as a whole begins to break down. And because the monastic Sangha has long been the most solid institution in this part of the world—the "glue" holding these societies together—any breakdown of trust in the Sangha threatens to cause other institutions to become unglued as well.

As the story of the Second Council shows (see Section 3.2.2), the governance of the Sangha is such that internal attempts to remedy this sort of breakdown require the cooperation of the entire Sangha, which is usually difficult to obtain. Thus reforms are usually spearheaded by outsiders: kings, often advised by monks with a reputation for having avoided the excesses of the merit economy. Scholars have proposed various theories to explain the motivation that would lead a king to initiate such reforms. A purely monetary explanation is that monastic reform would enable him to expand his tax base. The landholdings of the larger and more luxurious monasteries were not taxable, whereas monks who strictly observed the Vinaya would not accept gifts of farm land. And it is true that reform-minded kings have often confiscated property from large monasteries with weak claims to their land.

However, purely monetary concerns do not explain the repeated efforts to send monks abroad to establish new ordination lineages. These efforts are better explained as a desire to return to the roots of the religion so as to make a fresh start and reestablish trust. Ordination lineages are considered a direct line to the Buddha, a line maintained through the practice of the Vinaya. In fact, a passage from the commentary to the Pali Vinaya states that the Vinaya is the vital force of the religion. If the monks in a particular lineage no longer follow the Vinaya in a way satisfactory to their supporters, the lineage is judged to have lost its vital force. For monks to undertake the often perilous journey abroad, to abandon their seniority in the act of becoming newly ordained, and to return with a renewed dedication to practice and teach the Vinaya is a sign that they want to make a clean break with the recent past and to draw vital force from their closest possible contact to the Buddha himself. A king sponsoring such monks would then believe that he had established trustworthy recipients for his own acts of merit. He would also believe that he had provided his subjects with renewed reason to trust the religion that teaches them to look for happiness, not through indulging the desires that would lead to social disorder, but through the sociable practice of generosity, virtue, and meditation. Thus he would be fulfilling his role as a true king, in line with the belief—popular in the Theravāda world—that true kings are bodhisattvas.

These considerations are worth keeping in mind as we read the history of Buddhism in this part of the world.

7.2 BUDDHISM IN "FURTHER INDIA"

Southeast Asia. A Sri Lankan narrative tradition maintains that King Aśoka in 247 B.C.E. sent envoys to Suvaṇṇabhūma, which has been identified with the Mon country in Lower Burma (Myanmar) and central Thailand, but otherwise there is no written or archaeological evidence that Buddhism was practiced in the area at that early a date. Indian records dating from the first century B.C.E. indicate that Indian traders were familiar with the region, and within a short period of time the traders had begun exporting Indian culture to its people. By the first century C.E., the region's first Indianized Southeast Asian states—those whose rulers accepted Indian culture, including Brahmanical and Buddhist beliefs—appeared. These states included Śailarājā (known to history by its Chinese name, Funan), centered in the lower Mekhong Basin, in what is now Cambodia and southern Vietnam; Champa; the empires of Angkor and central Java; the Mon states in Lower Burma and central Thailand; and the Śrīvijaya empire, centered on the Malay Peninsula.

Once Brahmanism and Buddhism were established in the courts and began spreading to the populace, the religious history of the region up until the eleventh century C.E. differed little from that of India itself. Various forms of Buddhism—primarily Theravāda, Sarvāstivāda, Mahāyāna, and Vajrayāna—coexisted with Hinduism and indigenous animist beliefs. The question of which element in the mix was dominant where and at what time was largely a matter of the vagaries of royal patronage. There are only a few discernible patterns to this patronage. Buddhism tended to enjoy more consistent support in the areas closest to India—Burma, Thailand, and the Malay Peninsula; and, ironically, the largest and most enduring Buddhist monuments were built in kingdoms where Buddhism was only briefly the main recipient of royal patronage.

One of these monuments is Borobudur, built in central Java by the Śailendras around 800. This is a giant maṇḍala in stone, its bas-reliefs representing the quest for Awakening through the 10 stages of the bodhisattva path. The circumambulation path up the monument leads through walled corridors past more than 2,000 reliefs depicting scenes from Śākyamuni's life, the jātaka tales, and the *Gaṇḍavyūha Sūtra,* finally reaching a broad open summit covered with 72 small stūpas containing Buddha images surrounding a large central stūpa. The ascent is a symbolic journey through the world of appearances and into the boundlessness of Awakening.

While Borobudur was being built, Jayavarman, a Cambodian prince whom the Śailendras had taken hostage, returned to his homeland and proclaimed it independent, founding an empire that lasted until its capital, Yasodharapura, fell to the Thais in 1431. Its greatest architectural achievement was a series of temples and mausoleums built at the capital, known today as Angkor. Jayavarman brought with him from Java the cult of the god-king, the belief that the ruler of the country was an incarnation of Śiva, and most of the Angkor complex is dedicated to this cult. Not until the last great builder of Angkor, Jayavarman VII, ascended the throne in 1181 did Buddhist elements begin to appear in the royal temples.

Jayavarman VII was a devotee of Avalokiteśvara, the bodhisattva of compassion, and conceived of himself as a bodhisattva king. Whether this idea was derived from the *Daśabhūmika Sūtra,* from his predecessors' concept of god-king, or from both, no one knows. In any event, the concept was to have a long life in Cambodian and Thai politics. Modeling himself on Avalokiteśvara, Jayavarman VII stated in his inscriptions that he was sensitive to the sufferings of his people as if they were his own. His greatest architectural project, the Bayon, is a maze of towers covered on all sides with enormous masks of the bodhisattva—or perhaps the king himself—watching out over the populace. The bas-reliefs on the walls of the Bayon are unique in Angkor art in depicting the daily life of the common people and were perhaps intended to show the king's compassion for his subjects. His building program, however, seems to have overextended the empire's resources, for it was left unfinished, and no new temples were added to Angkor after his reign. A Mon monk is reported to have brought Theravāda to Cambodia during this period, but it did not become the state religion until the fourteenth century.

Sri Lanka. Prior to the third century B.C.E., Indo-Aryan clansmen came to the island from the Gangetic Plain, bringing with them brahmanical customs together with a north Indian language and political institutions. There is the possibility that they also brought along Buddhist monks. The Sinhala clan founded a royal dynasty and maintained ties with northern India. According to tradition, King Aśoka sent missionaries, headed by his own son, Mahinda, from the Theravādin center at Sanchi to convert the Sinhala king, Tissa, in approximately 247 B.C.E. The king accepted the faith quickly, built a large monastery—the Mahāvihāra—for the monks in his capital at Anuradhapura, and provided support for them to spread their teachings throughout the island. Within a few years, Mahinda's sister, Saṅghamittā, brought a shoot of the Bodhi Tree from Bodhgaya and founded the Sri Lankan branch of the Bhikkhunī Sangha.

In the first century B.C.E., an invasion by South Indian Coḷa forces was followed by a devastating famine; the Pali Canon, which was preserved solely through oral transmission, was nearly lost. Soon after Sri Lankan forces regained control of the island, the new king built a monastery in the capital, the Abhayagiri Vihāra, and awarded it to a monk named Mahātissa who had provided him with help during his military campaign. The Mahāvihāra, perhaps jealous for having lost its exclusive hold on royal support, suspended Mahātissa for unbecoming association with a layman. When one of Mahātissa's students protested the suspension, he was suspended as well. Viewing these acts as illegitimate, he and his friends formed a new sect with the continued support of the king. The Mahāvihārins, feeling threatened on several fronts, sent their best scholars to a cave in central Sri Lanka to write down the canon and the commentaries that had grown up around it. Not long afterwards, they regained royal patronage.

The split between the Mahāvihāra and the Abhayagiri Vihāra, which came to call itself the Dharmaruci sect, continued until the twelfth century C.E., with royal support alternating between the two. In the third century C.E., a third sect—the Jetavana Vihāra—split off from the Dharmarucis. Unfortunately, the only detailed accounts we have of these splits are the chronicles compiled by Mahāvihāra monks, and many scholars have doubted their impartiality. For instance, although the chronicles accuse the Dharmaruci monks of accepting non-Theravādin teachings, I-ching—a Chinese monk who visited the island in the seventh century—reports finding no differences among the teachings of the three sects. However, archaeologists have recently found eighth-century Mahāyāna inscriptions in stūpas belonging to both the Dharmaruci and Jetavana sects, so perhaps the Mahāvihāra chronicles are more accurate than scholars have thought. At any rate, the chronicles do show without a doubt that the Mahāvihārins saw their strength as lying in their conservative stance. In the second century C.E., they stopped adding new material to their commentaries, and eventually their reputation for conservatism spread to the Indian mainland. By the fourth and fifth century C.E., Mahāvihārin monks established a center in Bodhgaya. However, the Dharmarucis also maintained a reputation for the purity of their Vinaya. In the fifth century a group of Dharmaruci bhikkhunīs was invited to help establish the Bhikkhunī Sangha in China (see Section 8.4). Indian monks came to Sri Lanka to study in the schools of both sects.

One of these monks, Buddhaghosa, came to the Mahāvihāra from the Theravādin center in Kañcipuram and asked permission to translate the commentaries from Sinhala into Pali to make them available to an international audience. According to tradition, the elders of the Mahāvihāra asked him first to compose a treatise on Buddhist practice to test his understanding of the Dhamma. The massive treatise he composed in response, the *Visuddhimagga (The Purity Path),* so impressed them that they provided him with the commentaries together with all the scribes and other assistance he might need. Eventually, he collated the various Sinhalese commentaries and prepared Pāli commentaries to most of the books in the canon. They, together with the *Visuddhimagga,* have since come to define Theravādin orthodoxy up to the present, and in Sri Lanka and Burma are regarded as even more authoritative than the canon itself.

The *Visuddhimagga* takes its structure from seven levels of purity mentioned in a Pali Sutta (MN 24): purity in terms of virtue, mind, view, the overcoming of perplexity, knowledge and vision of what is and is not the path, knowledge and vision of the way, and knowledge and vision. These levels of purity in turn fall under a larger framework of the Threefold Training, with the first purity corresponding to virtue, the second purity to concentration, and the remaining levels of purity to discernment. Although the work contains detailed instructions for concentration practice, it is primarily a work of discernment in its approach to its topics, aiming to get at the *sabhāva* (essence) of each topic. For Buddhaghosa, *sabhāva* meant, not inherent existence, but simply the nature of individual phenomena when stripped of conventional presuppositions. This nature could be known by defining each dhamma in terms of four aspects: its characteristic, function, manifestation, and proximate cause. Thus, for example, to apply this method to discernment itself: The characteristic of discernment is to penetrate to the essence of dhammas, its function is to penetrate the darkness of delusion obscuring that essence, its manifestation is nondelusion, and its proximate cause is concentration.

Buddhaghosa claimed simply to be collating what was already contained in the Sinhalese commentaries, and only occasionally proposed his own opinions, clearly marked as such. There is no way of checking his work, however, as his source commentaries are no longer extant. A few fragments of non-Theravādin Mainstream materials predating his time, translated into Chinese, suggest that at least some of his positions at odds with the Pali Canon were already common to other Mainstream schools, and may have already been accepted in the Theravādin school as well. Still, even though we cannot say with absolute certainty whether he introduced changes into the Theravādin tradition or simply reflected changes already there, his works were so widely accepted in the Theravādin world that we can use them as guides to the state of Theravādin scholastic orthodoxy in the fifth and sixth centuries. What they show is that Theravādin scholasticism did not simply repeat the teachings in the Pali Canon, but rather had developed in original directions. For example, Buddhaghosa's works make a clear division between samatha (tranquility) and vipassanā (insight) meditation techniques. They also drop the canon's emphasis on whole-body breath awareness as the prime form of concentration practice (see Section 2.3.2), in favor of trance states acquired by gazing intently at objects of various colors, a technique that plays only a peripheral role in the canon. They then define jhāna in terms of these trance states, and change the instructions for breath meditation so as to induce such states. This shift in the definition of what constitutes jhāna has fed the controversy, still alive in the Theravāda tradition, as to the relationship between jhāna and mindfulness, and the question of how necessary jhāna is for the attainment of liberating insight.

After Buddhaghosa made the commentaries accessible to scholars in South India, Kañcipuram came to eclipse the Mahāvihāra as the main center of Theravādin studies. New scholars there provided commentaries to the texts that Buddhaghosa did not live to finish, and subcommentaries to the texts he did. In the centuries following Buddhaghosa, most of the records we have of Sri Lankan Buddhism concern not scholarship but economics. Beginning in the eighth century, the major sects found themselves embroiled increasingly in the running of the huge agricultural estates donated to them by kings, queens, and other members of the nobility. The monks, in gaining the control of irrigation works, became the primary landlords of the island, rivaling the kings in their economic and political power. Given this expanded economic base, the head monasteries of the sects followed the Indian example and developed into universities. The Dharmarucis followed the Indian model in maintaining fraternities of four major monastic lineages—Theravāda, Sarvāstivāda, Sāmmitīya, and Mahāsaṃghika—together with faculty versed in Mahāyāna and Tantric texts, while the Mahavihārins limited their curriculum to the Pali Canon and commentaries. However, the day-to-day life of the monks in both sects was similarly luxurious.

In reaction to this development, a wilderness-dwelling fraternity developed within the Mahāvihārin sect, and by the tenth century began winning royal support. The ruins of these wilderness monasteries show that they were considerably more austere than the monastic centers in the cities, except for one elaborate detail: The urinal stones are decorated with finely carved bas-reliefs of city monasteries and palaces. Apparently the wilderness monks enjoyed expressing their disdain for the luxurious life of their city brethren on a daily basis. A similar ascetic movement developed among the Dharmarucis, but the ascetics were expelled from the sect—an event that had important consequences in later centuries. After Anuradhapura fell to Coḷa forces in 1017, the Bhikkhunī Sangha died out in the ensuing political and social chaos, and the monastic estates were destroyed. When social order was restored, the Mahāvihāra forest movement emerged in the strongest position to lead the revival of Sri Lankan Buddhism and the strengthening of the Theravāda school throughout Southeast Asia.

7.3 THE THERAVĀDA CONNECTION

After the fall of Anuradhapura, a series of events in Burma and Sri Lanka set the stage for the Mahāvihāra Theravāda to become the predominant form of Buddhism in the area. In the middle part of the century, King Aniruddha (Anawrahtā) (r. 1040–1077) had brought most of present-day Burma, together with Nanchao in southern China, under the control of his kingdom centered in Pagan. With his base of power expanded, he embarked his people on a program of temple building that made Pagan one of the architectural glories of Southeast Asia. He is credited with bringing the Pali Canon to Pagan from Thaton in Lower Burma and with converting Burma to Theravāda, but archaeological evidence indicates that whatever it was he brought from Thaton, it was not pure Theravāda. Still, Theravāda must have been prominent in Pagan at this time, for in 1065 King Aniruddha received a request from King Vijayabahu I of Sri Lanka for help in reinstating a proper Theravādin ordination line on that island, and Pagan had the monks to send him.

King Vijayabahu had just succeeded, with Pagan's help, in driving the Coḷa forces from Sri Lanka and was establishing a new capital, not at Anuradhapura, but further inland at Polonnaruwa. Part of his program was to re-establish all three major Sri Lankan sects, but as there were not enough monks left on the island to conduct ordinations, he had to send abroad for new monks to reinstate a proper ordination line. The main Theravādin center of the time was the Coḷa port of Kañcipuram, but for obvious reasons he was not about to send an embassy to the Coḷas asking for monks, so he sent the embassy to his allies in Pagan instead. This is the first recorded instance of Sri Lanka's switching its religious focus away from India and to mainland Southeast Asia, and it was to establish a precedent that served both sides of the new connection well in the following centuries when India began exporting Islam instead of Buddhism and Brahmanism.

King Aniruddha complied with the Sri Lankan request by sending a contingent of monks, although there is some question as to whether the monks were native Burmese or Sri Lankans who had sought refuge in Pagan during the Coḷa invasions. In either case, the mission opened a line of communication between the two kingdoms—involving not only monks, but also religious texts, together with artistic and architectural styles—that was to last on and off for two centuries. The connection strengthened the Theravāda tradition in both countries.

Ironically, although Sri Lanka was originally on the receiving end of the help, it came to dominate the exchange of texts. King Vijayabahu's reign saw a renaissance of Pali studies, and a number of important works—including the *Abhidhammattha Saṅgaha* (*The Compendium of Abhidhamma*), which continues to be the basic text for Abhidhamma studies in Theravāda schools to this day—were composed. Elements of Sri Lankan history and mythology, together with the Sri Lankan recension of the Pali Canon, came more and more to dominate the murals in Pagan.

Sri Lankan dominance further increased under the reign of King Parakrāmabāhu I (1153–1186). By his time, the three Sri Lankan sects realized that, with their economic base still weakened, their only hope for survival lay in forgetting their ancient rivalry and uniting into a single order. Under the guidance of a Venerable Mahākassapa—an elder dwelling in a wilderness monastery outside of Polonnaruwa—and consciously following King Aśoka's example, King Parakrāmabāhu held a synod at which monks who did not go along with the unification were forcibly expelled from the monkhood. To prevent a grassroots revolt, the defrocked monks were offered high-paying jobs on the royal payroll. All the monks remaining in robes agreed to form a single order and to submit to a stringent code of conduct, based on the Pali Vinaya, but with a few modifications. Although each of the three sects maintained vestigial identities within the newly united order, the Mahāvihārin wilderness monks were nominally in charge.

Their position was further strengthened under the rule of Parakrāmabāhu II, who took the throne in 1236. The recent fall of the Buddhist centers in northern India was very much a concern in the king's mind, as he had no idea how much further the Muslims were planning to go in their conquests. A student of Venerable Mahākassapa, a Venerable Sārīputta, convinced the king that the Indian Buddhist centers had fallen because they had abandoned the original Buddhist teachings in their embrace of Mahāyāna and Vajrayāna. Therefore, he argued, the only way to protect Buddhism in Sri Lanka, and through it the king's position, was to revive the original teachings and to provide a system of governance to ensure that they were put into practice. The king complied by establishing a more efficient system for governing the Bhikkhu Sangha, which was now divided into village-dwellers and wilderness-dwellers rather than along the old sectarian lines. This was to provide the norm for monastic governance in Sri Lanka and Southeast Asia into the early twentieth century. To the new position of *mahāsāmī,* or great master of the order, he appointed Venerable Sārīputta who, with the assistance of a talented group of students, produced many religious and secular writings, including subcommentaries to Buddhaghosa's commentaries—and particularly the commentary on the Vinaya—to advance the Mahāvihārin cause. The views of Venerable Sārīputta and his school came to define Theravādin orthodoxy up through the early modern era, not only within Sri Lanka, but also in the states of mainland Southeast Asia that began looking to the Sri Lankan example for guidance in protecting Buddhism and stemming the Muslim tide in their countries as well.

The thirteenth century saw the beginning of Pagan's political decline, which was accelerated when Mongol forces looted the capital in 1287 and, in the course of their looting, destroyed the last remaining centers of the Theravāda

Bhikkhunī Sangha. By the beginning of the following century, a Mon kingdom in Lower Burma had split away from Pagan, which by the middle of the century was no longer an important power. Nevertheless, the connection between Sri Lanka and Burma remained, and the events of the eleventh to thirteenth centuries—the forging of this connection concurrent with the demise of Buddhism in India—shaped perceptions in Southeast Asia in a way that influenced events up to the recent past. (1) These events established Sri Lanka as a prime center of Theravādin orthodoxy and Pali scholarship, so that the destruction of the Buddhist homeland in northern India was less psychologically damaging for Southeast Asian Buddhists than it otherwise might have been; (2) they kept the traditions surrounding the Pali Canon alive, so that the canon and its commentaries became prime sources of inspiration, not only for the religious life of the area, but also for such aspects of secular culture as law and popular literature; (3) they established the tradition that, when the merit economy entered periods of crisis, wilderness monks could be relied on to help restore order; and (4) in tying the example of King Aśoka firmly to the furtherance of Pali studies and the maintenance of orthodox Theravādin ordination lines, these events created a model that rulers in Burma, Sri Lanka, and Thailand (which joined the connection in the fourteenth century after winning independence from the Khmers) followed through the twentieth century. Kings in these countries who founded new dynasties or expanded their empires often came to regard the re-establishment of Theravādin orthodoxy in their kingdoms as a means of making personal merit and stabilizing their political achievements. Every century from the thirteenth through the nineteenth witnessed at least one new ordination lineage established in at least one of the three major Theravādin countries, either drawing on lineages from one of the other countries in the connection or on local traditions of wilderness monks.

In the early fourteenth century, a wilderness-based version of the ordination line established by Parakrāmabāhu II was invited into Lower Burma by a Mon king, and into Thailand by the kings of Sukhothai and Chieng Mai, which had recently gained independence from the Khmers. Sukhothai abandoned Khmer architectural styles in favor of the style developed jointly by Pagan and Polonnaruwa, and quickly went beyond imitation to become a major center of Buddhist art. Its bronze Buddha images in particular are among the most graceful ever produced. Theravāda also spread to Laos, where it was quickly made the state religion.

In latter part of the fifteenth century, the monastic tradition in Pegu, Lower Burma, had declined to the point that King Dhammazedi of Pegu requested a new ordination line from Sri Lanka and forced the entire Sangha in his kingdom to take reordination in this new lineage. At about this time, Theravāda was also brought to the Dai tribes in southern Yunnan. Southern Vietnam, however, came under the control of the Chinese-dominated court from the north, which brought the entire country into the sphere of Chinese Mahāyāna. Thus from this point on, the religious history of Vietnam properly belongs with that of China (see Section 9.9), although a few pockets of Theravāda have continued to exist near Cambodia to the present.

In the mid-eighteenth century, tables were turned when—after the complete disappearance of the Sri Lankan Sangha—King Kīrti Śrī Rājasinha obtained help from the court at Ayudhaya (by then the new capital of central Thailand) in sending Pali texts and reinstating a proper ordination line in his kingdom. Later in the same century, the Burmese destroyed Ayudhaya, burning its libraries and melting its Buddha images down for their gold. When King Rāma I finally established a new capital at Bangkok in 1782, he began an active campaign to destroy all remnants of Tantric practices and beliefs—which he blamed for the fall of Ayudhaya—and sent emissaries to Sri Lanka for reliable editions of the Pali Canon. His grandson, Rāma IV, instituted a reform movement in the Thai Sangha by sponsoring a spread of the ordination lineage that King Dhammazedi of Pegu had brought from Sri Lanka four centuries earlier.

Modern scholarship has shown that the chroniclers of these reform movements tended to exaggerate the purity and success of the reforms. For example, European travelers to Ayudhaya in the seventeenth century reported that Tantric visualization exercises dominated the practice of meditation in the monasteries. Pali dhāraṇīs and visualization chants, evidently written to compete with Sanskrit Tantric dhāraṇīs in the fourteenth and fifteenth centuries, are still widely memorized and chanted throughout Theravādin countries today. Nevertheless, the consistent pattern of Theravādin reforms for nine centuries did succeed in keeping the traditions of Pali scholarship alive and in establishing Theravādin beliefs as the orthodoxy in Sri Lanka, Burma, Thailand, and other areas in their sphere of influence. This created a sense of cultural unity and continuity in these countries that outlasted the rise and fall of many political dynasties and may in part explain why—unlike Buddhists in Malaysia and Indonesia, which did not join the Theravāda connection—Buddhists in these kingdoms were the only ones in the Indianized states of the region able to resist the Islamic influences emanating from India through most of this period.

7.4 THE COLONIAL PERIOD

Given that the survival of this Theravāda-dominated syncretism depended to a large extent on royal patronage, it should come as no surprise that the colonial period (sixteenth–twentieth centuries) had an enormous impact on the status of Buddhism in these countries. Even in Thailand, the only country in the region that did not become a European colony, the European threat strongly affected the government's religious policy. Throughout the area, the spread of Western education and medicine deprived city and village monks of their traditional roles as teachers and doctors, leaving them a social role reduced to ritual functions based on a worldview that Westerners, and Christian missionaries in particular, began attacking as ignorant and superstitious. Still, the height of the colonial period (the nineteenth century) saw the rise of reformist movements in all the major Theravādin countries, as monks and their supporters sought a return to their roots as a way of resisting the European threat.

7.4.1 Sri Lanka

Of the three focal countries here, Sri Lanka suffered most from the colonial period. The Portugese (1505–1658) were the first Europeans to take power, seizing the lowlands, destroying monasteries, persecuting Buddhists, and forcibly converting them to Catholicism. Under this onslaught, the Sinhala kings withdrew to Kandy in the mountains, where they ruled from 1592 until 1815, supporting Buddhism insofar as their circumstances and resources would allow. When the Dutch and later the British replaced the Portugese as the dominant powers in the lowlands, their religious policy was somewhat more benign, but the schools and printing presses that the Protestant missionaries established under their rule were used to disparage Buddhism as the superstitious faith of ignorant masses. After the British took over the entire island in 1815, the level of scholarship and practice in the Sri Lankan Sangha—now deprived of government support—steadily deteriorated. Stripped of their traditional role as teachers, their medical knowledge discredited, monks found their social position increasingly curtailed.

Finally, in the 1860s, Mohoṭṭiwatte Guṇānanda (1823–1890), a Buddhist novice who had received his education in Christian schools, responded to the Christian attack by wandering throughout the country, engaging Christian missionaries in open debates. His campaign climaxed with a week-long debate in 1873 at which he was declared the winner. As a result, Guṇānanda's cause attracted large-scale support not only from fellow Sri Lankans, but also from Helene Blavatsky and Henry Steel Olcott, founders of the Theosophical Society. Blavatsky and Olcott came to Sri Lanka from America, declared themselves Buddhists, and campaigned to free Sri Lankan Buddhism not only from the oppression of the colonial Christian regime but also from what they regarded as primitive spirit cults, which had been a part of the Buddhist tradition from its earliest days on the island.

The Theosophists encouraged Sri Lankan lay people to play an active role in the revival of Buddhism, giving rise to what has been called Protestant Buddhism, both in the sense that it was a protest against Christianity and in the sense that it adopted many of the techniques and traditions of the Christian missionaries. As was the case with Protestant Christianity, Protestant Buddhism was spearheaded by educated lay people who took over the role of religious teacher from the monks and tried to strip away from the tradition any elements that had no basis in the early texts. As in any confrontation, Protestant Buddhists—led by a Sri Lankan protégé of Olcott and Blavatsky, Anagārika Dharmapāla—tended to define themselves in terms of the enemy. On the one hand, they stressed the scientific, rationalist side of Buddhism to counteract the charge that the religion was superstitious; while on the other hand, they defined Buddhist doctrines as repudiations of Christian doctrines. In their eyes, for instance, the not-self teaching (2.3.1) was a metaphysical doctrine denying the Christian concept of soul.

In some ways, Protestant Buddhism was simply the means by which lay organizations took over the old role of the Theravādin kings in trying to support the return of Buddhism to its original tenets. However, because monks were now no longer doctors and teachers, the movement had to expand the concept of Buddhist revival to cover not only the reform of the monastic Sangha, but also to deal directly with the education and uplift of the Buddhist laity at large.

In this it was to provide a model for Sri Lankan Buddhist movements throughout the twentieth century.

Because it was directed against European culture, the Buddhist cause became the rallying point for the nationalist, anticolonial cause as well. This had the effect of politicizing not only the lay Buddhist organizations but also the monastic Sangha. By the time independence was finally won after World War II, the monks had become so thoroughly involved in political activities that one faction actually planned and executed a political assassination in the early years of independence. This sent a shock through the country just as it was looking to Buddhism as a guide for the definition of national identity after more than four centuries of European rule.

7.4.2 Burma

The Burmese Sangha fared somewhat better than the Sri Lankan under British rule (1885–1948), perhaps because the British had learned from their mistakes in Sri Lanka, perhaps simply because colonial rule was shorter here. In fact, certain aspects of British rule were actually favorable for Buddhism—in some cases, intentionally so. Although the British refused to take up the king's role as watchdog of the Sangha, they arranged for monks to elect their own ecclesiastical leaders and allowed ecclesiastical examinations to be given on a regular basis. As a result, Pali studies—including the Burmese specialty, the Abhidhamma analysis of mind-states—continued unabated.

Another aspect of British rule beneficial to Burmese Buddhism was unintentional, and dated from the initial British attempts to conquer the country. In 1852, during the second Anglo-Burmese war, King Mindon seized power and sued the British for peace. Under the terms of the peace, the British took Lower Burma, leaving the king with only the upper half of the country. This put him in a precarious position, threatened not only by British colonial ambitions but also by the possibility that—in light of his having lost half of the country—his subjects might not view him as a legitimate ruler. To counter this second danger, he outdid his predecessors in trying to fulfil the traditional expectation that a legitimate king must embody all aspects of Burmese culture. Reasoning that Buddhism was the highest expression of Burmese culture, and vipassanā practice the highest expression of Buddhism, he was the first Burmese king to encourage vipassanā practice in his court. Monks were invited from the forest and quizzed as to the way they taught and practiced vipassanā; those whose methods satisfied the king were then requested to teach vipassanā to him and his courtiers. Similarly, a ten-precept nun was invited to teach vipassanā to his wives. In doing this, Mindon established a set of cultural expectations that survived throughout the colonial period and into the period of Burmese independence: that vipassanā could be identified with a particular method, that the method could be taught in condensed form to lay people, and that one of the duties of a highly placed Burmese was to foster vipassanā practice in a lay setting. After the fall of the monarchy in 1886, a successful Burmese merchant set up the first center specifically for lay vipassanā practice in his home compound in 1913. The movement remained small until the 1930s, when students of Ledi Sayadaw (1846–1923) and

Mingon Sayadaw (1868–1955), among others, helped set up many centers and produced many schools of thought as to what sort of method was a genuine vipassanā method, and what methods were "merely" samatha. When Burma gained independence, the U Nu government continued the vipassanā-sponsoring tradition by setting up its own vipassanā center in Rangoon. The continuity of the tradition is exemplified by the fact that the monk chosen to head the center, Mahasi Sayadaw (1904–1982), traced his practice lineage back to King Mindon's favorite forest monk, Thilon Sayadaw (1786–1860).

Despite this positive effect, British rule did have the negative effect of politicizing the Burmese Sangha, as it had the Sri Lankan. Unlike Sri Lanka, Burma possessed a tradition of easily obtained temporary ordination. When the British banned political gatherings, many nationalists took ordination to preach their political ideas to the laity who gathered at the monasteries for religious purposes. These nationalist monks played a prominent part in the early days of the independence movement, later faded into the background, and then reemerged as an ecclesiastical lobby after independence was won following World War II.

7.4.3 Thailand

As mentioned previously, Thailand did not come under colonial rule, although this is not to say that the survival of the Thai monarchy during this period was a foregone conclusion. With pressure from the British on the west and south, and from the French on the north and east, Thai monarchs had to follow a skillful campaign of external diplomacy and internal reform to remain in power. Religious reform was an important part of this campaign.

King Rāma IV (r. 1851–1868) had been ordained as a monk for nearly 30 years before ascending to the throne, and during that time had begun his own personal reform from within the Thai Sangha. The reform was called the *Dhammayut* (In Accordance with the Dhamma) movement, and entailed an unusual combination of strict adherence to the Vinaya and a more rationalist, critical attitude to the Suttas, Abhidhamma, and commentaries. It is hard to tell whether Rāma IV's historical perspective on the relative authority of the commentaries resulted from his contact with Westerners—he was an avid fan of Western science—or from a more traditional Thai skepticism toward the commentaries, which were primarily a Sri Lankan and Burmese enterprise. Either way, it set the tone for Thai Pali studies up to the present time.

The reign of King Rāma V (r. 1868–1910) was marked by a drive for centralization that weakened the Sangha in some respects but strengthened it in others. On the one hand, a secular educational system was established, taking the traditional role of teacher from the monks and placing it in the hands of lay teachers who received their orders from the central government. Thus, even though the Thais, unlike the Sri Lankans and Burmese, were not saddled with a Christian educational system, Thai monks were stripped of one of their most important social roles. When Western medicine began spreading through Thailand in the latter part of the 1800s, monks were deprived of yet another important social role, a fact that began to make them seem superfluous in the eyes of many educated Thais.

On the other hand, Rāma V, together with his half-brother, the Prince-Patriarch Vajirañāaṇa (1859–1921), succeeded in creating a national organization for the Thai Sangha, uniting all the various regional groupings except one—their father's Dhammayut movement—into a single sect, called the *Mahānikāya* (Great Sect). The Dhammayut was formally declared a separate sect, although both sects were placed under a single ecclesiastical authority. The Prince-Patriarch wrote a series of new textbooks reflecting a rationalist approach to the Dhamma and the legends surrounding the Buddha, favoring the Dhamma as taught in the early Suttas over beliefs based on the apadānas. These textbooks became the basis for nationally administered ecclesiastical exams that were meant not only to standardize knowledge of the Dhamma throughout the country, but also to form the prerequisite for advancement through the government's system of ecclesiastical ranks.

These reforms had their onerous side as well. Ancient, non-canonical texts from outlying parts of the country were brought into Bangkok for evaluation. If they conflicted with the new curriculum, they were burned. An important rule in the Vinaya was changed to forbid monks from holding ordinations unless authorized by the central authorities. Monks from outlying areas who posed a potential political threat to central power were summoned to Bangkok for questioning and sometimes placed under house arrest.

On the whole, though, the reforms succeeded in raising the general level of practice and study among the majority of monks, in managing to keep Buddhism respectable in the eyes of the more educated members of the society, and in countering the charges made by Christian missionaries that Buddhism was a religion of the ignorant and superstitious. At the same time, the central government's newfound strength enabled it to prevent the Thai Sangha from becoming politicized like those in Sri Lanka and Burma. Still, the reforms were unable to provide the village and city monks with new social roles to replace the ones they had lost to Western education and technology. In this respect the Thai Sangha was placed in the same quandary as its brethren in Sri Lanka and Burma.

7.5 THE POST-COLONIAL PERIOD

In the heady days following independence after World War II, lay organizations in Sri Lanka and Burma began a conscious policy of sponsoring Buddhism, in line with the traditional pattern of the Theravādin connection. In Burma, the most active organization in this regard was the government. From 1954–1962, the Burmese government sponsored a Sixth Buddhist Council, inviting religious leaders from all the Theravādin countries to reestablish contact and reedit their texts. Prior to that, the prime minister of Burma, U Nu, founded a government-sponsored meditation center in Rangoon and persuaded Mahasi Sayadaw to become the center's chief teacher. Mahasi's method of vipassanā equated mindfulness with a precise noting of fleeting mental and physical events, resulting in certain physiological and psychological reactions that were identified with the stages of insight as set out in the *Visuddhimagga*. U Nu planned to make the center the starting point for a reform of the entire Burmese Sangha, but fell from power before achieving his aim. Still, the center spawned many offshoots not only in Burma, but also in Sri Lanka, Thailand, Malaysia, and the West, making the Mahasi method one of the more prominent meditation methods in present-day Theravāda. U Ba Khin (1899–1971), Burma's accountant general in its first decade of independence, also established a meditation center in Rangoon, with himself as teacher. His method of practice, as taught by his student S. N. Goenka, has spawned centers abroad as well. The military junta that replaced U Nu originally espoused a purely secular ideology, but in more recent years has turned to advertising its support for the Sangha as a way of shoring up its crumbling popularity.

As for Sri Lanka, the government started a World Buddhist Fellowship in 1950 and began sponsoring an Encyclopedia of Buddhism, a still ongoing project that has won international respect for its level of scholarship. Monks were sent to study meditation at the Mahasi center in Burma to revive the almost moribund state of meditation on the island. Unfortunately, attempts to build a national Sri Lankan identity around Buddhism have exacerbated tensions between the Sinhala Buddhist majority and the Tamil Hindu/Islamic minority, resulting in many years of bloody civil war.

The most active role in the post-colonial Buddhist revival on the island has been played by non-governmental lay organizations, the most prominent of which is the Sarvodaya Shramadāna (Donation of Labor for the Uplift of the Masses) Movement. Founded in 1958, it has attempted to bring Buddhist ideals to bear on the material, social, and spiritual development of the Sri Lankan poor. Individuals have also fostered important changes. Recently, Ranjani de Silva sponsored efforts to revive the Theravāda Bhikkhunī Sangha by having Sri Lankan monks join forces with bhikṣuṇīs from Taiwan to provide full ordination to women from Sri Lanka and elsewhere. Ecclesiastical authorities in Burma and Thailand, however, have refused to recognize these ordinations as valid, and the Sri Lankan Sangha is divided on the issue.

The factors most influential in determining the postwar fortunes of Buddhism in this region, however, were beyond the control of any government or organization: over-population, industrialization, and urbanization. These had the effect of making popular Buddhism, with its strong ties to the needs of the rural agrarian class, seem increasingly irrelevant to growing numbers of people.

Even more radical social changes came with the Cold War. Communist takeovers in Laos and Cambodia destroyed organized religion in those countries, but in a strange spin-off of geopolitics, the Cold War resulted in a windfall of scholarly knowledge about Buddhist syncretism in this area, especially in Thailand. American military and political advisers, concerned with stabilizing Thai society to keep the country from falling to the communists, came to the realization that the most unstable societies in Asia were those where Christian missionaries had been most successful in winning converts. As a result, anthropologists received government grants to study the role of Buddhism in Thai society in hopes that knowledge of Thai village beliefs and of the monks' role would help in using the monks to mold public opinion. It is hard to tell what impact these studies played in the conduct of the Cold War. Thais, for instance, still laugh about their government's request in the 1950s that monks stop teaching the Buddhist ideal of contentment with few possessions on the grounds that it hampered economic development. Still, the anthropologists were working in the interests of science and their professional reputations, and their studies have left us a remarkably detailed picture of Theravādin Buddhist syncretism and its social role at a unique point in history.

The anthropologists discovered that the traditional distinction between village-dwelling and wilderness-dwelling monks is as valid as ever, but that urbanization has led to new varieties of Buddhist practice. Thus, in the following sections, which present a short summary of anthropological findings about Thai Buddhism, we will focus on three types of Buddhism: in the village, in the wilderness, and in the city. Bear in mind that the situations in Sri Lanka and Burma, although differing in details, follow similar overall patterns.

7.5.1 Buddhism in the Village

The primary focus of village Buddhism is the pursuit of merit. Within the village, the three canonical categories of making merit—generosity, virtue, and meditation—shape the practice of Buddhism both for monks and laity. Here we will look at Buddhism as practiced in a typical central Thai village to show how the Buddhism of a village *wat,* or temple/monastery, interacts with the other elements in the Thai belief system in the quest for merit.

The wat serves as the primary institution for facilitating the making of merit. For the typical Thai villager, a community is not civilized, an area is not settled, until a wat has been built and monks have taken up residence. The translation chosen for the word *wat*—temple/monastery—gives an idea of the dual function the institution plays. It is both a ritual arena for merit-making ceremonies and a place where monks may devote themselves to the meritorious activities of following the monastic code, studying the Buddha's teachings, and meditating as much as the circumstances of the village location will allow. Thais recognize the dual function of the wat by dividing it into two areas, the *Buddhāvāsa,* or dwelling of the Buddha, and the *Saṅghāvāsa,* or dwelling of the community of monks. In wealthier wats the two areas are clearly defined, sometimes separated by walls; in poorer wats they are not so clearly separated, but the concepts still apply to an intuitively felt sense of sacred space and dwelling space.

The Buddhāvāsa contains the main meeting hall of the wat, which invariably houses a Buddha image and the altars devoted to it. Other elements may include a library housing old texts, and a *chedi* (cetiya), or stūpa, which ideally will enshrine a relic of the Buddha or, failing that, copies of the Pali Canon together with consecrated objects. The Buddhāvāsa is the primary ritual arena of the wat and of the village as a whole. Here is where villagers gather to participate in communal merit-making ceremonies, such as making donations, taking the precepts, and listening to the Dhamma. The presence of the Buddha image or of the Buddha's relics is believed to heighten the power of the ritual—a belief owing its ultimate provenance to the apadānas. In fact, the influence of the apadānas on this part of village Buddhism is so strong that the major forms of adhikāra performed in the presence of the image or relics precisely imitate forms of adhikāra performed in the presence of the Buddha or of stūpas in the apadānas. People take refuge, take the precepts, and chant the Buddha's praise in the presence of the image.

They present the image with gifts of flowers, candles, lights, canopies, and pennants. They bathe the image with perfumed water and cover it with gold leaf. And, as the apadānas advise, they augment the merit planted in the Buddha-field by planting additional seeds of merit in the field provided by the monastic Sangha.

This is why the Saṅghāvāsa is a necessary adjunct to the Buddhāvāsa. The moral purity the monks gain by observing the monastic code makes them the ideal recipients of the gifts of the laity. Their celibate lifestyle frees them to devote their time to studying the Dhamma and other subjects that the laity have little time to pursue on their own. Thus the monks function both as the repository of merit that the laity can tap into by giving the monks support, and as the custodians of the knowledge valued in the smooth functioning of the community. In this respect, the monks form a ritual and, relatively speaking, literate elite, although it should be remembered that the monkhood is open to males regardless of social background, and most of the monks in a given village monastery are close relatives of the villagers. As noted above, the monks' role as the custodians of knowledge has grown smaller in the past century, but they are still the prime repository of traditional knowledge not taught in the government schools. They are also the primary counselors for problems on the personal, family, and communal level.

A third element in the wat—and which, in legal terms, makes it a wat—is the *sīmā,* or sacred boundary containing the ordination hall. The sīmā is considered so sacred that no political authority, not even the king, has jurisdiction over it. If a criminal takes refuge in the sīmā, the police have to ask permission of the wat's abbot before they can enter the area to catch him. In wats that make a clear delineation between the Buddhāvāsa and Saṅghāvāsa, there is some disagreement over which area the sīmā belongs to, but actually it belongs to both. Being the most sacred spot in the wat, it is where their functions merge on the highest level. On the one hand, the ordination hall is where the monks meet to conduct their communal business, such as the fortnightly recitation of the Pāṭimokkha. On the other, it is where very important merit-making rituals are held, such as Buddha-image consecrations and—the most important merit-making ritual, in which the dual functions of the entire wat as ritual center and monastic dwelling unite—the ordination ceremony by which a member of the community, with the support of his relatives and friends, offers himself up to become a monk to further his own pursuit of merit and to aid the community in theirs.

The high value placed on the monks as a repository of merit can be understood best by making a structural model of the Thai villager's view of the forces working on his or her life. On the first level are the empirical forces: the villager's position in society, the weather's influence over the success of the crops, and the cycle of life itself—a process of birth, aging, illness, and death. Because one is virtually powerless against these forces on the empirical level, one must tap into the power of the invisible forces controlling them.

These forces start with the spirits believed to inhabit the world, among them the deities guarding particular locations such as one's house or fields, wandering ghosts of the newly dead, ancestor spirits, fertility goddesses, and others. According to animist beliefs, these spirits have the power to affect the course of one's fortunes; they may work invisibly or else enter one's dreams, take possession of members of one's family, or communicate with spirit mediums to indicate their pleasure or displeasure with one's conduct. In dealing with them, one may try to tap into their power by promising to perform a certain favor if their help is forthcoming; one may appease their anger with offerings or, failing that, try to control them through rituals, spells, or talismans.

A second layer of invisible forces are those derived from Brahmanism. The Brahmanical gods are generally viewed as a higher level of spirits, to be handled with a higher level of offerings and rituals, but except on very important occasions they are rarely thought to be concerned with the affairs of villagers, as they have more important business to attend to. The Brahmanical forces that weigh most heavily on a villager's mind are astrology and numerology. The planets, which govern both systems, are conceived as gods more predictable and less capricious than the spirits, but at the same time less susceptible to offerings and rituals. Their beneficent influences may be tapped into by the proper scheduling of events. Their malevolent influences can be counteracted only by means of good luck, which may be fostered by such things as talismans, good luck rituals, lucky numbers, and auspicious colors.

Buddhism adds another set of gods and spirits to the invisible world, and—with the remnants of Tantrism—another element to the ritualists' repertoire. Its most important contribution, however, is a layer of force overarching all others: the principle of kamma, that one meets with events in line with the intentional quality of one's past and present thoughts, words, and deeds. Even gods, according to the canon, are subject to this law. From the orthodox point of view, this law invalidates the influence of the planets and lowers the status of the spirit world. However, from the syncretist point of view, kamma does not abrogate the lower levels of force; it simply provides another method for explaining and influencing them. For example, one's social position, the success of one's crops, and the vicissitudes of life in general can be attributed to one's accumulated good and bad kamma. The extent to which spirits meddle in one's life can be attributed either to one's general stock of merit or to particular actions of help or harm directed to a particular spirit in this life or the past. One's birth chart is essentially a diagram showing the strengths and weaknesses of one's kamma inherited from past lives. This being the case, an entire host of problems may be dealt with by adding to one's stock of merit in general or, in cases when a particular spirit is looking for repayment for past wrongs, making merit and dedicating it to the spirit. Thus, merit is power, a means for controlling the forces of the world on all levels so as to gain happiness in this life and the next. This explains the importance of merit in the eyes of the typical villager, and the need in human society for a place where merit can be most effectively made.

The fact that the doctrine of kamma lies over all other forms of power, however, does not mean that merit-making entirely supplants other means of trying to acquire power, such as occult rituals or propitiatory offerings. The drawback of merit is its general, rather than specific nature. There is no control over how quickly its results will be felt; it is the most invisible and impersonal of the invisible powers. Thus there are occasions—as when a spirit enters one's dreams and makes a specific demand—where the typical villager, instead of making merit, will turn for help to a ritual specialist, either lay or monastic.

General familiarity with rituals, both animistic and Brahmanical, has also influenced the typical villager's view of kamma in that merit is often seen as residing, not in the quality of the intention behind an action, but in the proper performance of acts that are defined as meritorious. This view differs radically from the view of kamma as expressed in the earliest layer of Suttas. However, it is often accompanied by a view of merit derived from the apadānas that is not purely ritualistic: Acts of adhikāra in the proper merit-field bear good fruit regardless of the intention, but even better fruit when done with an attitude of prasāda—confidence both in the fruitfulness of the act and the power of the merit-field—and still better fruit when the merit is intentionally dedicated toward nibbāna. Among villagers who have taken to heart the teachings of the reform curriculum established by Prince Vajirañāṇa or of the wilderness traditions, these views have been replaced or augmented with a third view: that merit is determined by the purity of one's intention. Although these views conflict on a theoretical level, the merit-making ceremonies held at the wat harmoniously accommodate them all. The act of merit-making is ritualized, while participants are also encouraged to develop a cheerful attitude of prasāda and to reflect on the quality of their intentions. In this way the external requirements of a ritualized view of merit are satisfied, while the inner requirements of an apadāna-based or Sutta-based view of merit are encouraged but not required.

A prime example of this sort of accommodation is the typical merit-making ritual on the morning of the Uposatha, which occurs on the days of the full, new, and half moons. The primary function of the ritual is to make merit by presenting food to the monks and listening to a sermon. Monks and villagers gather in separate zones of the main meeting hall. The general mood of the gathering is cheerful. Before the food is presented, the villagers pay respect to the Buddha image and request the Triple Refuge and Five Precepts from the chief monk. For those who have had recourse to animist or Brahmanical practices since the last Uposatha service, and who believe that their allegiance to the Buddha, Dhamma, and Sangha has thus been tarnished, the request for the Triple Refuge offers the chance to renew allegiance with no questions asked. For others, it is an opportunity to renew their sense of prasāda in the Triple Gem. The request for the Five Precepts serves a similar dual function. On one level it is ritualistic: A donation is said to bear the greatest fruit if both the donor and the recipient live by the precepts. For those who have little intention of trying to observe the precepts after leaving the monastery, the act of taking the precepts puts them "in possession of" the precepts at least while the donation is being given. For those who do intend to keep the precepts, the request is an opportunity to renew their dedication and make a fresh start if they have broken any precepts since the last Uposatha.

Once the preliminaries are completed, the villagers as a group make a formal declaration of donating their offerings to the Sangha. This is because the act of making a donation to the Sangha is more meritorious than that of donating it to individual monks. The declaration may be short or may last several minutes, mentioning the various benefits the donors hope to gain from their donation, the dead relatives with whom they wish to share the merit, and the various local, Brahmanical, and Buddhist deities and spirits they hope will rejoice in the merit of the act, ending with the wish that the merit will someday lead to nibbāna.

Only then is the food formally handed to the monks, who chant blessings rejoicing in the merit the villagers have made. The monks then eat while the villagers look on, chatting informally about the events of the past week.

After the monks have eaten, one of them delivers a sermon, often with the express purpose of fostering prasāda in the listeners' minds. The villagers then have their meal, and many of them return home at this point. Others stay for the morning chanting service. The texts of the service, compiled by Rāma IV while he was still a monk, include a reflection on the virtues of the Triple Gem for the purpose of developing prasāda, and a contemplation of the Three Characteristics for the purpose of developing saṁvega toward the sufferings of life. Some of the villagers understand the meaning, others don't, but they are convinced that by repeating and listening to the Pali phrases they are gaining merit by calming their minds and listening to the Dhamma in any case. This, according to a commentarial classification, would count as a form of meditation. Combined with the ritualized donation and precepts of the earlier part of the service, this makes the morning ritual, in the eyes of those who view merit ritually, a complete expression of the three major forms of making merit.

Sometimes the villagers will go—alone or in groups—to other parts of the country in search of monasteries offering more powerful merit-fields than those offered in their home monastery. In some cases, this will involve performing adhikāra in Buddha-fields: worshiping famous Buddha images or participating in the annual festivals at famous stūpas. In other cases, this will involve planting seeds of generosity in the merit-field believed to reside in monks or nuns famous for strong meditative attainments. These extraordinary trips have become more common in recent years, as Thailand's transportation network has improved. However, an individual's daily cultivation of merit still centers on ceremonies at the local wat, at home, or in the family's rice fields.

The ritualization of merit-making is most striking in the prime event drawing the villagers and monks together: the ordination of a new monk. In the Buddha's time, ordination involved the complete renunciation of family life and was expected to be a lifelong commitment. For Thai Buddhists, however, temporary ordination—usually lasting three months—is the norm rather than the exception, functioning as a rite of passage for young men and preparing them, ironically, for marriage. By ordaining they repay the debt they owe to their parents for the troubles and hardships involving in raising them; during their time as monks they prepare for adulthood by gaining the knowledge and strength of character they will need as they take on a wife and children.

Parents are said to acquire a vast store of merit by allowing a son to ordain. They become "relatives of the religion" and are guaranteed to meet with Buddhism again in future lifetimes. Because ordination usually occurs during the growing season, they hope that the merit of doing without their son's labor will bring them even more merit. As for the sons, they are given the time to study textbooks from the reform curriculum, which conclude with a section on Dhamma appropriate for householders. They also must develop the patience, propriety, and responsibility that adherence to the monastic code requires. Thus, at the end of the three months, after they have gone through a simple disrobing ceremony, they are considered "ripe"—knowledgeable and responsible enough to be eligible for marriage. They have also gained familiarity with the monks' life, which prepares them for their future role as supporters of the wat.

However, not all monks disrobe after three months. A small number stay on for longer periods, even for life, with many vocations open to them. To begin with, monkhood is one of the few avenues of social mobility open to a Thai villager. A monk may acquire an education from the school system set up especially for monks, leading all the way to university degrees (see Section 7.5.3). Upon graduation, he may disrobe and look for a job, or he may stay on in the monkhood and work his way up the hierarchy. Most of the recent Supreme Patriarchs of the Thai Sangha have been sons of peasants.

Alternatively, rather than taking the route of education—termed *ganthadhura,* the duty of books—a monk may seek out a meditation teacher and devote himself to *vipassanādhura,* the duty of insight. Fear of the dangers and hardships associated with a meditative life in the forest, though, usually leads the monk's relatives to discourage him from such a course.

A third course open to a monk is to stay on at his village wat, acquiring merit and whatever Buddhist or ritual knowledge he feels will be helpful to his fellow villagers. Thais in general, as their society undergoes rapid change, have a certain nostalgia for the folk figure of Luang Taa, the elderly village monk who may not have much of an education or a position in the ecclesiastical hierarchy, but who through the accumulated experience of his years in the monkhood is a source of consolation and wisdom for all who seek his advice. However accurate this nostalgic picture may be, it gives a good indication of the affection that Thais in general feel for their village monks as their partners in acquiring the merit that will lead to their long-term happiness and well-being.

Because the last living lineage of the Theravāda Bhikkhunī Sangha ended with the Mongol attack on Pagan in 1287, women generally do not now have the opportunity for ordination that men do. Thailand has communities of eight-precept nuns, either independent or attached to monasteries, but young women, unlike young men, are actively discouraged from ordaining. However, there are ways that a woman determined to devote herself to a religious life can circumvent her parents' objections. A common one is, when suffering from illness, to promise to a guardian deity that she will ordain; if she recovers, her parents usually respect her need to fulfil her promise. Failing this, a woman may postpone ordaining until her children are grown.

A nun's role is very different from that of a monk. Nuns play a very small part in the community's pursuit of merit, usually limited to chanting at funerals. This has both its drawbacks and its advantages. On the one hand, nuns usually draw their support from their immediate families. If no support is forthcoming, they must undertake work of various kinds to maintain themselves. If, however, a nun can obtain adequate material support, she will find that she has more free time than the typical village monk to devote to meditation and her own personal pursuit of merit.

For a woman who does not ordain, the center of her religious life is in the home. She may donate to the monks a share of the food she prepares, adding a religious dimension to her role in the kitchen. She may also use part of her share of the family income to sponsor merit-making ceremonies, the construction of religious edifices, and so on. If she has been initiated by a female ritual specialist, she may practice private rituals for her prosperity and safety and that of her family. Most importantly of all, she may train her children to live by the Dhamma. Thai villagers have not been exposed to books of political history, with their tendency to glorify the male role in public affairs at the expense of the female role in the family. The Pali Canon places a high importance on the role that parents play in the life of their children. Children are to regard their mother and father as their foremost teachers, and to treat them with the same respect due an arahant. Thus her role as a foremost teacher is where a Thai lay woman will commonly find her greatest source of merit.

When death comes to a Thai village, all elements of the popular religion shape the ensuing funeral. From the animist point of view, the main concern is to keep the spirit of the deceased from disrupting the community. Because the spirit is thought to hover around the dead body, cremation is the preferred means of disposing of the corpse. Once the body has been cremated, the spirit has its locus removed and is more likely to go on to its next life. To keep it under control before the cremation, the feet, wrists, and neck of the corpse are bound, a hex sign and other charms are placed on the chest before the coffin is closed, and people who attend the funeral will often repeat a silent charm to themselves as protection against the spirit. Although financial considerations often determine how long the funeral will last, animist considerations can also play a role, the general rule being that if the death was violent or sudden, the funeral should be held as quickly as possible, for the spirit in such cases is especially troublesome. Wakes are held to keep the body company at night, so that the spirit will not feel neglected and start prowling the village.

Brahmanical elements enter into the funeral arrangements primarily in the numerology. For example, monks are invited in even numbers, rather than the odd numbers used for auspicious occasions. Otherwise, Brahmanism's role at this time lies in coloring the attitude of people attending the funeral. Funeral rites, even the merit-making ceremonies connected with them, are classified by the official Thai Sangha text on rituals as *avamaṅgala,* inauspicious. This is a Brahmanical concept, for there is nothing inauspicious about death from a Buddhist point of view. Contemplation of death and even of corpses is one of the original Buddhist meditation themes for counteracting lust and complacency. However, from a Brahmanical point of view, any involvement with a corpse is polluting. Thus those who attend funerals must observe certain taboos. They may repeat charms to themselves to ward off ritual pollution; they are careful not to visit sick people on the way home from the funeral; and they may leave a small bowl of lustral water next to the door of their home compound before leaving for the funeral, using it to sprinkle their heads before entering the compound on their return.

The main component of the funeral rites is merit-making, which serves a dual purpose: to comfort the living and to dedicate the merit to the deceased so as to improve his or her chances for a good rebirth. Donations are presented to monks, sermons are given, and in particular, the monks chant, using a different set of chants from those used on auspicious occasions. Here, so soon after a death, chants referring to good fortune are judged inappropriate, so the Pali chants deal with the Three Characteristics, the ineffectiveness of spells and other human powers in the face of death, and the efficacy of good kamma in leading to a happy rebirth—topics that are consoling for those who have been devoting their life to the pursuit of merit. Passages from the Abhidhamma are also chanted, on the grounds that they are the highest level of Dhamma, and that listening to them will produce the highest level of merit, which is then passed on to the deceased.

Their inauspiciousness aside, funerals are among the main social occasions in the life of Thai villagers. If the deceased was well-loved or highly respected, the body may be kept for several months in a temporary mausoleum until the family—or the community as a whole, if the deceased was a monk—has saved up enough money for a ceremony lavish enough to express its regard and respect. When this is the case, the funeral is a remarkably cheerful affair. The bereaved have had time to get over their loss and can take satisfaction in the conviction that they are helping the deceased to a favorable rebirth. The communal nature of their merit-making renders even their own upcoming death less fearful, as they are assured of enjoying the fruits of their good kamma together with friends and family in the next life.

7.5.2 Buddhism in the Wilderness

As we have seen, the ritual life of village Buddhism closely follows the apadānas. However, some of the early Suttas and Vinaya texts present a very different picture of the ideal monastic life, one of meditation in the solitude of the wilderness. Members of the monastic Sangha—either as groups or as individuals—have often left their villages to follow the ideal embodied in these strata of the canon. And, following the example of Kings Parakrāmabāhu I and II, many rulers have looked to these wilderness monks for help in periods when the economy of merit centered in the villages and cities has threatened to break down. Examples include not only King Mindon of Burma, but also the kings of fourteenth and fifteenth century Chieng Mai and Sukhothai in Thailand. Some rulers looked without finding anything. Rāma V, while planning his reform program, had his Dhamma department survey the known wilderness monasteries throughout his kingdom in hopes of finding a meditation tradition worthy of royal patronage, but the survey turned up nothing but Tantric and Brahmanical practices. This convinced him that the path to nibbāna was no longer being pursued, and that the only avenue open to him was to support the study of the texts. Still, the noteworthy point is that the wilderness was the first place to which he turned.

The wilderness has long played an important, if ambivalent, role in the societies of South and Southeast Asia. On the one hand, it is a place of danger: wild animals, disease, outlaws, malevolent spirits, and treacherous temptations. On the other hand, it is where the Buddha attained Awakening, a place where truths transcending social conventions may be found and brought back to reform the social order. Throughout Theravādin history, the concept of wilderness Buddhism has carried the same ambivalence. On the one hand, the wilderness is a place of heterodoxy, where hermits and strange cults go to escape societal norms, and from which messianic movements arise to challenge the political order. On the other hand, the wilderness has spawned movements that reject the concerns of apadāna Buddhism and outdo the social norm in adhering to the Suttas and Vinaya.

This uncertainty as to whether the wilderness harbors orthodoxy or heterodoxy explains why the ruling elites tend not to look there for inspiration in stable times. But in unstable times, they are more willing to take the risk. Sometimes their motives for going to the wilderness are less than pure, as when King Mindon turned to wilderness monks for legitimization after his original ecclestiastical advisors had resigned their posts and retired to the Sagaing Hills in protest of his proposed monastic reforms. At other times, the motivation for looking to the wilderness may be more sincere, as was apparently the case with Rāma V, who had no issues with ecclesiastical authorities aside from their inability to organize proper monastic education systems. Either way, given that ruling elites go to the wilderness only when conditions are unstable, and given the extreme political and economic instability of post-colonial Asia, it is not surprising that wilderness movements have had a major voice in modern Thai Buddhism. Three examples will give some idea of the range of messages this voice has conveyed.

The oldest of the three is the Forest or *Kammaṭṭhāna* (Meditation) Tradition founded by Phra Ajaan Sao Kantasiilo (1861–1941) and Phra Ajaan Mun Bhūridatto (1870–1949) in the forests of northeastern Thailand. Members of this movement—mostly belonging to the Dhammayut sect, although there is also a Mahānikāya offshoot—are renowned for their asceticism, their strict adherence to the Vinaya, and their meditative powers. The movement took its original inspiration from a handful of texts resulting from missions to Sri Lanka sponsored by Rāma IV: a Thai synopsis of Buddhaghosa's Vinaya commentary, a chapter from the *Visuddhimagga* on the *dhutaṅga* or ascetic practices, and the canonical *Discourse on Mindfulness Immersed in the Body* (MN 119), which teaches breath meditation and contemplation of the unattractiveness of the body as means for developing concentration and insight. However, aside from questions of Vinaya, the movement has a strong anti-scholastic bent. Many of its members insist that their primary teacher has been the wilderness itself. One of their most distinctive teachings is that nibbāna is not an ending of awareness, but a pure awareness beyond the five khandhas. Although already present, this awareness is radically different from the khandhas and from mental stillness, and can be reached only through intense effort. A common analogy is that of salt water: The pure water already present within salt water cannot be obtained simply by letting the water sit still, but requires the effort of distillation.

The Kammaṭṭhāna movement kept to the forests of north and northeastern Thailand during the early years of its existence, both in search of solitude and to avoid the dragnet of the government's attempts at monastic reforms at the turn of the twentieth century. In the 1950s, however, it began to emerge from the forests and to attract a sizable following in central Thailand. Soon it numbered among its supporters members of the ruling elite, including the royal family.

Another wilderness movement was started by Buddhadāsa Bhikkhu (1906–1993) in the 1930s. Disappointed with the state of monastic education in Bangkok, Buddhadāsa acquired a complete edition of the Pali Canon and returned to an abandoned monastery near his home in southern Thailand.

There he studied and meditated in seclusion; after a few years he began publishing books and giving public talks, eventually filling an entire room in the Thai National Library with his books. He also founded a meditation hermitage, Suan Mokh (the Garden of Liberation), which spawned a branch specifically for Westerners interested in meditation. He is best known for his attacks on animist and Brahmanical elements in Thai Buddhist practice, his translations from the Pali Canon, his researches into breath meditation, and his original teachings on the doctrine of dependent co-arising. According to his view, kamma and the factors of dependent co-arising bear fruit only instantaneously, and not over time; the Buddhist doctrine of rebirth applies only to the arising of the sense of "me and mine" within the mind; and the question of rebirth after death is irrelevant to the Buddha's teachings. Nibbāna is the absence of any sense of "me and mine," first experienced temporarily in moments of mental stillness, and then gradually lengthened through practice. Buddhadāsa attracted a following primarily among the nonruling, educated elite.

A third wilderness movement is Khao Suan Luang (Royal Park Mountain), a women's practice center founded in western Thailand in 1945 by Upāsikā Kee Nanayon (1901–1979). Upāsikā Kee was best known for her austere life style and for her teachings that recommended restraint of the senses, strong concentration, and insight gained through direct contemplation of the arising and passing away of mental states. She began publishing transcripts of her talks for free distribution in 1954, and her books have attracted a wide following.

All three of these movements agree that modern Thailand would benefit from abandoning the astrology, the animist beliefs, and the ritualized approach to kamma present in popular Buddhism, from closer adherence to the Five Precepts, and from more meditation, both for the monks and the laity. They all tend to side with the Dhamma as taught in the early Suttas as opposed to the merit-making concerns of the apadānas. They also agree that the way to nibbāna is still open, in contradistinction to the view that became common after King Rāma V's survey, that nibbāna was no longer a realistic possibility. Otherwise, though, their prescriptions for modern Thai Buddhism differ considerably.

The Kammaṭṭhāna tradition maintains that a monk's primary duty is to abandon the defilements binding him to saṁsāra; he should concern himself with helping society only when he has put his own house in order. On a practical level, teachers in this tradition have advised their supporters among the ruling elite to eschew political corruption and to work for a more equal distribution of economic opportunity throughout the Thai countryside, but until recently they espoused no particular social or political program. After Thailand's economic collapse in 1997, however, the government—on the advice of the International Monetary Fund (IMF)—began relaxing rules against foreign ownership of Thai companies. Fearing that this would lead to the end of Thailand's independence, the most senior member of the Kammaṭṭhāna tradition—Ajaan Maha Boowa Ñāṇasampanno (b. 1913)—began a six-year national donation drive to establish a fund that would underwrite the Thai currency. Millions of dollars were raised, but Ajaan Maha Boowa's complaints about how the pro-IMF government was handling the funds he had raised was one of the factors leading to that government's downfall.

In contrast, Buddhadāsa was very vocal and confrontational regarding social matters from the beginning of his teaching career. Because selfishness lies at the essence of suffering, he taught, monks and laity alike should meditate to reduce the sense of "I," but they cannot truly comprehend "not-self" unless they devote themselves at the same time to a life of selfless social service aimed at returning society to the moral principles inherent in nature.

Upāsikā Kee's following has remained firmly apolitical, on the grounds that political confrontations would involve them in fruitless entanglements, but their mere existence as an active, highly visible community is in itself a repudiation of the limited role that mainstream Thai Buddhism has traditionally assigned to women.

These voices have in the past few decades found a significant hearing throughout Thai Buddhism and have begun to spark a renewed interest in meditation among monks, nuns, and lay people in rural and urban areas. At the same time, however, the message from these voices has been compromised somewhat by the fact that, as they grow more popular, wilderness movements become increasingly co-opted and domesticated. This pattern has occurred repeatedly in the past, and anthropologists have already noticed signs of its reoccurrence in the Kammaṭṭhāna tradition. The typical life story of a famous teacher falls into four phases: wandering through the forest; setting up a small, unofficial hermitage; developing the hermitage into an established monastery as the teacher gains renown; and finally enshrining the teacher's bodily relics in a stūpa after his death. With this fourth stage, apadāna patterns of merit-making begin to dominate the life of the monastery, especially during the annual commemoration surrounding the stūpa on the date of the teacher's passing away. In the past, when this process reached a point of total domestication, the traditional recourse was to look for new movements from the forest. At present, though, the forests are rapidly disappearing, and many people have begun to look to the concrete jungle of the cities to provide the next wave of reforms in Thai Buddhism.

7.5.3 Buddhism in the City

A great deal of Buddhism as practiced in Bangkok and other urban centers is simply village Buddhism transported to a new locale. However, the combined effects of globalization, Western-style education, and modern mass media have created new classes of urban Thais whose religious needs and expectations cannot be met by village Buddhism. Thus new forms of Buddhism have arisen in response. Here we will focus on three developments: the rise of monastic schools following the Western model; the rise of lay meditation groups; and the rise of new urban cults. We will also look at a recent controversy that pitted city monks against wilderness monks and poses questions for the future of Thai Buddhism.

Many of the older monasteries of Bangkok were established when urban Buddhism differed little, if at all, from village Buddhism. In recent decades, however, the example of Christian missionaries in establishing Western-style schools for the children of wealthy Thais has led many of the established monasteries to counter with an educational program of their own: establishing Western-style schools for monks and novices. What began as a few scattered schools has grown into an educational system paralleling that of the government, beginning with elementary schools and ending with graduate programs. These schools, for the most part, attract the sons of peasants and workers who cannot afford the costs of public education, and the background of these students is reflected in the fact that the Mahānikāya university for monks, Mahāchulalongkorn, has one of the most leftist student bodies in Bangkok. Many young men will ordain for the duration of their education and disrobe on graduation. Some conservative Thais have deplored the emphasis on worldly subjects offered at these schools, but the schools have succeeded in channeling donations from the upper classes to provide an avenue of upward mobility that otherwise would have been closed to the sons of poor families.

A development that responds more to the needs of the upper classes is the rise of lay meditation groups associated with government ministries, housing developments, universities, or corporations. Thus, the Ministry of Industry has a weekly meditation group, as do Esso and the Electricity Generating Authority of Thailand. Monks—usually from the Kammaṭṭhāna tradition—are frequently invited to teach to these groups; during their time in Bangkok, they tend to stay, not in established temples, but in small, unofficial hermitages built by lay supporters in quieter enclaves on the outskirts of the city. These hermitages are urban versions of the unofficial, makeshift monastic residences in the wilderness that housed the Kammaṭṭhāna movement during its formative years.

The most controversial development in urban Thai Buddhism has been the rise of new cults focused on monasteries that shape their programs specifically to meet the needs and expectations of the new middle and upper classes. The most successful of these cults is centered on Wat Phra Dhammakāya, established in 1975 on a large tract of land to the north of the city. Founded by two monks, Phra Dhammajayo and Phra Dattajīvo, under the spiritual guidance of a nun, Mae Chi Jan Khonnokyoong, the monastery takes its name both from a meditation technique and from a cosmological principle. Dhammakāya as a meditation technique is a practice whereby one visualizes a small crystal ball within the body and then visualizes an image of oneself inside the ball. The transparency of the image, together with its mode of dress, is taken as a sign of one's spiritual attainment. As a cosmological principle, however, the Dhammakāya is said to be the basic force that created the world. Shortly after the creation, it split into two halves: the white Dhammakāya, a force of good; and the black Dhammakāya, a force of destruction. According to the teachings of the cult, the black Dhammakāya is currently ascendant, and so the white Dhammakāya has been embodied in Phra Dhammajayo to save the world and to make the Dhammakāya temple the center of a new world Buddhism.

These teachings have sparked sharp controversy, as have the temple's methods of proselytizing. Following the lead of the many new religions in Japan (see Section 10.9), Dhammakāya applies the management and marketing techniques of a modern business corporation to the most popular layer of folk Buddhism: the economy of merit. Direct-marketing sales teams are trained to inform the public of opportunities to make merit with the temple and to enlist new members. Fund-raising efforts have been so successful that they raised 30 billion baht to construct an enormous stūpa meant to provide the movement with the perfections needed to ward off its enemies. Special opportunities to make merit and develop perfections are promoted in ways reminiscent of the promises found in the apadānas. Recently the temple offered a Millionaire Forever program, through which those who make a lifetime pledge of 1,000 baht per month to the temple's food fund are guaranteed to be millionaires every lifetime until they reach nibbāna. The temple advertises itself as the ideal merit-field: Not only is the leader of the movement an embodiment of a cosmological principle, but Mae Chi Jan, during her lifetime, was said to have frequent audience with the Buddha through her meditation, during which she could present him with rarefied versions of the offerings made to the temple.

Despite the controversy surrounding the temple's teachings and methods, they contain elements that appeal to many modern Thais. Contact with Western-style education and the Western mass media has given many Thais a sense of the powerlessness of their country as it is buffeted by amoral global economic forces beyond its control. At the same time, Bangkok's rapid growth has created a society that is increasingly impersonal and materialistic, devoid of any sense of purposeful community. Dhammakāya doctrine, however, promises the Thai nation a direct contact with the basic principle underlying the universe, together with a central role in the moral drama of the human race. Its merit-making celebrations and other programs create a happy, purposeful sense of community similar to that which we noted in connection with the early stūpa cult (see Section 3.7). In particular, although it has attracted few of the traditional elites, it has attracted many of the new elites made wealthy by the economic boom of the 1980s and 1990s, providing them with a public way of devoting their newfound wealth to a purpose larger than themselves. And the organization's very success breeds success. Obviously well funded—with a lavish, modern campus; a polite, educated, and disciplined staff; and a professional command of the mass media—the temple displays all the signs of having achieved the perfections that, as a merit-field, it promises to its followers.

Thus urban Thai Buddhism currently has three sorts of centers: traditional monasteries, unofficial mini-forest hermitages, and modern cult centers. For the past 40 years, the ecclesiastical authorities—who reside in traditional monasteries—have viewed the two alternative forms with waxing and waning concern, and have tried to exert more control over the situation. The current Sangha leadership, for example, claims to possess evidence that Phra Dhammajayo used Dhammakaya funds to buy land in his own name, and the case currently languishes in the courts. In 2002, an up-and-coming generation of Sangha leaders proposed legislation for tightening control over the Sangha, some of whose provisions would have meant the end of the Kammaṭṭhāna tradition and would have stifled the growth of any wilderness movement to take its place. The proposal was voted down in parliament, but the fight is not over.

However these issues are resolved, the stakes are high for Buddhism throughout the country. In the past, when settled areas were islands in the larger sea of wilderness, the wilderness always provided a source for individual or social reform when the state of the Sangha deteriorated in the cities. Now that wilderness areas have been reduced to islands in a sea of settled land, it is not clear that they will be able to continue playing that role.

8

Buddhism in Central Asia and China

CENTRAL ASIA

8.1 THE DHARMA TRAVELS THE SILK ROAD

Central Asia's contribution to the history of Buddhism lies largely in its role as an intermediary in the spread of the Dharma to East Asia and Tibet. However, beginning with the third century B.C.E. and lasting in some areas until the eleventh century C.E., people in the area practiced the religion for their own benefit, created Buddhist art for their own enjoyment and edification, and spread the Dharma not because it was an outside force flowing through their territory, but because it had made an important contribution to their own lives. Unfortunately, the ravages of weather and warfare have left few traces of Buddhism's former presence, but those traces attest to a vibrant and sophisticated culture.

The earliest archaeological evidence of any Buddhist activity in Central Asia consists of two Aśokan inscriptions in Afghanistan. Otherwise, there is no sign of Buddhist missionary presence in Central Asia during this time, although legends in the kingdom of Khotan, located in what is now the southern portion of eastern Turkestan, claim that Aśoka's son, Kustana, founded the kingdom in 240 B.C.E; and that Aśoka's great grandson, Vijayasabhāva, championed Buddhism there.

The earliest evidence for any Buddhist missionary activity in Central Asia dates from the Kushan empire, which we have discussed in Section 4.1. During its three centuries of rule, the Kushan empire ranked among the four major powers of the world, alongside Parthia, Rome, and China. In terms of cultural sophistication, it was the greatest empire Central Asia has ever seen. The stability it brought to the region facilitated the movement of goods and ideas along the major trade routes, including the north–south route from India into Bactria and Sogdia, and the east–west route from Persia into China, called the Silk Road after the most prized commodity that traveled west along the road.

After the fall of the Kushans in the middle of the third century, the region was fragmented politically and subject to occasional invasions by the Ephthalite Huns. The movement of ideas and goods along the Silk Road, however, increased. Originating in what is now western Iran and continuing south of the Caspian Sea, the Silk Road divided into two routes at Kashgar in the Tarim Basin, with a northern route leading through Samarkand and a southern one along the Amu River. The two routes reunited in northwest China at the city of Tun-huang, in Kansu province. Reports from Chinese travelers tell us that the city-states of Kucha, Turfan, and others along the northern route of the Silk Road belonged primarily to the Sarvāstivādin school, whereas Khotan was a stronghold of the Mahāyāna. Chinese travelers left detailed reports of the Buddhist festivals celebrated there and had high praise for the decorum and discipline of Khotanese monks. One of the few Buddhist texts undoubtedly composed in Central Asia—the *Book of Zambasta*—was written in Khotan. It contains an eclectic mix of Indian Buddhist myths and an idealist version of Yogācāra philosophy, maintaining that all dharmas, including ignorance and wisdom, are ultimately unreal. Fragmentary murals found in Khotan depicting maṇḍalas centered on Mahāvairocana suggest that Yoga Tantras also were practiced there.

During this period, Chinese pilgrims, convinced of the need to obtain Buddhist texts directly from India rather than through Central Asian intermediaries, began making the long, arduous journey overland to India. First among these pilgrims was the Chinese monk Fa-hsien, who reached India in 400 C.E. The last pilgrims were also the most famous: Hsüan-tsang and I-ching, who made separate journeys in the seventh century shortly before the Tibetans closed the route. This period also marks the high point in the history of the major translation center at Tun-huang. First settled by the Chinese during the Han dynasty (202 B.C.E.–220 C.E.), Tun-huang had for centuries been home to a cosmopolitan population. As the Chinese demand for Buddhist texts grew, monk-scholars of many nationalities formed translation teams to meet the demand. Prominent among these teams was the group of Indians and Chinese who gathered around Dharmarakṣa (b. 230), a native of Tun-huang born of Yüeh-chih parents.

Tun-huang became not only a translation center but also a center of Buddhist art, known especially for its cave temples. The largest of these is the Cave of a

Thousand Buddhas (Ch'ien-fo Tung), dating from 366 C.E. Today 492 caves still exist, with elaborately painted frescoes accompanied by statues ranging from barely 1 inch to 109 feet in height. More than six hundred additional caves are located in the surrounding region.

The seventh century was the beginning of a new period in Central Asian Buddhist history as Tibet suddenly rose to become the major power in the area. Originally the destroyers of the Buddhist monasteries and libraries they encountered in their conquests, the Tibetans quickly converted to the religion and became its avid protectors. Their first contact with Buddhism was in Khotan, but in 787 they captured Tun-huang. The Tibetan king at the time, an avid Buddhist, arranged for the learned monks at Tun-huang to translate Buddhist texts into Tibetan and to answer his questions on the Dharma. Murals in the Tun-huang caves attest to the Tibetan kings' having also sponsored Buddhist art at the center.

The Tibetan empire collapsed in the middle of the ninth century, with much of its Central Asian territory taken over by the Uighur Turks. Meanwhile, Islam had begun making mass conversions in western Central Asia in the eighth century, and by the eleventh had swept throughout the region. Only the Uighurs, who had converted to Buddhism from Manichaeism and had settled in Turfan, resisted Islamic influence. The Chinese recaptured Tun-huang in the eleventh century, but danger from marauding attackers forced them to seal a library in one of the caves. This was to have great consequences for the study of Buddhism in the twentieth century.

In the thirteenth and fourteenth centuries, the Mongols under Genghis Khan conquered the region, destroying whatever religious culture they found. Although they eventually converted to the Tibetan form of Buddhism (see Section 11.4), the Mongols made no effort to impose their religion on their subjects. Thus Central Asia remained Muslim. The Silk Road was reopened, with the Mongol chieftains boasting that an unescorted virgin with a hoard of gold could travel from one end of the road and arrive at the other with both gold and virginity intact. India, however, was no longer exporting Buddhism, so the Dharma no longer traveled the road. After the fall of the Mongol empire, the Silk Road fell into disuse as newly opened sea routes offered a passage that was quicker and safer.

This, however, was not the end of Central Asian Buddhist history. In 1907–1908, the sealed cave at Tun-huang was discovered and reopened, yielding an invaluable treasure of 20,000 drawings and manuscripts dating from the fifth through the eleventh centuries. Among them was the world's oldest printed book, a Chinese translation of the *Diamond Sūtra* dated to 868 C.E. The collection contained manuscripts in a variety of languages, both living and dead, ranging from translations, historical documents, contracts, and financial statements to songs, poems, and Sūtras. These texts have been extremely helpful for filling in gaps in Buddhist history, especially concerning the development of the early Ch'an school in China (see Section 8.5.5) and the first centuries of Tibetan Buddhism (see Section 11.2.1). More recently, manuscript fragments of Mainstream Buddhist canons dating from the first century C.E., the oldest known Buddhist manuscripts, have been found in Afghanistan. Thus, although Buddhism is no longer practiced in Central Asia, the traces of Buddhism preserved there continue to play a role in rewriting Buddhist history.

CHINA

8.2 A GRAND ASSIMILATION

The Chinese encounter with Buddhism is one of the most momentous stories of intercultural assimilation in human history. Buddhism is now such an integral part of Chinese culture that it is easy to forget that Buddhism was a very foreign import when it was first brought to China, and that five centuries passed before the Chinese felt that they had a full picture of what it had to offer. Of all the Asian civilizations to which Buddhism spread outside of India, China's was by far the most sophisticated, complex, and ethnocentric, with its own thoroughly developed system of social organization, religious ideology, and speculative thought. Nevertheless, many Chinese individuals felt that Buddhism had something new and valuable to offer them in terms of devotionalism, doctrine, meditation techniques, and the vocational opportunities offered by the monastic Sangha.

The Sangha, in particular, was Buddhism's most revolutionary contribution to Chinese society, as well as the most controversial. Chinese thought and practice had traditionally located the sacred within the realm of family, state, and social relationships, whereas the Sangha embodied the ideal of leaving not only one's home but also one's role within the civil society for the sake of inward cultivation. The Sangha, however, was not totally anti-family or anti-state. In India, in had become an intermediary for transferring merit to dead ancestors, and monastics had given help to royal courts, acting as advisers, diplomats, and ritual specialists. In China, members of the Sangha also took on these roles, but many court officials, offended by what they saw as the Sangha's baleful effect on family traditions and the state economy, found these efforts at conciliation even more insidious. For centuries, they protested the Sangha's power and occasionally succeeded in mounting purges. Nevertheless, the Sangha repeatedly revived and still exists in China, whereas the imperial courts are gone.

Many writers have stressed the extent to which the Chinese, in absorbing Buddhism into their culture, changed it and made it their own, adding elements borrowed from Confucianism, Taoism, and local spirit cults. Much of this adaptation is due to the sophistication of Chinese culture: Unlike other lands in Asia who adopted Buddhism, the Chinese did not regard it as a bringer of refined culture, for they had a strong sense that their culture was equally, if not more, refined. Thus Chinese converts to the religion had to explain it to themselves and their fellow Chinese in a way that would meet their own standards of intelligibility. Still, granted that Chinese Buddhists made changes in their religion, it is important not to underestimate their willingness for their religion to change them, as they made a sincere effort to master the practices of generosity, the Buddhist precepts, meditation, the close study of the texts, and the often strenuous demands of Buddhist devotionalism. Some Chinese Buddhists, braving many dangers, even journeyed overland or by sea to India to bring back the definitive word on the Dharma.

Many of the creative Chinese contributions to Buddhism were an effort, not to add something Chinese to Buddhism, but to work out tensions and fill in gaps already there within Buddhism itself. For instance, the great multisystem philosophical schools of Chinese Buddhism, so distinctively Chinese, owe their existence at least in part to the disorganized way Buddhism was brought to China. Individual missionary monks would arrive from India or Central Asia, advocating a wide variety of devotional and meditational practices, and promoting a random mixture of Mainstream and Mahāyāna texts, all claiming to originate from the Buddha. At the same time, the doctrines and practices of the religion were undergoing continual changes in India, sparking new waves of missionary activity, contradicting earlier ones. This forced the Chinese to construct their own frameworks to give order to the ensuing confusion, so that they could choose the most efficacious doctrines and practices for defining and meeting their needs.

Thus the process of assimilation went both ways. Had the Chinese not been able to translate Buddhist practice into terms familiar to themselves, the religion would have remained nothing more than an exotic curiosity. Had it not offered them something useful, new, and unique, they would not have even been curious. As we survey the history of the Chinese adaptation and assimilation of Buddhism, it is useful to keep these points in mind.

8.3 BUDDHISM ON THE FRINGES OF SOCIETY

Chinese Buddhists preserved a story that their religion was first brought to China at the instigation of an emperor of the Later Han dynasty, Ming Ti (r. 58–75 C.E.), whose curiosity about Buddhism had been piqued by a portentous dream. Historical records, however, indicate that the religion was more likely brought into Han China by Central Asian merchants, who set up monasteries in their enclaves in the major Chinese cities and invited Central Asian monks to staff them. The first reference to Buddhism in imperial historical records, nevertheless, does date from the reign of Ming Ti. The records tell of a Chinese nobleman who combined the "gentle Buddhist rites and fasts" with Taoist practices aimed at physical immortality. The first reference to the appearance of Buddhist statues in the imperial court, dating from the second century C.E., follows a similar pattern. A Taoist adept added Buddhist rituals to a program of Taoist rites to bless the emperor. The connection between Buddhism and Taoism was justified by a story that began circulating in China during this period, claiming that the Buddha was actually the Taoist sage Lao-tzu, who had gone west at one point in his career to teach the barbarians. The Buddhists may have originally welcomed this story, for it made their religion seem less of a foreign import. Eventually, as they began asserting their own separate identity, they found the story increasingly objectionable, but not until the thirteenth century were they able to establish once and for all that it was a fabrication.

The first reference to a Buddhist monastery in China, dating from the middle of the second century C.E., also contains the first explicit description of one of the Buddhist rites practiced during these first centuries: the washing of a Buddha-image, a rite that was to enjoy long-term popularity in East Asia (see

Section 8.7.3). The second century was also when the first Buddhist texts were translated into Chinese. The Parthian monk An Shih-kao reached the Chinese capital of Lo-yang in 148 and began translating a set of texts dealing with meditation practices, such as breath awareness, and numerical lists of Dharma topics, including the Wings to Awakening. An Shih-kao was not fluent in Chinese, so a strategy was devised whereby he would recite the text to a bilingual interpreter, who would then transmit it to a group of Chinese, who would then discuss points of interpretation and produce a polished final copy. This was the procedure that similar teams of translators were to follow until the seventh century. Another translator, Lokakṣema, was the first known Mahāyāna missionary. Working in Lo-yang between 168 and 188, he effected the first translation of a Perfection of Discernment text into Chinese and recruited the first Chinese monk.

The quality of the first few generations of translations was mixed, due to the inherent difficulty of translating into a sophisticated language such as Chinese, whose technical terms already packed a heavy load of connotations picked up from native philosophical traditions. Thus, for instance, in the early years the word *Tao,* the Way—which in Taoism meant the underlying essence of all things—was used to translate *bodhi, yoga, Dharma,* and *mārga* (path). Other inaccuracies in translation were products of simple misunderstanding: *Skandha* (aggregate), for instance, was rendered as *yin,* the passive or receptive principle of nature. Not until the early fifth century was a fairly standardized and reliable system of translation equivalents devised.

The early fifth century also marked the point when the first complete Vinaya texts were made available through the efforts of Tao-an and Kumārajīva in the north, and Fa-hsien, Guṇavarman, and Saṅghavarman in the south. Prior to that time, the lack of such texts had hampered the Chinese Sangha in its organization and development.

The Later Han regime fell apart during the latter half of the second century and ended in 220, to be followed by a period in which three kingdoms vied unsuccessfully to reunite the empire. During this period, Buddhism began gaining converts among the peasants, the lower bureaucrats, and even the courts. Central Asian Buddhist monks claiming psychic abilities won many converts. Images of Buddhas and bodhisattvas—especially Maitreya, Amitābha, and Avalokiteśvara—played a central role both in devotion and in meditation practice. In fact, the religion as a whole became known as the "religion of images". The cult of the Buddha image was reportedly responsible even for some of the royal converts to Buddhism during this period. For instance, Sun Hao (r. 264–280), ruler of the kingdom of Wu, was originally anti-Buddhist. When a Buddha image was found in the park of his harem, he had it moved to his urinal where he performed his own version of the rite of washing the image, much to the amusement of his courtiers. Immediately stricken with a painful and mysterious disease, the story goes, he had to submit to the power of the Buddha and accept the Five Precepts.

The work of translation and evangelizing continued through the third century, culminating in the period when the empire was briefly reunited under the Western Chin dynasty (265–316). Dharmarakṣa (see Section 8.1), "the bodhisattva from Tun-huang," worked in north China from 266 to 308, completing a large number of translations, including the first Chinese versions of the *Lotus*

Sūtra and the *Perfection of Discernment in 25,000 Lines.* Recent scholarship, however, has shown that many of his translations were less accurate than the work of translators in previous centuries. Nevertheless, he gave extensive lectures, attracted numerous converts, ordained monks, and founded monasteries. Although the sacking of the capitals at Lo-yang and Ch'ang-an at the end of the Western Chin period destroyed many of the monasteries he had founded, it caused his disciples to disperse to other parts of the country, taking his teachings along with them.

8.4 BUDDHISM ENTERS THE MAINSTREAM OF CHINESE CULTURE

In 318 the Western Chin dynasty fell as non-Chinese tribes living in Chinese territory conquered the northern half of the empire, driving the ruling elites south to the area of the Yangtze River. This event ushered in the period of the northern and southern dynasties (318–589), during which the southern half of the empire was ruled by a series of native dynasties, whereas the north fell under a succession of sinicized "barbarian" rulers. The political division of the empire was reflected in a cultural division. The south tended to follow more traditional modes of Chinese culture; the north was more open to outside influences.

Buddhism made enormous advances in gaining adherents in both north and south. The institution of the Sangha provided a haven for men and women from all levels of society, including those orphaned by the sporadic warfare as well as those whose general exposure to hardship inspired them with the desire for a religious vocation. The sense of dislocation suffered by the elites at this time resembled that felt in India at the time of the Buddha. Many began questioning their cultural ideology and found that Buddhism had satisfactory answers for their questions. As a result, Buddhism was increasingly accepted into mainstream Chinese culture and began to have a major influence on the life and values of society as a whole.

The period was notable for two major developments. One was the institution of a Buddhist nuns' order. In 317, Chu Ching-chien (circa 292–361) was the first Chinese woman to take the novice's precepts. When joined by 24 other like-minded women, she founded a convent in Ch'ang-an. Soon other convents were founded in both north and south China. Not until 434, however, was the Bhikṣuṇī Sangha established on Chinese soil, when a group of Sri Lankan bhikṣuṇīs came specifically for that purpose. The ordination line they established has lasted in Chinese communities in Taiwan, Hong Kong, and Singapore to the present day.

The founding of the Bhikṣuṇī Sangha was a momentous event in the history of China, as it opened up for women the possibility of an institutional religious vocation free from domestic duties. Women with literary or religious talents could now devote their time to study, meditation, and devotion. Many nuns gained renown for their mastery of classical Chinese literature as well as Buddhist texts. Unfortunately, the rules of their order required that their convents be built within city walls; they thus incurred all the disadvantages of being close to the centers of political power. Open to charges of corruption when they were perceived as wielding too much influence in the imperial courts, they were among the first to bear the brunt of any imperial crackdowns on Buddhist monastic orders.

The other notable development during this period was the widespread conversion of the ruling elites to Buddhism, beginning in the early decades of the fourth century. Particularly in the south, sons and daughters of noble families, many of whom had been orphaned during the warfare at the end of the Western Chin, entered the monastic orders. Already versed in the Chinese classics, their urbanity and erudition helped in spreading the religion among their fellow members of the nobility, as they brought home the point that a Buddhist could be "one of us." Although many of the elite monks took ordination because of a true sense of spiritual need, some were attracted to the monastic life as a new version of the traditional life of the retired scholar, who chose a lifestyle of rustic simplicity to devote himself fully to art, literature, and philosophical conversation. As a result, Buddhist themes began appearing in the traditional scholar's domains of painting and literature during the fourth century.

The conversion of the elites, together with the continued spread of Buddhist devotion among the lower classes, brought about a three-way split in the modes of Sangha life: large monastic estates patronized by the ruling elites, smaller village monasteries, and forest hermitages for monks who focused on meditation and/or literary pursuits. In principle, the Sangha, in contrast to Chinese society in general, was relatively free of class distinctions. People from the lower classes who showed intellectual promise could find in the monastic orders an opportunity for a literary education that was otherwise closed to them. However, there was a general tendency for members of the smaller village monasteries to remain illiterate, their Buddhism an amalgam of devotional practices and local spirit cults. Similarly, in the forest hermitages there was little concern for the Vinaya, and the monks tended to combine the methods of Buddhist meditation with traditional Taoist practices aimed at immortality. Unlike the great monastic estates, the smaller monasteries and hermitages remained outside the pale of government control. These tendencies characterized Buddhism for many centuries in both the north and south.

On the level of elite Buddhism, however, the northern and southern kingdoms differed widely. In the south, the monks and nuns who frequented the court were members of the Chinese elite, moving naturally among their own kind, speaking the same language and inhabiting the same intellectual universe as the members of the court. The sense of fellow identity they were able to cultivate enabled them to succeed in exerting the independence of the Sangha from the political realm without engendering any sense of threat. In 340 and again in 402, the question arose as to whether monastics should pay deference to the emperor, and on both occasions the ultimate decision was that they should not. Occasionally the sense of easy familiarity between rulers and the aristocratic monks backfired. Po Yüan, the first Chinese monk known to have developed a personal friendship with a member of the imperial house, so impressed his host that he was asked to leave the Sangha and join the court. When he refused, he was whipped to death. The same fate befell his brother. On the whole, though, the relationship between the Sangha and the southern rulers was stable and secure.

Not so in the north. Northern elite Buddhism was largely a continuation of the earlier pattern, in which missionary monks were of foreign extraction and depended largely on their psychic powers to gain favor with the court. A prime example was Fo-t'u-teng, who arrived in north China from Kucha around 310. He served as court advisor for more than 20 years, performing magic, forecasting the future, mitigating the excesses of the barbarian rulers, and training a cadre of disciplined and enterprising Chinese monks. Fo-t'u-teng had no pretensions to being a scholar. The Buddhism that grew under his influence stressed devotion and meditation, rather than intellectual sophistication. The lack of class and racial fellowship between monks and rulers, however, meant that the relationship in the north was more volatile than in the south, with the government alternating between lavish support for and severe repression of the Sangha. Twice—in 446 and 574—edicts were issued for the total suppression of Buddhism, in response to complaints from government officials that the Sangha was growing too strong. However, because none of the rulers involved controlled all of China, the monastics could escape with copies of their scriptures to other parts of the empire. In both cases the repression was short-lived, as Buddhism had acquired widespread popular support, and in both cases the ruling dynasties did their best to make up for the harm that had been done. In 460, for example, the ruler of the Northern Wei dynasty (386–534) undertook the creation of one of the world's great religious monuments, the cave temples of Yün-kang, as an act of expiation for the earlier persecution.

Another long-lasting contribution to Chinese Buddhism had been made earlier by the founder of the Northern Wei dynasty, who appointed a moral and learned monk to the civil service post of Sangha director, thus establishing government jurisdiction over the monasteries in his realm. This arrangement was followed by all succeeding dynasties up to the twentieth century. Unlike the monks in the south, the appointed monk did not fight for the Sangha's independence from the state but paid deference to the emperor, justifying his action by identifying the emperor as an emanation of the Tathāgata.

However, the most important development of this period, in both the north and south, was Buddhism's new prominence in Chinese intellectual life. The first step in this process, begun by the elite monks of the south during the fourth century, was to apply Buddhist ideas to issues that had been raised in Confucian and Taoist intellectual circles during the third century. Ultimately, proponents of this "Buddho-Taoism" began to realize that they were distorting the Buddha's message and so began efforts to understand Buddhism on its own terms. This prepared the way for the great monk-translator Kumārajīva, who arrived in Ch'ang-an and inaugurated a period in which scholars focused on mastering Indian scholastic treatises and finding order in the much more extensive picture of Buddhism that resulted.

8.4.1 Buddho-Taoism

To understand Buddho-Taoism and its impact on the subsequent centuries of Buddhist thought in East Asia, it is necessary to backtrack and deal in some detail with the issues of third-century intellectual life in China. The third century had been a period of great philosophical activity in China, one that was to determine the vocabulary and values the Chinese used in trying to make Buddhism intelligible to themselves for many centuries afterward. Trained bureaucrats focused on what was, for them, the central issue of philosophy: the art of government. Because they felt that any successful government had to harmonize with the principles underlying nature, their discussions modulated quickly from social philosophy to metaphysics and back. The event that sparked their philosophizing—termed *hsüan hsüeh* (Speculative Metaphysics)—was the fall of the Han dynasty: Why had the dynasty failed even though it had been run in accordance with the teachings of the Confucian classics? Was there something wrong with these classics, or had they simply been misapplied?

The masters of Speculative Metaphysics decided that the problem lay primarily in the interpretation of the classics and not in the classics themselves. They made a distinction between the basic principles underlying the insights of the classic thinkers and the way in which those principles had been expressed. The more an expression took into account the particulars of the situation it addressed, the farther it was from the basic principle. Thus these masters of Speculative Metaphysics developed a preference for what later generations came to call "sudden" expressions—those that expressed in most immediate terms the basic principles—over "gradual" expressions, which made use of expedient means that in some cases were a necessary bridge from the principle to a particular situation, but in other situations might prove misleading. This preference carried over into the study and practice of Buddhism and may explain why many Buddhist thinkers and meditators later tried so hard to avoid any indication that their teachings were "gradual."

Once the principle underlying the text was separated from its expression, the question arose as to how the principle was to be grasped. Here Wang Pi (226–249) and other members of the first generation of masters of Speculative Metaphysics (called the proponents of "nonbeing") borrowed a concept from the Taoist texts: that the realm of differentiated and nameable phenomena, which they termed *being,* came from a common principle that was undifferentiated and unnameable, which they termed *nonbeing. Nonbeing* was the essence of all phenomena, whereas *being* was the function of *nonbeing.* Words were adequate for expressing phenomena, but not for their underlying principle. Again, this distinction between essence and function, and the strong sense that words were incapable of expressing underlying essences, were to play a large role in Chinese Buddhist thought.

Because nonbeing was the ultimate principle underlying not only the universe but also any form of government that attempted to harmonize with nature, the way to intuit this principle was for the Ruler to attain a frame of mind in touch with the undifferentiated and unnamed. Thus attuned, he would be able to make spontaneous decisions that, in a natural pattern of stimulus and response between Ruler and heaven, would lead to the harmony of society and the world of phenomena in general.

This line of thinking sparked a reaction from a group of intellectuals, led by Juan Chi (210–263), who insisted that if the same principle underlay all beings and could be touched by a completely natural mind, everyone had the ability to touch it and the right to do whatever came spontaneously. These thinkers practiced what they taught and became known for flouting almost every social convention imaginable. Although their position was never widely adopted, it remained an undercurrent in Chinese society in the belief that people who behave unconventionally are either insane or else directly in touch with a higher principle. This belief also had an effect on attitudes toward unconventional Buddhist meditation masters in later centuries.

However, solid pillars of society, such as Hsiang Hsiu (circa 221–300), could not countenance this call for anarchy, so they reformulated the basic principles of Speculative Metaphysics in response. Because they used these new principles to interpret Taoist classics as a way of undercutting their opponents, their thought has been termed neo-Taoism. In their day, however, the neo-Taoists were termed the proponents of "being." Their basic position was that there is no single underlying principle of the universe, and no difference between essence and function. Words are thus perfectly adequate for expressing the essence of things. Each individual thing or living being arises spontaneously, uncaused, with its own allotted place in the totality of things, its spontaneous nature being to function in its allotted way. Good and evil for different individuals are thus relative to how well they follow their individual function. Only the Sage (Ruler) has the allotment to know the allotment of all individuals under heaven, and to lie above their relative norms of good and evil. Thus only he has the right to be in a natural relationship of stimulus and response with the forces of heaven.

This reformulation succeeded in closing the door on anarchy and defending the status quo. However, it could not account for the source of the allotment of things and made the basic structure of the universe seem arbitrary and amoral. It was with regard to this point that many Chinese thinkers at the beginning of the fourth century realized that Buddhism had something to offer to their discussion. The doctrine of karma and rebirth offered a moral structure to the universe and to the pattern of stimulus and response between humanity and its environment, at the same time accounting for the allotment of all phenomena. Chinese monks—such as Chi Tun (314–366)—also realized that the Perfection of Discernment doctrines of emptiness and the two levels of truth were relevant to the discussion. Some of them discerned that the doctrine of emptiness agreed with the teachings claiming that things had no underlying essence—although nothing arose spontaneously—in that all things were part of an interdependent causal web. Others viewed emptiness as the essence from which all things came—like the Tao—and to which they would all return. These views resurfaced several centuries later and formed the basis for the great doctrinal syntheses of the sixth to ninth centuries.

The important development in the fourth century, however, was that Buddhism gained recognition as a source of solutions for issues that had been plaguing Chinese thought. The contribution of Chinese monks to these issues was also momentous in sociological terms. It ended the bureaucratic monopoly on metaphysical speculation, bringing it into the religious cloister, where the goal of speculation was more personal than political. In principle it also opened the role of Sage—the wise person who could attain a state of mind in touch with the basic essence of the universe, which had long been the Ruler's monopoly—to men and women from all levels of society. At the same time, this opening of roles did not pose the threat of anarchy, because the nature of that essence was expressed through the workings of karma, and thus thoroughly moral.

In the course of making this drastic shift in Chinese intellectual life, some of the monks responsible for Buddho-Taoism began to realize how little they actually understood Buddhism. Chief among them were Tao-an (312–385) and his disciple, Hui-yüan (334–circa 416). Tao-an was the most illustrious of Fo-t'u-teng's disciples. Driven from Ch'ang-an by civil war, he established a center in the south and joined the Buddho-Taoist discussions. As he collected and cataloged copies of the scriptures to aid in his work, he was struck by the gaps and inconsistencies in the various translations then available. When in 379 he was captured by northern forces and taken back to Ch'ang-an at the request of the new emperor, a Tibetan, he went back with a plan. He opened the first translation bureau to be granted imperial support and succeeded in attracting not only Indian monks knowledgeable in Buddhist texts but also a high-caliber team of Chinese scribes. Monks were dispatched to Khotan to bring back reliable texts. In the few years before his death, the bureau was able to translate an important body of literature, mostly Sarvāstivādin. In this it laid the groundwork for the major accomplishments of Kumārajīva, the monk-scholar from Kucha who was to change the face of Chinese Buddhist doctrine.

8.4.2 The Rise of Buddhist Scholasticism

Kumārajīva (344–413) was brought to Ch'ang-an in 401 as bounty from a military conquest. The son of an Indian nobleman and a Kuchean princess, he had ordained as a novice at an early age and traveled to India, together with his mother, who had been ordained as a nun, where he was converted to Madhyamaka doctrines. Famous in China for his command of Buddhist doctrine even before his capture, Kumārajīva inaugurated an extensive translation project in cooperation with hundreds of monks. The quality of their work far surpassed that of previous translators in terms of accuracy, intelligibility, and elegance. Even though they were still flawed on technical points, many of these translations are highly regarded even today as exemplars of the old translation style, in preference to the later and more accurate new translation style developed in the seventh century by Hsüan-tsang (circa 596–664). Kumārajīva's lyrical version of the *Lotus Sūtra,* for example, has been chanted daily by millions of Buddhists throughout East Asia for centuries.

Kumārajīva's contributions to Chinese Buddhism, however, went beyond the translation of texts. He lectured his translation team and other audiences on the importance of understanding Buddhist ideas in their original doctrinal context. Although he translated a variety of Mahāyāna and—at the request of his captors—Mainstream texts, his specialty was Madhyamaka. In his commentaries, prefaces, and lectures, he gave his Chinese disciples a thorough grounding in the subject. Although his school of disciples was scattered by an invasion of Ch'ang-an in 420, this disbanding had the long-term effect of disseminating his ideas throughout China, inaugurating a new era in Chinese Buddhist studies. During the fifth and sixth centuries, monks formed study groups specializing in particular texts: Madhyamaka treatises, Vinaya texts (Sarvāstivādin and Dharmaguptaka), Yogācāra treatises, the *Lotus Sūtra,* and the *Mahāyāna Mahāparinirvāṇa Sūtra* (*or Nirvāṇa Sūtra* for short), among others. Even two Mainstream texts—the *Abhidharmakośa* and the *Satyasiddhi* (a text of the Bahuśrutīya offshoot of the Mahāsaṃghikas)—attracted followings, although these were eventually absorbed into Mahāyāna schools. Some monks specialized in single texts; others traveled from group to group to broaden their learning. Eventually these study groups either died out in China or else were absorbed into the multisystem schools of later centuries. A few of them were exported to Korea and Japan, where they have maintained a separate existence up to the present day.

Of these study groups, the one devoted to Madhyamaka treatises came the closest to becoming a distinct tradition. Termed the *San-lun,* or *Three Treatise,* tradition, the group took its name from three Madhyamaka treatises translated by Kumārajīva: the *Chung lun (Treatise on the Middle Way),* which contained Nāgārjuna's MMK together with a commentary by Piṅgala; the *Po lun (Hundred Treatise),* a commentary on the *Four Hundred Stanzas* by Āryadeva, Nāgārjuna's pupil; and the *Shih-erh men lun (Twelve Topics Treatise),* a text unknown in the Indian and Tibetan traditions. A fourth text that was also authoritative for the San-lun group was the *Ta-chih-tu lun (Great Perfection of Discernment Treatise),* a massive commentary to the *Pañca* attributed by Kumārajīva to Nāgārjuna. As we have noted (see Section 5.3.3), there is no evidence that Nāgārjuna actually wrote this text, and many scholars believe that it was at least partly composed by Kumārajīva himself. No works by later Indian Madhyamaka thinkers, such as Bhāvaviveka or Candrakīrti, were ever translated into Chinese, which explains why Chinese Madhyamaka studies developed in very different directions from those pursued in India and Tibet.

The respect for Buddhist texts paradoxically spawned a number of apocryphal translations—texts composed in Chinese that claimed to be translations from Sanskrit—as individual thinkers tried to bestow the authority of scripture on their own understanding of Buddhist doctrine. Foremost among these texts was *The Awakening of Faith in the Mahāyāna,* attributed to Aśvaghoṣa (see Section 4.5), which espoused a doctrine of the One Mind from which all things came. This text was apparently written in response to one of the major issues of the time—how to understand the various Buddhist theories of mind, and in particular the relationship between the fundamental basis of mind and phenomenal reality—and was to play a major role in shaping the Ch'an and Hua-yen schools.

As Chinese scholars gained greater familiarity with Buddhist texts during this period, they were confronted with further issues, among them the question as to whether some beings were ineligible for Buddhahood. This particular issue, sparked by an incomplete translation of the *Nirvāṇa Sūtra,* was settled only after a more complete translation of the text came to light. This incident demonstrated that not all available translations were totally reliable, and that there was a continued need to return to the source. However, even in the more trustworthy translations there were many points of contradiction. Because all the Sūtras claimed to come from the Buddha, many scholars sought a comprehensive system for resolving the differences among them. In their eyes, none of the Indian philosophical schools provided the framework they were looking for. The Mainstream schools could not accommodate the Mahāyāna teachings; Madhyamaka could not accommodate such teachings as the *Gaṇḍavyūha* vision of emptiness, or the tathāgata-garbha, which the Chinese interpreted as *fo-hsing* (Buddha-nature); and Yogācāra could not accommodate the universality of the Buddha-nature, as taught in the *Nirvāṇa* and *Lotus Sūtras.*

So these scholars turned from the scholastic treatises to the Mahāyāna Sūtras themselves, which furnished the rudiments of an explanation: The Buddha used his tactical skill to teach different doctrines to suit the conditions of his various audiences at different points in his career. This interpretation struck a responsive chord, as it fit in with the distinction, derived from Speculative Metaphysics, between basic principles and their expression. That the Mahāyāna Sūtras were the ones offering this explanation is one of the factors that assured the ascendancy of Mahāyāna over Mainstream in Chinese thought; that they were Sūtras espousing universal Buddhahood helps explain why this doctrine gained much more currency in Chinese than in Indian Mahāyāna.

One of the first proposals for ordering Buddhist doctrines based on this insight was offered by Hui-kuang (468–537). According to him, the Buddha taught four essential doctrines, in ascending order of sophistication: (1) the Abhidharma doctrine that phenomena arise in accordance with causes and conditions, a doctrine taught to counteract the view of spontaneous origination; (2) the Satyasiddhi doctrine that phenomena are no more than mere names, as they cannot exist independently of causes and conditions; (3) the Madhyamaka doctrine that even names are empty because there are no substantial phenomena underlying them; and (4) the doctrine of the ever-abiding Buddha-nature that constitutes the ultimate reality, taught by the *Nirvāṇa* and *Avataṃsaka Sūtras,* among others. This attempt to provide a comprehensive framework for all Buddhist teachings laid the groundwork for the great doctrinal syntheses of the Sui and T'ang dynasties.

8.5 THE SUI AND T'ANG DYNASTIES (581–907)

An avowed Buddhist—Wen-ti (r. 581–604)—succeeded in reuniting the empire in 589, partly through a conscious policy of promoting Buddhism combined with Confucianism as a unifying ideology. Although the Sui dynasty he founded fell in 617, the T'ang dynasty that replaced it lasted for almost three centuries. Thus Buddhism was faced with a new situation: For the first time since it had entered the mainstream of Chinese civilization, the empire was united. This proved to be a mixed blessing. In the area of doctrine and meditation practice, the Chinese finally mastered the Buddhist tradition and made it their own. Many of the great scholars and meditators whose reputations were to assume legendary proportions in Chinese Buddhism—Hsüan-tsang, Chih-i, Fa-tsang, Hui-neng, and Lin-chi, among others—flourished during this time. In the institutional area, however, because political power was concentrated in a single ruling house with authority over the entire empire, the Sangha was more exposed to the whims of a small handful of people. This was ultimately to prove disastrous.

Although Wen-ti had enforced throughout the empire the southern principle that monastics need not pay deference to government officials, he adopted the northern tradition of state control over the Sangha. The T'ang ruling house claimed to be descended from the Taoist sage Lao-tzu, so their general sentiments were not pro-Buddhist. A few of the rulers converted to Buddhism and lavished enormous donations on the Sangha, only to be followed by successors who felt the need to undo their predecessors' excesses and bring the religion back in line. In the first two centuries of the dynasty, however, anti-Buddhist measures were fairly circumscribed. The religion had broad support outside of the court, and rulers feared that excessively harsh measures would backfire.

One of the highlights of the first century of the T'ang occurred in 645, when the pilgrim-monk Hsüan-tsang (596–664) returned from his journey to India bringing more than 675 Buddhist texts. The story of his journey fired the imagination of the Chinese people, and they gave him a hero's welcome on his arrival at Ch'ang-an. Gaining imperial support for a translation team to render his collection of texts into Chinese, he ultimately converted the emperor, T'ai-tsung (r. 626–649), to Buddhism. Sadly, he lived to translate only a small portion of the texts he had brought back. His translation team was undoubtedly the most talented ever assembled on Chinese soil. He and his coworkers developed a new, more accurate vocabulary for rendering Buddhist ideas into Chinese, but only one text using this vocabulary—the *Heart Sūtra,* a compendium of Perfection of Discernment teachings—ever gained popularity. At his death, the reigning emperor, whose personal admiration for Hsüan-tsang did not extend to Buddhism, ordered the translation team disbanded and the remaining untranslated texts placed in an imperial library. They were never translated. The Yogācāra school founded by Hsüan-tsang—called Fa-hsiang (Dharma Characteristic)—survived no more than a century in China. This was due partly to its unpopular assertion that not all beings were eligible for Buddhahood, and partly to concerted attacks from the Hua-yen school, its major competitor for imperial patronage. However, the school did continue in Korea and Japan. Hsüan-tsang's influence on Chinese Buddhism lived on less in his scholarship than in the tales that developed around his journey, which provided the model for the classic novel *Journey to the West* (see Section 8.7).

Another landmark in the Buddhist history of the T'ang was the reign of Empress Wu (circa 625–706). Beginning her life in court as a concubine of Emperor T'ai-tsung and continuing as the major wife of his son, Wu Chao skillfully maneuvered herself into a position of power before her husband's death by eliminating her rivals. Not content to rule as regent for her son, she declared herself emperor and established a new dynasty. Unable to gain support from Taoists or Confucians, she sought to solidify her precarious position as a woman ruler by claiming to be the incarnation of Maitreya and actively cultivating the support of the Sangha, who obliged her by reporting omens and claiming to have discovered texts that justified her rule. Although much of this activity was of dubious benefit to the religion, she did sponsor important translation teams—on occasion working as a scribe herself—and actively patronized the Ch'an and Hua-yen schools.

After Empress Wu was driven from the throne in 705, a descendent of the original T'ang line, Hsüan-tsung (r. 712–756), came to power, determined to correct what he viewed as the Sangha's abuse of its privileged position. Although many imperially supported monasteries had used their wealth for charitable purposes, such as alms houses for the poor, there were genuine abuses that needed correcting. Many monks and nuns had become ordained simply to evade taxation and live comfortably off the generosity of lay donors. Some monasteries were blatant business enterprises, occupying prime commercial locations near markets. Others, called "merit cloisters", were tax havens for the aristocrats who had built them and who were still receiving proceeds from the land. One of Hsüan-tsung's first moves to regulate Buddhism was a "sifting and weeding" of the monastics on imperial rosters. More than thirty thousand monks and nuns were defrocked, approximately one-fourth of the registered monastics in the empire. Although Hsüan-tsung planned further moves against the Sangha, these were prevented by political developments.

Ironically, during this selective purge Hsüan-tsung had begun to patronize Tantric Buddhist missionaries, Indian initiates into the Yoga Tantras (see Section 6.2.1). Chinese Tantrism, called *Chen-yen,* or Truth-Word, flourished at the court for a little less than a century, during which time its initiates performed rituals for producing rain and protecting the state. Archaeologists have uncovered lavishly decorated caves west of Ch'ang-an in which some of these rituals took place. Upon the death of the last Tantric advisor to the court, Amoghavajra (705–774), Chen-yen died out in China, although it spawned schools in Korea and Japan, with its Japanese offshoot—Shingon—existing to the present day.

Hsüan-tsung's reign is regarded as the peak of T'ang art, poetry, and culture, but it also marked the beginning of the end of the dynasty. The debilitating An Lu-shan rebellion (755–764), together with widespread famine, left a large death toll and brought about a breakdown of administrative control. The rebellion did both immediate and long-term damage to the Sangha. The immediate damage lay in the destruction of many monasteries and the total demise of Hsüan-tsang's Fa-hsiang school. The long-term damage was caused by a government policy devised to raise money for the financially strapped imperial treasury. Official certificates granting permission to ordain were offered to anyone who would pay a flat fee. This reversed a centuries-long practice of tight state controls over ordinations, and huge numbers of people responded. Although the policy raised the needed funds, it continued unchecked for decades after the rebellion, decimating the tax rolls and filling the monasteries with tax dodgers. In 830 it was estimated that there were twice as many monks and nuns as there had been in 730. Even Buddhists were complaining that the policy was destroying their religion.

Clearly, something had to be done, but no ruler had either the desire or the will to effect any major restrictions until Emperor Wu-tsung (r. 840–846) came to the throne. A fervent seeker of immortality, Wu-tsung was driven more by religious zeal than by political considerations. When his Taoist priests convinced him that their efforts to make him immortal were being foiled by the preponderance of "black" in the empire—black being the color of the Buddhist monastic robes—he determined to wipe Buddhism from the face of China. In a series of edicts dating from 842 to 845, he succeeded in destroying more than 4,600 temples and 40,000 shrines across the empire, and forcing 260,500 monks and nuns back to lay life. The Japanese monk Ennin happened to be studying in China at the time and left behind a graphic account of the sufferings incurred not only by the Sangha but also by those who had come to depend on it. Slave families who had been assigned to monasteries were separated, and the poor were evicted from monastic alms houses. Military governors in a few regions resisted the edicts, and lay Buddhists gave shelter to some of the monks and nuns, but in general the purge was as thorough as any a pre-modern state could inflict on its citizens.

Shortly after his most strident anti-Buddhist edicts, Wu-tsung began suffering from the effects of his immortality medicines, issuing demands that live sea otters and the hearts and livers of 15-year-old youths and maidens be brought to the palace for his potions. Within a few months he was dead, poisoned by his quest for immortality, at age 32. Buddhists immediately interpreted his death as karmic retribution for his persecution of the religion. Whatever disdain later emperors may have felt for Buddhism, this perception may account for the fact that there were no more purges of the Sangha until the twentieth century.

Wu-tsung's successor, Hsuen-tsung (r. 846–859), attempted to reinstate the religion, although he proceeded cautiously in the face of continued anti-Buddhist feeling in the court. Nonetheless, he and his successors had managed to reopen monasteries and reordain large numbers of monastics when a second blow came in the form of the Huang Ch'ao Rebellion (875–884). Although this rebellion was not directed against Buddhist institutions per se, many monasteries were destroyed in the mayhem. After the rebellion, the power of the imperial house was so sapped that it could do little to help the Sangha. The dynasty fell in 907, and not until 970 was the empire reunited.

The double blow of persecution and rebellion at the end of the T'ang had a devastating effect on Chinese Buddhism. In particular, the destruction of monastic libraries meant that the great scholastic schools were damaged almost beyond repair. T'ien-t'ai and Hua-yen, the most important of the schools, revived somewhat in the Sung dynasty only because some of their texts had been sequestered in Korea. Even the traditions that depended more on oral transmission, Ch'an and Ching-te (Pure Land), were damaged as well. Of the nine Ch'an meditation lineages existing before the persecution, only two survived the end of the dynasty. The texts that had formed the theoretical basis for Pure Land practice were mostly destroyed. Nevertheless, even in their truncated form, these innovative schools continued to have an influence in later centuries. We can only conjecture what might have developed if more of their breadth and variety had been allowed to survive the end of the dynasty that had spawned them.

8.5.1 T'ien-t'ai

T'ien-t'ai (Heavenly Terrace), the first of the great multisystem schools, took its name from the mountain in Chekiang where its principal center was located. Although Hui-ssu (515–576) is honored as the school's founder, the first true architect of the T'ien-t'ai system was his student Chih-i (538–597). That system underwent change through the T'ang and Sung dynasties, with many of the changes reverently incorporated by T'ien-t'ai editors into their editions of Chih-i's writings. As a result, although the major outlines of the system can apparently be ascribed to Chih-i, it is difficult to determine which other elements of the system are genuinely his. Here we will give an sketch of the teachings that the T'ien-t'ai school has attributed to him, with the caveat that some of the teachings may actually postdate him by centuries.

As mentioned previously (see Section 8.4.2), the major issue facing Chinese Buddhist thinkers in the fifth and sixth centuries was how to find a comprehensive framework to encompass and explain the great variety of Buddhist doctrines and practices emanating from India. Chih-i offered a solution to this problem based on the insight that theory and practice could not be separated: The study of doctrine should ideally be undertaken in the context of practice, just as meditational and devotional practice is a means of gaining further understanding of doctrine. The need for practice comes from an inherent limitation in language: Ultimate truth lies beyond words. From this it follows that all true statements can at best be only partially adequate; their opposites may also be partially true. Thus the statements that come closest to expressing ultimate truth are the middle or "complete" ones that encompass seeming contradictions, pointing out how both sides of the contradiction are true although neither is fully true. From this principle, Chih-i was able to build a system of great complexity and subtlety for comprehending the entire range of Buddhist doctrines and practice.

Chih-i applied this approach to what he called the three discernments of Buddhism: the provisional discernment of existing dharmas, represented by the Abhidharmists; the ultimate discernment of emptiness, represented by Madhyamaka; and the middle or complete discernment of the *dharmadhātu* (Dharma-element), taught in the *Lotus, Avataṃsaka,* and *Nirvāṇa Sūtras.* This last discernment points directly at the highest principle underlying the cosmos, while at the same time comprehending the truth and limitations of the provisional and ultimate discernments. Chih-i was sophisticated enough to realize that even the complete discernment was not an entirely adequate expression of the Dharma-element; it was simply as close as language could get. Hence his insistence that study be paired with practice, for only then could complete Awakening be fully realized.

Chih-i classified both doctrinal teachings and meditational practices into three categories: *sudden,* those that pointed directly to the Dharma-element; *gradual,* those that used expedient means; and *variable,* those that mixed sudden and gradual approaches in a variety of ways. Encompassing all these approaches was the *complete* approach, which Chih-i tried to provide in his two great works: *The Profound Meaning of the Lotus Sūtra (Fa-hua hsüan-i),* dealing with doctrine; and *The Great Calming and Contemplation (Mo-ho chih-kuan),* dealing with meditation practice.

Chih-i followed a passage in the *Nirvāṇa Sūtra,* classifying the Buddha's teachings into five flavors corresponding to five dairy products. The first flavor, corresponding to milk, includes the very earliest Buddhist texts; the second flavor, the cream, includes the Sūtra Piṭaka; the third flavor, the curds, corresponds to the great Mahāyāna Sūtras, such as the *Śrīmālā* and the *Vimalakīrti-nirdeśa;* the fourth flavor, the butter, corresponds to the Perfection of Discernment Sūtras; and the fifth flavor, the ghee, corresponds to the *Nirvāṇa Sūtra* itself. Just as cream comes from milk, and curds from cream, and so forth, the later Sūtras come from the earlier ones, being neither identical with nor different from them. Chih-i, following traditions that had developed within China during his time, made two changes in this lineup. The first flavor, he said, was the sudden flavor of the *Avataṃsaka Sūtra,* which the Chinese believed was the first sermon the Buddha delivered immediately after his Awakening. It was called sudden both because it was as direct as possible an expression of the Dharma-element, and also because it made no concessions to the capacities of its listeners. Most who heard it were bewildered. Thus the Buddha retraced his steps and began formulating the body of gradual teachings that make up the Sūtra Piṭaka.

Chih-i's second main change in the lineup was to include the *Lotus Sūtra* under the fifth flavor as the most perfect expression of the Buddha's teachings. This was because it had the same "sudden" message as the *Avataṃsaka Sūtra,* but illustrated the message with expedient similes and explanations that made its meaning perfectly clear to all its listeners. Thus it represents Buddhist doctrine at its most complete.

As with all categories in Chih-i's thought, these flavors are relative: Because no words can adequately express the Dharma-element, all teachings are gradual to some extent; because all the teachings come from an Awakened mind, they are all partially sudden. This relativity is what gives Chih-i's categories, which otherwise would have become little more than sorting boxes, nuance and complexity. Because they are relative, they are also interpenetrating. The realization of this point constitutes the highest teaching: that principle cannot be found apart from phenomena. Even though distinctions are made between shallow and profound, and so forth, all truths are universally coextensive. The entire cosmos is immanent in a moment of thought and is perceived simultaneously by the Awakened mind as empty, substantial, both, and neither.

To show the way to this realization, Chih-i wrote the most extensive and comprehensive meditation guide that had ever appeared in China. Again, he made a distinction between sudden, gradual, and variable approaches. The gradual approach makes use of various expedient objects, such as the breath, *nien-fo* (the repetition of the Buddha's name), liturgy, or contemplation of the *Lotus Sūtra* (the method that had given rise to Chih-i's own first experience of great samādhi). The sudden approach focuses immediately on the Dharma-element as its object from the moment that bodhicitta occurs. Here again, the distinctions are relative. The Dharma-element is present in all mental moments; thus all meditation methods are in a sense sudden. Because in the ultimate sense the Dharma-element transcends the subject–object dichotomy, it cannot be an object. Thus all approaches are to some extent gradual. The complete approach, which follows on the sudden, entails contemplating the mind in all postures, simply viewing its passing states as partial expressions of the Dharma-element. However, Chih-i advised that contemplation of mind be practiced in conjunction with the more gradual methods; otherwise, simply viewing good and bad states coming and going, one might be misled into believing that there was no practical need to distinguish right and wrong. In this manner, his view of the total practice encompassed the particulars without denying their validity.

Issues of sudden and gradual, verbal doctrine and practice, and principle and phenomena coalesce in Chih-i's analysis of the question of the identity between the mind and the Dharma-element, which is the overarching framework of the

T'ien-t'ai system, working out in full detail the initial insight of the system, that study and practice cannot be separated. In the course of the practice, one proceeds step-by-step through six levels of identity, beginning with identity in principle—the identity that adheres between principle and phenomena in general, even before acquaintance with the Buddha's teaching. In the second level, one moves on to verbal identity, that is, the intellectual understanding that the mind and the Dharma-element are identical. On this level, one engages in a study of gradual, sudden, and complete teachings so as to perfect one's verbal understanding, at the same time learning the limits of language, thus appreciating the necessity for practice. The third through fifth levels correspond to the three stages of practice—gradual, sudden, and complete—culminating in the sixth level, ultimate identity, or the full attainment of Buddhahood. One had to understand these six levels at the outset, Chih-i maintained, for otherwise one would be led either to the arrogance of thinking that one was already fully identical with the Dharma-element before the practice, or into discouragement in thinking that one had nothing in common with the goal. Again, the complete view overcomes the limitations inherent in an either–or dichotomy, encompassing and transcending the partial truth and falsity of one-sided views.

Comparing these six levels with Asaṅga's teachings on the phases of discernment in the practice (see Section 5.3.2) shows how the outlines of Chinese Mahāyāna thought do not differ as radically from those of Indian Mahāyāna as many writers have assumed. The first level corresponds to Asaṅga's assertion that all dharmas are originally pure. The second and third levels correspond to his phase of preparatory discernment; the fourth level to the phase of nondual discernment; and fifth level to the phase of subsequent discernment, encompassing both the preparatory and nondual phases, and yielding ultimately in full Buddhahood, the sixth level in the T'ien-t'ai system.

T'ien-t'ai had a far-reaching influence on East Asian Buddhism. Its doctrinal synthesis framed the issues for all later efforts at explaining Buddhist doctrine. Similarly, its synthesis of ritual, liturgy, and devotional practices provided the framework for these aspects of Buddhist practice throughout East Asia. And its approach to meditation formed the matrix in which the Ch'an schools developed. Many later Ch'an meditation guides, even into the eleventh century, repeated verbatim large portions of an abbreviated version of *The Great Calming and Contemplation*. Unlike some of the later Ch'an schools, however, T'ien-t'ai did not deprecate gradual methods of teaching or practice. According to Chih-i, Buddhism was similar to a complete course of medical science. A person with a limited view might not see the necessity for certain medicines or techniques, but a truly skilled doctor knows the full range of illnesses and the need for a full array of techniques for dealing with them. However, the strength of the T'ien-t'ai system, its comprehensiveness, was also its weakness in that it required its followers to diffuse their energies in mastering all areas of doctrine and practice. This may be one of the reasons why, in the seventh century, many T'ien-t'ai monks went over to the newly developing Ch'an schools.

During the sixth century, however, Chih-i and T'ien-t'ai in general received strong support from the Sui royal house, which felt that the school's integration of southern scholarship with northern meditation and devotional methods paralleled its policy of political integration. The connection with the Sui, however, meant that the school was eclipsed during the early T'ang dynasty. In the eighth century, Chan-jan (711–782) revived the school in response to what he saw as the mistaken views of Hua-yen. Chan-jan was responsible for making the T'ien-t'ai a self-conscious school *(tsung),* and for reformulating Chih-i's views into a matrix that came to be the school's slogan: the five periods and the eight teachings. The five periods corresponded to the five flavors; the eight teachings were actually two lists of four categories. The first list consisted of four methods of teachings: *sudden, gradual, secret* (one teaching that meant different things to different groups), and *variable* (one teaching that gave sudden results to one group and gradual results to another). The second list consisted of four doctrines: *tripiṭaka* (doctrines particular to Mainstream Buddhism, such as the Wings to Awakening); *shared* (common to both the Mainstream and the Mahāyāna); *distinctive* (exclusive to Mahāyāna); and *complete* (totally comprehensive). In this manner Chan-jan sorted out three separate ways of classifying the Buddha's teachings—in terms of chronology, method, and doctrine—while at the same time tracing the complex relations among the three. Thus he managed to clear up an issue that the Hua-yen patriarch Fa-tsang had confused.

In the generations after Chan-jan, T'ien-t'ai scholars continued developing the school's doctrines, often incorporating Hua-yen teachings on Original Mind. The school was practically wiped out during the troubled years of the ninth century, however. Texts were destroyed, and not until the latter part of the Five Dynasty period (907–960) was the ruler of Wu-Yüeh, located in Chekiang, able to send to Korea for copies of T'ien-t'ai texts to be brought back to China. The Korean monk Chegwan (d. 971) not only brought the texts but also composed a short summary of T'ien-t'ai doctrines (mistakenly attributing Chan-jan's innovations to Chih-i), which became one of the standard texts of the school. Beginning in the eleventh century, T'ien-t'ai was established as the main surviving doctrinal school and T'ien-t'ai scholars during the Sung dynasty further refined the school's doctrines, falling into two factions over whether to remove the Hua-yen elements that had earlier been incorporated into the teachings. The school's earlier preeminence in meditation, however, was totally eclipsed by Ch'an.

8.5.2 Hua-yen

Hua-yen, the second great multisystem school, took its name from the *Avataṃsaka* (Flower Ornament or Hua-yen) *Sūtra*—a vast collection of Sūtras that had coalesced around the *Daśabhūmika* and *Gaṇḍavyūha Sūtras*—whose teachings formed the basis for many of the school's doctrines. The philosophical tradition that developed from the *Avataṃsaka* is only one aspect of its impact on Chinese Buddhism, which also included meditation practices, ascetic practices, thaumaturgy, and a cult of the book surrounding the text of the Sūtra itself.

The philosophical tradition of Hua-yen is difficult to define, not only because of the inherent complexity of its teachings, but also because those teachings changed so radically over the course of the three centuries from the school's first patriarch to its last. To convey a sense of this change, we will discuss the teachings of two patriarchs: the third, Fa-tsang (643–712), who was the school's first great architect; and the fifth, Tsung-mi (779–840), a Ch'an patriarch who recast Hua-yen thought in a way that made it relevant to Ch'an practice.

Fa-tsang differed with the T'ien-t'ai teachings on the issue of the One Vehicle taught in the *Lotus Sūtra* (see Section 5.2.3). According to T'ien-t'ai, the *One Vehicle* was a blanket term for the three vehicles of śrāvaka, pratyeka-buddha, and bodhisattva. According to Fa-tsang, the One Vehicle was actually a separate vehicle, superior to all the others. Although it shared some common points with standard Mahāyāna, it also possessed special doctrines of its own, which Fa-tsang identified with the teaching in the *Avataṃsaka Sūtra*. Whereas ordinary Mahāyāna Sūtras saw reality in terms of the unimpeded interpenetration of principle and phenomena, the *Avataṃsaka* saw reality in terms of the unimpeded interpenetration of phenomena with all other phenomena in the cosmos. The image illustrating this view is that of Indra's net: a net of fine filaments stretching in all directions with a jewel at each interstice. Each jewel reflects all the other jewels in the net, so that each reflects the reflections in all the other jewels, on to infinity. This viewpoint is said to be that of a Buddha. Thus, much of Fa-tsang's metaphysics is concerned with the phenomenology of Awakening: what the cosmos looks like to an Awakened one.

Fa-tsang's analysis begins with the teaching from *The Awakening of Faith* that describes how the entire cosmos comes from the One Mind expressed in two aspects: principle and phenomena. *Principle* here means the mind as understood from the perspective of Suchness, which transcends all dualities; *phenomena* means the mind as understood from the perspective of dependent co-arising. Each aspect has two sides: Principle is characterized both by immutability (it is unconditioned) and conditionedness (it finds expression in conditioned things); phenomena are characterized by quasi existence (they function in a causal network) and emptiness (they have no separate essence of their own). Fa-tsang then goes on to demonstrate that principle cannot exist separately from phenomena. In fact, principle and phenomena are two sides of one thing. The quasi existence of phenomena is nothing other than the conditionedness of principle. Following Nāgārjuna's identification of emptiness with the law of dependent co-arising, the emptiness of phenomena is nothing other than the immutability of principle. Thus there cannot be one without the other.

From this equation, Fa-tsang goes on to claim that the entire cosmos is identical with the mind and body of the Buddha Mahāvairocana—the cosmic Buddha that the *Avataṃsaka Sūtra* identifies as embodied in the universe as a whole (see Section 5.2.3)—for, according to him, the One Mind is Buddha-nature. Thus Buddha-nature is nothing other than the principle of dependent co-arising. This point underlies Fa-tsang's conceptual model for the distinctive view of the One Vehicle—what he called "the dependent co-arising of the Dharma-element." *Mahāvairocana* means Great Illuminator. The nature of the mind, from which the cosmos is made, is to reflect all that appears to it. Thus Fa-tsang's basic metaphor for the process of mutually dependent co-arising is that of light and mirrors. Causes penetrate their effects, just as light penetrates a mirror. Effects embrace their causes, just as mirrors contain all the light that penetrates them. From this conception of causality, Fa-tsang makes three assertions about the dependent co-arising of the Dharma-element: (1) All phenomena interpenetrate one another.

In other words, because each phenomenon is empty—that is, a result of the combined effects of all other phenomena—it is penetrated by all other phenomena and embraces them all. Because each has quasi existence, participating in the conditioning of all other phenomena, each phenomenon penetrates them all and is embraced by them all. Thus, (2) all phenomena are identical, in that each phenomenon functions in the same way. (3) Because the totality of each part already contains that part, interpenetration is repeated infinitely, as in the image of Indra's net.

Fa-tsang actively courted and won imperial patronage. According to his biography he explained the dependent co-arising of the Dharma-element to Empress Wu with a concrete image. In the middle of a room he placed a Buddha image and a lamp, representing the Buddha Mahāvairocana and the principle of dependent co-arising. He then placed mirrors in the 10 directions surrounding the Buddha image: the 8 major directions plus above and below the Buddha image. He then walked her around the room to show that each mirror (phenomenon) contained not only the Buddha image (principle) but also all the other mirrors (phenomena), and that their mutual interpenetration repeated infinitely.

Fa-tsang worked out other implications of the dependent co-arising of the Dharma-element in terms of three pairs of characteristics: totality and particularity, identity and difference, and unity and individuality. With regard to the totality of all phenomena, each phenomenon is both a particular within the totality and equivalent to the totality itself. The argument here is that because each part depends on the whole, it is also the sole cause of the whole. This is because the lack of any one part means that the whole is lacking. However, each part is simply a part, because a whole has to be made up of parts. Thus, Fa-tsang says, particularity and totality are equivalent in this view of reality. With regard to the relationship between particular phenomena, because the existence of each phenomenon is its function—and because the function of each is identical, to act as a cause of the whole—each phenomenon is identical with every other single phenomenon. But because the cosmos as we know it has to be made up of different parts, each phenomenon has to be different from others. Thus their identity comes from their differences. With regard to all other particular phenomena, each phenomenon unites with the others in forming the whole, and yet each must maintain its individuality, for otherwise there would be no factors to keep forming the whole. Thus their unity comes from their individuality.

Fa-tsang did not expect his listeners to fully understand his paradoxical teachings. In fact, he felt that it would enough for them simply to accept the teachings on faith. He saw the bodhisattva Path as consisting of 53 stages, but for him the tenth stage, accepting the dependent co-arising of the Dharma-element on faith, was the crucial one. As with the Mainstream Buddhist teachings (see Section 1.4.1), his view of the principle of interpenetration worked not only in the immediate present, but also across time. However, because he viewed the cosmos as already being identical with the mind and body of the Buddha Mahāvairocana, he regarded cause and effect as operating in both directions of time, forward as well as back: Because existence is function, the result is what makes the cause a cause, for without the result, the cause would not function as a cause, and thus would not exist as such. In this view, the attainment of the tenth stage already includes all the subsequent stages. On attaining this stage, one is already a bodhisattva and a Buddha. All that remains is to continue contemplating the emptiness and functioning of phenomena. Tranquility meditation, according to Fa-tsang, means viewing phenomena as empty. This gives rise to discernment, so that the mind does not dwell in saṁsāra. Insight meditation means to view emptiness functioning in the form of phenomena. This gives rise to compassion, in that all phenomena are identical, so that there is no dwelling in nirvāṇa. With a mind dwelling neither in saṁsāra nor nirvāṇa, one remains in the cosmos, acting out of wisdom and compassion, which is a Buddha's true function.

Like many Mahāyānists, Fa-tsang viewed it an act of selfishness for a bodhisattva to enter nirvāṇa, but he went further than most in decreeing a separate nirvāṇa a theoretical impossibility. According to him, there is no Unconditioned separate from the Conditioned. The universe already is the body and mind of the Buddha Mahāvairocana. Even if there were a separate unconditioned realm, no one could go there until the entire universe went, grass and insects included. Because every part is interpenetrated by, identical with, and in union with every other part, all parts would have to go together. And, given the dazzling and marvelous nature of dependent co-arising, there is no reason to go. One attains Buddhahood by appreciating the wonder of the universe; and one continues to live in it eternally, acting out of discernment and compassion, attuned to its infinite ramifications.

These, at least, were the intended implications of Fa-tsang's teachings. Chan-jan (see Section 8.5.1), however, saw other implications. Placed against the T'ien-t'ai doctrine of the six identities, Fa-tsang's assertion—that Buddhahood was implicitly attained at the stage of accepting the right view of the universe—equated the second stage of identity with the sixth. This, Chan-jan said, would lead to the danger of arrogance. One would feel that because one was already Awakened, there was no need to practice morality or any other stages of the Path.

The issues surrounding morality later inspired Tsung-mi's recasting of Hua-yen doctrine. Tsung-mi was a master of the Ho-tse school of southern Ch'an, founded by Shen-hui (see Section 8.5.5). All southern Ch'an schools taught a doctrine of sudden Awakening, according to which gradual practice could not give rise to a true understanding of the Buddha-nature. Because Awakening was unconditioned, gradual approaches to the immediacy of full understanding only got in the way. Thus some of the more radical Ch'an schools advocated the abandoning of moral norms and formal meditation practice altogether. Recognizing the danger in this approach, Tsung-mi sought a doctrinal justification for his conviction that sudden Awakening had to be followed by gradual cultivation—including observance of moral principles and formal meditation—in order to integrate that Awakening fully into one's life.

He found the justification he was looking for in the writings of Ch'eng-kuan, the fourth Hua-yen patriarch, and so went to study with him. In the course of his studies, he learned much that suited his purposes, but the doctrines that were the hallmarks of the Hua-yen school—the separateness of the One Vehicle, the superiority of the *Avataṁsaka Sūtra,* the interpenetration of phenomena with phenomena—struck him as irrelevant. Thus he eventually abandoned or downplayed them in his own writings. Nevertheless, later generations counted him as the fifth patriarch of the school, largely because of the extensive use he made of the writings of the earlier patriarchs even while putting them in a new framework. In this sense, Tsung-mi is an object lesson in how the schools of T'ang Buddhism developed in response to the concerns of their individual members.

Like Fa-tsang, Tsung-mi began with the theory, derived from *The Awakening of Faith,* of the One Mind already intrinsically Awakened at the basis of reality. Unlike Fa-tsang, however, he did not dwell on the interpenetration of phenomena, but instead closely followed the evolutionary scheme discussed in *The Awakening of Faith* to show how this One Mind gives rise to deluded experience. The process unfolds in 10 stages, analogous to what happens when a person falls asleep and dreams. In the first two stages, the purity of the tathāgata-garbha splits into two aspects: Awakened and unawakened. The unawakened aspect, the *ālaya-vijñāna,* is similar to a person simply falling asleep. In the next four stages, thought arises, followed by a perceived subject, perceived objects, and attachment to the basic elements (dharmas) of existence. This is analogous to the arising of dreams, along with dreaming consciousness, the perception of objects in the dream, and clinging to the things seen in the dream as real. In the next two stages there arises attachment to self, followed by such defilements as greed, anger, and delusion. This is similar to the dreaming person identifying with the person in the dream and feeling like and dislike for the objects in the dream. In the last two stages, karma is generated and one experiences the consequences. This is similar to the person in the dream acting in accordance with likes and dislikes, experiencing pleasure and pain.

Throughout this process, called nature origination, Tsung-mi follows *The Awakening of Faith* in asserting that the mind is still intrinsically Awakened in spite of the arising of delusion. The basic image, adapted from the *Laṅkāvatāra Sūtra,* is of an ocean: The water of the ocean is still intrinsically water even though wind makes it form into waves. Tsung-mi then develops this image to show how Buddhist practice reverses the process of delusion and brings the mind full circle back to the attainment of full Awakening. One learns the Dharma from one already Awakened and so realizes the true nature of the mind as being identical with the tathāgata-garbha. This is called sudden Awakening and is similar to the stopping of the wind. However, the inertia of the water continues forming waves. To calm down the waves, one must continue with gradual cultivation of one's sudden realization to bring it to completion.

Here Tsung-mi introduces a fivefold classification of Buddhist teachings designed to reverse the stages in the origination of delusion: (1) The teachings of human and divine beings, consisting essentially of the doctrine of karma and morality, overturn the process of generating karma and experiencing the consequences. (2) The Mainstream teachings then undercut one of the basic assumptions of the first category—the existence of a self taking rebirth—by analyzing the self into impersonal dharmas. This overturns the stages of defilement and attachment to self. (3) The Fa-hsiang/Yogācāra teachings of the three *svabhāvas* then serve to correct an assumption of the Mainstream teachings—that dharmas exist in an ultimate sense—by showing that they are simply projections of the ālaya-vijñāna. This overturns the stages of perceived subject, perceived objects, and attachment to dharmas. (4) The Perfection of Discernment teachings then show that the projecting ālaya-vijñāna is just as unreal as the projected subject–object dichotomy. Although this stage succeeds in establishing that the ālaya-vijñāna is not the ultimate reality, it does not show what that reality is. Thus the need for the fifth class of teachings: (5) the revelation of the (Buddha) nature in such texts as *The Awakening of Faith,* the *Avataṁsaka Sūtra,* and the *Lotus Sūtra.*

Tsung-mi maintains that classes (2) to (4) express their teachings in negative terms in order to rid the mind of its attachment to concepts. Only when the mind has completed its training in these classes is it ready for the positive language of class (5), which—following Shen-hui (see Section 8.5.5)—he says is ultimately expressed in a single word: *awareness.* Thus a full return to the awareness that constitutes the tathāgata-garbha can be attained only after a complete course of gradual cultivation, including training in morality and formal meditation. Tsung-mi treats the interpenetration of phenomena as little more than a footnote to the teaching of awareness, showing that he regarded it as an inappropriate teaching for people in lower stages of the Path and as ultimately irrelevant as a guide even to the advanced stage. The person who actually fathoms awareness will realize this aspect of reality without having to be told.

In this way, Tsung-mi was able to preserve the components of the traditional Buddhist path even in the light of the doctrine of sudden Awakening. However, the events of 845 effectively put an end to the Hua-yen school, destroying its texts and dispersing its followers. The Korean monk Ŭich'on (see Section 9.4.1) brought Hua-yen texts from Korea in the eleventh century, and a number of Ch'an monks wrote commentaries on them during the Sung and later dynasties. The lineage of patriarchs, however, was never revived. As we will see in the following chapters, Hua-yen played a more influential role in Korea and Japan.

8.5.3 Pure Land (Ching-te)

Pure Land—the practice aimed at gaining rebirth in a Buddha-field—was never a formal school or lineage in China. Instead, it was a broad movement that found a home in a wide variety of settings and enjoyed a long career as the most popular movement in Chinese Buddhism. The roots of the movement date back to the Later Han dynasty, when the *Pratyutpanna* (see Section 4.3.2) was translated into Chinese. In the fifth century, Hui-yüan (see Section 8.4.1) and his followers formed a society dedicated to gaining rebirth in Amitābha's paradise; Pure Land practices were also an integral part of T'ien-t'ai ritual and contemplative practice.

However, from the sixth to the ninth century a string of teachers specializing in Pure Land practice, and offering a specifically Pure Land doctrine, almost succeeded in making Pure Land an independent tradition, and definitely laid the groundwork for the Pure Land schools of Japan. The first of these teachers was a northerner, T'an-luan (476–542). T'an-luan received his religious vocation when, convalescing from a grave illness, he saw a vision of a heavenly gate opening before him. He turned first to Taoism and its prescriptions for attaining immortality; a treatise he composed describing a Taoist meditation technique is still extant. He then met the Indian monk Bodhiruci, who arrived in Lo-yang in 508. Bodhiruci convinced him that Buddhism had a superior method for gaining everlasting life and taught him the Amitābha texts. T'an-luan was converted and burned his Taoist books.

Like many meditation masters of the time, Bodhiruci advocated the use of *dhāraṇī* for concentration. T'an-luan's practice gradually developed into the *nien-fo* (recitation of the Buddha's name). The term *nien-fo* in T'an-luan's earliest writings referred generally to the practice of meditation. There are three possible meanings for the word *nien:* (1) concentration or meditation; (2) a length of time equal to one thought; hence, the expression *shih-nien* (10 *nien*) meant the length of time consisting of 10 thought-moments. This led eventually to a reinterpretation, as *nien* also means (3) vocal recitation, with the phrase *shih-nien* seen as meaning 10 recitations of the Buddha's name.

T'an-luan organized societies for recitation of Amitābha's name and propagated the Pure Land practice with great success. He also lay the foundations for its doctrine, declaring that even those who have committed evil deeds and atrocities are eligible for rebirth in the Western paradise if they sincerely desire it. However, those who revile the Dharma are excluded, he said, because blasphemy is not conducive to aspiration and because the karmic retribution for blasphemy is repeated rebirth in the lowest hell. Eventually, he came to advocate dependence on *t'a-li* (other power) rather than on *tzu-li* (one's own power), asserting that even the merit one seems to earn for oneself through nien-fo is facilitated by the overarching power of Amitābha's vows. Rebirth in the Pure Land and attainment of Buddhahood there are a result of this power. Thus, instead of meditation, the prime requisites of Pure Land practice became faith coupled with recitation of Amitābha's name.

These two points—recitation rather than meditation, and the inclusion of sinners with those who can benefit from Amitābha's vow—were the main Chinese departures from Indian Amitābha doctrines. T'an-luan's motive in explaining away the *Sukhāvatī-vyūha Sūtra*'s statement claiming that grave sinners are excluded from the effect of Amitābha's vow was his conviction that all living beings possess Buddha-nature, and thus none could be excluded from the bliss of his Pure Land. This conviction may account for the popularity of Pure Land in China.

By the sixth century, many Buddhists had become obsessed with the notion that the latter days of Buddhism had arrived. Indian texts, beginning with some of the Mainstream canons, distinguished two Dharma periods: the period of True Dharma (0–500 after the Parinirvāṇa [A.P.]), followed by a period of Semblance Dharma. To these two stages, Chinese texts had added a third period, that of the Latter-day or Degenerate Dharma, (expected to begin either 1000 or 1500 A.P., depending on the source, and lasting ten thousand years). Sixth-century Chinese dated the Parinirvāṇa at 949 B.C.E., which meant that the Latter-day Dharma would begin about 550 C.E. Thus there was a receptive audience for teachings and practices appropriate for a degenerate age, promising rewards in a better world. This was precisely what T'an-luan's Pure Land offered. It placed few intellectual or financial demands on its followers, and made no pretense that life in this world, even when in harmony with nature, could in any way be ideal.

The next great Pure Land masters were Tao-ch'o (562–645) and his disciple Shan-tao (613–681), who gave Chinese Pure Land its definitive shape. Shan-tao was the first Pure Land master to settle in the capital and was remarkably successful in spreading the faith there. Nien-fo was still the crucial religious act in his teaching—in fact, he recommended that it be repeated at all times, as a mantra—but he included other practices in addition to the recitation: meditation, morality, and scholarship. In this way he aspired to make Pure Land practice independent, rather than an appendage to other schools.

The last two great masters of this formative period were Tz'u-min (680–748) and Fa-chao (late eighth century). Fa-chao was the first Pure Land master to teach in the T'ang imperial court. His ecstatic method of reciting Amitābha's name in five rhythms, which he equated with the five wonderful sounds to be heard in Sukhāvatī, proved very popular.

The Pure Land teachers developed a large body of texts, not only to spread their teachings among the general populace but also to defend their practice from the attacks of the more philosophical schools. Pure Land philosophy adopted the distinction between principle and phenomena to explain the need for the nien-fo. Just as principle cannot be perceived without recourse to phenomena, they said, true Buddha-nature cannot be grasped without recourse to simple expedient means.

However, the nature of Pure Land practice was such that it needed no great masters or philosophical texts. Although the texts of the Pure Land masters were destroyed in the turmoil of 845, the practice was so widely diffused that, aside from Ch'an, it was the only Buddhist movement to survive the suppression relatively intact. Despite T'ang emperors' having followed it, neo-Confucian gentlemen, beginning with the twelfth century, disdained to participate in a practice that was both "vulgar" (because the common people adhered to it) and "foreign." Their wives, however, continued to recite *"na-mo a-mi-t'o-fo"* ("Homage to Amita Buddha") and taught it to their children. To this day, a shortened version of the phrase, *"O-mi-t'o-fo,"* is a common greeting and exclamation among older Chinese. No native Chinese god has ever commanded the universal worship that Amita has received. Even today, the faith is still strong among the vast majority of Chinese Buddhists, and *"na-mo a-mi-t'o-fo"* is chanted regularly in the daily liturgy of Ch'an monasteries.

8.5.4 The Three-Level Sect (San-chieh-chiao)

A related development during this period was the establishment of the Three-Level Sect (San-chieh-chiao). Like the Pure Land movement, this movement assumed the existence of three periods in the survival of Dharma after the Buddha's Parinirvāṇa. It took its name from its assertion that the three periods were characterized by the level of beings born during each. In the age of Degenerate Dharma, which had already arrived, beings were on so low a level that they were blind as to what the true Dharma might be. The sect's founder, Hsin-hsing (540–593), taught that in such an age even the basic distinctions of language were uncertain, and that the only spiritual certainty lay in an attitude of universal reverence for all beings.

From this principle, he drew several ethical imperatives. The first was that no one should teach the Dharma. The second was that no one should make distinctions or pass judgment on anyone. The third was that the one reliably true religious activity was to be generous—an imperative that applied to monks and laity alike. For Hsin-hsing, generosity lay at the heart of all the bodhisattva's perfections. Thus in 620 his followers in Ch'ang-an established an "Inexhaustible Treasury," a credit union and mutual financing society patterned after a model in the *Vimalakīrti-nirdeśa Sūtra*. This project soon assumed enormous proportions. Capital accumulated at a rate defying the ability of accountants to keep track of it. Funds were dispersed for such projects as temple repair, relief for the sick and homeless, and religious rituals throughout the empire. According to accounts of the time, loans were always repaid when due, even though no interest was charged and no legal contracts were required of the borrowers.

Had the sect kept to its imperatives it might have stayed out of trouble, but it broke them by criticizing other people for not observing them as well. In particular, it began denouncing Sangha authorities as bogus monks who were enriching themselves by teaching a bogus Dharma. In response, these authorities sent appeals to the government to rein in the sect, appeals that were heeded only during reigns when the emperors were Buddhist and felt a personal responsibility to the Sangha. Finally, in 725, Hsüan-tsung dissolved all of the sect's monasteries, having closed the Inexhaustible Treasury in 721. The memory of the Treasury, however, has remained as a model and inspiration for Buddhist charitable organizations throughout East Asia up through the present.

8.5.5 Ch'an

The Ch'an (Dhyāna) school—better known in the West by its Japanese name, Zen—is the meditation tradition with the longest documented history in the Buddhist world. Throughout its history it has gone through periods of decline alternating with periods of renewal and reform, with each period of renewal rewriting the history of the school in line with its perception of contemporary issues facing it. Because of their polemical intent, these revisions have tended to obscure the school's actual history, but the Tun-huang documents have helped to uncover a more objective portrait of its early generations.

Ch'an is sometimes presented as a quintessentially Chinese form of Buddhism. However—regardless of how "Chinese-ness" might be defined—it is important to notice the elements of the Ch'an tradition that have parallels with the meditative traditions in other Buddhist cultures. We have noted (see Section 7.5.2) a tendency among Buddhist meditative traditions to become domesticated as the attainments of their teachers become widely known. In most cases, the traditions then die out within a few generations as material prosperity smothers the authenticity of the practice. Most extant early Ch'an writings date from the two main periods during which the tradition became domesticated: the period from the mid-eighth to the mid-ninth century, and then again from the late tenth through the twelfth. This may simply be a historical accident, in that writings from other periods may have been destroyed, but comparison with the Kammaṭṭhāna tradition suggests that this may not be an accident after all. A meditative tradition would tend not to leave written records until it became so famous that it felt compelled to define and defend its teachings beyond the immediate circle of person-to-person contact. The material support attendant on fame might also create factions within the tradition, as different groups jockeyed for support, and this would require the tradition to sort out which of its various lineages had deviated from the "authentic teaching" of the practice.

Further comparison with the Kammaṭṭhāna tradition reveals another point in common: an ambivalent attitude toward established scholarly traditions. Meditative traditions must use the terminology established by the scholarly tradition to discuss their teachings and gauge their meditative experiences, but they may find the fashions of scholarship inimical to their approach. Scholars may champion spurious texts or mistaken interpretations of legitimate texts. On a more subtle level, even when scholarly theories are essentially correct, the tendency to focus on theory—and the attendant pride that can often develop from mastering theory—may obscure the direct experience of what the theory describes. These two concerns—to defend the school's doctrines and practices from outside attack and inner deviation, and to prevent later generations from focusing on theory to the exclusion of seeing into their own minds—account for much of the form and content of Ch'an literature.

The literature produced during the two periods of the school's domestication exhibits two approaches to these concerns. In the long run, the literature produced during the second period—which we will consider in Sections 8.6.1 and 8.6.2—was far more successful than that produced during the first. In fact, not until the second period did Ch'an actually become a unified school with an established body of doctrine and legendary tradition. Prior to that, the "school" was more a loose family of lineages, each with its own fluid amalgam of teachings and traditions, scattered through mountainous regions in central, southeastern, and southwestern China. Even after its establishment as a distinct school, Ch'an continued to split over several recurrent issues, the most prominent of them being the question of whether Ch'an practice was in harmony with traditional scriptural doctrines or was something entirely separate and unique.

The first Ch'an masters to gain widespread popular attention were members of the East Mountain School of Hupeh province, Hung-jen (circa 600–674) and his student Shen-hsiu (circa 606–706). Hung-jen attracted dozens of students, but not until 700, when Empress Wu invited Shen-hsiu to teach in the imperial palace and—in a dramatic display of veneration unprecedented for an emperor—publicly bowed down to his feet, did the school attain national prominence. Shen-hsiu wrote a number of texts describing the doctrines and practices of his school. Other students of Hung-jen also wrote texts, recording Hung-jen's teachings and those of his predecessors, establishing a lineage going back through Mahākāśyapa to the Buddha himself. Some of them claimed that this lineage was transmitted through Bodhidharma, a fifth-century South Indian monk famous for his meditative prowess. In an attempt to compensate for the school's lack of any clear basis in a particular Buddhist text, they also connected Bodhidharma with the *Laṅkāvatāra Sūtra*. Although modern scholarship indicates that the school's connections with Bodhidharma, and his with the *Laṅkāvatāra*, were tenuous at best, later legends surrounding Bodhidharma claiming him as the First Patriarch of the school played a central role in the developing Ch'an mythology. According to the reckoning of the East Mountain School, Hung-jen was the Fifth Patriarch of the school, and Shen-hsiu the Sixth.

The most important doctrine for the school was the teaching of the Buddha-nature immanent in all living beings. Different members of the school dealt in different ways with the practical implications of this teaching, and in particular with the question of how to regard mental defilements in light of the Buddha-nature's intrinsic purity. Shen-hsiu approached the problem from two angles. When describing the practice from the outside, he stated that the pure mind and the defiled mind, though conjoined, were essentially separate, each with its own intrinsic reality. Neither generated the other. Thus the goal of the practice was to rid the mirror-like pure mind of any impurities. When describing the techniques used to rid the mind of its impurities, however, he recommended that the meditator regard the impurities as essentially unreal. Some of the practices he taught implied a sudden approach to Awakening; others, a more gradual approach.

Shen-hsiu's school remained popular in the capital for several generations, but its popularity attracted controversy. In 730, a monk named Shen-hui (684–758)—a former student of Shen-hsiu and of Hui-neng, another student of Hung-jen—mounted a campaign attacking Shen-hsiu and his followers, whom he called the Northern School, for teaching a limited gradualistic and dualistic approach to the practice. Shen-hui insisted that the doctrine of the Buddha-nature's essential purity meant that mental impurities were nonexistent, and that expedient efforts to remove those impurities were a distraction rather than a help in awakening to that nature. Shen-hui produced new and more dramatic stories of Bodhidharma to support his position on sudden or unmediated Awakening, and insisted that Hui-neng, about whom almost nothing is known, was Ch'an's actual Sixth Patriarch.

Shen-hui was less a meditation teacher than an evangelist, focused on organizing ordinations and winning recruits to his Southern School. Although the emperor in 796 posthumously declared him the true Seventh Patriarch, he maintained this title only in the Ho-tse school he founded, which did not last beyond the persecutions of 845.

Shen-hui's attack on gradualism, however, had a lasting effect on Ch'an rhetoric. No Ch'an school after his time openly advocated any doctrines or practices that might be labeled "gradual." The term *Southern School* came to stand for any Ch'an lineage that taught a sudden Awakening, although records from Tun-huang show that the Northern School taught a type of sudden Awakening as well. All the schools that lasted into the Sung dynasty claimed to be Southern, accepting Hui-neng as the Sixth Patriarch, and passing over Shen-hui in almost total silence. As for the Northern School, it continued until the tenth century, when it died out with the end of the T'ang.

In 780, one of the Southern Schools—the Ox-head School—composed the *Platform Sūtra* to advance its interpretation of the distinction between the Northern and Southern Schools, at the same time providing Hui-neng with an attractive mythology. Whatever its historical accuracy, the *Platform Sūtra* became one of the most influential texts in the development of southern Ch'an. Part of its appeal lay in its dramatic presentation of the "transmission" of the Dharma from Hung-jen to Hui-neng. Hung-jen, the story goes, asked his students to write poems on the wall to show the extent of their Awakening. Based on the poems submitted, Hung-jen would then choose his Dharma-heir. Shen-hsiu, considered the prime candidate for succession, wrote the only poem, which recommended a "complete" practice—in T'ien-t'ai terms—of clearing away the obstructions that block the recognition of Awakening in all things. The body, the poem said, was the Bodhi tree, and the mind was a stand for the mirror of Awakened awareness, from which the dust should continually be removed. Hui-neng, an illiterate layman working in the monastery kitchen, heard of the poem and asked to have his rebuttal written next to it. There are various recensions of the rebuttal, but all agree on the central image: Originally bodhi has no tree, the mirror has no stand, Awakening is originally pure, so where could dust arise? Hung-jen realized that Hui-neng alone was ready to fathom the teaching on emptiness and non-abiding, and so at night secretly invited him into his chambers and read the *Diamond Sūtra* to him. Immediately, Hui-neng "received" the Dharma—that is gained Awakening—and so Hung-jen bestowed his robe on him as a sign of the transmission of the Dharma. The practice of a teacher ceremonially transmitting the Dharma to a student dates back to such texts as the *Pratyutpanna* (see Section 4.3.2), but the *Platform Sūtra* succeeded in enshrining this practice in Ch'an ideology, where it has continued to play an important role to the present day. It also helped to establish the *Diamond Sūtra* as one of the school's primary texts, and the Perfection of Discernment teaching on non-abiding as one of the school's primary teachings.

The practical implications of Hui-neng's poem are contained in the *Platform Sūtra*'s sudden teaching of "no-thought." No-thought does not mean putting a stop to thoughts. Instead it means allowing successive thoughts to follow one another without interruption or without abiding. If a single thought were interrupted, the dharma body would be detached from the physical body, creating—in the image of the poem—a duality of "mirror stand" and "tree," providing a place where thoughts could abide. If a single thought were to abide, succeeding thoughts would pile up, creating bondage. But when thoughts are allowed to flow without interruption or without abiding, that is simply the functioning of Suchness, which forms the essence of this thought-stream. There would then be no bondage to clear away, for the "bondage" had simply been the piling up of thoughts that were originally pure and now were allowed to flow. Thus, on realizing no-thought, one realizes Suchness and attains the status of Buddha.

The Sūtra incorporates its teaching of no-thought into its definition of *tso-ch'an* (sitting meditation), which it expands on the *Nirvāṇa Sūtra*'s assertion that concentration and discernment are identical. According to the *Platform Sūtra,* sitting (corresponding to concentration) means not a physical posture, but the state of no-thought in any and all circumstances; meditation (corresponding to discernment) is the state of seeing Suchness without confusion. Thus concentration (the functioning of Suchness) is the essence of discernment, and discernment (the seeing of Suchness) the function of concentration.

The Sūtra offers no further details as to whether this approach was to be combined with formal meditation techniques, or if it implied a rejection of techniques altogether. Various Southern Schools took up different sides on this question, but evidence suggests that the mainstream position retained formal techniques as the backbone of the practice, using the sudden perspective as a corrective to the pitfalls that formalism might entail. At the same time, the schools provided differing interpretations of the crucial poems in Hui-neng's story. For instance, Tsung-mi, who traced his lineage back to Shen-hui, interpreted the poems as expressing the difference between gradual and sudden practice—rather than the Ox-head

School's distinction between complete and no-thought practice—an interpretation that has proven influential to the present day.

These debates continued until the persecutions of 845, although some lineages managed to stay in the mountains and avoid the controversy. In terms of their later influence, the most important of these provincial lineages hailed from the southeast, one beginning with Ma-tsu (709–788), whose first two generations of students included many who were to become famous in later Ch'an mythology, among them Huang-po (d. 850), Lin-chi (d. 866); and another beginning with Tung-shan (807–869). According to that mythology, these Ch'an masters developed a new teaching style that made heavy use of paradox, iconoclasm, cryptic statements, shouts, and beatings to jolt their students into a state of non-dual *chien-hsing* (in Japanese, *kenshō*), or seeing-nature, in which there is no duality between the seeing-awareness and the Buddha-nature seen. Although documents dating from the time of Ma-tsu and Tung-shan confirm the importance of *chien-hsing* in their teaching, the accounts of their unorthodox teaching methods were not written down until the tenth century, and so there is some doubt about the accounts' reliability. They may well be accurate, simply reflecting the fact that monks in the ninth century had different views from monks in the tenth century about what deserved to be written down, but no one now can know for sure. By the twelfth century, Five Houses had developed within the Ch'an school, three of them tracing their lineage back to Ma-tsu (most prominently the Lin-chi house) and one—the Ts'ao-tung house—to Tung-shan. However, historical records from the late T'ang show virtually no division among these lineages during the eighth and ninth centuries. Students of one master often studied under other masters with no sense of having crossed sectarian boundaries.

Because these provincial lineages avoided the capital, they were best positioned to survive the Huang Ch'ao Rebellion. In fact, they were the only lineages in any major school, meditative or scholastic, to continue unbroken through the turmoil at the end of the T'ang.

8.6 THE SUNG DYNASTY (970–1279)

The Sung dynasty witnessed a major restructuring of Chinese society, as the agrarian feudal economy of previous dynasties developed into an urban economy administered by a centralized bureaucracy. The major intellectual concern of the times was to recast Chinese culture into a comprehensive, harmonious form that could serve as a unifying ideology for the newly consolidated state. The emphasis on harmony and unity is understandable, considering the preceding centuries of warfare and upheaval. To ease the sense of alienation that such a major social shift might cause, writers of this period harked back to the golden age of Chinese civilization during the T'ang, which they claimed to be preserving even as they molded it into a radically new form.

These trends influenced Buddhism on many levels. On the level of popular devotion, the various pantheons of Taoist immortals, Buddhist bodhisattvas, and local spirits were organized in the popular imagination into a bureaucratic hierarchy, mirroring the political process occurring on Earth. Although this process had begun under earlier dynasties, it was finalized only during the Sung. For instance, the deities associated with the afterlife were organized into the ten courts of the underworld that would determine a dead person's state of rebirth. Funeral rites were thus arranged with an eye to helping the departed one negotiate the schedule of court hearings, corrupt bureaucrats, and other legal hurdles faced after death.

On the institutional and doctrinal levels, the early Sung rulers were concerned with placing the Sangha on a more stable, rational basis. To standardize the teaching, the government printed many Buddhist texts, including a Chinese Buddhist Canon, based on a core canon defined and compiled during the T'ang by the monk Chih-chung (fl.669–740). This was a massive undertaking requiring 11 years and 130,000 wood-printing blocks. To standardize practice, the government established large monastic estates, termed "public monasteries," with government support balanced by standardized discipline and strict government controls over ordinations and the selection of abbots. A small number of these monasteries were designated as Vinaya monasteries, the only places where ordinations could be conducted. These functioned more or less as boot camps for new monks who would then take up residence in the other monasteries. To provide a standard code for these centers, the Vinaya expert Yüan-chao (1048–1116) eventually established a Vinaya (Lü) school, based on the commentaries that the T'ang scholar Tao-hsüan (596–667) had written on the Dharmaguptaka Vinaya. This established the Dharmaguptaka Vinaya as standard in Chinese monasteries, a position it has held up to the present.

8.6.1 Ch'an Politics

The question of who would be put in charge of the remaining monasteries led to intense political jockeying between the two main surviving T'ang schools: Ch'an and T'ien-t'ai. Ch'an prevailed for several reasons. To begin with, it could produce records to show that its lineage, unlike T'ien-t'ai's, had not lapsed during the persecution of 845. In fact, the T'ang-Sung interregnum—called the Five Dynasties period (907–960)—which had laid to waste all the other schools of Chinese Buddhism, had been a fertile period in the history of Ch'an. To escape the turmoil that was engulfing most of China, thousands of monks from the southern Ch'an lineages had taken refuge in present-day Fukien, a relatively peaceful enclave in southeastern China. Forced into close proximity, they began to view themselves as a unified school. Threatened with the potential for total political chaos, they began writing down their oral traditions as a way of preserving them for future generations. Their writings focused on tales of the unorthodox ways in which the Ch'an masters of the past embodied the principle of nonduality through nonsequiturs, ambiguous statements, and outrageous actions. Many of these tales depicted encounters in which masters employed these unorthodox methods to spark *chien-hsing* in their students. Although the monks' initial motivation may have been simply to preserve these teachings, they also used these *ku-tse,* or ancient precedents, to flesh out the Ch'an lineage accounts, called lamp records, to demonstrate in detail the various ways in which the light of *chien-hsing* had been passed from generation to generation. The earliest extant example of this style of lamp record was *The Collection of the Patriarchal Hall,* compiled in 952 by Ching-hsiu Wen-t'eng.

With the beginning of the Sung dynasty, Ch'an monks produced new lamp records—far more extensive in content and literary in style—to promote the school's good reputation in the eyes of the imperial court. The first of the new lamp records was *The Transmission of the Lamp* (1004), compiled by Yung-an Tao-yüan for the edification of the emperor during the Ching-te reign. This codified the Ch'an lineage in a form that was to become standard throughout the remaining history of the school, tracing the transmission back not only to the Buddha but to seven Buddha's before him. Although Tao-yüan wrote this record to illustrate the principle of the harmony between Ch'an and written teachings, a younger monk, Yang-I (971–1020) rewrote the preface to make it accord with the first phrase of what became the official slogan of the Ch'an school under the Sung: "A special transmission outside the [written] teachings; not setting up scriptures; pointing directly at a person's mind; seeing into its nature and attaining Buddhahood." In other words, Ch'an was special because it was a nonverbal mind-to-mind transmission that did *not* accord with the written teachings. This principle was further promoted in other texts, most importantly *The Record of the Extensive Transmission,* complied in 1036 by Li Tsun-hsü. According to this record, the mind-to-mind transmission between the Buddha and Mahākāśyapa was totally nonverbal: The Buddha picked up a flower while instructing the assembled monks; Mahākāśyapa was the only monk to smile; and so the Buddha announced that he was transmitting to him the treasury of the true Dharma-eye, the wondrous mind of nirvāṇa.

This notion of a nonverbal transmission was popular with the imperial court in that it provided a convenient rallying point for unifying divergent interpretations of the Dharma. All were free to intuit the nonverbal level in their own terms. At the same time, it satisfied the conviction, dating back to the time of Speculative Metaphysics, that nonverbal intuition characterized the clearest understanding of the highest principles.

As a result of the Ch'an campaign for imperial support, the vast majority of public monasteries were designated Ch'an monasteries, with only a small minority left as teaching monasteries, headed by members of the T'ien-t'ai school. In a large sense, however, this was a hollow victory for the Ch'an monks. Life at the two types of monasteries differed little, in that both were run on the same tight schedule of study and meditation. The only differences were that ku-tse were read at the formal meetings in the Ch'an monasteries, whereas Sūtras and scholastic treatises were read at similar meetings in teaching monasteries; and the designation of the monastery was what determined the lineage from which the abbot would come. Even in Ch'an monasteries, many monks devoted a good amount of their time to the study of formal doctrine, such as Hua-yen texts, as well as to non-Buddhist topics, such as Confucianism, literature, and painting. Thus, despite the school's new slogan, most Ch'an monks were extremely cultured and well read.

Only a small cadre of monks actually studied with the abbot of a particular monastery, the remaining monks being free to come and go. Many of them actually spent their time traveling among Ch'an and teaching monasteries to broaden their education. This gave rise to the system of the three *men* (traditions) that identified a monk's affiliation: *lü-men* (the disciplinary tradition in which he had been ordained); *tsung-men* (his lineal tradition, that is, the Ch'an lineage under which he first received tonsure and meditation training); and *chiao-men* (his doctrinal lineage, that is, the school of formal doctrine under which he had studied).

8.6.2 Ch'an Meditation

Despite the institutionalization of Ch'an, the practice of meditation continued to develop in new ways. Here again, the ku-tse played a prominent role, perhaps best understood in light of the T'ien-t'ai classification of gradual, sudden, and complete methods of meditation. Gradual methods consist of the tactical skills employed to bring about the nondual realization of the Dharma-body in the sudden method, which in the Ch'an terminology would correspond to *chien-hsing*. The complete method integrates the nondual perspective with the world of phenomena, to avoid what, in the Mahāyāna perspective, is the error of seeing the dual and nondual as separate in any way.

Ku-tse were first used in Ch'an meditation as a complete method. Meditators who had realized *chien-hsing* would lecture on the ancient precedents, exploring the ramifications of how nonduality was best expressed in the world of dualistic appearances. These lectures, later transcribed as commentaries, could also serve as proof to others that the lecturer was operating from the same complete perspective as the ancient master in the ku-tse. The first Ch'an master known to have used this method was Yün-men Wen-yen (864–949) during the Five Dynasties period. In the early Sung, Fen-yang Shan-chao (947–1024) was the first to collect commentaries of this sort. In his *Record* he appended verses and commentaries to 200 old cases and 100 new cases of his own invention. This was the format later followed by the great compilations, such as the *Emerald Cliff Record,* compiled by Yüan-wu K'o-ch'in (1063–1135), and the *Gateless Barrier,* by Wu-men Hui-k'ai (1183–1260), which superseded Fen-yang's *Record* as the school's classic texts.

In writing commentaries on the ancient precedents, the Ch'an masters were following a tradition with roots in the T'ien-t'ai school. As we have noted previously, the T'ien-tai school held that the most complete statements of truth were self-contradictory, operating on many levels of meaning. Thus, as part of their studies, T'ien-tai monks would write commentaries on specific complete statements, usually drawn from the Perfection of Discernment literature. Ch'an commentators, in following this tradition, introduced two innovations: The passage to be commented on came from native Chinese encounter dialogues, rather than abstract foreign texts; and the purpose of the commentary was not to explain the encounter to a person immersed in duality, but to pass judgment on the encounter from a complete standpoint. In some cases, this would involve approving of the master's action in the encounter and then expressing the master's point of view in totally different words, often employing references from classical Chinese literature even more cryptic than the original encounter. In other cases, the commentator would find fault with the master and then suggest how genuine nonduality would have been expressed in the situation. This tendency for commentators to pass judgment on the ku-tse may account for the name that these cases developed by the twelfth-century: *kung-an,* public legal cases, which led to the Japanese form, *kōan.*

At some unknown point in the early Sung, Ch'an masters began assigning these cases to their students prior to the students' first Awakening. In T'ien-t'ai terminology, this was tantamount to using a complete method to function as a gradual method. Ch'an masters writing in the early twelfth century mentioned that the practice was already well established by their time, but gave no indication of how the cases were used in this way. Thus we do not know how this approach was defended against possible attacks that it constituted sneaking a "gradual" method in through the back door.

However, in the late twelfth century, two pre-Awakening methods were articulated: the Silent Illumination *(mo-chao)* method of the T'sao-tung master, Hung-chih Cheng-chüeh (1091–1157), and the Kung-an Introspection *(k'an-hua)* method of the Lin-chi master, Ta-hui Tsung-kao (1089–1163), a student of the author of the *Emerald Cliff Record.* The writings of both masters indicate that they articulated their methods in response to a widespread fashion among monks and lay literati to write commentaries on kung-ans as a purely literary exercise, with some even equating the act of artistic creation to Awakening itself. In counteracting this fashion, however, Hung-chih and Ta-hui proposed radically different approaches.

By their time, encounter-dialogue kung-ans had been supplemented with catch-phrase kung-ans, which consisted of cryptic statements devoid of narrative context. Typical catch-phrase kung-ans included, "Your self before the empty aeon [i.e., prior to any point in time]," "Why did Bodhidharma come from the West?" "She keeps calling out to [her maid] Hsiao-yü although nothing's the matter." Hung-chih's biography relates that he gained Awakening when his master asked him to explain "your self before the empty aeon." Just as Hung-chih was about to formulate an answer, his master hit him with a stick and Hung-chih gained Awakening. Apparently the import of this Awakening experience was that the answer to the kung-an lay not in the verbal answer, but in the state of still awareness preceding verbalization. Hung-chih thus taught a method in which one looked for one's Buddha-nature in a state of absolute mental stillness and clarity—"like a censer in an old shrine," "like a man who doesn't take a single breath"—in which the words of the kung-an were allowed to drop away into the vast, radiant stillness.

Ta-hui, without questioning Hung-chih's personal Awakening, strongly objected to the Silent Illumination teaching method in that it could easily lead to a dead-end stillness, devoid of understanding. To avoid this pitfall, and at the same time to avoid the dangers of over-intellectualizing, he proposed a method of focusing on the *hua-t'ou* (critical phrase) in a dialogue, converting it from *ssu chü* (a dead utterance) to *huo chü* (a live utterance). His favorite dialogue for this purpose was this: "A monk asked Chao-chou: 'Does even a dog have Buddha-nature?' Chao-chou answered: 'No' [Chinese: *wu;* Japanese: *mu.*]" In this example, the critical phrase is the single word, *wu.* Ta-hui recommended holding this word in mind with total single-mindedness, without trying to explain it, without trying to locate it at any particular point in either in body or mind, without lapsing into unconcern or vacuity, without latching onto "mind," without waiting for Awakening. With all these avenues cut off, and with no alternatives offered as to what to do, the meditator—if sufficiently earnest in pursuing this *wu*—would enter a state of "great doubt," that would eventually ripen into a nonduality of *wu* and the totality of body and mind. As Ta-hui explained, "Everywhere people say that when you become still you will become Awakened. I say that when you become Awakened you will become still."

Ta-hui's initial descriptions of this method were contained in his letters to lay literati, but his first student to achieve Awakening through this method was a nun, Miao-tao. Eventually the method was adopted by monastics in all the Ch'an schools, including the T'sao-tung, where it totally eclipsed the practice of Silent Illumination. Ta-hui's attacks on Silent Illumination were so effective that, like the term "gradual approach," this term never again had a positive meaning in the Ch'an tradition. At the same time, because his approach to the kung-an denied all conceivable avenues of methodical effort, he himself was able to fend off charges of gradualism.

In addition to their general influence on Ch'an meditation, Yüan-wu, Hung-chih, and Ta-hui were also notable for being the earliest known Ch'an masters to have left numerous female Dharma-heirs, chief among them being Ta-hui's student, the nun Ting-kuang, who became a successful teacher in her own right.

8.6.3 The Rise of Neo-Confucianism

Although Buddhist practice continued to develop throughout the Sung dynasty, by the twelfth century Confucianism had come to dominate the standard ideology of the imperial bureaucracy. In part, this was because Buddhism was doctrinally no longer a growing force. Lay support was still strong, but no new texts were being translated, so there was no challenge to create new multisystem syntheses. Buddhism, Taoism, and Confucianism were viewed as static traditions, and the question was how to integrate them into a single ideology that would prevent the sectarian conflicts that had proven so divisive in the past. This boiled down to the question of which tradition among the three would be paramount.

Confucianism had the advantage. Even during the periods of strongest government support for Buddhism, Confucianism had provided the ideology for the day-to-day running of the empire. Of the three traditions, it gave the highest priority to the maintenance of family and state. The Confucians were also able to point to aspects of Buddhism that made it untrustworthy as a guide for bureaucrats. They cited kung-ans to show that Ch'an was amoral; they pointed to historical instances when the fervor of Buddhist popular devotion had been detrimental to the economic interests of the state. In particular, a memorial written during the T'ang dynasty by a Confucian scholar, scathingly critical of the excesses surrounding the public worship of a Buddha relic in 819, became required reading for all potential government officials.

Perhaps the most successful strategy adopted by the Confucians was to take attractive and useful elements of Buddhist doctrine and graft them onto their own, creating a neo-Confucianism. For instance, they initiated government-sponsored social programs—from public clinics and cemeteries to housing for the aged, infirm, and orphans—to embody the Buddhist principle of compassion unlimited by social barriers. The most important of the Sung neo-Confucians was Chu Hsi (1130–1200), who drew on the writings of Chan-jan and Tsung-mi to offer a moralistic, practical philosophy integrating the Buddhist doctrine of self-cultivation with the worldly wisdom and humanistic values of Confucianism. Thus, although Buddhism eventually lost the battle to become the dominant ideology of the Sung bureaucracy, certain Buddhist doctrines helped shape the ideology, where they were enshrined as basic principles in the inherited wisdom of Chinese civilization.

8.7 THE RELIGION OF THE MASSES (1279–1949)

Except for the brief interlude of the Yüan dynasty (1279–1368), when Mongol forces ruled China, the government bureaucracy and monastic system devised during the Sung proved remarkably stable and secure. The major long-term effect of the Mongol rule on Buddhism was in driving a number of Ch'an monks into exile in Japan, thus establishing the Lin-chi (Rinzai) lineage there. Otherwise, the development of Buddhism in China from the thirteenth to the twentieth century was largely an uninterrupted process characterized by several long-term trends. Lay organizations became more prominent in Buddhist circles, engaging largely in charitable work. Pure Land became overwhelmingly the religion of the uneducated masses: the poor, women, children, and merchants without a Confucian education. Any young man training to be a Confucian bureaucrat had to unlearn the faith learned at his mother's knee. Pure Land began to play a more dominant role in the Ch'an monasteries during the Ming dynasty (1368–1644), when the nien-fo was combined with kung-an practice, and monastics adopted the slogan that Ch'an and Pure Land were essentially one. The most popular kung-an at this time was: Who in the mind is reciting the nien-fo? Ch'an retained some of its intellectual respectability among the educated elite, primarily as a lively, private alternative to the public bureaucratic orthodoxy. A gentleman might be a Confucian in the way he conducted government and family affairs, but a "Ch'annist" in his private moments as a poet or artist. In this way Buddhism functioned as an unthreatening counterbalance to the institutions and ideology of the Confucian state.

The peaceful coexistence of Buddhism and Confucianism during the Ming dynasty is best illustrated by the great novel that appeared at this time, *The Journey to the West*. Although the novel is loosely based on the story of Hsüan-tsang's pilgrimage to India and contains many figures from the Buddhist pantheon and Chinese folklore, the author, Wu Ch'eng-en (1500–1582), was a Confucian. The Buddhist virtues he teaches in the novel are essentially those where Buddhism and Confucianism concur. The monk Yuan Chuang (Hsüan-tsang) and his companions are allegorical figures. The monk represents moral conscience; the resourceful yet mischievous magical monkey-king, Sun Hou-tzu, is human nature with all of its weaknesses and potentials; the pig fairy, Chu Pa-hsieh, embodies greed and other base motives. In the course of the adventures, the monkey-king learns self-discipline, loosely defined so as to fit either the Buddhist or neo-Confucian mode, to tame his wayward tendencies. In this manner, the Buddhist reader is taught Confucian ideals in a palatable way—a fine example of a Confucian turning the Mahāyāna strategy of tactical skill to his own uses.

As the religion of the masses, Buddhism also became the religion of the disaffected. Some of the lay Buddhist organizations—such as the White Lotus Society, loosely connected with the T'ien-t'ai school—actually staged insurrections against the Mongol and Manchu rulers. The White Lotus rebellion at the end of the eighteenth century (1796–1804) took 10 years to suppress. A few temples, such as the center at Shao-lin, trained monks in the martial arts, but the Sangha as a whole remained aloof from such affairs.

Modern historians have written disparagingly of the lack of dynamism and creativity in Chinese Buddhism from the late fourteenth to early nineteenth century, but there were attempts at revitalization during both the Ming and the Manchu Ch'ing (1644–1912) dynasties. The Pure Land/Ch'an synthesis during the Ming not only produced figures famous in China, but also spawned new schools of "Ming Ch'an" in Japan and Vietnam. Tibetan monasteries were opened in the capital during the Ch'ing dynasty as the emperors assumed the role of patron to the various Tibetan sects (see Section 11.4), and in this way elements of Vajrayāna practice were reintroduced both to the court and to the general society. Perhaps the most wide-ranging reform during these centuries followed the T'ai-p'ing rebellion (1850–1864). The rebels, fervent Christians, had looted and burned most of the great monasteries in the areas they occupied. In shocked response, lay and monastic Buddhists rebuilt the monasteries, formed scripture-printing societies and study clubs, and started schools. Some young monks who acquired modern ideas through lay-initiated schools agitated for social revolution and participated in the overthrow of the Manchu dynasty in 1911. However, these radicals were not supported by the majority of the Sangha, who believed that monastics should stay out of politics and study the scriptures rather than modern secular subjects.

The Nationalist regime in mainland China (1912–1949) fluctuated between mild hostility and mild support for Buddhism, but generally allowed Buddhists a freedom they had not enjoyed during Manchu rule, when all private associations had been under suspicion of treason. Statistics released in 1930 claimed that there were 738,000 monastics and 267,000 Buddhist temples in China. This was by far the largest clergy in China, or in any national church in the world. The majority did not live in strictly run monasteries, but at least fifty thousand did. Although Buddhism was not a prominent force in national life, Republican China—insofar as it was religious—was more Buddhist than anything else, and Buddhist religious life still followed many of the same patterns as it had for centuries.

8.7.1 Religious Life: Devotional

Buddhist religious life had taken some distinctive directions in China. Some scholars have attributed these developments to Taoist or other local influences, but the picture is far more complex than that.

Devotionalism, for instance, was much stronger among Buddhists—lay and monastic—than among Taoists. Buddhist devotional cults grew rapidly from the time of the fall of Han through the Three Kingdoms and Six Dynasties period (220–584). The most popular objects of devotion were Kuan-yin (Avalokiteśvara, who metamorphosed from male to female during the Sung dynasty), Amitābha, and Maitreya. Kuan-yin was popularly reputed to save one from dangers here on Earth, whereas Amitābha and Maitreya welcomed one to their realms of happiness after death. There was also a cult of the arhat Piṇḍola Bhāradvāja (see Section 3.3.3). According to Sarvāstivādin tradition, the Buddha had assigned him the duty of looking after the religion as punishment for having exhibited his psychic powers to lay people. Monasteries often contain *lohan* (arhat) halls to house representations of him and other arhats, despite their belonging to a Hīnayāna tradition.

As in other Buddhist countries, the geography of China was made sacred through the reputed presence of great Buddhist beings. In particular, four great bodhisattvas were believed to have made China their home: Samantabhadra (Chinese: P'u-hsien) on Mount Omei in Szechuan in the south; Kuan-yin on Mount P'u-t'o on an island near Chekiang in the east; and Kṣitigarbha (Chinese: Ti-tsang) on Mount Chiu-hua in Anhui in the west. However, the most famous of the bodhisattva abodes was Māñjuśrī's (Chinese: Wen-shu), on Mount Wu-t'ai in Shansi in the north. Prior to the fifth century, this mountain had been renowned for its natural anomalies, such as blossoms raining down from the heavens, hot springs on mountain peaks, and rainbow clouds. By the middle of the sixth century the belief developed that Māñjuśrī had made his home there, a belief fostered by a passage in the *Avataṃsaka Sūtra* stating that the bodhisattva dwelled in a "cold mountain" in the Northeast. By the eighth century, Mount Wu-t'ai was attracting Buddhist pilgrims from as far away as India in hope of visions of the great bodhisattva, who would reveal himself either majestically—as a blazing ball of light or a young prince riding the clouds astride a golden-haired lion—or covertly, as a beggar or old man mysteriously wandering the slopes. Legends attested that a Kashmiri Tantric monk, Buddhapāli (Chinese: Fo-t'o po-li), had succeeded in entering Māñjuśrī's secret cave and continued to serve there as his acolyte. Over the centuries, hundreds of temples were built on the slopes of the mountain, often in response to visions received there, and the center flourished even when Buddhism was in decline elsewhere in the country.

The sacred geography of these bodhisattva mountains is often replicated on the altars of East Asian Buddhist temples. The north–south pair of "inspiring" bodhisattvas— Māñjuśrī and Samantabhadra—tend to flank Śākyamuni, whereas the east–west pair of "protecting" bodhisattvas—Kuan-yin and Kṣitigarbha—tend to flank Amitābha.

As has been the case elsewhere in the Buddhist world, relic worship has long been popular in China. Popular relics include a finger bone of the Buddha presented to an emperor of the T'ang dynasty. In addition, the Chinese have developed a cult around the entire mummified bodies of especially revered monks or nuns. The mummy with the longest known continuous history, dating back to 713 C.E., is that of Hui-neng, the Sixth Ch'an Patriarch, whose body did not decay after death. Covered with lacquer, it exists to this day in a grotto in south China. The early biographies of monks and nuns, dating from the Later Han dynasty to the Liang dynasty (150–519), tell of monks or nuns whose bodies also did not decay. Eventually it became part of a postmortem test of a revered monastic's spiritual attainments. The body would be placed in a large urn and checked after a certain length of time. If it had not decayed, he or she was regarded as truly worthy of veneration.

8.7.2 Religious Life: Monastic

Members of the Chinese Sangha did not, as a rule, wander for alms. Instead, they were supported by income from monastic landholdings or by gifts from lay donors. Some Ch'an texts from the eighth and ninth centuries mention monks working in the fields. Having a choice in their food, and sometimes a role in its production, all monastics ultimately became strictly vegetarian, a practice that sets East Asian Buddhism apart from the monastic orders in other Buddhist countries. Some scholars trace this practice to Taoism, although Indian Mahāyāna Sūtras, such as the *Nirvāṇa Sūtra,* indicate that vegetarianism may also have had its roots among Mahāyāna monastics in India.

The practice of monastics' following Taoist diets—such as eating nothing but pine needles—can, of course, be attributed unequivocally to Taoist influences. However, some unusual diets can be traced to Buddhist sources. A diet of fragrant oil was observed by the few monastics who, in the early centuries of Chinese Buddhism, practiced self-immolation inspired by a passage from the *Lotus Sūtra,* describing bodhisattvas who set fire to their bodies as an offering to the Triple Gem. Although there is good reason to believe that the compilers of the *Lotus Sūtra* meant the passage to be taken figuratively, a small number of monastics took it literally and practiced self-immolation at night, making their bodies into lamps as a way of offering light to others and demonstrating their total commitment to the Dharma. So far as is known, this suicide by fire was practiced only in areas within the Chinese cultural sphere (see Section 9.10). A vastly attenuated form of this practice, still common today, is that of monastics using incense to burn marks on their heads at ordination as a sign of dedicating their bodies to the Triple Gem.

Over the centuries, the Sangha in China developed a family and clan system parallel to the secular clans of blood lineages, with an elaborate hierarchy of relationships based upon tonsure, the first act required of one leaving the household life. The newly tonsured individual moved from secular to Buddhist family complete with "father," "uncles," "brothers," and "cousins" (these male terms were used among both monks and nuns). This practice had both Chinese and Indian precedents, as the newly ordained monks and nuns in India were also told to regard their preceptors as their parents.

8.7.3 Religious Life: Lay

Lay practices attested to in early times and continuing to modern days include the Lantern Festival, which has no Indian counterpart; the Buddha's birthday; the Ghost Festival; vegetarian feasts; image processions; and the release of living beings. As is the case with Buddhist festivals elsewhere (see Sections 2.6.2 and 3.7), these public festivals all are very joyful.

The Lantern Festival takes place on the fifteenth day of the first lunar month. The legend behind the festival alleges that, to determine whose doctrine was true and whose false, three altars were once set up: one for Buddhist scriptures, one for Taoist scriptures, and one for local gods. These were set on fire, and only the Buddhist scriptures did not burn. The reigning emperor then ordered that, to commemorate the day of the trial by fire, lamps were to be lit symbolizing the great light of Buddhism. This day also marks the conclusion of New Year celebrations.

The Buddha's birthday is celebrated on the eighth day of the fourth month. It is also known as the day for bathing the Buddha, in commemoration of the devas' having bathed him immediately after his birth. A tiny image of the baby Buddha is placed in a basin of fragrant water, often with flower petals in it. The baby Buddha stands with his right arm upraised as he announces that this is his final birth. Worshipers ladle three dippers full of water or tea over the image, pay reverence three times, then ladle three dippers more.

The Ghost Festival is the fifteenth day of the seventh lunar month. Patterned on the *Ullambana Sūtra* (a text composed in China), it commemorates the arhat Maudgalyāyana's (Chinese: Mulien) search in hell for his mother. Lanterns are lit, placed on little boats, and set adrift on a river. If there are no rivers, lanterns are made for the occasion and lit for everyone's enjoyment. The festival, although a commemoration of the dead, is a happy get-together. Sermons are given for the benefit of the dead, to give them proper direction in their sojourn after life, keeping them from becoming malevolent and thereby dangerous to the living. Donations are made to the Sangha and the merit then shared with the dead. In this way, the Sangha functions as an intermediary in the cult of the family. Although some writers have assumed that this role is peculiar to the East Asian Sangha, as a concession to Confucian values, texts from the Mainstream canons, such as the *Petavatthu* (see Section 3.1), indicate that the Sangha has played this role from the very early centuries of the religion.

Vegetarian feasts are meals donated by a lay person to accomplish a karmic purpose or to fulfill a vow. Donors invite a certain number of monks or nuns to these meals for a certain number of consecutive days, often seven. Lay societies also hold communal vegetarian meals, which take on the aspect of a church potluck supper. Image procession is simply the parading of an image of the Buddha or a bodhisattva either around a temple or monastery grounds, or through the streets of a village or town. The occasion can be the Buddha's birthday or any other special event.

Releasing living beings is an ancient practice. Monastic compounds have ponds in which the laity put fish, turtles, eels, and other aquatic creatures originally destined for the cooking pot. Caged birds are also released, the lay devotee buying them from a vendor and then setting them free.

The general acceptance of the doctrine of universal Buddhahood, and the attendant belief that all true Buddhists must take the bodhisattva path, means that dedicated lay Buddhists are expected to abide by the bodhisattva precepts. These are set out in the apocryphal *Scripture of Buddha's Net* at ten: the five Mainstream lay precepts—refraining from killing, stealing, illicit sex, telling lies, and intoxicants—plus five more—refraining from speaking of others' sins, from praising oneself and blaming others, from greed, from anger, and from slandering the Triple Gem.

In the worldview of a typical Chinese lay Buddhist, karma is not necessarily the primary explanation for the vicissitudes of life. There are also the forces of *yin* and *yang*—the cosmic principles of receptivity and activity—as well as the world of spirits and of one's ancestors. If a person is taken ill, his or her family might resort to a spirit medium to see which variety of force is causing the particular illness, and then take appropriate action: making merit to improve a poor stock of karma, making offerings to spirits or ancestors, resorting to a geomancer to bring the yin and yang forces in the environment back into balance, or seeking out a doctor to deal with the physical causes of the disease. Thus a person who participates in a Buddhist ritual is not necessarily a committed Buddhist; by the same token, a committed Buddhist might find it advisable at times to hire the services of a non-Buddhist ritual specialist. The Buddhist techniques for dealing with the invisible forces acting on life, then, are simply one set of alternatives among many that an individual may choose to follow on an ad hoc basis, much as he or she might choose to take Western or Chinese medicine depending on the nature of a particular disease. This ad hoc approach to religion in dealing with mundane issues is especially noticeable in China because the traditional alternatives to Buddhism are also organized religions, but it is typical of the relationship between Buddhism and spirit cults throughout the Asian Buddhist world (see Sections 7.5.1, 9.5, 10.4, and 11.5).

8.8 MODERN CHINESE BUDDHISM

When the Communists took control of the mainland in 1949, monks and nuns were treated as social parasites. Buddhist properties were confiscated in 1951 and many monastics were massacred or imprisoned. Among those who survived, younger monastics were returned to lay status; older ones were put to work farming, weaving, running vegetarian restaurants, or teaching school. Ordination was discouraged, and the Sangha became an institution of the aged.

In 1953 the government established a Chinese Buddhist Association to impose direct control over Buddhist institutions. Famous and beautiful old temples were maintained at government expense, Buddhist art works were safeguarded, and sites such as the Yün-kang caves were designated national treasures. However, the Cultural Revolution (1966–1976) signaled an abrupt return to destruction. Rampaging Red Guards targeted Buddhist sites as remnants of the feudalistic past that stood in the way of their new order. Many monks and nuns fled China for Hong Kong and Taiwan.

Currently, however, the government has eased its policy of religious repression. Temples and shrines ransacked during the Cultural Revolution are being rebuilt, often with the help of donors from Taiwan, Hong Kong, North America, and Japan. Defrocked nuns and monks, no longer routinely denounced as "parasites," are being allowed to resume monastic lives. The motivations here are both spiritual and economic. Those who persisted in their Buddhist faith are now more free to practice. The government, however, has an eye on the tourist trade.

The island of Taiwan was not occupied by the Communists after the revolution, and so it experienced no abrupt severing of Buddhist or other Chinese traditions. The old guard of the Nationalist party, though primarily Christian, portrayed itself as the caretaker of China's cultural heritage, using Confucian values to encourage popular support for its policy of constant preparedness for war. Buddhism was treated as largely irrelevant to the needs of the times. Now, however, a number of factors—the changing of the guard, the relaxing of military policy, and the fast-growing economy—have contributed to a strong Buddhist revival, to the point where Taiwan currently has the most vibrant Buddhist community in East Asia. The growth of the economy in particular has provided surplus funds that can be devoted to religious projects, while at the same time inspiring a sense of alienation from the widespread greed unleashed by material progress. This sense of alienation has led many to search for the solace offered by a variety of lay and monastic Buddhist organizations.

Foremost among these organizations is Fo-kuang Shan (Buddha Light Mountain), founded in 1967 by Master Hsing Yun. Espousing what it calls Humanistic Buddhism, this organization seeks to shift Buddhism's focus from the supramundane to the mundane, to create a Pure Land on Earth utilizing the advantages of modern material progress tempered by Buddhist values. Thus, for instance, it recommends seeking economic advancement through the practice of generosity, virtue, and nien-fo meditation; once wealth and status are gained, they are to be used with the compassion of a bodhisattva. To implement its vision, the organization runs a large orphanage, several old-age homes, mobile medical care units, and various Buddhist colleges and universities. It has many branches worldwide, including a lavish monastery outside of Los Angeles.

Buddhism has proven to be particularly attractive to women in Taiwan, who have been joining the Sangha to an unprecedented degree. In a society that does not espouse equality of the sexes as an ideal, much less a reality, the life of a nun offers an autonomy otherwise unavailable to women. Buddhist groups also attract many lay women who view Buddhism as a spiritual refuge and enthusiastically devote their services to its advancement.

Chinese communities scattered throughout Southeast Asia are also experiencing a Buddhist revival. Greater access to books, both in Chinese and English, has disseminated knowledge not only of previously obscure aspects of Chinese Buddhism, but also of non-Chinese Buddhist traditions. As a result, lay organizations devoted to Theravādin or Tibetan practice have sprung up in Singapore, Malaysia, and Hong Kong, as well as Taiwan; and Chinese natives of these countries have ordained in Theravādin and Tibetan orders.

8.9 A BUDDHIST CHARITABLE ORGANIZATION

One of China's most distinctive contributions to Buddhism has been its tradition of Buddhist charitable organizations, which we have already noted in Sections 8.5.4 and 8.7. At present, one of the more notable examples of this tradition is the Buddhist Compassion Relief Love and Mercy (T'zu-chi) Foundation, founded in Taiwan in 1966 by a nun, Dharma Master Cheng Yen.

Born in 1937, Cheng Yen's early life was blighted by her having inadvertently contributed to the death of her father. She sought solace in the teachings of various religions, but only the Buddhist teaching of responsibility for one's own karma gave her any satisfaction. Still, there was much in the general practice of Chinese Buddhism, with its appeals to Buddhas and bodhisattvas for help, that struck her as superstitious. Rather than beseeching a bodhisattva for help, she resolved to become one herself. In 1962 she left home in hopes of ordaining. Shortly before a mass ordination in Taipei the following year, a famous scholar agreed to sponsor her.

She then retreated to a small temple, isolated in the mountains, near the east coast city of Hwalien. Her style of teaching, using simple, modern language to explain abstract concepts, and her personal determination to work for her own livelihood soon attracted a small but dedicated following. In 1966, struck by the sufferings of the poor aborigines in her area—and in particular by their inability to gain admission to the local hospital for medical care—she resolved to establish a charitable fund to help them. Asking advice from some Catholic nuns, she was told that Buddhism was a poor basis for charitable work, as it was a passive religion that ignored the needs of others. Stung by this remark, she gathered her five disciples and thirty supporters and had them join in a resolution that they would become "Kuan-yin's watchful eyes and useful hands," so that the world would never call Buddhists a passive group again.

From these small beginnings, the foundation has grown into an organization numbering three million followers in Taiwan, plus many thousands of Chinese around the world. In Taiwan, the active work of the foundation is carried out by three thousand "commissioners," volunteers who collect donations, propose and personally carry out specific projects, and conduct follow-up studies on the results. Their projects include modern hospitals that charge no admission fees (a novelty in Taiwan) and offer free care for those who cannot pay, a nursing college, and a medical school and research center. They also offer food and housing assistance to Taiwan's poor and needy as well as disaster relief throughout the world. Their activities have recently spread to America, where they have provided aid for the inner-city poor and relief to Californians made homeless by the fires of 1993 and 2003. In addition—in response to what many Asians view as the greatest crime in American society—they have provided companionship for neglected patients in old-age homes.

The stated aims of the foundation are platonic—Truth, Beauty, and Goodness—but in more practical terms it hopes to benefit both the recipients and the donors of the aid. For the recipients, the aim is to make them self-reliant, if possible, and in a position to become charitable themselves. For the donors, the aims are more complex and are related to Master Cheng Yen's view of the function of the "Love and Mercy" in the foundation's title. Using the classical symbol of the dusty mirror, she says that the purity of Buddha-nature within each person is clouded by the dust of petty, selfish defilements. Positive cultivation means washing the defilements away with merciful conscience and selfless love. When the dust is gone, the inherent love and mercy of the Buddha-nature will shine through. Thus love and mercy are both a means of self-cleansing and a natural expression of one's inner nature once it is cleansed.

In this sense, the opportunity to give aid is a chance to cleanse one's own heart, and for this reason the members of the foundation are exhorted to honor and be grateful to those they are able to help. Volunteers who assist in the hospitals and other activities of the foundation are taught to do their work with an absorbed, observant state of mind, reflecting on the range of suffering inherent in the human condition, so that they will be able to abandon their own petty greed, aversion, and delusion, thus feeling greater appreciation for their own families. In a pattern of mutual reinforcement, this creates a healthier family environment, which in turn makes it easier for one to contribute further to aiding the greater family of the entire sentient realm.

Master Cheng Yen and her followers tend to regard many of the ritual traditions of Chinese Buddhism with some disfavor. As one of her followers has remarked, "We don't believe in burning incense or in similar rituals, since good deeds mean much more than creating smoke." Some Taiwanese have objected to this aspect of the foundation, saying that Master Cheng Yen is founding a new school of Buddhism, but she claims simply to be bringing Buddhism back to its original form, plain and down-to-earth. This view is reflected in the foundation's buildings, which replace the ornate intricacy of traditional Chinese temple architecture with clean, unadorned lines and spacious, well-lit rooms. For many Chinese in this and other new Buddhist organizations, this is the new face of Buddhism in the twenty-first century.

9

Buddhism in Korea and Vietnam

9.1 A FOCAL POINT FOR UNITY AND DIFFERENCES

The cultures of Korea and Vietnam have long existed in an organic relationship with that of their dominant neighbor, China. Both countries adopted the Chinese form of writing, which enabled them to participate fully in Chinese literary culture. China's centralized government bureaucracy served as a model for Korean and Vietnamese rulers, with Confucianism providing the underlying ideology. Chinese models also influenced their arts and technology.

Within this organic relationship, Buddhism played a paradoxical role, both contributing to the sense of cultural unity with China and providing a focal point for differences. For instance, Chinese movements such as Pure Land and cults such as the worship of Kuan-yin became dominant in both countries, but the influence was not entirely one-sided. One of the early Buddhist missionaries in China, K'ang Seng-hui (d. 280), was born in an Indian trading community located in Chiao-chih, in present-day northern Vietnam, and received his initial training in a Buddhist monastery established by Indians there. Chiao-chih also served as a center where texts brought overseas by Indian monks would be translated into Chinese. During the fourth century, Chinese monks unable to go to India for Buddhist training and texts would study in Chiao-chih instead. Korean monks wrote some of the earliest Ch'an texts, and one, Musang (circa 694–762), even headed a Ch'an school in Szechuan. Korean scholars played a prominent role in formulating Hua-yen and Fa-hsiang doctrine. We have already noted how Chegwan (8.5.1), a Korean, helped revive the T'ien-t'ai school in China during the Five Dynasties period.

Despite these connections, the fact that Buddhism's roots lay outside of China allowed it to serve as a rallying point for Korean and Vietnamese nationalists opposed to Chinese military incursions. Temples in Korea were dedicated to the protection of the military and were assumed to ward off attacks. During the sixth century Korean Buddhists came to believe that their country had been Śākyamuni's home in a previous lifetime. Thus they claimed a special connection with Buddhism; the Chinese, in their eyes, did not transmit a new doctrine to them, but simply reminded them of their own heritage. To emphasize the connection, members of the Silla royal house were named after Śākyamuni's relatives, and many Korean kings consciously followed the model of the wheel-turning monarch (see Section 2.2) as a way of securing the loyalty of their subjects. As for the Vietnamese, they dedicated Buddhist stūpas to national heroes and heroines who had fought off Chinese invaders, and believed that the Buddhist guardian deity of the north, Vaiśravaṇa (see Section 1.4.1), also protected them from their northern neighbor.

Both countries differed from China in another important respect: size. Neither was able to sustain the diversity of schools that had flourished in the much larger Chinese context. As a result, Buddhists in both countries have had an active tendency toward syncretism and eclecticism, in the belief that religious differences should not be allowed to stand in the way of national unity.

KOREA

9.2 THE THREE KINGDOMS PERIOD (18 B.C.E.–688 C.E.)

The history of Korea as a distinct cultural entity began in the first century B.C.E. as rival clans led by warrior aristocracies competed for control of the Korean peninsula. Eventually three clans emerged victorious, establishing the separate kingdoms of Koguryŏ, Paekche, and Silla.

Each kingdom had its own unique responses to the entrance of Buddhism, but with certain patterns in common. Like the northern Chinese courts with whom they had close connections, the royalty of each kingdom viewed Buddhism as a cult offering supernatural protection for the nation through its connections with powerful Buddhas and bodhisattvas. Each viewed Buddhism as a potential force for internal unification and pacification as well, because it offered a moral ideology that could supersede the more divisive mythologies associated with rival clans. Kings and other members of the royal families entered the Sangha as monks and nuns, and actively disseminated the religion to the general populace, who integrated it with their native shamanic beliefs. Symbolic of this integration was the tendency to build Buddhist temples on secluded mountain tops. Korean shamanism had placed great faith in the power of mountain spirits, who often took the form of demonic tigers. By laying claim to the homes of these spirits, Buddhists hoped to appropriate their powers.

Koguryŏ (37 B.C.E.–668 C.E.) The territory of the Koguryŏ kingdom covered the northern portion of the Korean Peninsula, overlapping parts of modern China. Traditionally, Buddhism's entry into the kingdom is placed in the year 372, the second year in the reign of King Sosurim. A monk from China, Sundo (Shun-tao), is credited with introducing Mahāyāna at the behest of the Chinese king Fu Chien. There is evidence, however, that a native Koguryŏ Sangha had developed prior to this date. Scholars have speculated as to whether this Sangha received its Buddhism directly from Central Asia rather than through China, but the evidence is inconclusive. At any rate, Sundo's mission does seem to represent the introduction of the religion to the Koguryŏ court. Within 20 years after his mission, nine temples were established in the capital of Kuknaesŏng (Tong'gou, China). Shortly before the kingdom fell, Buddhist monks formed a militia for its protection, establishing a pattern that was revived in later periods of Korean history.

Paekche (18 B.C.E.–660 C.E.) In the southwest portion of Korea, the kingdom of Paekche arose shortly after Koguryŏ. The Paekche king granted official recognition to Buddhism in 384, following the arrival of an Indian monk who had traveled to Paekche via China. The first temple was built the following year. In the sixth century, the Paekche monk Kyŏmik traveled to India to pursue Vinaya studies. He returned to Paekche in 526, accompanied by the Indian monk Paedalta (Sankrit:*Vedatta). Together they established a productive translation institute in the capital, Wiryesong (near Seoul). As a result of their work, Kyŏmik is regarded as the father of Vinaya studies in Korea. Paekche was especially active in exporting Buddhism and other aspects of Chinese culture and technology to Japan. One of the most prominent nuns of this period, Pŏpmyŏng, was a native of Paekche who traveled to Japan in 655 and achieved fame for her ability to cure illness by chanting the *Vimalakīrtinirdeśa Sūtra*. Her regional Korean accent is said to be responsible for the way the Japanese chant Chinese Sūtra passages to this day.

Silla (57 B.C.E.–668 C.E.) Situated in the mountainous hinterlands of southeast Korea, Silla was the most isolated of the three kingdoms and thus the last to officially recognize Buddhism. The missionary monk Ado (born circa 357) is said to have dazzled the Silla court with his miraculous powers, while "flowers rained from Heaven whenever he preached." Other sources credit a monk from Koguryŏ with introducing Buddhism to the Silla kingdom in the fifth century. Buddhism did not become the state religion until the sixth century, however, largely because the government was less centralized than in the other two kingdoms, and the aristocracy put up more resistance to what it viewed as a political tool for strengthening royal power. Legends state that in 527 the Buddhist devotee Ich'adon conspired with his uncle the king to remove aristocratic opposition to the religion by becoming a martyr. The solar eclipse that followed his execution convinced the people of the power of the Dharma. Within 25 years after

Ich'adon's death, scores of Silla aristocrats had become Buddhist converts. Scholars have pointed out, though, that the Silla aristocracy also had political motives for embracing the religion as a way of fostering diplomatic ties with China.

9.3 THE UNIFIED SILLA DYNASTY (668–918)

In the seventh century, the Silla kings succeeded in conquering their neighbors by playing them off against the Chinese. The unification of the peninsula paved the way for an outstanding period for Korean culture, in which syncretic tendencies, paralleling the political unification of the country, were dominant. Elements from Confucianism, Buddhism, Taoism, and native shamanism were merged in a common religious ideology, with Buddhism playing primarily a cultic role. The opportunity to make merit with the monastic Sangha, and the ability of the Sangha to intercede with Buddhas and bodhisattvas, were seen as guaranteeing the stability and security of the nation.

An instance of this syncretic pattern appears in the *hwarang* (flower squires), a select corps of aristocratic youth who were sent to an exclusive military academy as a means of providing the nation with a civilized elite. Although the moral code they adhered to was primarily Confucian, they adopted the bodhisattva Maitreya (Mirŭk-bosal) as their patron deity.

Maitreya was popular on other levels of society as well. In contrast to the situation in China, his cult was never superseded by that of Amitābha. In fact, one of the distinctive features of the Korean Pure Land (Chŏng-t'o) movement has been its recognition of Maitreya and Amitābha as equals. During the Silla period, the Maitreya cult involved two modes of movement, serving two functions in the society. In the "descent" mode, kings and would-be kings portrayed themselves as incarnations of Maitreya in order to justify their claims to power. In the "ascent" mode, other members of society sought to attain Maitreya's abode in the Tuṣita heaven after death. Other members of the Buddhist pantheon who became popular included Bhaiṣajyaguru (Yaksa-yorae); Amitābha (Amita-bul); Avalokiteśvara (Kwansé ŭm-bosal); and Kṣitigarbha (Chijang-bosal). The historical Buddha, Śākyamuni (Sŏkkamuni), was also accorded the highest reverence, as were his purported relics, such as skull fragments, teeth, and bits of clothing. Temples were built specifically to house these relics, as well as to channel their powers to individual devotees and to the country as a whole.

The Buddhist pantheon inspired monumental works of art, such as the cave temple at Sokkuram. Begun in 751, it was inspired by the cave temples of China, yet reflects a Korean aesthetic. The main Buddha image, a seated Śākyamuni Buddha nearly ten feet tall, is surrounded by statues of various bodhisattvas and disciples. Many wooden temples were built but have not survived the ravages of time.

On the doctrinal level, early interest focused on the *Avataṃsaka* and *Lotus Sūtras.* Ironically, it was during this period of unification that, under the influence of trends in China, Korean Buddhism split into five doctrinal schools: Vinaya (Kyeyul chŏng), Nirvāṇa (Yŏlban chŏng), Dharma Characteristic (Pŏpsŏng chŏng/Haedong), Hua-yen (Wonyung chŏng/Hwaŏm), and "Old" (pre–Hsüan-tsang) Yogācārin (Pŏpsang chŏng). Ch'an (Sŏn) and T'ien-tai (Ch'ŏnt'ae) also came to Korea during this time, although the latter did not become well established until the following dynasty. Chen-yen (Sinan) was popular with the royal family, but the fall of the dynasty apparently brought about the end of the school as well.

9.3.1 Hwaŏm (Hua-yen)

Of the doctrinal schools, Hwaŏm became the most important. Its Korean systematizer, Ŭisang (625–702), studied in China as a disciple of the second Hua-yen Patriarch, Chih-yen (602–668). Ŭisang not only introduced Hwaŏm to Korea, founding the school's Korean headquarters at Pusok Temple, but also continued to shape its doctrine in China through his correspondence with Fa-tsang (see Section 8.5.2).

Another Korean monk who influenced Hua-yen/Hwaŏm doctrine both in China and Korea was Ŭisang's friend and fellow student, Wŏnhyo Daesa (617–686). Koreans generally regard Wŏnhyo as one of their great philosophers, and his career is remarkable for the way in which his life mirrored his thought. Trying to unite all the diverse Buddhist schools, he delineated two main approaches to Awakening: the analytic approach, in which one tried to develop the full range of perfections, and the synthetic approach, in which one tried to return to the One Mind. He then worked out a scholarly method using the two approaches to analyze all issues in Buddhist thought, after which he synthesized them by showing how each approach contained the other in a totally unhindered way. After he had written 240 volumes applying his method to major Mahāyāna texts, his principle of unhindered thought led to a life of unhindered action. Fathering a son with a widowed princess, he abandoned his robes and began wandering, teaching that meritorious and demeritorious action were one and the same for the truly wise person. He used song, music, and dance to spread Pure Land teachings among the common people, and made a career of bringing the Dharma into brothels and taverns.

9.3.2 Sŏn (Ch'an)

Pŏmnang (fl. 632–646), a Korean disciple of Fourth Ch'an Patriarch Tao-hsin (580–651), is credited with bringing Ch'an to his homeland, although his lineage soon died out. Other Ch'an lineages arrived later, becoming organized into the *kusan* (Nine Mountains) system by the early tenth century. Almost all were founded by disciples trained in the tradition of Ma-tsu Tao-i (see Section 8.5.5), and like the Ch'an monks of the Five Dynasty period, they were inspired by stories of Ma-tsu's iconoclastic behavior. As a result, they soon found themselves at odds with the five doctrinal schools. Frustrated by the obstacles the schools placed in their way, some of them began mounting direct attacks on their opponents. Thus as the Unified Silla dynasty drew to a close, Korean Buddhism found itself radically split between textual study and practice, the widespread perception being that the two approaches were irreconcilable.

9.4 THE KORYŎ DYNASTY (918–1392)

Under the Koryŏ dynasty, Buddhism continued in its cultic role as the state religion, reaching a high point in its Korean history. The founding king of the dynasty, Wang Kon (T'aejo, r. 918–943), regarded the Dharma as the foundation for his rule, and instituted an examination system for Buddhist monks, modeled on the Confucian civil-service exams, that provided avenues for monks to become advisers to the court.

Perhaps the main reason for government patronage of Buddhism was an unstable military situation that plagued the dynasty and fueled the perceived need for supernatural assistance. The most striking monument to this perceived need is the Korean Tripiṭaka. Around the turn of the eleventh century, Korea was harassed by the Khitans, an invading tribe from Manchuria. By royal decree, a complete canon of all available Chinese and Korean Buddhist texts was compiled and carved in wooden printing blocks in hopes of securing Śākyamuni's protection for the country. The project—utilizing more than eighty thousand blocks—took two decades to complete, but had little effect on the ongoing warfare. The Khitan menace did not end until 1218, when the tribe was stamped out by the Mongols, who posed an even bigger threat to the peninsula and actually put the Tripiṭaka blocks to the torch. In 1236, a royal decree ordered that another set of blocks be carved. Again, the more than eighty-one thousand blocks completed in 1251 did not immediately drive away the Mongols, although the country suffered less than many others from Mongol depredations. Eventually Mongol power in Korea began to wane in the 1350s, and ended altogether in 1381 with the downfall of the Yüan dynasty in China. This second set of blocks has survived to the present, and in the early twentieth century formed the basis for the massive Japanese Taishō edition of the Chinese Canon.

Benefiting from strong political patronage from the Koryŏs, monasteries grew in size, wealth, and influence. Many became major landholders, with large numbers of serfs. Some even embarked on commercial ventures such as alcohol, noodle, and tea production, while monks became embroiled in court politics. Sŏn monks in particular were well known for their mastery of geomancy, which involved them in construction projects and ceremonies, pulling them away from their meditation practice. As had happened in many other countries, worldly success began to taint the Korean Sangha. This sparked a backlash from both inside and outside the Buddhist community. Confucians mounted their usual attacks on the religion as a whole, whereas Buddhist government officials accused individual monks of ordaining not for spiritual reasons but merely to avoid military service and to exploit the lucrative potential of monastic life. In the tenth century, the government instituted a series of restrictions to limit the participation of monks in secular affairs; in the twelfth century, it ordered that all monks breaking their precepts be forcibly disrobed.

In the midst of the political and ecclesiastical turmoil of the period, three Korean monks—Ŭich'on, Chinul, and T'aego—applied working models from China to raise the standards of the religion and to heal the split between doctrine and practice that had begun under the previous dynasty. Their efforts, which transformed the original divisions of "five teachings and nine mountains" (major Sŏn temples) into "five teachings and two sects," have shaped Korean Buddhism ever since.

9.4.1 Ŭich'on

Ŭich'on (1055–1101) began his life as a royal prince. At the age of 11 he entered a Hwaŏm monastery; in 1085 he went to China to collect texts and further his education. There he studied widely with noted masters from various schools, but was especially drawn to T'ien-t'ai. He vowed to the memory of Chih-i that he would expound the school's doctrine in his homeland, viewing it as the ideal means to synthesize competing traditions by avoiding the pitfalls inherent both in study without practice (represented by the five orthodox schools) and practice without study (represented by Sŏn). In particular, Ŭich'on criticized contemporary Sŏn practitioners for abandoning what he saw as their school's original reliance on study as a basis for meditation.

Enjoying the advantages of royal patronage, Ŭich'on's order soon flourished, attracting members from all quarters of the Buddhist community. His early death, however, put a halt to his attempted unification of Korean Buddhism. Instead of unifying Korean Buddhism, Ŭich'on succeeded simply in adding one more school to the already crowded field. Nonetheless, his example provided important lessons for the more successful reformer, Chinul, one century later.

9.4.2 Chinul

Chinul (1158–1210; posthumously named Pojo) was largely responsible for molding Sŏn into its present form. As a result of his efforts, almost all of Korean Buddhism is now in a sense Sŏn.

Severe childhood illness provided the occasion for Chinul's entry into the monkhood. When all attempts at healing failed, his father promised his son to the Sangha if the Buddha would provide a cure. The cure came, and so Chinul received tonsure at the tender age of 7, followed by the novice precepts at age 15. Bound to no permanent teacher, he began practicing meditation from an early age based on his own reading of texts. This combination of scholarship and practice, rare in his days, was to provide the pattern for his life and teachings.

In 1182, the young Chinul traveled to the capital to sit for the Sŏn examinations. Although he passed them easily, he was disgusted with the worldly climate surrounding them and so made a pact with a handful of fellow examinees to retreat into the mountains and start a reform-minded religious society, the Concentration and Discernment Community, for both lay people and monastics. This was to be the first such society in Korea, although it followed a pattern popular in China since the fifth century. Delays in setting up the community set him on an itinerant life. In the course of his wanderings he settled in the extreme southwest, where he experienced the first of his three major meditative insights. Each insight came as a result of reading a text, a fact that underscored his conviction that doctrinal knowledge and meditative experience were meant to go hand in hand. His first insight came from a passage in the *Platform Sūtra* that identified the mind with the self-nature of Suchness. The insight this gave him into his own mind convinced him of the truth of the *Platform Sūtra*'s teaching on the unity of concentration and discernment, and of Tsung-mi's teachings on sudden Awakening and gradual cultivation. His second insight came while reading a commentary on the *Avataṃsaka Sūtra* that identified the original mind with the discernment of universal brightness that awoke suddenly and completely to the Dharma-dhātu (Dharma-element), or the true nature of reality. This insight underscored for him the essential unity of Hwaŏm doctrine and Sŏn practice.

Soon after this second insight, Chinul's Concentration and Discernment Community became a reality in 1188. By 1197 the community had become well known throughout Korea, attracting large numbers of followers from all walks of life. To accommodate their growing numbers, the group chose Sŏng-gwang Mountain as the site for an enlarged temple. Chinul's third and definitive insight came during a short retreat he took en route to the new center. Although the political situation in Korea had curtailed contacts with China, Chinul had somehow gained access to the *Record* of Ta-hui Tsung-kao (see Section 8.6.2), whose distinction between live and dead utterances sparked Chinul's final experience of Awakening. This final Awakening, however, did not erase Chinul's respect for the texts that had inspired his earlier insights. For him, understanding the meaning of words as dead utterances remained a necessary precursor to approaching them as live utterances so as to understand the process of verbalizing and then reach the radiance of the mind that lay beyond meanings and words. As a result, Chinul continued to use all three texts that had inspired his Awakenings as the basis for his instructions to his students. His combination of *Platform Sūtra* and Hwaŏm doctrine with kung-an practice set the pattern for the Chogye Order he helped spawn.

The name of the order came from the royal decree, promulgated after Chinul arrived at his new center, that renamed the mountain *Chogye,* after Hui-neng's mountain home in southern China. The temple on Chogye/Sŏnggwang continued to function as Sŏn headquarters for more than three hundred years; the community continues to thrive today. When Chinul died in 1210, he was succeeded by his favored disciple, Chin'gak Hyesim (1178–1234), who consolidated his master's efforts, attracted students from all the Sŏn schools and the scholastic sects, and assured the acceptance of kung-an meditation as the principal Sŏn practice.

9.4.3 T'aego

A native of Kwangju in southern Korea, T'aego Pou (1301–1382), reconciled Chinul's Chogye sect with the remaining Sŏn practitioners of the Nine Mountains system on the basis of the personal Lin-chi (in Korean, Imje) transmission he brought back from China. Although Chinul provided the philosophical basis for the Chogye Order, some Korean monks today regard T'aego as the order's true founder by virtue of his direct link to Chinese Ch'an.

T'aego was ordained at the age of 13 and experienced a first glimmering of Awakening in his twenties. At the age of 37 he realized great Awakening after meditating on the famous "Wu" kung-an (see Section 8.6.2). Three years later he began a vastly successful teaching career. During a visit to China (1346–1348) he studied with great Chinese masters both north and south. Of these, Shih-wu,

Eighteenth Patriarch in the Lin-chi lineage, certified T'aego's Awakening and convinced him to return home to spread the Dharma.

Back in Korea, T'aego lived a quiet life on Mount Sosol. The surrounding environment was anything but quiet, though, as the Yüan dynasty was coming to an end in China. For the Koryŏ king Kongmin (r. 1351–1374), this presented a golden opportunity to reassert Korean independence from the Mongols and to consolidate his power within his realm. In the year he assumed the throne, he called T'aego to the capital. Whatever the king's motives for the summons—a desire for Buddhist wisdom or to tap into T'aego's popularity—T'aego took advantage of his new position both to lecture the court on the moral imperatives of power and to petition the king's help in unifying the fragmented Sŏn establishment. Impressed with T'aego's petition, the king appointed T'aego to the position of Royal Teacher in 1356 for the express purpose of carrying out the proposed unification. T'aego based his efforts for a unified Sŏn both on personal transmission through kung-an practice and on the monastic ordinances then current in China.

In typical Ch'an-Sŏn fashion, T'aego balanced his concern for proper form and discipline with iconoclastic rhetoric. The record of one of his lectures to the royal court depicts him as reverently offering incense to the Buddha and then taking the abbot's high seat to proclaim that all the scriptures and the Three Vehicles are just "piss left behind by an old barbarian." After serving as Royal Teacher off and on for 10 years, T'aego eventually sought refuge in monastic retirement. At death he was granted the title of Sŏn Master of Perfect Realization. Several Sŏn lineages claim him as a common ancestor.

9.5 THE YI/CHOSŎN DYNASTY (1392–1910)

The Yi dynasty, which bestowed the name Chosŏn (Land of Morning Calm) on the country, replaced Buddhism with neo-Confucianism as the state ideology. Buddhist monks were forced into seclusion in the mountains, leaving the political field to scholar-officials. As a result, Korean monks—unlike many of their Japanese brethren—do not play a major ritual role in the life of the Buddhist laity to this day.

The transition to this new situation was gradual. The founder of the Yi dynasty, a former general under the Koryŏ kings, actually incorporated Buddhist elements in his new order. However, internal and external political factors favored the neo-Confucians. On the internal level, the new regime needed to counteract the lingering power of those still loyal to the former dynasty. On the external level, it needed the support of China's neo-Confucian Ming dynasty to maintain power.

Thus during the reign of the third king of the dynasty the government began taking active measures against the Buddhists. Lands and servants were confiscated, temples closed, and Buddha images melted down to make weapons. Members of the social elite were forbidden to ordain, and existing monks were pressured to disrobe.

Conditions improved somewhat under later kings. The fourth king, Sejong (r. 1419–1450) advocated a phonetic Korean script, Han'gŭl, which contributed greatly to the popularization of Buddhism by enabling Koreans to read Buddhist literature without having to learn Chinese or Sanskrit. King Sejong also consolidated the Korean Sangha into two schools: the Sŏn school, which included not only Sŏn but also Ch'ŏnt'ae; and the Doctrinal (Kyo) School, which included Hwaŏm and three other schools.

During this period Korea was plagued by invading forces, both Japanese and Manchu. Buddhist monks, following a tradition established during the Koguryŏ kingdom, assumed a military role. The Sŏn master Sŏsan Hyujŏng (1520–1604), for example, led 5,000 of his comrades against the Japanese. Although the Koreans succeeded in driving the Japanese from their territory, the monks' involvement in the war effort incited the Japanese to burn many major monasteries to the ground.

Despite its waning influence in the court, Buddhism maintained its support among the populace, in part because of its willingness to accommodate indigenous shamanism. As a result, the elite linked Buddhism and shamanism as traditions equally to be avoided. In his satirical tale, "The Story of a Yangban," Pak Chi-won (1737–1805) pokes fun at the attitude of a proper Confucian-trained court official: "When ill, do not call a shaman; when sacrificing, do not invite monks."

In the nineteenth century, growing Christian influence in the country sparked a small Buddhist backlash. Ch'oe Che-u (1821–1864; also known as Ch'oe Sūn) founded the Eastern Learning (Tonghak) movement in response to the Western Learning (Sŏhak) movement associated with Catholicism. Also known as the Religion of the Heavenly Way (Ch'ŏndogyo), his movement incorporated meditation practices somewhat influenced by Sŏn, with Confucian, Taoist, and native shamanic doctrines. Another reaction to Western influences was Won Buddhism, founded in 1916, which added Christian doctrines to the traditional Korean eclectic mix.

Meanwhile, beginning in the late nineteenth century, traditional Sŏn was experiencing a revival, largely through the efforts of Kyŏng Ho (1849–1907) and his student, Mang Gŏng (1872–1946). Mang Gŏng in particular was notable for his role in teaching Sŏn not only to monks but also to nuns and lay people. Of his 25 Dharma heirs, four were nuns. One of them, Manseŏng (1897–1975), established what is now the most highly reputed nunnery in the country, T'aeseŏng-am, on the outskirts of Pusan.

9.6 JAPANESE RULE (1910–1945) AND ITS AFTERMATH

In the late nineteenth century, Japan began actively modernizing along Western lines and mounted a program of military expansion that led, among other conquests, to the annexation of Korea in 1910. At home, the Japanese government had followed a policy of using Buddhism to mold public opinion, and it followed a similar policy in Korea. At first, Korean Buddhists were pleased by the Japanese support for their religion. However, they felt betrayed upon learning of

Japanese plans to subjugate the Korean Sangha to the Japanese Sōtō Zen sect. As a result, monks became increasingly involved in efforts to oppose colonial power.

The Japanese countered by pressuring the Korean Sangha to abandon its vows of celibacy, following the Japanese model, by reserving high ecclesiastical positions and abbotships at the most prestigious monasteries for noncelibate monastics. Celibate monks gradually became a minority, until in 1926 the colonial government required Korean abbots to remove all rules against marriage among the clergy. The result was a marked change in the character of Sangha life, as the mundane pressures of supporting a family placed new burdens on the monks. The communal conditions that had allowed monasteries to accumulate goods and property began to break down. Most important from the Japanese point of view, family responsibilities gave the monks less time for political activity.

One positive result of the Japanese occupation was that the threat of total Japanese domination moved the Sŏn and Doctrinal schools to patch up their differences. In 1935, after seven years of negotiations, the two schools formally merged into the Chogye Order, realizing the centuries-old dream of a united Korean Sangha. The union, however, was short-lived. After independence, the order was badly split between a small rural minority who had managed to preserve their celibacy throughout the Japanese occupation and the majority who had abandoned their celibate vows. The celibate monks fought to regain control of the monasteries that had gone over to the married priests, and in 1954, after the end of the Korean War, they finally won government support for their cause. Married priests were expelled from the order and formed their own separate T'aego Order. All major monasteries now are in Chogye hands, but tensions between the two groups remain strong to this day.

9.7 BUDDHISM IN MODERN KOREA

The success of South Korea's economic policy is changing the country so drastically that it is difficult to point out any clear trends in contemporary Buddhism, aside from two facts: An increasing proportion of the country is reported to be Buddhist, and Korean nuns now play an increasingly prominent role in Sangha affairs. In addition to the Chogye and T'aego Orders, there are 16 "homegrown" sects, including Won. Mirroring the split between the Chogye and T'aego monks, Korean nuns now have two independent orders. The larger one, formed in 1985, is affiliated with the Chogye Order; the smaller one, founded in 1972 and heavily involved in social work, is affiliated with the T'aego Order. As for North Korea, lack of information makes it difficult to assess the position of Buddhism there, but Buddhists are probably not free to practice.

Ordination in South Korea is controlled by government regulations. Educational standards for both monks and nuns are becoming more stringent, with a high school diploma now a minimum requirement. Once a year, candidates from various masters are convened for joint ceremonies lasting several days. In 1982, the practice of dual ordination for nuns (see Section 3.3.2) was revived by the Chogye Order after a 100-year lapse. Once ordained, monastics spend three to five years studying Chinese language and Buddhist Sūtras. More Sangha members are also pursuing higher degrees beyond the temple, even going abroad for study.

A movement has begun to attract young people to Buddhism at the lay level. This includes a network of Sunday schools for children on the Christian model. Massive efforts are underway to translate Sūtras and related texts into Han'gŭl, making them more accessible to the average reader, and the Korean Tripiṭaka is being put into a computer format. Monks and nuns also devote themselves to social services. Perhaps because the nuns have traditionally played a more prominent role in offering pastoral help to the laity, they are now in the forefront of finding new ways to serve the fast-changing society: counseling prisoners, running homes for the aged, hosting radio shows, offering healing through meditation, and providing instruction in such arts as painting, flower arranging, and music as forms of spiritual training.

Korean Buddhists are actively proselytizing not only at home but also abroad. Most prominent in this regard has been the Chogye monk, Seung Sahn (b. 1927), famous for his teaching of "don't-know mind." His Kwan Um School, founded in 1983, now claims more than fifty affiliated groups throughout Europe and the Americas.

Not all is rosy, however. The wealth and power won by the Chogye Order have led to charges of financial and political corruption coming from within the order itself. In the late 1970s, as a reaction to the Christian churches' support for political dissidents, the government began promoting Buddhism as an expression of Korean identity, and the order established a Monks' Militia for National Defense. Accusations that the upper echelons of the order have funneled Sangha funds to sympathetic politicians have given rise to concern that the pattern of the Koryŏ dynasty will be repeated, whereby government patronage proves detrimental to the religious life of the Sangha.

9.8 LIFE IN A SŎN MONASTERY

Despite the rapid secularization of Korean society, the Korean Sangha is probably the strongest monastic institution in East Asia. Life in the traditional Sŏn monasteries and nunneries continues largely unchanged from the pattern it has followed for centuries, providing an accurate picture of conditions in the Sung monasteries on which they were modeled. As a result, these institutions offer an important corrective to many of the stereotypes about Ch'an/Zen/Sŏn that fill the popular press. Reading the teachings of the ancient Ch'an masters, one would assume that they avoided books entirely and lived totally spontaneous, iconoclastic lives. Upon visiting a Sŏn monastery, however, one discovers that the monks devote their early years to a thorough study of the classical texts, and that throughout their monastic careers they adhere to a strict code of discipline and etiquette. As we noted in Sections 8.6.1 and 8.6.2, most extant Ch'an literature was composed during a period when life in Ch'an monasteries had become extremely formalized. In Korean monasteries we can see living examples of how Ch'an life and literature were originally designed to interact, each providing a corrective for the shortcomings of the other.

Four large forest monasteries exist in Korea today. Located on hillsides sheltered by mountains in remote areas of the country, their location reflects not only the principles of Chinese geomancy—which maintains that mountains provide protection from baleful influences—but also the geographical isolation imposed on Buddhist institutions under the Yi dynasty. In theory, each monastery preserves the four strands of tradition that have come to define Korean Buddhism—Sŏn, Hwaŏm study, Vinaya, and Pure Land—although the balance among these strands differs from monastery to monastery. In some, seminaries are maintained, offering the traditional curriculum established during the Yi dynasty, whereas others place more emphasis on meditation. All preserve traces of Hwaŏm doctrine in their formal organization. Sinuous paths winding from shrine to shrine among the buildings replicate the Hwaŏm dharmadhātu maṇḍala, a diagram that outlines the unimpeded interpenetration of phenomena (see Section 8.5.2). The monastic population is divided into two classes: the scrutinizers of principle, or meditators and scholars; and the scrutinizers of phenomena, or the support corps. The interaction between these two groups is an object lesson in Hwaŏm doctrine, forming a dharmadhātu maṇḍala in the four dimensions of space and time.

Each monastery is divided into several compounds, each of which is a monastery in miniature. One compound is also set aside for nuns who wish to study with the resident Sŏn master. Although they come together for the daily ceremonies of the monastery, contact between the monks and nuns is strictly curtailed. Within their compound the nuns lead a life similar to that of the monks.

Korean folk wisdom traditionally recognizes five possible reasons for taking on the life of a monk: a sense of vocation, the fulfillment of a vow (as in the case of Chinul), family pressure, failure in love, or laziness. The fulfillment of a vow does not appear to play a role at present, and only the most devout Buddhist families would consider the life of a monk a desirable vocation for one of their sons, but the other incentives are still in force. Ironically, the sense of vocation felt by young men seeking ordination now often stems from the rampant Westernization of the country, as university students become disillusioned with the Western approach to philosophy that dominates the modern educational system and view ordination as a way to reconnect with Korea's ancient roots. The call to ordain can also come from personal experience in modern warfare, as happened in the late 1970s, when many Vietnam War veterans became monks. Young men who come to the monkhood with a sense of vocation tend to be more idealistic than their brethren, but practical experience shows that initial motivation does not necessarily determine how successful a monk's career will be.

That career goes through several stages, beginning invariably in the support corps of the monastery. The candidate spends the first six months as a postulant, working in the kitchen, the latrines, and the monastery's fields. Not only does this provide the manual labor needed to keep the monastery self-sufficient, but it also tests the stamina and commitment of the newly arrived devotees. The postulants are also expected to study basic chants and the Vinaya. As a result, their days—from the wake-up call at 3:00 A.M. to lights-out at 9:00 P.M.—are full, with little time for rest. If they last the six months, they are invited to ordain as novices, receiving the Ten Precepts (3.3.2), although here the vow to abstain from eating in the afternoon is changed to a vow to abstain from keeping domestic animals. At the end of the ordination ceremony, the novice's change in status is marked by his taking a wick, placing it inside his forearm, lighting it, and letting it burn down to the skin, as a symbol of nonattachment to the body. When the wound forms a scab, some novices have been known to pick at it, to enlarge the scar, as a badge of their bravado.

Novitiate ordination carries a tacit agreement to contribute another three years of service to the monastery, usually as an attendant to the senior monk who sponsored one's ordination. Formal studies begin, focusing on chants, ritual performances, and Vinaya. Learning also proceeds on a more informal basis through interaction with senior monks. This is the period during which the young monk's sense of family identity switches away from his biological family and becomes attached to the brotherhood of his institution. After three years, the novice is eligible to ordain as a bhikṣu. This involves a ceremony where he vows to observe the 250 precepts of the Mahīśāsaka Vinaya. In practice, no one expects the monks to observe the precepts related to the mendicant life—such as the prohibitions against eating after noon, eating stored-up food, handling money, and digging in the soil—but all monks are required to observe strictly the four rules entailing expulsion (see Section 3.3.1).

Bhikṣu ordination marks the point when the ordinand has committed himself to the monkhood for life. Although disrobing is possible, it is considered a great disgrace, unlike in Thailand and Burma. The other primary change in the life of the new ordinand is that he now has the right to travel and undertake studies at other monasteries, changing from a scrutinizer of phenomena to a scrutinizer of principle, as he has now paid his debt to the home institution. Most monks go to seminary, where they study Chinese language as well as basic texts in Sŏn and Hwaŏm doctrine. Those who take the complete course of study, which lasts 12 years, are eligible to become teachers themselves, either in a seminary or in programs of outreach to the laity. Other monks, after studying the *Record* of Ta-hui Tsung-kao, begin training in meditation.

Training begins in a meditation hall, which occupies its own separate compound in the large monasteries, aloof from the compounds of the support corps. In fact, most meditating monks stay away from their home monasteries to escape the pressure to return to the support corps. As a result, the contingent of meditators living at a monastery at any one time are there as privileged guests, with few assigned jobs. Despite their heavy schedules of practice, meditators as a group are remarkably independent, beholden only to their own sense of devotion to the practice.

For six months out of the year, during the periods of "slackened rule"—roughly August to November, and February to May—the meditators are free to come and go, and to schedule their individual practice as they see fit. Intensive retreats, called periods of "binding rule," are held during the summer and winter months. During these retreats the meditators are expected to stay put. Sessions are typically three to four hours long—beginning at 3 A.M., 8 A.M., 1 P.M., and 6 P.M.—subdivided into 50-minute periods of seated meditation alternating with 10 minutes of walking meditation. Lying down is prohibited except during breaks before breakfast and in the evening. Work assignments are minimal so that the meditators may devote their full energies to meditation. The most arduous period of training is the week of "ferocious effort" immediately prior to the celebration of the Buddha's Awakening (the eighth day of the twelfth lunar month, which usually falls in January). The entire period is one extended meditation session. No one sleeps; breaks are taken only for meals. In this way the participants re-enact the Buddha's all-out practice prior to his Awakening.

Although meditators will often choose to enter retreat at a particular monastery because of the reputation of its Sŏn master, few have close contact with him. The meditator is free to choose his own kung-an and to find his own techniques for focusing on the "critical phrase" (see Section 8.6.2) so as to maintain the mind in the "great doubt" where Awakening can be reached and then matured. The master will give a formal lecture once every two weeks and will conduct required private interviews once or twice during the retreat, but that is usually the extent of his interaction with the itinerant group that has taken up residence in the meditation hall. A meditator may schedule an interview with the Sŏn master at any time, but young monks are usually too timid to do so, whereas older monks often feel that the master has nothing to teach them that they have not already heard. The fact that Korean meditators are encouraged to stick to one kung-an for life may be a factor here. As a result, a master may spend his career teaching all the active meditators in the country without leaving behind a single personal disciple.

Periodically, the strict division between meditators and support corps is put aside, in keeping with the principle of unimpeded interaction. All able-bodied monks are called out to help with planting and harvesting in the monastery's fields, to fight forest fires, or to help with labor-intensive jobs in the kitchen, such as pickling vegetables or making Chinese dumplings. The lunar New Year, shortly after the period of ferocious effort, brings a three-day respite in the schedule, during which all the monks feast together, sing songs, and play games. At the end of these periods, the division of labor resumes.

If, after several years, a monk finds that he is suited to the meditative life, he will abandon the meditation-hall circuit and retreat to a forest hermitage to develop his meditation in isolation, returning to the large monasteries when he feels the need for group support to reinvigorate his practice. If his understanding develops sufficiently, he may eventually return to his home monastery, where he may be elected to one of the subsidiary positions of authority in the meditation compound, or even to the position of Sŏn master when the office falls vacant.

By far the vast majority of Korean monks, however, do not meditate. Either they never attempt the meditative life to begin with, or find that it does not suit them when they do. Thus they remain in or return to the support corps of their home monastery, filling positions in the kitchen, the field, or the office, perhaps even being elected to the position of abbot, going into retirement when too old to work. In this respect they carry out a tradition of specialization within the Sangha that goes back not only to Sung China, but to the earliest centuries of Indian Buddhism, whereby a minority concentrated on gaining Awakening in this lifetime, while others facilitated that effort in hopes of acquiring merit for future lives.

As with all traditional institutions, the great Korean monasteries have found their very existence challenged by changes in modern society. One major disruption has been land reform, which has severely reduced the land holdings that used to provide their primary source of income. As a result, the monasteries have had to organize lay support groups in the major cities to ensure their financial survival. This outreach to the laity has entailed new responsibilities for the senior monks, as they must make periodic teaching visits to groups scattered throughout the country and provide lay retreat sessions on their monastic campuses. Another change has been wrought by the new tendency among the urban population to regard the monasteries as tourist spots. In some cases, the impact of tourism has proven so disruptive that monasteries have abandoned their campuses to the tourists, building unassuming retreats for monks and nuns even farther away in the mountains. Because the monastic alternative is still attracting candidates, though, solutions will probably be found to these problems, so that Korea will continue to provide, perhaps in altered form, environments conducive to a life of Buddhist practice.

VIETNAM

9.9 TWO STREAMS OF BUDDHISM CONVERGE

Vietnam as a political and cultural entity is largely a product of the modern era. For centuries the country now known by that name was divided politically and culturally into two parts, north and south. The earliest archaeological evidence for Buddhism in this area dates from the first century C.E.; the first written evidence, from the latter part of the second century.

As we have already noted in Section 7.3, southern Vietnam belonged to the area of "Further India" until the fifteenth century, and so received its Buddhism from Indian sources. Northern Vietnam belonged to the Chinese cultural sphere—and at times was actually part of the Chinese empire—since the third century B.C.E., but it, too, originally received its Buddhism via Indian traders monks and actually helped spread the religion to China in the third century C.E. Eventually Chinese Buddhism came to dominate the country, although scholars disagree as to when full dominance was achieved. Some say no earlier than the fifteenth century; others, no later than the sixth. The mixed evidence indicates that sinification was a gradual process.

The history of Buddhism in northern Vietnam, prior to the annexation of the south, can be divided into two periods, from the second to the tenth centuries, and from the tenth through the fifteenth. The first period covers the centuries during which northern Vietnam, called Chiao-chih, was under Chinese control; the second period covers the centuries of independence.

Records indicate that during the rule of Shih Hsieh (r. 187–226), the Han governor of Chiao-chih, Central Asian and Indian monks famed for their meditation and magical attainments were roaming the country, and that Shih Hsieh availed himself of their powers. Legends dealing with this period indicate a strong connection between Buddhism and local spirit cults. Perhaps the most famous of these legends concerns Man Nương, the daughter of an ascetic, who learned various dhāraṇīs from a wandering Indian Buddhist monk, including those for making rain. One day a typhoon uprooted a gigantic banyan tree, depositing it at the gate of Shih Hsieh's palace. Three hundred men tried unsuccessfully to remove the tree, but only when Man Nương came along and gave it a playful tap did it budge. She then revealed that years previously she had entrusted a daughter, conceived through magic, to the tree. The part of the tree that had grown up around where she had placed the daughter was then carved into four Lady Buddha images: the Dharma-Clouds, Dharma-Rain, Dharma-Thunder, and Dharma-Lightning. Man Nương herself was then revered as a Mother Buddha. Government records indicate that even during the Later Lê dynasty, when Confucianism had come to dominate the court, Dharma-Clouds would be escorted to the capital in times of drought for the emperor to invoke in a ritual for making rain.

During the T'ang dynasty, Chiao-chih was an embarking point for Chinese monks who traveled to India by sea. Buddha images dating from this time have been unearthed in the area, showing a strong similarity to the images at Borobodur (see Section 7.2). In this they differ from the Gandharan images popular in China at the time, leading scholars to speculate that Buddhist influences arriving from the south by sea were still stronger in Chiao-chih than those coming overland from the north.

Ironically, Chinese influences did not come into clear dominance in this area until after the Vietnamese had achieved political independence from China. When the Đinh dynasty (969–980) gained independence, Buddhism was proclaimed the national religion. Archaeologists, having unearthed Đinh dynasty steles inscribed with mantras, have concluded that Tantrism had made its way to Vietnam by the tenth century, but nothing in the mantras indicates that they are anything more than early Mahāyāna dhāraṇīs, as they contain no specific Vajrayāna elements.

Buddhism maintained its dominant position through the Former Lê dynasty (980–1009), the Lý (1010–1225), and well into the Trần (1225–1400). The Lý dynasty, in particular, was strongly Buddhist, as the founder of the dynasty had been a temple orphan and appointed Buddhist monks to his governing council to help ensure that the spirits of the land and waters were favorable to his regime. Despite its Buddhist leanings, the Lý dynasty tried to forge a national culture from all the diverse elements in Vietnamese society; its policy of eclecticism in religious matters set the standard for subsequent dynasties.

In the later part of the Lý dynasty, the polished literature of Sung dynasty Ch'an began to receive an enthusiastic reception in the Vietnamese court. This enthusiasm grew stronger in the Trần dynasty, when monks of the Lin-chi sect arrived from China to instruct court officials. Although their practices never took root in Vietnam, Ch'an sentiments came to dominate Vietnamese literary works. One of the Trần emperors, Trần-Nhân-Tôn (1258–1308), an accomplished poet, abdicated his throne to start a Ch'an (in Vietnamese: Thiền) school of his own—the Trúc Lâm (Bamboo Grove) school—although it apparently lasted only three generations.

Within the court, Thiền was viewed as the *New Buddhism,* as opposed to the *Old Buddhism* of the general populace. The members of the court, however, did not abandon Old Buddhism. Instead, they simply added a sensitivity to Thiền literary themes to their earlier practices and beliefs. This can be seen clearly in the *Thiền Uyển Tập Anh,* or Outstanding Figures in the Thiền Community *(Thiền Uyển* for short), composed in 1337. The *Thiền Uyển* was an attempt to portray Vietnamese Buddhist history as a series of Thiền lineages dating back to the Third Ch'an Patriarch, claiming that the New Buddhism actually had its roots in the distant Vietnamese past. When this text was rediscovered in the early twentieth century, it was read as straight history, but recent scholarship has demonstrated that its encounter dialogues and transmission stories are largely borrowed from Chinese lamp records, and that the purported ancient Thiền lineages probably never existed.

However, the legends recorded in the *Thiền Uyển* are valuable in painting a picture of Buddhist life and values in the fourteenth century. When stripped of Ch'an elements, they portray a Buddhism of Sūtras rather than of scholarly treatises or schools. An individual monastic might chant dhāraṇī Sūtras for gaining magical powers, read the *Diamond* and *Hua-yen* Sūtras for philosophy, and recite the *Lotus Sūtra* as a devotional text. There were no specific schools or lineages surrounding these texts. Individual monastics were free to draw on whatever literature they found inspiring, developing their own individual approach which, in some cases, earned them the respect of their fellow Buddhists. When we examine the standards by which monks or nuns were considered worthy of respect, we find that they differ little from the standards used in other Asian Buddhist countries, whether Theravāda, Mahāyāna, or Vajrayāna.

Monks or nuns were respected for two major reasons: the intensity of their practice or the compassionate use of their powers. In the prior category, an individual might be respected for strong asceticism or for long hours given to meditation. For instance, Bhikṣuṇī Diệu-Nhân (1043–1115) was an adopted daughter of Emperor Lê Nhân Tôn (r. 1072–1127). When widowed at an early age, she retired to a convent and became famous for her imperturbability in the face of hardships. A woman of few words, she was once asked why she taught so little Dharma. Her reply: "The Path is fundamentally wordless."

In the latter category—the compassionate use of one's powers—a monk or nun might become famous for helping the general populace or for acting as an advisor to the court. Helping the general populace might involve teaching the Dharma, using psychic powers to heal disease or make rain, or using persuasive powers to inspire people to undertake public works, such as building bridges or repairing roads. Acting as an advisor at court might include not only forecasting the future and using psychic powers to ward off invaders, but also teaching the Dharma and giving sagely advice. Thảo Đường, for instance, was captured as a prisoner of war in Champa in 1069 and eventually became teacher to his captor, Emperor Lý Thánh Tôn (r. 1054–1072). He is credited with teaching three stages in nien-fo practice: reciting the Buddha's name while focusing the eyes on a physical Buddha image; reciting the Buddha's name while focusing the mind on a mental image of the Buddha; and "reciting the Buddha's name while meditating on the quintessence of the Buddha," that is, avoiding any visualization of a Buddha or any assumption of a self doing the reciting or visualizing.

Monks summoned to court, however, were often admired for resisting the summons, a sign that they were not attracted to wealth and fame. For instance, when Huệ Sinh (d. 1063) was summoned to court, he told the messenger: "You've seen a sacrificial animal, haven't you? At first they dress it in embroidered silk and feed it nice, sweet grass. But when they drag it into the royal temple, it can't gain its wish to be even an orphaned animal at that point, much less anything better."

Perhaps the most dramatic legend of an eminent monk is that of Đạo Hạnh (d. 1117), who has a shrine to his memory to this day. When Đạo was a young man, his father was murdered at the instigation of a government official. The corpse, floating down the river, stopped before the official's palace, rose up out of the water, and pointed at the palace for a full day before the current pulled it away. Planning revenge, Đạo went off into the mountains and recited a dhāraṇī Sūtra 108,000 times, causing a guardian deva to appear to him. The deva promised help, and when vengeance was done, Đạo ordained as a monk, perhaps out of remorse. He used his psychic powers to help people of all sorts, and once burned off a finger to bring rain. It so happened that the emperor at that time was heirless. Learning of a young child who demonstrated psychic powers, including intimate knowledge of the imperial family, the emperor wanted to make the child his heir. Đạo heard of this and, convinced that the child was a demon, defeated the child in a battle of dhāraṇīs. Having deprived the emperor of a prospective heir, however, he was obliged to take rebirth as the heir himself. Calling his students together, he told them of his karmic obligations and then passed away. The teenage emperor, Lý Thần Tông (r. 1128–1138), was believed to be Đạo Hạnh reborn.

In 1407, Chinese forces invaded Chiao-chih and ruled it for 20 years. When the Later Lê dynasty (1428–1788) regained independence, it followed the example of the Ming officials it had just expelled in establishing Confucianism as the official ideology of the court. The vast majority of the populace, however, remained Buddhist, with Pure Land increasingly the dominant practice.

The Later Lê dynasty also annexed the Indianized Champa kingdom, based in central Vietnam, beginning a process whereby the sinified culture of the north came thoroughly to dominate the south. Completed in the eighteenth century, this process brought almost all of Vietnamese Buddhism, aside from a few Theravādin enclaves along the Cambodian border, under Chinese influence. The imperial court, however, did not exert government control over religious orders, and there was no national organization of the monastic Sangha. Thus the principle of eclecticism continued to hold sway in religious matters, following the slogan, "Many directions but one destination."

Two reform movements marked the later centuries of the premodern period. The first came in the latter part of the seventeenth century, when Chinese monks led by Nguyễn Thiêu (d. 1712) fled to central Vietnam to escape the Manchu invasions ushering in the Ching dynasty. With the support of the princes of Hue, they established the Lâm-Te (Lin-chi) school, which has survived into the modern period. A "Ming Ch'an" school, Lâm-Te advocates the combined use of kung-ans and nien-fo. In terms of dress, ritual, and daily routines, it closely resembles the Japanese Ōbaku sect (see Section 10.7), another "Ming Ch'an" school founded at approximately the same time.

In the eighteenth century, the Lâm-Te school spawned an offshoot founded by Liêu Quan (d. 1774), a second-generation disciple of Nguyễn Thiêu. Liêu Quan was an active proselytizer who toured the country, giving lectures and offering to reordain monks and nuns whose practice had grown lax and who wanted to make a fresh start in their vows. To emphasize the fact that he was reviving Thiền, rather than imposing Chinese Ch'an on his fellow Vietnamese, he proclaimed a new lineage starting with himself. Once reordained, the new members of the school were allowed to continue their meditation—Theravāda or Mahāyāna—as before. In this sense, the Liêu Quan ideology was less a Thiền school than a movement for voluntary rededication to the religious practice of one's preference. As a result of this eclectic nationalism, the Liêu Quan school quickly became the dominant lineage in Vietnamese Buddhism and maintained that position until the Communist takeover in the twentieth century.

9.10 THE MODERN PERIOD

Under the French rule of Vietnam (1883–1939), Catholic missionaries won many converts, especially in the south. At the end of World War II in 1945, Vietnamese forces declared independence, but the French did not relinquish control until 1954. With independence, the country quickly fell into a devastating civil war between a Communist north and an anti-Communist south.

The most graphic symbols of Buddhist reaction to the war were the monastics who practiced self-immolation as a way of calling world attention to their double plight: the suffering caused both by the war and by the pro-Catholic south Vietnamese government's persecution of Buddhists. Many of the monastics who gave their lives in this way were Theravādin, but the historical precedent for their actions came from China (see Section 8.7.2), where self-immolation had once been a devotional practice. In the context of the Vietnam War, however, its impact was more political. Pictures of burning monastics provoked the United Nations into investigating the Vietnamese government's history of religious persecution and played a contributing role in the downfall of the Diệm regime.

Perhaps the most eloquent Vietnamese Buddhist spokesman during this period was the Thiền monk, Thích Nhất Hạnh (b. 1926), who in 1964 founded the School of Youth for Social Service and the Tiế'p Hiê'n Order (Order of Interbeing), dedicated to the cause of peace and social rehabilitation. Seeing the destructiveness that ideological fanaticism can cause, the order adopted as its first precept the principle: "Do not be idolatrous about or bound to any doctrine, theory, or ideology, even Buddhist ones. All systems of thought are guiding means; they are not absolute truth." Working together with other monks and nuns—in particular, the nun Chân Không (Cao Ngọc Không; b. 1938)—Nhất Hạnh organized such projects as rebuilding bombed villages, starting farmers' cooperatives, and establishing clinics. After making a trip to the United States to plead for peace, however, he was declared persona non grata by both the northern and southern regimes. In exile he continued his antiwar activities; after the Communist victory, he helped in efforts to rescue the massive exodus of boat people fleeing Vietnam between 1976 and 1978; recently he has begun holding meditation retreats worldwide for Vietnamese refugees and American Vietnam War veterans as a way of healing the wounds left by the war.

Thích Nhất Hạnh still lives in exile in a monastic community called Plum Village in France, with branch monasteries in Vermont and California at which he trains monks and nuns in hopes that they will someday be allowed to return to Vietnam. A prolific scholar, writer, and poet, he has produced numerous volumes on the theme of "engaged Buddhism," the blending of meditation with social service. For Nhất Hạnh, these activities are two sides of a single practice: the breaking down of barriers between mind and object, inner and outer, self and other. Central to his teaching is the notion of "being peace." To help the cause of peace, one must embody inner peace in every act of body, speech, and mind. To gain this inner peace, it is necessary to practice mindfulness, which Nhất Hạnh defines as the ability to appreciate the miracle of each present moment as it happens, to accept and embrace even negative things so as to discover their positive uses. In this way, suffering is not to be escaped from, but to be transformed. Rather than trying to leave saṁsāra, one breaks down one's defensive barriers so as to enter into the interrelatedness of all things. With this insight, one can take the wisdom and compassion used in pacifying one's own greed, anger, and delusion, and use them to pacify the forces of greed, anger, and delusion in the world at large. In this way, Nhất Hạnh gives Fa-tsang's view of interrelatedness (see Section 8.5.2) a political slant.

Within Vietnam, the Communists won the civil war in 1975. Despite the antireligious ideology of the Communist state, 80 percent of the population is currently estimated to be Buddhist. A state-sponsored Vietnam Buddhist Church was established in 1975, but many dissidents have resisted government control. Prominent among the resistance organizations is the Unified Buddhist Church of Vietnam (UBCV), a union of Theravāda and Mahāyāna groups. Officially banned in 1981, the UBCV marshaled the support of overseas Vietnamese to pressure the government into reinstating it. Its concerns include the release of imprisoned activists and the return of confiscated Sangha properties. Although the situation for Buddhism is still uncertain, the dissidents take comfort in Buddhism's having outlived many other regimes in its past, and so feel that time is on their side.

10

Buddhism in Japan

10.1 THE CULT OF CHARISMA

Prior to the importation of Buddhism from Korea and China, Japan had no speculative tradition of its own. However, it had developed a unique approach to the role of religion in political and cultural life that shaped the way it adopted and adapted Buddhism. Pre-Buddhist Japanese religion centered on the worship of *kami:* beings (spirits, people, animals), objects, and places possessing charismatic power. This charisma was perceived to have not only a religious dimension, but political and aesthetic dimensions as well. The long-term historical impact of this perception has tended to blur the line between religious and political life on the one hand, and between religious and aesthetic sensitivity on the other. The interpenetration of these three dimensions can be regarded as a distinctive feature of Japan's contribution to the Buddhist tradition.

Kami worship interpenetrated political life in that the basic unit of political organization—the *uji* (tribe or clan)—was defined by all members of the clan, whether related or not, owing ultimate allegiance to the same kami. The political leader of the clan was also the clan's chief priest and sometimes its shaman, conducting rituals with the aim of appeasing the clan's kami and augmenting his or her own charisma (Japan from early on had a tradition of strong female rulers). In some cases, the leader became so charismatic as to be identified with the kami itself. A true leader was supposed to be particularly sensitive to the kami's wishes and to rule the clan accordingly. Thus ritual and political administration were viewed as two facets of a single process. Because the kami were numerous and essentially amoral, with no established order among them, this system was inherently unstable and fractious. One of the principal problems in unifying Japan as a country thus lay in establishing a fixed narrative cycle to explain the hierarchy among the kami so that the various clans could be brought into a hierarchical relationship as well. The truth of these narratives was tested in the battlefield, and a shift in the balance of power would be reflected in a retelling of the relevant narrative.

In the sixth century, as Japan became exposed to the religions of Korea and China, the imperial uji began to look to Buddhism and Confucianism to shore up its ideological credentials. This seems to have been due both to the Sui dynasty's success in using these two religions to unify China, and to the claims made by both religions that they were based on universal principles, rather than uncertain narratives. Buddhism functioned primarily as a state religion for its first six centuries in Japan, and—until the rise of the Tokugawa shogunate in the seventeenth century—it predominated over Confucianism in the state ideology. Buddha images were worshiped as the highest kami, and powerful monastic centers—often built on mountains known for their powerful kami—maintained elaborate ritual calendars that were believed to protect the interests of the government and the nation as a whole.

Buddhism's desired role as a unifying force in society was complicated by its having split into several schools—in some cases worshiping different Buddhas—prior to its arrival in Japan. Thus it could function as a force for disunity as well as unity. The court tended to favor syncretic, all-inclusive forms of Buddhism, but because state Buddhism could not meet the religious needs of the entire society, there also developed independent popular Buddhist and folk-Buddhist sects around charismatic individuals. The possibility that these breakaway sects could function as rebellious uji and thus threaten political stability, explains the vehemence with which the establishment has from time to time suppressed such movements. In fact, one of the great ironies of the history of Buddhism in Japan is that, although the Japanese originally imported Buddhism as a means of fostering national unity, what they made of it proved so divisive that the political establishment eventually decided to suppress it.

On the aesthetic side, early Japanese poetry addressed to the kami of natural objects fostered the idea that religious sensitivity and aesthetic sensitivity to the beauties of nature were two sides of a single faculty. The leader of an uji, expected to be especially sensitive to the charisma of the kami, was also expected to have a highly developed aesthetic sense. Artistic sensitivities, and the disciplines that fostered them, were thus regarded as credentials for leadership. As the various forms of Buddhism came to Japan, the aristocracy was especially attuned to the style of each form, assuming that the essential message of the teaching could be intuited from its style, much as the character of another person could be intuited through the aesthetic appreciation of an object that that person had made. Thus each school of Buddhism became associated with a particular style: Shingon was sumptuous, Tendai and Zen were spare and vigorous. These styles had a strong influence on Japanese arts and crafts. Particular skills, such as the tea ceremony and the training of warriors, adopted the Zen style and were pursued as *ways* (*dō* or *tō*, from Chinese *tao*), similar to the ways of Buddhism (*Butsudō*) and *Shintō*, the name given to the various sets of beliefs surrounding the kamis.

The cult of charisma came to surround these aesthetic disciplines so strongly that the belief arose that the discipline of the craft or skill enabled one to develop one's spirit to the same pitch of sensitivity that could be achieved through overt religious training. In Buddhist terms, this belief was strengthened in the medieval period by the development of the doctrine of "original Awakening," the belief that everything in the universe, even grass and trees, is already pure and Awakened by its very nature. Thus an aesthetic sympathy for the beauty of even an ordinary object was regarded as a function of a mind already attuned to its own Awakened nature, and in this way aesthetics maintained its strong religious overtones in the Buddhist context. Although the doctrine of original Awakening lost currency in the eighteenth century, its impact on Japanese aesthetics has continued to the present day.

10.2 THE IMPORTATION OF KOREAN BUDDHISM

Buddhism was probably first brought to Japan by Korean immigrants who settled in the Asuka-Nara area of central Japan. The first recorded contact on the royal level, however, was in 552, when King Syŏng-myŏng of Paekche sent Buddhist statues and Sūtras to the Japanese imperial court, motivated in part by hopes of forging an alliance with the Japanese against his Silla rivals. The Korean case for Buddhism was that the Triple Gem functioned as a very high level of universal kami. If worshiped, it would safeguard the nation. Thus, from the very beginning, the Japanese regarded Buddhism as a political force, centered in Buddha images, and embroiled it in political controversies. The ambitious Soga clan, descended from Korean immigrants, championed the Buddhist cause and obtained the right to build a temple to house a Buddha image, at the same time arranging to have the first Japanese monks and nuns ordained. When a plague then broke out, anti-Soga forces claimed that the worship of foreign kami had angered native kami. To appease the native kami, they drowned the image in a canal and forced Buddhist nuns to disrobe. When this had no apparent effect on the plague, the image was fished out of the water and Buddhists were allowed to resume their practice.

The Sogas eventually came to dominate the imperial court, thus assuring Buddhism's adoption as a state religion. The individual most instrumental in this adoption was Prince Shōtoku (573–622), who was later regarded as the founder of Japanese Buddhism. As regent for Empress Suiko (r. 592–628), he formulated in 604 Japan's first constitution, a statement of governing principles covering the areas of ethics, religion, and the psychology of leadership. The constitution combined elements from Buddhism, Confucianism, and kami worship, foreshadowing the way in which these three traditions were to interact as the national ideology for the following millennium. Shōtoku advocated the Triple Gem as the highest refuge for all beings; only by taking refuge in it could morally crooked people be motivated to become straight. Straightness, however, was a function of the Confucian principle of propriety, which required one to adhere closely to the duties of one's social position. Finally, the citizenry were called on to continue worshiping the kami to keep the male and female forces of the cosmos in balance and to ensure the proper course of the seasons.

To implement the Buddhist side of his policy, Prince Shōtoku imported Korean artisans to build temples—including the Hōryū-ji, the oldest surviving temple complex in the nation, with what are now among the oldest wooden buildings in the world—along with Korean monks and nuns to staff them. Three Japanese nuns—Zenshin, Zensō, and Eizen—were sent to Paekche in 587 to study the Vinaya. On their return in 590, they established an ordination center for nuns. Prince Shōtoku himself studied under Hye-cha, a monk from Koguryō, and is credited with writing commentaries on Mahāyāna Sūtras.

In bringing Buddhism to Japan, the Koreans also brought elements of Chinese culture, such as the Chinese writing system, which the Japanese adopted for their own language. Because Buddhist Sūtras were written in Chinese, the Japanese realized that they might do better to establish direct contact with China rather than go through Korean intermediaries. This realization, together with the desirability of establishing commercial ties with a China newly reunited by the Sui dynasty, inspired Prince Shōtoku to initiate diplomatic relations with the Sui court in 607 and to send talented young monks and scholars there to study. Although his untimely death aborted many of his policies, these contacts with China shaped the political and cultural future of Japan as a whole. On the one hand, they provided the catalyst for the emergence of a pro-Chinese, anti-Soga clan, the Fujiwaras, who were to dominate the court through the Heian period. On the other hand, the contacts set the stage for the wholesale importation of Chinese Buddhism and other features of Chinese culture, which provided the Japanese with models for what civilization should be. Thus Chinese Buddhism came to supplant the Korean models that Shōtoku himself had followed.

10.3 THE IMPORTATION OF CHINESE BUDDHISM

Under Emperor Temmu (r. 672–686), a Chinese form of government was instituted, including laws for the support and control of religion. As a result, Buddhist temples came under the jurisdiction of the Department of Kami Affairs, which exerted tight control over who could obtain ordination and where. This was to ensure that Buddhism would not develop into a force inimical to the state interests.

Meanwhile, a number of Chinese Buddhist schools had been imported to Japan, with little or no modification. In 625, a Korean monk who had studied in China introduced the San-lun (in Japanese, Sanron) and *Satyasiddhi* (Jōjitsu) traditions (see Section 8.4.2). In 658, two Japanese monks who had studied under Hsüan-tsang introduced the study of Vasubandhu's *Abhidharmakośa* (Kusha). Another Japanese monk went to China in 653, studied the Fa-hsiang (Hossō) teaching under Hsüan-tsang for more than ten years, and then introduced it to Japan. Other Koreans as well as Japanese returned from China and reinforced these initial transmissions. Kusha, Jōjitsu, and Sanron were never more than curriculum subjects, but Hossō became a wealthy, politically influential school and has maintained an institutional existence to the present day.

In 710 the imperial court was moved to Heijō-kyō (Capital of the Peaceful Citadel) at present-day Nara, where a city based on the design of the Chinese capital at Ch'ang-an had been laid out. The Hua-yen (Kegon) school was introduced from China and rapidly became influential. The Hua-yen world view was adapted to political ideology by equating Vairocana, the Cosmic Sun Buddha, with the emperor, whose uji claimed to be descendants of the sun. The principle of unimpeded interpenetration of phenomena was proclaimed the model for Japanese society, in hopes that the various ujis would interact harmoniously. Kegon, like Hossō, has continued as a school up to the present.

Throughout the Nara period, the number of Buddhist temples continued to grow. In 741, Emperor Shōmu ordered every province to construct a temple and pagoda with at least twenty monks and ten nuns. Shōmu's consort, Empress Kōmyō, converted her father's residence into the chief convent for the country. In 752, Tōdai-ji (Great Eastern Temple), the largest wooden structure in the world today, was designated the head temple in Nara. Two years later, the Chinese Vinaya master Ganjin established an ordination center there. In keeping with the laws passed under Emperor Temmu, the government permitted ordinations only at approved centers, which were intentionally kept limited to a few. Although the purpose of this restriction was to keep tight rein on the Sangha, in practice it led to strongly organized sects, with branch temples in the provinces dependent on the head temple to provide properly ordained monastics, and the head temple dependent on the local temples for income.

Nara Buddhism was primarily a state cult, with little impact on the general populace, but Buddhist ideas and practices at this time did begin to penetrate Japanese folk religion in three forms. The first was the *Jinenchishū* (Nature Wisdom school), whose members—some of them Buddhist monks—sought Buddhist-like Awakening in the mountains and forests using non-Buddhist, "natural" ascetic practices. The second form included *ubasoku* (from the Sanskrit *upāsaka*)—the "private monks" or "unordained monks"—charismatic religious leaders who combined Buddhist teachings with native Japanese shamanic practices such as healing and divination. In this form we can see the predecessors of the new religions of the nineteenth and twentieth centuries. The third form, which was also to have long-term impact, was the integration of Buddhist and Shintō beliefs. Certain kami were alleged to have encouraged the construction of Buddhist temples, in return for which they were declared to be bodhisattvas, so that shrines to them could be constructed in the temple compounds. This arrangement was later given a theoretical justification in the ninth century, when both the Tendai and Shingon school explained that the Shintō kami were actually Emanation Bodies (see Section 5.2.1) of the great Cosmic Buddhas.

During this period, Buddhism's main impact on lay life, at least in aristocratic circles, was in its advocacy of non-violence. Hunting for sport was abandoned, and cooks began to develop a Japanese vegetarian cuisine. The artisans imported from China to work on temple construction also influenced Japanese arts and crafts not only in temples but also in the court and in private homes.

Close relations between state Buddhism and the court thoroughly politicized the former. The *inke* system, whereby wealthy clans could receive income from land donated to monasteries, meant that monasteries became closely tied to the interests of their sponsors. The *insei* system, whereby an emperor could abdicate the throne, ordain as a monk, and yet continue to rule from behind the scenes, brought political intrigue directly into the monasteries. The government decrees ordering a certain number of men ordained as monks every year ensured that the monasteries would remain fully staffed, but also brought into the orders men with no real religious vocation. Eventually, a monk by the name of Dōkyō, having worked his way up the political hierarchy as the paramour of the Empress Kōken (r. 749–758), was accused of trying to usurp the throne. Although banished after the empress's death, he was apparently not the last monk to get overly involved in political affairs, for in 794 the capital was removed to a remote place to isolate the government from the political influence of the Nara monasteries. Ten years later it was again moved, to Kyōto, thus beginning a new era in Japanese history.

10.4 THE HEIAN PERIOD (804–1185)

In 788, a young monk named Saichō (Dengyō Daishi, 767–822) left Nara and established a new monastery on Mount Hiei—a mountain northeast of Kyōto noted for its powerful kamis—with the intention of creating a community that would adhere strictly to the Vinaya. When the new capital was established in the city in 804, Saichō won the patronage of the emperor, who sent him to study in China. During his year there he was trained in Chen-yen, the bodhisattva precepts, the Northern and Ox-head Schools of Ch'an, and T'ien-t'ai in particular. On his return, he combined these with Shintō elements into a single system, *Tendai,* which was thus broader in scope than its Chinese namesake. This system was the first of two distinctly Japanese attempts to amalgamate various Buddhist teachings into comprehensive One Vehicle schools. Saichō kept his monks in seclusion on Mount Hiei while they underwent a 12-year period to cultivate the three requirements of "the true path of the complete teaching": discipline, meditation, and study. Some of his graduates stayed on the mountain, whereas others left to serve the state as scribes, engineers, and teachers.

One of the characteristics distinguishing Saichō's teachings from those of the mainland T'ien-t'ai school was his focus on fully realizing the One Vehicle as taught in the *Lotus Sūtra.* To avoid any Hīnayānist taint contained in the Mainstream Vinayas, he campaigned to get an ordination center using purely bodhisattva precepts established on Mount Hiei; but, due to the opposition of the Nara clerics, the center was authorized only in 827, five years after his death. His followers continued to root out Hīnayānist elements from their practice, and in the tenth century went so far as to rephrase the act of homage to the Triple Gem, replacing homage to the Buddha with homage to Amitābha (in Japanese, Amida), homage to the Dharma with homage to the *Lotus Sūtra,* and homage to the Sangha with homage to Kuan-yin (in Japanese, Kannon).

Mount Hiei became the primary monastic center in Japan until its destruction at the end of the sixteenth century. In its heyday, it housed thirty thousand monks and contained more than three thousand buildings. Its shrines to Buddha images and kamis formed a central complex for ritual practices for the Japanese court and aristocracy. The fusion of Buddhist and Shintō rituals in these complexes meant that Buddhist monks played an important role in developing the rites and beliefs of Shintō during the medieval period. Close association with the imperial court, however, focused the practice of inke and insei on Mount Hiei, engendering the kind of political intrigue that Saichō had left Nara to avoid. The vast amount of wealth donated to the temple required that some of the monks be armed to protect it from thieves. Nevertheless, even as the center became renowned for its political intrigue, it also maintained its vitality as a religious institution, creating some of the most original and influential doctrines of the medieval period.

Shingon was the other new One Vehicle Buddhist school, and the only Tantric school to survive in East Asia. Shingon (in Chinese, Chen-yen) was brought to Japan by Kūkai (Kōbō Daishi, 774–835), a remarkably erudite and talented man. In addition to founding the Shingon school, for example, he devised the *kana* syllabary that greatly simplified the reading and writing of Japanese. He also opened the first school in Kyōto for the poor. Like Saichō, he had gone to China in 804, seeking to find order among the plethora of Buddhist schools. Unlike Saichō, he saw the highest expression of the Buddha's teachings not in the *Lotus Sūtra,* but in Yoga Tantra. For him, Tantra was the direct teaching of the Dharmakāya, while the non-Tantric Sūtras were simply the word of the Emanation Body, Śākyamuni. On returning from China, he founded the great monastic center at Mount Kōya—which, like Mount Hiei, had been known for its powerful kami and remained closed to women until very recently. He later founded a second center, the Tōji, in the capital, as he began developing a following in the imperial court. Writing prolifically on Buddhist theory and practice, he drew up a map of the spiritual path in ten stages of increasingly profound insight into the already-Awakened nature of one's own body and mind. The first stage was the "goat level" of totally undeveloped realization, while the remaining nine corresponded to various Confucian, Brahmanical, and Buddhist schools. The tenth and topmost realization, perfecting those below it, was the realization of the "glorious mind, most secret and sacred," to be found only through the Tantric practice taught in Shingon.

Like Chen-yen, Shingon was based on Tantras of the Yoga class, which imitate the body, speech, and mind of the Buddha Mahāvairocana, "The Great Sun," so as to assume the identity of that great being (see Section 6.2.1). However, Kūkai elaborated the theoretical side of Yoga Tantra in much more detail than had his Chinese predecessors. Adopting a Hua-yen teaching, he postulated Mahāvairocana as the entire cosmos itself, in both its physical and mental aspects. On an impersonal level Mahāvairocana was all six great elements: earth, water, fire, air, space, and consciousness. On a personal level, he was expressed in terms of body, speech, mind, and action. Mahāvairocana's speech, for example, consisted of mantras coupled with all the colors, forms, and sounds of the cosmos, as symbolically interpreted by the Tantric initiate.

Kūkai taught that each living being is a microcosm of the Dharmakāya, and although the various aspects of Mahāvairocana are all in perfect union and harmony on the macrocosmic level, they are in disharmony in the microcosm of the individual. The word *disharmony* is carefully chosen here, for even in disharmony the original nature of the individual is already Awakened. The purpose of practice is thus not to remove defilements from the microcosm but simply to bring the microcosm into tune with the macrocosm and to realize the original Awakened identity between the two. The first step is to observe the Vinaya precepts, so as to bring one's actions into harmony with macrocosmic action. The next is to bring body and speech into harmony through the use of the mudrās and mantras taught by Mahāvairocana. Then, by absorbing one's mind in these physical manifestations along with visualization of chaste but colorful maṇḍalas, total harmony can be attained as one realizes that Mahāvairocana's Body of Principle—that is, all that is to be realized—has all along been identical with the Body of Wisdom that attains the realization.

Kūkai's interpretation of Buddhist cosmology resonated well with native Japanese beliefs, which helps account for its quick acceptance by the imperial court. The solar imagery and pantheism in his portrait of Mahāvairocana corresponded with the ancient imperial sun cult, and his emphasis on form, color, and sound as means of expressing religious truths—especially in the sumptuous and sonorous rituals he devised for the court—satisfied the traditional Japanese sense that art and religion are essentially one. During his lifetime, Shingon eclipsed Tendai in popularity, although its popularity declined somewhat after his death, partly because Shingon produced no new leaders of Kūkai's caliber. Nevertheless, the school remained a major religious and political force until the civil wars of the fifteenth century and continues to be moderately popular even to this day.

In response to the success of Shingon, Tendai monks in the late Heian and Kamakura periods began developing a Tantric system of their own—called *Taimitsu*—based on interpreting the *Lotus Sūtra* as a Tantric text. A central element in this interpretation was the adoption of a Mahāyāna doctrine from outside the *Lotus Sūtra,* that of the *tathāgata-garbha.* As we noted in Section 5.2.3, the earliest expressions of this doctrine used similes that could be interpreted in at least two ways: the tathāgata-garbha, like a child in a womb, represented Awakening as a hidden potential; or, like honey in a beehive, it represented Awakening as a hidden actuality. Early Tendai doctrine, to the extent that it addressed the issue, interpreted the tathāgata-garbha in the first sense. Taimitsu, under the influence of Kūkai's teachings, interpreted it in the second sense but with a further expansion: Not only was the individual mind already Awakened, so were all phenomena in the cosmos. The central element in secret Taimitsu transmission was thus the revelation of the original Awakened nature of all things. In this light, Buddhist practice—instead of being a gradual path that eventually yielded Awakening—was one that began with the recognition of a liberation already present. Different lineages of Taimitsu transmission then gave different interpretations to how the remainder of one's practice was to be conceived. Some of the more antinomian lineages maintained that the recognition of one's original Awakening was enough to make all of one's subsequent actions, no matter how impure they might seem in traditional terms, automatically pure. More orthodox lineages maintained that continued practice through discipline, meditation, and study was required for deepening and strengthening one's faith in one's Suchness and one's discernment of nonduality. In either case, though, the essential view of the practice was not one of effort toward a future goal but as confirmation of a liberation that is already present. This picture of the path was to have a profound effect on the independent schools that developed simultaneously with Tendai original Awakening thought.

Although both Tendai and Shingon saw their primary role as ministering to the ritual needs of the court, they also began to participate in the spread of popular Buddhism. The Heian period witnessed the emergence of *shugenja,* or mountain ascetics who combined Buddhism and shamanic practices, like the ubasoku of the Nara period, and who affiliated themselves, albeit loosely, with the two new schools. Tendai also played an important role in the rise of Japanese Pure Land Buddhism. The *nembutsu* (nien-fo), or repetition of the name of the Buddha Amida, had very early formed a part of the Tendai synthesis, where it functioned primarily in rituals for the dead and as a means of gaining merit devoted to the attainment of nirvāṇa. Tenth-century Kyōto, however, suffered a string of natural disasters that were interpreted as signs that the Mappō—the age of Degenerate Dharma, when people would be unable to practice under their own power—was near at hand. This inspired a number of Tendai monks to divorce the nembutsu from its context in the Tendai synthesis and to recommend that it be made the sole focus of practice for the sake of attaining Amida's Pure Land (Jōdo). One of these monks, Kūya (903–972), danced in the streets singing simple hymns about Amida and organized self-help projects among the common people. Another, Genshin (942–1017), wrote an influential treatise, *The Compendium of Rebirth,* advocating the nembutsu because it was open to all: saint and sinner, monk and lay person, man and woman, emperor and peasant. Genshin was followed by Ryōnin (1072–1132) who, like Kūya, spread the practice of nembutsu in song, attracting followers in court and countryside. Not until the Heian period had ended, however, did Pure Land become a separate school.

A major source for seeing how Buddhist ideas percolated into day-to-day religious life of the Heian period is the popular literature that began developing at this time. For example, one of its early masterpieces, *The Tale of Genji,* by Lady Murasaki Shikibu (978–circa 1025), presents a worldview that combines karma and spirit agency in a way similar to what we noticed in Thai popular Buddhism (see Section 7.5.1). Calamities—from earthquakes to marital spats—are blamed on the influence of angry spirits, called *goryo.* To appease these spirits, festivals are held, partly to entertain them with shows of wrestling, dancing, music, archery, and horse racing; partly to exorcise them with Buddhist and Shintō rituals. Karma plays an integral role in Murasaki's plots, in that good and bad fortune are traced back to the characters' own actions, either in present or past lives, but it is viewed less as a means of shaping the future than as a fatalistic force bringing rewards or punishments from the past. Romantic entanglements, for instance, are predestined and thus unavoidable. The ancient Chinese view of the sins of the parents being inflicted on their children also plays a role: A bastard son is cursed by his parents' adultery. Thus the characters are essentially helpless, "bits of driftwood in a floating world"—an image that was to have a lasting influence on subsequent Japanese literature.

10.5 THE KAMAKURA PERIOD (1185–1333)

Toward the end of the twelfth century, courtiers and provincial warriors became involved in a series of battles that led to a decisive victory for the warriors in 1185. This ushered in a new era for Japan, politically, socially, and culturally. Political power was now in the hands of the *Bakufu* (tent government) or shogunate, which moved the seat of government to Kamakura. While the warriors ruled, the emperor and his court remained in Kyōto, where they were allowed to "reign," in a ritual sense, deprived of any real power. Emperors sporadically attempted to regain control of the government, but feudal military rulers remained in power until the mid-nineteenth century.

During this period, a new middle class began to develop, with newfound time to devote to religious pursuits, thus bringing to Buddhism its own varied needs and expectations. Both the Tendai and Shingon schools developed in new directions to respond to these needs and expectations, and thus they remained the preeminent Buddhist institutions in the country. The Kamakura period, for example, was when Tendai original Awakening thought developed into its final form. It was also a period in which precept reform became a widespread movement across sectarian lines, as monks tried to revive among themselves the ideal of a pure and orderly life based on the Vinaya, at the same time organizing precept ordination for groups of lay people as a means of strengthening their karmic connection with the Dharma. Many of these groups would then engage in charitable work. Although none of these groups became independent religious organizations, they established precedents for Buddhist charitable organizations into modern times.

However, during the Kamakura period there were individuals who, for personal or political reasons, left the existing institutions and formed marginal independent schools of their own, often advocating a single practice, rather than the broad range of practices taught by Shingon and Tendai. These schools remained small during the Kamakura period but gained prominence in the following centuries.

There is some irony in presenting the founders of these schools in this section, as they were only briefly if at all popular during the Kamakura period, and when their schools did become popular in succeeding centuries, the thought of the founders was often changed beyond recognition by the schools' new leaders. However, there is no understanding the schools without knowing something of the founders, and there is no understanding the founders without viewing them in the context of their time.

10.5.1 Zen

Overcoming strong opposition from Mount Hiei, Myōan Eisai (1141–1215) established the first Zen (in Chinese, Ch'an) temple in Kyōto, in 1202, after having received the seal of transmission from a Lin-chi master in China in 1191. Eisai himself, though, was essentially a Tendai adherent. Of his extant writings, only one piece deals with Zen—recommending it as a tool for unifying the nation—whereas his remaining writings focus on restoring Tendai to its earlier stature. Dissatisfaction with the eclecticism of Eisai's Zen led a number of monks in the following generation to travel to China on their own to receive transmission of a less adulterated teaching to bring back to Japan.

The first to do so was Dōgen Kigen (1200–1253). Born into an aristocratic family but then orphaned at age 6, Dōgen was ordained a monk at age 14 at Mount Hiei. An extremely precocious child, he quickly mastered Tendai doctrine but then left Mount Hiei after his preceptor had been removed from his post. He studied with students of Eisai but was dissatisfied with his training, so in 1223 he left for China, where he eventually began intensive practice under the Ch'an master Ju-ching (1163–1228) and had an Awakening experience that he called "the dropping away of body and mind." In 1227 he returned to Japan to spread his vision of the true Buddhist teaching to counteract what he regarded as the gross misunderstandings of Buddhism rampant there. Although he first settled near Kyōto, ecclesiastical politics forced him to retreat to the mountains far to the northeast of the city, where he founded a temple, Eiheiji. There he lived until his death from tuberculosis at age 53.

Dōgen was a prolific writer, authoring kōan (in Chinese, kung-an) commentaries, meditation manuals, and treatises on monastic discipline, along with many essays and poems. Although some of his writings are straightforward, many are extremely prolix, pushing language and logic to the breaking point. Modern writers have advanced the thesis that this kind of Zen writing by Dōgen and others was meant to stymie all attempts at logical analysis, forcing the mind to abandon rational thinking, but Dōgen himself maintained that this is not the case. There is a logic to Awakening, he maintained, but it requires a special kind of thinking. He hints at the nature of this thinking in his guide to Zen meditation, the *Fukan-zazengi* (the *Universal Guide to the Principles of Zen Sitting*). After detailing the proper physical environment and bodily posture for meditation, he advises: "Think no-thinking. How is no-thinking thought? Nonthinking." The *Fukan-zazengi* gives no further explanation, and on the surface these instructions would seem to echo the Platform Sūtra's teachings on no-thought, the practice of allowing the thought stream to continue with no interruption and no abiding. In this light, nonthinking would be the practice of not interrupting the thought stream. However, Dōgen's many other writings on meditation portray a very different picture of what "nonthinking" might mean.

For example, in one of his most massive works—*Shōbōgenzō,* or the *Treasury of the True Dharma-Eye*—he recommends that a meditator practice *shikantaza* (just sitting). But instead of simply allowing thoughts to flow while just sitting, nonthinking must detect and question many subtle unspoken presuppositions that could hide behind ordinary thinking, providing an abiding place for thought. Only then can one just sit. In one of the *Shōbōgenzō* essays, "Zanmai-Ōzanmai" ("The King of Samādhis' Samādhi"), Dōgen shows how nonthinking might function in this case: "What is the sitting itself? . . . Is it doing something? Is it not doing anything? Do we sit in the sitting or in our body and mind? Or do we sit dropping off sitting in the seated body and mind, or is sitting still something else? We must investigate these and countless similar details. . . . There is sitting of the mind, which is different from sitting of the body. There is sitting of the body, which is different from sitting of the mind. There is sitting of dropping off the body and mind, which is different from sitting of dropping off the body and mind. . . . You must thoroughly investigate perception, intention, and consciousness." In this case, nonthinking functions more like "dethinking," deconstructing any and all potential unspoken assumptions where thought might abide. And this is why Dōgen's writings can be so difficult, for they often are examples of nonthinking in action.

In his kōan commentaries, Dōgen applies nonthinking to classical kōans, but he makes clear that the purpose of asking these questions from all possible sides is not to abide with the answers, but to become more and more familiar with the dynamic of nonthinking here and now. In this way, he says, full familiarity with or authentication of Dharma-nature—the dropping away of any abiding in body or mind—is to be found in the process of cultivating nonthinking, not as its end result.

This teaching of "cultivation as authentication" is Dōgen's contribution to the discussions surrounding the issue of original Awakening. As we noted previously, a primary issue engendered by the original Awakening doctrine was that of the function of practice: If the mind is already Awakened by nature, what is the purpose of practice? Dōgen's journal of his sojourn in China indicates that he took the question of original Awakening to his teacher, who categorically rejected the idea that ordinary awareness is already Awakened. Nevertheless, Dōgen's own Awakening experience under his teacher's training showed him that Awakening is not a static state produced at the end of practice; instead, it was expressed in the nonthinking that formed the heart of the practice all along. Thus he later formulated the position that the cultivation of the path is, in and of itself, the authentication of Awakening. Instead of waiting to attain Awakening at the end of the Path, one should look to see it authenticated as the process of correctly cultivating the path itself.

True to his penchant for nonthinking, Dōgen demolished both sides of the question as to whether transmission outside of the texts was related to transmission in the texts. Still, especially in his later writings, he often quoted from not only the Mahāyāna Sūtras, but also the Chinese Āgamas, or translations of the Sūtra Piṭaka. Like his teacher, he insisted that he was transmitting not a Zen or Ch'an school, but simply the true Dharma-eye, the true Buddha way.

Nevertheless, soon after his death, Dōgen became regarded as the founder of the Sōtō (in Chinese, T'sao-tung) school of Zen. The Fourth Sōtō Patriarch, Keizan Jōkin (1268–1325), simplified the doctrine and practice of the school, dropping Dōgen's complex approach to kōan study in favor of a return to Hung-chih's method of Silent Illumination (see Section 8.6.2), which Dōgen had criticized vehemently. At the same time, Keizan added Shingon and kami ritual elements to make the school more popular with peasants and the rural aristocracy. His program was so successful that Sōtō became known as "farmer's Zen." Although the school became one of the largest in Japan, it never developed centers near the capital and so failed to become popular among the aristocratic elite. Dōgen's thought was virtually forgotten, even in his own school, from the fifteenth to the eighteenth century. Gentō Sokuchū, nominated to become abbot of Eiheiji in 1795, further expunged Dōgen's tradition from the school by forbidding kōan study entirely. Only in the past century have scholars resuscitated Dōgen's writings and made the wide range of his thought and practice available to the Japanese intellectual mainstream.

Soon after Dōgen returned from China, he was followed by a number of Chinese and Japanese masters who brought Rinzai Zen (in Chinese, Lin-chi Ch'an) to Japan. Most of the Chinese masters were refugees from the Mongol invasions of China or—in following generations—members of Lin-chi lineages that were out of favor with the new Yüan dynasty. Unlike Dōgen, many of these teachers followed the later Sung Ch'an tendency of combining their teachings with neo-Confucian social and political doctrines, and so were willing to act as scribes and teachers of Chinese culture for their aristocratic supporters. This helped make Rinzai popular with the ruling classes. Rinzai was quickly accepted by both the shogunate and the imperial court, a fact that helped the school withstand the political pressures exerted by the more established schools. The only Rinzai school established in the thirteenth century that is still extant today is the Ō-Tō-Kan school, founded by Nampo Jōmyō (1235–1309), who emphasized classical kōan study and resisted the temptation to combine Rinzai teachings with those of other Buddhist or Confucian schools. His follower, Shūhō Myōchō, organized the first systematic program of kōan study in Japan and founded the Daitoku-ji temple in Kyōto, which is today the head temple of the Rinzai school, justifiably famous for the quiet sophistication of its buildings and gardens.

10.5.2 Pure Land

Belief in the imminence of the Mappō—the age of Degenerate Dharma—continued to gain credence into the Kamakura period, leading to the formation of three major popular schools that have continued up to the present time. The history of these schools is especially interesting in that they give us the earliest detailed records of the way in which Japanese religious groups formed around charismatic leaders and suffered at the hands of the authorities.

The first of these schools was the Jōdo-shū (Pure Land sect), founded by the Tendai monk, Hōnen (1133–1212). Strongly influenced by the views of the Chinese Pure Land master Shan-tao (see Section 8.5.3), Hōnen wrote a long work systematizing Pure Land doctrines under the title, *The Treatise on the Selection of the Nembutsu of the Original Vow* (1197). As was the case with his Pure Land predecessors, such as Kūya and Genshin, Hōnen viewed the nembutsu as a single practice that could fulfill a wide range of purposes. Not only could it lead to rebirth in Amida's Pure Land, but it could also bring about a realization of one's Buddha-nature, provide protection from worldly calamities, grant salvation to one's dead relatives, and eradicate one's own sins.

A charismatic leader, Hōnen practiced what he preached—chanting the nembutsu up to 70,000 times a day—and drew disciples from all levels of society, including aristocrats and samurai. Of these the most important was the Fujiwara regent, Kujo Kanezane (1148–1207), whose enthusiastic support greatly advanced the position of the school. Hōnen might have followed the example set by Kūya and Genshin, who had remained in the Tendai fold, had he not gotten into trouble with the Tendai establishment on two counts: He was extremely popular, and his enthusiastic claims for the all-encompassing powers of the nembutsu could be interpreted as granting license to sin, as all wrongdoing could supposedly be cleansed by chanting. Hōnen himself adhered closely to what he regarded as the spirit of the Vinaya, but his insistence that the practice of nembutsu was sufficient for salvation, with no need for meditation or merit making, led many of his followers to interpret his doctrine as a release from moral strictures. In 1207, when four of his followers were executed for alleged indiscretions with ladies of the court, he was stripped of his monastic title and ordered into exile, together with a handful of his closest disciples. The order was rescinded in 1211, but he died soon thereafter. Fifteen years after his death, in 1227, his *Treatise on the Selection of the Nembutsu of the Original Vow* was publicly burned on the grounds that it was a threat to the Dharma.

Shinran (1173–1262), the inspiration of the Jōdo-shin-shū (True Pure Land sect), was one of the disciples ordered into exile with Hōnen. Although he had no intention of founding a separate school, dramatic visions inspired him to make two important changes in the tradition—one institutional, the other doctrinal—that led his followers to form a separate institution. The first vision came while Shinran was still a Tendai monk. After 20 years on Mount Hiei, grappling with the constraints of celibacy, he experienced a dream revelation in which the bodhisattva Kannon promised to come to him in the form of a young woman whom he should marry. Shinran did as he was told and for the remainder of his life assumed the status of "neither monk nor layman," which accurately describes the married clergy of the school that took him as its inspiration. These clerics continued to live in temples and perform religious services, but also led a family life and expected the eldest son to take over the temple from his father.

Shinran's place of exile was the northern province of Echigo, where he propagated the nembutsu among the general populace. Because Hōnen died soon after both of them were pardoned, Shinran did not return to Kyōto, but traveled through the towns and villages of east Japan, spreading the teaching and founding *dōjō nembutsu* (nembutsu temples). During this period he had his second major revelation: that the saving grace of Amida required only one nembutsu. This provided Shinran's answer to a question that had divided members of the Pure Land school for decades: How many times was it necessary to repeat the name of Amida in order to be assured a place in his paradise? The *Sukhāvatī-vyūha Sūtra* (see Section 5.2.2) stated that one need repeat Amida's name only 10 times to qualify for the benefit of his saving vow, whereas Shan-tao had recommended repeating the nembutsu as a mantra as many times as possible throughout the waking day.

Shinran's position—formulated in his work, *Teaching, Practice, Faith, and Attainment* (1224)—was that the original question had been misconceived. The nembutsu was not a means of earning one's way to the Pure Land, for such a view involved a total misunderstanding of the true nature of Amida as an embodiment of the Tathāgata. By nature, the Tathāgata is *jinen hōni,* or "that which becomes such on its own." Any effort to influence the Tahtāgata through one's practice is a misguided attempt to force oneself onto that which cannot be forced. Similarly, however, any belief in one's original Awakening is misconceived, for the Tathāgata, though found inwardly, can be experienced only as something totally other. Thus the only course open to the sincere practitioner is to develop a profound sense of one's own sinful inadequacy, abandoning all sense of *jiriki* (self-power) and nurturing faith in the grace of Amida's *tariki* (other-power). Even one's ability to accept Amida's grace has nothing to do with one's own merit, but is a result of Amida's grace as well.

In this context, one nembutsu is enough to acknowledge and accept Amida's grace; the remaining repetitions are simply to express gratitude to the Tathāgata. Although Shinran's thought presents a radical break both with gradualist depictions of the Buddhist path and with the Tendai depiction of the path as a confirmation of one's original Awakening, it does parallel original Awakening thought in that the one moment of true practice—in this case, the full acceptance of tariki—is enough to make contact with the Tathāgata within. The remainder of one's practice is simply the deepening of that acceptance.

Shinran's frequent references to himself as having sinned in taking on a wife must be viewed in the context of his radical emphasis on faith. Evil individuals who recognize their evil nature, he said, are more likely than good individuals to be born into the Pure Land, for the good are deluded by the pride they take in their virtue, and thus are blocked from accepting the gift of grace.

Shinran's doctrine, like Hōnen's, opened itself to all sorts of abuses and misinterpretations. His own son, Zenran, preached such an inflammatory version of the teaching as to make it an outright invitation to sin—on the grounds that the best way to reduce one's pride was to engage in evil—and Shinran eventually had to sever all relations with him. Dōjō leaders were accused of treating the school's funds as their own, and government officials intervened in 1235. Shinran returned to Kyōto in that year and lived quietly to the age of 90. Only after his death did his followers organize themselves into a school.

10.5.3 Nichiren

Nichiren-shū, the third Mappō school formed during the Kamakura period, was the first major school of Japanese Buddhism with no foreign antecedents, and the first to be named after its founder. The son of a fisherman, Nichiren (1222–1282) was ordained at the age of fifteen and given the name Renchō (Eternal Lotus). As he grew older, he became greatly concerned with the calamities befalling the nation and the imperial family, convinced that they had a religious cause. Thus he resolved to study all of the Buddhist teachings to find the solution to this problem and to save the nation from what he saw as imminent disaster.

His studies eventually took him to Mount Hiei, where he was drawn by the nationalistic elements in Saichō's teachings. He came to the conclusion that Saichō had been right in basing his teachings on the *Lotus Sūtra,* but wrong in adding to it teachings from other Sūtras and schools. Only the *Lotus Sūtra,* Nichiren felt, contained the unadulterated true Dharma. All other Buddhist teachings were not only wrong, but actually evil in that they obscured and distorted the truth, advocating the worship of false Buddhas. The chief culprit in this regard was the Pure Land movement. The calamities befalling the nation and the imperial family could be traced to the emperor's having allowed false Dharma to be propagated in the country. The only solution was to punish the evil individuals who were responsible, and to bring the entire nation to the worship of the truth as contained in the *Lotus Sūtra*. As a result of this realization, Renchō took on the name Nichiren, or Sun Lotus, thus combining the symbols of the two concerns foremost in his mind—the *Lotus Sūtra* and the Japanese nation—with the intention of showing that hope for salvation lay in their union.

The practice Nichiren recommended to replace the nien-fo was to recite the *daimoku,* or title of the *Lotus Sūtra*—"Namu Myōhō-renge-kyō," Homage to the Scripture of the Lotus of the Perfect Truth—in full confidence that the daimoku contained the totality of all Buddhist teachings and practices. Nichiren wrote extensively to demonstrate that the chanting of the daimoku was the actualization of the highest level of meditation in the T'ien-t'ai system, the single thought-moment comprising the 3,000 realms of being. It contained all good precepts and the merit gained by observing them, and transferred to all who embraced it the practices undertaken by the Buddha and his ensuing Awakening. Nichiren also formulated a maṇḍala, called the *gohonzon,* toward which one was to face while chanting the daimoku. The gohonzon depicted the daimoku flanked by the names of two eternal Buddhas and surrounded by the names of the ten levels of being, symbolizing the power of the daimoku as an Awakening penetrating all of the cosmos. Later generations in the Nichiren school developed the Tantric implications of Nichiren's teachings as one mantra (the daimoku), one maṇḍala (the gohonzon), and one mudrā (the añjali, or in Japanese, *gasshō*).

Nichiren attracted a following largely through his courage and the incandescent intensity of his personality. His life was reportedly marked by omens and portents, and he was hailed as a great diviner when the Mongol invasion that he had predicted in 1260 and 1268 was actually attempted in 1274. His utopian vision predicted that Japan, by following his teaching alone, would become a Buddha-field on Earth, from which the revived and purified Dharma would spread to the rest of the world. Later in life, he became convinced that he was an emanation of the bodhisattva Viśiṣṭacārita (Superb Conduct); his followers were equated with the bodhisattva hosts whom Śākyamuni summoned out of the earth with the command to worship and protect the *Lotus Sūtra.*

As might be expected, Nichiren ran afoul of the authorities for his inflammatory accusations. He was twice exiled and once narrowly escaped execution, but from his viewpoint each suffering was a glorious martyrdom. He died in poverty and relative obscurity, but his school grew in the following centuries and continues to thrive at present.

10.6 THE MUROMACHI PERIOD (1336–1603)

After an abortive 3-year period of imperial rule, a new shogunate established its capital in Kyōto in 1336, ushering in a new period in Japanese history that witnessed the gradual collapse of the estate economy, to be replaced by a loose system of semi-autonomous villages. This social change was reflected in the religious scene, as some of the marginal schools of Kamakura Buddhism, reinterpreted for the new situation, began to attract large followings who found the single-practice approach advocated by these schools consonant with their perceived religious needs. At the same time, Rinzai Zen began to replace Tendai and Shingon as the school with the closest ties to the ruling house. The possibilities opened by these changes in the social and religious realm, however, were thwarted by famine and a devastating series of civil wars. By the end of the Muromachi period, all Buddhist schools aside from Sōtō and Rinzai had formed armed societies to protect their interests, only to be slaughtered by the hundreds of thousands. This effectively destroyed Buddhism's credibility as an instrument of national unity.

The first shogun's religious adviser, Musō Soseki (1275–1351), was a Rinzai monk who had also received training in the Tantric traditions. After spending his youth in seclusion, he became one of the most politically active monks in Rinzai history, numbering not only shoguns but also emperors among his pupils. He thus cemented the bond that had been developing between Rinzai and the ruling classes during the Kamakura period, making Rinzai the new de facto state religion. Although he himself was respected as a serious meditator, the school he founded quickly became immersed in the political and cultural life of the capital. Zen monasteries mounted trade expeditions to China to help strengthen the financial base of the new government; monks served as diplomats, accountants, and teachers of Chinese arts and culture, neo-Confucianism in particular.

With few exceptions, the Zen of the Muromachi period is remembered more for its contributions to the arts than for its meditative rigor. Classical kōan cases were used, not for meditation training, but as literary and educational devices. Zen monks became renowned for their skill in the arts of poetry, flower arrangement, garden design, painting, calligraphy, and *chadō* (the cult of tea). In doing so, they developed a fastidious style, blending the sophistication of Chinese and Kyōto court culture with the austerity and attention to subtle detail that they saw as distinctively Zen. As education and opportunities for social mobility became more widely available during this period, this style proved immensely popular not only among the ruling classes, but also among the newly enfranchised, who adopted a self-consciously rustic version of the Zen style as a badge of their newfound status and cultural sophistication. It was thus that Zen began to percolate throughout Japanese culture as an attitude: the belief that anything, if done in the proper style with the proper frame of mind, was an expression of Zen.

The aristocratic Zen style was best expressed in the *nō* drama, particularly in the plays of Zeami Motokiyo (1363–1443), which developed at this time. The structure of nō drama in general is based on the Mahāyāna assertion that beings suffer if they see saṁsāra as separate from nirvāṇa, but can gain tranquillity if they can break through dualities to realize the nirvāṇa in saṁsāra here and now. Zeami's plays drew on incidents that conveyed Buddhist themes, including the teachings of Tendai, Shingon, and Pure Land, while the aristocratic Zen style provided the stark stage settings and the overriding aesthetic. In his theoretical writings on nō, Zeami maintained that the training of the nō actor was analogous to that of a Zen monk. Each performance of a play was part of the ongoing training in which the actor, while acting, was to attain a particular state of mind as a result of the performance. In Zeami's phrase, the performance is the seed, while the mind is the flower. Thus the actor was to direct his efforts at his own state of mind, rather than at pleasing the audience. If the audience was sufficiently sensitive, it would be able to intuit the actor's success at internal transformation, but even if it couldn't, the true measure of the actor's performance would be something he could gauge from within. The state of mind that Zeami called the ideal "flower" had three characteristics: deep poetic emotion expressed with elegance and acute sensitivity; utter transcendence and unapproachability (symbolized by the image of the "sun at midnight"); and beauty enhanced by being made subtle and elusive ("the moon veiled by a wisp of cloud"). Later writers, such as Komparu Zenchiku (1405–1468), made the Zen–nō connection even more obvious as they fashioned their dramas around explicit Zen themes.

The most famous Zen meditator of the Muromachi period was the Rinzai monk, Ikkyū Sōjun (1394–1481). The illegitimate son of an emperor, Ikkyū was forced into a Rinzai monastery at the age of 5 to escape the political intrigues of the court, only to encounter the political and sexual intrigues of monks close to the court and the shogunate. Trained in a Kyōto temple to be an accomplished poet, he eventually left the capital to undergo kōan training in a provincial center, where he claimed to have gained Awakening. His uncompromising temperament, however, led him to rebel against the hypocrisy he saw around him, both in the capital and in the provinces. He began using his poetic skills to mount scathing attacks on the "leprous and perverted" Zen establishment. He also flagrantly broke monastic rules as a form of protest, eating meat, drinking alcohol, and even fathering a child.

Styling himself a "crazy cloud," Ikkyū frequented the company of disreputable commoners and was not averse to taking ruffians and street-walkers as disciples. Nevertheless, he insisted on rigorous standards of meditation practice. His distinctive contribution to Zen thought was his doctrine of "the red thread of passion," in which lust became the testing ground for the doctrine of the nonduality of the realm of Awakening and the realm of desire. In his old age Ikkyū wrote erotic poetry comparing his mistress, Lady Mori—a blind street singer, some forty years his junior—to the Buddha. Later generations of Zen practitioners revered him, but he left no Dharma heir.

During the fifteenth century, the sophisticated Muromachi aesthetic was reduced to a thin veneer over a society that was essentially falling apart. Bloody power struggles rent the shogunate; famines and epidemics led to peasant uprisings. The ruinous Ōnin War (1467–1478) effectively brought an end to central control, and provincial warlords began asserting their independence. Merchants and artisans in the cities and towns formed guilds centered on Buddhist temples and Shintō shrines to defend their interests. Rennyo (1415–1499), the Eighth Patriarch of the Jōdo–shin–shū school, organized his followers into a feudal state that was protected by peasant armies; the other Pure Land schools and the Nichiren school soon followed suit, staging peasant revolts to assert their interests.

In the sixteenth century, a string of warlords tried to reunify the country, only to find their path blocked by the armed Buddhist groups. Oda Nobunaga (1534–1582) was especially ruthless in his suppression of Buddhist institutions, burning the monastery at Mount Hiei and putting its monks to the sword. He also attacked the Shingon stronghold on Mount Kōya and suppressed the Nichiren and Pure Land armies. In one province alone (Echizen) he is said to have slaughtered thirty to forty thousand followers of the Jōdo–shin–shū Ikkō (Single-minded) sect. Rinzai Zen, like Sōtō, escaped his ire largely because it remained unarmed and also because it had begun to decentralize, spreading out to the country after many of its main monasteries in Kyōto were destroyed during the Ōnin War. Nobunaga's successor, Toyotomi Hideyoshi (1536–1598), was somewhat less savage in his policies, disarming rather than killing the peasantry, although he too attacked rebellious monastic communities, such as the Shingon center in Negoro. National unification finally came under Tokugawa Ieyasu (1542–1616), who moved the capital to Edo, modern-day Tokyo, and opened a new era in Japanese history.

10.7 THE TOKUGAWA PERIOD (1603–1868)

The Tokugawa shogunate was more than just another feudal regime. It was a military dictatorship with an all-embracing ideology aimed at the total restructuring and control of Japanese society. The ideology was founded on Confucian ideals. The role of the government was to be based not on the power of ritual, but on the order of heaven, which was immanent in the natural norms implicit in human, social, and political order. Society was to be divided into rigidly defined classes, and the duty of each citizen was to fulfill the obligations of his or her class. Religions were allowed to function to the extent of supporting this order, but were not to pass judgment on the government or disturb social peace and unity in any way.

The rise of Confucianism under the Tokugawas can be explained both by what was perceived as the Buddhist-inspired disunity of the previous century, and by the success of the Ming dynasty in using neo-Confucianism to unite China. Neo-Confucian scholars in Japan separated themselves from the Zen monks who had been their teachers, and devised an anti-Buddhist, pro-Shintō version of their philosophy to serve the new government's needs.

On the surface, Tokugawa policy seemed to support Buddhism. All families were required to register as members of a Buddhist temple; an edict was published, denouncing the activities of Christian missionaries, and noting that Japan was essentially a Buddhist and Shintō nation. In actuality, the registration of families was a means of keeping tabs on the population and preventing proselytizing by any religious group. No one was allowed to change religious affiliation without the entire household's changing. Monks became not only census takers but also government informers. Although the state used Buddhist institutions as an arm of its policy, it gave them no financial support.

Deprived of their political influence, many Buddhist groups attempted a self-purification through a return to their roots. Shingon scholars, led by Jiun Sonja (1718–1804), retreated to the mountains and wrote voluminous commentaries on Sanskrit texts as part of their effort to uncover the True Dharma-Vinaya. Tendai scholars abandoned the medieval teachings of their school in favor of the "pure" teachings of Sung T'ien-t'ai scholars. Individual monks in the Sōtō school began the gradual recovery of Dōgen's teachings.

Most of the religious innovations of this period were initiated in the Rinzai school. In 1654, Yin-yüan Lung-ch'i (Ingen Ryūki, 1592–1673) came to Japan and founded a Ming Ch'an school, the Ōbaku school, which combined Rinzai and Pure Land teachings. This inspired Rinzai monks to examine and reformulate the foundations of their practice. In the provinces, for instance, Bankei Yōtaku (1622–1693) taught that Rinzai practice consisted simply of letting things be while one dwelled in the innate "knowingness" of the mind, which Bankei equated with the Unborn Buddha-mind.

Diametrically opposed to Bankei's approach was that of the most influential Zen practitioner of this period: Hakuin Ekaku (1686–1769). An extremely high-strung, sensitive child, Hakuin entered the monkhood at an early age and vigorously pursued kōan study under numerous masters. Controversy has ensued over whether any of his masters certified his *satori* (Awakening), but the broad nature of his training enabled him to devise a comprehensive system of kōan study, drawing on many traditions, that has shaped the universal Rinzai curriculum ever since.

Hakuin's teachings drew both on his own dramatic experiences as a meditator and on his extensive readings in the literature of the Ch'an/Zen school and the Chinese Āgamas. Following the example of Ta-hui (see Section 8.6.2) he advocated an intense involvement with one's kōan, leaving no time for art, literature, or other secular pursuits. This involvement had to be based on a strong moral foundation and required three basic attitudes: great belief in the kōan, great questioning of one's assumptions, and great aspiration and perseverance. These attitudes were to be encouraged by frequent *dokusan* (interviews) with the teacher. Two features, however, made Hakuin's approach distinctive. The first was in advocating a strong physical involvement with the kōan. After beginning with breath meditation, the meditator was to fill the energy-center of the lower abdomen with vital force, and then to confront the kōan right there, not simply with the mind, but with the energy of the mind and body together. This energy would then help to maintain the three basic attitudes needed to arrive at *kenshō* (see Section 8.5.5), the realization of nonduality between the mind/body and the kōan itself. This is where the second distinctive feature of Hakuin's teaching would come into play, that of *kōjō,* or "going beyond." After attaining kenshō, one should not abide there, but instead should take on additional kōans as further challenges. Thus, unlike kung-an practice in Korea—where "going beyond" involves delving deeper into one's initial kung-an—the Rinzai curriculum based on Hakuin's teachings involves tackling many kōans, and not just one.

The principle of kōjō is embodied in this curriculum in many ways. For instance, kōans are divided into five stages of difficulty to teach specific lessons on the interpenetration of principle and phenomena: the Apparent within the Real, the Real within the Apparent, Coming from within the Real, Arrival at Mutual Interpenetration, and Unity Attained. Interestingly enough, the names of these stages are drawn from the writings of the Ts'ao-tung monk, Tung-shan (see Section 8.5.5). Each major kōan within these stages is broken into a main case following by "checking questions." Thus, in the famous Mu kōan, the story of Chao-chou's saying "No!" forms the main case. Once this case is "kenshō-ed," the meditator might be asked such checking questions as, "After seeing Mu, what is your proof?" "Seeing Mu, how did you free yourself from life-and-death?" "One time Chao-chou answered, 'Yes!' What about that?" The purpose of these questions is to force the meditator to see how the nonduality of kenshō penetrates different aspects of the world of duality. And the teacher is to assess his students' answers to these questions, not by their words, but by their capacity as manifest in their total comportment in body and mind.

Although there is no way of knowing the extent to which the modern Rinzai curriculum is faithful to the details of Hakuin's practice, the principles underlying the curriculum can all be cited in his writings. And one of the best-known first-stage kōans in the Zen tradition can definitely be traced to him: "What is the sound of one hand?"

During the Tokagawa period, the Zen influence on aesthetics continued. Reflecting Rinzai's new social status, tied more closely to commoners, the Tokagawa Zen style was totally dominated by its more rustic version, in which spiritual significance was sought in the most ordinary, mundane details, rather than in fastidious sophistication. The best exemplar of this style is the poet Matsuo Bashō ("Banana Tree," 1644–1694), the foremost practitioner of the art of haiku poetry. Assuming in the fourth decade of his life the persona of a wandering Zen monk, he wrote travel essays recording aesthetic experiences analogous to satori, attempting in short impromptu verses to capture the transcendent in a single cluster of images. His aesthetic emphasized the values of lightness, contented solitude, and an appreciation of the commonplace. For example, late in his life he composed this reflection on not-self: "On this road/with no traveler/autumn night falls."

Another development in the Tokugawa period that was to have a long-term effect on Japanese Buddhism was the work of the nationalistic scholar Yamaga Sokō (1622–1685), who formulated the ideals of *bushidō* (the Way of the Warrior). This was a code of military virtues, drawn from various strands of Japanese tradition, intended to justify the continued existence of a largely idle samurai class. In essence, bushidō was a Confucian code, in that the warrior's duty was to be as effective as possible in going to battle for his ruler. Although it had no relation to Buddhist ethics, bushidō adopted a Zen style: a quick and total awareness of the present, so free from distracting thoughts and dualisms that the swordsman attained a state of *mushin* (no-mind), at one with his sword. Japanese writings on Rinzai Zen that appeared in the West in the early twentieth century asserted a deep connection between Rinzai and bushidō, but the warrior code itself never gained popular currency or connection with Zen institutions in Japan itself until the end of the nineteenth century.

At the beginning of the nineteenth century, pressures from inside and outside Japan made the tight Tokugawa control over the society increasingly untenable. Millennial cults appeared, and pro-Shintō factions, formulating a new unitary philosophy of Shintō, asserted their independence from the Confucian ideologues who had previously supported them. In 1868 they restored the imperial system by bringing the Meiji emperor to power.

10.8 STATE SHINTŌ IN CONTROL (1868–1945)

The Shintō forces behind the Meiji restoration were initially hostile to Buddhism, viewing it as a decadent foreign influence that had polluted the original purity of Japanese culture and prevented the modernization of the Japanese state. After passing a law separating Buddhism and Shintō, the new government pursued an active policy of persecuting Buddhists, denouncing their traditions, expropriating temple lands, and converting Buddhist temples into Shintō shrines. A decree went out that Buddhist monks of all schools should be allowed to marry; at the same time, the monks were pressed into service to teach the new state religion—State Shintō—throughout the countryside. Only the intervention of a foreign businessman saved Prince Shōtoku's Hōryū-ji (see Section 10.2) from being turned into kindling wood for a public bath. The anti-Buddhist fervor peaked in 1871, after which it became clear that the policy of outright suppression was counterproductive. Some of the policies were dismantled—monks no longer had to propagate Shintō—but the decree allowing marriage remained. At present, there are very few celibate monks in Japan except for young men in training, although the nuns' orders have maintained their celibate vows.

Toward the end of the nineteenth century, the state mounted an expansionist, militaristic policy that eventually led Japan into a long string of wars: the Sino-Japanese War (1894–1895), the Russo-Japanese War (1904–1905), the annexation of Korea (1910), World War I, and the invasion of Manchuria followed by World War II. This new national mission provided the context in which a new generation of Buddhist scholars—mostly educated in the institutions of Western learning established by the Meiji government—began a concerted effort to reclaim Buddhism's place in Japanese culture. To do so, they had to redefine the Buddhist tradition in a way that would make it respectable, not only to Japanese nationalists, but also to the younger generation educated in Western rationalism and science. This Japanese redefinition of Buddhism in the light of Western thought was simply one instance of a trend sweeping throughout Asian Buddhism at the time, but its imperialistic overtones gave it a tenor all its own.

Borrowing a page from the European Enlightenment (see Section 12.2), the proponents of *shin bukkyō* (New Buddhism) distinguished the monastic institutional form of Buddhism from its original and pure principles. Contemporary Japanese Buddhist institutions, they conceded, were decadent and corrupt, but the original principles of the religion were consonant with modern ideals—humanistic, cosmopolitan, and socially responsible—that would aid the nation in its efforts toward modernization. At the same time, following the Social Darwinists, they insisted that the turmoil of Japanese history, including the recent Shintō suppression of Buddhism, had ensured that only the fittest and most developed expressions of Buddhism had survived on Japanese soil. The obvious contradictions in these two positions they reconciled by appealing to a Japanese version of the racism rampant in the West at the time. The Japanese, they insisted, had a unique talent for combining refined aesthetic/religious sensitivity with ruthless courage, and thus had managed to remain true to the inner essence of Buddhism while simultaneously taking it to a heightened pitch.

Zen priests, such as Kōsen Sōon (1816–1892) and his student Shaku Sōen (1859–1919), insisted that Rinzai Zen in particular, when stripped of its institutional forms, embodied the essence of Buddhism with a purity matched nowhere else. This essence consisted of a direct experience attained through a radically empirical and scientific inquiry into the true nature of things. In fact, the total stripping away of all conventionalities was in and of itself Zen. Thus the New Rinzai took the more iconoclastic side of Zen and made it represent the whole tradition, while dismissing as historical baggage the institutional forms that had balanced that iconoclasm and formed its reason for being. To answer Western charges of the effeminacy of Oriental culture, these priests also insisted on Zen's ties with the bushidō code of manly self-sacrifice, discipline, and single-minded fearlessness. Thus Zen was the ultimate expression both of the spirit of Buddhism and of the unique strengths of the Japanese race. As a political creed, New Rinzai answered Japan's need for a national ethos, immune to Western criticisms, that would support the national war effort and justify the disregard of conventional morality in its political designs on its spiritually "effete" neighbors. As the movement developed, its advocates began to view themselves as guardians of the primary essence of all world spirituality, and Japan as the vanguard of the spiritual regeneration of the human race. As part of their program, they sent one of their lay students, D. T. Suzuki (1870–1966), to promote Zen in the West in the early twentieth century.

The books and courses offered by the New Buddhists were so successful that government ideologues began to reassess Buddhism's role in Japanese history. As a result, they came to glorify the Rinzai contribution to the Way of the Warrior and the Muromachi aesthetic as signs of Japan's innate racial and cultural superiority. Rinzai monks were called on to teach the Zen aesthetic to members of the society as a way of fostering national pride, and to teach meditation as a way of instilling the single-minded "no-mindedness" of the Way of the Warrior—not only to soldiers, but to all whose total commitment would be needed to support the war effort. Monks from all Buddhist schools were also called on to justify militarism as a spiritual duty by teaching that the "bodies and hearts broken by war" were a noble sacrifice to a greater cause. The monks, aside from a handful of pacifists, did not refuse.

Until its collapse during World War II, the militaristic policy was a stunning success. Nevertheless, it created severe dislocations in Japanese society, which led to new religious movements centered on charismatic leaders. The number of quasi-religious groups skyrocketed from 98 in 1924 to more than 1,000 in 1935. Many of these movements were suppressed during World War II, but a handful of them emerged from the war with a renewed vigor and went on to dominate Japan's postwar religious scene.

10.9 MODERN URBAN BUDDHISM

Japan's defeat in World War II, together with the subsequent American occupation and rapid postwar industrialization, brought about radical changes in the nation's religious life. Defeat discredited religious institutions that had collaborated with the government's war effort. Occupation made American notions of religious freedom, democracy, and the separation of church and state the law of the land. Industrialization and urbanization fostered the breakdown of family and village social structures. These factors combined to undermine traditional Buddhism and to spark a phenomenal growth in the new religions, some of which incorporated Buddhist elements.

In 1945, the occupation force dissolved the official structure of State Shintō; in 1946, the emperor publicly denied his divinity; in 1947, the traditional system of interlocking households was dismantled, so that individuals were no longer bound by their family religion. A policy of land distribution was enacted to help create the stable middle class that a secure democracy would require, but this involved confiscating much of the land that had provided the income for Buddhist temples. The combined effect of these directives was to create, for the first time in Japanese history, a totally secular government; to give individuals total religious freedom; and to force many Buddhist priests into taking on lay occupations to support their families, thus limiting their time and ability to meet the new religious needs of the laity.

The government pursued its new secular role with the single-minded determination it had applied to its earlier religious and militaristic goals. As was traditional in Japanese society, it functioned essentially as a federation of ujis, although now the ujis were industrial conglomerates. The perceived lesson of the war was that pure spirit alone could not overcome technological superiority, so the government's efforts were now aimed at technological and economic progress. Much of Japan's postwar economic success can be traced to the combination of Zen concentration and Confucian devotion to one's social duty that had marked the Way of the Warrior. Zen monks were again called upon to teach meditation, this time to corporate workers and executives so that they would be able to devote themselves totally to their sales and production goals. Traditional manuals on military strategy were studied as guides to capturing domestic and foreign markets.

This single-minded focus on economic success has created one of the most secular societies on Earth. Polls indicate that large numbers of Japanese do not view themselves as belonging to any particular religion. Interest in traditional Buddhism is largely confined to two widely disparate groups: (1) the rural agricultural classes, who look to Buddhist institutions for the same services they have performed for centuries; and (2) the urban intelligentsia, who look to Buddhist thought as a model for creating distinctively Japanese forms of such Western enterprises as critical philosophy and psychotherapy.

For the remainder of society, though, traditional Buddhism has lost much of its appeal, except as a relic of Japan's cultural past. "Funeral Buddhism" is the name many people use to refer to the traditional schools, in light of the ritual role to which many of the priests have been reduced. Many Japanese people point to their continued appreciation of art and the beauties of nature as a sign that their religious sensitivities have not atrophied, but this simply means that they are still sensitive to the old notion of kami. Because the ujis currently in power, unlike the ujis of the past, are devoted to no kami, many Japanese have turned to the new religions of charismatic leaders to provide them with the traditional connection between their religious and social/political life, that is, to ujis that have reestablished the kami connection.

The postwar growth of the new religions came in two waves: first, during the rapid industrialization following the Korean War, and then during the dislocations of the 1980s, when the conglomerates that had once promised their workers lifetime job security began to abandon the home labor force in search of cheaper labor abroad. The first wave involved what were termed *shinkō shūkyō* (the new religions); the second, *shinkō shinkō shūkyō* (the new new religions). Both waves consisted of widely disparate groups, some claiming connections with Buddhism, others not, but what they have in common is a modern urban version of a pattern typical of traditional Japanese folk religions: utopian, sometimes apocalyptic, visions; direct connection with divinities or divine agents; healing—now expanded to include not only physical healing but also psychological healing and subsequent social and economic success; and a concern for physical and mental purification. Where these new religions differ from older Japanese folk religions is in their use of modern organizational skills and the mass media to win and maintain their followings. They are essentially ujis, but the pattern for a successful uji is now no longer the tribe, but the modern industrial corporation.

The three most successful of the new religions were associated with the Nichiren school: Sōka Gakkai (which we will discuss in the next section), Risshō Kōsei-kai, and Reiyūkai. Of the new new religions, the most notorious has been Aumshinrikyō, which gained international notoriety after an urban guerrilla attack on the Tokyo subway in 1995. The most successful of the new new groups, however, has been Kōkufu-no-Kagaku, or the Institute for Research in Human Happiness. This was founded in 1986 by Ryuho Okawa, a self-proclaimed incarnation of a "core spirit" named El Cantare, whose previous incarnations include the Buddha and Hermes, the Greek god of the sun. Ryuho's teachings, as presented in the book, *Laws of the Sun,* combine the apocalyptic forecasts of Nostradamus (the group has produced a popular movie on this theme) with the laws of the Buddha for a new age: self-reflection and conservative living in line with the Noble Eightfold Path. In ancient Japan, Ryuho's solar pretensions would have been sufficient grounds for execution, but in modern Japan they pass simply as a sentimental connection with the kami that inspired Japan's past imperial glories.

10.10 A RELIGION OF SELF-EMPOWERMENT

Sōka Kyoiku Gakkai, the Value-Creation Education Society, was founded in 1937 by Tsunesabarō Makiguchi (1871–1944), a reform-minded educator who had developed a theory of education as a means of creating personal and social values. Drawing on four sources—cultural geography; the thought of the American pragmatist, John Dewey; the thought of the American sociologist, Lester Ward; and Nichiren thought and practice—Makiguchi taught that the ideal education should foster within a student a set of values that would allow for the pursuit of individual happiness, personal gain, and a sense of social responsibility to combine harmoniously in fostering a harmonious community. As Sōka Kyoiku Gakkai grew in the prewar years, the emphasis shifted from educational to religious concerns, reflected in the society's publications, which reported the personal benefits that its members had gained from Nichiren practice. However, when the society protested the government's plan to unite all Nichiren sects during the war, the government disbanded the society in 1943 and, denouncing its entire leadership as "thought criminals," threw them into jail.

Makiguchi died there of malnutrition a year later, but one of his followers, Josei Toda (1900–1958) had a religious experience after chanting the daimoku more than two million times, which inspired him to work for the revival of the society on his release. In 1951 he registered the society as a lay religious group subject to the ritual authority of the Nichiren-shō-shū sect, at the same time dropping the Kyoiku (Educational) from its name, indicating that the emphasis was now totally religious. Toda's religious experience while in prison had shown him that the earlier society had not been single-minded enough in its devotion to the *Lotus Sūtra,* so this became the primary focus of the re-formed group.

Although the *Lotus Sūtra* has many elitist passages, Toda emphasized the passage in which bodhisattvas are called out of the earth to protect the Sūtra. In his eyes, these earth-bodhisattvas represented the poor and disenfranchised, and so that was the level of society among which he proselytized. As a tactical skill in responding to the needs of his listeners, Toda advocated directing the chanting of the daimoku toward this-worldly rewards: job promotion, financial success, family harmony, and the alleviation of physical and psychological ills. Once these small desires were satisfied, he felt, they could be transformed into the "great desire": the salvation of all. Thus he stressed repeatedly that chanting the daimoku was not sufficient for true happiness. It had to be accompanied by *shakubuku,* or proselytization, to convert the entire world to the one true form of Buddhism, thus ushering in a Pure Land on this very Earth.

Under Toda's leadership, Sōka Gakkai's aggressive efforts at shakubuku became notorious, as they sometimes bordered on physical and psychological intimidation. This aggressiveness can partly be explained by the intense belief that Toda engendered among his following concerning three points: that their true happiness depended on successful shakubuku, that their success in shakubuku was a measure of the sincerity of their motives, and that any resistance to shakubuku was inherently evil, and so should be overcome by all possible means. Although some potential converts were repelled by Sōka Gakkai's tactics, many others were drawn into the organization by its dynamic sense of purpose and by its members' earnest reports of the benefits they had gained from the practice. When Toda died in 1958, the organization claimed a membership of more than 750,000 families.

In 1960, Toda's handpicked successor, Daisaku Ikeda, assumed leadership of the organization, a position he still holds. This change in leadership coincided with a shift in the concerns of the Sōka Gakkai membership. As Japan grew increasingly affluent, more and more of the organization's members, in addition to seeking relief from specific worldly problems, began searching for a more meaningful life in general. At the same time, having survived the disgrace of defeat and occupation, Japanese society as a whole felt more confident about assuming its proper role in the world. These two trends influenced many of the changes that Ikeda made in the organization. Under his leadership, the Sōka Gakkai has grown from a national to an international religion with a membership in the millions, branches on all the populated continents, and an especially strong presence in Brazil and the United States. At the same time, it has developed a more moderate approach to and understanding of its "great desire." The tenor and techniques of shakubuku have been moderated, particularly in developed countries, and the goal of the organization has been changed to disseminating knowledge about, rather than converting the world to, Nichiren Buddhism. Ikeda has also revived the educational element of Makiguchi's original vision, opening a Sōka high school in 1968, a Sōka university in 1971, and the Sōka University of America in southern California in 1987. And, in line with Makiguchi's vision of value-creation as a means to a harmonious society, Ikeda has defined the organization's goal as world peace. As a means to this end, he founded a political party, the Kōmeitō (Clean Government Party) in 1964. However, when the other new Japanese religions banded with the Liberal Democrat and Democratic Socialist parties to protest this violation of the principle of the separation of church and state, formal ties between the organization and the party were severed in 1971.

As Sōka Gakkai developed into an international organization, tensions grew between it and the parent Nichiren-shō-shū sect over their relative roles, and in 1991 the sect excommunicated the entire organization. The split was bitter and still excites strong feelings on both sides, but in many ways Sōka Gakkai—now Sōka Gakkai International (SGI)—has greater freedom to adapt to the demands of the modern world. Lay volunteer leaders perform many of the ritual functions that were once reserved for Nichiren priests; the organization has become more democratic, with leadership roles increasingly filled by women; it has dropped its old confrontational attitude to other religions, engaging more in interreligious dialogue; and its formulation of its vision for the world—peace and prosperity through inner transformation—has assumed a more humanistic tone.

Still, the *Lotus Sūtra* remains the central focus of SGI religious life. Inner transformation still depends on the contact that the daimoku provides to the eternal Buddha-nature. This point can be illustrated by the schedule of a typical SGI meeting. After chanting excerpts from the *Lotus Sūtra,* the participants face the gohonzon and engage in a long and rhythmically exciting repetition of the daimoku. This is followed by individual silent prayers to direct the power of the chanting to specific ends. Then there is a short presentation by one of the group leaders, who might read from Nichiren's teachings or Ikeda's writings. Finally there is a group discussion, in which participants make testimonials or bring up problems from their job or family life that have a bearing on their practice. Group leaders are instructed not to try to solve these problems, but to remind the individual that, because they come from his or her own karma, he or she has the power to change them. Also, the problem should be seen as a gift to bring about personal growth. Through the chanting of the *Lotus Sūtra* and the daimoku, individuals can tap into the universal principle of the Buddha-nature, thus empowering themselves to "transmute poison into medicine." This emphasis on self-empowerment explained much of Sōka Gakkai's phenomenal growth in postwar Japan, just as it explains the organization's success in gaining converts among the disenfranchised throughout the world.

Scholarly discussions of the new Japanese religions have tended to focus on two questions: What do the religions represent, and what do they augur for the future? The second question is impossible to answer with any certainty, but an answer can be found for the first. The development of almost all of these movements falls into two phases: the first, in which charismatic leaders provide a personal spiritual connection to deal with immediate crises; and the second, in which the larger issues of the perfection of the personality and the improvement of society can be more systematically addressed once the crises have passed. Some of the new religions, such as Risshō Kōsei-kai, experienced a sharp break between the two phases. Others, such as SGI, have made a more gradual transition. The first phase represents a revival of the traditional uji in a form least integrated with the rest of society. The second phase represents a combination of the uji ideal of devotion to the clan and the clan's deity, with congruent elements from neo-Confucianism. Although some of the new religions use Buddhist terminology to describe their teachings during this phase, the basic pattern of religious life is Confucian. There is no role for the monastic Sangha, and solitary meditation is discouraged except as a means of strengthening the mind in pursuit of this-worldly ends. Lay people take full responsibility for their ritual obligations to their ancestors, secular life is the ideal arena for religious practice, and one's perfection as an individual is to be found by sincerely fulfilling one's social duties so as to bring about the perfection of society as a whole. By adopting this neo-Confucian pattern, these new ujis have integrated peacefully with the rest of society and have taken on the status of established religions. Thus, even when they are nominally Buddhist, they represent—in both phases of their development—the ascendancy of pre-Buddhist and non-Buddhist elements in Japanese religious life.

11

Buddhism in the Tibetan Cultural Area

11.1 A VAJRAYĀNA ORTHODOXY

The Tibetan cultural area covers the lands in which the Tibetan form of Vajrayāna became established as the dominant religion. This includes not only Tibet, but also the Himalayan valleys immediately bordering on Tibet—such as Ladakh, Spiti, Bhutan, Sikkim, and Mustang in northwestern Nepal—as well as areas further afield that the Tibetans converted to their form of Buddhism, such as Mongolia, the Buryats in Siberia, and the Kalmyks in the steppes north of the Caspian Sea.

To say that Vajrayāna is the dominant form of Buddhism in this area does not mean that a majority of the people engage in Vajrayāna practice, simply that Vajrayāna doctrine and practice have provided the framework by which the vast majority understand the methods and goals of Buddhist practice in general. In this framework, the three main vehicles—here termed Hīnayāna, Mahāyāna, and Vajrayāna—are defined in terms of the vows they require. Monastic Hīnayānists vow to follow the Vinaya, while lay Hīnayānists vow to follow the precepts. (This definition explains why the only parts of the Mainstream canons well represented in the Tibetan canon are Vinaya texts, and why Hīnayāna in the Tibetan context cannot be equated with Theravāda or Indian Mainstream Buddhism.) Mahāyānists take bodhisattva vows, and Vajrayānists supplement their bodhisattva vows with the specific vows of their Tantric initiations. Further it is understood that these vows are based on ascending levels of motivation, with the Mahāyāna vows involving more compassion and tactical skill than the Hīnayāna vows, and the Vajrayāna more than the Mahāyāna. These levels of motivation are in turn related to ascending levels of spiritual capacity.

Tibetan Buddhists, regardless of how they label their individual practice, agree that Vajrayāna is the superior path, but they differ in how they regard the relationship among the three paths. One view holds that all three are valid paths to Awakening, while another holds that Hīnayāna and Mahāyāna are practical expedients for those who are not yet ready for the Vajra path, but who will someday take it up when they are ready. There is also some disagreement as to whether the vows of the higher paths include or abrogate the vows of the lower path. In other words, some hold that a practitioner must still abide by Hīnayāna vows even when observing Vajrayāna vows, whereas others hold that this is not necessary.

Tibetan Vajrayāna is not a carbon copy of Indian Vajrayāna. Tibetan scholars and practitioners have provided new texts, commentaries, and practices to augment and synthesize the wide variety of Vajra traditions they inherited from India. A few modern scholars have tried to trace some of these innovations to pre-Buddhist shamanic traditions in the Tibetan cultural area, but the similarities between shamanism and some aspects of Vajrayāna make it hard to trace influences clearly to one source or the other. In fact, these similarities apparently contributed to the introduction of Vajrayāna into Tibet, for many of the Tibetan lay men who helped introduce Buddhism from India were shamans who had gone to India to learn siddhis. An additional difficulty in trying to trace the influences behind Tibetan innovations lies in the fact that our knowledge both of Indian Vajrayāna and pre-Buddhist Tibetan religion is far from complete. However, as we will see, with the possible exception of Dzogchen meditation practices (see Section 11.2.2), most Tibetan innovations can be traced to tensions already present within what we know of Indian Vajrayāna itself.

Even the way the Tibetans have fashioned their own distinctive view of their religious history is shaped by assumptions inherited from the primary Indian Vajrayāna practice, *sādhana*. This practice, in which the practitioner takes on the identity of a divine being, tends to blur the lines between individual identities. This tendency has fostered the creation of traditional histories in which important individuals are regarded as emanations of great deities, bodhisattvas, and Cosmic Buddhas acting out an epic drama for the protection and prosperity of the Tibetan nation and its Buddhist religion. Although modern secular scholarship might question these histories, their influence is an important historical fact in and of itself, and must be kept in mind when trying to understand how Tibetan Buddhism has developed over the centuries.

11.2 THE DHARMA COMES TO TIBET

What little is known of pre-Buddhist Tibetan religion indicates that it dealt with what were later called the four ways of gods and men: divination, exorcism, magical coercion, and the guidance of the human spirit after death. A cult centering on the divinity of the king involved elaborate sacrifices for the maintenance of the king's power while he was alive, and for the provision of his eternal happiness in heaven after death. Ritual experts were hired for both sorts of occasions, and some seem to have acted as the king's advisers in the day-to-day running of the kingdom. Scholars have suggested that this pattern, which focused political and sacred power on a single figure, set the stage for the later period in Tibetan history when monasteries assumed the role of noble families, and their abbots the role of kings, but as we shall see, there were also other reasons for this later development.

Considering Tibet's proximity to India, Buddhism reached it remarkably late. The Tibetans themselves recorded that Buddhism was introduced twice into their country, first in the seventh to ninth centuries, and then again beginning at the end of the tenth, with a period of anti-Buddhist persecution in between. We must qualify this scenario, however, by noting that it covers only the periods in which the rulers of Tibet took an active interest in propagating Buddhism, and that the persecution was more antimonastic than anti-Buddhist. From the seventh century until the Muslim conquest of India, a fairly constant stream of individual Tibetans braved the Himalayan passes to acquire initiations and instructions from the siddhas in northeastern India and Kashmir. Their interest in siddhis contrasted with the interests of the kings who sponsored the importation of Buddhism into Tibet, who showed little if any interest in Vajrayāna, and in some cases openly opposed it.

11.2.1 First Propagation

The first king traditionally credited with bringing Buddhism to Tibet was Song-tsen Gam-po (Srong-brtsan sgam-po; d.circa 650). King Song-tsen inherited a united Tibetan kingdom from his father and started Tibet on a campaign of imperial conquest that made it the dominant power in Central Asia, with control over the Silk Road, until the middle of the ninth century. Traditional histories record that he had two Buddhist wives, a princess from China and one from Nepal, and to please them he built Tibet's first Buddhist temple, the Jo-khang in Lhasa. Later Tibetan historians identified King Song-tsen as an emanation of Avalokiteśvara, and his Chinese wife as an emanation of the female bodhisattva, Tārā. Inscriptions dating from his reign, however, make no mention of Buddhism. After his reign, Lhasa began attracting Buddhist monks whose homelands had been decimated by the Tibetan conquests, but these monks, together with the handful of Tibetan monks they had managed to ordain, were later forced to leave Tibet after being blamed for a smallpox epidemic in the capital. Nevertheless, they left behind a legacy of texts that served to convert the first Tibetan monarch whose interest in Buddhism has corroborating historical evidence: Trisong Detsen (Khri-srong lde-brtsan; r. 755–circa 797).

Tibet's imperial power reached its peak during Trisong Detsen's reign, which coincided with the An Lu-shan rebellion in China (see Section 8.5). Tibetan armies occupied the Chinese capital at Ch'ang-an in 763, and captured Tun-huang, the great Buddhist translation center on the Silk Road, in 787, after which scholars there turned to translating Chinese Buddhist texts into Tibetan for their new overlords. Trisong Detsen took advantage of this situation to send emissaries to India, China, and Central Asia to obtain Buddhist texts, to invite Buddhist scholars to the Tibetan court, and to submit lists of questions on

Buddhist doctrine to any renowned scholars who were unable to make the trip. One such list has been found in the caves of Tun-huang. It is a remarkable document showing that (1) Yogācāra was the primary school of Buddhist thought entering Tibet during this period, and (2) the king had a sophisticated grasp of its teachings and controversial points. This may explain why later Tibetans regarded him as an emanation of Māñjuśrī.

The king was also responsible for starting the great Sanskrit-Tibetan-Chinese lexicon, the *Mahāvyupatti,* designed to standardize the translation of Buddhist texts into Tibetan. Tibet, unlike China, had virtually no native philosophical tradition, and so Tibetan equivalents could be freely assigned to Sanskrit terms with little danger of being misinterpreted in light of non-Buddhist connotations. Coming through a consistent lexicon, Tibet translations can be somewhat stilted and unnatural, but they are very reliable in representing the Sanskrit originals. Thus they have been an invaluable tool for modern scholars trying to reconstruct Sanskrit texts that were otherwise lost.

Two other major events in the history of Tibetan Buddhism occurred during King Trisong's reign. The first was the building of the monastery at Sam-ye (bSam-yas), southeast of Lhasa, a process that took a total of 12 years, from 763 to 775. The great Indian scholar, Śāntarakṣita (see Section 6.1), was invited from Nalanda to preside over the founding of what was to become Tibet's first native monastery, but a series of natural disasters, which the anti-Buddhist faction at court attributed to his presence in the country, forced his return to India. Before leaving, however, he counseled the king to invite to Tibet an Indian siddha, Padmasambhava, who would tame the local gods and demons, making them more amenable to the establishment of Buddhism on Tibetan soil. The king followed his advice, and Padmasambhava accepted the invitation. Tibetan traditions report that Padmasambhava was a fabulous wonder worker, subduing a vast number of demonic forces and forcing pledges from them to protect Tibetan Buddhism.

Construction was then resumed on the monastery at Sam-ye, complete with a meditation retreat: an institutional solution to the problem of combining the dual vocations of study and meditation that was to become standard in Tibet. Śāntarakṣita was invited to its consecration, and the king swore in an edict, still extant, that Tibet would dedicate itself in perpetuity to the support of the Triple Gem. At the same time, seven hand-picked members of the Tibet nobility, called the Seven Elect, were ordained to form the first native Tibetan Sangha. The Mūlasarvāstivādin Vinaya was chosen as the guide for monastic discipline. This is one of the few Mainstream texts to be translated into Tibetan and has formed the disciplinary code for all Tibetan monastic orders ever since. Life at Sam-ye was patterned on that of the great Buddhist universities in India: large, organized communities dependent on land grants for their continued existence. This established a pattern that has shaped the Tibetan Sangha ever since.

Historical records have little more to say about Padmasambhava after the consecration of the monastery at Sam-ye, but Tibetan legends credit him with spending decades in Tibet, subduing gods and demons throughout the land. Tibetans regard him as a second Buddha, eclipsing Śākyamuni in his importance for their country. In later centuries the Nyingma order claimed him as their founder and as the conduit—from the great Cosmic Buddha, Samantabhadra—of their central meditation tradition, Dzogchen (rDzogs-ch'en, The Great Wholeness).

However, Padmasambhava had little influence over the policies adopted at Sam-ye. The king appointed a council, composed of the chief monks, to oversee the translation of Buddhist works into Tibetan and, in particular, to prevent the translation of Tantras. The large number of Tantras translated into Tibetan during this period were thus the result of independent efforts, and not of royal sponsorship.

The second major event occurring during Trisong Detsen's reign is the Great Debate on the issue of sudden versus gradual Awakening, held at Sam-ye from approximately 790 to 792. Historical sources covering this event are contradictory, some even suggesting that no direct debate was held, but rather that different scholars from India and China were invited to present their positions separately to the king. One of the few sources dating from the time of the debate—the report of Hwa-shang Mo-ho-yan, the major Chinese participant and a student of the Northern School of Ch'an—claims that the Chinese defense of sudden Awakening won the king's favor. Later Tibetan sources, however, all maintain that the Chinese lost the debate and that the king banned any further Chinese missionary activity in the country. There is good evidence that this ban was never enacted. However, the accepted version of the event had an important effect on later Tibetan thought and in fact is a major source for our understanding of the issues alive in the period during which this version crystallized, the thirteenth and fourteenth centuries, and so we will discuss it in connection with that period.

Two of Trisong Detsen's successors, his son and grandson, continued his enthusiastic support of Buddhism. The grandson, Ralpachen (Ral-pa-can; r. 823–840) even appointed a Buddhist monk as his chief minister. However, this appointment, together with the growing power of the Buddhist monasteries in general, appears to have been unpopular with members of his court, for in 840 both the king and his chief minister were assassinated. Ralpachen's brother, Lang Dar-ma (gLang Dar-ma), came to the throne and proceeded to suppress the monasteries. He is depicted in the traditional histories as an anti-Buddhist fanatic, although Tun-huang records show him as opposed not to the religion per se, but simply to what he perceived as the inordinate power that the monasteries had begun to acquire based on their land grants. He in turn was assassinated by a Buddhist monk—the assassination was later justified on the grounds that it was an act of kindness to prevent the king from creating further bad karma—and the ensuing political chaos brought about the end of the Tibetan empire and any semblance of centralized control in Tibet. The monasteries were depopulated, and thus ended the period of the First Propagation.

Traditional histories depict the period between the First and Second Propagations as a dark age with little or no Buddhist activity. Other sources indicate that—although the political order was too fragmented to provide any support to Buddhism, and the monasteries were largely abandoned—individual Tibetans continued the independent pursuit of Vajrayāna practices, and some of them made the trip to India for further initiations and texts. One of the most famous practitioners of this time was Ma-cig (Ma-gcig, The One Mother; 1055–1145), a nun who left the order in search of Vajrayāna instructors. After suffering from a variety of ailments caused by empowerments received from improperly initiated adepts, she eventually met up with an adept who had studied with Abhayākaragupta in Nalanda and who was able to diagnose the cause of her trouble. After arranging for her to undergo an elaborate ceremony of atonement, he became her new principal partner, and from that point onward she met with nothing but success. Eventually her fame eclipsed his; Tibetans continue to venerate her as an emanation of Tārā to this day.

Without royal patronage to encourage monastic discipline, transgressive practices began to flourish. In the latter part of the tenth century, as various minor Tibetan kingdoms began to attain a measure of stability, the new kings came to regard this situation with concern, seeing the misuse of Tantra as detrimental to the moral fiber of their societies. Their concern is what led to the Second Propagation of the Dharma.

11.2.2 The Second Propagation

This movement began in the newly stabilized kingdoms to the south of Mt. Kailāśa in the extreme southwest of Tibet, as the central area around Lhasa was still in disarray. The prime mover in this Buddhist renaissance was the king of Purang, Yeshe-od (Ye-shes-'od), who abdicated his throne in favor of his son and took ordination in order to devote himself fully to the Buddhist revival. He wrote an ordinance denouncing sexual yoga and animal sacrifice as practiced during his time, and set forth the principle that only those practices clearly derived from Indian Buddhist texts should be accepted as true Dharma. This principle formed the guiding standard behind the entire Second Propagation.

Yeshe-od's major act was to send a group of followers to Kashmir to collect Buddhist texts. One of the two survivors of this mission, Rinchen Zangpo (Rin-chen bzang-po; 958–1055), took several further trips to India to invite Indian scholars to Tibet and to collect additional texts. He, his Indian colleagues, and his students were responsible for such a large number of translations, and of such high quality, that he earned the epithet of "The Great Translator" in Tibetan history. The range of their translations provided the framework for what was eventually to become the Tibetan Canon (see Section 11.3.2).

After Yeshe-od's death, his grandson, O-de ('Od-lde), invited the great Indian scholar, Atīśa (982–1054) from the university at Vikramaśīla, near Nalanda, to help spread the Dharma in Tibet. This was perhaps the most influential single event in the propagation of the Dharma into Tibet, as Atīśa not only founded the first of the great Tibetan monastic orders, but also provided a philosophical framework for absorbing Tantric rituals into Mahāyāna practice in a way that did not violate the monastic rules. The order he founded together with his Tibetan disciple, Dromtön ('Brom-ston; 1003–1065), was called the Kadam (bK'gdams, Bound to [the Buddha's] Command), which became renowned for its high standard of scholarship and strict adherence to the Vinaya. His major philosophical work, written specifically for use in Tibet, was called the *Bodhipathapradīpa,* or Lamp on the Path to Awakening. In this work, Atīśa divided human beings into three levels, based on their motivation in their search for happiness: nonreligious people, who aim only at pleasures in this life; Hīnayānists, who work only for their own Awakening; and Mahāyānists, who work for the Awakening of all. For Atīśa, the ideal Mahāyānist is a monk who devotes himself to developing the perfections, while at the same time engaging in whatever Tantric practices do not violate his monastic vows. Thus, in his eyes, Vajrayāna practice, rather than supplanting or offering an alternative to the Mahāyāna path of perfections, is simply an auxiliary to that path. Although this understanding of the relationship between Mahāyāna and Vajrayāna satisfied Atīśa's royal sponsor and proved influential in later Tibetan history, it was supplemented by other understandings as well, in particular the positions of Munidatta and Abhayākaragupta that we noted in Section 6.2.2. Atīśa's analysis of the place of Hīnayāna in the scheme of Buddhist practice, however, became standard in all schools of Tibetan Buddhism.

The layered nature of Atīśa's thought is best illustrated by his analysis of the bodhisattva path into three stages: developing saṁvega to renounce the world of saṁsāra, developing prasāda to arouse the thought of Awakening (bodhicitta), and attaining a correct view of emptiness. Viewed from an academic standpoint, this is a fairly standard interpretation of Mahāyāna thought. At the same time, however, it also follows the process of generation in sādhana. The renunciation of the world corresponds to the adept's renunciation of the everyday level of experience to enter into the maṇḍala he or she is visualizing. The arousing of the bodhicitta corresponds to the adoption of the deity's mind-set. The correct view of emptiness corresponds to the "recollection of purity," in which the adept stops to reflect that all levels of reality—everyday and visualized—are equally empty of any self-nature, so as to prevent the mind from placing any thought-constructs on the ritual experience before proceeding with the remainder of the ritual. This pattern of layered philosophical and ritual meanings can be found not only to Atīśa's thought, but also in the thought of many other Tibetan authors.

Traditional histories cite Atīśa's gifts to Tibetan Buddhism in other areas as well. Regarded as a student of Nāropā (see Section 6.2.2), he is remembered as the conduit of a great number of Tantric initiation lineages. He is also credited with importing the cult of Tārā, which was to become Tibet's most widespread bodhisattva cult; and with introducing the practice of *lo-jong (blo-sbyong),* or thought-transformation, a set of principles designed to rid the practitioner of the habit of cherishing self, so as to develop the selfless, compassionate attitude of a bodhisattva.

The Second Propagation continued until the decimation of Buddhism in northern India and Kashmir, and was largely a story of how the Kadam movement interacted with other Vajrayāna lineages being brought from India during this period and the earlier Buddhist traditions derived from the First Propagation. Many Tibetans continued traveling to India to collect texts and initiations throughout this period, but two in particular stand out: Drok-mi ('Brog-mi, Nomad) and Marpa. Drok-mi (992–1074) collected a large number of initiations while in India, principally from the lineage of the siddha Virūpa. After his return to Tibet, another Indian, Gayadhara, sought him out and gave him exclusive rights to grant initiations in his lineage in Tibet as well. One of Drok-mi's disciples, Kon-chog Gyalpo (Dkon-mchog Rgyal-po), established a monastery in Sakya (Sa-skya); his son, adopting the discipline of the Kadams, became the first hierarch of the Sakya Order, which was to become the dominant political power in Tibet in the thirteenth and fourteenth centuries.

As for Marpa (1012–1096), he originally began studying with Drok-mi but objected to the latter's high initiation fees and so went to India to acquire initiations on his own. He is said to have studied primarily with Nāropā, who taught him the *Cakrasaṃvara Tantra.* On his return to Tibet, Marpa married and set himself up as a householder, revealing his mastery of the Tantras only to a chosen few. His main student was Milarepa (Mi-la ras-pa, Cotton-clad Mila; 1040–1123), who was to become one of the most beloved figures in Tibetan history. Mila, as a youth, had learned magic in order to take revenge on a wicked uncle who had dispossessed and mistreated Mila's widowed mother. Seized with remorse after destroying his uncle, he sought first to expiate his bad karma and then to attain liberation. At 38 he became Marpa's disciple. For six years the master put him through harsh ordeals before finally granting him the initiation he sought. Milarepa spent the remainder of his life meditating in the caves and wandering on the slopes of the high Himalayas. After a long period of solitude, he gradually attracted many disciples and worked wonders for people's benefit. A story of Milarepa's life, composed in the form of an autobiography in the fifteenth century, is one of the great classics of Tibetan literature.

Milarepa's primary student was Gampopa (Sgam-po-pa; 1079–1153), a monk of the Kadam lineage who at age 32 heard of Milarepa from a beggar and acquired his teachings in 13 months of study. Milarepa taught Gampopa a version of the Mahāmudrā, called *Sūtra Mahāmudrā,* that could be attained through a union of the male and female energy channels in the body, thus not violating Gampopa's vows of celibacy. This method eventually became one of the dominant meditation methods in Tibet. An entire book, though, could be written on the various permutations it underwent as it was passed down from master to master and school to school, combining with Dzogchen and other methods.

Gampopa's combination of Kadam monastic discipline and Mahāmudrā meditation formed the basis for a new school, the Kagyü (bKa' brgyud, the Followers or the Transmitted Command). His disciples split into five subschools, chief of which was the Karma school. Various other small schools and monastic orders formed as the Kadams combined with other Tantric lineages newly arrived from India—including one lineage that traced itself back to Nāropā's sister, Nigumā, and another that adopted Yogācārin doctrines—but none of them gained prominence.

Some of the older Tantric lineages, however, refused to submit to the new reform movement. These were composed largely of lay practitioners whose traditions included not only Indian Buddhist texts but also native texts, doctrines, and practices—such as Tantric rituals centered on native Tibetan deities—for which no Indian texts could be cited as precedents. The question of how to meet the challenge of the reform movement's new standards and at the same time maintain their old traditions brought these lineages together into two broad camps that eventually developed into two loosely organized lineages of their own. One was the Bon lineage, which identified itself with pre-Buddhist Tibetan religion. Maintaining that the Śākyamuni of the reform movement was an imposter Buddha, the Bons claimed to have inherited the lineage of the true

Buddha, named Shenrab (gShen-rab, Best of Holy Beings), a native of a land to the west of Tibet called Ta-zig (possibly present-day Tadjikistan). Thus they had no need to justify their traditions as coming from India. As a result they developed a tradition that combined Buddhist teachings—generally following the Yogācārins—and older shamanic beliefs, including a myth of the universe as created from light.

The other camp, who agreed that they and the reformers worshipped the same Buddha, called themselves the Nyingma (rNying-ma, Ancient) school. This school maintained the authenticity of its native texts in that they had been hidden by Padmasambhava and later discovered by spiritual adepts. Eventually this tradition of *termas* (gter-ma)—hidden treasure texts reputedly placed underground, underwater, in the sky, or in "mind" (conceived as the Dharmakāya)—spread to other schools as well. In the eyes of some, termas discovered by *tertons* (gter-ston), or treasure-finders, were a more profound transmission than texts with an established historical pedigree.

The primary Nyingma terma of this period was the *Mani Kabum* (Maṇi bka' 'bum), which set forth the proposition that all interpretations of the Buddhist path were equally correct, and that the ultimate realizations produced by these paths were all equivalent. It also set forth a system—which was to influence all subsequent Nyingma thought—whereby the highest level of Tantra was divided into three sublevels, with the Nyingma/Bon form of meditation, Dzogchen, forming the highest of the three.

Dzogchen, unlike most other methods of Buddhist meditation, asserted that Awakening wasn't "brought about" at all. Awareness in and of itself, the Nyingmas said, was already innately pure and nondual, and all that needed to be done in order to realize its innate purity and nonduality was to let thought processes come to a stop. The approach they prescribed was thus one of spontaneity and nonstriving, effortlessly abiding with the "Primordial Basis." They offered no analytical path for how to do this, though, for they said that any analysis would simply add to the mind's thought processes. The obvious parallels between the Dzogchen and Ch'an doctrines of spontaneity have caused some scholars to assume that Ch'an was the source for the Dzogchen tradition, but early Dzogchen documents from the tenth and eleventh centuries show the very real differences between their school and Ch'an, which was also practiced in Tibet at that time.

By the end of the Second Propagation there were four major schools of Buddhism in Tibet—the Kadams, Sakyas, Kagyüs, and Nyingmas—along with four minor schools that have not survived into the modern era. In addition to the four major Buddhist schools were the Bon, who maintained a separate religious identity despite the many doctrines and practices they held in common with the Nyingmas. The Kadams, Sakyas, and Kagyüs had well-established monastic orders both for men and women, with the Kadams the strictest in terms of maintaining their celibacy. The Nyingmas and Bons did not develop monastic orders until the fourteenth and fifteenth centuries.

No hard and fast lines existed between the various Tibetan schools, largely because of the tendency for individual monks, nuns, and lay adepts to travel about, gathering up instructions and initiations from as many authorized teachers—termed *lamas* (bla-mas)—as possible, regardless of affiliation.

11.3 THE PERIOD OF CONSOLIDATION

During the first two centuries after the decimation of Buddhism in northern India in the early thirteenth century, the Tibetans succeeded in consolidating their religion into the form it was to maintain, largely unchanged, until the early twentieth century. This involved four processes: studying the history of Buddhism so as to provide a background for textual study, gathering texts to form a standard canon, establishing doctrinal syntheses to interpret and accommodate the many schools of thought inherited from the two propagations, and forming a political system that reflected the increasing institutional power of the monastic communities.

11.3.1 Historical Issues

The first task confronting the scholars of this period was to establish a standardized canon from the mass of texts they had inherited from the two propagations of Dharma; this, in turn, required that they research the history of Buddhism, both in India and Tibet, to provide a framework for their textual studies. In part, these researches were motivated by a genuine quest for historical truth, and the resulting histories remain among the most reliable sources for modern historical study of Buddhism's last centuries in India. However, the fact that the two propagations of Dharma to Tibet had resulted in two distinct camps of thought meant that partisan concerns—in which the historians tried to find precedents for their own camps' positions—occasionally eclipsed their concern for factual truth. As a result, the scholars came to focus on a handful of specific incidents within Tibet itself that they polemicized to the point where it is virtually impossible to determine what actually transpired during the events in question. The histories written during this period, though, provide excellent source material for studying the issues that were uppermost in the historians' own minds.

One prime example of this phenomenon was the controversy that developed over the correct record of the Great Debate held at Sam-ye in 790–792 on the issue of sudden versus gradual Awakening. The crux of the debate—if in fact it did occur—was not so much over the sudden or gradual nature of Awakening as it was over how necessary morality and analytical insight were in bringing Awakening about. This was a primary point of disagreement between the two major camps: the old schools, following their practice of Dzogchen, maintaining that simply stilling the processes of thought is enough to realize Awakening; the newer schools, following their monastic teachings, maintaining that morality and analytical insight were indispensable components of the path. Thus the two camps focused on what support they could find for their positions in King Trisong Detsen's handling of the case. It is interesting to notice how, in the course of the controversy, the battle lines were redrawn, with the Karma school and its practice of Sūtra Mahāmudrā finding itself lined up with the Nyingmas. This regrouping was to last up through modern times.

The controversy began with Kunga Gyaltśen (Kund-dga' rGyal-mtshan; 1182–1251), leader of the Sakyan school, who is one of the few figures in Tibetan history to be remembered primarily by his Sanskrit name, Sakya Paṇḍita. Sakya Paṇḍita depicted the Chinese side of the Great Debate as identical with the

Sūtra Mahāmudrā and "Chinese" Dzogchen methods of meditation that were being propagated during his time. According to him, Trisong Detsen clearly repudiated the Chinese position, forbidding that it ever be taught in Tibet again. This, he said, was proof that Sūtra Mahāmudrā and Chinese Dzogchen were invalid as well.

To counter Sakya Paṇḍita's attack, the Nyingmas presented their own interpretation of Trisong Detsen's reign, in which the king's daughter, Yeshe Tsogyel (Ye-shes mTsho-rgyal), was Padmasambhava's primary consort, and the king himself was a trained Dzogchen adept. In addition, the twelfth century Nyingma historian, Nyang Nyi-ma 'od-zer, provided an alternative version of the outcome of the debate, in which Trisong Detsen decreed that the gradual and sudden approaches to Awakening were essentially the same, the gradual mode being generally preferable simply because it was better suited for people of ordinary talents, whereas the sudden method was better for those with extraordinary talents. Thus, according to this account, both sides emerged victorious from the debate.

Butön (Bu-ston; 1290–1364), a monk from an independent branch of the Kadams, later reasserted Sakya Paṇḍita's position in his definitive history of Buddhism, and this was to become the position accepted by Tibetan officialdom. Hwa-shang, the Chinese representative at the debate, came to be depicted as a buffoon in the dances staged by the state to celebrate the Tibetan new year, although this development was due as much to Tibetan nationalism as it was to historical beliefs. Nevertheless, the Nyingmas continued to uphold their version of the debate, and the matter was left at an impasse.

11.3.2 Texts

Scholars worked throughout the thirteenth century to gather, standardize, and collate the various texts that had been brought over from India and translated into Tibetan since the earlier compilation of a Tibetan Canon in the ninth century. The connection between this process and that of historical research is shown by the fact that the collation was completed in the beginning of the fourteenth century by Butön, the author of the definitive history of Buddhism mentioned previously. Butön's Canon consisted of two parts: the *Kanjur* (bKa'-'gyur), which contained the word of Śākyamuni and other Buddhas; and the *Tenjur* (bsTan'gyur), which consisted of later treatises not only on Buddhist doctrine, but also on other subjects—such as medicine, astrology, grammar, and so on—that had been taught in the great Buddhist universities during the period when Tibetans were gathering texts there. The Kanjur fell into six parts: the *Mūlasarvāstivādin Vinaya,* the *Perfection of Discernment Sūtras,* the *Avataṃsaka Sūtra,* the *Ratnakūṭa Sūtra* (a collection of 49 Mahāyāna Sūtras compiled by a Chinese scholar), other Sūtras, and Tantras. Very few Mainstream Sūtras made their way into the collection. The first printed Kanjur was completed in Peking in 1411, and the first complete printings of the canon in Tibet were done at Narthang in 1742, utilizing 108 volumes for the Kanjur and 225 for the Tenjur.

Butön did not include Nyingma Tantras in his compilation of the canon, so in the fifteenth century a Nyingma scholar, Ratna Lingpa (Ratna gLing-pa; 1403–1478), collected the Nyingma texts then available in a work called the *Nyingma Gyudbum* (rNying ma rgyud 'bum), or 100,000 Nyingma Tantras.

11.3.3 Doctrinal Systems

The compilation of a standardized canon was only the first step toward resolving the most bewildering problem facing Tibetan Buddhists during this period, that of finding order in the welter of conflicting doctrines and practices contained in the legacy of Sūtras, Tantras, and treatises they had inherited from the past. Many monks of high intellectual caliber attacked the problem, but only two provided syntheses that were to prove enduring, forming the two basic approaches to doctrine and practice that have continued to characterize Tibetan Buddhism up through the present.

The first of the two was the great Nyingma scholar, Longch'en Rabjam (Klong-ch'en rab-'byams; 1308–1363), who produced a series of texts called the Seven Treasuries, presenting the Nyingma path of practice, and Dzogchen in particular, in light of scholastic Indian Buddhist philosophy. Longch'en Rabjam was less interested in systematizing Buddhist doctrine as a whole, however, than in systematizing Dzogchen theory and practice. He held to the Nyingma position that all Buddhist teachings, no matter how contradictory they might appear on the surface, were equally valid as alternative approaches to the truth, suitable for different temperaments, but that they all were ultimately inadequate as descriptions of the realizations to be gained through the practice of Dzogchen. However, by his time a variety of Dzogchen traditions had developed, and he felt called upon to impose some order on them.

He ultimately delineated three valid Dzogchen traditions, two lower ones tracing their lineage from a Chinese monk in Kashmir, and a higher one founded by Samantabhadra and brought from India to Tibet by Vimalamitra. The higher one taught two approaches to Awakening—both equally effective, but the second the more spectacular of the two. The first, a "sudden" method, was *trekchö* (khregs chod, cutting through rigidity), in which one simply broke through to the innate purity and simplicity of awareness and then stabilized one's ability to remain in touch with that purity. The second, a more "gradual" method, was *tögal* (thod gral, passing over the crest), in which yogic techniques were used to stabilize the attainment of light, acquired in the earlier stages, to the point where one attained the rainbow body, whereby one's physical body would dissolve into light after death.

These practices may have been shamanic in origin, related to the Bon myth of the creation of the world from light, but Longch'en defined them in Buddhist terms, identifying the pure awareness realized in trekchö with the Dharmakāya, and the rainbow body attained in tögal with the sambhogakāya, or Enjoyment Body. However, like one of the sixth-century Indian Yogācārin schools, he was careful to point out that the Dharmakāya was not identical to the storehouse consciousness (see Section 5.2.3a), for unlike the storehouse consciousness it has been pure and nondual all along. Thus a recurrent question in later Dzogchen teachings has been how to distinguish between the two in practice.

Longch'en Rabjam's systemization of Dzogchen has remained definitive up to the present, but it did not satisfy those thinkers who took seriously the inconsistencies they found among the various schools of Buddhist thought. At the same time, his life—he reportedly sired a number of illegitimate children—did not provide a satisfying model for those who wanted to follow the celibate monastic life. Only later in the fourteenth century did Tsongkhapa (Tsong kha-pa; 1357–1419), a native of northeast Tibet, formulate a system accommodating both of these concerns that was to win widespread approval.

Tsongkhapa had become a novice in boyhood and received Vajrayāna initiations before traveling to central Tibet. There he studied the exoteric Mahāyāna treatises for years and visited all the notable centers of learning, regardless of their affiliation, his special interests being logic and Vinaya. Taking full ordination in the Kadam order at age 25, he began to ponder the central question of Mahāyāna philosophy: the meaning of the doctrine of emptiness. Did it completely negate the validity of conventional norms and reality—including other Buddhist doctrines—or did it leave them intact? After years of study and meditation, he was introduced to a text by Candrakīrti (see Section 5.2.3) and in 1398 this inspired a vision in which he saw all Buddhist teachings as mutually reinforcing rather than contradictory. According to his vision, the doctrine of emptiness, if properly understood, did not invalidate ethical norms, logic, or the doctrine of dependent co-arising. This realization formed the basis for the remainder of his life's work.

Tsongkhapa's *Sung-bum* (gSung 'bum), or Collected Works, total well over 200 titles. They cover the entire range of Buddhist philosophy and Tantric practice under the rubric of Atīśa's threefold analysis of the Buddhist path—renunciation, bodhicitta, and right view concerning emptiness—with a special emphasis on the last category. According to Tsongkhapa, the emptiness of the exoteric Mahāyāna treatises was in no way different from or inferior to the emptiness induced by Tantric practices; in fact one needed to have a proper understanding of emptiness, arrived at through logic and textual study, for one's Tantric practice to succeed. Logic was needed because it made clear the "object of negation," that is, precisely what was and was not negated by the doctrine of emptiness. Textual study was needed for the same reason, for as one worked through the various formulations of Buddhist doctrine produced over the centuries, one's understanding of emptiness would gradually become more subtle and precise.

Tsongkhapa rated, in ascending order, the various schools of Buddhist thought known to him, as follows: Vaibhāśika, Śautrāntika, Yogācāra, and Madhyamaka. He further divided the Madhyamaka school into two subschools, Svātantrika Madhyamaka and Prāsaṅgika Madhyamaka, the former composed of thinkers like Bhāvaviveka and Śāntarakṣita, who used inferential arguments to establish their positions; and the latter (and higher of the two schools) exemplified by Candrakīrti, who saw that a higher understanding of emptiness precluded the use of such arguments.

The rating of all these schools was based on the thoroughness with which the school understood the doctrine of emptiness, although Tsongkhapa saw the higher schools as perfecting rather than negating the lower ones. Śautrantika and Vaibhāśika he faulted as giving too much reality to mental objects; Yogācāra he faulted as giving too much reality to mind. For him, Prāsaṅgika Madhyamaka provided the Middle Way in that it did not negate too little, as did the earlier Buddhist schools, nor did it negate too much, as did some of Tsongkhapa's contemporaries, who saw emptiness as negating moral norms and other conventional truths.

To implement his proposed course of study, Tsongkhapa founded a monastic university on Mt. Ganden (dGa'-ldan), near Lhasa, in 1409. Soon his students founded two additional universities, also near Lhasa, at Dre-bung ('Bras spungs) in 1416, and Sera (Se-rwa) in 1419. In their heyday, the three universities housed a total of more than 20,000 monks. Their curriculum started with basic study in logic and then proceeded through what were termed the *five great texts:* six to seven years on Asaṅga/Maitreya's *Abhisamayālaṃkāra,* a text on the bodhisattva path; two years on Candrakīrti's *Madhyamakāvatāra,* a commentary on Nāgārjuna's MMK, to introduce the proper understanding of emptiness; two years on Vasubandhu's *Abhidharmakośa;* and two years on a Vinaya commentary by Guṇaprabhā. Each year throughout the course of study, time would be taken out to review the fifth great text, Dharmakīrti's major work on logic and epistemology.

The curriculum as a whole was an attempt to recreate the atmosphere of the great Indian universities. The student body in each university was divided into two debating teams, who were encouraged to be ruthless in their attack of each other's positions. The course of study would culminate in several years of review before the student would attain his *geshe* (dse-bshes, Refined Knowledge) degree and participate in a final debating contest. This contest ultimately grew into a major national event, with each year's winner becoming a national hero.

Throughout the course of study, the monks also pursued preliminary Tantric practices. Only after the completion of their studies, however, were they allowed to pursue higher Tantric practices on full-scale retreats. Tsongkhapa insisted on strict adherence to the monastic discipline throughout the course of the practice. Although he did not deny the possibility that one might be able to practice the Mahāyoga or Yoginī Tantras with a karma-mudrā (see Section 6.2.2), he set out a stringent—virtually impossible—list of qualifications that both partners would have to fulfill if they did not want their practice to lead them to hell. As a result, his followers for the most part stuck to the celibate jñāna-mudrā path.

Tsongkhapa's program was so distinctive that it developed into a new school—the Gelug (dGe-lugs, Virtuous Ones)—and so popular that it took over the Kadam school and in effect replaced it. His program also influenced studies in the other major schools as well. The curriculum he set out remained unchanged until Lhasa fell to the Chinese in the middle of the twentieth century, and is still followed in Gelug monasteries scattered throughout the world. When Tibetan Buddhism spread to Mongolia and Siberia in later centuries, the Gelug curriculum formed the heart of the movement. Although it succeeded in producing a line of brilliant scholars and academicians, it precluded any new syntheses in Tibetan monastic academic circles. In the later centuries of Tibetan Buddhism, the creative impulse tended to come instead from sources that found their inspiration in Longch'en Rabjam's more eclectic approach.

11.3.4 Politics

Tibet, in inheriting the tradition of the monastic universities from India, inherited a logistical problem as well: how to maintain these large institutions. Unlike the early Buddhist monks, the students at the Tibetan monasteries could not rely simply on the alms they might gather, for in many cases they formed enormous communities. The problem of maintaining these communities—many of which became well-endowed—as stable institutions with a minimum of hardship and dissension, became a major political issue on both internal and external levels.

On the internal level, the primary question was how to provide for a smooth transition in the leadership. In some of the orders, such as the Sakyas, this problem was solved by making the highest office hereditary, passing from uncle to nephew. In others, such as the Karmas and eventually the Gelugs, a more innovative approach was adopted, whereby the leader, at death, would intentionally reincarnate in such a way that he would resume leadership after his reincarnated form, a *tülku* (sprul-sku), gained maturity.

The tülku tradition originated in the Karma subschool of the Kagyüs. One of Marpa's reputed magical skills had been the ability to transfer his spirit to animate a fresh corpse. An Indian play, the *Bhagavadajjukīya* (Master-Mistress), shows that this skill was reputed to yogins as early as the second century, and exploits it for comic effect, but the skill had a serious purpose, which was to cheat death. If one were approaching death oneself, one could continue life in a younger body of one's choosing. Marpa had been unable to pass along this particular skill to any of his followers, but the tradition of its existence led the second hierarch of the Karma school, Karma Pakśi (1204–1283)—reputedly skilled at both Mahāmudrā and Dzogchen practices—to attempt to inject his spirit at death into the corpse of a boy. He failed in his attempt and ended up injecting his spirit into the womb of an expectant mother. After his rebirth, he was able to recount the details of his experience and ultimately was accepted as the next leader of the Karma school.

As this tradition became standard in the Karma school, it spread to positions in other orders and monasteries as well, until eventually there were more than 300 recognized tülkus in Tibet. The dying leader would leave signs to indicate the location of his or her next rebirth, followers would attempt to interpret the signs and find the child who fulfilled them, and then bring up the child until it was old enough to resume authority. This method had a number of advantages in that it freed the school or monastery from having to depend on the uncertain ability of a single family to provide it with a string of suitable incumbents, while at the same time arranging for talented children to be groomed for leadership from an early age. However, it was also was open to serious abuses, especially in the case of wealthy or politically powerful institutions, where differing factions might propose different children as the genuine tülku, or where the regents might refuse to pass power along to the tülku when the latter reached maturity.

The tülku tradition was originally explained as an application of the doctrine of rebirth, although the political complications that sometimes grew out of the tradition inspired some new interpretations of the rebirth doctrine. The most striking example of this was a case in Bhutan where three children were proposed by different factions as the rightful hierarch of the Drugpa ('Brug-pa) branch of the Kagyüs in charge of that country. The final decision was that the previous hierarch had split his body, speech, and mind among three incarnations, and that the speech and mind incarnations should assume authority. From that point onward, this tülku developed a habit of making this three-way split. However, in the seventeenth century the tülku tradition began to combine with the tradition of bodhisattva emanations, and thus was explained in terms of the nirmāṇakāya theory. As a result, tülkus who turned out to be obvious poor choices could be removed from office on the grounds that their bodhisattva had abandoned them.

Questions of internal politics, however, were relatively mild in comparison to external politics. As we have noted, monks have participated in Tibetan politics from the time of the First Propagation; their erudition made them ideal diplomats, much like the clerics of medieval Europe, and in this they followed a precedent established by their forerunners in India and Central Asia. They also followed a Pāla precedent—the priest–patron relationship—whereby the patron would reward a monk's political work by granting him or his monastery full rights over a gift of land, free from taxation, thus making the monastery the governing power in a small fiefdom. By the thirteenth century, some of these fiefdoms were no longer small, and the fact that they were the only institutions in the country transcending the clan level made them major players on the political scene.

Ultimately, one of the orders, the Sakya school, parlayed this position to full sovereignty over Tibet by transposing the priest–patron relationship to the international level. In 1247 the ruling clans of Tibet realized that the Mongols, who by then had become the dominant power of Central Asia, were planning to invade. In order to prevent this catastrophe, they sent Sakya Paṇḍita (see Section 11.3.1) to negotiate a truce with the Mongol ruler, Ködön Khan. Sakya Paṇḍita was famed not only for his scholarship but also for his practical wisdom, which he used on this occasion to play both sides to his advantage. By offering Tibet's submission to Mongol rule, he persuaded the Khan not to invade Tibet. He then persuaded the Khan to place him and his descendants in the position of viceroys over the entire country.

Scholars have argued that the long intermingling of politics and religion in Tibetan history from pre-Buddhist times has inclined the Tibetans to see nothing wrong with the notion of a monk as ruler of their country, but Sakya Paṇḍita's actions on this occasion were extremely unpopular with his countrymen. The Sakyans were able to use their power to their advantage in the short run, waging war on and destroying any monasteries who opposed them, but their rule was short-lived, ending in 1354 as their patrons, the Mongols, also fell. Nevertheless, they set a precedent. During their reign, other schools tried to follow their example by establishing their own priest–patron relationships with the Mongols. After their reign, the Kagyü school affiliated with the clan who overthrew the Sakyas briefly achieved ascendance. However, the Gelugs benefited most in the long run from the Sakyan precedent. The story of how this happened takes us into a new era of Tibetan history.

11.4 THE AGE OF THE DALAI LAMAS

The Gelug monasteries, in carrying on the traditions of the Indian universities, continued the tradition of producing missionaries as well. In 1578, Tsongkhapa's third successor as head of the school, Sonam Gyatsho (bSod-nams-rgya-ntsho; 1543–1588), converted the Mongol ruler, Altan Khan, to Buddhism. This set into motion a process whereby the Mongols and other inhabitants of the Central Asian steppes took on the Gelug system of monastic education and came to regard Lhasa as the cultural and religious capital of their lands. The Khan bestowed the name of Dalai Lama (Ocean [of Wisdom] Teacher) on Sonam Gyatsho, but because Gyatsho was regarded as the tülku of his two predecessors, he became known as the Third Dalai Lama, with the title of First and Second granted retroactively to them.

The Fourth Dalai Lama was born in the family of the Mongol Khan, but not until the reign of the Fifth Dalai Lama (1617–1682) did this priest–patron relationship bring political power to the Gelugs. With the help of Mongol troops, the Fifth Dalai Lama defeated his enemies in central Tibet and became ruler of the entire country. His policies forced monks of other politically active sects to take refuge in outlying areas of Tibet, Sikkim, and Bhutan, but he was very generous with sects exhibiting no political ambitions. In particular, he showed a great interest in Nyingma doctrines—he was reputed to be a Dzogchen adept—and bestowed on the Nyingma order property he had seized from the Kagyüs. Proclaiming himself an emanation of Avalokiteśvara, he built an enormous maṇḍala-palace on a hill overlooking Lhasa and named it the Potala, after the mountain in southern India reputed to be Avalokiteśvara's home. Thus he became the first figure in Tibetan history to combine the traditions of tülku and bodhisattva emanation in one person.

Nine years after the Manchus took power in China in 1644, the Fifth Dalai Lama visited Peking and established a special priest–patron relationship with the new dynasty, thus setting the stage for the Gelugs to rule Tibet well into the twentieth century. With considerably more skill than the Sakyas—and considerably more luck, in that their patrons held power for an unusually long time—the Gelugs were able to use Chinese power to keep their political enemies under control, while using their own diplomatic skills to keep the Chinese from interfering excessively in Tibet's internal affairs. The priest–patron relationship lasted until 1951, but the different views held by both sides on what that relationship implied meant that it was always precarious.

Only two of the Fifth Dalai Lama's successors, however, shared his political acumen. During the reigns of the Sixth through the Twelfth, most of the political power was held by the Gelug regents. The Sixth Dalai Lama, born to a Nyingma family, proved remarkably unsuited for monastic life; he is credited with authoring a series of erotic poems based on his exploits in the brothels of Lhasa. His fellow lamas debated on how to deal with the situation, finally deciding that Avalokiteśvara had abandoned him and entered another lama. Before they could act, however, the Mongols attacked Lhasa, killed the regent, and kidnapped the Dalai Lama, who died in captivity. The Seventh and Eighth Dalai Lamas preferred quiet contemplation to politics, the Ninth through the Twelfth died in childhood.

The Thirteenth (1874–1933) survived the perils of childhood in the Potala only to become enmeshed in international politics, as the British and Chinese both invaded Lhasa during his reign. Seeing the long-term threat to his country if it did not modernize, he strengthened the civilian branch of the government service, raised a standing army, and instituted a number of other modernizing reforms that—after initial resistance—gradually became very popular. As he approached death, however, he could see that his reforms were too little too late; his death was accompanied by bad omens that left the populace dispirited. The Fourteenth Dalai Lama (b. 1935), enthroned in 1950 just before the Chinese communists invaded Tibet, was forced to flee the country in 1959 as the Chinese set about systematically destroying all vestiges of Tibetan culture. Setting up a Tibetan government in exile in Dharamsala, India, he has worked tirelessly to provide support for Tibetan refugees scattered throughout the world and to build unity among the lamas of the various Tibetan schools. Realizing that the only hope for the survival of Tibetan Buddhism lies in developing an international base of support, he has also disseminated Buddhist teachings to the world at large. He is currently one of the most—if not the most—visible and influential exponents of Buddhism on the world stage.

This survey of the political fortunes of the Dalai Lamas over the past four centuries has bypassed the religious developments of the period largely because most of the religious innovations of this period occurred outside of the Gelug school, whose rigorous system of education tended to preclude innovation. The primary religious development of this period was the growth of the Nyingma eclectic school of thought, and its permeation into the other non-Gelug orders. The Nyingma monastic order grew considerably as a result of the Fifth Dalai Lama's support in the seventeenth century, and the school produced one of its greatest thinkers and meditation masters in the following century, Jigme Lingpa ('Jigs-med gLing-pa; c. 1730–1798). Jigme Lingpa—reportedly as a result of mind-to-mind transmission from Longch'en Rabjam—streamlined and ritualized the latter's guides to Dzogchen with an eye to making them more accessible, forming the basis for all Dzogchen practice ever since. He taught that individually interpreted self-discipline was more important than monastic discipline in the pursuit of the path, and that the ultimate truth could not be captured or even approached by any verbal formulation.

These points formed the rallying point for the Ri-med (Ris-med, Unrestricted) movement that began sweeping through the non-Gelug orders in eastern Tibet in the middle of the nineteenth century. This movement was unrestricted in three ways: It drew on the traditions of all the monastic and Tantric lineages, regardless of affiliation; it offered to the general public initiations that had been kept as closely guarded secrets for many centuries; and it devalued the monastic disciplinary rules, in particular the rules concerning celibacy. Several reincarnate lamas who joined the movement, such as the Fifteenth Gyalwa Karmapa (1871–1922), abandoned their celibate practices and took on consorts for the first time in their tülku line. Although the Ri-meds drew their leaders from the Sakyas, Kagyüs, Nyingmas, and even the Bons, the movement was primarily a triumph of Nyingma eclecticism, in that it emphasized Dzogchen as an element in all true Buddhist practice and supported the idea that all interpretations of Buddhist doctrine are equally valid, with no one version in a position of orthodoxy above any others.

Although the Ri-med movement was originally nonpolitical, it ran into trouble in the early twentieth century as the Gelugs began viewing it as a threat to the Thirteenth Dalai Lama's drive to centralize Tibet. The Gelug representative in eastern Tibet, Pabongkha (P'awongk'a) Rimpoche (1878–1943) tried to thwart the movement, but the Chinese intervention in the 1950s defused the conflict. Virtually all of the Tibetan lamas now teaching internationally are students of either Pabongkha Rimpoche or the Ri-meds.

11.5 THE DYNAMICS OF TIBETAN RITUAL

Tibetan religious thought and practice revolve around Tantric ritual. Unless one is acquainted with the ritual patterns, it is impossible to understand the tradition at all. Although we have already discussed Tantric ritual in Chapter Six, the Tibetans have added their own elements and interpretation to the ritual. Thus their distinctive amalgam deserves a separate discussion, which we will attempt here.

As we noted in Section 11.2, indigenous Tibetan religion involved four activities: divination, the ushering of the spirits of the dead to the afterlife, exorcism, and coercion. Of these, divination is the only practice where pre-Buddhist forms of spirit possession still predominate. Tibetans may resort to mediums, termed *lha-pa* (god-possessed) or *dpa' bo* (heroes), although there are milder forms of divination, such as astrology, brought over from India, that they may resort to as well. These mediums are used by people on all levels of society. In 1959, for instance, the decision for the Dalai Lama to flee the advancing Chinese troops was made by the State Oracle.

A manuscript found at Tun-huang suggests that, in pre-Buddhist times, the purpose of ushering spirits of the dead to the afterlife was primarily to make sure that they stayed put and did not return to bother the living. This practice has long since been brought into the framework of Tibetan Buddhist theory through the *Bardo T'ödröl*—known in the West as the *Tibetan Book of the Dead*—which is chanted for the first 49 days after a person's death to help him or her circumvent the fruits of karma and safely negotiate the hazards of the postdeath *bardo,* or intermediate state. Ideally, given this guidance, the spirit may escape the need for rebirth altogether; failing that, it can be directed to a decent rebirth. This guidance is intended primarily for those who have not mastered Vajrayāna ritual, for the adept should have sufficiently mastered the bardos experienced during life so that the death bardo should pose no problems.

There are four bardos in all: the mental space between two events, the space between two thoughts, the space between sleeping and waking (the dream bardo), and the space after death (the death bardo). In all of these spaces, which form the openings toward expanded states of consciousness, there is an intense experience of clear light that, if one is unfamiliar with it, can be terrifying. Tibetans feel that if one feels terror at the light after death, one will not be able to deal skillfully with the various possibilities for rebirth. Thus the highest aim of all religious practice is to familiarize oneself thoroughly with the "child light" appearing in the bardos that can be experienced during one's lifetime, so that one will skillfully let it be subsumed into the "mother light" appearing at death. In this way one can master the rebirth process, if one has inclinations toward being a tülku or a bodhisattva, or escape it entirely if not.

For most people, though, their ability to negotiate the dangers of the spirit world around them is of more immediate concern than their fate after death.

These issues are covered under the topics of exorcism and coercion. Little is known about how Tibetans handled these issues before the propagation of Buddhism, although the Tun-huang manuscript mentioned previously suggests that one of the reasons the Tibetans adopted Buddhism was because it appeared to have more effective techniques for dealing with these problems. On the simplest level, the doctrine of karma explains how one's good acts may protect one from the uncertainties of the spirit realm. In this sense, the popular Tibetan view of merit is much like what we have already seen in Thai popular Buddhism (see Section 7.5.1): Merit is viewed as a form of power that can override but does not necessarily abrogate the power of the spirit world. In response to this belief, Tibetans have devised a number of distinctive methods for increasing one's stock of merit. For people in general, these can include repeating Avalokiteśvara's mantra, *Oṃ maṇi-padme hūm* (Oṃ jewel in the lotus hūṃ); writing mantras on flags, which are considered to repeat the mantra in one's stead each time the flag flaps in the wind; and spinning "prayer wheels" containing mantras inscribed on slips, which are thought to repeat the mantra each time the wheel is spun. Another popular form of acquiring merit is going on pilgrimages to pay respect to important religious sites.

More elaborate are the rituals performed by Vajrayāna initiates, whose professionalism in this area has few parallels in other Buddhist cultures. These initiates come in a wide variety of forms—celibate monks and nuns, noncelibate lay practitioners, and solitary hermits—but here we will focus on the rituals in a typical moderate-sized monastery to give an idea of how one community has developed a coherent religious and ritual life from the variety of models available in the Vajrayāna tradition. The monastery—a Kagyü provincial center influenced by the Ri-med movement and located in eastern Tibet—is no longer functioning, but its survivors have transported its practices to northern India and continue to maintain hope that they will someday be allowed to return and rebuild what they have lost.

The monastery was located in a valley surrounded by low, grassy hills. A large walled compound, it contained two main temples where group rituals were held, workshops for the creation of ritual implements, and row houses capable of housing 300 monks. Further up the hill was a hermitage where the monks were expected, at least once in their lives, to go on a retreat lasting for three years, three months, and three days. In permanent residence at the hermitage were 13 yogins, termed *vidyādharas,* who spent their entire lives following the example of Milarepa. If one of them died, one of the ordinary monks who showed the proper talent was assigned to replace him so as to keep the number constant.

Because families in the area were expected to donate a set number of their young sons to become monks—a so-called "monk tax"—to keep the monastery's population at a viable number, not all of the monks showed a religious avocation. However the practical running of the monastery offered plenty of activities for those who were less religiously inclined. It needed craftsmen to provide a steady output of ritual implements, and security guards to protect the monastery from bandits and thieves. Almost all the monks kept their own dairy cattle, tended gardens, and were expected to provide and prepare their own meals. Aside from maintaining celibacy, they led lives little touched by the

Mūlasarvāstivādin rules they studied. Their support came from their families and from fees for their performance of rituals for the local laity. Generally free to come and go, they were subject to the rule of the abbot only if they happened to take him as their Tantric master. The temple as a whole, in addition to receiving donations from lay supporters, sponsored trading ventures and caravans to supplement its income.

As one observer has noted, Vajrayāna practice is a performing art, and the life of the monks was devoted to becoming skilled performers. This involved learning not only the techniques of the art, but also the proper altruistic motivation for performing it. A society believing firmly in the reality of ritual power could not wisely support its practice by anyone who did not have the proper motivation. Young monks, in addition to taking minor roles in the morning and afternoon group rituals, devoted their time to learning the basics of classic Tibetan. At the age of 20, they began their education in the colleges associated with the temple. Unlike the great Gelug universities in Lhasa, the course here took only 8 to 10 years, although it covered the same five basic texts. Here the emphasis was less on mastering the controversies that had built up around the texts over the centuries in the pursuit of the correct "object of negation," than on gaining familiarity with their basic ideas. On completing this course, the monk took a three-year training course in ritual techniques: mudrās, chanting, the making of offerings, the performance of ritual musical instruments, ritual dancing, and the painting of maṇḍalas. The painting of maṇḍalas was particularly important, for it aided the monk in the process of visualization so central to sādhana practice.

On completing this course, the monk was encouraged to begin his retreat, for only on retreat could he devote himself full-time to the mastery of the ritual, and only on completing the retreat could he be considered a lama. The training here would begin with an initiation—given by a lama, who in the course of the ceremony identified himself with the central deity of the ritual—authorizing the trainee to attempt the ritual. Without this authorization, a trainee who attempted the ritual would be considered a trespasser and would not be safe from having the ritual power backfire on him. Prior to the initiation, the trainee would have to supplement his monastic and bodhisattva vows with the vows listed in the Tantra that provided the instructions for his sādhana practice. These would include injunctions against speaking ill of one's lama, speaking ill of women, divulging secret doctrines to the uninitiated, being friendly with evil people, or dwelling among Hīnayānists.

Once the initiation was granted, the trainee would further prepare and purify himself for the ritual with the four common and uncommon preliminaries. The common preliminaries, so-called because they were common to all Mahāyāna practitioners, were reflections on the difficulty of attaining a human birth, on death and impermanence, on the principle of karma, and on the horrors of rebirth in saṃsāra. The uncommon preliminaries, exclusive to Vajrayāna practice, consisted of a series of purification rites accompanied by visualizations. The trainee visualized the field of hosts—the assembled deities and lamas of his lineage—and prostrated to them 100,000 times. He then visualized the primary deity of his ritual and recited the deity's 100-syllable mantra 100,000 times. He offered the maṇḍala 100,000 times to his lama lineage, and finally, through prayer and yoga, made their empowerment enter into himself 100,000 times. At the conclusion of each stage, he absorbed the maṇḍala into himself. This process completed, he was prepared to take on the central ritual.

Vajrayāna deities have both a personal and an impersonal aspect, and thus the basic pattern of the ritual consisted of an offering, to arouse the deity's heart, and an evocation, in which one used the deity's mantra to coerce the impersonal power set in motion by the deity's original vow or pledge to become a deity or to protect Buddhism in the first place. The deities who were the focus of these rituals fell into three classes, called the Three Basic Ones, which for many Vajrayāna practitioners superseded the Triple Gem in immediate importance. The three classes were members of one's lama lineage (including one's personal lama), high Vajrayāna patron deities—subsumed under the five Buddha clans (see Section 6.2.1)—and ḍākinīs. To this list were added the "Lords," fierce patron deities of the particular monastery or school, who had their own special rituals that had to be practiced 20 hours every day by a monk especially assigned to the task in a dark, ferociously decorated room. If these rituals were not carried out, the Lord would turn against the monastery.

From its beginning, Vajrayāna has maintained that two elements make its Tantric practice distinctively Buddhist: its underling motivation—compassion—and its discernment of the emptiness that lies at the heart of the practice. Thus the central ritual, each time it was performed, was bracketed by mantras representing the Three Sacred Things: awakening bodhicitta and contemplation of emptiness beforehand, and dedication of merit afterward. One standard list of the steps in the "awakening bodhicitta" stage included mantras for homage, offering, confession of sins, rejoicing in the merit of others, an entreaty that the deity reveal the Dharma, a prayer that the deity not pass away into nirvāṇa, and dedication of one's own merit. The "contemplation of emptiness" stage was a mantra referring to emptiness; while reciting it, the practitioner was supposed to reflect quickly on the proper meaning of the concept. In this and all the other steps of the ritual, the practitioner was to develop speed and accuracy not only in the repetition of the mantra and the performance of the mudrās, but also in the processes of visualization and contemplation that were supposed to accompany them, thus engaging his entire body, speech, and mind in the ritual world. In this way, the performance of the Three Sacred Things repeatedly made real to the practitioner the principle that compassion and discernment should underlie his exercise of ritual power.

The ritual proper was the process of generation, which involved three steps: visualizing the deity's maṇḍala, abandoning one's own world and identity so as to assume the deity's identity through the power of the mantra, and the "recollection of purity." The assumption of the deity's identity, or "pride," was crucial in that one could not expect to control the deity's power unless one became the deity. The recollection of purity—another reference to emptiness—was essential for returning to the emptiness from which the deity had sprung so that one could make contact with the source from which all things come, and thus be able to exercise power over them.

The element of choice now came into the ritual, for one could now decide what to do with one's acquired power. A traditional text lists two basic uses for ritual power, extraordinary and ordinary. The one extraordinary use is the attainment of the Innate Union of Clear Light and Emptiness, which is accomplished through the process of perfection. Various texts explain this stage in different ways, depending on how much emphasis they lay on physical yoga or the analytical insight needed for the proper apprehension of emptiness. Essentially it was a process whereby one coerced one's way into the deity's awareness of emptiness—called its knowledge body, as opposed to its mantra body, assumed in the process of generation—and so immersed oneself in the emptiness of Awakening.

In the ordinary uses of ritual power, one generated the deity once again, this time in front of one, and then directed it into an object (say, a flask of water to be used for its ritual power), a person (such as a new initiate), or into the sky (as when one wanted to drive away a hailstorm). These ordinary uses of power came in three levels: high, medium, and low. The high level attainments were particular abilities that sprang spontaneously from one's karmic background; the medium attainments covered all the classic powers of Indian yoga—such as clairvoyance, the ability to read minds, and so on—plus practices from traditional Tibetan shamanism. The lower attainments covered the four functions of the krīya Tantras that have been discussed in Section 6.2.1. The potential that these powers could be grossly misused was one of the reasons why compassion was so emphasized in the preliminary vows and the framework of each ritual performance.

Because the Three Basic Ones contained such a wide range of personalities, different deities were employed for different ritual ends. For instance, Tārā was used primarily in rituals with a directly compassionate purpose; her fierce aspect, Kurukullā, was called on for more aggressive purposes, such as the subjugation of spirits. Thus a monk, to enlarge his ritual repertoire, would try to master the mantras of as many deities as possible while on retreat; when he left retreat, he continued to collect initiations, as he could afford, from wandering monks visiting his monastery or from lamas he sought out on his own. The remainder of his life would be devoted to finding a balance between the ordinary and extraordinary uses of his powers, weighing his supporters' needs for his ritual help against the time he needed to devote to his own pursuit of Awakening.

Life in a Tibetan nunnery was organized around lines similar to those for a monastery, with the same division between ordinary nuns and those on retreat. The main monastic orders all had affiliated nunneries, although bhikṣuṇī orders were never established in Tibet. Some independent nunneries were run by highly regarded female tülkus. With rare exceptions, they tended to have fewer opportunities than monks for gaining an academic education; they also tended to be less sought after than monks for their ritual powers. This was for two reasons: (1) Aside from rituals associated with Tārā, men in general were considered more capable masters of ritual power than women; (2) nuns tended to have smaller incomes than monks, because they had fewer supporters seeking their services, which meant that they could not afford the fees charged for the more powerful initiations. This was a vicious circle, because those without the powerful initiations would then tend to attract less support. Thus, as is the case with nuns in Thailand, Tibetan nuns had more time than the monks to devote to private meditation and the extraordinary uses of their ritual powers. This pattern still holds in the Tibetan nunneries set up in India, although the steady influx of refugee nuns from Tibet has imposed added burdens on institutions already at a severe financial disadvantage. However, thanks to the efforts of the international Tibetan Nuns Project, many of the nuns in India now enjoy more opportunities for education and practice than they did in their homeland.

11.6 A TRADITION AT THE CROSSROADS

The Chinese suppression of Tibetan Buddhism in the 1950s and 1960s was unusually cruel, insulting, and thorough. Nuns were raped, monks were tortured and killed, and almost all of the monasteries and nunneries were razed to the ground. Prayer books were used as shoe linings, mattress stuffing, and toilet paper; printing blocks for religious books were used to pave roads. As we noted in Chapter 8, after the death of Chairman Mao the Chinese began pursuing a policy of guarded religious tolerance throughout their country, and to some extent applied this policy to their colony of Tibet as well. As a result, authorities gave permission for a few monasteries to resume functioning and for a handful of religious monuments to be rebuilt. Mongolia followed suit with a similar policy of tolerance, with the result that the country is currently enjoying a Buddhist revival. However, in Tibet the Chinese policy of tolerance has been severely restricted because Tibetan monasteries have proven to be hotbeds of anti-Chinese nationalist sentiment. A constant stream of monks and nuns continue to risk the dangers of the Himalayan passes in order to make their way to safety in Bhutan and India rather than let themselves be subjected to the continued brutality of the Chinese garrison.

At the moment, the best hope for the survival of Tibetan Buddhism lies in the monasteries and nunneries being built in India, and among the groups of meditation students and supporters gathering around refugee lamas throughout the West. Western children have begun to be recognized as tülkus, much as happened in Mongolia in the seventeenth century. It remains to be seen whether this will lead eventually to a priest–patron relationship that will return the Tibetans to power in their country—using Western media and academia to shape world public opinion so that one of the major world powers will act as the patron—or to the development of a new home base for Tibetan Buddhism in the outside world.

12

Buddhism Comes West

12.1 EUROPE'S EARLY CONTACT WITH BUDDHISM

Prior to the opening of sea routes from Europe to Asia, the story of Europe's contact with Buddhism was one of historical oddities and undocumented possibilities. Among the possibilities, it is known that there was fairly extensive trade between India and the Mediterranean area in the era of the Greek city-states and the Roman Empire. This has led scholars to conjecture about whether the Platonic and Gnostic doctrines of the transmigration of souls originated in India, and also whether the references to Buddhism in the writings of Clement and Origen—two early Alexandrian fathers of the Christian church—can be taken as evidence that King Aśoka's emissaries to the Mediterranean countries actually reached their destination (see Section 3.4). There is also the question of whether the Egyptian Desert Fathers were influenced by Buddhists or members of the other Indian śramana movements. Because the Desert Fathers were the direct inspiration for the first Christian monastic orders, it is possible that Christian monasticism derived indirectly from the same sources as did Buddhism, if not from Buddhism itself. Finally, there is the possibility that the Christian cult of relics was originally inspired by the Buddhist example.

Among the documented oddities, modern scholarship has revealed that in the sixteenth century the Catholic church unwittingly included the Buddha in its list of saints. The saints Barlām and Josaphat (a corruption of the word *bodhisattva*) derive from the Buddha legend, which had become increasingly garbled as it traveled west from India through Georgia and, in the tenth or eleventh century, began spreading throughout Europe.

Beginning in the thirteenth century as a result of the Crusades, Europeans gradually began to travel overland to Asian Buddhist countries, primarily as occasional ministers to the Khan or—like Marco Polo—as adventurous merchants. When Vasco da Gama discovered oceangoing routes in 1497, he opened Asia to European religious and commercial interests, the primary religious interest being to convert Asians to Christianity. The zeal for this mission led Jesuits to travel to India, Japan, and China in the sixteenth century, and Tibet in the seventeenth. These missionaries made detailed studies—sometimes quite accurate—of the religions they were trying to supplant, although their reports often languished, unread, in the Vatican until the twentieth century. Early European colonizers viewed it as their God-given duty to convert the natives to Christianity and stamp out heathenism. From this attitude came the atrocities the Portuguese committed against Sri Lankan Buddhists during their control of the island during the sixteenth and seventeenth centuries (see Section 7.4.1).

Later colonizers tended to be more mixed in their attitudes toward Asian customs and religions. While many continued to regard the colonizing of Asia as a means for spreading the Gospel, largely through education and medical care, some of them wrote glowing accounts of the highly civilized, rationally organized societies they encountered in Asia. These accounts had a telling effect in Europe, as they opened the European mind to the possibility that Europe was not the only truly civilized society on Earth. Cultural relativism—the view that cultural values and institutions were not absolutes, but were relative to geographical, historical, and other factors—thus came to be more widely accepted in European intellectual circles by the seventeenth century. This set the stage for the revolution that was to reshape Western culture at the same time it was to shape all serious Western encounters with Buddhism up to the present day. That revolution was the European and American Enlightenment of the eighteenth century.

12.2 THE AWAKENING MEETS THE ENLIGHTENMENT

The Enlightenment was essentially a campaign made by a loosely organized confederation of intellectuals—including Voltaire, Hume, Kant, Diderot, Franklin, and Montesquieu—to liberate Western society from what they considered the intellectual and political tyranny of the past. Tyranny in the intellectual sphere, for most of them, meant Catholic control over Western thought, although some of them went so far as to equate this tyranny with the Christian mind-set itself. In the political sphere, they discerned tyranny chiefly in institutions and policies serving the narrow, shortsighted interests of a privileged few. To free the West intellectually, they advanced the view that only the scientific method, or the rational analysis of empirical data, could provide absolutely true knowledge. All other sources of knowledge—and religious sources in particular, many of them said—were culturally relative. Thus their intellectual manifesto was an amalgam of empiricism, cultural relativism, pluralism, and eclecticism. Their political manifesto, however, dealt more in absolutes: the belief that the "science of humanity"—the empirical study of human society through the fledgling disciplines of psychology, comparative sociology, and secular history—could yield abstract laws that would have the force of mandates for social reform. Among the absolutes they proposed as possessing scientific validity were liberty, equality, and the doctrine of human rights. Although they recognized a potential conflict between their political absolutes and intellectual relativism, they were hopeful that with the advance of the social sciences these conflicts could be resolved. With the passage of time, however, the conflicts became more marked and have consumed Western civilization ever since.

One of the unforeseen effects of the Enlightenment was its role in the introduction of Buddhism to the West. (1) It provided the rationale for the collection, translation, and study of Buddhist texts, along with the excavation of Buddhist archaeological sites, at the same time providing the framework for understanding the resultant body of knowledge. (2) Even before Westerners began converting to Buddhism, the Enlightenment opened the minds of individual Westerners to the possibility that an Eastern religion might make a useful contribution to their personal eclecticism. (3) It was responsible for creating splits in Western culture that led Westerners to look to Buddhism as a potential means of healing the splits. And, (4) it sanctioned the attitude that if Buddhism did not actually offer the solutions that Westerners were seeking to solve their own cultural crises, they had the right to reform the religion in line with their own values so that it would, and that in doing so they would be making a positive contribution to the progress of the human race. These four strands of influence, in their various combinations, account for much of the complex interaction between Westerners and Buddhism during the past two centuries. Because a strictly chronological survey of this process would be little more than a jumble of facts, the following sections will present a thematic analysis instead.

12.2.1 Buddhism and the Science of Humanity

The Europeans who in the late eighteenth and early nineteenth centuries began the serious recovery of Buddhist texts and archaeological sites in Asia were motivated by two missions. The first was to learn enough about the customs of the nations coming under their power that they could design an enlightened form of colonial rule, one that would combine rational European principles with a sensitivity to local conditions. The second was to add to the body of data available to the growing science of humanity so that a more comprehensive view of the varieties of human experience could place the science on a more solid basis. Initially, in their view, Buddhism formed only a few scattered pieces of the larger puzzle of Asian culture they were trying to comprehend, and they often confused Buddhism with other traditions. Not until 1844 did the French philologist Eugene Burnouf put the pieces together, concluding that certain religions discovered in China, Tibet, India, Sri Lanka, and Southeast Asia were in fact branches of a single tradition whose home was in India. Burnouf thus laid the foundation for Buddhology, the scholarly study of Buddhism, which has since spread throughout the West, engaging scholars in the fields of philology, comparative religion, history, sociology, psychology, philosophy, and anthropology. Buddhology has also become fashionable in the East, with Japan and Sri Lanka currently providing some of the most prolific members of the field.

In the latter part of the twentieth century, Buddhology—like many other academic disciplines—became something of an end in itself, with little thought for its role in the society at large. However, the twin impulses that originally led to this professional activity—political and social-scientific—are still active to some extent. Buddhologists have occasionally been called upon to help Western governments with foreign-policy decisions and to train diplomats going to Asia. Discoveries about Buddhism continue to shape the science of humanity, especially in the "caring professions." The medical profession, for instance, has adopted elementary techniques from Buddhist meditation to treat hypertension and enable patients to cope with chronic, severe pain. Some psychotherapists now recommend Buddhist meditation to their patients, practice it themselves, and advertise their personal meditation background as part of their professional credentials. Social workers in prisons and inner-city neighborhoods have adopted similar techniques to help their clients handle stress.

But although Buddhism has had some influence on the science of humanity, the influence has been greater the other way around. This is especially true in the field of the psychology of religion. In shaping the way educated Westerners regard the nature and aims of religious life, this discipline has played a major role in determining how Buddhism is perceived in the West, which of its branches and doctrines have proven most popular, and which doctrines have had to be recast in order to make them palatable to Western tastes.

Two contradictory features of the psychology of religion account for this influence. On the one hand, because the psychology of religion draws its raw data from religious traditions all across the world, it can claim for its theories a scientific breadth and objectivity that no culture-bound tradition can claim. On the other hand, the concepts it uses to explain those data are drawn from familiar Western intellectual traditions and thus make intuitive sense to Westerners in a way that concepts from other cultures would not.

There are several branches of thought within the psychology of religion, but the one most influential in shaping Western attitudes toward Buddhism is the humanistic strain developed in William James's *The Varieties of Religious Experience* (1902), Carl Jung's *Modern Man in Search of a Soul* (1933), and Abraham Maslow's *Religions, Values, and Peak-Experiences* (1970). These writers evaluated religions, not in terms of their truth claims, but in terms of their psychological effect on the individual. The ideal religion, they maintained, centers on peak experiences of oneness that overcome both internal divisions within the psyche and any sense of separateness from the external world. These peak experiences should then lead to plateau experiences, in which the feeling of internal oneness and external connectedness is carried into daily life as an on-going process of personal integration. James stressed that this integration should include a heightened sense of individual morality and social responsibility. Jung, however, stressed the importance of fluidity: the ability to deal spontaneously and creatively with the uncertainties of life without trying to force confining certainties on them.

For all three of these writers, however, the internal and external integration of the personality was a lifelong process that would never achieve perfection. They believed that a wide variety of teachings and practices could aid in this integration; and for them, the differences among these teachings and practices were immaterial, for the true essence of religion lay in their common pragmatic uses.

Although James, Jung, and Maslow drew their data from a wide range of world religions, the underlying categories of their thought derived from Western philosophy and religion. The pattern of peak and plateau experiences derived ultimately from the Methodist doctrine of conversion and sanctification. The high value placed on feelings of internal oneness and external connectedness derived both from the Pietist traditions of Christianity and the thought of the European Romantics. Romanticism and American Transcendentalism also accounted for the notion that the perfection of the individual is an on-going process, rather than an achievable goal, and that the highest expression of that process lies in the element of play and spontaneity.

Although this branch of the psychology of religion is not the only discipline that has influenced the way Buddhism is understood in the West, its theories have shaped many of the ideas espoused by Western converts to Buddhism, regardless of school. For example, they have led to the assumption—widely accepted but unsupported by the earliest accounts—that the Buddha's Awakening was a generic peak experience. Secondly, they help explain why Mahāyāna has proven more popular than Theravāda in the West. Many Mahāyāna doctrines—as expressed in writings intended for the West—parallel the assumptions that have shaped psychology of religion as a discipline. When Zen was first presented to the West, the emphasis on satori paralleled the belief that dramatic experiences lay at the essence of the religious life. Its emphasis on spontaneity and play, and its rejection of set moral guidelines, follow many of the Romantic ideas advocated by Jung and his followers. Its insistence that the sage "return to the marketplace" after Awakening parallels the belief that religious experience proves its worth by contributing to the welfare of the everyday world.

In addition, the positive Hua-yen interpretation of dependent co-arising resonates better with the Romantic notion of interconnectedness than does the more negative Theravādin interpretation. The Perfection of Emptiness emphasis on "coursing the way of the bodhisattva," rather than arriving at nirvāṇa as a set goal, parallels the notion that religious life is a continual move toward perfection rather than its attainment. Furthermore, the bodhisattva's talent at "coursing" rather than taking a stance echoes the fluidity of the well integrated personality: the metaphor of the religious life as a free-form dance is popular in Western Buddhist writings. Finally, the Mahāyāna emphasis on nonduality resonates with the belief that the aim of religion is to overcome divisions both internal and external. And its acceptance, within that nonduality, of contradictory teachings as skillful means for moving toward perfection parallels the view that multiple religious truths can be psychologically healing for individuals of different types.

Although these resonances between Mahāyāna doctrines and the assumptions of the psychology of religion have helped popularize Mahāyāna in the West, they have also helped distort its interpretation here. Many Mahāyāna doctrines that do not resonate with these assumptions—such as the doctrine of rebirth implicit in the bodhisattva vow—tend to be ignored, while those that do resonate are often portrayed as identical with, rather than merely similar to, these assumptions.

Even in non-Mahāyāna circles, the psychology of religion has inspired the reshaping of Buddhist doctrines that do not parallel its assumptions. Perhaps the most striking instance of this tendency has been the reshaping of the not-self doctrine among Theravādin converts. Because traditional Theravādin interpretations of this doctrine deny the assumption that religion's role is to create an integrated sense of self, most Western teachers of Theravādin vipassanā methods have simply dropped them. For instance, they qualify the interpretation that there is no self to mean no *separate* self, thus showing an affinity, not with Theravādin tradition, but with Romantic assumptions latent in Western psychology. The same tendency can be found in the writings of Western converts to Zen and Tibetan Buddhism as well.

Thus the science of humanity has played a paradoxical role in the introduction and adoption of Buddhism in the West. On the one hand, Buddhologists have exposed Westerners to the wide variety of Buddhist traditions. At the same time, psychologists of religion have used information from these traditions to support their theories, which has had the effect of exposing their readers to Buddhist ideas in an atmosphere of at least guarded respect. On the other hand, these same psychologists have subjected Buddhist ideas to their own views on the nature and aims of religious life. As a result, Buddhist doctrines at odds with these views have tended to disappear from Western Buddhism. Furthermore, because these psychologists regard doctrines as a secondary and inessential part of religion, they have provided justification for those who knowingly drop or change Buddhist doctrines as they present the tradition to their Western audience.

As we will see in this chapter, Western Buddhism is far from monolithic. Still, the science of humanity has shaped an emerging consensus among Western Buddhist converts as to the nature and aims of their adopted religion. At present, this consensus is a prime feature that defines Western Buddhism as a product of the West.

12.2.2 The Appropriation of Buddhist Ideas

Before Westerners could convert to Buddhism, however, they first had to be open to the idea that it held valid lessons for them, even if they had no intention of converting. This, in turn, required the climate of tolerance and eclecticism provided by the Enlightenment. Many early Buddhologists were Christian apologists whose avowed purpose in studying Buddhism was to discredit it. Others, however—such as T. W. Rhys Davids, who founded the Pali Text Society in 1886—were more steeped in Enlightenment values and presented Buddhism to their readers and listeners as a faith-free rationalism whose tenets could easily be integrated into the Victorian cult of heroic agnosticism.

For a large part of the nineteenth and twentieth centuries, however, the most creative answers to the question of what Buddhism has to offer the West have come from outside the academic world. Some of these answers have been only tangentially related to actual Buddhist teaching, but they touch on almost all areas of Western intellectual and artistic life. A thorough account of this process would fill a book, so here we will simply note a few of the more striking examples.

The German philosopher Arthur Schopenhauer (1788–1860) was the first Westerner to declare publicly his affinity for Buddhism, seeing in the First Noble Truth an expression of the thoroughgoing pessimism he advocated in his own philosophy. Schopenhauer in turn influenced Richard Wagner, who in the latter part of his life tackled the project of writing an opera on the life of the Buddha but was stymied by the problem of finding a *leitmotiv,* a dramatic and musical theme, for a character free from passion, aversion, and delusion.

Neither Schopenhauer nor Wagner was a Buddhist in the sense of taking refuge in the Triple Gem, but the eclecticism they exemplified has played a prominent role in the West's appropriation of Buddhist ideas. A modern example of this trend is the role that Zen has played in the art and aesthetic theories of avant-garde composers such as John Cage, and of writers such as Allen Ginsberg, Jack Kerouac, Gary Snyder, and J. D. Salinger. Salinger's novel *The Catcher in the Rye* (1951), for instance, is structured as a kōan meditation on the question, "Where do the ducks in Central Park go in the winter?" No answer is given, of course, and the resolution of the kōan lies in the lessons in compassion that the main character has learned by the end of the book.

In many cases, the appropriation of Buddhist ideas has led to what might be called "extrapolated Buddhism," in which Buddhist themes are taken out of their original framework and extrapolated to radically different contexts. An extreme example of this tendency is the way Catholic contemplatives have adopted Zen teachings and techniques to aid them in the search for God. Pioneers in this process were Father Hugo Enomiya-Lassalle (1898–1990), a German Jesuit missionary to Japan, and Thomas Merton (1915–1968), an American Trappist monk. Father Lassalle underwent kōan training, became recognized as a master in 1978, and later returned to Europe, where he led Zen retreats drawing kōans from the Bible. Awakening, he taught, was a culturally neutral experience that could be interpreted in terms of any worldview. Thus, for a Christian, it could lead one "along the line that ends in the vision of God." Another extreme in extrapolated Buddhism is found in commercial advertisements exploiting Buddhist themes, such as saṁsāra to sell perfume, and nirvāṇa to sell everything from Caribbean cruises to grapefruit juice.

At present, though, the eclectic approach to Buddhism is most widely embodied by so-called "nightstand Buddhists": people who, without identifying themselves as Buddhist, keep a book or two of Buddhist teachings on their nightstands or participate in Buddhist retreats, looking for Buddhist answers to their spiritual questions, Buddhist or not. This sort of eclecticism, of course, is nothing new in the Buddhist tradition. We have seen it in every part of Asia that the Buddhist religions have called home. What is unique to the West is the way the science of humanity is used to extol eclectics as more true to the Buddhist spirit than those who are single-mindedly committed to a particular Buddhist tradition.

Two types of arguments are generally cited to support this position. The first, drawing on history, cites the way people throughout Asia have adapted Buddhism to suit their home cultures by mixing it with local elements (although this point is commonly phrased to give the impression that Buddhism is what did the adapting). This precedent is then said to justify Western efforts of a similar sort. The second sort of argument, drawing on the psychology of religion, goes deeper, saying that eclecticism is truer to the original and central experience of the religion than are the teachings that have grown up around it. Thus Stephen Batchelor's *Buddhism without Beliefs* (1997), reviving the cult of heroic agnosticism, argues that an agnostic attitude toward issues such as karma and rebirth is closer to the Buddha's original "existential, therapeutic, and liberating agnosticism" than is belief in the Buddha's recorded teachings on those subjects. The ideal agnostic Buddhist should reject any consolation that might be gained from traditional teachings, and should look instead to such sciences as astrophysics, evolutionary biology, and neuroscience for answers to questions on the source and aims of life. Other writers have offered different arguments for the superiority of eclecticism. Given the legacy of the Enlightenment in Western culture, more are likely to appear.

12.2.3 The Crisis of Cultural Relativism

Closely related to the issue of eclecticism is that of cultural relativism. The eighteenth-century Enlightenment advanced the argument that reason and empiricism offered the only absolute truths, whereas the truths of religion were culturally relative. Although this argument did not convince everyone in the West, it did create a cultural crisis in terms of how the breach between reason and religion could best be healed. Some early Buddhologists indicated their feelings on the matter by referring to the Buddha's Awakening as his "enlightenment." In the late nineteenth century, a number of writers, including Sir Edwin Arnold in his poem *The Light of Asia* (1879), explicitly advanced the case that Buddhism—with its tolerance, its rejection of blind faith, and its invitation for all to test its doctrines in the light of experience—was much better suited than Christianity to heal the breach. The spread of Western science and rationalism to the East meant that Eastern thinkers were confronted with the same problem, and many of them came to the same conclusion: Buddhism, when stripped of its cultural accretions, was the most scientific of all religions. In 1893, when Buddhist reverse missionaries came to America to participate in the first World's Parliament of Religions, this was the central theme of their message, and it remained a strong theme in the writings of Buddhist polemicists throughout the twentieth century. K. N. Jayatilleke, for instance, devoted books to the assertion that Buddhism was an early version of logical positivism; and his student, David Kalupahana, has been even more vocal in attempting to prove that the Buddha and Nāgārjuna operated from the same presuppositions as Jamesian pragmatism. A more modern version of the same theme animates the writings of Fritjof Capra and Gary Zukav, who see parallels between the discoveries of quantum mechanics on the one hand and the insights of Madhyamaka and Zen on the other. These parallels, they claim, prove that the breach between scientific method and religious inspiration has been healed.

For many Westerners in the twentieth century, however, this theme has seemed irrelevant at best, because the work of Nietzsche, Freud, and their contemporaries at the turn of the century used reason and empirical findings to question whether reason and empiricism themselves were psychologically and culturally relative. What human beings think they perceive and what they regard as reasonable, these thinkers argued, is shaped by their psychological and cultural background; thus any abstractions based on reason and perception must be culturally relative as well. Westerners who accepted these arguments found themselves faced with the question of how experience freed from the taint of cultural prejudices might be achieved. In the early part of the century, continental European philosophy—existentialism and phenomenology in particular—grappled with this issue; by midcentury, Gestalt psychotherapy was experimenting with methods to bring the mind back to a pure state of cognition, free from the inhibitions of social and psychological structures. Meanwhile, Asian Buddhists who were aware of these trends had begun proselytizing in the West, presenting Buddhist meditation as an alternative route in the search for an awareness untainted by culture.

In 1905, Shaku Sōen (see Section 10.8), the New Rinzai delegate to the World's Parliament of Religions, had been invited to return to America to teach Zen. The visit resulted in three of his closest disciples' coming to America. One, Nyogen Senzaki, founded Zen groups from the 1920s to the 1950s on the West Coast. The second, Sokei-an, founded a Zen group in New York City in 1930 (the Buddhist Society of America, which became the First Zen Institute of America). The third, D. T. Suzuki (see Section 10.8), became—through his writings and personal influence—the primary interpreter of Zen to the West during his lifetime. His influence is felt to the present day. Suzuki's writings on Zen fell into two contradictory categories. One insisted that Zen could not be properly understood or practiced outside of the Buddhist context. The other maintained that the essence of Zen was transcultural or, as he put it, that "Zen is the ultimate fact of all philosophy—that final psychic fact that takes place when religious consciousness is heightened to extremity. Whether it comes to pass in Buddhists, in Christians, or in philosophers, it is in the last analysis incidental to Zen." The essence of Zen, in this light, lies in an aesthetic and spiritual realization of the beauty and perfection innate in each fleeting moment, no matter how ordinary that moment may seem to common perception.

This second category of Suzuki's writings was by far the more influential. His separation of Zen from Zen Buddhism gave rise to the impression that Zen might hold the answer to the search for pure, unfettered experience. From this it followed that Zen's connections with aspects of Buddhist doctrine problematic to the modern, relativistic Western mind—such as the teachings on karma and rebirth, the seeming nihilism of nirvāṇa, and the role of ethics on the path—were simply cultural baggage that could be dispensed with at will. This opened the Buddhist fold to a group of thinkers and artists who felt little or no allegiance toward the Buddhist tradition per se. At the same time, Suzuki's portrayal of meditation as the realization of the beauty to be found in the midst of the ordinary has had an overwhelming influence on how meditation has been taught in the West—an influence that has extended not only to Rinzai Zen, but also to Sōtō, Sŏn, Thiền, Dzogchen, and even Theravādin vipassanā.

In the 1960s, Thomas Kuhn's landmark book *The Structure of Scientific Revolutions* (1962) furthered the crisis of cultural relativism by advancing the thesis that even the physical sciences are not purely empirical, but are shaped by intellectual presuppositions, called paradigms, that determine how empirical data are selected and ignored. At the same time, the rise of the drug culture exposed large numbers of Westerners to aspects of expanded consciousness and intensified perception that went beyond standard paradigms in psychology and logic, and that had obvious parallels with Buddhist and Hindu teachings on the nature of the mind. These were among the main factors leading to an explosion of interest in the possibility of unconditioned experience to be found within the mind, and two Asian Buddhist teachers came to America in time to direct part of the force of this explosion into the practice of Buddhist meditation.

One of these teachers was Shunryu Suzuki-roshi (not to be confused with D. T. Suzuki), a priest of the Sōtō Zen tradition who founded the San Francisco Zen Center in the early 1960s. His teachings made it clear to his students that many of the formalities of Sōtō practice were not mere cultural baggage, but had an intrinsic relationship to the attainment of what he called Big Mind. Suzuki-roshi's concept of Big Mind—as explained in his book *Zen Mind, Beginner's Mind* (1970)—referred to the innate oneness of consciousness from which all beings are born and to which all return after death. The purpose of meditation, he said, was to realize the perspective of Big Mind in all one's activities and perceptions so as to be able to maintain one's composure in the midst of change and to be open to the innate perfection of each moment as it passed. The image he used to illustrate this concept was Yosemite Falls. The drops of water leave the oneness of the river as they fall over the rock ledge, only to rejoin that oneness at the bottom of the cliff; Zen enables one to remain upright through the interval of separation and fall. Thus the freedom offered by Zen was one to be found within the world, and not by escaping it. Although Suzuki-roshi insisted that the insights of Zen were radically different from those induced by psychedelic drugs, some Americans could see in his depiction of meditation a safe, disciplined method for stabilizing mental states that they had already encountered in their exposure to psychedelic substances.

Although he stressed the necessity of the formalities of Zen practice, Suzuki-roshi declined to establish an ethical code for his students, on the rationale that ethics were relative to culture. Such a code, he said, would have to be developed gradually over time through trial and error, as Western practitioners applied the perspective of Big Mind to the affairs of their daily life. Again, even though Suzuki-roshi insisted that Americans might end up needing more rules than the Japanese, his general ethical relativism had an obvious appeal to the generation that had pushed through a revolution in American sexual mores.

The other teacher who had a large impact on the spread of Buddhism at this time, Chögyam Trungpa, took an even more radical approach to the question of ethics. Trained in the Tibetan Ri-med (Unrestricted) movement (see Section 11.4), Trungpa viewed ethical norms as part of the "bureaucracy of the ego" that meditation was intended to overthrow. As was the case with both Suzukis, he taught that the purpose of meditation was to attain intensified perception in this life, freed from the strictures of the ordinary mind, although—following his Dzogchen training—he viewed this level of perception as a realization of the light innate in all things. His proposed method of attaining this free mode of perception was a typically Tibetan emphasis on the centrality of the teacher–student relationship, expressed in the terminology of Gestalt psychotherapy. The ideal relationship was of a "raw, naked" variety, in which the teacher called into question all of the student's ego defenses and ruthlessly stripped them away so as to leave only the pure nature of the mind. Trungpa's writings—in particular, the book *Cutting through Spiritual Materialism* (1973)—were quite popular, and his frank rejection of ethical norms notorious. In addition to founding the Naropa Institute, a center for Buddhist studies in Boulder, Colorado, he established a network of meditation groups and retreat centers throughout the United States and Canada.

The general mood of cultural relativism affected even the conservative Theravādin meditation methods that began appearing in the West in the 1970s. In 1975 a group of Americans—including Joseph Goldstein, Sharon Salzberg, and Jack Kornfield—who had studied the Mahasi Sayadaw method of vipassanā meditation in Asia (see Section 7.5), established the Insight Meditation Society in central Massachusetts. Through their work, this society has become the major lay center for the practice of vipassanā in the West. Although they have enforced the Five Precepts (see Section 3.3.5) during their retreats, not until the early 1990s did the group formally adopt a code of conduct for its teachers outside of the retreat context. Based on the Five Precepts, the code reflected their desire to make the precepts more appropriate to "this particular time in history and in this specific cultural setting." The precept against use of intoxicants, for example, was changed to forbid only the misuse of intoxicants. The precept against illicit sexuality was changed to forbid sexual exploitation, which in practical terms meant that a teacher should observe a three-month moratorium after a retreat before entering into a sexual relationship with a former student. After some controversy over whether the precept against killing would cover abortion and the killing of insect pests, the group agreed to leave these particular issues unsettled for the time being.

Meanwhile, in 1977, Sumedho Bhikkhu, an American trained in the Thai forest tradition (see Section 7.5.2), was invited to establish a Theravādin monastery in England. His chief monastery, Amaravati, now has three branches in other parts of England, as well as affiliates in Switzerland, Italy, Australia, New Zealand, and North America. Although the monks and nuns at these monasteries have made only slight adjustments to their precepts, eclecticism and cultural relativism play a role in the Dharma they teach. The purpose of religious practice, according to Venerable Sumedho, is to realize the ultimate reality found by transcending one's cultural conditioning. He calls the Buddhist approach to this process the practice of being, rather than trying to become, enlightened. It involves maintaining a reflective attitude toward the way events arise and cease in the body and mind in the present, and opening to the space of peaceful emptiness that contains their arising and ceasing. He adds, however, that contemplative traditions in all major religions can lead to the same state. Thus one's choice of a religious path is a matter of personal preference, as no one religion can claim to possess the only true way. What matters most is trust in the conventions of one's chosen tradition and full devotion to a life of wisdom. In saying this, he breaks from the traditional Theravāda assertion that nirvāṇa is unlike the goals of other religions, and that the Noble Eightfold Path is the only way there.

Suzuki-roshi died in 1971, and Chögyam Trungpa in 1987. Both had appointed American Dharma heirs shortly before their deaths; both heirs quickly became involved in sex scandals and were eventually removed from their appointments by their respective organizations. Soon similar scandals in other Zen, Sŏn, and Tibetan centers, involving Asian as well as American teachers, brought home that these were not isolated instances but part of a general pattern: the unsettled questions of whether a person officially recognized as Awakened is subject to ethical norms; whether "officially recognized" Awakening is a valid institution; and whether the authority in a practice group is to be invested in the teacher or in the group as a whole. The role that cultural relativism had played in bringing these groups into existence made it difficult to call upon any fixed ethical norms to resolve these questions. Some members maintained that such norms are part of the puritanical tradition that American Buddhists should abandon, whereas others pointed out the central role that ethics has played in Buddhism from its earliest days. Thus, the crisis of cultural relativism that brought many to the practice of Buddhist meditation in the first place has now become a crisis within Western Buddhism itself.

12.2.4 Calls for Reform

Like their Enlightenment forebears, Western Buddhists have combined their cultural relativism with a fairly absolutist program for institutional reform. The Enlightenment's belief that absolute truths could be found through the social sciences has long given Westerners a strong sense that not only their own culture, but also the cultures of other people, should bend to the findings and hypotheses of these disciplines. As Westerners began entering the Buddhist fold, this attitude led them quickly to call for reforms, subjecting what they viewed as Buddhism's relative truths to the absolute truths of their vision of comparative religion, history, psychology, and other social sciences.

This Western tendency has been present since the nineteenth century. Henry Steel Olcott and Helena Blavatsky, the American and Russian founders of the Theosophical Society, sailed to Sri Lanka in 1880 and amid much publicity became the first Westerners to take refuge in the Triple Gem (see Section 7.4.1). They quickly assumed the role of Buddhist leaders, recommending such extensive reforms to remove what they viewed as superstitious elements in Sri Lankan Buddhism that most of their newfound following eventually left them. Other Western reformers took the anticlericism they had inherited from the Enlightenment and focused it on Buddhist monks. In the 1920s, Caroline A. F. Rhys Davids, president of the Pali Text Society, argued that all great religions must be life-affirming. The life-negating ideas she saw in early Buddhist texts—such as nirvāṇa and not-self—were thus obviously monkish inventions that could not possibly have come from such a great religious figure as the Buddha. As a result, she said, the job of a Western Buddhologist was to ferret out the few remaining glimmerings of the original teachings and to expose all life-negating elements as later interpolations. Throughout the first half of the twentieth century, Westerners who went to Asia in search of Buddhist truths—including Alexandra David-Neel, Dennis Lingwood (Saṅgharakshita), and Ernst Hoffman (Lama Anagarika

Govinda)—lectured their Asian hosts on how monasticism had perverted the Buddha's doctrines. Although a number of Westerners, beginning in 1900, went to Asia for ordination, not until the 1950s did any of them submit to long-term training under an Asian Buddhist master on Asian terms. Prior to that, all Western bhikṣus had either returned to the West soon after ordination or had established their own centers in Asia where they could study and practice the Dharma as they saw fit, thus effecting their own personal reforms in the tradition.

Since the establishment of Buddhist centers in the West in the latter half of the twentieth century, the clamor for reform has become more widespread and intense. Some of the proposed reforms simply combine various Buddhist traditions, a combination now possible because, for the first time since Buddhism left India, all surviving Buddhist schools speak a common language. Whether or not this eclecticism becomes institutionalized, it is already a fact of life, with Theravādin vipassanā teachers studying Dzogchen, Zen priests studying the Pali Canon, Tibetan lamas quoting Zen masters in their talks, and practicing Buddhists of all schools reading books by Buddhist masters of every tradition available. Some books have argued that this fact of life should become the norm. Joseph Goldstein's *One Dharma* (2002), for instance, maintains that a pragmatic borrowing from many Dharma paths, rather than an exclusive attachment to a single one, is the true expression of the teaching central to all Buddhist traditions: liberation through nonclinging.

Other de facto reforms have integrated Western values into Buddhist practice. These include the increasing role played by women in running Buddhist organizations and by laity in teaching and practicing meditation. These reforms, however, are not without precedent in the Asian traditions (see Sections 10.5.2 and 10.10). A more distinctly Western reform is the development of "engaged Buddhism," which calls on Buddhist practitioners to prove the worth of their practice in this-worldly terms by engaging in social and environmental reform. Although many of the pioneers of engaged Buddhism, such as Thích Nhất Hạnh and Sulak Sivaraksa, are Asian, their inspiration seems to have come from the Christian social activists of the nineteenth century. Members of the movement, in an effort to give it more specifically Buddhist roots, have identified the doctrine of dependent co-arising with the Romantic ideal of interconnectedness. Because interconnectedness implies mutual responsibilities and duties, they argue, the true test of Buddhist practice lies in its ability to "get off the cushion" and work for social and economic policies that respect the planet as a whole.

A deeper reform, though, has gone virtually unnoticed: the redefinition of the Third Refuge, the Sangha, to include all people who practice Buddhist meditation, regardless of whether they regard themselves as Buddhist or not. This concept was introduced in the 1950s by Saṅgharakshita, was fostered in the following decades in particular by Chögyam Trungpa and Thích Nhất Hạnh (see Section 9.10), and is now accepted by many Western Buddhists of all schools. Thus the popular notion of Sangha in the West now covers an area wider than that of even the classical notion of pariṣad (see Section 2.4), including in the Third Refuge people who have not taken refuge themselves. This has also changed the notion of the kind of refuge one might expect from the Triple Gem—in this case, the psychological support offered by those sympathetic to one's chosen path.

It is too early to tell whether these reforms will become distinctive, long-term features of Western Buddhism or are simply part of a passing phase. But a number of writers have advanced the case that the reforms should become normative—not only for Western Buddhism, but for Asian Buddhism as well. The most comprehensive and systematic argument for this case has been presented by a student of Chögyam Trungpa, Rita Gross, in her book *Buddhism After Patriarchy* (1993). Following the classical pattern of Enlightenment scholarship, Gross's absolute values are abstractions drawn from the study of history, psychology, and comparative religion. She argues that Buddhism, like all other religions, must accept that it is a system of myths with no absolute claims to scientific or historical truth. It should also abandon as inappropriate any concepts of dualistic, other-worldly freedom—such as a nirvāṇa beyond this world—and reject as irrelevant such questions as rebirth and the individual's preparation for death. Instead, it should focus on its sufficient role: mandating gender equality and providing a psychological grounding of wholeness, balance, tranquility, and deep peace so that one may (1) find the freedom within the world by developing composure amid change, (2) communicate with and provide comfort for other people, and (3) develop a sense of care and appreciation for the Earth. Any Buddhist doctrines, practices, or institutions that de-emphasize this role for the sake of other goals, she argues, are holdovers from a patriarchal mind-set that should be dropped from the tradition altogether.

Another reformer using social science paradigms to rethink the Buddhist path is Jack Kornfield. In his book *A Path with Heart* (1993), he combines his background in meditation and humanistic psychology (particularly the work of Maslow) with his extensive reading in comparative religion to present a picture of the Buddhist path that transcends the limitations he claims are inherent in all practice lineages. Spiritual practice, he says, should center on issues of relationship and personal integration. Many would-be meditators are so wounded psychologically by modern society, however, that meditation alone cannot deal effectively with these issues in their lives. Thus they might benefit by combining humanistic psychotherapy with their meditation. This does not mean that one gets one's psychological house in order and then strikes out for nirvāṇa. Rather, one should use psychotherapy step-by-step along one's way to heal the mental wounds uncovered in meditation and to integrate newfound insights into one's life. Although Kornfield warns against becoming obsessed with goals in the practice, he concludes his discussion with a personality profile of the type of maturity that spiritual practice should produce: a sense of the sacred that is both integrated and personal; an embracing of opposites; an attitude of nonidealism, kindness, immediacy, questioning, flexibility, and ordinariness; and the ability to express these qualities in the entire range of one's relationships—to one's family, one's sexuality, the community, the environment, politics, money—every being and action. Spiritual practice begins and culminates, he claims, in the simple presence of intimacy. The ultimate test of the success of one's practice should be the ability to love well, live fully, and let go.

Other reformers limit themselves more to institutional restructuring. For instance, there are attempts to revive the Tibetan and Theravādin Bhikṣuṇī Sanghas and to design new formats for teaching and practicing meditation so that lay people may practice without sacrificing their families and careers. However, there is wide disagreement among reformers as to what in the Buddhist tradition is dispensable and what needs to be retained. Even the doctrine of rebirth, one of the few common denominators among the various Asian traditions, is controversial in Western Buddhist circles. Commentators writing on the Western Buddhist movement as a whole, when trying to define its unifying thread, are often reduced to saying that "the essence of Buddhism is an inexpressible living force" or "the Zen that tries to define itself isn't true Zen." This suggests that the frequent attempts to define Western Buddhism in neat formulae are misguided. Not only is it too early to tell what directions Western Buddhism will take, it's also important to remember that those directions will have to remain plural if Buddhism is to continue to speak to the diversity of the West.

12.3 THE VARIETIES OF BUDDHISM IN NORTH AMERICA

Although trends from the Enlightenment have played a major role in shaping Western Buddhism, Western Buddhism is only one part of Buddhism in the West. This is an important distinction. Many Buddhists practicing in the West closely follow the precedents established by their Asian traditions, either ignorant of Enlightenment values or consciously rejecting them. Thus to gain an overall perspective of Buddhism in the West, we must fit their practices, together with those of Western Buddhists, into a larger landscape.

Scholars have proposed a variety of typologies to chart this landscape. One focuses on ethnic identity—Asian versus Western Buddhism. Another focuses on modes of transmission: import Buddhism (which came West because Westerners were interested in it); export Buddhism (whose transmission to the West was fueled by a missionary impulse in Asia); and baggage Buddhism (brought by Asian immigrants who came to the West for nonreligious motives). These typologies, however, are too simple to take in the actual complexities of the landscape, and in some cases actually obscure important features. For instance, many Asian Americans find themselves attracted more to "Western" forms of Buddhism than to the Buddhism of their parents. Western Zen, often classed as import Buddhism, actually owes its existence to many individual Asian monks who came to America and worked hard in obscurity before Zen was "discovered" in the 1950s. Thus a more comprehensive map requires approaching the landscape from a variety of angles, covering at least three sets of variables: the nature of the parent traditions in Asia; the mode of transmission; and the types of Western religion onto which the Asian traditions have been grafted and have begun to take root.

Here we will focus primarily on Buddhism in North America, as it constitutes Buddhism's most variegated landscape in the West. And we will present the different sets of variables as a series of questions, because the main interest in establishing these sets lies in the follow-up questions concerning the implications of each variable for survival.

12.3.1 Parent Traditions

The first sets of questions concern the parent traditions. North America is now home to all the major divisions of Buddhism currently extant in Asia, along with many of the minor ones. Despite the variety of these traditions, they can be sorted along two spectrums.

The first spectrum runs from traditions centered on monastics to those centered on lay people. Because monastic traditions have never been strong in North America, monastic Buddhist traditions face an immediate issue: how much they will have to alter their traditions in order to survive in this culture. Theravādins and Tibetan groups have so far been very conservative in instituting changes. Others have been more experimental. For instance, Zen Mountain Monastery in upstate New York has instituted married monastics, and is working out their impact on recruitment and community discipline. The monastery is also following the example of Christian monasteries by operating businesses to supplement its income.

Lay-centered organizations face another problem: how to formulate a code of ethics and ensure capable leaders to carry on the tradition when the current generation dies out. For lay Zen groups, this means interpreting the meaning of transmission: Does passing the traditional kōan program guarantee the ability to train students in an American context? Vipassanā groups, which have broken off from their parent monastic traditions, face a different question: how to design programs and set standards for turning meditators into meditation retreat leaders.

The second spectrum for sorting parent traditions runs from faith-centered teachings to meditation-centered teachings. In North America, meditation-centered teachings tend to attract a clientele from a higher income bracket: those with the time and disposable income to devote to intensive retreats. These groups also tend to espouse a white culture—which they themselves call, with chagrin, the "upper-middle way"—in which people of color do not feel at home. Some of these centers, most notably Spirit Rock, founded by Jack Kornfield, have begun taking steps toward diversification, and many voices have called for more. Traditions that are more faith-centered or mix faith with meditation practices tend to attract followers from a larger variety of income brackets and ethnic groups. Sōka Gakkai, for instance, is the only Buddhist tradition that has attracted a large number of African Americans and Hispanics.

Groups of both sorts in this second spectrum face unique problems in training and attracting the children of their members. Faith-based groups have to present their faith as reasonable in a modern context. Meditation-centered groups have to devise programs for meeting children's needs that cannot be addressed by meditation, and for accommodating the noise and energy level that children inevitably bring to centers originally designed for quiet and calm. They also must try to balance the desire of many meditating parents not to "impose" their religion on their children, with the children's need for firm values to hold to.

12.3.2 Modes of Transmission

The prime question to ask about the mode of a Buddhist tradition's transmission to America is whether it came through the organized efforts of an institution in Asia. If it did, the immediate questions concern how much the parent organization's control is compatible with the survival of the movement in America.

A follow-up question is whether the organization has focused its attention primarily on Asian immigrants and their children. If so, the immediate question is whether the parent organization is traditional or modern in its emphasis.

The primary traditional organization in this category is the Jōdo-shin-shū sect, which founded the Buddhist Churches of America (BCA) prior to World War I. Of all the major Asian American Buddhist groups, it has the longest track record in facing the issues encountered by every immigrant group in America: how to negotiate the gap presented by the second generation. First-generation immigrants tend to view their religion as a means for maintaining contact with their home culture. Their children, however, tend to regard their inherited religion as problematic when trying to combine their American identity with the values taught by their parents. A typical pattern, repeated with every wave of immigration to North America, is that second-generation immigrants tend to reject their parent's cultural values, whereas third-generation immigrants often try to recover what their parents rejected. The history of the BCA, however, has been complicated by several factors, including the mass deportation of its members to prison camps during World War II. Also, the drive to attract members of the younger generation, and to recruit non-Japanese Americans, has run against the requirement—imposed from Japan—that all its ministers learn Japanese and spend many years training there.

Three modern Asian Buddhist movements have proselytized among Asian Americans. Fo-kuang Shan and the Buddhist Compassion Relief Love and Mercy Foundation (see Section 8.9) have concentrated on the Chinese American community; Dhammakāya, on Thai Americans. Their success so far has relied on the syntheses they have forged in Asia between Western and Asian values. These syntheses have attracted educated immigrants repelled by what they regard as superstitious elements in their traditional heritages. The question is whether they will provide the right mix to attract second-generation immigrants and non-Asian Americans.

Of the groups that have focused organized efforts on attracting non-Asian converts, four stand out: Sōka Gakkai, the Tibetan lineages, Thích Nhất Hạnh's organization, and the Goenka-U Ba Khin vipassanā movement. All four are spearheaded by charismatic leaders and will soon face the issues that any such movement must face when its leaders pass away: Should the leader's message remain unaltered, or should the organization be allowed to change? The Goenka movement has already made steps in the first direction. All its retreats are taught by video tapes of its leader; facilitators play a carefully scripted role. Sōka Gakkai has headed cautiously in the other direction. Since the split with the Nichiren priesthood in 1991, Sōka Gakkai America has been allowed to take on a somewhat more active role in shaping its future.

The Tibetan groups already have an established pattern for passing on charisma from one generation to the next. Their unique issue lies in having come to America with a dual purpose: religious and political. They have actively sought widespread support for Tibetan independence and the monasteries they have established in India, which has led them to cast their teachings in an extremely accessible form. However, they rarely encourage Western followers to ordain, and only a few of the recognized Western tülkus are in line for leadership roles. Whether this policy will change depends on the political fate of Tibet.

As for Buddhist traditions that have come to America without organized proselytizing from Asia, they fall into two main categories: immigrant Buddhism and convert Buddhism. Immigrant Buddhism is what Asian immigrants have brought along with them as they come to America for nonreligious purposes: work, education, or political asylum. The most prominent groups in this category are the more than 150 loosely organized Theravādin temples serving Southeast Asian immigrants and refugees that have appeared throughout the United States and Canada since restrictions on Asian immigration were lifted in the 1960s. Convert Buddhism is what has resulted as individuals or small groups of Asians come to America to teach Buddhism, or individual Americans have gone to Asia and brought Buddhism back on their return. Most Zen and Sŏn groups, practitioners of the Mahasi Sayadaw method of vipassanā, and Western monastics trained in the Thai forest tradition fall into this category.

Both categories, as they enter their second generation, face the same basic issue: the extent to which they will want to maintain their independence or will feel the need to form regional or national organizations to establish standards and prevent fragmentation. For the Theravādin immigrant temples, this problem is compounded by the second-generation issues encountered by all immigrant groups. For the convert groups, many of which have already begun Westernizing their teachings and practices in the first generation, the question for the second generation is how they will handle the fragmentation that has already appeared among three subgroups: those who are content with the amount of Westernization already introduced, those who want more, and those who feel it has gone too far. An example of a community trying to forge a tight organization is the San Francisco Zen Center, which as a result of the scandals following Suzuki-roshi's death (see Section 12.2.3) has established a clear-cut system of community governance and is currently standardizing its founding teacher's legacy in print. On the less standardized end of the spectrum is the White Plum lineage established by Maezumi Roshi (1931–1995), who founded the Zen Center of Los Angeles in 1967. His immediate students run the gamut from Charlotte Joko Beck, who has renounced what she regards as Zen's patriarchal trappings, and Bernard Tetsugen Glassman, who has established an inner-city bakery and taken up clown-training as an extension of Zen, to John Daido Loori, who has founded a monastery more conservative than that of his teacher. The second generation of the lineage already includes a rabbi and a Jesuit priest.

As long as Buddhism remains popular, and the American religious landscape undergoes no major changes, there will be room in American Buddhism both for standardized organizations and for independent groups on the fringe. How each mode will affect the practice of the Dharma, however, only time will tell.

12.3.3 Grafting onto American Roots

Mainstream religion in America falls into certain discernible modes. A few of the more prominent ones are *liberalism* (which interprets religious traditions in light of Enlightenment and Romantic principles), *fundamentalism, social activism, pietism* (religion as the cultivation of feelings rather than adherence to specific beliefs), *nature mysticism, occultism, cultural religion* (the cults surrounding media heroes and heroines), *the religion of self-culture* (the various self-improvement and New Age movements descended from Transcendentalism), and *civic religion* (the cult surrounding the spiritual mission of the nation and its government in world history). More on the fringe of the American landscape are *ethnic religions, ecstatic religions*, and *monasticism*. Buddhism is already established in the ethnic and monastic modes, although its uncloistered monasticism is novel in America. The test of whether Buddhism will become a mainstream American religion will be the ability of American Buddhists to express their religion within the established mainstream modes.

Already they have made great strides in this direction. We have noted in Section 12.2.1 the existence of liberal Buddhism, as influenced by theories in the psychology of religion. The work of the Buddhist Peace Fellowship, one of the few truly ecumenical American Buddhist organizations, is an example of Buddhist social activism. The growing literature on mettā (the cultivation of loving-kindness) resonates with American pietism. American Buddhists advocating Deep Ecology espouse nature mysticism; Tantra has been grafted onto American occultism; a handful of Buddhist teachers, such as the Dalai Lama and Thích Nhất Hạnh, have become cultural heroes; and vipassanā is an important component in the religion of self-culture.

However, there are areas where Buddhism has not established roots. As of yet, there is no American Buddhist fundamentalism. More importantly, Buddhism has largely been excluded from civic religion. Most Buddhist groups have shown little interest in this area, whereas those who have shown strong interest are either ignored or rebuffed. Congressional candidates from both major U.S. political parties have visited ethnic Buddhist temples in search of the ethnic vote, which often involves showing furtive respect to Buddha images. But during the 1996 U.S. presidential campaign, Fo-kuang Shan's donations to the Democratic Party sparked a racist reaction and a congressional investigation. In 2002, when the Gelug leader, Lama Zopa, suggested that the White House invite Tibetan practitioners to chant in support of the war on terrorism and economic recovery, the suggestion was ignored. A small Buddhist meditation group meets in the Pentagon, but conservative Christian groups using the same room feel compelled to exorcise any traces of the meditation after the Buddhists have left.

Historically, Buddhism's ties with governments in Asia have been a mixed blessing, and American Buddhists may decide to avoid civic religion entirely. However, the process of grafting their religion onto other American roots is sure to create issues they cannot avoid. As the BCA has discovered, acculturation is an unending process. When they first organized, they tried to fit in with the American mainstream by calling their organizations "churches" and adopting a Protestant style of worship on Sunday morning, with black-robed ministers and hymns set to Western melodies. These adaptations are now, for non-Japanese Americans, among the least attractive features of the organization. Succeeding generations in the BCA have found that they must keep discovering new ways to keep abreast of changing American religious trends. Such changes are sure to continue into the future, and all Buddhist groups will have to formulate their responses. So far, a great deal of energy and creativity have been devoted across the board to making the Dharma accessible to Americans. The question then becomes: When does American Buddhism become so American that it ceases being Buddhist?

Buddhists in Asia have had to face a similar question throughout the history of the tradition. And usually, independently minded individuals, rather than organizations, have spearheaded a return to the roots of the tradition. They have done so in three ways: by returning to the parent land(s), by turning to ancient texts, and by going into the wilderness. At present, there are still strong traditions in Asia to which American Buddhists can turn for inspiration, and ancient Buddhist texts are increasingly available in the West. There is no pre-existing American tradition of wandering religious mendicants onto which wilderness Buddhism can graft, however, and so far only a few small groups have made efforts to plant Buddhism in the wilderness. But it would seem that a homegrown tradition of wilderness Buddhism could perform a crucial role in keeping the Buddhism in American Buddhism alive.

It's also likely that individuals, rather than organizations, will play an important role in keeping the American side of Buddhism creative. As we have seen in earlier chapters, Buddhist religions have rarely demanded sole allegiance from their followers. This attitude sits well with the eclecticism we have noticed in Enlightenment and Romantic views on religion, and studies have shown that it is characteristic of Buddhists in America across the board. The vast majority of them do not identify solely with a particular organization, feeling quite free to adopt beliefs and practices from a wide range of Buddhist and non-Buddhist sources. This, in fact, may be Buddhism's most obvious fit into to the current American religious scene, as it harmonizes with the eclectic attitudes toward religious identity that have developed since the 1960s. These attitudes make it easy for a Thai engineer to cross the racial divide by attending a course at a predominantly white vipassanā center, for a vipassanā teacher with breast cancer to cross the cultural divide by invoking the protection of Kuan-yin, or for a former Zen monk to cross the sectarian divide by teaching Biblical stories as kōans to ministers and rabbis. This sort of boundary-crossing plays havoc with the neat typologies that scholars like to draw, but it lies at the heart of how Buddhism has entered mainstream American culture. In all likelihood, it will also characterize Buddhism's survival in America: less as organizations concerned with survival than as sets of practices and teachings that continue to meet people's needs. Some people will reformulate Buddhism to meet their pre-existing conceptions of their needs, just as others will look to pre-existing Buddhist teachings to articulate what their needs are. The combination of the two will determine the directions in which Buddhist religions develop in America.

An Overview of the Three Major Canons

A. The Pali Canon: The *Tipiṭaka* ("Three Baskets")

   I. *Vinaya-piṭaka* ("Basket of Discipline")

      1. *Sutta-vibhaṅga* ("Analysis of the Text")—the rules of the Pāṭimokkha codes with explanations and commentary.

         a. *Mahāvibhaṅga* ("Great Analysis")—the 227 rules for monks.

         b. *Bhikkhuṇīvibhaṅga* ("Nuns' Analysis")—the 311 rules for nuns.

      2. *Khandhaka* ("Groupings")

         a. *Mahāvagga* ("Great Chapter")—rules for ordination, Observance Day, Rains Retreat, clothing, food, medicine, and procedures of the Sangha.

         b. *Cullavagga* ("Lesser Chapter")—judicial procedures, miscellaneous rules, ordination and instruction of nuns, history of the First and Second Councils.

      3. *Parivāra* ("Appendix")—summaries and classifications of the rules. This is a late supplement.

   II. *Sutta-piṭaka* ("Basket of Discourses")

      1. *Dīgha-nikāya* ("Collection of Long Discourses")—34 Suttas.

      2. *Majjhima-nikāya* ("Collection of Medium Discourses")—152 Suttas.

      3. *Saṁyutta-nikāya* ("Collection of Connected Discourses")—56 groups of Suttas.

4. *Aṅguttara-nikāya* ("Collection of Item-more Discourses")—more than 2,300 Suttas grouped by the number of factors in their topics.
5. *Khuddaka-nikāya* ("Collection of Little Texts")
    a. *Khuddaka-pāṭha* ("Little Readings")—a breviary.
    b. *Dhammapada* ("Verses on Dharma")—423 verses in 26 chapters.
    c. *Udāna* ("Exclamations")—80 exalted pronouncements of the Buddha, with circumstantial tales.
    d. *Itivuttaka* ("Thus-saids")—112 short Suttas.
    e. *Sutta-nipāta* ("Collection of Suttas")—short Suttas, mostly in verse.
    f. *Vimāna-vatthu* ("Tales of Heavenly Mansions")—gods tell the deeds that earned them celestial rebirths.
    g. *Peta-vatthu* ("Tales of Ghosts")—how various persons attained that unfortunate rebirth.
    h. *Thera-gāthā* ("Verses of the Elders")—stanzas attributed to 264 early monks.
    i. *Therī-gāthā* ("Verses of the Eldresses")—stanzas attributed to 73 early nuns.
    j. *Jātaka* ("Lives")—tales ostensibly reporting the former lives of the Buddha. The verses in each tale are supposed to have been uttered by the Buddha, and so are considered canonical; but the 547 tales themselves are extracanonical.
    k. *Niddesa* ("Exposition")—verbal notes to part of the *Sutta-nipāta*.
    l. *Paṭisambhidā-magga* ("The Path of Discrimination")—scholastic treatment of doctrinal topics.
    m. *Apadāna* ("Lessons")—the Buddha and the arhats describe how acts of merit under previous Buddhas set them on the path to Awakening.
    n. *Buddhavaṃsa* ("Lineage of the Buddhas")—lives of 24 previous Buddhas, of Śākyamuni, and of Maitreya, presented as being told by Śākyamuni.
    o. *Cariya-piṭaka* ("Basket of Conduct")—verse retellings of jātakas illustrating the Bodhisattva's practice of the perfections.

III. *Abhidhamma-piṭaka* ("Basket of Higher Dharma")
1. *Dhamma-saṅginī* ("Enumeration of Dharmas")
2. *Vibhaṅga* ("Analysis")—more on sets of dharmas.
3. *Dhātu-kathā* ("Discussion of Elements")—lists of physical and mental elements.
4. *Puggala-paññatti* ("Designation of Persons")—classifies types of individuals according to their spiritual traits and stages.
5. *Kathā-vatthu* ("Topics of Discussion")—arguments about theses in dispute among the early Mainstream schools.

6. *Yamaka* ("Pairs")—arranged in pairs of questions; deals with distinctions among basic sets of categories.
7. *Paṭṭhāna* ("Conditional Relations")—24 kinds of causal relation and their almost infinite permutations.

B. The Chinese Canon: The *Ta-ts'ang-ching* ("Great Scripture-Store")
The first printed edition, produced in Szechuan in 972–983 C.E., consisted of 1,076 texts in 480 cases. The standard modern edition is the *Taishō Shinshū Daizōkyō* (*Ta-ts'ang-ching* newly edited in the Taishō reign-period). Published in Tokyo, 1924–1929, it consists of 55 Western-style volumes containing 2,184 texts. A supplement consists of 45 volumes. The following analysis is of the Taishō edition.

I. *Āgama* Section, Vols. 1 and 2, 151 texts. Contains the Long, Medium, Mixed (Connected) and Item-more Āgamas (Nikāyas), plus some individual texts corresponding to parts of the Pali Khuddaka.
II. Story Section, Vols. 3 and 4, 68 texts. *Jātakas,* lives of various Buddhas, fables, and parables.
III. *Prajñā-pāramitā* Section, Vols. 5–8, 42 texts.
IV. *Saddharma-puṇḍarīka* Section, Vol. 9, 16 texts. Three complete versions of the *Lotus Sūtra,* plus some doctrinally cognate Sūtras.
V. *Avataṃsaka* Section, Vols. 9 and 10, 31 texts.
VI. *Ratnakūṭa* Section, Vols. 11–12, 64 texts. A set of 49 Mahāyāna Sūtras, some in more than one translation.
VII. *Mahāparinirvāṇa* Section, Vol. 12, 23 texts. The Mahāyāna account of Śākyamuni's last days and words.
VIII. Great Assembly Section, Vol. 13, 28 texts. A collection beginning with the Great Assembly Sūtra, which is itself a suite of Mahāyāna Sūtras.
IX. Sūtra Collection Section, Vols. 14–17, 423 texts. A miscellany of Sūtras, mostly Mahāyāna.
X. Tantra Section, Vols. 18–21, 572 texts. Vajrayāna Sūtras, Tantras, ritual manuals, and spells.
XI. Vinaya Section, Vols. 22–24, 86 texts. Vinayas of the Mahīśāsakas, Mahāsaṃghikas, Dharmaguptakas, Sarvāstivādins, and Mūla-sarvāstivādins. Also some texts on the Bodhisattva discipline.
XII. Commentaries on Sūtras, Vols. 24–26, 31 texts on Āgamas and on Mahāyāna Sūtras, by Indian authors.
XIII. Abhidharma Section, Vols. 26–29, 28 texts. Scholastic treatises of the Sarvāstivādins, Dharmaguptakas, and Sautrāntikas.
XIV. Madhyamaka Section, Vol. 30, 15 texts.
XV. Yogācāra Section, Vols. 30–31, 49 texts.
XVI. Collection of Treatises, Vol. 32, 65 texts. Works on logic, anthologies from the Sūtras, and treatises.
XVII. Commentaries on the Sūtras, Vols. 33–39, by Chinese authors.

XVIII. Commentaries on the Vinaya, Vol. 40, by Chinese authors.
XIX. Commentaries on the Śāstras (Treatises), Vols. 40–44, by Chinese authors.
XX. Chinese Sectarian Writings, Vols. 44–48.
XXI. History and Biography, Vols. 49–52, 95 texts.
XXII. Encyclopedias and Dictionaries, Vols. 53–54, 16 texts.
XXIII. Non-Buddhist Doctrines, Vol. 54, 8 texts. Sāṃkhya, Vaiśeṣika, Manichean, and Nestorian Christian writings.
XXIV. Catalogs, Vol. 55, 40 texts. Successive catalogs of the Canon beginning with that of Seng-yu published in 515 C.E.

C. The Tibetan Canon

I. *Bka'-'gyur* (*Kanjur;* "Translation of Buddha-word"). The number of volumes and order of sections differ slightly from edition to edition. The following is according to the Snar-thang (Narthang) version.
   1. *Vinaya,* 13 vols.
   2. *Prajñā-pāramitā,* 21 vols.
   3. *Avataṃsaka,* 6 vols.
   4. *Ratnakūṭa,* 6 vols. A set of 49 Mahāyāna Sūtras.
   5. *Sūtra,* 30 vols., 270 texts, almost entirely Mahāyāna.
   6. *Tantra,* 22 vols., over 300 texts.

II. *Bstan-'gyur* (*Tenjur;* "Translation of Teachings"). In the Peking edition, this consists of 224 volumes and 3,626 texts, divided into:
   1. *Stotras* (hymns of praise), 1 vol., 64 texts.
   2. *Commentaries on mantras,* 86 vols., 3,055 texts.
   3. *Commentaries on Sūtras,* 137 vols., 567 texts.
      a. *Prajñā-pāramitā* commentaries, 16 vols.
      b. *Madhyamaka* treatises, 17 vols.
      c. *Yogācāra* treatises, 29 vols.
      d. *Abhidharma,* 8 vols.
      e. Miscellaneous, 4 vols.
      f. *Vinaya* Commentaries, 16 vols.
      g. Tales and dramas, 4 vols.
      h. Technical treatises: logic (21 vols.), grammar (1 vol.), lexicography and poetics (1 vol.), medicine (5 vols.), chemistry and miscellany (1 vol.), supplement (old and recent translations, indices; 14 vols.).

Pronunciation Guide

As a pan-Asian religion, Buddhism has made use of the major languages of an entire continent. None of these languages is natively written in the Roman alphabet, but all can be transliterated into it. Each system of transliteration carries its own set of pronunciation difficulties. The following guidelines are intended simply to help the student overcome some of the more blatant hurdles to approximating correct pronunciation. They are not complete phonetic guidelines.

Sanskrit and Pali. A few basic rules for pronouncing words in these languages are as follows:

1. Marked vowels: A bar (called a macron) over a vowel makes it long, both in quality and in the length of time it is pronounced:

   ā as in "father"

   ī as in "machine"

   ū as in "rule"

2. Unmarked vowels:

   a as in "about"

   e as in "they"

   i as in "is"

o as in "go"

u as in "rhubarb"

3. Unmarked consonants are generally pronounced as they are in English, with a few exceptions:

   c as in "ancient"

   k unaspirated as in "skin"

   kh aspirated as in "backhand"

   ñ as the *ny* in "canyon"

   p unaspirated as in "spot"

   ph as in "upholstery"

   t unaspirated as in "stop"

   th aspirated as in "Thomas"

4. Double consonants—**kk, mm, nn, pp**—should be pronounced distinctly as double, like the *nn* in "unnecessary."

5. Retroflex dots under letters—such as **ṭ, ḍ, ṇ**—mean that those letters should be pronounced with the tip of the tongue curled back up into the middle of the mouth, giving them a nasal quality. Exceptions to this rule:

   ṣ is pronounced as the *sh* in "sheep"

   ḷ is pronounced as the *l* in "apple"

   ṛ is pronounced as the *ri* in "rig"

   ṃ is pronounced as a humming sound, pronounced in the nose and the back of the mouth, much like the *ng* in "sing"

6. Other marked consonants:

   ṅ is pronounced as the *ng* in "sing"

   ś is pronounced as the *sh* in "sheep"

Chinese. Aside from modern place names, like Beijing, Chinese words in this book are transliterated using the Wade-Giles system. A few peculiarities of the system are as follows:

1. Initials:

   ch unaspirated as the *c* in "ancient"

   ch' as the *ch* in "chest"

   hs as the *sh* in "shirt"

   j as the *sur* in "leisure"

k unaspirated as in "skin"

k' aspirated as the *k* in "kin"

p unaspirated as in "spot"

p' aspirated as the *p* in "pot"

t unaspirated as in "stop"

t' aspirated as the *t* in "top"

ts/tz as the *ds* in "reads"

ts'/tz' as the *ts* in "its"

2. Vowels and finals:

a as in "father"

ai as the *i* in "high"

ao as the *ou* in "out"

ei as the *e* in "they"

en as the *un* in "unable"

eng as the *ung* in "rung"

i as in "sit"

ih as the *ur* in "church"

ou as the *o* in "go"

u as in "rhubarb"

ü as it is pronounced in German

ui as the entire word "way"

Japanese. The transliteration system used in this book is the Hepburn system, which has few peculiarities, but the following principles should be kept in mind:

1. Vowels are pronounced as in Italian. Thus **o, e, i, a** are sounded as in "do, re, mi, fa," although the **e** in "re" should be short and clipped. **U** is generally like the *u* in "rhubarb," although often, especially at the end of a word, it is barely pronounced at all. Vowels written with macrons—**ō** and **ū**—have the same quality as if they were written without macrons, but are sounded for a longer period of time. **Y** is pronounced as in "quickly," and not as in "why."

2. Consonants:

r as the unaspirated *tt* in the American pronunciation of "little"

g as in "go"

3. Double consonants—**kk, nn, pp**—should be pronounced distinctly as double, like the *nn* in "unnecessary."

Tibetan. Like English, Tibetan has a spelling system in which many of the consonants are silent. The Wylie transliteration reproduces all of the letters used to spell a word, but is absolutely useless as a guide to pronunciation. In this book, words and names are introduced in a phonetic rendering, followed by the Wylie transliteration in parentheses, after which the phonetic rendering is used alone. Vowels and consonants in the phonetic rendering are pronounced much as they are in English; vowels with an umlaut—**ü** and **ö**—are pronounced as they are in German.

Korean. Vowels and consonants in the standard Korean transcription system are pronounced much as they are in English, with the following peculiarities:

ae as the *e* in "they"

e as in "let"

ch' unaspirated as the *c* in "ancient"

ch as in "chop"

t' unaspirated as the *t* in "stop"

t as in "top"

Vowels with a breve are pronounced as follows:

ŏ as the *o* in "song"

ŭ as the *u* in "curl"

ŭi as the *i* in "machine"

Vietnamese. During the French colonial period, the Vietnamese adopted a modified form of the Latin alphabet, using a complex system of diacritical marks to indicate subtleties of tone and vowel length. A reasonable approximation of correct pronunciation—disregarding those subtleties—can be achieved by keeping the following rules in mind.

1. Vowels:

a as in "father"

â as the *u* in "hurt"

e as the *a* in "at"

ê as the *e* in "they"

i as in "fit"

o as in "song"

ô as the *o* in "go"

u'o' as the *u* in "bull"

y as the *e* in "me"

2. Consonants:

c as the unaspirated *k* in "skin"

ch at the beginning of a word is pronounced as in English. At the end of a word it is extremely clipped, like a *t* or a *k*.

d as the *y* in "you"

đ (Đ) as the *d* in "do"

nh as the *ny* in "canyon"

t unaspirated as in "stop"

th as in "Thomas"

Glossary

The following list covers foreign-language and specialized terms, along with the names of major bodhisattvas, celestial Buddhas, and cosmic Buddhas that appear in the text.

Often our English equivalents for specific terms carry connotations unwarranted for a different worldview. Thus, to understand Buddhist worldviews, it is necessary to understand the terms expressing those views in context. For this reason, the following glossary is an interlocking one. Many of the key terms are explained using other terms explained elsewhere in the glossary. If not already known, these other terms—which are italicized—should be consulted as well.

Unless otherwise noted, all foreign-language terms are in Sanskrit. When the Pali form of the term—used in Chapter Seven—is sufficiently different from the Sanskrit as to cause possible confusion, the Pali form follows in parentheses. A word immediately following in quotation marks is the literal English meaning of the term, but not necessarily a good translation equivalent. Generally, the first word that follows the literal equivalent is the translation equivalent chosen for this text.

Abhidharma (Abhidhamma). "Higher dharma." Lists classifying the wide variety of doctrinal terms found in the early Mainstream Sūtras into orderly categories.

Abhidhamma Piṭaka. Collection of seven works of the *Theravāda* school, categorizing the teachings in the *Sutta Piṭaka* of the Pali Canon; one of the three traditional portions of the Pali Canon.

Adhikāra. Act of service to an Awakened being, contributing to one's *pāramitās*.

Āgama. Grouping of *Sūtras* in the *Sūtra Piṭaka* sections of the Chinese canon.

Akṣobhya. "Imperturbable." A celestial *Buddha* ruling over a *Buddha-field* to the east. The earliest references to Akṣobhya maintain that he achieved Buddhahood by having made a vow in a previous lifetime never to be angered. In the Mahāyoga *Tantric* systems, Akṣobhya and his fierce Vajra family occupy the center of the maṇḍala, expressing the *Vajrayāna* doctrine that awakened forms of wrath are ultimately based on nonanger.

Ālaya-vijñāna. Storehouse consciousness. The *Yogācārin* teaching of a level of consciousness that contains the seeds of past karma together with pure seeds that will eventually lead to Awakening. In some teachings, this is equated with the *tathāgata-garbha.*

Amitābha. "Unlimited Light." A celestial *Buddha* ruling over *Sukhāvatī*, a *Buddha-field* to the west, the basis for the Pure Land schools in East Asia. Amitāyus (Unlimited Lifespan) is another name for the same Buddha. His Chinese name is A-mi-t'o; his Japanese name, Amida.

Anātman (Anattā). Not-self. A term applied to all phenomena, fabricated or unfabricated, to which one may develop a sense of self-identification. In the *Sūtra Piṭaka,* the anātman teaching is used as part of a strategy to undercut all craving and attachment for the *skandhas*. Around the beginning of the common era, it came to take on the status of a metaphysical doctrine denying the existence of a self or soul underlying the phenomena of experience.

Anitya (Anicca). Impermanent; inconstant. An attribute of all conditioned phenomena.

Añjali. Gesture of respect made by placing the hands palm-to-palm in front of the heart, in front of the face, or over the head.

Anubhāva. Inspiring power, either of a great being (such as a Buddha) or of the vows one makes to become a great being.

Anuśaya. Latent tendency; obsession. Mental predispositions, similar to the *āsravas,* that prevent *bodhi*. There are many lists of these tendencies; a standard list contains seven: sensual passion, resistance, views, uncertainty, conceit, passion for becoming, and ignorance.

Arhat (Arahant). "One who is deserving (of reverence), worthy"; a person who has attained *nirvāṇa,* destroyed the *āsravas,* and who is destined for no further rebirth. In the Mainstream schools, this term is applied both to the *Buddha* and to the highest level of his noble disciples *(śrāvaka);* in the *Mahāyāna* schools, it is applied only to the highest level of śrāvakas.

Āsrava (Āsava). Binding influence; effluent; pollutant; fermentation, the ending of which is equivalent to attaining the goal of Buddhist practice. Listed either as three or four: sensual passion, becoming, (speculative views), and ignorance.

Avadāna (Apadāna). "Lesson," a text extolling the rewards that come from performing *adhikāra* in a *Buddha-field*. Avadānas were among the last texts added to the *Sūtra Piṭakas* of the early canons, and Buddhists in South Asia continued to compose them through the fifteenth century C.E.

Avalokiteśvara. "The Lord Looking Down." A bodhisattva believed to inhabit Amitābha's Buddha-field, renowned for giving help to those in danger. A variant name—*Avalokitasvara,* where *svara* means sound, voice—underlies the Chinese short name Kuan-yin, "sound-regarder." In South Asian art he is usually represented as a bejewelled lay man wearing a high crown bearing a cross-legged image of *Amitābha*. He often holds a lotus in his hand. In the *Vajrayāna* he came to be represented with eleven heads, or with four, ten, twelve, twenty-four, or a thousand arms ready to help people in trouble. In Tibet, he is revered as the country's patron, protector, and founder of the Tibetan race. In East Asia, Avalokiteśvara was eventually represented as a woman, the Chinese calling her Kuan-yin; the Japanese, Kannon; the Koreans, Kwanum; and the Vietnamese, Quan-âm.

Avidyā (Avijjā). Ignorance, particularly of the Four Noble Truths. This is the root cause of *duḥkha* and the first link in the causal chain of *pratītya-samutpāda* leading to recurrent rebirth in *saṃsāra;* its opposite is *bodhi* or *prajñā.*

Bardo (Tibetan). Intermediate state. There are four in all: the mental space between two events, the space between two thoughts, the space between sleeping and waking (the dream bardo), and the space after death (the death bardo). Each of these spaces can form the opening to altered states of consciousness.

Bhikṣu (Bhikkhu). Buddhist monk.

Bhikṣu Sangha. The Order of Buddhist monks.

Bhikṣuṇī (Bhikkhunī). Buddhist nun.

Bhikṣuṇii Sangha. The Order of Buddhist nuns.

Bodhi. Awakening. Comprehension of the nature of conditioned reality and direct experience of the Unconditioned.

Bodhicitta. Thought or mind (aspiration for) *bodhi.* In *Mahāyāna* practice, this is the mental attitude the candidate arouses when aspiring to the *bodhisattva* path.

Bodhisattva. A being dedicated to becoming Awakened (achieving *bodhi*). In the *Sūtra Piṭaka,* this term is applied to Gautama prior to his Awakening. In *Mahāyāna* the term applies to (1) those who have aroused *bodhicitta* and (2) those who have attained *bodhi* but who have taken a special vow to continue being reborn into *saṃsāra* so as to deliver others from their suffering by aiding in their attainment of Awakening as well.

Bon (Tibetan). A semi-indigenous religion of Tibet that combined elements of Buddhism from the First Propagation with native shamanic practices and beliefs.

Brahmā. A god; inhabitant of the heavens of form or formlessness. A state to be attained through the practice of *dhyāna* and the development of the four "Brahma-vihāras" (Sublime Attitudes): good will, compassion, appreciation (or sympathetic joy), and equanimity.

Brahman. Ritual priest of the Aryan religious tradition, continuing into classical times as the upper, sacerdotal caste of the Hindu social system. Related religion: Brahmanism.

Buddha. Awakened One. One of several titles from Indian religious tradition that Gautama claimed as the result of his Awakening (see also, *Tathāgata*). Later Buddhist tradition recognized three types of Buddhas: samyak-sambuddhas, rightly self-awakened teaching Buddhas; pratyeka-buddhas, "private" Buddhas who gain Awakening without a teacher but are unable to formulate teachings to show the path to others; and śrāvaka-buddhas, or arhats. According to Mainstream theory, there can be only one samyak-sambuddha at a time; Gautama is the fourth of our current era and will be followed by the final one of the era, Maitreya; also, there are no pratyeka-buddhas when the teachings of a samyak-sambuddha are still extant. According to *Mahāyāna* theory, there are innumerable world systems in the cosmos; although each may be home to only one Buddha at a time, they may all contain Buddhas simultaneously.

Buddha-field (Sanskrit, *buddha-kṣetra;* Pali, *buddha-khetta*). In the *avadānas,* this term denotes the fertile ground surrounding a *Buddha* or his relics that enables "seeds" of merit to bear abundant fruit. In *Mahāyāna,* it denotes the separate cosmos in which a celestial Buddha resides. In East Asian Buddhism, a Buddha-field in this latter sense of the term is called a Pure Land.

Buddhology. (1) Theory of Buddhahood. (2) The academic study of Buddhism.

Caitya (Cetiya) (Thai, chedi; Burmese, zedi). A memorial shrine, especially to the *Buddha* or his disciples, containing relics, sacred objects, or sacred texts. Buddha images are also classed as caityas.

Ch'an (Chinese). The first syllable of the Chinese word Ch'an-na, which transliterates the Sanskrit *dhyāna*. Originally, this referred simply to one of several vocations open to a monastic. During the T'ang dynasty, several Ch'an lineages developed. Those that survived into the Sung dynasty were regarded as "houses" of a more-or-less unified Ch'an school.

Chien-hsing (Chinese). An experience of nondual awareness.

Cult. Although this term has acquired a negative connotation in many contexts, in the context of this book it is used strictly in its neutral sense as a system of worship or devotion surrounding a person, god, or venerated object.

Daimoku (Japanese). The title of the Lotus Sūtra—"Namu Myōhō-renge-kyō," Homage to the Scripture of the Lotus of the Perfect Truth—chanted in the Nichiren school of Buddhism and in the new religions derived from it.

Ḍākinī. A powerful female deity, capable of flight, associated with Buddhist and non-Buddhist Tantric traditions and derived from earlier pre-Aryan Indian folklore.

Dependent co-arising. See *pratītya-samutpāda.*

Deva. A deity; inhabitant of the heavens of sensual pleasure, the realm of form, or the formless realms.

Dhāraṇī. "Holding;" a spell or incantation, often formed of syllables from passages or lists of Dharma-topics, and said to "hold" the power of those topics. Used to fix the meditator's mind, to invoke a god or goddess (see *mantra*), to generate beneficial *karma* or power, or to function as a basis for insight into the emptiness of phenomena.

Dharma (Dhamma). This word has many meanings in Buddhist texts, depending on context. Meanings occurring in this textbook are: (1) Dharma, the teaching of the *Buddha;* the practice of those teachings; the attainment of *nirvāṇa* as a result of that practice; moral law; and (2) dharmas, the basic constituents of all phenomena, mental or physical, in the conditioned realm.

Dharma-kāya. "Dharma-body." In Mainstream schools, Dharma-kāya denotes the entirety of the Buddha's teachings; in *Mahāyāna* teachings, Dharma-kāya denotes the cosmic principle of *bodhi* embodied by the *Buddha* and to the principle of Buddhahood, which in some schools of *Mahāyāna* thought is innate in all beings.

Dhyāna (Jhāna). Meditative absorption; steady, mindful concentration in a single physical sensation or mental notion. Sometimes used to mean meditation in general, rather than specific states of absorption.

Duḥkha (Dukkha). "Dis-easeful;" usually translated as suffering, ill, or stressful. One of the common characteristics of all conditioned reality; as the First Noble Truth, duḥkha denotes all the suffering resulting from *avidyā, tṛṣṇā,* and attachment to the five *skandhas.*

Gohonzon. A *maṇḍala* used in Nichiren Buddhism, composed of the title of the Lotus Sūtra (the *daimoku*), flanked by the names of two eternal Buddhas—Śākyamuni and Prabhūtaratna—*bodhisattvas,* and the names of the ten realms of beings, symbolizing the power of the *daimoku* as an Awakening penetrating all of the cosmos.

Guru. Spiritual teacher; mentor.

Hīnayāna. The Small ("Inferior") Vehicle or Course. The *Mahāyāna* pejorative to denote (1) the paths of practice aimed at becoming an arhat or pratyeka buddha, and (2) schools of Buddhist thought that did not accept the *Mahāyāna Sūtras* as authoritative.

Jhāna. See *dhyāna.*

Jñāna-mudrā. An imagined partner used in transgressive forms of *Tantra.* See *karma-mudrā.*

Kami (Japanese). Spirit; charismatic force, object, or being.

Karma (Kamma). Intentional act, performed by body, speech, or mind, which—in line with the intention it embodies—will result in happiness or *duḥkha* in this or a future rebirth, or will lead beyond rebirth to *nirvāṇa.*

Karma-mudrā. An actual flesh-and-blood partner used in transgressive forms of *Tantra.* See *jñāna-mudrā.*

Kenshō (Japanese). "Seeing-nature." An experience of the nonduality of one's mind-body and the object of one's meditation.

Kṣitigarbha. "Earth Womb." A bodhisattva of non-Indian provenance who became popular in East Asia. In art, he is depicted as a bhikṣu. Called Jizo in Japan, he is there venerated as the protector of children, aborted fetuses, and those who have fallen into hell.

Kuan-yin (Chinese). The Chinese translation of Avalokiteśvara, the *bodhisattva* of compassion. During the Sung dynasty, (960–1279), this *bodhisattva* changed from male to female. Kuan-yin is petitioned for earthly boons such as money, good luck, and children, as well as for safety on voyages.

Lama (Tibetan). Spiritual teacher; mentor; master of *Tantric* ritual (Sanskrit *guru*).

Madhyamaka. "Middle School," so-called because it taught a doctrine of *śūnyatā* as a middle position between being and nonbeing; a *Mahāyāna* school based on the writings of Nāgārjuna.

Mahāvairocana. See *Vairocana.*

Mahāyāna. The Great Vehicle or Course. The *bodhisattva* path and the teachings advocating the practice of that path.

Mainstream. The form of Indian Buddhism that did not accept the *Mahāyāna Sūtras* or *Tantras* as the definitive word of the *Buddha.*

Maitreya (Metteyya). "Friendly One." The next Buddha to appear in our world.

Maṇḍala. A stylized realm representing a deity's field of power, used in *Tantric* meditation and ritual.

Māñjuśrī. "Sweet or Gentle Glory." A bodhisattva renowned for his wisdom. In art, he is depicted as a bodhisattva bhikṣu, with a five-pointed coiffure or tiara, a sword (to cut ignorance) in his right hand, a book (the *Prajñā-pāramitā*) in his left, and a lion for his mount.

Mantra. "Instrument;" short verse or collection of syllables used to evoke a deity, gain protection against evil or adverse forces, or as a meditation object, especially—but not exclusively—in *Tantra.*

Māra. "Destroyer, Tempter," the personification of evil or attachment to conditioned reality; the god of desire and death; defilement and the *skandhas* as personifications of obstacles to release from *saṃsāra.*

Mudrā. Sign, seal token; especially a position of the fingers and hands characterizing images of the *Buddha* or other Buddhist figures and practiced in tantric ritual performance.

Nāga. A magical serpent, capable of assuming human form.

Nembutsu (Japanese). Japanese translation of the Chinese *nien-fo.*

Neo-Confucianism (Chinese). A renewal and development of Confucianism in the Sung dynasty (960–1279), inspired partly in reaction to Buddhism but also incorporating many Buddhist ideas. This "new" Confucianism received definitive interpretation in the hands of Chu Hsi (1130–1200) and remained the official state orthodoxy until the Republic (1912).

Nien-fo (Chinese). "Reciting Buddha's name, recollection of the Buddha." A meditative practice with roots in the Mainstream canons that played a prominent role in the development of the *Mahāyāna.* In China, this practice focused largely on the practice of reciting the name of the *Buddha Amitābha* as a means of gaining rebirth in his *Buddha-field.*

Nikāya. (1) Grouping of *Sūtras* found in the *Sūtra Piṭaka,* also called Āgama; (2) school of Early Buddhism.

Nirmāṇa-kāya. The "Emanation-body" of a *Buddha.* According to *Mahāyāna* thought, this corresponds to a human Buddha's physical body and to the apparitions of him that may appear to human beings in visions or dreams.

Nirvāṇa (Nibbāna). "Unbinding, the extinguishing of a fire." Metaphorical name for the Buddhist goal, conveying connotations of stilling, cooling, limitless emancipation, and peace; release from the limitations of *saṃsāra* through the extinguishing of the "fires" of passion, aversion, and delusion, and through the ending of the *āsravas.*

Pāramitā (Pāramī). "Supremacy;" perfection, practice of a virtue to the point of supreme perfection, leading to arhatship or Buddhahood.

Parinirvāṇa (Parinibbāna). Total *nirvāṇa;* denotes (1) the attainment of release from *avidyā, tṛṣṇā,* and attachment to the five *skandhas;* and (2) the utter release from *saṃsāra* attained at the death of a *Buddha* or *arhant.*

Perfection of Discernment. In this text, the translation equivalent for the Sanskrit term *prajñā-pāramitā.*

Phenomenology. Study of the phenomena of consciousness as they are directly experienced, without reference to the question of whether or not they correspond to anything outside of experience.

Poṣadha (Uposatha). Observance Day, determined by the phases of the moon. For the laity, these days are times to observe the eight precepts and listen to the Dharma; they occur on the days of the full, new, and half moons. For monastics, they are times to listen to the Prātimokṣa, occurring on the days of the full and new moons.

Prajñā (Paññā). Discernment; wisdom. Understanding of the true nature of reality, leading to release from bondage to *saṃsāra.*

Prajñā-pāramitā. The perfection of *prajñā.* The *Mahāyāna* designation of the supreme degree of *prajñā;* also the designation of a class of *Mahāyāna Sūtras* that define this discernment as seeing (1) the nonarising of dharmas and (2) the fact that all *dharmas* are empty of *svabhāva.*

Prasāda (pasāda). A clear sense of serene confidence.

Prātimokṣa (Pāṭimokkha). The code of monastic discipline.

Pratītya-samutpāda (Paṭicca-samuppāda). Dependent co-arising, also translated in other works as dependent origination, conditioned genesis, and variations on these. The specific formula analyzing the preconditions (nidāna) in the causal loops connecting *avidyā* with the consequents of birth, aging, death, and the whole mass of samsaric *duḥkha.*

Private Buddha (Pratyeka-buddha). See *Buddha.*

Sādhana. A ritual invocation in which one assumes the identity, powers, and knowledge of a deity. A central feature of *Vajrayāna* practice.

Samādhi. Concentration; a mindful state characterized by singleness of object, calm, stability, and absence of distraction; Right Concentration is equivalent to the four states of *dhyāna.*

Śākyamuni. "Sage of the Śākyan Clan." An epithet for the most recent *Buddha.*

Samantabhadra. "Entirely Auspicious." A bodhisattva representing tactical skill, often represented as seated on an elephant. In the *Gaṇḍavyūha* (Flower Array) *Sūtra,* he appears as the greatest of all the bodhisattvas, a tradition that became very popular in China and Japan, and that was also portrayed in the top level of bas-reliefs on the great Javanese stūpa, Borobudur. In East Asian temples, Samantabhadra is often paired with Mañjuśrī. In Tibet, he is regarded as the great Cosmic Buddha who founded the tradition of Dzogchen meditation.

Sambhoga-kāya. The "Enjoyment-body;" the glorified body that a *Buddha* attains as a reward for his *bodhisattva* practices, a transfigured form that the great *bodhisattvas* apprehend when they see him.

Saṃsāra. "The wandering-on;" the round of death and rebirth, into which beings driven by craving *(tṛṣṇā)* are repeatedly born; characterized as *anitya, duḥkha, anātman,* and *śūnya.*

Saṁvega. A sense of alienation, awe, shock, and dismay over the futility of life as it is normally lived, combined with a strong sense of urgency in trying to escape from the trap of futility.

Sangha. Community. This word has two levels of meaning: (1) on the ideal (ārya) level, it denotes all of the *Buddha*'s followers, lay or ordained, who have at least attained the level of *srotāpanna;* (2) on the conventional (samvṛti) level, it denotes the Orders of *Bhikṣus* and *Bhikṣuṇīs.*

Satori (Japanese). Awakening.

Shintō (Japanese). Native, pre-Buddhist beliefs in Japan, centered on the worship of *kami.* These beliefs, and their corresponding cults, were developed as part of Japanese Buddhism in the medieval period, but regained their separate identity—at the same time as they were organized into a unitary set of beliefs and practices—only in the nineteenth century.

Siddha. A ritual adept devoted to the practice of *sādhana.*

Siddhi. A power attained through the practice of *sādhana.*

Śīla. Morality, virtue; precepts of behavior conducive to the development of *samādhi* and *prajñā.*

Skandha (Khandha). "Heap, mass, aggregate." A term to indicate that all factors with which one might identify as one's "self" are in fact impermanent, causally produced aggregations. The five skandhas are (1) form (rūpa, the body or physical skandha), (2) feeling (vedanā), (3) perception, mental label (saṃjñā), (4) thought formations (saṃskāras, plural), and (5) sensory consciousness (vijñāna). These five skandhas constitute the phenomenal world-and-person; are the five bases for clinging to (taking sustenance from) conditioned existence, resulting in continued rebirth; and are characterized by *anitya, duḥkha,* and *anātman.*

Śramaṇa (Samaṇa). "Striver." A member of of the renunciant sects of early India (after 800 B.C.E.) whose rule usually required abandoning social and ritual status and whose doctrines denied the validity of Vedic revelation in favor of truths directly discovered from nature through the use of reason or meditative experiences. The early Buddhist etymology for this word comes from "sama," which means "in tune," in the sense that the proper śramaṇa way of life was in tune with what was naturally right.

Śrāvaka (Sāvaka). "Listener." A disciple of the Buddha. In Mahāyāna teachings, this denotes a person who has taken the path to arhatship, rather than the Mahāyāna path.

Śrāvakayāna. "The vehicle of discipleship," a term for the path to arhatship.

Srotāpanna (Sotapanna). Stream-winner, one who has entered the stream leading to *nirvāṇa,* will never relapse, and is destined to be reborn at most seven more times, never in any of the lower realms; the lowest of the four grades of Noble Disciples or saints, which are in ascending order:
(1) srotāpanna, (2) sakṛd-āgāmin (sakadāgāmin), once-returner, one who will have to be reborn in the human world only once more to become an *arhat,*
(3) anāgāmin, nonreturner, one who will never have to be reborn in this world but will be spontaneously reborn in the highest Brahma realms, there to attain *nirvāṇa,* and
(4) *arhat,* one totally freed from the processes of renewed becoming and birth.

Sthavira (Thera). "Elder." See *Theravāda.*

Stūpa. Memorial shrine or reliquary, especially to a deceased *Buddha* or *arhat.*

Sukhāvatī. "Happiness-having;" Pure Land or *Buddha-field* of the *Buddha Amitābha.*

Śūnyatā. "Emptiness." In the Sūtra Piṭaka, this term is used as an attribute of phenomena—stating that they are empty of self or anything pertaining to self—and as a mode of perception, in which phenomena are viewed simply in terms of what is absent or present to awareness, without adding anything or taking anything away. The philosopher Nāgārjuna later expanded these two meanings. As an attribute of phenomena, he wrote, emptiness meant that phenomena had no "own-nature," *(svabhāva);* as a mode of perception, it meant the relinquishment of all views. Nāgārjuna's treatment of this topic, combined with the *Perfection of Discernment* teaching on the non-arising of *dharmas,* formed the cornerstone for the major schools of *Mahāyāna* thought.

Superknowledge (Sanskrit, abhijñā). Knowledge attained through meditation. The six superknowledges listed in the Pali Canon are (1) psychic powers, (2) clairvoyance, (3) knowledge of others' minds, (4) memory of one's former lives; (5) clairvoyance, and (6) ending of the *āsravas.* Only the last attainment is considered transcendent.

Sūtra (Sutta). A Buddhist text, especially a dialogue or discourse attributed to the *Buddha.*

Sūtra (Sutta) Piṭaka. The collection of discourses included in the early Mainstream canons.

Svabhāva. "Own-nature." In Mainstream *Abhidharma* theory, this is the defining characteristic that distinguishes one dharma-type from all others. Nāgārjuna and *Mahāyāna* thinkers attacked this notion on the grounds that no phenomenon dependent on conditions could have a nature of its own.

Tantra. Ritual manual; also, the ritual described in such a manual. The philosophy and path of practice surrounding the use of Tantras has, in the modern period, received the name of Tantrism.

Tantrika. A practitioner of Tantra.

Tao (Chinese). The Way, the order of the universe, the way one ought to act to be in harmony with the cosmos. A native Chinese concept used to translate a number of Buddhist terms, including *bodhi, Dharma,* and mārga (path).

Taoism (Chinese). A complex of several systems of practice all claiming as authoritative the early works attributed to Lao-tzu and Chuang-tzu, including philosophical Taoism, alchemical Taoism, and magical or popular Taoism, the latter two being very much interested in physical immortality.

Tārā. A female bodhisattva, manifesting the protective aspect of Buddhahood, especially popular in Tibet.

Tathāgata. "He who has come or gone thus (that is, on the path of all the *Buddhas*)," or "He who has reached or become what is really so, the True." The term the texts depict the *Buddha* using to speak of himself after Awakening.

Tathāgata-garbha. The "womb or embryo of Tathāgatahood"; the innate potential for Buddhahood that, according to some *Mahāyāna* schools, is present in all beings.

Terma (Tibetan). Hidden treasure texts reputedly placed underground, underwater, in the sky, or in "mind" by spiritually advanced beings, and discovered by later generations.

Theravāda (Pali for Sthaviravāda). The Teaching of the Elders. An early Buddhist sect that became established in Sri Lanka at the Great Monastery of Anurādhapura about 240 B.C.E., later to become the dominant form of Buddhism in Sri Lanka and Southeast Asia.

Theravādin. One who holds to the teachings of the Elders.

Tripiṭaka (Tipiṭaka). "Three Baskets"; early Buddhist Canon, composed of collections of *Sūtras, Vinaya,* and *Abhidharma.* The Pali Canon is the only complete early Canon still extant. In extended usage, this term also applies to later comprehensive collections of Buddhist texts, such as the Tibetan, Chinese, and Korean Tripiṭakas, even though these collections are not divided into three collections.

Tṛṣṇā (Taṇhā). "Thirst," craving, the cause of *duḥkha.* Includes craving for sensuality, for becoming, and for nonbecoming.

Tülku (Tibetan). The reincarnation of a spiritually advanced person, usually a *lama,* who on maturity resumes the office of his/her previous incarnation. In some cases, the tülku is regarded as the *nirmāṇa-kāya* of a *bodhisattva.*

Uji (Japanese). Clan; tribe.

Upaniṣad. Sanskrit speculative texts, the earliest of which were roughly contemporaneous with early Buddhism; later accepted into orthodox Brahmanism and Hinduism.

Vairocana. "Illuminator." The cosmic *Buddha* that the *Gaṇḍavyūha* and *Daśabhūmika Sūtras* identify as embodied in the universe as a whole. In the Caryā and Yoga *Tantras,* Vairocana occupies the center of the maṇḍala. Also called Mahāvairocana, "Great Illuminator."

Vajra. Diamond; thunderbolt. A symbol of unfettered spiritual power used by the *Vajrayāna* to denote both the means of the practice, in which the *vajra* stands for firm compassion, and the goal, in which the Vajra Realm stands for the ground of all Buddhahood.

Vajrayāna. Adamantine Vehicle or Course. Path of *bodhisattva* practice, originally formulated in approximately the seventh century C.E., claiming to be faster and more direct, if somewhat riskier, than older *Mahāyāna* practices.

Vidyādhara. "Wizard." In Indian mythology, *vidyādharas* were a race of beings with magical powers living in the Himalayas, often the focus of *sādhana.* In Tibetan *Vajrayāna,* a *vidyādhara* is a *yogin* who has taken up permanent residence in the meditation hermitage of a monastery.

Vihāra. Monastic residence.

Vinaya. Monastic discipline.

Vinaya Piṭaka. Collection of texts containing rules for monastic discipline included in the early canons.

Vipaśyanā (Vipassanā). Insight. This term covers (1) particular forms of meditation that are said to provoke insight into the three characteristics of *anitya, duḥkha,* and *anātman,* and (2) the insight itself.

Wat (Thai). Temple-monastery complex.

Wings to Awakening (Sanskrit, bodhipakṣya-dharma; Pali, bodhipakkhiya-dhamma). Seven sets of *dharmas,* totaling 37 factors in all, that the early canons identify as constituting the essential part of the *Buddha's* teaching: (1) the four foundations of mindfulness, (2) the four right exertions, (3) the four bases for attainment, (4) the five strengths, (5) the five faculties, (6) the seven factors of Awakening, and (7) the Noble Eightfold Path.

Yogācāra. "Yoga practice." *Mahāyāna* school of meditative practice and the scholastic theories that developed around that practice.

Yogācārin. Follower of the Yogācāra School.

Yogin (feminine, **yoginī**). Practitioner of yoga and meditative self-discipline.

Zen (Japanese). Japanese pronunciation of the Chinese *Ch'an.*

Select Bibliography

This selection is drawn primarily from the large academic literature on Buddhism, augmented with popular works where the academic literature has gaps. These works provide material that will supplement the discussion in this textbook, in some cases agreeing with the interpretations presented here, in some cases not. Citations are gathered under the chapters to which they are most relevant, preceded by a list applicable to the entire book or to large parts of it.

GENERAL BOOKS ON BUDDHISM

Auboyer, Jeannine. *Buddha: A Pictorial History of His Life and Legacy*. New York: Crossroad, 1983.

Basham, A. L. *The Wonder That Was India*. New York: Macmillan, 1954.

Bechert, Heinz, and Richard Gombrich, eds. *The World of Buddhism: Monks and Nuns in Society and Culture*. London: Thames and Hudson, 1984.

Cabezón, José Ignacia, ed. *Buddhism, Sexuality, and Gender*. Albany: SUNY Press, 1992.

Conze, Edward. *Buddhist Scriptures: A Bibliography*. Edited and revised by Lewis Lancaster. New York: Garland, 1982.

Gethin, Rupert. *The Foundations of Buddhism*. Oxford: Oxford University Press, 1998.

Katz, Nathan. *Buddhist Images of Human Perfection: The Arahant of the Sutta Piṭaka Compared with the Bodhisattva and the Mahāsiddha*. Delhi: Motilal Banarsidass, 1982.

Kitagawa, Joseph, and Mark Cummings, eds. *Buddhism and Asian History*. New York: Macmillan, 1989.

Lancaster, Lewis. "Buddhist Literature: Its Canon, Scribes, and Editors." In *The Critical Study of Sacred Texts*. Edited by Wendy D. O'Flaherty. Berkeley: Berkeley Religious Studies Series, 1979, pp. 215–229.

Liebert, Gosta. *Iconographic Dictionary of the Indian Religions*. Leiden, Netherlands: E.J. Brill, 1976.

Lopez, Donald S., Jr., ed. *Buddhism in Practice*. Princeton: Princeton University Press, 1995.

———, ed. *Buddhist Hermeneutics*. Honolulu: University ofHawaii Press, 1988.

Malalasekera, G. P., ed. *Encyclopedia of Buddhism*. Colombo: Government of Sri Lanka, 1961.

Nattier, Jan. *Once Upon a Future Time*. Berkeley: Asian Humanities Press, 1991.

Pal, Pratapaditya. *Light of Asia: Buddha Śākyamuni in Asian Art*. Los Angeles: County Museum of Art, 1984.

Reynolds, Frank E. *Guide to the Buddhist Religion*. Boston: G. K. Hall, 1981.

Schober, Juliane, ed. *Sacred Biography in the Buddhist Traditions of South and Southeast Asia*. Honolulu: University of Hawai'i Press, 1997.

Snellgrove, David L., ed. *The Image of the Buddha*. Tokyo and New York: Kodansha International/UNESCO, 1978.

Sponberg, Alan, and Helen Hardacre, eds. *Maitreya: The Future Buddha*. Cambridge: Cambridge University Press, 1988.

Strong, John. *The Experience of Buddhism: Sources and Interpretations*. 2nd edition. Belmont: Wadsworth, 2002.

Sutherland, Stewart, et al. *The World's Religions*. Boston: G. K. Hall, 1988.

Warder, A. K. *Indian Buddhism*. 2nd ed. Delhi: Motilal Banarsidass, 1980.

———. *Indian Kāvya Literature*. Six volumes (to date). Delhi: Motilal Banarsidass, 1972–1992.

Williams, Paul, and Anthony Tribe. *Buddhist Thought: A Complete Introduction to the Indian Tradition*. London: Curzon, 2000.

Zwalf, W. *Buddhism: Art and Faith*. London: British Museum Publications, 1985.

CHAPTERS ONE AND TWO: THE BUDDHA'S AWAKENING AND THE BUDDHA AS TEACHER AND POWER FIGURE

Bodhi, Bhikkhu. *The Connected Discourses of the Buddha*. Boston: Wisdom Publications, 2000.

Collins, Steven. *Selfless Persons: Imagery and Thought in Theravāda Buddhism*. Cambridge: Cambridge University Press, 1982.

Cook, Elizabeth, ed. *Holy Places of the Buddha*. Berkeley: Dharma Publishing, 1994.

Cummings, Mary. *The Lives of the Buddha in the Art and Literature of Asia*. Ann Arbor: University of Michigan, Center for South and Southeast Asian Studies, 1982.

Gethin, R. M. L. *The Buddhist Path to Awakening: A Study of the Bodhi-Pakkhiya Dhamma*. Leiden, Netherlands: E.J. Brill, 1992.

Gunaratana, Henepola. *The Path of Serenity and Insight: An Explanation of the Buddhist Jhānas*. Delhi: Motilal Banarsidass, 1985.

Jayatilleke, K. N. *Early Buddhist Theory of Knowledge*. London: George Allen and Unwin, 1963.

Johnston, E. H., trans. *The Buddhacarita, or, Acts of the Buddha*. 3rd ed. Delhi: Motilal Banarsidass, 1984.

Harvey, Peter. *The Selfless Mind*. London: Curzon, 1995.

Kalupahana, David J. *Causality: The Central Philosophy of Buddhism*. Honolulu: University Press of Hawaii, 1975.

Karetsky, Patricia Eichenbaum. *The Life of the Buddha: Ancient Scriptural and Pictorial Traditions*. Lanham, Maryland: University Press of America, 1992.

Ñanamoli, Bhikkhu. *The Life of the Buddha According to the Pali Canon*. Kandy, Sri Lanka: Buddhist Publication Society, 1978.

Ñanamoli, Bhikkhu and Bhikkhu Bodhi. *The Middle Length Discourses of the Buddha*. Boston: Wisdom Publications, 1995.

Strong, John. *The Buddha: A Short Biography*. Oxford: Oneworld, 2001.

Thanissaro Bhikkhu. *The Mind Like Fire Unbound: An Image in the Early Buddhist Discourses*. Barre, MA: Dhamma Dana Publications, 1993.

———. *The Wings to Awakening: An Anthology of the Buddha's Teachings from the Pali Canon*. Barre, MA: Dhamma Dana Publications, 1996.

Walshe, Maurice O'Clarke. *The Long Discourses of the Buddha*. Boston: Wisdom Publications, 1995.

CHAPTER THREE: THE DEVELOPMENT OF EARLY INDIAN BUDDHISM

Chakravarti, Uma. *The Social Dimensions of Early Buddhism*. Delhi: Oxford University Press, 1987.

Chau, Thich Thein. *The Literature of the Personalists of Early Buddhism*. Translated by Sara Boin-Webb. Delhi: Motilal Banarsidass, 1999.

Hirakawa, Akira. *Monastic Discipline for the Buddhist Nuns: An English Translation of the Chinese Text of the Mahasaṃghika-Bhikṣuṇī-Vinaya*. Patna, India: Kashi Prasad Jayaswal Research Institute.

Jones, John Garrett. *Tales and Teachings of the Buddha: The Jātaka Stories in Relation to the Pali Canon*. London: George Allen & Unwin, 1979.

Lamotte, Etienne. *History of Indian Buddhism: From the Origins to the Saka Era*. Louvain-La-Neuve, Belgium: Institut Orientaliste, 1988.

Mitra, Debala. *Buddhist Monuments*. Calcutta: Sahitya Samsad, 1971.

Norman, K. R. *The Elders' Verses II: Therīgāthā*. London: Luzac and Company, 1971.

———. *Pali Literature, Including the Canonical Literature in Prakrit and Sanskrit of All Hīnayāna Schools of Buddhism*. Weisbaden, Germany: Otto Harrassowitz, 1983.

Nyanatiloka. *A Guide through the Abhidhamma Piṭaka*. Kandy: Buddhist Publication Society, 1971.

Olivelle, Patrick. *The Origin and Early Development of Buddhist Monachism*. Colombo, Sri Lanka: Gunasena, 1974.

Prebish, Charles S. *Buddhist Monastic Discipline: The Sanskrit Pratimokṣa Sūtras of the Mahasaṃghikas and Mūlasarvāstivādins*. University Park: Pennsylvania State University Press, 1975.

Ray, Reginald A. *Buddhist Saints in India: A Study in Buddhist Values and Orientations*. Oxford: Oxford University Press, 1994.

Snodgrass, Adrian. *The Symbolism of the Stūpa*. Ithaca: Cornell University Southeast Asian Studies Program, 1985.

Strong, John. *The Legend of King Aśoka*. Princeton: Princeton University Press, 1983.

Thanissaro Bhikkhu. *The Buddhist Monastic Code*. Two volumes. Valley Center, CA: Metta Forest Monastery, 1994; 2001.

Tharpar, Romila. *Aśoka and the Decline of the Mauryas*. Delhi: Oxford University Press, 1983.

Walters, Jonathan S. "Stūpa, Story, and Empire: Constructions of the Buddha Biography in Early Post-Asokan India." In *Sacred Biography in the Buddhist Traditions of South and Southeast Asia*. Edited by Juliane Schober. Honolulu: University of Hawai'i Press, 1997, pp. 160–192.

Wijayaratna, Mohan. *Buddhist Monastic Life According to the Texts of the Theravāda Tradition.* Translated by Claude Grangier and Steven Collins. Cambridge: Cambridge University Press, 1990.

Zysk, Kenneth G. *Asceticism and Healing in Ancient India: Medicine in the Buddhist Monastery.* New York: Oxford University Press, 1991.

CHAPTER FOUR: THE PERIOD OF THE THREE VEHICLES

Conze, Edward, trans. *The Perfection of Wisdom in Eight Thousand Lines.* San Francisco: Four Seasons Foundation, 1973.

Garfield, Jay L. *The Fundamental Wisdom of the Middle Way: Nāgārjuna's Mūlamadhyamakakārikā.* New York: Oxford University Press, 1995.

Harrison, Paul, trans. *The Samādhi of Direct Encounter with the Buddhas of the Present* Tokyo: The International Institute of Buddhist Studies, 1990.

Kalupahana, David J. *Nāgārjuna: The Philosophy of the Middle Way.* Albany: SUNY Press, 1986.

Khoroche, Peter, trans. *Once the Buddha Was a Monkey: Ārya Śūra's Jātakamāla.* Chicago: University of Chicago Press, 1989.

Kloppenborg, Ria. *The Paccekabuddha, A Buddhist Ascetic.* Leiden, Netherlands: E.J. Brill, 1974.

Napper, Elizabeth. *Dependent-Arising and Emptiness.* Boston: Wisdom Publications, 1989.

Nattier, Jan. *A Few Good Men: The Bodhisattva Path according to The Inquiry of Ugra (Ugraparipṛcchā).* Honolulu: University of Hawai'i Press, 2003.

Potter, Karl H., ed. *Encyclopedia of Indian Philosophies.* Volume VII, *Abhidharma Buddhism to 150 A.D.* Delhi: Motilal Banarsidass, 1996.

Robinson, Richard H. *Early Mādhyamika in India and China.* Madison: University of Wisconsin Press, 1967.

Verardi, Giovanni. *"Homa" and Other Fire Rituals in Gandhāra.* Naples, Italy: Instituto Universitario Orientale,1994.

CHAPTER FIVE: EARLY MEDIEVAL INDIAN BUDDHISM

Anacker, Stefan. *Seven Works of Vasubandhu.* Delhi: Motilal Banarsidass, 1984.

Cleary, Thomas, trans. *The Flower Ornament Scripture.* Boston: Shambhala, 1983.

Conze, Edward, trans. *The Large Sūtra on Perfect Wisdom.* Berkeley: University of California Press, 1975.

Dreyfus, Georges B.J. *Recognizing Reality: Dharmakīrti's Philosophy and Its Tibetan Interpretations.* Albany: SUNY Press, 1997.

Dreyfus, Georges B.J., and Sara L. McClintock, eds. *The Svātantrika-Prāsaṅgika Distinction.* Boston: Wisdom Publications, 2003.

Eckel, Malcolm David. *To See the Buddha: A Philosopher's Quest for the Meaning of Emptiness.* Princeton: Princeton University Press, 1992.

Frauwallner, Erich. *Studies in Abhidharma Literature and the Origins of Buddhist Philosophical Systems.* Translated from the German by Sophie Francis Kidd. Albany: SUNY Press, 1995.

Gómez, Luis O. *The Land of Bliss: The Paradise of the Buddha of Measureless Light.* Honolulu: University of Hawai'i Press, 1996.

Huntington, C. W., Jr. *The Emptiness of Emptiness: An Introduction to Early Indian Mādhyamika.* Honolulu: University of Hawai'i Press, 1989.

Hurvitz, Leon, trans. *Scripture of the Lotus Blossom of the Fine Dharma (The Lotus*

Sūtra). New York: Columbia University Press, 1976.

La Vallée Poussin, Louis de, trans. *Abhidharmakośabhasyam*. Translated from the French by Leo M. Pruden. Berkeley: Asian Humanities Press.

Nagao, Gadjin. *Madhyamika and Yogācāra: A Study of Mahāyāna Philosophies*. Albany: SUNY Press, 1991.

Powers, John, trans. *Wisdom of Buddha: The Saṃdhinirmocana Sūtra*. Berkeley: Dharma Publishing, 1995.

Pye, Michael. *Skilful Means: A Concept in Mahāyāna Buddhism*. London: Duckworth, 1978.

Sutton, Florin Giripescu. *Existence and Enlightenment in the Laṅkāvatāra-sūtra: A Study in the Ontology and Epistemology of the Yogācāra School of Mahāyāna Buddhism*. Albany: SUNY Press, 1991.

Tatz, Mark, trans. *The Skill in Means (Upāyakauśalya) Sūtra*. Delhi: Motilal Banarsidass, 1996.

Thurman, Robert, trans. *The Holy Teaching of Vimalakīrti: A Mahāyāna Scripture*. University Park: Pennsylvania State University Press, 1976.

Williams, Paul. *Mahāyāna Buddhism: The Doctrinal Foundations*. Routledge & Kegan Paul, 1989.

Willis, Janice Dean. *On Knowing Reality: The Tattvartha Chapter of Asaṅga's Bodhisattvabhūmi*. New York: Columbia University Press, 1982.

CHAPTER SIX: BUDDHISM IN LATE MEDIEVAL AND MODERN INDIA

Das Gupta, Shashibhusan. *Obscure Religious Cults*. Calcutta: Firma K. L. Mukhopadhyay, 1969.

Davidson, Ronald M. *Indian Esoteric Buddhism*. New York: Columbia University Press, 2002.

Dowman, Keith. *Masters of Mahamudrā: Songs and Histories of the Eighty-Four Buddhist Siddhas*. Albany: SUNY Press, 1985.

George, Christopher S. *The Caṇḍamahāroṣana Tantra*. New Haven: American Oriental Society, 1974.

Kinnard, Jacob N. *Imaging Wisdom: Seeing and Knowing in the Art of Indian Buddhism*. London: Curzon, 1999.

Lorenzen, David L. *The Kāpālikas and Kālamukhas: Two Lost Saivite Sects*. Berkeley: University of California Press, 1972.

Śāntideva. *The Bodhicaryāvatāra*. Translated by Kate Crosby and Andrew Skilton. Oxford: Oxford University Press, 1995.

Snellgrove, D. L. *Indo-Tibetan Buddhism: Indian Buddhists and Their Tibetan Successors*. Vol 1. Boston: Shambhala, 1987.

———. *The Hevajra Tantra*. Oxford: Oxford University Press, 1959.

Tribe, Anthony. "Mantranaya-Vajrayāna—Tantric Buddhism in India." In *Buddhist Thought: A Complete Introduction to the Indian Tradition*. Paul Williams and Anthony Tribe. London: Curzon, 2000, pp. 192–244.

CHAPTER SEVEN: BUDDHISM IN SRI LANKA AND SOUTHEAST ASIA

Adikaram, E. W. *Early History of Buddhism in Ceylon*. Dehiwala, Sri Lanka: Buddhist Cultural Centre, 1994.

Aronson, Harvey B. *Love and Sympathy in Theravāda Buddhism*. Delhi: Motilal Banarsidass, 1980.

Bartholomeusz, Tessa J. *Women under the Bo Tree: Buddhist Nuns in Sri Lanka.* Cambridge: Cambridge University Press, 1994.

Blackburn, Anne M. *Buddhist Learning and Textual Practice in Eighteenth-Century Lankan Monastic Culture.* Princeton: Princeton University Press, 2001.

Bond, George. *The Buddhist Revival in Sri Lanka.* Delhi: Motilal Banarsidass, 1992.

Brereton, Bonnie. *Thai Tellings of Phra Malai: Texts and Rituals Concerning a Popular Buddhist Saint.* Tempe: Arizona State University Program for Southeast Asian Studies, 1995.

Bunnag, Jane. *Buddhist Monk, Buddhism Layman: A Study of Buddhist Monastic Organization in Central Thailand.* Cambridge: Cambridge University Press, 1973.

Carrithers, Michael. *The Forest Monks of Sri Lanka.* Delhi: Oxford University Press, 1983.

Gombrich, Richard F. *Buddhist Precept and Practice.* Delhi: Motilal Banarsidass, 1991.

———. *Theravāda Buddhism: A Social History from Ancient Benares to Modern Colombo.* London: Routledge & Kegan Paul, 1988.

Gombrich, Richard F., and Gananath Obeyesekere. *Buddhism Transformed: Religious Change in Sri Lanka.* Princeton: Princeton University Press, 1988.

Gómez, Luis O., and Hiram W. Woodward, eds. *Barabudur: History and Significance of a Buddhist Monument.* Berkeley: Berkeley Buddhist Studies Series, 1981.

Gunawardana, R. A. L. H. *Robe and Plough: Monasticism and Economic Interest in Early Medieval Sri Lanka.* Tucson: University of Arizona Press, 1979.

Holt, John Clifford. *Buddha in the Crown: Avalokiteśvara in the Buddhist Traditions of Sri Lanka.* New York: Oxford University Press, 1991.

Houtman, Gustaaf. *Mental Culture in Burmese Crisis Politics.* Tokyo: Institute for the Study of the Languages and Cultures of Asia and Africa, 1999.

Kornfield, Jack. *Living Dharma: Teachings of Twelve Buddhist Masters.* Boston: Shambhala, 1996.

Mendelson, E. Michael. *Sangha and State in Burma.* Ithaca: Cornell University Press, 1975.

Ñāṇamoli Thera, trans. *The Path of Purification (Visuddhimagga).* Kandy: Buddhist Publication Society, 1991.

Strachan, Paul. *Pagan: Art and Architecture of Old Burma.* Whiting Bay, Scotland: Kiscadale Publications, 1989.

Strong, John. *The Legend and Cult of Upagupta: Sanskrit Buddhism in North India and Southeast Asia.* Princeton: Princeton University Press, 1992.

Swearer, Donald K. *The Buddhist World of Southeast Asia.* Albany: SUNY Press, 1995.

Tambiah, Stanley. *Buddhism and Spirit Cults in Northeast Thailand.* Cambridge: Cambridge University Press, 1970.

Taylor, J. L. *Forest Monks and the Nation-state.* Singapore: Institute for Southeast Asian Studies, 1993.

Trainor, Kevin. *Relics, Ritual, and Representation in Buddhism: Rematerializing the Sri Lankan Theravāda Tradition.* Cambridge: Cambridge University Press, 1997.

CHAPTER EIGHT: BUDDHISM IN CENTRAL ASIA AND CHINA

CENTRAL ASIA

Beckwith, Christopher I. *The Tibetan Empire in Central Asia.* Princeton: Princeton University press, 1987.

Emmerick, R. E. *A Guide to the Literature of Khotan.* Tokyo: Reiyukai, 1979.

Snellgrove, David L. *Indo-Tibetan Buddhism: Indian Buddhists and their Tibetan Successors.* Vol. 2. Boston: Shambhala, 1987.

CHINA

Buswell, Robert E., ed. *Chinese Buddhist Apocrypha*. Honolulu: University of Hawai'i Press, 1990.

Ch'en, Kenneth. *Buddhism in China: A Historical Survey*. Princeton: Princeton University Press, 1964.

———. *The Chinese Transformation of Buddhism*. Princeton: Princeton University Press, 1973.

Cook, Francis H. *Hua-yen Buddhism: The Jewel Net of Indra*. University Park: Pennsylvania State University Press, 1977.

Donner, Neal, and Daniel B. Stevenson. *The Great Calming and Contemplation: A Study and Annotated Translation of the First Chapter of Chih-i's Mo-ho Chih-Kuan*. Honolulu: University of Hawai'i Press, 1993.

Ebrey, Patricia Buckley, and Peter Gregory, eds. *Religion and Society in T'ang and Sung China*. Honolulu: University of Hawai'i Press, 1993.

Faure, Bernard. *The Rhetoric of Immediacy: A Cultural Critique of Chan/Zen Buddhism*. Princeton: Princeton University Press, 1991.

Gernet, Jacques. *Buddhism in Chinese Society: An Economic History (5th to 10th c.)*. Translated by Franciscus Verellen. New York: Columbia University Press, 1995.

Gregory, Peter N., ed. *Tsung-mi and the Sinification of Buddhism*. Princeton: Princeton University Press, 1991.

———, ed. *Traditions of Meditation in Chinese Buddhism*. Honolulu: University of Hawai'i Press, 1986.

———. *Sudden and Gradual: Approaches to Enlightenment in Chinese Thought*. Honolulu: University of Hawai'i Press, 1987.

Haar, B.J. ter. *The White Lotus Teachings in Chinese Religious History*. Leiden, Netherlands: E.J. Brill, 1992.

Hakeda, Yoshito, trans. *The Awakening of Faith*. New York: Columbia University Press, 1967.

Heine, Steven, and Dale S. Wright, eds. *The Kōan: Texts and Contexts in Zen Buddhism*. Oxford: Oxford University Press, 2000.

Hsu Sung-peng, *A Buddhist Leader in Ming China: Life and Thought of Han-Shan Te-Ch'ing, 1546–1623*. University Park: Pennsylvania State University Press, 1979.

Kieschnick, John. *The Eminent Monk: Buddhist Ideals in Medieval Chinese Hagiography*. Honolulu: University of Hawai'i Press, 1997.

Lai, Whalen, and Lewis R. Lancaster, eds. *Early Ch'an in China and Tibet*. Berkeley: University of California Press, 1983.

Lopez, Donald S., Jr., ed. *Religions of China in Practice*. Princeton: Princeton University Press, 1996.

Mair, Victor H. *Painting and Performance: Chinese Picture Recitation and Its Indian Genesis*. Honolulu: University of Hawai'i Press, 1988.

McRae, John R. *The Northern School and the Formation of Early Ch'an Buddhism*. Honolulu: University of Hawai'i Press, 1986.

———. *Seeing Through Zen: Encounter, Transformation, and Genealogy in Chinese Chan Buddhism*. Berkeley: University of California Press, 2003.

Naquin, Susan, and Chun-fang Yu. *Pilgrims and Sacred Sites in China*. Berkeley: University of California Press, 1992.

Powell, William F. *The Record of Tung-shan*. Honolulu: University of Hawai'i Press, 1986.

Robinson, Richard H. *Early Mādhyamika in India and China*. Madison: University of Wisconsin Press, 1967.

Shahar, Meir, and Robert P. Weller, eds. *Unruly Gods: Divinity and Society in China*. Honolulu: University of Hawai'i Press, 1996.

Sommer, Deborah, ed., *Chinese Religion: An Anthology of Sources*. New York: Oxford University Press, 1995.

Teiser, Stephen F. *The Ghost Festival in Medieval China*. Princeton: Princeton University Press, 1988.

———. *The Scripture on the Ten Kings and the Making of Purgatory in Medieval Chinese Buddhism*. Honolulu: University of Hawai'i Press, 1994.

Tsai, Kathryn Ann. *Lives of the Nuns: Biographies of Chinese Buddhist Nuns from the Fourth to Sixth Centuries.* Honolulu: University of Hawai'i Press, 1994.

Weinstein, Stanley. *Buddhism under the T'ang.* Cambridge: Cambridge University Press, 1987.

Yu Chun-fang. *The Renewal of Buddhism in China: Chu-hung and the Late Ming Synthesis.* New York: Columbia University Press, 1980.

Zürcher, Erik. *The Buddhist Conquest of China: The Spread and Adaptation of Buddhism in Early Medieval China.* Leiden, Netherlands: E. J. Brill, 1972.

CHAPTER NINE: BUDDHISM IN KOREA AND VIETNAM

KOREA

Buswell, Robert E., Jr. *The Korean Approach to Zen: The Collected Works of Chinul.* Honolulu: University of Hawai'i Press, 1983.

———. *The Zen Monastic Experience: Buddhist Practice in Contemporary Korea.* Princeton: Princeton University Press, 1992.

Cleary, J. C. *A Buddha from Korea: The Zen Teachings of T'aego.* Boston: Shambhala, 1988.

Lancaster, Lewis R., and C. S. Yu, eds. *Assimilation of Buddhism in Korea: Religious Maturity and Innovation in the Silla Dynasty.* Berkeley: Asian Humanities Press, 1991.

———, eds. *Introduction of Buddhism to Korea: New Cultural Patterns.* Berkeley: Asian Humanities Press, 1989.

Mu Soeng. *Thousand Peaks: Korean Zen—Tradition and Teachers.* Cumberland, RI: Primary Point Press, 1991.

Park, Sung Bae. Buddhist Faith and Sudden Enlightenment. Albany: SUNY Press, 1983.

Tae-heng Se Nim. *Teachings of the Heart: Zen Teachings of Korean Woman Zen Master Tae-Heng Se Nim.* Occidental, CA: Dai Shin Press, 1990.

VIETNAM

Chân Không. *Learning True Love: How I Learned and Practiced Social Change in Vietnam.* Berkeley: Parallax Press, 1993.

Nguyen, Cuong Tu. *Zen in Medieval Vietnam: A Study and Translation of the Thiền Uyển Tập Anh.* Honolulu: University of Hawai'i Press, 1998.

Nhât Hạnh, Thích. *Vietnam: Lotus in a Sea of Fire.* New York: Hill and Wang, 1967.

Taylor, Keith Weller. *The Birth of Vietnam.* Berkeley: University of California Press, 1983.

Thien-Tam, Thich. *Buddhism of Wisdom and Faith: Pure Land Principles and Practice.* Sepulveda, CA: International Buddhist Monastic Institute, 1991.

CHAPTER TEN: BUDDHISM IN JAPAN

Abe, Ryūichi. *The Weaving of Mantra: Kūkai and the Construction of Esoteric Buddhist Discourse.* New York: Columbia University Press, 1999.

Bielefeldt, Carl. *Dōgen's Manuals of Zen Meditation.* Berkeley: University of California Press, 1988.

Bodiford, William. *Sōtō Zen in Medieval Japan.* Honolulu: University of Hawai'i Press, 1993.

Colcutt, Martin. *Five Mountains: The Rinzai Zen Monastic Institution in Medieval Japan.* Cambridge: Harvard University Press, 1981.

Dobbins, James C. *Jōdo Shinshū: Shin Buddhism in Medieval Japan*. Bloomington: Indiana University Press, 1989.

Groner, Paul. *Saichō: The Establishment of the Japanese Tendai School*.Berkeley: Berkeley Buddhist Studies, 1984.

Hardacre, Helen. *Kurozumikyo and the New Religions of Japan*. Princeton: Princeton University Press, 1986.

Heine, Steven. *Dōgen and the Kōan Tradition*. Albany: SUNY Press, 1994.

Ketelaar, James Edward. *Of Heretics and Martyrs in Meiji Japan: Buddhism and Its Persecution*. Princeton: Princeton University Press, 1990.

Kraft, Kenneth. *Eloquent Zen: Daito and Early Japanese Zen*. Honolulu: University of Hawai'i Press, 1992.

———, ed. *Zen: Tradition and Transition*. New York: Grove Press, 1988.

LaFleur, William. *The Karma of Words: Buddhism and the Literary Arts in Medieval Japan*. Berkeley: University of California Press, 1983.

McMullin, Neil. *Buddhism and the State in Sixteenth Century Japan*. Princeton: Princeton University Press, 1988.

Payne, Richard K., ed. *Re-Visioning "Kamakura" Buddhism*. Honolulu: University of Hawai'i Press, 1998.

Reader, Ian, and George J. Tanabe, Jr. *Practically Religious: Worldly Benefits and the Common Religion of Japan*. Honolulu: University of Hawaii Press, 1998.

Ruppert, Brian. *Jewel in the Ashes: Buddha Relics and Power in Early Medieval Japan*. Cambridge: Harvard University Press, 2000.

Sanford, James H. *Zen-man Ikkyū*. Chico, CA: Scholars Press, 1981.

Stone, Jacqueline I. *Original Enlightenment and the Transformation of Medieval Japanese Buddhism*. Honolulu: University of Hawai'i Press, 1999.

Tanabe, George J., Jr. *Myoe the Dreamkeeper: Fantasy and Knowledge in Early Kamakura Buddhism*. Cambridge: Harvard University Press, 1992.

Yampolsky, Philip B. *The Zen Master Hakuin: Selected Writings*. New York: Columbia University Press, 1971.

CHAPTER ELEVEN: BUDDHISM IN THE TIBETAN CULTURAL AREA

Beyer, Stephan V. *The Cult of Tārā*. Berkeley: University of California Press, 1973.

Cabezón, José Ignacia. *Buddhism and Language: A Study of Indo-Tibetan Scholasticism*. Albany: SUNY Press, 1994.

Cozart, Daniel. *Highest Yoga Tantra: An Introduction to the Esoteric Buddhism of Tibet*. Ithaca: Snow Lion Publications, 1986.

Dowman, Keith. *Sky Dancer: The Secret Life and Songs of the Lady Yeshe Tsogyel*. London: Routledge & Kegan Paul, 1984.

Dreyfus, Georges B.J. *The Sound of Two Hands Clapping: The Education of a Tibetan Buddhist Monk*. Berkeley: University of California Press, 2003.

Gyatso, Tenzin, Dalai Lama XIV. *Freedom in Exile*. New York: HarperPerennial, 1990.

Havnevik, Hanna. *Tibetan Buddhist Nuns: History, Cultural Norms, and Social Reality*. Norwegian University Press: The Institute for Comparative Research in Human Culture, 1989.

Kapstein, Matthew. *The Tibetan Assimilation of Buddhism*. Oxford: Oxford University Press, 2000.

Karmay, Samten Gyaltsen. *The Great Perfection: A Philosophical and Meditative Teaching of Tibetan Buddhism*. Leiden, Netherlands: E.J. Brill, 1988.

Lhalunga, Lobsang P. *The Life of Milarepa: A New Translation from the Tibetan*. Boston: Shambhala, 1977.

Napper, Elizabeth. *Dependent-Arising and Emptiness*. Boston: Wisdom Publications, 1989.

Powers, John. *Introduction to Tibetan Buddhism*. Ithaca: Snow Lion Publications, 1995.

Rhie, Marylin M., and Robert A. F. Thurman. *Wisdom and Compassion: The Sacred Art of Tibet.* New York: Harry H. Abrams, 1991.

Samuel, Geoffrey. *Civilized Shamans: Buddhism in Tibetan Societies.* Washington: Smithsonian Institution Press, 1993.

Snellgrove, David L. *Four Lamas of Dolpo.* Cambridge: Harvard University Press, 1967.

———. *Indo-Tibetan Buddhism: Indian Buddhists and their Tibetan Successors.* Vol. 2. Boston: Shambhala, 1987.

Taring, Rinchen Dolma. *Daughter of Tibet.* London: Wisdom Publications, 1986.

Tsering Shakya. *The Dragon in the Land of the Snows: A History of Modern Tibet Since 1947.* New York: Columbia University Press, 1999.

Tucci, Giuseppe. *The Religions of Tibet.* Berkeley: University of California Press, 1980.

Willis, Janice D. *Feminine Ground: Essays on Women and Tibet.* Ithaca: Snow Lion, Publications, 1989.

CHAPTER TWELVE: BUDDHISM COMES WEST

Batchelor, Stephen. *The Awakening of the West: The Encounter of Buddhism and Western Culture.* Berkeley: Parallax Press, 1994.

Droit, Roger-Pol. *The Cult of Nothingness: The Philosophers and the Buddha.* Translated by David Streight and Pamela Vohnson. Chapel Hill: University of North Carolina Press, 2003.

Fields, Rick. *How the Swans Came to the Lake: A Narrative History of Buddhism in America.* Boston: Shambhala, 1992.

Friedman, Lenore. *Meetings with Remarkable Women: Buddhist Teachers in America.* Boston: Shambhala, 1987.

Lang, David Marshall. *The Wisdom of Balahvar: A Christian Legend of the Buddha.* New York: Macmillan, 1957.

Lopez, Donald S., Jr., ed. *Curators of the Buddha: The Study of Buddhism under Colonialism.* Chicago: University of Chicago Press, 1995.

Numrich, Paul David. *Old Wisdom in the New World: Americanization in Two Immigrant Theravada Buddhist Temples.* Knoxville: University of Tennessee Press, 1996.

Prebish, Charles S., and Kenneth K. Tanaka, eds. *The Faces of Buddhism in America.* Berkeley: University of California Press, 1998.

Seager, Richard Hughes. *Buddhism in America.* New York: Columbia University Press, 1999.

Tsomo, Karma Lekshe. *Sakyadhita: Daughters of the Buddha.* Ithaca: Snow Lion Publications, 1988.

Tweed, Thomas A. *The American Encounter with Buddhism, 1844–1912.* Chapel Hill: University of North Carolina Press, 2002.

Tweed, Thomas, and Stephen Prothero, eds. *Asian Religions in America: A Documentary History.* New York: Oxford University Press, 1999.

Tworkov, Helen. *Zen in America.* New York: Kodansha America, 1994.

Five periodicals dealing with Buddhism in the West may be of interest to students. They are *Buddhadharma: The Practitioners Quarterly; Inquiring Mind; Insight Journal; Shambhala Sun: Creating Enlightened Society;* and *Tricycle: The Buddhist Review.*

Index